ERASED

# Erased

## A HISTORY OF INTERNATIONAL
## THOUGHT WITHOUT MEN

PATRICIA OWENS

PRINCETON UNIVERSITY PRESS

PRINCETON & OXFORD

Copyright © 2025 by Princeton University Press

Princeton University Press is committed to the protection of copyright and the intellectual property our authors entrust to us. Copyright promotes the progress and integrity of knowledge created by humans. Thank you for supporting free speech and the global exchange of ideas by purchasing an authorized edition of this book. If you wish to reproduce or distribute any part of it in any form, please obtain permission.

Requests for permission to reproduce material from this work should be sent to permissions@press.princeton.edu

Published by Princeton University Press
41 William Street, Princeton, New Jersey 08540
99 Banbury Road, Oxford OX2 6JX

press.princeton.edu

All Rights Reserved

ISBN 978-0-691-26644-2
ISBN (e-book) 978-0-691-26682-4

British Library Cataloging-in-Publication Data is available

Editorial: Rebecca Brennan and Rebecca Binnie
Production Editorial: Jill Harris
Jacket Design: Heather Hansen
Production: Erin Suydam
Publicity: Kate Hensley and Kathryn Stevens
Copyeditor: Tash Siddiqui

Jacket image: Courtesy of the LSE Library

This book has been composed in Arno

Printed in the United Kingdom

10 9 8 7 6 5 4 3 2 1

For my beloved mother, Margaret Murphy Owens

# CONTENTS

# ILLUSTRATIONS

ACKNOWLEDGEMENTS

MANY PEOPLE AND INSTITUTIONS supported the research and writing for this third book—and first monograph—of the Leverhulme Trust Research Project on Women and the History of International Thought (RPG-2017-319). It was an honour, and the highlight of my career so far, to work with Kim Hutchings, Katharina Rietzler, Sarah C. Dunstan and Joanna Wood, the interdisciplinary collaborators, on the 'WHIT Project'. I am especially grateful to the Leverhulme Trust for its generous financial support; to our Project Advisors, David Armitage, Bob Vitalis and Penny Weiss; and earliest advocates with the Trust, Glenda Sluga and Andrew Hurrell. Sharon Krummel at Sussex and Dawn Tohill at Oxford offered brilliant administrative support.

I am forever indebted to my longtime readers, intellectual guides, and friends Michael Jago, Lene Hansen, and Helen M. Kinsella, who commented on the book in its entirety, as did Clare O'Connor, Isabelle Napier, Glenda Sluga, Kim Hutchings, Aden Knaap, and Molly Cochran. Katharina Rietzler, Morgan Dacosta, Tarak Barkawi, Debbie Lisle, Madeleine Herren, Waltraud Schelkle, and Katharina Engel commented on specific parts. I cannot thank them enough, nor the many interlocuters during presentations of portions of the book at Sydney, Harvard, McGill, the European University Institute, Copenhagen, Oxford, Cambridge, School of Oriental and African Studies, Edinburgh, St Andrews, Swansea, Glasgow, Royal Military College Sandhurst, London School of Economics, Kent, Sussex, the Institute for Historical Research, Oxford's Meeting Minds Festival, and conferences of *Millennium: Journal of International Studies*, the International Studies Association, the British International Studies Association, the Mexican International Studies Association, and the Britain and Ireland Association for Political Thought.

Many other historians, political theorists and scholars of International Relations (IR) engaged directly with the WHIT project across several fora, all of whom profoundly influenced my thinking. They are Barbara D. Savage, Cynthia Enloe, Adom Getachew, Duncan Bell, Vineet Thakur, Robbie Shiliam,

Helen McCarthy, Jeanne Morefield, Keisha N. Blain, Meera Sabaratnam, Charlotte Lydia Riley, Laura Sjoberg, Or Rosenboim, Ayşe Zarakol, Immi Tallgren, Anne Phillips, David Long, Catherine Lu, Tamson Pietsch, Vivian M. May, Christopher J. Finlay, Manjeet Ramgotra, Mona Siegel, Luke Ashworth, Imaobong Umoren, Geoffrey Field, Su Lin Lewis, Anne-Sophie Schoepfel, Juliette Gout, Lauren Wilcox, Catia Confortini, Craig Murphy, Jan Stöckmann and Tomás Irish.

The book could not have been written without the work of countless archivists and librarians, and various family members of some of the figures discussed. I am indebted to Cathie Wilson and Elizabeth Thomas, Rachel Wall's niece and sister, who spoke to me at length. Cathie hosted me in her home and allowed access to Rachel's papers, now deposited at St Hugh's College, Oxford. Music historian Martha Stonequist was a generous source of knowledge about her grandmother Lucie Barbier Zimmern. Susan Strange's two oldest children, Giles Merritt and Jane Streatfeild, shared their memories and reflections. Agnes Headlam-Morey's nephew, Peter Headlam-Morley, kindly corresponded with me, and Meike Fernbach translated Agnes's surviving letters to her German mother. I am grateful to Anthony Rayne for permission to quote from the papers of his great-aunt and godmother, Dame Margery Perham; to Cathie Wilson for permission to quote from Rachel Wall's papers; the Isaiah Berlin Literary Trust for permission to quote from Berlin's papers; and to Polly Watson Black for sharing a photograph that includes her father Adam Watson and Coral Bell.

For their assistance, knowledge and permission to quote from archives, I am extremely grateful to Anna Towlson, Gilliam Murphy, and especially Daniel Payne at LSE Library; Simon Bailey, Anna Petre, Michael Hughes, Faye McLeod, Katherine O'Donnell, and Alice B Millea at the Bodleian Library, Oxford; David Bates and Malcolm Madden at Chatham House Library; Annabel Valentine, Dan Mitchell and Robert Winckworth at University College London Special Collections; Jacqueline Cox and the Syndics of Cambridge University Library; Julie Archer and Catrin Griffiths at Aberystwyth University; Melanie Owen at the National Library of Wales; Hannah Westall, Mathilda Watson, and the Mistress and Fellows of Girton College, Cambridge; Anne Thomson and Frieda Midgley at Newnham College, Cambridge; Sophie Bridges and Nicole Allen at Churchill Archives Centre, Cambridge; Amanda Ingram, Nora Khayi, Matthew Chipping and the Principal and Fellows of St Hugh's College, Oxford; Anne Manuel and Kate O'Donnell at Somerville College, Oxford; Oliver Mahony at Lady Margaret Hall and St Hilda's College,

Oxford; Aimee Burlakova at St Antony's College, Oxford; Anne-Marie Purcell at Royal Holloway, University of London; Paul Barnaby and Danielle Spittle at Edinburgh University Library; Simone Amis at Sussex University Library; Heather Personage at Nottingham Trent University Library; James Peters at Manchester University Library; Stephanie Rolt, keeper of the Westfield College archives at Queen Mary University of London; Gillian Long at School of Slavonic and East European Studies Library; Christopher Gilley and Anna Cartwright at Durham University Library; Beth Lonergan at the Australian National University archives; Ellen Shea at the Schlesinger Library at the Radcliffe Institute for Advanced Study, Harvard; Eric Dillalogue and Sarah Heim at the Kislak Center, Penn Libraries; the librarians and archivists at the University of Aberdeen; the Rockefeller Archive Center, New York; the Schomburg Center for Research in Black Culture in New York; the Tamiment Library and Robert F. Wagner Labor Archives at New York University; the Wiener Holocaust Library; and the Bancroft Library/Special Collections in California, Berkeley.

I'm grateful to the Bodleian Library, the Mistress and Fellows of Girton College, Emily Craker, Chatham House, Julian Brigstocke, the Meitner-Graf Estate, LSE Image Library, Western Michigan University Archives & Regional History Collection, the Principal and Fellows of St Hugh's College, Getty Images, Lambeth Archives, Cathie Wilson, and Polly Watson Black for permission to reprint images of Lucie Zimmern and the Geneva School of International Studies, Margery Perham, Mary and Hedley Bull, Florence Melian Stawell, M. G. Jones and Eileen Power, Margaret Cleeve, Elizabeth Wiskemann, Lucy Philip Mair, Eileen Power, Merze Tate, Agnes Headlam-Morley, Claudia Jones, Rachel Wall, the LSE International Relations Department, Susan Strange, and the British Committee on the Theory of International Politics.

Most of the archival and other primary research was caried out before the Covid-19 pandemic, multiple lockdowns, and homeschooling. However, for research funds to work around cancelled archival visits and lost research time, I'm extremely grateful to Oxford's Social Science Division allowing Toni Čerkez in Aberystwyth, Natasha Shoory in Durham, and Rowena Squires and Ben Tan in Cambridge to copy and send missing papers. I also benefited enormously from Oxford graduate research assistance from Isabelle Napier, Morgan Dacosta, Caiban Butcher, and Philip Xing. Several scholars kindly responded to specific questions and queries, sharing their expertise, including Vanessa Ogle, Cornelia Navari, Ian Hall, Nat Dyer, Jenny Mathers, Ken Booth, Bob Vitalis, V. Spike Peterson, Martin Ceadel, Adam Roberts, Christopher

May, Alison Phipps, Stephen Legg, Mick Cox, Timothy Rood, Roger Tooze, Lou Pauly, Edward Maltby, and Filippo Costa Buranelli.

During 2019–20, the WHIT Project relocated from Sussex to Oxford. I am so grateful to former Sussex colleagues and friends, many of whom commented and advised on the earliest stages of the WHIT Project, including Anna Stavrianakis, Synne Dyvik, Rorden Wilkinson, Jan Selby, Paul Kirby, Melanie Richter-Montpetit, and Louiza Odysseos. Somerville College and Oxford IR provided a congenial home. I am especially grateful for the intellectual culture and friendship fostered by Jan Royall, Lois McNay, Eddie Keene, Sudhir Hazareesingh, Louise Fawcett, Kalypso Nicolaïdis, Jeannie Morefield, Meera Sabaratnam, Sophie Smith, Neta Crawford, and Andy Hurrell.

I am incredibly grateful to Rebecca Brennan at Princeton University Press for her enthusiasm and support in getting this book out, and the anonymous reviewers for the Press. I'm also grateful to Rebecca Binnie for editorial assistance at the Press. For excellent editorial production and copyediting, I thank Jill Harris and Tash Siddiqui, and for the index I thank Kathleen Strattan.

Some paragraphs of the material are reprinted from my research and writing in Patricia Owens and Katharina Rietzler, 'Polyphonic Internationalism: The Lucie Zimmern School of International Relations', *The International History Review*, vol. 45, no. 5 (2023), pp. 623–624; and Patricia Owens, 'Images of International Thinkers', *Review of International Studies* (2024).

I am forever grateful for the love of my family, Clare, Maggie, Edie, Jane, Fiona, and Margaret.

*Brighton and Oxford*
January 2024

ERASED

# The Gender of International Thought

IN 1929, a former classics don at Newnham College, Cambridge published the first book of a new and highly distinctive genre, an historical survey of international thought.[1] *The Growth of International Thought* was the first English-language book to coin the term, but as historian Glenda Sluga has recently pointed out, this was not the book that Florence Melian Stawell had intended to write.[2] The idea came from Stawell's mentor, fellow Australian émigré and classicist, Gilbert Murray, Oxford's Regius Professor of Greek. Asked by the publisher to review Stawell's proposal for a different book, a popular history of the League of Nations, Murray seized the project for himself and suggested she write a history of international thought instead. Within a year, Stawell had written that book. Murray never wrote his on the League.

At the very origin of twentieth-century Anglophone histories of international thought we find a gendered intellectual appropriation. Entirely by chance, a sixty-year-old woman who shared her life with another woman and who left academia due to ill-health inaugurated a genre from which she and all other women, people of colour, and those living non-heteronormative lives would be erased.

'How often does History go wrong owing to this sort of thing? And what was the cause of such an omission?',[3] Alice Maud Allen asked in her biography of 'international thinker' Sophy Sanger.[4] Like Stawell, Sanger studied at Newnham, Cambridge's oldest women's college, and became Britain's leading expert on international industrial law, one of the most significant and effective dimensions of the League of Nation's work.[5] 'The "queer foreigners" . . . must have thought her a queer representative of Great Britain', Allen wrote of her life companion.[6] While Allen was 'Chef de la Division Domestique',[7] Sanger took a second law degree, founded her own journal, *The World's Labour Laws*, and was a key architect of the creation and conception of the International Labour Organization (ILO). 'We determined to make our friendship and alliance as near a marriage as we could', Allen later recalled: 'we would give . . . love and care for one another, companionship, faithfulness, security, each putting the other first. We would share our incomes and whatever we possessed; and create for one another a home . . . And we brought one another happiness'.[8] Much to Maud Allen's feminist rage, Sophy Sanger was later marginalised from the ILO by less knowledgeable men who took credit for her work and ideas.[9] With *Sophy Sanger: A Pioneer in Internationalism* Allen determined to write Sanger—and herself—back into histories of international thought. Some international intellectual history is a labour of queer love.

This book is a history of international thought set in Britain during the twentieth century. It focuses on a cohort of women and their ideas on international relations, including international organisations, anticolonial organising and non-Western powers, colonial administration, the British Empire and its collapse, and the new science of international relations. Outside the academy, women of world-historical significance educated tens of thousands of Black and brown Britons on international relations and mobilised them to political action. In universities, think tanks, and summer schools, a new field of knowledge was built on the intellectual labours of women historians and classicists; scholars of international law, international institutions and colonial administration; information managers, educators, and intellectual entrepreneurs on the margins of academe. All these thinkers were drawn to the magnificent and destructive fact that there are multiple and different kinds of polities interacting in the world, to the fact of international relations.

This book is about a cohort of women intellectuals, but also how—like Stawell and Sanger—they were written out of histories of international thought. Like many other academic fields, International Relations (IR) presents its own history as almost entirely homosocial, a conversation between elite white men. This is an old story, of course, that feminist historians have exposed many times in philosophy, law, the sciences, and the arts. But IR's is a more paradoxical story of gendered power, knowledge, and erasure. Women were there from the start. The new field relied on the intellectual labours of women, figures who were influential and well known in their own time, but were only later devalued, ignored, and erased.[10]

This is the feminist history that I set out to write, an alternative genealogy of women intellectuals in a male-dominated world operating in a less male-dominated field. However, it turns out that one cannot write this history, or at least I cannot write this history, without discerning something else with wider implications for understanding the gendered history of knowledge. During the 1950s, with Britain violently clinging onto empire, and when Maud Allen was writing about Sophy Sanger, a small number of university men attempted to redefine the academic field in opposition to the forms of international relations expertise, to the writings, genres, and research methods in which women international thinkers had excelled. The attempt to forge IR as a separate academic field in Britain in the middle decades of the twentieth century was a highly gendered but also racialised project with major implications for its long-term intellectual standing.

The academic field of IR has come a long way since the 1950s. Yet, its standing and legitimacy is still questioned. Some of its best-known practitioners lament that IR is 'backward', without the intellectual standing of philosophy or history.[11] Its 'big names' are almost entirely unknown outside the field.[12] As I researched the ideas and the lives of women international thinkers, and how they were erased, I realised that their story revealed the main sources of IR's failure as an intellectual project. As scholars and publics still struggle to make sense of plurality on a worldwide scale, recovering the women against whom the academic field was defined is of enormous relevance. It not only reveals the gendered, racialised, and methodological roots of IR's intellectual failures, but potential sources of its renewal as Britain continues to reckon—and not reckon—with the legacies of empire in public and intellectual life.

## The History of International Thought without Women

Almost a century after Florence Melian Stawell's 1929 book, women and people of colour are still rarely at the centre of histories of international thought.[13] Even Stawell's own cast of thinkers in *The Growth of International Thought* was entirely male and Eurocentric. The academic field tasked with writing intellectual and disciplinary histories of international relations offers a similarly patrilineal story about 'white man's IR', of 'fathers' 'master-debating' the 'seminal' thinkers.[14] The works and ideas of men appear as if from nowhere or emerge only in conversation with other white men in a game of intellectual influence.[15] Even the few belated attempts to address the entrenched neglect of women tokenise one or two. These women, in turn, are usually presented as precursors to feminist IR, as if women can only teach men about gender.

Generations of feminist historians and theorists have shown that when women and people of colour are absent from intellectual histories it is not because they were missing, but because they were erased. The patrilineal story is entirely inadequate for understanding the thinkers, genres, and intimate conditions of intellectual production.[16] The absence of women and people of colour in intellectual histories is never evidence of intellectual deficit, that they could not think very deeply.[17] Rather, overwhelmingly white male authors equivocated, deeply attached to a fantasy of the superiority of white men and to their own selective ignorance. Even as some identified IR as a failed intellectual project, others had little interest in undoing the racialised and disciplinary boundaries between women's intellectual history and histories of international thought, or interweaving interpersonal, institutional, and intellectual histories.[18]

This book examines a much wider variety of political, professional, intimate, and intellectual contexts and genres of international thinking. It does not centre the usual cast of white men or ignore the personal and the intimate contexts of intellectual production. It focuses on the women whom many of these men and later intellectual historians marginalised to produce an all-white male canon.[19] It examines the operations of gendered, racial and other hierarchies in the production of international thought in imperial Britain and in historical writing on this thought.[20] It draws on and extends the work of feminist intellectual historians and theorists to write a new kind of critical disciplinary history.

Historians have already shown that 'international relations' was a highly feminised field from its heyday in the first decades of the twentieth century.[21] Women were some of the most active agents of the new internationalism in anticolonial and feminist struggles, including at the League of Nations.[22] They thought about international relations in academia, journalism, philanthropy, political parties, summer schools, think tanks, or advocacy organisations such as the League of Nations Union and International League for Peace and Freedom. They wrote the first English-language book to coin the term 'international thought', as we have seen, but also some of the earliest textbooks and model international relations syllabi. Two wealthy sisters and a brother established the world's first IR professorship. Women pioneered the information services on which the new science was built and some of the methodological approaches to which it would turn.[23]

Because the early science initially had no single home in one university department or form of disciplinary training, international relations lacked some of the more entrenched patriarchal networks of the older disciplines of history, philosophy, and law.[24] It was thus an intellectual and practical field in which some women could get ahead. They founded the best-funded international relations institute in the interwar United States and were among the earliest cohorts of interdisciplinary scholars appointed to the first IR departments in Britain.[25] Oxford and Edinburgh's first women professors, Agnes Headlam-Morley and Elizabeth Wiskemann, and Oxford's first African–American graduate student, Merze Tate, were all scholars of international relations. IR's first spousal hire was the husband of Lilian Friedländer, the first women appointed to an IR department, who was once in sole charge of its teaching.

This book returns to key moments and locations in the formation of IR as a separate university field in twentieth-century Britain to show the centrality of gender relations to this project. I return to some of the highest profile and influential women in the early field, including Oxford's Montague Burton Professor of IR for over thirty years, Agnes Headlam-Morley, and Margaret Cleeve, the head of the Information Department at Chatham House for twenty-five years. I show that women were the leading international thinkers of their generation across the four decades of the mid-twentieth century. These were Margery Perham, the most important white public intellectual on the British Empire; Claudia Jones, a British subject from Trinidad who theorised and educated ordinary people about class, gendered, and racialised oppression on a global scale; and Susan Strange, the dominant persona in the IR university profession in the 1970s and 1980s.

Intimate life is a fundamental part of the history of international thinking. I show how the early cross-disciplinary science relied on feminised labour, including assistant lectureships in support of male professors, the domestic and familial support of wives and social capital of their *salons*, and research assistance, sometimes carried out by wives and mistresses.[26] One wife and interwar IR's most vilified woman, Lucie Zimmern, shaped the course of IR history as protagonist in a major debate on the nature of international relations and how it should be taught. During the effort to create IR as a separate university subject after World War II, women scholars such as Lucy Philip Mair were marginalised from the largest university departments of IR in Britain and later erased from their histories. Some, like Lilian Friedländer, left academia entirely or, like Lucy Mair, moved to a different department as intellectual fields were reorganised during decolonisation. Others such as Eileen Power and Merze Tate were writing on international relations in locations that are entirely missing or neglected in disciplinary histories.[27]

I show that the project for a 'separate IR' initiated in the 1950s by a few London-based men followed a masculine and imperial imperative to develop an abstract sociological 'theory' of international society, elevating forms of sociology that were already passé. One of these men, Charles Manning, quite literally imagined the new IR teacher as a 'Superman'.[28] This project for a separate IR was deeply ideological, defined against multiple feminised, racialised and methodological Others: against historical and political analyses of empire; against popular writing aimed at wider publics and children; against a 'middle-aged spinster'[29] diplomatic historian and disciplined historical method; against a wife of a canonical thinker; and against the 'voice of Portia', Shakespeare's capable cross-dressing heroine from *The Merchant of Venice*.[30] By the 1980s, one woman, Susan Strange, variously seen as an honorary gentleman, superwoman and Queen Bee, fashioned herself as an iconoclastic outsider on a patricidal mission to reinvent IR again.

If we want to understand the history of international thinking during the twentieth century, and especially the formation of a separate university subject in Britain, then we must understand how it was gendered.[31] We have to look not just to the earliest university departments and think tanks, not just lecture halls, academia, tangible scholarly achievements and new degree programmes. We must look to women's colleges (including their hiring practices and heavy teaching burdens), summer schools, departments of music and history, professors' homes, hotel rooms, concert halls, *salons*, and independent journalism. We must examine the accidents and contingencies, including illness, ableism, the effects of mental-health crises, and several early deaths on the development of the field. We must examine the roads not taken, the course proposals that went nowhere and the book projects never completed. We must look at the minutiae of university operations and workings of power and the many disciplines, fields, and methodological approaches sidelined. We cannot fixate on the homosocial relations between professional men. We must examine the personal and the intimate, heterosexual power couples, marriages and affairs, trailing spouses and self-sacrificing 'spinsters'[32] devoted to an intellectual cause, heteronormative lives and intimate partnerships between women. Many wives and assistants were not amanuenses, secretaries transcribing the work of the so-called 'fathers of international thought' but international thinkers themselves. In contrast to the discourse of 'fathers' or 'masters', the history of international thinking was more marital and domestic than patrilineal, something carried on between husbands and wives, lovers and intimate partners, between siblings, and occasionally fathers and mothers.

## Women (and White Men)?

This project began as a feminist recovery of figures written out of the history of an intellectual field in which they were prominent. However, not all readers will sympathise with the focus on women. Why define a cohort of thinkers in gendered terms? Unless we assume that only white men wrote anything important on international relations, then on one level the question answers itself. As I was coming up as a young scholar in the early 2000s, I found it very difficult to respect or admire the men I was told formed the intellectual history of my field. In retrospect, this may be why I wrote my first book on Hannah Arendt's international thought.[33] I do not respect or admire everything about the cohort of women in this book, nor strongly identify with all aspects of their work. Yet their recovery is necessary in the first instance to better understand the actual history of the field and to rectify an epistemic injustice.[34]

Except it is not that simple. Many queer and gender theorists argue that recovery history and genealogical approaches not only risk hagiography but also representing a continuous past of 'women thinkers' or 'women's experience', which reinforces binaries of sex and gender that we ought to reject.[35] Certainly one risk in feminist recovery is that it simply recuperates (mostly) elite white women from the condescension of elite white men.[36] We might condemn the sexism and patriarchy that shaped women's intellectual production, yet does it follow that we recover these figures primarily *as women*? During the research for this book, the political and intellectual stakes of the 'woman question' in Britain became even greater. In the name of defending biological and sex-based women's rights, small gains in trans rights, trans recognition, and gender-affirming healthcare were rolled back. As violent assaults on trans, non-binary, and queer communities increased, feminist movements split, and feminist collaborations ended.

To write an intellectual history that centres figures who were defined as, read as, and marginalised as women, who defined themselves as women, does not conflate gender with biological sex. This book does not revolve around a stable ontological subject. Woman is a subject constructed through history, not biology.[37] All of the figures in my cohort understood themselves as women. At least one briefly experimented with their gender identity and, in their own writing on feminist movements around the world, never used the term 'women' universally.[38] Many in my cohort lived queer lives, though none were trans, non-binary, or genderqueer as far as I know. The operative question is not whether my cohort are essentially part of a group defined in terms of sex. It is how the gender binary shaped the production and reception of international thought. All of them operated in professional and intellectual contexts that were fundamentally structured around gender difference and patriarchal and heterosexist norms. The challenge is to write a history that does not impose gender or other sexual conventions on figures who may not accept them nor reproduce the hierarchies that shaped the conditions and the reception of their work.

I acknowledge the limits of the category of historical women and the genealogical recovery that I have attempted. Though I am interested in how my cohort performed and expressed gender as a form of opposition to, resistance to, and complicity in patriarchal, racist and class structures, I do not subject their gender and/or sexual identities to radical questioning.[39] Such a book could certainly be written, as could a book on the male homosocial desire, bonding rituals and identity politics that produced IR's all-white male canon.[40] However, we cannot do justice to these figures as historical subjects without also understanding how they were positioned and read *as women* and how this was fundamental to their work and the history of the wider intellectual field.

But not only as *women*. I do not argue that gender is the most important thing about my cohort. For obvious reasons in a study that encompasses the greatest expansion and contraction of the British Empire, their international thought and its reception were equally shaped by structures and ideologies of race, empire, and class, as well as heteronormativity, that is, intersecting and multiple positionalities.[41] Florence Melian Stawell's *The Growth of International Thought* was a product of her class privilege and status as a white Australian settler abroad. Maud Allen's intellectual biography of Sophy Sanger was a celebration of a middle-class social reformer just as concerned with countering proletarian revolution as international action on the wrongs of child labour and the dangers of white phosphorous.

Some figures were reluctant to define themselves in gendered terms and, like Susan Strange, were indifferent and sometimes hostile toward feminist movements. It would be equally anachronistic to describe others, like Stawell and Allen, as representing some timeless lesbian identity when female friendship was a bedrock of women's intellectual life, or even label them queer as biographical subjects. Then as now, many women chose not to marry men because, as Allen wrote, 'the conditions of marriage at the time seemed to them intolerable'.[42] However, the near-total erasure of all women, queer, and non-binary people from international intellectual history invites the recovery of some not only as *women*, but as figures who were in intellectual and often intimate and sexual partnerships with other women. After Stawell resigned her Newnham College lectureship due to ill health she could keep writing on international relations because of the loving support of her partner Clare Reynolds. Maud Allen's intellectual history of Sophy Sanger is a queer labour of love not because they were sexually intimate—that we cannot know—but because they lived non-heteronormative lives.

As a practice of intellectual and political resistance, still others defined themselves primarily in racial and class terms. Born in Trinidad, Claudia Jones did not receive formal education beyond high school, yet became an original theorist of the 'triple oppression' of Black working-class women and disseminator of Black Atlantic thought in the British metropole. She also died prematurely and penniless. Most other figures were relatively privileged, certainly compared to Jones, including African–American Merze Tate. A lighter-skinned Black woman who grew up on a family-owned farm in the American mid-West on land previously stolen from Native Americans, Tate was a member of the first African–American sorority, Alpha Kappa Alpha, that funded her first year at Oxford. Unlike IR's intellectual and disciplinary historians, I do not conceive international thinking in Britain as 'white'.

Many dozens of thinkers could have been included in this book. I limit the study to those I consider the eighteen most important for understanding the gendered and racialised history of international thinking in twentieth-century Britain. I examine twelve in most detail: Lucie Barbier Zimmern, Margery Perham, Eileen Power, Lucy Philip Mair, Lilian Friedländer Vránek, Merze Tate, Agnes Headlam-Morley, Claudia Jones, Margaret Cleeve, Coral Bell, Rachel Wall and Susan Strange.[43] I also discuss F. Melian Stawell, Elizabeth Wiskemann, Gwladys Jones, Sibyl Crowe, Lilian Knowles, and Betty Behrens.

What makes these figures a cohort? They are all twentieth-century intellectuals born in imperial metropoles or colonies and were defined and read as women. They all thought deeply about international relations in the early to long mid-twentieth century and all spent a substantial portion of their intellectual lives in Britain. They worked in or around academe or related professional fields like think tanks, summer schools, and journalism. All but one, Claudia Jones, had connections to the new intellectual field-in-formation of international relations. I include Jones as the most effective originator and disseminator of Black Atlantic thought in Britain after her deportation from the United States in 1958. The treatment and later reception or non-reception of every one of these thinkers shaped the development of the academic field of IR, yet with only one exception none have received the recognition they deserve. I suggest that recovery history can also illuminate seemingly 'exceptional' thinkers like Susan Strange that intellectual and disciplinary historians thought they knew well.

These figures are also a cohort because with only a few exceptions they were all deeply historical thinkers with a commitment to historical methods. More so than in the United States, international relations began in Britain as a cross-disciplinary field with its closest ties to history. Contrary to frequent claims that international relations in Britain was far more historical than American political science, a low bar given the dominance of rationalist approaches, historical methods were slowly sidelined in the post–World War II project to forge a 'separate IR'.[44] By training or temperament, members of my cohort were highly skilled and creative historians, often seeking to pioneer new approaches to history including moving away from Eurocentrism. They practised international thinking as diplomatic and contemporary historians; social, economic, and world historians; classicists and historical comparativists; or as a form of political education. I show that their historical sensibilities partly account for their marginalisation from IR and their erasure from its intellectual history.

I do not seek the inclusion of my cohort in a new, presumably more 'inclusive' IR canon as if the current racial and gendered hierarchies of the field could be undone in this way.[45] Nor are they presented as figures to emulate, unsung heroines, saints, or victims, even as some faced a near-constant barrage of misogynist and racist abuse. They do not represent a women's 'tradition' of international thought. There are obviously some common themes across their work—for example, Perham, Friedländer, Power, Strange, Jones and Wall all criticised political-science notions of state sovereignty. Yet there is little commonality in their politics, which extend from high Tory appeasement, anticolonial Black Marxism, conservative and liberal imperialism, socialist and feminist internationalism, conservative realism, and antiracist geopolitics.[46] Though many were historians, they were also anthropologists, classicists, an international lawyer, a political economist, a musician, a journalist and an information manager. Instead of looking for a woman's tradition of international thought, or forebears of something now called 'historical IR', I recover my figures as living people, flawed and active agents in their own lives and the intellectual lives of others, and sometimes by interactions with leading 'IR men'.[47] I read them all in the context of a larger history of international thought, the intellectual project for a 'separate IR', and as offering different potentialities and missed opportunities for this field still in formation.

The book is both a recovery history and a critical history of a scholarly field. It turns out that much of the history of 'British IR' is a story of men who hated women, and the intellectual and institutional legacies of misogyny and racism in its earliest institutions, including Chatham House, the British Coordinating Committee for International Studies (BCCIS), founded in 1928, the Department of International Studies (later Relations) at the London School of Economics (LSE), founded in 1927, and the British Committee on the Theory of International Politics, founded in 1959. I confess that I would rather not attend to the men and their networks. Yet I could not write a gendered history without also addressing the men who used their power to create and defend personal fiefdoms, to marry or begin affairs with students or assistants, to commit intellectual amicicide, to consolidate their scholarly identity by caricaturing, ignoring, erasing or gender-typecasting women. There was an emotionally abusive husband, a doctoral supervisor who threatened to throw his graduate student down the stairs and declined to pass her dissertation. There was a male professor who refused to appoint women to academic posts or acknowledge women's scholarship, another who bullied a woman out of her job for having too many children, another who appropriated a woman's idea for a book, and an outright plagiarist of women's work.

Some readers may be impatient with the attention paid to some of these men. They are only discussed when necessary to hold them accountable for their actions and to uncover some of the lesser-known aspects of their intellectual milieux. I could not write the story of British IR without the men who were dependent on a racialised and heterosexual gender order that pushed out women and elevated white male mediocrities, or who vilified some women. Some men were good mentors and tried to support their intellectual partners, wives and/or women students. In a reversal of the usual gendered plagiarism, one husband, Alfred Zimmern, may have co-written a book that was published solely in his wife's name. Others recognised some of the most exceptional women, like Eileen Power and Susan Strange, as their intellectual equals. Gilbert Murray claimed for himself Stawell's idea for a book on the League but was a strong supporter of women's suffrage and education, and a Council member of Somerville, one of Oxford's first women's colleges, and an early mentor to Lucy Philip Mair.[48]

Not all the men were mediocrities, misogynists, and racists. However, one figure stands out as all three. He also happened to do more than anyone to shape twentieth-century British IR.[49] Charles Manning (1894–1978) was a white supremacist South African legal scholar who held the most senior position in Britain's largest IR department for thirty-two years, the Montague Burton Professorship of IR at the LSE. He was also a leading figure at BCCIS, founded in 1928 by the League of Nations International Institute of Intellectual Cooperation to advance IR teaching and research.[50] Manning was also singularly influential over the careers and thinking of leading men associated with the British Committee on the Theory of International Politics.

Manning published little but devoted himself to establishing international relations as a separate university subject. Under his influence, an interdisciplinary field that included disciplined and trained historians, lawyers, anthropologists, classicists, and others was transformed into a field with no specialist methodological training at all. He conceived the new IR specialist as a 'Superman', meaning an expert in no one scholarly method or discipline, rather an amateur in them all.[51] British IR's intellectual standing and even legitimacy never recovered, and its relation to its two closest disciplines, political science and history, never settled. Some of Manning's modes of thought are still present in the norms of the field today.

This book presents new evidence for IR's intellectual failures and its remedies. I return to key moments in the 1930s, 1950s and 1970s to show the marginalisation of women, people of colour, and historical method narrowed IR's intellectual resources and impoverished its work. It is no coincidence that Manning refused to hire a single woman to a permanent post, married one of his undergraduate students, and erased from his department's history the woman who did much of its IR teaching for almost two decades. Even some of IR's earliest leading men, including historians E. H. Carr and Martin Wight, became alienated from the field, abandoning IR to return to history.

Histories of thought matter because they draw intellectual and methodological boundaries around a scholarly field, shaping its present and future. Intellectual and disciplinary histories are legitimation projects; they deplete or enhance a field's intellectual resources by introducing novel themes, temporalities, and geographies. Recent historiography has challenged the long-held view that IR's intellectual history is a series of 'great debates' beginning in the 1920s when so-called 'realists' and 'idealists' debated the merits, morality, and possibilities of the League of Nations. There has been much focus on the post–1945 American moment, including how realism's reimagining of empire was constituted in the exile of central European Jews.[52] Others have shown how projects of imperial reform were central to early visions of the new intellectual field, demoting the significance of the world's first IR professorship, established in the small Welsh seaside town of Aberystwyth in 1919.[53]

My cohort poses further challenges to IR's intellectual histories and founding myths, including the singularity of IR's leading men and the exceptionalism of one woman; the subliminal feminisation of 'idealism'; the existence, location, content, and protagonists of any 'first great debate' in IR, nuancing what such a debate could be; the myth that British IR's leading men bequeathed a historical field; and the significance of powerful intellectual currents coming from across the Atlantic. Not American realism, but the exilic Black Atlantic tradition offered Britons a different vision of empire, Britishness, international relations, and the public audiences for international thought. None of this cohort were obsessed with defining themselves against American political science. To them, depending on class, nation, and racial position, the United States was variously a place of birth and early childhood, a nation steeped in white supremacy and expulsion, a source of students, a location of scholarships and career advancement, and an intellectual culture in need of tutoring or friendly critique.

In the specifically British imperial context, this cohort also challenge assumptions about the disciplines, locations and genres of international thinking. Oxford and Cambridge, including their independent self-governing and multidisciplinary women's colleges, become more significant; Aberystwyth and LSE become less so; and the most interesting international thinking at these institutions is found outside their IR departments. To some extent, this is a very English and, to a lesser extent, Welsh story. But the cohort also raises questions about Britain as a multiracial and imperial formation, the significance of decolonisation and the new territorial and racial definition of Britain as post-imperial and white to the relatively belated establishment of British IR's first professional organisation. Whether they identified as IR scholars or not, they offer a different genealogy of international thinking not as saviours of contemporary IR, but in revealing intellectual paths taken and not taken, profoundly shaping the professional development and historical self-understanding of a field still struggling with its identity.

## Methods and Outline

Much of the empirical record for this book was assembled from scratch using primary, predominantly archival sources. To begin to identify women teaching international relations in the academy, I combed through institutional records and lecture lists of the major locations of IR teaching, including in Oxford, Cambridge, London, Aberystwyth, Edinburgh, and Manchester; identified over one hundred different sets of papers in over twenty locations ranging from personal papers, personnel files, correspondence, lecture notes and other teaching materials. Other primary sources include dozens of books, hundreds of academic journal and newspaper articles, book reviews, teaching materials, internal university memos, journalism, radio addresses, images, memoir and autobiographical writing, speeches, poetry, obituaries and oral histories, some newly created through the Leverhulme Project on Women and the History of International Thought.[54]

I deal with various sources in different ways. Oral histories are a valuable window into one person's memory of historical events, not objective fact; they augment rather than underpin my account of an historical moment or figure. Autobiographical writing is not only a source of information. It is also a writing of the self in ways that can shape the development of an intellectual field. I also combine archival and visual analysis of photographic images to show how some in my cohort crafted their own identity and persona, how they fashioned themselves through their choice of clothes, posture, body language, facial expression, how they looked at the camera, how they performed gender, race, class, and intellectual power.[55]

Some of my thinkers are well known outside IR and are subjects of full-length biographies. I draw on these and other secondary literature to supplement my reading of primary sources and my own arguments about, and contextualisation, of these thinkers.[56] I account for my cohort's intellectual production on international relations but also present them as biographical and historical subjects with intimate lives. However, my account of their intimate worlds is obviously incomplete, and I refrain from speculating about their inner lives.

I encountered the commonplace methodological hurdles of feminist recovery, including partial, incomplete, or non-existent papers, and other forms of gendered erasure, including research and writing by wives or mistresses who received little or no credit for their work. My findings are clearly shaped by the intersectional oppressions that produce different forms of inclusion and exclusion in archives and other primary sources. Some personal papers were never kept and will never be recovered. Some, like Agnes Headlam-Morley's, were held (until very recently) with their father's; or, like Lucie Zimmern's, subsumed and uncatalogued with their husbands; or, like Rachel Wall's, saved in the private family home of a loving niece hoping one day that an historian would ask to see them. For some figures, the sources are abundant, and I could have written more. In one case, Zimmern's, they are so abundant that—given her proximity and influence on interwar IR's leading man—her erasure from IR's history continues to shock.

Most of my cohort worked in or were connected to elite British higher education, a setting both of new freedoms for some women and of colonial subjugation for others. In both Britain and the United States, women and Black people entered the academic profession through the historically Black and/or women's colleges created in the late nineteenth century. It is not surprising that Robert Vitalis's recovery of a counter-discourse to white supremacist IR in the United States centred on a cohort of African–American scholars at the historically Black Howard University and their links to the wider Black intellectual world.[57] This study similarly recovers historical women's colleges, among other locations, as sites of women's international thought, including one of Vitalis's lead protagonists, Merze Tate.

I do not assume that the academy is the only or best location of international thinking, on the contrary; only that recovery history must include women both in and outside of this setting. My focus on thinkers of the 'British world' does not indicate that other national–imperial contexts are less important, or that the intellectual field emerged in the imperial centre rather than in and with its peripheries.[58] Neither the British nor the American cases are universal models against which comparable histories in other locations should be understood to converge or diverge.[59] I neither wish to exaggerate or downplay the significance of Britain to the wider intellectual field. However, my reading of the distinctiveness of British IR's development is different to existing accounts. Some of the limitations of this study are imposed by the class and racial hierarchies of academe, in which only some exceptional women of colour could transgress with great difficulty and at great personal cost, and some by my own limitations as a scholar. There is much more scope to explore the international thinking of differently racialised and nationalised women in the British world, both inside and outside academe, and histories centring different imperial, national, and postcolonial contexts.[60]

The book is structured broadly chronologically with chapters arranged thematically around one or more thinkers. Chapter 1 returns to a familiar moment and location in disciplinary histories, the Welsh town of Aberystwyth, where two wealthy sisters and a brother established the first professorship of International Politics. We begin here not to reinstate 'Aber 1919' as IR's founding moment. It was the founding moment and location not of an academic discipline but of a love story, a marriage, and an intellectual partnership that upends numerous assumptions about the thinkers, locations, possibilities, and racial politics of interwar IR. We find the future wife of a canonical thinker, one half of IR's first celebrity power couple, practising her distinctive and original approach to international relations *before* the first IR department was established. Lucie Barbier Zimmern became the originator—and initial victor—of a debate with one of American IR's 'founding fathers', Nicholas Spykman, on how IR should be taught. In Aberystwyth, we also find IR's first spousal hire, the husband of Lilian Friedländer, the first woman appointed to an IR department, illuminating diverging professional trajectories from heterosexual marriage.

International thinking in Britain during the twentieth century is obviously bound up with imperial reform and the management of global decline. Easily the most important white British historian, commentator, and public intellectual on twentieth-century empire and decolonisation was Margery Perham. Yet while intellectual and disciplinary historians have paid much attention to empire, there has been little to no engagement in IR with this most important thinker on empire at its end.[61] Perham's marginalisation delayed by decades IR's reckoning with empire, including its legacies and critics. More than any other British thinker closely associated with the new IR field, Perham engaged extensively with Black interlocuters, including radical Black intellectual traditions, as will be seen in chapters 2 and 8. She also bridged the intellectual and institutional gap between the two generations of men on whom IR's intellectual and disciplinary historians have obsessed, the interwar imperial founders of British IR's earliest scientific institutions and the post–World War II men of the British Committee on the Theory of International Politics.

Dismissed as unscientific propaganda, and almost entirely neglected in IR's intellectual and disciplinary histories, white women's popular writing on international and imperial affairs was responsible for the first English-language book to use the term 'international thought'. Chapter 3 discusses this genre through the early work of Eileen Power and F. Melian Stawell. It shows some of British IR's most important founding institutions and research methods were defined in gendered opposition to this popular form of writing. The science of international relations was consolidated not in universities, but through the painstaking work of documentation, collecting, arranging, reading clippings from the national and international press, and the organisation and maintenance of reliable facts in libraries of documents and statistics at Britain's most influential international relations 'think tank',

Chatham House, all overseen by Margaret Cleeve. No other figure is so closely associated with the success of a central institution of British international relations that was also major location of women's intellectual labour. Cleeve's case, and the army of backroom Chatham Houseworkers and researchers she oversaw, illuminates changing valuations of professional worth and gendered politics of memorialisation and non-memorialisation in early white women's IR.

A new science of international relations was forged at Chatham House under Margaret Cleeve. Yet the question of IR's standing as a separate university subject remained an open question in the 1930s. Mary Gwladys Jones was teaching International Law and Organisation at Cambridge, likely drawn into the subject through her intimate friendship with Eileen Power. The course was dropped in 1945 due to doubts among historians about the intellectual rigour and presentism of the new science. Chapter 4 further develops the themes of intimate relationships and conflicting visions of the new field through the first women appointed to IR's earliest departments. As a teacher of a considerable proportion of students in the largest IR department, Lucy Philip Mair had a clear vision of IR teaching, but it was very different to the senior male colleague who later erased her and her subject of colonial administration from IR's history. We examine the highly gendered reasoning of the London-based scholars *au fait* with fragments of sociology which they used to justify IR as a separate university subject.

During the 1920s and 1930s, the vanguard of international thinking at LSE was not in the then International Studies Department, and certainly not by its Montague Burton Professor. It was by Eileen Power, a social and economic historian in the Department of History. Chapter 5 discusses the most extraordinary and methodologically consequential marginalisation from the project for a separate IR. Power was no more peripheral to the interwar field than numerous of her male contemporaries who are repeatedly analysed in histories, having won the male game of intellectual influence. As an economic historian writing histories of the transition from a medieval pluriverse of empires to a world of national–imperial states, Power's scholarship at the intersection of world history and international relations anticipated the second generation of the *Annales* school, which influenced world systems theory, and calls into question the later attempt to justify a separate IR on a radical distinction between sociology and historical method. Power also belied the schism between Economics and Politics necessary for Susan Strange's later project for a new International Political Economy (IPE).

Both Eileen Power and the LSE men of the British Coordinating Committee for International Studies agreed on the limits of traditional approaches to diplomatic history that exclusively focused on the doings of diplomats and other 'great men'. Yet Power also understood the indispensability of the historian's craft and the many ways to study diplomacy. Chapter 6 examines Merze Tate's three hard years as the first African–American to earn a graduate degree at Oxford. Her training in diplomatic history was the grounding for her later antiracist approach to geopolitics. At Oxford, Tate faced the vicissitudes of graduate supervision, institutional blundering and the personal and intellectual risks of extreme financial precarity, racism and the burden of racial representation. She went on to become one of the most significant international thinkers of the twentieth century not because she studied at Oxford but despite it.

Chapter 7 turns to Tate's uncredited supervisor at Oxford, and the second most vilified woman in British IR, Agnes Headlam-Morley, whom I read alongside her colleague, Sibyl Crowe. Given her standing as Oxford's Montague Burton Professor of IR for three decades, Headlam-Morley became the caricature of the 'diplomatic historian' for the IR men trying to establish a separate subject, and the scapegoat for Oxford's delay in developing an IR graduate degree. I challenge the presumption in existing histories that it was a lack of entrepreneurial ambition or supposed commitment to a narrow form of diplomatic history that explains Headlam-Morley's alleged refusal to 'develop' IR. Rather she was the gendered foil and constitutive Other for the intellectual projects and insecurities of some of early IR's leading men. If IR failed as an intellectual project, then how, we might ask, do their intellectual projects and legacies measure up today?

Under Headlam-Morley's reign, imperialism remained a core international relations subject at Oxford, often taught by the university's 'sentinels of the British Empire'.[62] Chapter 8 returns to the twentieth century's most important white British intellectual on decolonisation, the Establishment's authoritative voice on empire. We focus on Margery Perham's skill at acknowledging and deflecting Britain's imperial crimes, her intellectual and emotional performance of white Britons' moral anguish and effort to assuage Britain's wounded dignity. We also examine Perham's account of the political psychology of anticolonial critique and consciousness of her own and white Britain's racial positionality. Ironically, Perham's assimilation of empire's loss, and influence on some of British IR's leading men, lay the groundwork for her own erasure from the field and for Susan Strange's project for a post-imperial IR.

In the post-war American academy, race and empire were expunged from IR by the marginalisation of African–American intellectuals.[63] With fewer Black and brown thinkers in the British academy, the white men of BCCIS and the British Committee need only ignore the 'other special relationship' between Britain and racialised thinkers of the Black Atlantic.[64] In refusing this political and intellectual gift of Black radical thought, the source of some of the most penetrating analyses of twentieth-century world politics, IR's early men further impoverished the field.[65] If, for many of its early founders, the task of the new field was to shape public opinion, then without question Claudia Jones was the most impressive and consequential figure in this vein. Chapter 9 examines Jones's international thought and pedagogy in the two institutions she founded after her deportation and exile to London.

By the 1950s and 1960s, a new generation of white women was making its way in the academy. Chapter 10 contrasts the stories of Rachel Wall and Coral Bell to illuminate different political and intellectual trajectories for the field at its elite locations and the benefits and risks of male patronage. Seeming stories of professional 'failure' and personal heartbreak are as revealing of the ableist and gendered history of a field and its criteria of failure and 'success' as cases of professional triumph and recognition. They also reveal intellectual paths not taken and the effects of accidents and contingencies, including the decision of whom to love.

The most conventionally successful figure in the history of British IR is the only woman to come close to receiving the recognition she deserves. However, Susan Strange's intellectual labours alone do not explain her legacy and reception. Strange's active fashioning of her own intellectual persona, including her deployment of sex and gender in autobiographical writing, was crucial to how she was read and received. Chapter 11 tells this story through what was most exceptional about Strange, not that she was a woman, but that she was a mother of six children who worked for pay. The most interesting aspects of Strange's persona, her iconoclasm and irreverence toward IR's male mediocrities and rational-choice theory, helped fashion a post-imperial British IR that also upheld some of its other more conservative norms.

The conclusion reflects on the three main sources of British IR's failure—methodological, racist–imperial, and patriarchal—and what the intellectual traditions, genealogies, and resources recovered in this history contribute to conversations about IR's futures.

# 1

# Aberystwyth 1919: A Love Story

But have you met Sir Alfred's Wife?

—J.F.F.[1]

Columbus didn't discover America. I discovered America.

—LADY LUCIE ZIMMERN

ABERYSTWYTH HAS NOT fared well in new disciplinary histories of International Relations (IR). Scholars used to believe that IR's origins were in the noble venture behind the world's first IR chair, established in 1919, the Woodrow Wilson Professorship at University College of Wales in Aberystwyth.[2] Three Welsh sibling philanthropists, Gwendoline, Margaret, and David Davies, wanted to honour Wilson who, as president of the United States, presided over the Paris Peace negotiations and championed the League of Nations. The siblings contributed equally to the 20,000 pounds of their vast inherited wealth to honour the memory of fallen students in World War I and to support the study of the world's myriad post-war problems.[3] The donor's first choice as inaugural holder of the chair was Alfred Zimmern, drafter of the Foreign Office proposal for the League of Nations, renowned international relations educator, and recent divorcé.[4]

In IR's disciplinary history, the Wilsonian moment was also the 'Aberystwyth moment'.[5] But Wilson's 'peace' was a peace among white nations, and the university teaching on international relations, which preceded 1919, was rooted in race science, inter-imperial rivalry, and colonial administration.[6] Few textbooks now centre Aberystwyth 1919, noting that IR's first journal, *The Journal of Race Development*, was established in the United States in 1910. At its centenary in 2019, Aberystwyth's IR doctoral researchers called on their department to dissociate from Wilson, following Princeton's decision to remove the white supremacist and segregationist's name from its School of Public and International Affairs.[7] At the time of writing, the department still honours Wilson's name.

In pointing to empire and race as IR's more immediate and telling origins, the new historiography has demoted Aberystwyth and the 'myth of 1919', often gleefully.[8] For an academic department in a small town whose attractiveness to faculty and graduate students in no small measure has hinged on its heritage, there is a lot at stake for Aberystwyth in the new disciplinary history. Hence in a sharp rejoinder, Aberystwyth Professor Ken Booth accused IR's new historians of sexism, conceptual confusion, and sanctimony. Some only mention David Davies and ignore Gwendoline and Margaret as 'midwives at the birth of IR'.[9] Yet Aberystwyth's own David Davies Memorial Institute does the same.[10] In a telling use of the passive voice, Booth conceded that some 'skeletons' in Aberystwyth's closet 'have been exposed'. But skeletons 'are artifacts of their time and as such need a certain understanding'.[11] IR's founding in 1919 may not have been 'a virgin birth', Booth noted, because the 'sources of international thought' have 'ancient and multiple sites' and 'stretch back through the centuries'.[12] Yet, 'IR', he insisted, was 'born as an institutionalized academic *discipline* in 1919'.[13]

This is doubtful. Aberystwyth was only *one* location in the emergence of a new intellectual and interdisciplinary field in formation whose intellectual and institutional roots preceded 1919. This is not because the first attempt to think about, across, and beyond borders stretches into the distant past 'lost in time'; the question is when, why, and where particular intellectual fields and new discourses become subjects of university enquiry.[14] The creation of a chair and even a cross-disciplinary department does not equate to founding an 'academic discipline', as if a university professorship or even the organised university teaching of a subject is 'synonymous with a discipline'.[15] As historian Jan Stöckmann has recently pointed out, this is to 'underestimate the intellectual and practical traditions that gave rise to the study of IR'.[16]

The discourse of 'international relations', the origins of the university teaching and research in this field, are not 'lost in time'. They have a specific origin and location in Europe and North America between the late nineteenth and early twentieth century.[17] The world-historical context for the rise of this new field were multiple and converging: the closing of imperial frontiers and a new world order that had to be understood and managed as a whole, the emergence of non-European imperial powers, anticolonial movements, revolutionary workers and women. The problem of international relations is not ancient, but modern.

Yet those who mock the 'myth of 1919' should not be so satisfied. In dislodging Aberystwyth's place from the centre of IR's origins they have missed one of the most interesting and important stories in IR's intellectual and disciplinary history, a story that precedes 1919. This story is fundamental to understanding Aberystwyth's significance, but also one of the most widespread and now obsolete claims about IR's intellectual history: that the main story of the field is progression through a series of 'great debates' beginning in the 1920s between so-called 'Wilsonian idealists' who sought to reform great power politics through international institutions and hard-headed 'realists' more 'directed toward building up an empirical or causal science' to study the relations between great powers.[18] This was followed by a debate between social science behaviourists and more historical traditionalists in the 1950s and 1960s; an 'inter-paradigm debate between realists, liberals and Marxists in the 1970s and 1980s; and between rationalists/positivists and post-positivists in the 1990s and 2000s'.[19]

It is now widely agreed that the so-called first 'great debate' was a myth invented in the 1940s by self-described realists seeking to justify their dominance of IR in the United States.[20] This is broadly correct. Yet if the criterion for the existence of a debate is a 'series of exchanges between interlocuters holding opposing "idealist" and "realist" points of view', then such a debate did, in fact, occur in the 1920s.[21] It took the form of a power struggle for intellectual and administrative control over the most influential educationalist projects of interwar IR in Geneva, when the boundaries between the feminised arts and internationalist pedagogy and IR as a masculine social science came into conflict. In purely intellectual terms, the most significant event for interwar international intellectual history in Aberystwyth in 1919 was not the appointment of Alfred Zimmern to the Wilson Chair in April. It was in December, when Aberystwyth's leading musical persona Lucie Barbier invited Zimmern to deliver the opening remarks before a concerto played by Barbier's friend, the 'world famous' French pianist and conductor Alfred Cortot. Having recently returned from Palestine, Alfred Zimmern duly obliged. Madame Barbier, soprano, pianist, and orator, then took the stage, introducing the programme of music to an 'enormous crowd'.[22] Soon after, perhaps even on stage, Zimmern and Barbier fell in love. Aberystwyth 1919 was not a Wilsonian moment. It was the Lucie Barbier moment.[23]

## IR's First Power Couple

The university teaching of International Relations in Aberystwyth did not have an auspicious start. After less than two years as the inaugural Woodrow Wilson Professor, Alfred Zimmern resigned, claiming to have 'been seriously misled as to the academic standing' of the college and the quality of its students: 'the work could be done by a Schoolmaster'. It was 'neither possible nor desirable' to teach international relations to undergraduates.[24] Yet Zimmern's employers knew that he did not resign because of the alleged quality of Welsh students, or even of his own accord. As numerous disciplinary histories have noted, Zimmern was forced to resign. Never mentioned is that Aberystwyth's better known and more controversial figure, Madame Lucie Hirsch Barbier, was also forced out. The renowned internationalist resigned the Woodrow Wilson Chair because he fell in love with the wrong woman.

Lucie Hirsch was born in Besançon, France in 1875. Her father, Maurice Hirsch, converted from Judaism to Protestantism in 1881, when she was six, becoming a Protestant pastor. Her Huguenot Swiss-born mother, Olympe Flotron, was a teacher.[25] Hirsch attended the Lycée Molière in Paris and studied music at the Sorbonne, specialising in soprano and piano in a period of musical and artistic renaissance in France. In 1901, she made her singing debut in England at the Royal Albert Hall and married French scholar André Barbier in 1902. As a 'trailing spouse', Lucie Barbier followed André to lectureships at the University College Wales at Bangor, to Manchester in 1903, then the University College in Aberystwyth in 1909.

In Manchester, Barbier became executive secretary of La Société de Concerts Français, Britain's most active branch outside London. In a period of political, musical and artistic renaissance in France, Barbier was a leading figure in the musical 'Entente Cordiale' between Britain and France, the cultural accompaniment to the new alliance cemented in 1904. After France's humiliating defeat in the Franco-Prussia war, and as 'an ardent French patriot',[26] Barbier wanted to supplant German hegemony in classical music and contribute to greater cross-cultural understanding, to new internationalist ideas about peace, and to cultural diplomacy. 'Let us, then, have good music from all parts of the world', she claimed in 1911, 'the beautiful has no nationality'.[27] She organised concerts and gave lectures on French music, using her contacts with celebrated French composers and musicians.[28]

After moving to Aberystwyth in 1909, Lucie Barbier took control of musical affairs and continued her cultural and geopolitical mission. She became assistant lecturer in music at the college, teaching French music, singing, and conducting, and founding and directing Aberystwyth's musical club. In west Wales, she knew exactly whom to cultivate. In 1911, Barbier invited the most artistic of the wealthy Davies siblings, Gwendoline, to perform violin as a study in one of Barbier's lectures and developed a relationship with the philanthropic sisters. During World War I, she organised concerts to raise funds for Belgian refugees and wrote to *The Guardian* about the 'plague' of Germans in Alsace.[29]

Long before the world's first IR professorship was founded through the Davies's patronage, Barbier persuaded the sisters to donate 75,000 pounds to fund a new Department for Instrumental Music. Barbier directed the money—considerably more money than the Wilson endowment, and originally given to her musical club—toward a new university department in support of her own political and aesthetic vision of international relations: musical cultural diplomacy would help bring 'peace in the world'.[30] Later, in 1951, she told an interviewer that music and world politics were 'her life' and 'closely allied'. 'Both Arts of movement—they are meditation put into movement, and are almost always truthful'.[31]

The Frenchwoman's home was considered a 'cultural Mecca' in the Welsh town, yet her preference for French music upset many locals.[32] Given Lucie Barbier's dominance of the classical music scene, she faced numerous 'accusations and insinuations', above all, favouritism toward French musicians and teachers. Many locals are reported to have found the Frenchwoman physically and intellectually 'frightening or overwhelming'.[33] They struggled with 'her animated gesticulating style of talking'.[34] Three decades later an historian of Welsh music was informed 'that her pale auburn hair, which was abundant, wobbled and sometimes fell down when she was excited; and some remember not only the cottage-loaf top to a generous figure, but also the loose Magyar frock girdled with decorative beads and a mincing walk'.[35]

In an open letter to the editor of the college paper, likely orchestrated by Lucie Barbier, her students mounted a strong defence against 'accusers' who had 'not always kept within the bounds of courtesy'. There would be no Department of Instrumental Music without Barbier's efforts, and the French professors were selected by Gwendoline Davies herself, who wished the students to receive instruction in French.[36] Art and music were also central to the Davies sisters' progressive vision of 'social services for South Wales and international peace for all'.[37] They were early benefactors of Lucie Barbier's brand of cultural internationalism. David was more interested in sport.

## 'Nasty Woman'

Both Alfred Zimmern and Lucie Barbier were in their mid-to-late forties, and Alfred was already divorced when the couple met.[38] The scandal was that Lucie was still married to Aberystwyth's Professor of French Literature. André and Lucie Barbier had two daughters, Edith and Evelyn, by then aged seventeen and twelve. In the summer of 1920, Lucie informed André that she wanted a divorce and 'in a very straight forward manner and very firmly', André later recalled, Alfred declared his intention to ask Lucie 'to share his life' as soon as she was free.[39] André initiated divorce proceedings in France on the grounds of desertion. The divorce was granted in his favour. Edith remained with André who was left in dire financial straits, paying off Lucie's debts, according to their granddaughter.[40]

The private affair, resolved by the divorce, became a scandal in the conservative and Methodist town. 'Local' members of the College Council were outraged at Zimmern's behaviour.[41] In March 1921, the Council established a Special Committee to enquire into 'certain circumstances' and make a recommendation about Zimmern's tenure of the Wilson Chair.[42] Given the dubious grounds for asking for his resignation, let alone firing him, the Special Committee chose to make no recommendation, referring the matter back to the College Council.[43] Zimmern had broken no law and, according to one Council member, the only grounds for asking him to resign was in 'the interests of the students and to prevent a very difficult and almost impossible situation'.[44] By April, locals on the Council had become 'very alarmed'[45] and 'restive'[46] at the delay in removing Zimmern, threatening to pass a motion calling for his resignation.

Initially, Zimmern resisted efforts to remove him on the basis of 'idle gossip'.[47] David Davies, college vice-president, warned that the very effort to force Zimmern out made it more likely that he would stay.[48] André Barbier had asked his ex-wife not to return to Aberystwyth and matters were 'raised to a high pitch' when the Zimmerns, now married, took rooms in the Queen's Hotel on the seafront and met with students.[49] Some thought Zimmern should be warned that his presence was 'not desirable'.[50] One anxious local wrote to Davies that 'there would not be the same objection if Prof. Zimmern came alone. I should be glad to have your advice . . . in the event of their . . . continuing to invite young and immature students to their rooms'.[51] Yet, replied Davies, Zimmern had just as much right as anyone to stay at the hotel. 'I am not a Trade Union leader . . . I cannot suggest any means of prevention as I presume that picketing would hardly be dignified'.[52]

By June 1921, the Council was desperate to find some evidence to use against Zimmern, inviting André Barbier to a special meeting to reveal details of the divorce.[53] André claimed that 'certain things took place which would be extremely unpleasant to me and to the children . . . I wanted it to be possible for my children to respect their mother all their lives'.[54] Despite the Council's apparent interest in her private life, Lucie Zimmern was not invited to address the meeting. She had resigned her college position in 1920, and she and her youngest daughter became financially dependent on Zimmern. All formal Council deliberations and internal correspondence concerned Alfred. Lucie mattered only because she had been Barbier's and was now Zimmern's wife.

Alfred was invited to speak and was proud and combative. He refused to 'allow anybody to criticise' his 'private affairs or conduct', or to speak about his wife. His written statement focused entirely on the college's failure to meet the academic standards he had been led to expect, reminding the Council that the Davies siblings had approached *him* to take the chair.[55] Zimmern's only consideration when contemplating whether to 'shake the dust of Wales from my feet' was intellectual, the poor 'academic standing in this college'.[56] He would henceforth spend more time on his international travel and expected that on his return he would 'find that steps have been taken to enable me to undertake the teaching side of my work'.[57]

Within three weeks, Zimmern had resigned. The International Politics Department's main news to the College's Court of Governors in 1922 was that a group of women students organised year-long study circles to address international problems, culminating in a summer conference attended by around thirty-five students.[58] Two years later, Zimmern's successor, historian Charles Webster, awarded Lillian Friedländer the Wilson Studentship for her MA degree.

It is difficult to assess whether the already existing local resentment toward Lucie shaped the College response to the 'Zimmern affair'. Probably with the small-town xenophobia and misogyny of some of its residents in mind, Alfred's *Impressions of Wales*, published in 1921, extremely harshly pointed to the 'jealousies and suspicions which run riot in Welsh life'. Too many in Wales suffered a 'dislike of outstanding personalities' and, compared to Scotland, Wales was 'much more timid, more imitative, more backward in every respect'. Its universities were 'too weak, too unassuming, too mediocre, to establish living contacts with the thought of the wider world'.[59]

Of all the figures in this book, Lucie Zimmern's physical and intellectual presence and ambitions elicited the most openly misogynistic and xenophobic tirades. Chaim Weizmann, future first president of Israel and former colleague of André Barbier's at Manchester, thought it was 'awful' that Alfred and Lucie were married. She was a 'terrible witch'.[60] Her father had converted from Judaism to Protestantism and Weizmann blamed Lucie for Alfred's estrangement from political Zionism. Tory feminist and anti-Semite Nancy Astor claimed 'Zim' had 'been had!'. Alfred threatened to sue Astor for libel and never spoke to her again.[61] People found Lucie 'ambitious',[62] 'abrasive',[63] and 'overpoweringly verbose and enthusiastic'.[64] For some, she was interwar IR's 'nasty woman'.[65]

Yet almost as soon as she left Aberystwyth, and for almost three decades, Lucie Zimmern was a sought-after public speaker on international affairs, lecturing around the English-speaking world on topics related to music and international relations, the status of women, and her original subject of Anglo-French relations. Press reviews were full of praise of her oratory skills, describing her as 'cultured and charming';[66] 'warm and vivacious';[67] 'an accomplished scholar in world affairs';[68] 'well-read and cultured';[69] 'a woman with a vibrant personality, and great cerebral capacity',[70] 'a brilliant woman . . . who can talk like chain lightening';[71] 'the "hit" of the evening'.[72] Lecturing with 'Gallic fire', Lucie was often 'received with more enthusiasm than' Alfred.[73]

The moralism and misogyny of some Aberystwyth 'locals' may be criticised today, as could Alfred's unforgiving response. Yet the patriarchy that excluded her from the college deliberations is paralleled in contemporary IR historiography, even works centring Alfred. If referred to at all, Lucie Zimmern is usually only mentioned as the cause of Alfred's resignation from the Wilson Chair.[74] Sometimes she is not named but referred to as Alfred's 'wife'.[75] IR historiography has scarcely moved beyond centring the singular white male canonical thinker.[76]

Yet the moral panic that forced Alfred Zimmern out of the Wilson Chair meant that Aberystwyth lost not only 'the most influential representative' of interwar IR.[77] They lost Lucie Zimmern and IR's first power couple, 'internationally noted authorities',[78] even celebrity speakers, teachers, and writers who co-founded the Geneva School of International Studies in 1923. They also lost the main protagonist, and initial victor, in what might be thought of as IR's first 'great debate'. Her victory was local and short-lived, and Lucie Zimmern was written out of the history of the field. But recovering her story also offers an alternative genealogy of approaches to IR that includes not only Lucie and the Davies sisters, but also African–American Merze Tate.

## Polyphony in Geneva

The Geneva School of International Studies, often referred to as the Zimmern School, ran for sixteen years between 1923 and 1939, and was Lucie's as much as Alfred Zimmern's creation, a product of their marital and intellectual partnership.[79] However, Lucie was the largest single influence on the school's organisation, conception, and delivery of its core teaching programme and what was most distinctive about its intellectual agenda. Her centrality is captured in the school's archive, and visually represented in Figure 1.1., a black-and-white group portrait, which Lucie Zimmern was likely responsible for organising, staging and preserving.

Lucie Zimmern was highly conscious of herself as a figure of historical importance, ensuring her letters, concert programmes, newspapers and other clippings related to the La Société de Concerts Français were bequeathed to her granddaughter, a musical historian, who deposited them at the National Library of Wales.[80] After Alfred's knighthood in 1936, Lady Zimmern actively curated her famous husband's archive, ensuring that a considerable collection of her own papers, correspondence, unpublished writings, and clippings were preserved with his. The collection should be considered joint papers instead of just Alfred's.[81]

In the portrait, Lucie sits front-and-centre surrounded by tutors and students, her head slightly tilted toward Alfred, who sits to her right. She is in Geneva by virtue of their marriage, officially only 'assistant to the director'. But this is not merely an image of a wife and assistant. She was centre stage at the school itself: its five main subject groupings were Economics, Psychology, Law, Seminar, and 'Mrs. Zimmern'.[82]

One of numerous internationalist educational initiatives of the 1920s, the Zimmern School was the most influential during its time. The Zimmerns attracted numerous high-profile figures to lecture, including John Maynard Keynes, Jane Addams, Halford Mackinder, Arthur Salter, Rachel Crowdy, and Lewis Mumford. They also invited junior academics associated with the new IR field, including Lilian Vránek, née Friedländer, assistant lecturer at Zimmern's erstwhile department in Aberystwyth, and Agnes Headlam-Morley, later Alfred's successor as Oxford's Montague Burton Chair.[83] The school was a product of the Zimmerns' intellectual and pedagogical agendas, but also of the internationalist educationalist moment and of American philanthropy. The school's Executive Committee was based in New York, with a large proportion of women members, including Virginia Gildersleeve, co-founder of

FIGURE 1.1. Geneva School of International Studies c.1930s. Photographer Unknown. Courtesy of Bodleian Library, University of Oxford

the International Federation of University Women, with her partner, Caroline Spurgeon.[84] Students were multinational, multiracial and mixed-gendered, though heavily reliant on numbers from the United States. In 1936, the school admitted seventy-six students from twenty-six 'different nationalities', including twenty-four from the US, six English, one Scot, one Welsh and 'four of Asiatic racial cultures' (meaning China, India, Syria, and Iran).[85] Forty-one students were identified as men and thirty-five as women. By 1937, the school admitted seventy-eight students from twenty-three countries, nearly 40 percent identified as women.[86] Its deputy director was Yale Professor Nicholas Spykman, a 'decisive' figure in the dominant realist approach to American IR after World War II.[87]

On a basic level, Lucie Zimmern oversaw the school's day-to-day activities and—irritating Deputy Director Spykman—occasionally used the director's office during Alfred's frequent trips to the International Institute of Intellectual Cooperation in Paris. She organised the school's practical and promotional work, including securing its premises, fundraising, initiating alumni associations, soliciting numerous messages of support, as well as editing and writing for the School's bilingual journal, *Comprendre*. She roped in members of her family and, on Lucie Zimmern's insistence, the school's location was Geneva's Conservatoire of Music.[88] According to one former student, the building's 'accustomed sounds of vocal and instrumental efforts were replaced by reverberations from lectures, discussions, arguments'.[89] But the choice was more than metaphorical.

Drawing on her own concept of 'polyphonic thinking',[90] the pedagogy and intellectual agenda of the Geneva School was the most refined and developed expression of Lucie Zimmern's conception of polyphonic internationalism. Polyphony indicates more than the simple notion of multiplicity, the existence of more than one culture or peoples. It represented plurality, the existence of many *kinds* of cultures that required harmonisation. As one student recalled, quoting Lucie, 'music appreciation is just as essential to world peace as is the study of international problems . . . "If you can't sing in harmony or feel the rhythm of a piece of music, you don't have polyphonic souls, and if you don't have polyphonic souls [then] you can never understand world problems"'.[91] Constant intellectual and cultural exchange was the necessary underpinning of international harmony, or in Lucie's term, 'a synchronization of syntheses'.[92] As she wrote in 1928: 'We must aim at a society which will be a diversity, not a uniformity, a harmonization, not a standardization, an orchestra, not a masculine solo'.[93]

Lady Zimmern saw herself as a highly trained and skilled cultural diplomat. She had already put her ideas into practice through her cultural diplomacy with La Société de Concerts Français and as director of musical affairs in Aberystwyth. A later biographical sketch, almost certainly drafted by Lucie, described her qualifications to lead in international relations pedagogy: Lady Zimmern's 'interest in æsthetic values has enabled her to understand the psychology of nationality in its different manifestations, and thus to break down the barriers of misunderstanding and suspicion'.[94]

With her teaching, Lucie Zimmern claimed to take students on a personal and spiritual, as well as intellectual, transformation. 'International interdependence cannot be *preached*', she explained in her 1932 book, *Must the League Fail?* 'It has to be experienced'.[95] Later, in 1951, she argued that the League of Nations failed 'because there were fifty-two different nations represented with fifty-two different points of view. "It was like a fugue with fifty-two voices juxtaposed with no harmony". What was needed was a Symphony which has the discipline of form which is necessary in world politics. It is a discipline yet it is wide, and can comprehend almost any expression. International law or the policeman is the conductor; He beats the time'.[96]

Lucie Zimmern's teaching at the school encompassed two overlapping subjects, 'The Comparative Study of Nations' and 'Beauty, Music, and Internationalism'. In the first strand, she took the lead in the school's study of what Alfred described as 'the deeper national forces which color the whole mental life and outlook of . . . various peoples'.[97] Hence, while students were taught 'the technical aspects of international relations', including international economics, law, and organisation, the school was also 'devoted to the culture and institutions of the various nations, as being the more fundamental cause of international differences'.[98] In Lucie's classroom, this incorporated gender, race, class, religion, history, and culture. Students were expected to examine their own prejudices, asking how their 'qualities of thought' were 'traceable' to the national histories and cultures, including on questions of language, 'Jews', and 'N——'.[99] Students attended evening lectures on 'Eastern thought', focusing on Chinese and Indian intellectual traditions.[100]

In this strand of teaching, Lucie Zimmern was seeking to create in miniature what had to be achieved in international relations itself. One student described the experience as like living 'in a new kind of community . . . Everything is seen in a new perspective, a perspective in which what used to look like insurmountable barriers between nation and nation, race and race, class and class, are seen as integral and interesting parts of the language of our diversified world'.[101] For both Zimmerns, the school's main purpose was not to transmit basic knowledge of the major trends in international relations. Rather, it was to stretch the mind. 'This "stretching"', the Zimmerns explained, 'was not simply the result of the impact of new ideas through lectures and formal discussions. It was the result of living for eight weeks in a new kind of community'.[102] As Merze Tate described the school's philosophy after attending in 1931, 'what is most needed for the understanding and practical handling of international affairs is neither the development of special discipline, nor the imparting of information of current events but a method of approach combining the knowledge and high standards of the specialist with a constant sense of the variety and complexity of the modern world'.[103]

In the second strand of teaching, Lucie Zimmern delivered lectures on 'The International Aspect of Music', 'Discs, Radio, and the Cinema', 'Beauty, Music and Internationalism', and 'The Place of Beauty in International Studies'. For students to literally experience the sounds of internationalism, she organised evening recitals of music from around the world, often providing the musical accompaniment herself.[104] But cultural internationalism required more than dabbling in the life of other cultures, she insisted. 'I am afraid that many think that by dressing up in costumes of other countries and singing their songs that they are internationally minded . . . and that peace is something they may snatch off a cloud; whereas the study of international relations means years of work and discussion'.[105] Aligning with wider forms of interwar cultural internationalism, 'the harmony of sounds' was the necessary accompaniment and generator of a 'harmony of spirits' in international affairs.[106] Conservatoire director and Lucie's friend, Henri Gagnebin, composed music for a School anthem, 'Canticum Scholae Genavensis'. Students sang the Latin words written by Alfred, including 'Harmonize Asians, Europeans, Africans',[107] and folksongs from around the world, including the African–American spiritual, 'Old Black Joe'.[108]

In Aberystwyth, Lucie Barbier had an institutional affiliation at the college and was a celebrated *salonnière*. After Lucie left Aberystwyth, and without institutional affiliation but through her marriage to Alfred, she repurposed her musical, organisational, and oratorial skills to forge a different pathway to influence in the early IR field, including inviting selected students and tutors to the Zimmerns' Geneva apartment. Their *salon*, where she presided, 'makes a most brilliant evening. They are delightful'.[109] Some imagined the Zimmerns to have 'exercised an almost mystical clairvoyance'[110] and were viewed as quite the double-act, with Lucie an 'excellent complement' to Alfred.[111] Alfred, in turn, gained social capital from his relationship to Lucie. Agnes Headlam-Morley, who had tutored at the Zimmern School in 1930, described one such scene in her inaugural lecture as Oxford's Montague Burton Professor of IR. Lady Zimmern, she recounted, 'gave us a little homily on the spread of reason and harmonism in the modern world', followed by a piano playing in her drawing room. 'Egged on by her daring', a young German whose views she had previously challenged was 'found playing the piano in her drawing room . . . he played with a fire he had not known before . . . In time she said a generation would grow up to whom war was impossible, unthinkable'. This was not 'crude and naïve', Headlam-Morley maintained, 'it was enlivened by wit and enriched by understanding'.[112]

## Lucie Zimmern v. Nicholas Spykman

Lucie Zimmern's *salon* was a major location and source of her intellectual power. But her cultural programme was not simply her way to repurpose her musical training in a semi-academic setting of a Summer School and the private space of her *salons*. It was integral to the school's pedagogical rationale. 'The school . . . is alive, sensitive, delicately poised, animating', one student wrote. 'Hardly ever does one see a great idea worked out . . . with such command over the instrument, with such flair for the rhythm of things'.[113] For Lucie, her great idea also demonstrated the limits of the purely academic approach to international relations teaching, favoured by her nemesis Deputy Director Nicholas Spykman, a Dutch–American sociologist who migrated to political science. In a 1928 essay, she claimed that it was 'not so much in the classroom or in the degree lists . . . but in the after careers of the students and, above all, in the homes of the professors themselves' that the real fruits of teaching can be witnessed.[114] The sentiment was reiterated by unnamed 'tutors', possibly written by Lucie Zimmern. Her informal discussion groups followed by a recital, they claimed, is 'one of the best ways of introducing that friendly spirit of human intercourse . . . [which] is not so easily kindled in a lecture room'.[115]

Having seen and experienced Lucie's polyphonic internationalism firsthand, Agnes Headlam-Morley could not 'talk of Sir Alfred without thinking of Lady Zimmern'.[116] Unfortunately for him, Nicholas Spykman could not say the same; 'to know her is never to forget her', as one interviewer said.[117] Like so many others who encountered Lucie, Spykman was clearly troubled by how she used her marriage to pursue her own intellectual agendas, which conflicted with his own. Lucie Zimmern was already a figure of influence and persuasive power before she came into conflict with Spykman, 'applying her ideas on music in an entirely original manner in the field of international fellowship', she claimed.[118] But, in 1927, after just three years as deputy director, Spykman resigned from the school, citing a conflict with Lucie Zimmern.

The report Spykman wrote outlining his grievances has not survived, likely expunged from the school's surviving papers. However, they are summarised in a response written by unnamed 'tutors', a document almost certainly initiated and even likely written by the Zimmerns themselves and preserved in the school's archives.[119] Based on this document, Spykman's complaints were twofold. Lucie was too influential at the school and, as a result, its programme was not what he had arranged with Alfred when he agreed to be deputy director.[120] Spykman claimed to have written a general outline for the Geneva School that was adopted by the school's Executive Committee in New York. Like Spykman's report, the outline does not survive, but the claim is confirmed in an undated memorandum, retained in the school's papers.[121] For Spykman, the school's practices and organisation in no way reflected what he had set out to the Executive Committee.

The Zimmerns responded that Spykman's plan was merely 'an American presentation of the programme', not the school's founding document. The school's 'spirit and raison d'étre' was outlined in Alfred Zimmern's *Learning and Leadership*.[122] Alfred invited Spykman to 'collaborate with *himself and Mrs Zimmern* in pursuing their common educational aims and methods on terms of comradeship and of an equality as complete as his sole responsibility for the educational work of the School permitted'.[123] Spykman was accused of trying to run the school 'on militaristic lines'; attempting to place the tutors 'under his orders' and giving 'a vexatory importance to administrative and material details, and to matters of hierarchy'.[124] When tutors refused to comply, 'Spykman ceased to entertain personal relations' with them, withdrew, and contributed 'little or nothing to the intellectual life of the School'.[125] Recalling Lucie's students in Aberystwyth who claimed that her accusers had 'not always kept within the bounds of courtesy', some tutors noted that Spykman's male American secretary 'fell short of observing the elementary requirements of politeness'.[126]

The Zimmerns attributed Spykman's apparent unwillingness to collaborate in a spirit of equality to a specifically *American* problem. American students and tutors had 'united their complaints as well as their undisguised indifference toward the spiritual life of the school'.[127] Some students complained that the programme was less 'a course of study' and 'much more an intellectual and spiritual experience',[128] others that lectures 'did not provide enough facts',[129] and with Spykman suggesting that 'the personality of the speaker was . . . more important' than their subject.[130] Still others objected to Lucie Zimmern's refusal to provide a 'unified method of approach' in her teaching. But this 'would have defeated the aims of the seminar', she responded. 'Diversity and disharmony' were deliberately pursued instead of 'efficiency and homogeneity'.[131] American students and staff made little effort to understand what constitutes 'the originality of the environment to which they have come',[132] or how to make use of 'the wealth of information in the lectures . . . It may be that the methods of Oxford, Cambridge, or the Ecole Normale Superieure in Paris, require more individual initiative from the student'. Americans should only come to Geneva when 'they are able to assimilate the subtler shades of the presentation of facts to which European students are accustomed'.[133]

The Zimmerns were more defensive and less convincing in their reply to Spykman's second main complaint: officially only 'assistant to the director', Lucie effectively 'undertook the duties of general executive manager', causing a 'conflict of functions' with Spykman. This was a potent and dangerous line of attack for the Zimmerns. There was a regular hint of scandal around Lucie's influence on Alfred. Nancy Astor accused Lucie of damaging Alfred's career.[134] Lucie was described as a 'political liability' when he lost an election to the House of Commons in 1924.[135] Because most of Alfred's correspondence was sent to and from the Zimmerns' residence in Oxford, not Balliol College, one historian of IR at Oxford described Alfred as 'uxorious', as if his working from home could only be a product of Lucie's power over Alfred and nothing to do with their intellectual collaboration.[136]

On the one hand, the Zimmerns were keen to establish the independence of Lucie Zimmern's ideas and expertise. In the preface to her 1932 book, Lucie wrote that she wished 'to acknowledge help given to her in putting her ideas into shape and suggestions received from one or two friends . . . but she alone is responsible for every statement in the book, which is the fruit of observation and reflection extending over many years'.[137] However, there is evidence that Alfred Zimmern, a hugely prolific author, had a literal hand in writing *Must the League Fail?* Among Alfred's papers there is an undated near identical handwritten manuscript on letterhead from the Geneva Federation and Geneva School. The title of the handwritten version uses the Latin plural Vigiles, meaning 'vigilant *people*', and may refer to Lucie and Alfred, suggesting co-authorship.[138]

It is not difficult to imagine the Zimmerns discussing the League of Nations and deciding that Lucie's intellectual standing would increase with a book under her name. Either way, this appears to be one of those rare occasions where a husband's single or co-authored work is passed off as the wife's instead of the reverse. As Alfred wrote in the preface to his 1953 work, *The American Road to World Peace*, the book 'was thought out and has reached written form in constant co-operation with my wife, as has been the case in all our educational work. It is impossible to separate her part in it from mine'.[139]

Despite such open acknowledgements of their intellectual partnership, Spykman's complaint, and the Zimmerns' response, indicate their vulnerability on the question of their collaboration, its potential to damage Alfred's reputation and the Zimmerns' joint projects. Against all the evidence, the Zimmerns claimed that the disagreement was 'one purely between Mr Zimmern and Professor Spykman and would have arisen in any case, and no doubt sooner, had Mrs Zimmern not been there'.[140] They declared that Lucie's duties were 'minimal'; she undertook no activities in the Conservatoire; and she never used Alfred's office when he was away.[141]

The ill-tempered row between Spykman and Lucie Zimmern was more than a personality clash that spilled over to students and colleagues. It was a clash between Spykman's vision of IR as an American social science and

Lucie's polyphonic internationalism in a semi-academic space. In other words, it was debate over the nature of international relations and how and where it should be taught. Their conflict, also partly fought through their students and colleagues at the Geneva School, was over the maintenance of academic hierarchy and professional boundaries against an approach that blurred boundaries between professional and familial worlds. It was also a methodological and normative conflict, the difference between international relations as technical and factual knowledge and between a more artistic, cultural and even spiritual experience that could lead to a political transformation if the attitudes, temperaments and culture of individuals and groups could be changed.[142] It was also about content, between the relations between states versus an approach to international relations that included questions of race, gender, and class.

Lucie Zimmern won the debate with Spykman because she was married to the Geneva School director and knew how to operate. Spykman resigned. Yet, as all IR students know, 'realism' won in the end. Unlike Spykman and the other male writers of the IR canon, Lucie Zimmern never had a hand in writing the history and myths of the field. To be sure, recent historiography has derided the notion that IR's intellectual history is best understood as a series of 'great debates' beginning in the 1920s between idealists and realists. No idealist–realist debate could have occurred in the 1920s because most realists—Carr, Morgenthau, Schwarzenberger, and Spykman—all 'wrote in the 1930s and 1940s'.[143] The debate myth was created after 1945, a fabrication of the realist ascendency in the United States.[144] E. H. Carr's caricature of international reformers (and revolutionaries) as 'idealists' in *The Twenty Years' Crisis*, published in 1939, was adopted by a new generation of realists, including Spykman, to explain and justify their dominance in the revamped IR discipline in the United States.[145] 'Idealism' 'is a realist category of abuse'[146] that, as discussed in chapter 4, was most effectively propagated by E. H. Carr, a man with a reputation for spousal abuse.

Recovering the Zimmern–Spykman debate is obviously not intended to rehabilitate the realist story. But if we take seriously their confrontation, then we have a more nuanced understanding of what early IR was and the marginalised Others on which the later field was built. By 1935, Spykman was co-founder and director of the Yale Center for International Studies, which became the preeminent centre for IR in the United States, where several of realism's 'founding myths' were created.[147] According to Yale men Arnold Wolfers and Lawrence Martin, 'international relations as a special field of study made its appearance . . . as a fruit of Wilsonian idealism' and was superseded in the 1930s by the 'new realist school of thought'.[148] When two Chicago men, Morgenthau and Thompson, forging their new field in the 1950s, sought to establish an IR canon, they selected writings by Nicholas Spykman and *Alfred* Zimmern to represent these two contrasting approaches to the 'science of international politics'.[149]

Perhaps Wolfers, Martin, Morgenthau, and Thompson were unaware of Lucie Zimmern. But her forgetting was necessary for their all-male IR canon. However, in 1936, when Spykman outlined his plans for his new IR teaching programme at Yale, his project was clearly defined in opposition to what Lucie Zimmern had fashioned in Geneva. Spykman had created something, he explained, with 'an outlook different from the one involved in a purely cultural education'; to focus on such 'finer things in life' was like 'the masculine equivalent of a girls' finishing school'.[150] Instead Spykman designed an IR programme for the 'Yale man' a 'well-rounded' career course, incorporating foreign service, business, teaching and research, but also sublimating race and empire.[151]

## Racialised Polyphony in Geneva

As Robert Vitalis has shown in detail, when Nicholas Spykman and his realist collaborators defined American IR as the study of the relations between white nation-states several leading African–American intellectuals writing on race and empire, including Alain Locke, Ralph Bunche, and Merze Tate, were pushed out of the field. Hence what is most distinctive and important about the Zimmern School in the interwar period was not that much 'attention was given to the American N——',[152] as Merze Tate reported after attending the 1931 session. Or even that students learned about racial injustice in the United States.[153] Race and empire were core teaching and research subjects in the early IR field and the dominant ethos was white supremacist. The Zimmern School's significance is that at the height of the Harlem Renaissance, African–American artists and intellectuals were invited to perform and give talks as part of Lucie Zimmern's polyphonic internationalism, and this drew one of the most interesting and important twentieth-century scholars of international relations into the field.

According to her biographer, Merze Tate only enrolled in the Zimmern School in the summer of 1931 because, during her own European travels, she met African–American performer Grace Walker on her way to lecture on African–American literature and art at the School.[154] Intrigued by an approach to international relations that centred race, Tate joined Walker, who had studied in Cambridge and London, and enrolled at the Geneva School. Pianist Lorenza Jordan Cole, also on scholarship in London, performed a recital featuring works of Nathaniel Dett, the composer, pianist, and teacher, and the acclaimed Samuel Coleridge-Taylor, who combined African and European classical traditions. Percival Parham sang Black spirituals, which Grace Walker interpreted and contextualised with 'beautifully appropriate' words, also introducing students to the poetry of Claude Mackay and Langston Hughes, among others.[155] 'They were royally received', Tate recalled, 'and the audience refused to leave the auditorium even after encores'.[156] One student from Aberystwyth thought the concert 'almost defies description'. Walker, Cole, and Parham 'entertained us with music which was exclusively the product of their race'.[157]

These mid-week recitals were not an add-on to the programme. For many students, they were the 'most fundamentally international experience' of their time in Geneva.[158] The inclusion of African–American artists was intended as a kind of antiracist politics. Lucie Zimmern's students were taught that race was the most 'important and difficult' international problem.[159] They attended lectures on the 'problem of racial differences', incorporating 'race from the point of view of physical characteristics', the 'question of racial superiority' and the 'problem of racial mixture'. Tate attended a lecture from an American sociologist who, she later wrote, spoke 'squarely and tactfully' on 'The N—— Problem in the United States'.[160] The psychologist and 'physiologist' Ross A. McFarland lectured on 'the role of culture in racial and national differences'.[161] Where Spykman's academic approach to IR had no place for cultural production and almost entirely expunged race and empire, these were central to Lucie Zimmern's polyphonic internationalism. But her celebration of racial and cultural difference was entirely compatible with empire's racial hierarchies and the cultural appropriation of African and African–American art.[162]

Lucie's harmonic model of international order aligned with Alfred's belief that the 'fundamental cause' of international conflict was the clash over ideas, national cultures, institutions, and mentalities, rather than white supremacy, imperialism, and class conflict.[163] 'That is why', Alfred wrote in 1927, 'the interpretation of the varieties of national temperament and experience' was so 'prominent' at the school.[164] The Zimmerns clearly viewed African–Americans as having reached a higher cultural plain, able to contribute to what Lucie conceived as 'the symphony of a world orchestra'.[165] This was especially so when they performed work inspired by classical European traditions; Samuel Coleridge-Taylor was known as the 'Black Mahler'.[166] Yet Alfred opposed African political independence. Based on the surviving records of the school,

African–American artists were invited to perform classical music or 'traditional' spirituals, which could be analysed and interpreted by Black artists. But lectures on the 'race problem' were delivered by white social scientists.[167] Students learned that race was the most important international problem, but concluded that the main cause for 'blind feeling of hatred and aversion' in the United States was the large number of 'n—— . . . In fact, the question of numbers seems to be a prime factor in all racial and national minority questions', rather than white supremacy and racial capitalism.[168] Still, by 1951, Lucie Zimmern was describing 'American jazz rhythms' as 'wonderful . . . someday they will be the materials for great music'.[169]

Lucie Zimmern's comparative politics teaching and cultural programming aligned with Alfred's rejection of the principle of state sovereignty and advocacy for a new international order based on a federation or 'post-racial Commonwealth'.[170] Both Alfred and Lucie believed that culturally mature nations, including many without their own state, could unite under and within multinational empires or as colonies. Real self-determination was not independence from imperial rule, yet when 'a nation, or national group, is free . . . to develop its own life and culture. Only in this way', Lucie's students recounted, 'can it really be free to co-operate, and to contribute its share to the . . . world orchestra'.[171] Lucie's polyphonic internationalism taught students to 'de-emotionalize politics, and to de-politicize nationality. Not our State, but our culture and tradition were to be the objects of our affection and devotion. The State should be the object of our criticism; let us be loyal to it, but we should refrain from political flag-waving'.[172] To cultivate a deep appreciation for one's own and others' national cultural traditions was to *depoliticise* national sentiments. Cultural, not political Zionism was Alfred's model for imperial reform and a new world order led by the English-speaking peoples.[173]

## Another Marriage Story

Unlike Lucie Barbier Zimmern, whose IR expertise was earned through work in cultural diplomacy and teaching, the first woman appointed to an IR department was academically trained to a postgraduate level in the new subject and at two major British centres of IR research—the London School of Economics (LSE) and Aberystwyth—and *her* husband, Jirí Vránek, was IR's first spousal hire. Lilian Friedländer taught at the Zimmern School, and her husband was Alfred Zimmern's personal secretary in Geneva. Alfred later appointed Jirí Vránek as secretary to the IR section of the International Committee on

Intellectual Cooperation in Paris. Friedländer wrote on the core subject of international organisation and Rockefeller and Carnegie funded her advanced training in international law. For the year preceding E. H. Carr's arrival as Aberystwyth's Woodrow Wilson Professor in 1936, Friedländer was in sole charge of IR teaching at Aberystwyth. Could Friedländer become Aberystwyth's—and IR's—first women professor and one half of IR's second power couple, with her husband as the trailing spouse?

Born to a North London Jewish family from the then Prussian city of Königsberg, Lilian Friedländer graduated from LSE in 1923 with a B.Sc. in political science, winning the Gladstone Memorial Prize for the best dissertation. Within a year of starting her Wilson Studentship in 1924, Friedländer became assistant lecturer to the new Wilson Professor, Charles Webster, replacing Sydney Herbert during a year of Rockefeller-funded leave to study immigration in the United States. She lectured on comparative politics and international relations, including her emerging specialism of the International Labour Organization (ILO). Drawing on her contacts from work with the Women's International League for Peace in Geneva, she started an interdisciplinary discussion group on the League's Economic Conference. In 1926, College Vice-President David Davies roped Friedländer into helping to host delegates from 122 countries attending a meeting of the International Federation of League of Nations Societies, which included coach tours of the Welsh countryside where women in villages were expected to wear 'Welsh national dress'.[174]

After Herbert's return, and the end of her first stint at Aberystwyth in 1926, Friedländer pursued an academic career in the US for three years. Supporting herself with savings and work for Baltimore's League of Nations Association, she first studied international law at John Hopkins with Frank Goodlaw, an expert on colonial administration, supporter of racial segregation, and first president of the American Political Science Association.[175] Her second year was funded through an international law fellowship from the Carnegie Endowment for International Peace during which she researched the admission of new states to the League of Nations, publishing the results in the *British Yearbook of International Law*.[176] In common with much international thought in the 1920s and beyond, Friedländer drew attention to the limits of nineteenth-century legal conceptions of sovereignty and recognition, which after 1920 had been effectively replaced by admission to the League.[177] She thus concurred with Irish Free State arguments that its sovereignty and international personhood should be recognised given Ireland's *de facto* independence from Britain and its treaty-making powers.[178]

Supported by the Rockefeller fellowship for 1928–9, Friedländer turned her attention to the internationalisation of labour regulation. This was not merely technical cooperation on 'industrial questions' across borders, dealing with minimum standards concerning child and immigrant labour, the length of the working day, unemployment, accidents and social insurance. 'Revolution', Friedländer wrote, 'was in the air, and the statesmen feared that any day the tide of Bolshevism might sweep in from the east'.[179] International and industrial relations questions were closely linked, with the tax-avoiding clothing magnate Montague Burton simultaneously endowing professorships in both of these fields.[180] Friedländer analysed the ILO's difficulties in agreeing minimum labour standards because of the United States' federal and decentralised character.[181] She supported an international labour parliament, and compared the problem of regulating labour standards in the US and the ILO itself. In both locations the 'relics of the theory of sovereignty have strayed from the realms of pure political science into an economic field where they are more than ever meaningless and cumbersome'.[182]

The recipient of numerous prizes and awards, Friedländer had two journal articles to her name, and her intellectual trajectory was promising. She had studied in Switzerland, Czechoslovakia, Germany, and the United States, and her work was funded by the main philanthropic organisations supporting the new IR field. Webster invited Friedländer to return to Aberystwyth in 1930 after Herbert moved to the History Department. Yet in marrying an 'alien'—Jirí Vránek was a Czech national from Southern Bohemia—Friedländer lost her British nationality. Only in 1948 did British women gain the right to their own nationality, but her more immediate problem was how to accommodate both her and her husband's careers. Jirí Vránek published less and received fewer prizes than Friedländer, though he had a Ph.D. in political science from Prague. According to a student yearbook, Jirí was 'intensely interested in the problems of international cooperation and understanding . . . He has a great craving for social affairs and nothing is as entertaining to him as a young lady'.[183] After a period of research in the United States, Friedländer only agreed to return to Aberystwyth if Vránek could share her job. Webster agreed to 'Mrs Vránek's' request. After lecturing for a term in Prague, Jirí was allowed to share Lilian's lectureship in Aberystwyth.[184]

'Dr. Vránek' made most of his connection to Lilian. In 1931, the two were reappointed for a further two years and both were invited to tutor at the Zimmern School in Geneva.[185] Lilian took two terms of sick leave during the 1931–2 academic year, and Jirí covered her teaching and other activities.[186]

In 1932, he stood in for the Wilson Professor at meetings of the British Coordinating Committee for International Studies (BCCIS) attended by Arnold Toynbee, Charles Manning, Margaret Cleeve, and Alfred Zimmern, whom he had assisted in Paris.[187] Jirí was invited to represent BCCIS on the International Editorial Committee for the Lexicon of Political Terms.[188] In 1934, Alfred appointed Jirí as secretary to the IR section at the International Committee on Intellectual Cooperation, and he resigned his Aberystwyth job-share.[189] With Jirí away, and now recovered from illness, Lilian was in sole charge of teaching IR in Aberystwyth in 1936, with the support of clerk–librarian 'Miss. J.E. Morris'. IR was still not a full degree course in Aberystwyth, with only nine undergraduates and one MA student, 'Miss A. D. Hooper', who wrote a thesis on the League of Nations' work on the traffic in opioids.

Lilian Vránek welcomed the latest Wilson professor, E. H. Carr, to the seaside town, giving him a guided tour around what she called 'the cramped, shabby, ill-equipped quarters'. It was a 'melancholy' experience, she later recalled.[190] We do not know what Lilian Vránek made of Carr's reorganisation of Aberystwyth's IR curricula, which demoted the League of Nations to only one among several elements of the study of relations between states and elevated international theory 'since Machiavelli'.[191] We also do not know what this Jewish woman made of Carr's inaugural lecture, which supported the appeasement of Adolf Hitler.[192] Nor do we know whether Carr would have renewed Vránek's lectureship had she wanted to remain working with him.

Within a year of Carr's arrival, Lilian Vránek left Aberystwyth to join Jirí in Paris, ending her career as a university teacher and researcher on international relations. No other woman was appointed to the International Politics Department in Aberystwyth until 1978, when defence analyst Edwina N. Moreton taught in the department for two years. Aberystwyth did not appoint its first woman IR professor, Jenny Edkins, until 2004. Certainly, her marriage and the war, and possibly E. H. Carr, combined to end Friedländer's academic career and Aberystwyth lost its second IR 'wife'. The International Committee on Intellectual Cooperation closed in 1940 and Jirí and Lilian's wartime activities are unknown. They are named in a database of Holocaust survivors whose property was confiscated during the Nazi occupation of 'the so-called Protectorate' of Bohemia and Moravia.[193] E. H. Carr spent six productive years at Aberystwyth, resigning in 1947 'after being cited as co-respondent in a divorce petition—a second Woodrow Wilson Professor to fall foul of the Nonconformist conscience'.[194]

Having lost her British citizenship upon marrying Jirí, Lilian Vránek was re-admitted to British nationality in 1947. The notice in the *London Gazette* described her as an assistant in the Books Department of the British Council, which was created in 1934 to promote Britain's cultural relations abroad.[195] She later worked for the British Embassy in Rome, for which she received an MBE in the 1968 New Year honours list, and remained in Italy for the rest of her life.[196] She died in 1999 at the age of ninety-eight and is buried in Rome's cemetery for non-Catholics alongside Shelley, Keats, and Antonio Gramsci. Since 2000, Aberystwyth has awarded the Lilian Friedländer Prize to MA students who have 'demonstrated academic excellence', 'contributed to departmental life or demonstrated great personal strength during their studies'.[197]

## Conclusion

The new IR historiography has responded to the 'myth of the first great debate' by historicising realism and recovering more diverse forms of interwar international thought. This has largely, though not entirely, centred on other white men.[198] Feminist and postcolonial scholars have long pointed to the importance of realism's constitutive Others, feminised and racialised 'idealisms'.[199] Christine Sylvester suspected that in the realist parody 'women' were always 'the model for idealism'.[200] In a seminal essay, J. Ann Tickner showed how Hans J. Morgenthau's 'six principles' of political realism were rooted in ideologies of hegemonic masculinity.[201] Drawing on and extending feminist political theory, feminist and postcolonial scholars have identified a distinctively IR tradition of misogyny at the ideological and conceptual level. We should also examine the concrete historical events and personalities through which the realist caricature of 'idealism' emerged.

There was no 'first great debate' as realists have understood it, of course. But there was a debate in the 1920s over the nature of IR, its proper subject matter, professional norms, and methodology. It did not occur on the pages of journals or books. It was in the semi-academic space of an internationalist education project, in classrooms, hotel rooms, and a concert hall. In retrospect, we can read the Spykman–Lucie clash as a debate between a so-called 'realist' and what in both orthodox and revisionist literature would later be called an 'idealist', but without any mention of Lucie. If IR scholars are looking for a 'first' great debate, then the Spykman–Lucie clash was it, and it prefigured the terms of later so-called 'great debates' in IR.

Spykman rejected Lucie Zimmern's polyphonic internationalism not because it was culturally, intellectually, and racially elitist, but rather because it was the wrong kind of elitism and racism. It was too cultural, too feminine, too concerned with the League of Nations, and not academic and methodologically rigorous enough. Polyphonic internationalism was an eclectic and flawed attempt to teach questions of race, class, and gender in the new field of international relations. As discussed later, its limits are best exposed in contrast to Claudia Jones's founding of perhaps the most powerful and effective form of polyphonic internationalism in history, the Notting Hill Carnival in London.

Lucie Zimmern's most important legacy for IR is whom she attracted to the new field. When Merze Tate happened to meet Grace Walker on her way to Geneva, IR's intellectual and disciplinary history was set on a new course. Tate dropped her plan to read French in Paris and switched subjects, applying to study IR at Oxford with Alfred Zimmern, and completing her studies under Agnes Headlam-Morley. Merze Tate's formative years at Oxford are discussed later, but is unlikely that Tate would have gone to Geneva and chosen international relations as her field without Lucie's polyphonic internationalism.

As prologue to continued debate around IR's intellectual pluralism, the obvious question is what IR might have become, including at Aberystwyth, had Lucie Zimmern not been marginalised from post-war IR, and then written out of its intellectual and disciplinary history. We cannot know. Yet she matters not only because she broadens and deepens IR historiography to include a wife of the 'canon' and the sources and locations of international thought. She matters too as an original practitioner and theorist of an eclectic, heterodox approach, the roots of which pre-date 1919, and which was distinct from and in some ways ahead of the 'post-positivist' theories by which Aberystwyth remade its name in the 1990s.[202] Unlike much of the 'critical IR' of this period, Lucie Zimmern centred questions of race and invited leading African–American speakers. The field might have turned to aesthetics much earlier than it did.[203] The 'Zimmern affair', if by that we mean the basic fact that Alfred resigned from IR's first chair, is rightly a footnote in IR's disciplinary history.[204] Lucie is not, and neither is Lilian Friedländer.

# 2

# This White, English, Self-Loved, Cultivated Self

ONE OF THE MOST important institutions for early research on international relations in Britain was born of multiple crises of empire. As new disciplinary historians have shown, the defining military confrontation for the creation of the British (later Royal) Institute of International Affairs (RIIA) was not World War I, but the Second Boer War in Southern Africa (1899–1902).[1] During that campaign, the British used scorched-earth tactics and mass concentration camps to defeat Boer guerrillas, generating widespread revulsion in Britain and around the world. Britain's elites grew increasingly anxious about the quality of what was perceived as Britain's racial stock, continual rebellions in the colonies, and increasing geopolitical competition from Germany, Japan, and the United States. Alfred Milner, Governor of the Cape Colony and High Commissioner for Southern Africa, his secretary, Lionel Curtis, and colonial administrator Philip Kerr founded the Round Table movement in 1909 to advance schemes of imperial reform, including the merger of the four settler colonies of southern Africa into the racially segregated Union of South Africa in 1910.

For the 'Milner group', the union was the model for a reformed British Empire in an era when imperial conquests were coming to an end: a federation of self-governing white 'Anglo-Saxon' dominions.[2] Imperial frontiers were closing; colonial administration and inter-imperial relations had to be managed on a worldwide scale. The language of 'international relations' captured new thinking on inter-imperial and interracial relations across the world as a whole.[3] Emerging from the Round Table's project for imperial union, Lionel Curtis famously proposed a series of affiliated institutes for the scientific study of 'international relations' at the sidelines of the Paris Peace negotiations in

1919.[4] The British (later Royal) Institute of International Affairs was established in 1920 with associated institutes established in Canada (1928), Australia
(1933), New Zealand (1934), South Africa (1934), and India (1935).[5] Later
known as Chatham House, the RIIA's policy-relevant studies on international
relations would support the (horizontal) solidarity of white English-speaking
nations, but also the (vertical) governance and education of newly enfran-
chised workers and women.

New disciplinary histories focus on imperial men like Curtis and Kerr who
established some of early IR's dominant institutions in Britain. For this generation of Milner's men, the new intellectual field was obviously and intimately
connected to the management of empire.[6] Unsurprisingly, the major academic
centres of international relations research, Oxford, London School of Economics (LSE) and Aberystwyth, later taught colonial administration as part
of the international relations curricula into the 1920s and 1930s, much of the
teaching done by women. We have a small literature on how the men of
the Rockefeller Foundation-funded British Committee on the Theory of International Politics, established in 1959—figures like Martin Wight and Hedley
Bull—contributed to the *neglect* of empire and neo-colonial relations in IR in
the 1960s and 1970s, discussed further in chapter 8.[7] Yet we have no account
of the intellectual and institutional links between these two generations, the
Milner men and the mid-twentieth-century men of the British Committee, a
period spanning the 1930s to the 1970s.

The figure bridging these two generations, the leading white British thinker
on empire from the 1930s to the 1970s, is Margery Perham.[8] She first made her
name and reputation as a respected interlocutor and gentle critic of the Edwardian generation of imperial men. She described Lionel Curtis as possess-
ing a 'splendid head' and 'almost mystical aura. One felt it was bordering upon
*lèse majesté* to disagree with him'.[9] Yet she did. She was the more liberal heir
and anointed successor to the principal agent of British rule in Africa of his
generation, Lord Frederick Lugard.[10] By the late 1940s and 1950s, when Perham's ideas on imperial government had superseded those of the Round
Table generation, she became mentor and patron to one of the most revered
international theorists in post-war Britain, Martin Wight, influencing his
ideas on trusteeship and international society. His views of Perham capture
much about her stature, her influence on him, and the misogyny she faced.
The Australian Mary Bull, another 'IR wife', was Perham's long-term researcher, collaborator and later expert on the historical figure of Perham

herself, after she followed her husband Hedley Bull from Sydney to Oxford in 1953. After her death in 2021, Mary Bull's personal copy of the catalogue of Perham's voluminous papers was advertised and sold (to me) from the 'library of Hedley Bull'.[11]

Given her level of expertise and influence on the most important international relations question of the twentieth century, it is astonishing that Margery Perham is so marginal in IR's intellectual histories, even those centring Britain.[12] No other figure came close to shaping British official and public opinion on the empire at mid-century, or—with the exception of international historian Arnold Toynbee—achieved the same level of fame and influence on an international relations question across such a long period of time. The towering figure in the academic, policy, and media field of imperial management, Perham and her major subjects of empire and decolonisation are fundamental to understanding the conditions for the relatively belated establishment of an IR discipline (actually semi-discipline) in Britain in the 1970s, two decades after the United States, when the British International Studies Association was founded.

Though she was almost certainly the British imperial thinker of her generation, Perham was never retrospectively recognised as part of 'early IR', nor were the numerous other scholars of the international relations of empire and colonial administration.[13] Perham's erasure from IR's intellectual history also effected an erasure of Lucy Philip Mair, who taught colonial administration as IR at the LSE. More importantly, Perham's loss from IR's intellectual canon was not only a loss of her subjects, but a loss of what president of the West African Students Union H. O. Davies called 'the most wanted critic of West Africans'.[14] Perham was official Britain's enlightened and knowledgeable conscience on empire. As postcolonial scholar Priyamvada Gopal has recently observed, in this role she actively engaged with anticolonial critique, all the better to reform the empire, to increase its virtues and longevity.[15] In no sense was Perham a model white interlocuter. Yet her erasure from IR, and hence her absence as a serious interlocuter for British IR, also indirectly delayed IR's reckoning with Black internationalism and anticolonial thought. Examining the limits of Perham's intellectual and political praxis as a white ally sheds light on her intellectual formation, but also the racial positionality and privileges of 'white women's IR'.[16] Given Perham's significance, and the scale of her intellectual production across four decades, she is discussed across two chapters, here and in chapter 8.

## Margery Perham and her Motorbike

Even as a child, Margery Perham claimed to be 'romantically drawn to Africa'.[17] She was born to a middle-class family in Bury, Lancashire on September 6, 1895, the youngest of seven children, and attended St Stevens College, an institution for girls run by the St John Baptist Clewer Sisterhood with a mission to serve the poor. She won an open scholarship to St Hugh's College, Oxford and was one of only four students to receive a first in modern history in 1917, though as a woman she could not formally receive her Oxford degree.[18] She was the youngest lecturer and only woman on the History Faculty at Sheffield, a position she held—unhappily—for four years. She became severely depressed from overwork, loneliness, and the death of her closest brother at the Battle of the Somme. When Perham's doctor advised a year's sabbatical and rest, she travelled to Hargeisa, Somaliland in 1921 to stay with her sister, Ethel, a Christian missionary working in British East Africa for the past decade.

Perham arrived in Somaliland when the question of British colonial control was both political and familial. Ethel's husband, Major Henry Rayne, was District Commissioner and had participated in the final crushing of Somalia's Dervish fighters, and previously fought in the Boer War. Perham accompanied Rayne in his Commissioner activities, surveying the terrain and its people from the vantage of official colonial power. She was briefly infatuated with Rayne, and she later elevated the District Commissioner to the highest status in the moral economy of colonial administration.[19] No matter the machinations in London, or the racism of white settlers, these men of good faith, humane administration, and service represented all that was best in the empire.

On her return to England, Perham attempted to resume her normal academic life; she made friends, she 'experimented with a motor-bike until it crashed', she later recalled, 'and then with a horse, which it didn't . . . But this was not enough. I wanted to *do* something about Africa'.[20] The crush on her sister's husband quickly ended, as did the experiment with the motorcycle. She had fallen in love with 'Africa'. 'I live on one plane—it is Africa always for me—I work, sleep, seek personal encounters, play games, enlarge my general knowledge, save my strength and money for Africa'.[21]

The image of Perham on her return from Africa (figure 2.1) captures how many contemporaries saw the 'handsome, six-foot-tall woman'.[22] She was considered 'strikingly' good looking, 'naturally' handsome 'amply proportioned, elegant and well-dressed'.[23] She had a 'controlled vitality', was a 'confident and masterful speaker', appearing 'more like an eloquent athlete than a don'.[24] She

FIGURE 2.1. Margery Perham. Photographer Unknown. Courtesy of Bodleian Library, Oxford

was 'formidable'.[25] The author of one 1961 profile described her as both 'immensely attractive' in her youth, and still attractive into her sixties. Martin Wight thought the author should delete 'immensely', and that 'handsome' was 'a happier word' to describe her in later life.[26] During the young Perham's first Africa trip, 'with a strong body', she claimed, 'I indulged in my greatest desire, that for physical achievement'.[27] The athleticism and physicality in the image points to a sexualised and highly gendered reading of her search for African adventure. Her biographer writes of 'Perham's rapturous—even semi-erotic—welcoming of her new life'.[28] The Model 16H Brooklands Special Norton motorcycle was literally a temporary stand-in for what had become her real vocation: 'Africa'.

The image also conveys Perham's racial and colonial privilege at the start of what would become a glittering career working 'on Africa'. The motorcycle frame appears low because of Perham's height but also because the Model 16H, introduced in 1921, during Perham's first Africa trip, was newly designed with a lower frame sufficient for Britain's relatively well-maintained roads. The 'H' stands for 'Home'. The higher frame of the older Model 17C was designed for the rougher roads and tracks of the colonial empire. 'C' is for 'Colonies'.[29] Perham's physical command over her motorcycle, her windswept appearance and outdoor attire, reproduce the colonial trope of the intrepid white woman in Africa embracing risk with the costume to match.[30] In a 1974 interview on her retirement, Perham continued to fashion herself as a bold explorer, presenting a picture of herself, in 'high leather boots, the breeches, the short circular khaki skirt, the becoming double terai hat . . . above all the rifle over the shoulder and the pistol under the pillow'.[31]

Initially, Perham articulated her intellectual and emotional response to the colonial frontier in a novel, *Major Dane's Garden*, published in 1925. Set in British Somaliland, the book included lengthy discussions of the tension between military repression and 'native' development, a kind of substitute for the doctorate she never wrote.[32] *Jose Vine*, a second novel published in 1927, was more autobiographical, about a close relationship between a brother and a sister, his death in the war, and unrequited love.

By 1924, with her new field of imperial governance, Perham left Sheffield to become tutor in modern history at St Hugh's, her former women's college at Oxford. She lectured on 'Problems of Colonial Administration', 'Problems of Race and Government in Africa', 'The Colonial Empire', and 'British Policy towards Native Races'. She spent vacations visiting the League of Nations headquarters in Geneva, where she became close to Lord Lugard, then British representative on the League's Mandates Commission which oversaw the colonies of the empires defeated in World War I. The League Covenant, Perham later claimed, 'was the expression of a general desire to secure better dealings between peoples: it applies to colonial no less than European relations'.[33] However, she opposed any notion of the League overseeing an international administration of all colonies, not because it would weaken Britain's empire, but because: 'Backward people are very "human" and extrovert: an international government might prove cold and rigid and so arrest their psychological adjustment to civilisation. At the worst, it might prove itself effective mainly in securing equal rights in exploitation and in prolonging imperialism by syndicating it'.[34]

Lugard and Philip Kerr supported Perham's application for a Rhodes Travelling Fellowship for a two-year global research tour between 1929 and 1931.[35] Like the diplomat's daughters Agnes Headlam-Morley and Sybil Crowe, Perham devoted considerable time to thinking and writing about the life and work of a 'great man' she revered.[36] After Lugard's death in 1945, as the first director of Oxford's Institute of Colonial Studies and with the assistance of Mary Bull,

Perham meticulously researched Lugard's official biography, published in two books of 750 pages, and edited his diaries in four volumes.[37]

During her Rhodes-funded travels, Perham developed the lineaments of her distinctive and more liberal approach to race and imperial governance, particularly on the question of white settlers. Her first academic book, *The Protectorates of South Africa*, published in 1935 as an exchange of letters with Lionel Curtis, staked out her more liberal position on African rights and critique of unfettered settler domination.[38] South African premier J.B.M Hertzog's Afrikaner supremacist views were even more extreme than former prime ministers, Louis Botha and Jan Christian Smuts. Perham loathed how Afrikanerdom spoke about and treated Black Africans; the British government had betrayed native peoples, and its own liberal traditions, she believed, when it handed control of native policy to the South African Parliament.[39] Black Africans might not yet be ready for independence, Perham claimed, but neither should they be subjected to unfettered settler minority rule. She criticised Curtis's call to transfer the Protectorates to the Union of South Africa to avoid a rift within the Commonwealth. Nonetheless, Lugard and Kerr also supported Perham's appointment to Oxford's first research lectureship in colonial administration, funded by Rockefeller, in 1935. As one of Oxford's leading 'sentinels of empire', Perham was clearly shaped by Oxford's long tradition of imperial history. She also influenced and redefined it.[40]

By 1939, Perham had dispensed entirely with undergraduate tutoring, becoming the first Official Fellow of Nuffield, a graduate-only college in Oxford, which 'was built around her'.[41] During the war, the British information service tasked Perham with shifting opinion on the empire in the United States. She duly toured the US, speaking at universities and luncheon clubs, and writing for *Foreign Affairs*.[42] Perham played on white America's racial anxieties to explain and justify Britain's predicament in Africa. She evoked white settler fears that if Britain removed its 'arbitral power', then this would lead to their 'utter submergence . . . under a vast flood of barbarism', evoking witchcraft, tribal war, 'cannibalism and ritual murder and the pawning of children'.[43] Perham also appealed to the United States' 'continental strength' and geopolitical interests, which required a close association with 'Britain's heterogeneous dominions and dependencies' all over the world. The British Empire was 'a setting and a training ground for weak and immature groups' that would all need to be incorporated into a new world order after the war.[44] She reminded her American readers that the way Britain handled the predicament—future self-rule by Africans not yet fit for the task—would largely determine whether power in Africa would be seized by radicals or handed to moderates willing to remain tied to 'the West'.

Perham tutored Americans on their continued need for the British Empire. But, in turn, she was adamant that Britain itself had to face up to its diminished global power and engage in significant imperial reform. Because Britain's 'white colonies' had acquired dominion status it was only a matter of time before the 'brown or black ones' achieved the same.[45] Perham always maintained that the colonial situation 'has to be read in the light of the total situation of the ruling power which in turn must be seen in its world context'.[46] In a talk to the BBC Home Service in 1943, Perham was explicit:

> we ought to face the fact that our power is not what it was. Great nations have lately come forward into world affairs: some of them are enemies who are covetous, some of them are friends who are critical. We have got to reckon with both as well as with the colonial peoples themselves . . . It is . . . plain realism to say that we have to shift the basis of our empire still more from power to service.[47]

For Perham, the world-historical event that came to symbolise the need for an entirely new approach to Britain's empire was the 'loss' of Singapore to the '"coloured" people' of Japan in February 1942, the largest British surrender in history.[48] The loss of Britain's largest military and economic base in Southeast Asia broke the 'spell of our invincibility . . . and has sent an almost involuntary thrill of response through many coloured nationalists subjected to white rule'.[49] Independence was inevitable; Britain needed to get ahead of the process.[50] As historian Caroline Elkins has put it, 'at this moment, the empire didn't need Churchill; it needed Perham and her crafting of new ideas and language'.[51]

## 'The Most Wanted Critic of West Africans'

The distinction between white settlers and British colonial authority in the metropole allowed Margery Perham to carve out a reputation as a defender of African rights against what she described as 'a highly organized, ceaselessly alert group of shock troops'.[52] Despite the British government's insistence on prioritising Kenya's native population, the colony was totally dominated by white settler interests and defended by figures such as writer, broadcaster, and daughter of white settlers, Elspeth Huxley. Huxley's first book was a hagiography of settler leader Lord Delamere, which Perham called 'the best apologia for white settlement that has been written'.[53] Like Curtis, Huxley was a perfect interlocuter and foil for Perham, their exchanges also published in book form in 1944 as *Race and Politics in Kenya*. Like her engagement with Curtis, Perham opposed Huxley's call for more powers for white settlers. In this context, 'self-government' amounted to minority rule underpinned by racial discrimination and, as Perham put it, the 'capitalist exploitation of one race by the other'.[54] Any 'anti-white distrust' from native peoples was understandable given the uncompromising nature of white domination.[55] However, Perham rejected the re-expropriation of land. Instead, colonial authorities should utilise all the resources of state planning and intervention to rebalance Kenya's economy, society, and government, and educate native populations 'in the early formative stage of their kindergarten in civilisation'.[56]

Perham was both repelled by and sometimes attracted to white settler life. Her strongest identification was racial: 'to feel the sense of singularity, of enhanced personality that comes from having a white skin among dark millions'.[57] Perham was always utterly explicit about the racial politics of colonialism, anticolonialism and postcolonial international relations, sometimes to the exclusion of all else, including the relation between racialisation and capitalism. For Perham, race and racism were not ideological or structural. They were personal, psychological and even existential. In 1961, she could confess to deep fear at the prospect of leaving 'the relative civilization of Aden' to travel to Somaliland. 'I do not think it was ordinary physical fear', she claimed, 'it certainly was not sexual fear. I think it was the fear that myself, this white, English, self-loved, cultivated self, would in some way be lost, overwhelmed, cut off from its base among tens of thousands of other human beings, who were not necessarily inferior, but utterly alien and uncomprehending'.[58] Racial difference, for Perham, produced an unquestioned Otherness and a basic sociological reality.

Perham regularly commented on physiognomy and the racialised appearance of Africans[59] and African–Americans, including during her visit to Howard University, the preeminent African–American institution of higher learning, which she visited during her 1929 tour.[60] The 'strikingly' good-looking Perham was obsessed with physical appearance. According to Martin Wight, she possessed a 'considerable streak of feminine vanity', evidenced in 'the photographs of herself among the illustrations to the Lugard book'.[61] Another of her assistants noted that Margery and her sister 'regarded it almost a calamity . . . not to be good looking',[62] and she conceived of 'good looks' in highly racialised terms. Perham conceived of racial prejudice as natural and something to be overcome. During her first US tour, she claimed that she had to 'face up to the n——'; 'this race business . . . must remain the main theme of all my thoughts while I am in America'.[63] In a 1936 review of Zora Neale Hurston's influential study of Black folklore, *Mules and Men*, Perham thought that despite 'all its fashionable glamour' and 'all the prestige of Paul Robeson', 'black America' was 'still mysterious'.[64]

The context of Perham's first serious engagements with anticolonial and Black internationalism was fascist Italy's colonial–fascist invasion of Ethiopia in 1935. Italy's attack on one of only two free African states was a watershed moment in global Black consciousness, galvanising resistance to European colonialism.[65] In *The Times*, Perham made much of Ethiopia's symbolic status. It was not 'the last unclaimed slice of Africa', but a 'symbol to Africans throughout the world'.[66] In an essay for *The Spectator* titled 'The Colour-Challenge', Perham alerted readers to something unprecedented in 'world history, ominous or promising according to the point of view', to 'huge demonstrations' in Africa and the United States, meetings in London organised by the International Friends of Abyssinia, the arrival of Syrian and Egyptian troops in support of the Ethiopian army, offers of assistance from the Levant, and an Ethiopian mission to Japan.[67] She later described the rebellions in the West Indies as 'much more than a question of labour', but of empire.[68]

Perham corresponded with some of Emperor Haile Selassie's most prominent white international supporters, including Sylvia Pankhurst, who was highly critical of Perham's 1948 book, *The Government of Ethiopia*,[69] written when she was later advising the Colonial and Foreign Office. Perham condemned the Italian invasion, though she praised its modernising effects, for breaking the 'crust of tradition'.[70] Pankhurst accused Perham of an 'inexcusable' libel, falsifying facts when she suggested that Selassie had come to power though orchestrating a coup against Zewditu, Empress of Ethiopia and first female head of an internationally recognised African state.[71] 'Did you realise who would make use of your work?' Pankhurst wrote to Perham after the Italian government cited her book in its colonial propaganda.[72]

At this world-historical moment of Black political organising in the mid-1930s, Perham began to develop one of the most enduring tropes in her writing on anticolonialism. In Ethiopia 'lies the one opportunity for Africans to civilize themselves', she claimed: 'A free Abyssinia, civilized by the common altruistic services of the Western powers—what a great human experiment that would be! It would also help to give Africans all through the world the thing they most need for their own sakes and our own—racial self-respect'.[73] Much later, in 1964, she would still write of the 'almost intolerable sense of anguish for the sufferings of Ethiopia, and of shame at our country's handling of the affair'.[74] However the distinctively Black political consciousness mobilised against colonialism, fascist and otherwise, was later reduced to the psychological response to an objectively inferior social status. Perham's longstanding explanation for radical anticolonialism, by which she meant criticism of Britain that was not 'constructive and judicial',[75] was a 'deep bitterness' among educated Africans at their 'sense of inferiority' and the 'handicap of a black skin'.[76]

For the next three decades, Perham was engaged with a series of Black interlocuters through speaking invitations, book reviews, correspondence with figures such as C.L.R. James, George Padmore, and Harold Moody, numerous prefaces and introductions to books by African writers, and in her own extensive publications.[77] In 1936, she reviewed Padmore's *How Britain Rules Africa*, yet she did not engage with his detailed history of Africa's conquest and partitioning, nor his main argument about Britain's methods of economic exploitation, the role of finance capital in African colonies, direct and indirect rule, or his claim that colonialism in Africa was the 'breeding-ground' of fascists.[78] Instead, she took Padmore to task for making no mention of the 'backwardness of Africans, their social atomization and savagery', despite Padmore opening with reference to so-called African 'backwardness'. Refusing to engage with the intellectual substance, Perham instead claimed the book's importance was in what Padmore 'tells the N—— world to draw from the Abyssinian tragedy, that, at this turning-point in the relationship of Black and White, Mussolini is to be thanked for undeceiving the subjects of France and Britain as to the character of their masters'.[79] Perham concluded that the book was a 'disappointment. Is it, perhaps, too soon to expect something constructive and judicial from a member of a rightly indignant race?'[80]

At Padmore's request, Perham agreed to circulate copies of the International African Service Bureau's magazine, *International African Opinion*, edited by C.L.R. James.[81] In 1939, Perham heard Padmore speak, describing him as 'self-possessed' and 'impressive', but also 'v. belligerent', an 'agitator type'. The 'sensible' Africans 'didn't speak at all'.[82] Perham's 'review' of *How Britain Rules Africa* was one of the few occasions she engaged with Black Marxist thought. However, in a 1944 essay for *Foreign Affairs*, Perham claimed that the 'strongest attacks on imperialism from an economic point of view, inspired by a communist doctrine, seemed to come from N—— intellectuals who have grievances of their own against white capitalism'.[83] Indeed, she was at pains to draw a distinction between anticolonial left criticism of what she called 'white capitalism' and of the British Empire itself. As a white woman of the liberal left, wanting major economic reform and redistribution, she thought that much of the communist critique of imperialism was 'justified'.[84] Hence, to readers of *Foreign Affairs* she could present Black critique of the British Empire as an 'ideological safety-valve' for the more justifiable 'grievances' against 'white capitalism'.[85] Any convergence between critiques of capitalism and colonialism, she claimed, was because Western communists 'taught' Indians and Africans 'to express their indictment of capitalist-imperialism in common terms'.[86] Yet, in the end, Perham's differentiation was a distinction without much difference.

Perham's clear preference was to engage with 'moderate' African leaders, whose voice she lifted while warning them to exercise restraint. Thus, in contrast to Padmore, she thought Akiki K. Nyabongo's *Africa Answers Back* was a 'gentler comment', dealing 'with racial misunderstandings, rather than with those deep conflicts of interest'.[87] She saw herself as antiracist, even a white ally if that meant alliance in the gradualist project of African self-government in the Commonwealth, joining Harold Moody's reformist League of Coloured People, and attending a speech by Paul Robeson in 1934, alongside Eslanda Robeson, Winifred Holtby, and Jomo Kenyatta, with whom she also corresponded. Perham wanted to undermine what she saw as white Britons' 'uncritical and generalised attitude of superiority towards Africans', which was 'an excuse for the less defensible activities of imperialism'. She challenged the notion that African backwardness was permanent, a fact on which white Britons were 'apt to lean a little too hard in order to make ourselves comfortable in a difficult situation'.[88]

To this end, Perham edited a collection of life stories, *Ten Africans*, including an essay by a 21-year-old Kofoworola Aina Moore, the first African woman to graduate from Oxford in 1935, and friend of Merze Tate.[89] Perham and Tate overlapped at Oxford but there is no record of them meeting. One Africanist scholar praised Perham's anthology as an 'authentic living document of African personality'.[90] However, Nigerian critic Louis Mbanefo observed that for 'the first time', Perham, 'desists from wielding the pen herself, preferring to watch Africans writing about themselves . . . African readers may hope that this method of giving the African a part will be extended to other fields than mere biography . . . But the African needs to understand the Englishman just as much as he needs to be understood'.[91]

Perham regularly gave invited talks to African student groups in London and was becoming a target of anticolonial critique herself.[92] According to Nigerian nationalist, journalist, lawyer, and then president of the West African Students Union (WASU), H. O. Davies, Perham's talk on 'The Democratization of Empire' drew 'an unusually large number'. Davies described

Perham as a 'prolific writer on Africans' who 'always had sordid topics' and was 'disliked by Africans'. After her talk, she was 'bombarded with critical questions, and tirades on some of her past press publications. One question after another was a lambast . . . [with] several students trying to put their questions at the same time. The whole affair seemed like a declaration of war against the most wanted critic of West Africans'.[93] As chairman, Davies was 'greatly embarrassed' and hastily ended the Q&A on the pretext that Perham had to catch a train. In the preface to her 1941 primer on British history in Africa written for Africans, *Africans and British Rule*, she was likely referring to this WASU event: 'some Gold Coast men are very strong politicians and trained lawyers, and they pressed me hard in argument'.[94] In 1936, she gave another talk to WASU on 'African Criticisms of International Relations'.

Perham imagined *Africans and British Rule* as a kind of letter to African readers, welcoming replies and questions.[95] Among her qualifications to teach African history to Africans she included her conversations with African leaders and students, including 'two or three educated women', visits to Aggrey House, a hostel for African students in London, and her talks at WASU. She had also 'read books by Africans: Padmore, Azikiwe, Mockerie, Kenyatta, Kayamba, Jabavu, and others'.[96] *Africans and British Rule* set the tone for Perham's overall approach to criticising and defending the British Empire. She admitted that imperial rule was obtained by force and had cruelly exploited African peoples. Yet Britain's was still the most 'checked and softened' empire in history.[97] Perham had asked her African readers to find some sympathy for Britain's plight: 'You must try to understand our difficulties as well as our faults'.[98] The real question now was how quickly Africans could develop political maturity. It gave Perham 'great pleasure' to declare that there was no evidence of any inherent racial inferiority. Africans were 'now free to prove to the world' their ability 'to progress'.[99] Britain itself, and those in the white settler colonies, had to face up to the facts, past and present: 'the strongest men and the strongest nations are those with the courage to face the truth'.[100]

White settlers succeeded in briefly banning *Africans and British Rule* in Kenya due its alleged anti-settler bias and call for greater African representation. In the League of Coloured Peoples *Newsletter*, the book was also condemned by St. Lucian LSE economist, W. Arthur Lewis. The book, he wrote, was,

not merely smug and self-satisfied: it reeks of that self-conceit which typifies the colonial Englishman and which is doing more than anything else to poison the relations between the races . . . The book will go down well in the Colonial Office; it will please the settlers and doubtless be subsidised by one or two colonial governments. Africans fortunately are accustomed to being insulted. They will merely hope that Miss Perham will have learned a little manners before she settles down to write her next apology for imperialism.[101]

By the middle of the 1940s, Perham was exactly where she wanted to be, charting what she saw as the realistic middle course between the 'extremes' of white settlers and anticolonial intellectuals. A progressive though gradual move toward African self-rule was the only justifiable course, given what she never questioned—the fact of African backwardness and the relative benevolence of the British Empire. As she later wrote in 1951, the British policy of 'gradualism', 'so logical and defensible', was the 'compromise between two extremes', which 'thus runs against the opposition of black and white in Africa. It is too quick for the whites; it is too slow for the Gold Coast Africans today and will be too slow for those of Kenya tomorrow'.[102]

## Women's Intellectual Life as Sexual Displacement

Perham's gender was inseparable from her position as the Establishment's authoritative voice on empire. She deployed her sex, and ideas of sex difference, to influence the management of imperial rule. While she continually pushed for reform, Perham celebrated British colonial paternalism and masculine virtues. Because of its physical strain and violence, she thought colonial administration was 'a man's job', ideally one educated at Oxford in one of her colonial service schools, their qualities of 'courage and physical prowess' already refined in elite private schools.[103] These men had their faults, she later noted, like excessive concern with hierarchy, but 'his too unoccupied wife' suffered from that 'even more'.[104] Perham became a kind of 'godmother' to the Colonial Service in the final decades of colonial rule.[105] Her works were required reading for colonial service cadets, generations of whom she taught.

Perham's strategy to influence the men of late empire was to pursue a balanced, tempered critique of the worst excesses of settler colonialism that neither threatened the empire's gender order or the masculinity of its administrators.[106] She gently cajoled officers of state and earned their respect. Like Susan Strange, discussed later, she seemed to prefer the company of men and was sceptical of the women's liberation movement.[107] Perham was appointed to the African Women's Education Sub-Committee because she was a woman, though she was not very interested in women's education and did not centre African women in colonial welfare policy. According to her research assistant Martin Wight, Perham 'is nothing so vulgar as a feminist. She is not interested in women as a class. The right she has implicitly fought for is the right of first-class women to be treated as equals by men . . . Like Queen Elizabeth the First, equal rights plus feminine appeal'.[108]

In *Native Administration in Nigeria*, Perham suggested that the women's movement was a 'sudden strain thrown upon primitive communities by the strong, all-embracing pressure of European influence'.[109] According to a former student, Perham 'despised her women's college, St Hugh's, and thought that Nuffield . . . was paradise in comparison',[110] but this was likely more to do with location, money, the absence of undergraduates, and the prestige of her unique status at Nuffield. As Wight observed, she was 'the first woman fellow of the first College in either Oxford or Cambridge to mix the sexes . . . Perham presiding at dinner at Nuffield High Table, in the warden's absence, a senior fellow, is something without precedent and still without parallel in Oxbridge, and she carries it off as effortlessly as if she were Catherine the Great'.[111] As an exceptional woman of a certain class, she could nudge colonial policy in a different direction, while retaining her influence and access. Of course, her desire to move policy towards more welfare and colonial development can be read in gendered terms as can her partial truth-telling on the need for Britain to accept its diminished global standing and description of Britain as 'colonial foster-mothers' to newly independent African states.[112] Where Susan Strange did not think of imperial–international relations in explicitly gendered terms, as discussed in chapter 8, Perham conceived imperialism through the lens of sexual relations.

Depending on her age, Perham was viewed by imperial men as their teacher, biographer, translator, 'potentially meddlesome woman', therapist, or virgin spinster workaholic.[113] Like Lucy Philip Mair, who taught colonial administration at LSE, Perham never married or had children. It was likely inconceivable to Perham that she could marry a man and operate at such a high professional level. Yet, despite all the talk of her physical attractiveness and prowess, Wight questioned whether it was 'a marriageable attractiveness'.[114] Like her Oxford colleague Sibyl Crowe, Perham kept a series of companionable dogs—Agnes Headlam-Morley preferred cats—and she was committed to animal welfare, writing to *The Times* about the fate of millions of battery hens as 'little white boiler corpses'.[115] Perham devoted herself entirely to work and, according to her biographer at least, remained a 'lifelong spinster unlucky in love'.[116] Her many research assistants liked to gossip about whether she was a virgin, concluding that she was. Colleagues and assistants were fascinated by her sex life, or lack thereof, and the degree to which her obsession with work was a substitute for heterosexual marriage and children, an expression of her sexual desire, her 'feminine energy', or 'the redirection of a multifarious psycho-sexual drive'.[117]

In the sexist discourse of Perham as a virgin spinster, her high-profile career, like the 'experiment' of the motorcycle, was a sexual displacement activity. This is how one of Perham's (male) friends in the Colonial Office described and thereby reduced her intellectual accomplishments. For all her achieve-ments, she remained like 'a housewife', Perham recounted, 'eager to sweep and scrub and manage the world'. Africa was supposed to be my 'house, my hus-band and my children, and . . . I conscientiously wear myself out according to the ancient tradition of all serving women'.[118] Working under Perham's patron-age for a number of years, Martin Wight rejected any notion that she was just like any 'female welfare-worker, all goodwill and platitudes'.[119] Perham too vociferously rejected any domestic analogy for her work world, even as she promoted and defended a racialised heteronormative order premised on do-mestic arrangements that she herself relied on.

Like many of her male peers such as Arnold Toynbee and Alfred Zimmern, Perham's work was supported by the extensive domestic and administrative labours of women. After World War II, when Perham's sister left her philan-dering husband, the sisters lived together for the rest of their lives. Wight observed that the family support for Perham was 'almost over-intense . . . Margery's own career seems, from early days, to have been the most impor-tant thing for all her relatives'. She was the family 'matriarch, if matriarch is the right word for a child-less chieftainess'.[120] Ethel managed all the domestic arrangements and chores, while Perham's research was supported by an army of mostly female assistants, including Mary Bull, wife of Hedley Bull. Wight clearly resented the patronage of 'this sublime and difficult woman'. He encouraged the author of a profile of Perham to mention 'the most obvious, perhaps hackneyed joke' about her, that she had become a version of 'She-who-must-be-obeyed', the white African queen in Rider Haggard's Victorian-era colonial erotic and romance novels.[121] In the effort to present Perham an 'an example of the great woman', Wight continually reached for the gendered typecast. Perham was 'She' and a child-less chieftainess, but also an aunt-figure out of P. G. Wodehouse; the mythical figures of Valkyrie or Sibyl; or Catherine the Great.[122]

FIGURE 2.2. Mary and Hedley Bull, with Emily and Martha, January 28, 1967. Photographer Unknown. Courtesy of Emily Craker

Unlike Wight, Mary Bull became an expert on both colonial administration and the figure of Margery Perham. Mary worked on and off with Perham from 1954, after the Bulls moved to Oxford, which 'provided not only an interesting occupation, but a reasonable salary', Mary later recalled. 'As we both had been brought up to frugal habits, Hedley never worried about money or domestic matters again'.[123] Bull's research work for Margery Perham included 'crawling around Rhodes house checking references', 'hunting for elusive documents', and 'carrying out "Girl Friday" tasks'.[124] Perham may have been 'very motherly towards' Mary, another 'IR wife'.[125] Yet through her apprenticeship with Perham, Bull also became an expert on colonial administration, that is, 'a scholar in her own right', as only Coral Bell has pointed out in print.[126] Named assistant editor of the first three volumes of Lord Lugard's diaries, with Perham, Mary is named joint author and co-editor of the fourth instalment. Perham insisted on referring to her as 'Mrs. Hedley Bull' in the acknowledgements to the early volumes of Lugard's diaries, against her assistant's preference for 'Mary Bull'.[127] Bull also authored a short book, *The Medical Services of Tanganyika in 1955*; wrote on indirect rule in Northern Nigeria for Perham's *Festschrift*;

co-edited, co-introduced and wrote for a journal special issue on Perham; and reviewed Perham's posthumously published *West African Passage*.[128]

## Conclusion

In many ways, Margery Perham could be conceived of as an exemplary thinker for what became of IR. When she expressed private doubts as to her intellectual purpose, she did so precisely in the terms that defined what would become British IR's dilettante character, that is, in 'a sort of uneasy and outside position, balanced between sociology and history, between theory and practice . . . My work, whatever it is', Perham feared, 'is extensive and superficial. It covers all aspects of half Africa. It is all at secondhand—picking other men's brains or reading their books. More than ever—I know it now—I have neither the industry nor the method to master or even to keep pace at present standards'.[129] Perham was too harsh on herself. The recent focus on the Edwardian founders of Chatham House and the endless attempts to revive or reconfigure the so-called 'English School', as the heirs to the British Committee on the Theory of International Politics became known, has obscured the one white British thinker on late empire of world historical significance. Yet her marginalisation in IR's intellectual histories is over-determined. She was a woman, an historian, and an expert on the empire during the transition to independence. As discussed in chapter 8, Perham's work of intellectualising and emotionally performing white Britons' moral reckoning with the empire and its loss helped to create the intellectual space for British IR's re-founding as a semi-discipline in the 1970s, shortly after Perham's retirement.

# 3

# The House that Margaret Built

## WHITE WOMEN'S HOUSEWORK
## IN IR'S BACKROOM

LIONEL CURTIS'S PROJECT for a cross-disciplinary 'science' of international relations in the 1920s and 1930s helped to fashion a new kind of international relations expertise.[1] Drawing on research practices refined in South Africa as part of the Milner group project of imperial reform, discussed in chapter 2, Curtis founded Britain's most influential international relations 'think tank', the Royal Institute of International Affairs (RIIA), later known as Chatham House. The defining research methodology of the new Establishment institution was simple enough: the peer review of independent 'fact-based' and often collectively authored and/or anonymised research. Supporting its claim to independence, the Royal Institute refused all government finance, though received funding from banks, corporations, and philanthropic organisations like the Rockefeller Foundation and Carnegie Endowment.[2] Chatham House claimed not to promote any one set of foreign-policy ideas or express an opinion on specific questions. It would gather and disseminate reliable factual knowledge on contemporary international relations on which policymakers, journalists, teachers, and members of the public could base their policies and opinions.

The reputation of the Royal Institute, its funding model, and its political projects were understood to rest on the quality of the factual information that it produced and the excellence of the research it organised and published. In this regard, the most important figure in the history of international relations research at Chatham House was not Lionel Curtis, 'the third-class scholar who became a Fellow of All Souls', Oxford.[3] It was the 'spinster with a thorny exterior', Margaret Cleeve, head of its Information Department.[4] If Curtis was the

63

'founding father' of a particular kind of scientific expertise in international relations, then Cleeve was its 'mother': equally nurturing, stern, and self-sacrificing. Cleeve was hailed inside Chatham House as second only to Curtis as having done 'more than anyone else to promote the institute's standing as the leading centre for the study' of international relations.[5] But more than Curtis, Cleeve oversaw the management, expansion, editing, and dissemination of Chatham House knowledge in its defining first three decades. In 1950, at the peak of Cleeve's influence, Susan Strange, who later worked at Chatham House for fourteen years, described it as the dominant British research institution in international relations.[6] Cleeve's Chatham Housework underpinned every basic activity for which the institution became famous: 'meetings and discussions; research by groups and by individual scholars; publications; the provision of information; the maintenance of a reference library on international affairs'.[7]

The language of science at Chatham House amounted to peer review, emphasis on 'facts', and coyness about its political agenda. Curtis and Cleeve's vision of a science of international relations was gendered, raced and classed not primarily because it was first imagined by elite white men in South Africa. It was because of the gendered, classed, and racialised Others against which it was defined and the labour of those on which it relied, an army of backroom workers and information entrepreneurs, primarily middle-class white women. Margaret Cleeve's work not only illuminates the role of international relations think tanks as a location of women's intellectual labour.[8] She is a case study of an indispensable but overlooked persona in the history of the scientific study of IR, that of the selfless woman utterly devoted to the cause and on whom major institutions depended. Examining Cleeve, and some of the figures she employed, illuminates the gender and class order at Chatham House, including the labour practices of a small number of 'big men' and much larger armies of women staff, intimate relations between these men and their researchers, and the changing valuations of the professional worth of information management on international affairs. Cleeve's importance was well understood at her retirement in 1956 both by its 'big men' and the mostly women staff. Internal Chatham House discussions about whether to honor Cleeve after her death in 1967 reveals much about the later devaluation of Cleeve's work and the gendered politics of memorialisation, then and now.

The mode, method, and content of early scientific studies on international relations depended on a gender order at Chatham House. But it was also a response to the wider popular contestation of international relations at the start of the twentieth century. In addition to coordinating Britain's white settler dominions, the popularisation of opinions on imperial and international affairs was the other major context for the institutionalisation of the scientific study of international relations at Chatham House.[9] One of the main targets of its ire was the League of Nations Union (LNU), Britain's leading voluntary society advocating on behalf of the League.[10] Cambridge classicist Florence Melian Stawell's idea to write the urtext of international intellectual history, *The Growth of International Thought*, rather than her original proposal for a popular history of the League, had come from Gilbert Murray, co-president of the LNU as well as Professor of Greek.[11] Stawell was an LNU member. Before lecturing on international relations and colonial administration at the London School of Economics (LSE) from 1928, Lucy Philip Mair, another classicist from Newnham College Cambridge, worked at the LNU for five years as publicity secretary, head of the Intelligence Department, lecturer, and representative at the Assembly of the League in Geneva. Mair is discussed in chapter 4.

After World War I, increasingly organised colonised populations, workers' movements, and suffragists were disseminating their competing and sometimes overlapping visions of world order—liberal socialist, anticolonial, and feminist—in newspapers and pamphlets, all challenging the notion that diplomacy was the preserve of elite white men.[12] The LNU was not the most radical of these movements, yet it was the most influential. In 1923, Kathleen Conyngham Greene's memorandum, 'The British Public and the League of Nations', a product of Curtis's peer review method at Chatham House, complained that LNU-sponsored writing was so pervasive that most British people thought the organisation was synonymous with the League itself; 'practically all the knowledge' British people have comes from LNU 'propaganda for what is called "the League idea"'.[13] In over-emphasising the League's social and humanitarian work, the LNU and its propagandists had 'taken up an attitude like that of the Naval Officer who shows his wife or his mother over a ship of war and calls her attention to the excellent baths, kitchens and pianos to divert her attention from the fact that all ships of war are built to carry big guns and that if these were fired in anger he might be in danger of being hurt'.[14] Where the LNU was spinning 'a web of sentimentality' around the League, Chatham House claimed to educate the 'public' by pointing to such objective facts.

The class project of Chatham House was implicitly and euphemistically acknowledged in its own account of itself. As Margaret Cleeve wrote, 'foreign affairs would no longer be left in the hands of a few diplomatists and experts, . . . the "man on the street" . . . would demand a say in their conduct'.[15] Cleeve's 'man on the street' encompassed not just white working-class men, but also women struggling for the vote. The claim to produce scientific work, in other words, rested on a dubious yet effective distinction between reliable 'facts' and the political 'opinion' of more leftist and feminist agitators, some more radical than others. Chatham House was the product of an imperial imagination and a response to the democratisation and feminisation of international relations expertise, including more openly political and popular forms of internationalist writing aimed at ordinary citizens, teachers, and school-children. Much of this work was written by women seeking to foster a 'lifelong habit of taking an interest in international relations', as economic historian Eileen Power wrote.[16]

Yet if we examine the writing of figures such as Florence Melian Stawell and her contemporary Eileen Power, then the distinction between internationalist writing aimed at ordinary citizens and children and scholarship of the highest order was less clear cut. Educated at elite women's colleges in Cambridge and considered among the best thinkers of their generation, Stawell and Power disrupt 'early IR's' binary distinction between scientific work and popular writing on international affairs, a distinction that was also foundational to the British Coordinating Committee for International Studies (BCCIS), founded in 1928 as part of the League of Nations interdisciplinary International Studies Conference, discussed further in chapter 4. Stawell and Power also destabilise heterosexist, as well as male homosocial norms, in international intellectual history. Where professional and personal boundaries were blurred in the largely heterosexual order at Chatham House, Stawell and Power suggest that homosocial relations between women and non-heteronormative lives were important networks and contexts of international thought.

## Kitchens and Pianos v. Big Guns: The Science of IR versus Popular Pedagogy

In the early 1920s, the best international relations book for teens, according to Eileen Power, was *Patriotism and the Fellowship of Nations: A Little Primer of Great Problems* by F. Melian Stawell.[17] Stawell's 1916 book was a plea for restraint in British foreign policy and for international and imperial reform, for the establishment of an international court, international council, international police, and the moderation of class war through a fairer distribution of wealth. Like the founders of Chatham House and its affiliated institutions in the white settler Commonwealth, Stawell evoked the common bonds of respect and affection between Britain, Australia, New Zealand and Canada, 'links by which we may hope to build up a chain of Humanity'.[18] The moral case for colonisation went beyond the crass notions of 'might is right', she argued, to avoid anarchy and barbarism. Performing moral anguish at empire's violence, Stawell claimed that Britons must remember and admit 'alas!' the 'terrible cruelties' and wider international conflicts caused by colonisation.[19]

F. Melian Stawell lived a privileged life, the youngest daughter of ten children, born into a wealthy and political family in the white settler colony of Australia. Her father, Sir William Stawell, was the Chief Justice and Lieutenant-Governor of Victoria. Stawell's mother, Mary Frances, later Lady Stawell, came from 'a long line of accomplished public servants . . . and the women (wives and mothers) . . . were more than their equals'.[20] F. Melian Stawell was among the first of six women permitted to attend the University of Melbourne that her father had co-founded and was then admitted to Newnham College, Cambridge in 1889. Despite not being recognised as a member of the university and attending lectures only if individual male dons allowed, Stawell was 'lauded by the men of Cambridge (one of whom described her as a Greek God incarnate)'.[21] Her father likely approved. So obsessed with the ancient Greeks was he that he named his youngest daughter after the inhabitants of Melos, the island whose women the Athenians famously enslaved during the Peloponnesian War. Stawell graduated in the First Division of the Classical Tripos, was appointed classics lecturer at Newnham, and her many doings were proudly reported in the Australian press.

In common with many interwar international thinkers, including her mentor, Gilbert Murray, Stawell combined her interest in contemporary world politics with classical training and scholarship, writing prolifically on both.[22] For her, like so many white British international thinkers including Alfred Zimmern, 'the script was Greek'; some of Stawell's interpretations and translation of ancient texts remain standard works.[23] The work for which she is known today, *The Growth of International Thought*, located in antiquity the germ of two ideas that Stawell claimed would be the foundation for international peace in the twentieth century, 'arbitration between equals and confederacy on equal terms'.[24] Yet, she lamented, any cooperation among Greek city states only seemed possible when they were 'united against another enemy, the Persian . . . "the foreigner"'.[25]

Stawell's script was also feminist and settler colonial. She hailed Thucydides's history of the Peloponnesian War as 'one of the strongest indictments against

FIGURE 3.1. Florence Melian Stawell c.1890s. Photographer Unknown. Public domain

war ever written'.[26] Yet she also turned to the equally powerful 'voice of reason and pity'[27] in the Euripides play *The Trojan Women*. Euripides famously recounted the Peloponnesian War from the perspective of the Melian women survivors of the slaughter, the 'conquered . . . are the heroic figures in the drama'.[28] Even Stawell's middle name recognised the conquered inhabitants of Melos. But as the granddaughter of white settlers, race and empire were also the foundation of Stawell's Eurocentric and teleological account of the history of international thought in which colonised populations were 'savages' and the underlying principles of true internationalism had 'been felt, sometimes clearly, more often dimly, by all the best thinkers of Europe'.[29]

Stawell was set for an illustrious career as a scholar of ancient Greece and the new imperial internationalism. Yet her Cambridge lectureship was cut short because of ill health, limiting her influence on the development of international thinking at Cambridge and beyond. She moved to London, living at the edges of the Bloomsbury circle, and associating with Virginia Woolf, Bertrand Russell, and G. Lowes Dickinson. She also lectured for the LNU and Morley College for Working Men and Women, founded in 1889 by feminist and social reformer Emma Cons and the first such college to admit women and men on equal terms.

At her death in 1936, Stawell was compared to the figure 'seated in a boat with a globe on her knee, in an allegorical picture by Giovanni Bellini now in the Accademia at Venice'.[30] This black-and-white portrait (Figure 3.1.) captures an androgyny or perhaps Stawell's queerness. She looks directly at the camera with worried eyes and a serious expression, a strong jawbone, thick neck, and hair pulled back. According to the *Australian Dictionary of Biography*, Stawell 'died unmarried'.[31] But she had a lifelong relationship with Clara (Clare) Reynolds, whom she met at Cambridge and with whom she lived continuously from 1921 until her death. Cambridge women's colleges were locations of passionate, sometimes queer bonds. At Newnham, Stawell developed an intense relationship with Mary Parker Follett, then visiting from Harvard Annex, later Radcliffe College. Stawell sparked Follett's interest in international relations, leading to Follett's 'masterpiece' on domestic and international reform, *The New State*.[32] At Follett's death in 1933, Stawell wrote her obituary, which, unlike her own in the *Australian Dictionary of Biography*, included Follett's long-term relationship with a woman, Isobel Briggs Myers.

F. Melian Stawell could make her way outside the academy because of her elite education, class and colonial privilege, and the life she made with Clare Reynolds. Not born into the same class privilege, Eileen Power pursued her internationalist projects and scholarly work from the relative safety of a lifelong career in academe. Born in 1889, the eldest of three sisters, Power came from a middle-class Anglo-Irish family based in Cheshire. Her mother died when she was fourteen, and Power was estranged from her stockbroker father who was convicted and imprisoned for fraud. Two spinster aunts saved the sisters from financial ruin, funding their education at Oxford High School for Girls. Power won a clothesworkers' scholarship to read History at Girton College, Cambridge where she worked for its branch of the National Union of Women's Suffrage Societies and received first class honours in 1910. Power won a Gilchrist Fellowship the following year to study at the Ecoles des Chartes in Paris at a time when French historians were experimenting with narrative history and the intersection of history and the new social sciences. Power returned to a two-year fellowship at LSE, funded by feminist Charlotte Payne Townsend Shaw, during which Power researched a pathbreaking study of the socio-economic life of medieval nunneries.[33] Power returned to Girton in 1913, becoming its director of history and one of the first women to lecture at Cambridge.

During the next three decades, and as discussed further in chapter 5, Eileen Power became a dominant figure in the historical profession in Britain and the most sophisticated international thinker at LSE in the 1920s and 1930s. While scholarly research, Power wrote, 'is the thing I <u>really</u> care about',[34] she was a politically engaged intellectual and was one of the leading writers and broadcasters of popular internationalism for ordinary public audiences, including school-children.[35] She was also deeply involved in the revision of school textbooks toward a greater focus on international affairs, editing and writing the preface and forward to the second edition of *A Bibliography for School Teachers of History*.[36] She collaborated with the Women's International League to influence history teaching in schools because they were 'the engine-rooms in which power is created'.[37] In December 1931, the director of the International Institute of Intellectual Cooperation, Henri Bonnet, invited Power to serve on a committee of experts to revise textbooks 'from the point of view of internationalism'.[38] G. P. Gooch chaired, and Eileen Power was secretary to the British National Committee of International Cooperation.[39] Power taught for the Workers' Educational Association and regularly lectured at the LNU.[40] She was treasurer for the Union of Democratic Control and had close links with Virginia Gildersleeve and her partner Caroline Spurgeon's International Federation of University Women' (IFUW) that grew out of the British Federation's Committee on International Relations. Gildersleeve, a medievalist like Power, was the only women included among the United States delegates to the 1945 San Francisco United Nations Conference. She invited Power to lecture at Barnard College in the spring of 1930.

Kathleen Conyngham Greene's Chatham House memorandum compared the League's social and humanitarian work to the baths, kitchens and pianos on a warship, a mere distraction for navy wives and mothers from the big guns on board.[41] But Eileen Power understood the importance of the 'kitchens of History'.[42] Her highly acclaimed *Medieval People*, published the year after Greene's memorandum and reprinted in ten editions, argued that while due recognition should be paid to the fact and ferocity of big guns, the social labour of ordinary people toiling in kitchens were also part of the story of world politics. Within the context of imperial and civilisational hierarchy— Power was no anticolonial thinker—she sought to include peoples and topics unjustly excluded from the historical record, particularly women and workers. She thus developed a form of internationalist social history that emphasised major economic transformations that shaped peoples' lives across the world and the interconnections across borders. The co-development of social and world history was Power's response to what she saw as the common origins of World War I in nationalism and class war.

For Power, the dual realities of class conflict and international relations demanded new forms of historical writing—social and world history—that would contribute to political and international transformation, but also a new form of historical pedagogy in the classroom. To avoid 'international or class war', history teaching must 'show mankind its common heritage in the past and its common hopes for the future'.[43] Children had to understand their own 'country within the larger whole of mankind, swept by great movements common at least to Europe'.[44] Presaging her later critique of the dominance of political and nationalist modes of historical writing, Power argued that most children across Europe thought of people in other nations as either '"the enemy" or "the allies," in the long series of struggles'.[45] Instead, national history should be taught within a 'framework of international history' so that children saw their own country not as [an] isolated planet moving through space', but part of a 'firmament of peoples'.[46] Stressing sameness and interdependence could produce solidarity across borders. Social and internationalist history was the necessary underpinning of a new form of world citizenship as given expression in the League.

As with her lecture notes and unpublished manuscripts, we are left with only some of Eileen Power's writings and broadcasts which survive in her papers. Yet as writer Francesca Wade has also noted, 'a large and important facet of her legacy is intangible, residing in the form of impressions made on children in their formative years'.[47] With her younger sister, Rhoda Power, '*doyenne* of BBC schools broadcasting between the 1920s and 1950s', Eileen recorded radio broadcasts and co-authored numerous books, including *Boys and Girls of History*, *Cities and Their Stories*, and *Twenty Centuries of Travel*.[48] Part of the Britain and World History Series, the latter surveyed how the Romans, Anglos, Saxons and Normans came to Britain; how Marco Polo went to China and Eastern goods came to England; how the Cabots sailed to America and Drake sailed around the world; how the East India Company 'went to India', Captain Cook sailed to New Zealand and Australia, and Livingstone and Stanley 'explored' Africa.[49] In 1934, the sisters lectured for the BBC on the Age of Discovery and the old civilisations of America, the relations between Europe and the Turks, the Mogul Empire in India, the Manchu Empire in China, and strong men in Japan. They lectured on 'Liberty, Equality, and Fraternity' without mentioning Haiti, and the American and Industrial Revolutions without mentioning slavery. Power told British children about the rise of the workers, endorsing Robert Owen over Karl Marx because 'most of the workers of Europe have preferred to go quietly on, getting equality bit by bit through their unions and Parliaments'.[50] She told them that the world was 'tied together' by 'the trade roads, the land roads and the sea roads . . . So silk and spices and plants got carried about all over the world, and religion and mathematics and stories and designs got carried about all over the world too. And every person or thing or thought that moved along the roads was like another little thread tying the world together'.[51]

With her numerous radio broadcasts and textbooks, Eileen Power was clearly more active and successful than related efforts by the British

Coordinating Committee for International Studies (BCCIS) to revise school textbooks. The BCCIS men were far less effective, in part, due to the premature death of S. H. Bailey, the LSE IR man most interested in the subject, but also because Power was more intellectually dynamic.[52] Eileen Power got on with the work of rewriting school textbooks while the BCCIS men were talking about it. As discussed further in chapter 5, she led innovative cross-disciplinary work at the intersection of social, world, and economic histories of international relations.

Power's erasure from IR's intellectual and disciplinary history was almost certainly shaped by her place in the gender order, in addition to her premature death from a sudden heart attack in 1940. Power performed a gender identity that was unusual in the context of male-dominated academe, though more common in Bloomsbury where she spent her adult life.[53] Unlike the self-reliant 'bluestocking' stereotype ('very learned, very excellent, very tiresome'[54]), many of whom never left their women's colleges, Power enacted a version of femininity that did not conceal her beauty and that attracted both women and men.

Power is often remembered more for her attractiveness and teaching than her scholarly work, and the fact that she was a woman was hardly ever ignored.[55] Contemporaries routinely commented on her 'beauty and grace',[56] her elegant and 'attractive'[57] appearance and her 'personal charm'.[58] Power was 'beautiful and erudite', 'exceptionally charming'.[59] Her Bloomsbury apartment was full of 'beautiful things, mostly Chinese' and her dresses were 'glittering'.[60] 'Eileen', said one admirer, 'you look like Semiramis', the only woman ruler of the Syrian Empire. 'I thought I looked like a Professor of Economic History', she replied.[61] 'Everyone had fallen in love' with Power.[62] Her most intimate friendship was with Girton College woman and historian Gwladys Jones, one-time international hockey player, who loved Power 'uniquely and possessively' and with whom she occasionally shared a bed.[63] Gwladys Jones succeeded Power as Girton director of history and it is no coincidence that she authored the second book of *The New World History Series*, covering 1485 to 1688, after Power authored the first, 'from the beginning to 1485'.[64] It is likely that Power's singular influence led Jones, the one-time historian of eighteenth-century English Charity Schools in Ireland, to become the main lecturer on the new subject of international relations at Cambridge for almost two decades until 1945 when historians voted to discontinue the subject, as discussed in chapter 4.[65]

During travels around China in 1929, the married international historian Arnold Toynbee also became 'spellbound' with Power. According to his

FIGURE 3.2. M. G. Jones and Eileen Power 1909. GCPH 10/25/24.
Photographer Unknown. Courtesy of the Mistress and Fellows of
Girton College, Cambridge

biographer, Power seemed to Toynbee 'delightfully responsive' to his 'grand
ideas on the clash of civilizations in the Far East'.[66] Yet Power's own early
writing on China as a 'third civilisation', neither East nor West 'yet both'[67] was
more interesting. Power's writing on China aligned not only with Orientalist
tropes of the erotic allure of the East, as discussed further in chapter 5, but the
fluidity of her own gender performance.[68] In order to travel through the Khy-
ber Pass in the early 1920s, Power disguised herself and passed 'as a man' in
what she described as 'a sort of hermaphrodite process'.[69] In her poem, 'Pekin',
originally published in the feminist journal *Time and Tide* in 1925, Power
imagined herself as a 'mandarin' living in 'yellow-roofed Pekin', with 'a lady
bright/ More beautiful than pale starlight/ And she should love me all the
night . . . / And sometimes she would dance for me'.[70] On learning that Power

was (briefly) engaged to a British diplomat during their travels together in China, Arnold Toynbee went to her adjoining room to profess his love, begging Power to call off the engagement. Power dispatched him instantly; he consoled himself by writing Greek verse about a man conquering the 'primaeval Bull' within.[71] A few years later, Toynbee divorced his first wife, Rosalind Murray, daughter of Gilbert, and married his research assistant at Chatham House.

## Then Being a Woman

With the arrival of Arnold Toynbee as research director in 1923, Chatham House activities expanded and Margaret Cleeve was soon in charge of the defining aspect of its work, the production and dissemination of reliable and objective knowledge on international affairs as a counter to the increasingly widespread 'propaganda' written in favour of the League of Nations project by figures such as Power and Stawell. Under Cleeve, Chatham House became the world leader in the documentation and analysis of major international developments. As Katharina Rietzler has recently pointed out, 'the business of foreign affairs think tanks was deeply entwined with practices of the retrieval, selection, preservation and analysis of primary sources'.[72] In this setting, reliable information was 'a highly prized commodity in a historical context that preceded the 1970s information revolution'.[73]

Little is known of Cleeve's early life except that she was well travelled. Born in 1895, she lived in Singapore as a child, visiting China and Japan, living in France from 1917 and moving to the United States in 1919. Cleeve was at Wellesley in the spring of 1921 when her friend, Eleanor Cargin, wrote to say that there was a 'niche' for her at a new Institute in London where she was the first organising secretary. Cleeve left on the first vessel she could find, 'a cattle boat which was making her last trip from Boston to Liverpool',[74] to become assistant secretary at the then British Institute for International Affairs, based in a single office near Victoria Station in London. Cleeve oversaw the institute's first move into five rooms at the Institute of Historical Research in London and then to the new building, Chatham House in St James's Square in 1923 while Curtis 'was busy arranging the partition of Ireland'.[75]

Margaret Cleeve was the main information entrepreneur, providing the raw materials for international relations research and teaching at a time when there was no real competitor to Chatham House, at least in Britain, and when information management generated its own international professional networks. The skilled work of documentation, the multilingual work of reading, collecting and arranging press clippings from around the world, organising library collections, documents, statistics, and memoranda, and the editing of journals of international affairs: these were fundamental to the production and legitimacy of new 'scientific' knowledge and teaching in the new field. This was the core source material, the archive, for the study of international relations as contemporary history in both think tanks and the wider academy. At Aberystwyth, for example, the Department of International Politics had its own library, 'dominated by the sombre ranks of black-bound volumes of the complete proceedings of the Council, Assembly and agencies of the League of Nations', organised and maintained by the 'formidable' Elizabeth Morris.[76]

Cleeve represented Chatham House on the Council of the National Central Library, the League of Nations Union Library Committee, and the Publications Committee of the Institute of Pacific Relations, one of the leading international relations think tanks in the United States.[77] According to Lionel Curtis, 'almost all of the important publications of the institute have passed through' Margaret Cleeve's 'hands'.[78] She was accordingly elected a member of Chatham House in 1930 with Curtis's nomination describing her qualifications as knowledge of national and international institutions for the study of international relations, and 'teaching, discussion, research and publications, including library and information services'.[79] From 1932 to 1957, Cleeve edited the Institute's flagship journal *International Affairs* when its book review section was considered the 'best of its kind in the world'.[80] She was fastidious in maintaining proper standards, once deleting contemporary historian and journalist Elizabeth Wiskemann's use of the word 'scurrilous'.[81]

Under Cleeve, the Chatham House press-cutting service was 'the envy of all working in our field'.[82] To maintain this lead, Cleeve travelled to European capitals on reconnaissance missions and to arrange publication exchanges.[83] She visited the International Colonial Institute in Brussels in 1930, but with no reference library, bibliographies or even advice on publications Cleeve was unimpressed.[84] The library at the French Ministry of Colonies consisted of only two small underground rooms with shelves 'bulging with unbound papers'. The Deutsche Hochschule fur Politik was more impressive, and Cleeve made detailed records on its methods of filing and storing press clippings. 'The cuttings are filed in cardboard boxes with a front flap. These stand one on top of the other on the shelves, and the total amount of cuttings possessed by the Hochschule were contained in a space of about 10ft.–12ft. long and 5ft.–6ft. high. The cuttings are pasted on foolscap sheets, long cuttings being pasted on the back. If a cutting is many columns wide, it is pasted longwise. Subjects are kept in different folders'.[85] The distinctive Chatham House method of folding clippings made its way into IR lecture halls. Years later, one LSE student could still recall the sound of her professor, Charles Manning, folding and unfolding press cuttings 'in Chatham House fashion . . . tut-tut-tut-tut'.[86]

Cleeve was a fixture in Britain's small academic IR scene of the 1920s and 1930s. She was secretary of the British Coordinating Committee for International Studies (BCCIS), founded in 1928, the same year that women gained the vote on equal terms with men. The Coordinating Committee claimed to represent 'all institutions in Great Britain providing for the scientific study of International Relations',[87] which initially comprised only four institutions, the International Politics Department in Aberystwyth (founded in 1919), Chatham House (founded in 1920), the Department of International Studies at LSE (created in 1927), and Oxford's Montague Burton Professor of IR (established in 1930). In the interwar period, BCCIS simply echoed Chatham House: the study of international relations should be as 'objective' and ethically neutral as possible, with 'propaganda sedulously avoided'.[88] BCCIS members also singled out the LNU and its 'great mass of pamphlets', which had 'destroyed the market for non-propagandistic publications'.[89] According to LSE lecturer S. H. Bailey, a member of the LNU, this could only be remedied by training 'more graduates with a scientific outlook on and knowledge of international relations'.[90] The ability to introduce international relations as a subject in the schools, as well as the universities, 'depended largely upon combining a scientific approach with a new technique of presentation'.[91]

As BCCIS secretary, Cleeve organised the 1933 conference on 'International Studies in Great Britain', the year she was awarded an O.B.E. in the New Year honours list. She was Chatham House representative at the International Studies Conferences (ISC), established in 1928, and organised the eighth ISC conference at Chatham House in 1935. She was unimpressed by the preparatory work for the tenth conference in Paris. 'The idea is alright, the general setting is alright, the actual practice is not', she complained. 'If we could have one big man the thing would be pulled up'.[92] She attended the conference but was uninspired by Charles Manning's 'impassioned speech'. He 'always did defeat interpreters and precis writers'.[93] However, she worked with Manning, Alfred Zimmern, and Lilian Friedlander's trailing spouse Jirí Vránek on the Editorial Committee for the English edition of the *Lexicon of Political Terms*. She also produced the memoranda on the history of Chatham House study groups, which remains an important source for historians of international thought.

FIGURE 3.3. Margaret Cleeve (front left), with Harry Snell and John Power. The other woman is unknown. Photographer Unknown. Courtesy of Chatham House

By the early 1930s, institutes affiliated to Chatham House were established in Canada, Australia, New Zealand, South Africa, and India. As 'Deputy Director General'[94] in all but name, Cleeve travelled to discuss the formation of one last branch to 'complete the circle', in Newfoundland in 1938.[95] Newfoundland acquired dominion status in 1907 yet surrendered independence after economic collapse in 1933. Its precarious status defeated efforts to establish a separate branch of the institute, and it later joined the Canadian Federation in 1949. Cleeve, nonetheless, made the most of her North America trip, including visits to the Halifax and Ottawa branches. The first meeting women were permitted to attend at any Canadian affiliate was an event in Cleeve's honour.[96] Unfortunately, Cleeve complained, dinner conversation was 'desultory'. 'Then being a woman I had to go with the wives and next thing was a room full of important-looking men and we plunged in'.[97] The 'we' was likely Cleeve and the men.

Things improved in New York, where almost half the guests at the welcome party for Cleeve were women, including employees of the Institute of Pacific Relations, the Rockefeller Foundation, the Council on Foreign Relations, and the Foreign Policy Association.[98] Cleeve held meetings at all the major international relations think tanks and funders as well as the League of Nations

Association and American Institute of Public Opinion. In Washington, she took meetings at Carnegie, Brookings, the Pan-American Union, the Library of Congress, and Department of State Library.[99] On her return, Chatham House asked the Rockefeller Foundation to fund a yearlong sabbatical for Cleeve for more research and travel, though funds were not forthcoming in 1939.[100] At the outbreak of the world war, Cleeve became acting director of Chatham House for two years and then deputy secretary from 1941. Her wartime work included organising courses for eleven thousand officers and men in the British, Canadian, and US armies.[101]

## Chatham Cathouse

Chatham House was more open to women as international relations experts than its Canadian affiliates and the Council on Foreign Relations in New York.[102] Today, Chatham House's official history mentions that a 1931 six-course dinner for donors, all men, elicited '10 letters of complaint from female members'.[103] Presumably they objected to being excluded from the dinner, not that it was paid for by South African diamond money. As already discussed, the institute's 'scientific' method was defined, in part, against more popular 'propagandistic' writing, often written by women. Yet, aspects of this scientific approach made it easier for some women to break into the world of international relations scholarship when opportunities in the academy were restricted.

Chatham House's study groups gave women (usually subordinate) roles in collaborative research. In Curtis's earlier iteration, the purpose of collective work was to obscure individual authorship. Accordingly, Round Table members 'would define a problem, Curtis would produce hundreds of interleaved mimeographed copies of a draft for circulation and written comment among groups throughout the Dominions, and in the light of the replies would produce an anonymous final version'.[104] At Chatham House, advisory committees held meetings, determined topics for research, and brought in leading experts to advise on drafts before a final report was produced and circulated. One of the most important early works to emerge from this method was the 'monumental' 1,837-page *African Survey* in 1938, proposed by South African politician Jan Smuts, led by Lord Hailey, an administrator in British India, and financed by the Carnegie Endowment.[105] As authorities on colonial administration, Lucy Philip Mair and Audrey Richards worked on the *African Survey*, and Margery Perham was consulted. Writing in 1936, Mair described it as 'bloody hard work but interesting and instructive and I think Hailey really is a Great

Man'.[106] International lawyer and later president of the International Court of Justice, Rosalyn Higgins, and international political economist Susan Strange were leading study groups in the 1960s and 1970s.

Individual women writers were also commissioned to produce book-length works on international relations, among them Elizabeth Wiskemann, Higgins, and Strange, Lucy Philip Mair, Elizabeth Monroe, Muriel Grindrod, Doreen Warriner, Miriam Camps, Merle Lipton, Dorothy Pickles, Barbara Ward, and Sheila Grant Duff.[107] Wiskemann and Monroe owed their reputations as leading writers on the contemporary history of international relations to works commissioned by Chatham House. Wiskemann gave up a temporary post teaching history at Newnham College, Cambridge for a commission to write her first book, *Czechs and Germans*, in the space of a year. The book examined the economic, cultural, and political problems of Czechoslovakia, emphasising the 'many centuries of struggle' between Slavs and Germans in the territories and intransigence from both sides, though sympathising with the Czechs. The book was widely praised and described, in the context of Hitler's world policy, as the 'most objective, painstaking study now existing' on one of the most urgent international questions.[108]

Despite writing some of the best-selling and most highly regarded works on contemporary international relations, Wiskemann was never financially secure, with Chatham House paying a pittance, a mere 200 pounds for *Czechs and Germans*.[109] As noted in chapter 4, Wiskemann's academic career was blighted by the misogyny of her doctoral supervisor, who threatened her with violence, and, against the view of her other examiner, refused to award her a doctorate. She managed to eke out a living from journalism, work for Chatham House, taking in lodgers to her home, and later teaching at the universities of Edinburgh and Sussex.

On one level, the RIIA's gender 'inclusion' was tokenistic when, for example, Cleeve proposed a delegation including Lionel Curtis, Philip Kerr, Alfred Zimmern, 'A Conservative, An economist, An Admiral, Air Force, and Woman ("probably 2")', likely herself plus one.[110] Yet, according to Cornelia Navari, a Chatham House researcher for four years in the mid-1960s, co-editor of a volume on its history, and now a leading IR scholar, 'Chatham House was absolutely dominated by women. There were very few men. Women really ran the place . . . all these biddies' (a term for interfering older women).[111] But Chatham House also offered Susan Strange a full-time research position in 1964 after she was pushed out of her IR lectureship at University College London (UCL) by the misogyny of the male IR professors, as shown in chapter 11.

Most women were employed as part of the institute's information management practices.

Under Cleeve's reign, the management of information on international relations depended on the labours of women administrators and staff researchers, in part, because their feminised labour was made cheap. As Cleeve wrote to Ivison Macadam, the institute's director, in 1937, 'I am afraid there will always be something wrong with men at that salary. It's a pity I have set my heart on one!'[112] Few women staffers had degrees before World War II, except those working in the Press Library. According to Navari, the Press Library was 'stuffed with little girls just down from Oxford and Cambridge' working temporarily until they got married.[113] But most women who took on more senior staff roles were unmarried, figures such as Cleeve, Dorothy Hamerton, Anne Campbell, Maggie Eveling, and Eileen Menzies.

The most delicate and disruptive sexual relationships at Chatham House was not an openly same-sex relationship among two women staffers, according to Navari. Rather it was that between one of Chatham House's 'big men', in one case its director, and one of the long-term women staffers in secretarial and assistant administrative roles who would then be favoured. Women staffers were subordinate to the smaller number of 'great men' but equal in status vis-à-vis the men who, in Navari's evaluation, were generally 'very kind and considerate', the type 'who bought their assistants scarves when they went abroad . . . It was the women vis-à-vis one another that was the problem'.[114] She described Chatham House as sometimes like 'a real cathouse'.[115] Navari's account is obviously partial, but it points to the centrality of gender relations to Chatham House.

Other professional and sometimes romantic opportunities came through work on the Institute's main flagship publications, especially the *Survey of International Affairs*.[116] Women researched and co-wrote the annual *Survey*, including Veronica Boulter, Rachel Wall, Sheila Harden, and Coral Bell. As discussed in chapter 10, Bell and Wall later took prestigious positions in academe. The *Documents of International Affairs* were selected by Margaret Carlyle, Denise Folliot, and later Navari, and *The Annual Register of World Events* and *The World Today* were selected and co-edited by Cleeve's successor as editor of *International Affairs*, Muriel Grindrod. Like Cleeve, Veronica Boulter was especially well known for her devotion to Chatham Housework. One of the RIIA's first employees from 1920, Boulter described herself as a naturally shy 'back room girl'.[117] She became secretary to Arnold Toynbee from 1924 and immediately began working with him on the *Survey*, work entirely dependent on the press clippings and information department run by Cleeve. However, with a first-class degree from Newnham College, Cambridge, Boulter was dissatisfied with assisting Toynbee. Within two years, she and Toynbee were co-authoring the *Survey* and numerous other works until their retirement in 1956.[118]

Boulter denied any impropriety in the relationship prior to Toynbee's divorce from Rosalind Murray in 1946. Rosalind, daughter of Gilbert Murray, was not as interested in, or in total agreement with, Toynbee's ideas as Boulter, who would make it her life's work to support his scholarship and reputation.[119] Boulter was the first but not the only researcher to become intimately involved with the Chatham House research director. Rachel Wall's long-term and ultimately destructive affair with Toynbee's successor, Geoffrey Barraclough, briefly advanced her professional career yet led to private despair and later contributed to her professional downfall at Oxford. Unlike Toynbee, Barraclough did not leave his wife. Like Boulter, Wall promoted her lover's approach to international relations as contemporary world history. However, four decades younger than Boulter, Wall's career path and later professional and personal independence from Barraclough, discussed in chapter 10, makes Boulter and Cleeve the most instructive case studies of the selfless woman entirely devoted to the work of a great IR institution.

According to Toynbee's biographer, Boulter's 'life *was* her work. Housekeeping bored her. She was indifferent to food and dress'.[120] She worked harder than Toynbee on his work and reputation, and his dependence on Boulter's emotional and intellectual labours was far greater than her dependence on him.[121] Boulter's work for and with Toynbee was underpinned by her views on the right gendered division of labour, and belief in a 'women's proper function' and skills, which she saw as different but 'complementary' to men's.[122] In practice, this discourse of difference propped up and covered for Toynbee's propensity to grand sweeping generalisations, which Boulter did her best to support with closer historical detail. Boulter also eschewed any attention or fame for her research with Toynbee, despite the so-called 'gentle giant's' efforts to accord recognition to 'his lady'.[123] Boulter likely found a 'vicarious realisation for her ambitions in Toynbee's success'.[124] To that end, she spent considerable time curating Toynbee's legacy, both before and after his death in 1975, collecting and organising his voluminous papers on which his biographer and numerous scholars have depended, usually without recognising their reliance on Boulter's work.[125] As with Patricia Pugh's four-year project of cataloguing the papers of Margery Perham, the Bodleian Library retained Boulter's original numbering in the collection of Toynbee's papers.

## Conclusion

Like Veronica Boulter, Margaret Cleeve dedicated herself to intellectual work on international relations, not for the advancement of a single man and his ideas, but for the institution of Chatham House itself. 'To say that Miss Cleeve was devoted to her work', wrote Director General Ivison Macadam in her *Times* obituary, 'is a gross understatement—she *lived* for it and no sacrifice was too great to ensure that high standards were maintained in every branch of its work'.[126] At a presentation for Cleeve to mark her twenty-fifth year at Chatham House, its chairman, Waldorf Astor, marvelled at Cleeve's 'capacity for over-working and yet not breaking down'.[127] For Helen Liddell, then secretary of the Information Department, 'It is Chatham House first and all the time and never Miss Cleeve'.[128] The methods, the productivity, the reputation of Chatham House was built up under her 'selfless devotion',[129] her painstaking, often 'gruelling work'.[130] According to then director, Kenneth G. Younger, 'it was very largely due to' Margaret Cleeve that the entire 'Research programme of Chatham House maintained a reputation for scholarship and objectivity'.[131] The library, in particular, 'was sacrosanct', recalled one former staffer, 'our girl-ish laughter was always silenced there'.[132] Cleeve ran a 'hard school', according to one apprentice.[133] She had 'little patience with shoddy work',[134] maintaining 'the strictest discipline' and the highest 'standards of accuracy and atten-tion to detail'[135] 'at all costs'.[136]

Praise of this kind, focusing on selflessness, devotion, and headmistress-like discipline, is clearly gendered, not least given assumptions about the painstak-ing nature of information management and editing. Cleeve's contribution to Chatham House was monumental. Cleeve was behind the work of *the* leading institution for international relations research in Britain for three decades. There is no other figure so closely associated with the success of a major institution of British international relations, not even Lionel Curtis himself. Toynbee's connection with the *Survey of International Affairs* comes closest, but its importance soon ended after he and Boulter retired. In contrast, the institution that Curtis and Cleeve built up remains a significant institution for the study of international relations today.

In 1967, Lois Simpson, former head of the Press Library at Chatham House, wrote to her former boss, Ivison Macadam, suggesting that the organisation endow a research prize in honor of Margaret Cleeve. In obituaries and speeches, current and former directors had waxed lyrical about Cleeve's sin-gular influence when Chatham House was Britain's leading institution for international relations research. She had been head of Chatham House's all-important Information Department, its acting director general during World War II, and deputy director general in all but name for thirty years.[137] Everyone inside the institution was aware of her work ethic and selfless devotion; only its founder, Lionel Curtis, rivalled Cleeve's influence. Kenneth G. Younger claimed that it was Cleeve's 'industry and intellectual integrity . . . more *than any other single factor*' that ensured 'Chatham House studies and publications maintained a consistent standard of scholarship and a reputation for accuracy'.[138] Yet when it came to honouring her with more than words, the discourse by which she was seemingly recognised and valued—selflessness, efficiency, consistency, accuracy—was easily flipped.

Younger submitted three reasons why Cleeve should not be memorialised with a research prize in her name. First, twelve years after her retirement and at her death, she was not well enough known among the general membership of Chatham House; only older members and a 'limited number of former staff' still knew of Margaret Cleeve. Second, the quality of Cleeve's work did not justify such an honour. 'Efficient and dedicated as she was', Younger wrote to Andrew Shonfield, director of studies, 'I know she was criticised a good deal at the time'. The Chatham House research programme 'was becoming too solid and unimaginative under her guidance',[139] 'careful rather than distinguished'.[140] Finally, the effort involved in recognising Cleeve was just too much for the men tasked with doing so, the job would be 'rather a bore';[141] just 'another considerable chore', repeated Shonfield, quickly detecting the vibe.[142] Prizes 'are very inconvenient to administer' and 'a millstone around the neck'.[143] Asked to advise, Oxford historian Alan Bullock concurred. A Margaret Cleeve Prize for Research would 'very soon become an embarrassment to everybody'.[144]

All three grounds for rejecting a Cleeve Prize were gendered in assumption and execution. Only a few old members and (women) staff still cared about Cleeve, not the people that mattered. Cleeve herself was somehow responsible for the mediocrity of mid-twentieth-century research at Chatham House when, by the late 1960s, the organisation was floundering because of Britain's diminished world role. No one associated with international relations as a separate subject in this period, including those associated with the British Co-ordinating Committee for International Studies (BCCIS) and Chatham House, produced genuinely first-order scholarship at this time. But with vague and unattributed memories ('she was criticised a good deal at the time'), Cleeve is reduced to a competent administrator ('solid', 'unimaginative', 'careful'). She was not someone genuinely 'distinguished' and thus deserving memorialisation. Worst of all, given Cleeve's own work ethic, Younger and Shonfield were unwilling to make the effort on her behalf, or for the members of staff who might be gratified by recognition of one of their own.

In the late 1960s, none of the 'big men' at Chatham House supported a Margaret Cleeve Prize. Something changed in 2022. At a time when organisations gain credit for 'diversity' and 'inclusion' work, Chatham House belatedly inaugurated the first Margaret Cleeve Lecture to recognise her 'lasting legacy to Chatham House'. The context was the organisation's centenary re-examination of its own history and new work on women and the history of international thought.[145] In exchange for membership of the Margaret Cleeve Circle, people can bequeath a legacy from their estate. Recognising Cleeve is no longer an 'embarrassment to everybody', but good for the institute's reputation and potentially its budget. In 2021, Oxford's Nuffield College similarly inaugurated a Margery Perham Society for individuals who leave financial bequests to the institution. In addition to receiving tax advantages, members are invited to Nuffield for an annual lunch.

Often it is the institutions where women international thinkers worked, more than intellectual and disciplinary historians, that have attempted to keep alive their memory. As noted throughout this book, both well-known and lesser-known figures have been honoured with prizes, buildings, and sometimes whole institutes in their name. When slavers' statues are coming down, and when Rhodes still stands, when the legacies of international and global history are a central focus of public and intellectual debate, the politics of memorialisation matter. But the timing, context, and selectivity of some prizes and awards is also revealing, with a flurry in the 2000s and when 'diversity and inclusion' was entirely compatible with existing class, gender, racial, and national hierarchies of the modern neoliberal academy.

# 4

# No International Relations
# without Women

But what manner of man is this teacher, and where can he be come by . . .
What can one man expect to do among so many sorts of expertise? . . . Can
anyone who claims to be teaching such a subject avoid becoming suspect
as a charlatan?

—CHARLES MANNING[1]

WHEN HISTORIANS EXAMINE intellectual fields though the life and work of
those erased, new themes, genres, and locations are reintroduced, and others
are demoted in significance. Examining women's thought places Cambridge's
presumed relative unimportance as a site of international thinking in a new
light; Oxford emerges as a far more important location than previously
assumed; and the two 'separate IR' departments, Aberystwyth's Department
of International Politics and the London School of Economics' (LSE) International Relations Department, emerge as less significant or singular.[2] Indeed,
these were simply not home of the best and most interesting international
thought in early- to mid-twentieth-century Britain. Economic historian Eileen
Power became one of the earliest and most successful proponents of a historical sociology of world politics, which she developed not in the IR Department
but in LSE's Department of History. Offered lectureships at both LSE and
Cambridge in 1921, she chose LSE, in part because Cambridge dons had just
voted—again—to deny women full university membership. The decision was
celebrated by a mob of 1400 male students rioting and smashing up Newnham,
Cambridge's oldest women's college.[3]

Cambridge's assumed relative lateness to the new field of international relations is usually attributed to Cambridge historians' concerns about IR's tendency to dilettantism and presentism.[4] However, from 1926, and for almost two decades, Mary Gwladys Jones, a fellow of another women's college, Girton, and intimate friend of Eileen Power, taught a year-long undergraduate lecture course on international law for the Faculty of History.[5] In both Oxford and Cambridge, the faculties organise lectures and admit and teach graduate students, and the self-governing colleges admit and teach undergraduates. In 1932, Jones broadened the lecture course to 'International Law and Organisation', emphasising developments after World War I, and de-emphasising diplomatic history. Within two years it was easily the most popular of the three 'alternative subject' papers in the history degree.[6] In addition to academic authorities, Jones assigned various contemporary political and legal texts, including the League Covenant, the Statute of the Permanent Court of International Justice, the Polish Minorities Treaty, and the Monroe Doctrine. Students learned about the laws of war in relation to neutral parties, the difference between colonial mandates and protectorates, and how to evaluate philosopher Immanuel Kant's essay 'Perpetual Peace'.[7] They read E. H. Carr, Alfred Zimmern, Lauterpact, Gathorne-Hardy, Brogan, Hailey and Lugard, but no women, at least not in 1942.

During a review of history papers in 1945, most History Faculty voted to eliminate Jones's course, despite its popularity with the students. According to Jones's faculty colleague Herbert Butterfield, she had 'watered down' the paper to include topical information on efforts at international reform at the League of Nations and this had attracted students who enjoyed 'wishful thinking' about the League. Instead of training them in the rigours of historical research, the course produced students with a more polemical type of mind. Had Jones retained the technical emphasis on interstate law, the course would more likely have survived.[8]

Butterfield's comments on Gwladys Jones's paper, delivered at the fourth conference of the British Coordinating Committee for International Studies (BCCIS) in 1949, was less special pleading for his own subject or method. It was a plea for technical training of *some* kind. His main target was not Jones; he did not even mention her by name. It was the wider project for a separate IR led by Charles Manning, the Montague Burton Professor of IR at LSE.

For Manning, IR scholars were specialists by subject, not method. They need not be trained in nor held accountable to the scholarly standards of its 'under-pinning'[9] or 'companion disciplines', such as history, law, economics, or political science.[10] At any given time, IR scholars could draw on knowledge and techniques from any of them to elaborate on various aspects of international relations. Manning literally envisaged the new IR man as a kind of 'Superman', 'like the one foreseen by Nietzsche, he will have to bred . . . from among the new generation'.[11] Butterfield's plea was for students of international relations to be trained in the methods of one or other of its constituent disciplines. 'I prefer any of the separate techniques to a pretended combination of them'.[12] Without training in the 'precise technique' and rigour of historical or some other method, IR could only produce 'dabblers' and a 'journalistic type of thinking'.[13]

As head of the largest concentration of IR scholars in Britain for three decades, Charles Manning succeeded in his project of turning the study of international relations from a field practised by scholars with disciplinary training in history, classics, law, and anthropology into a field that required no methodological training at all. As one of Manning's successors as LSE Montague Burton Chair and a former journalist approvingly noted in 1989, 'International relations stands as the one social science with barriers to entry so low that anyone can jump them'.[14] To some extent, then, Butterfield's prophesy was correct. In the face of 'so many sorts of expertise',[15] Manning's Superman would be a 'dabbler'. Yet concerns among Cambridge historians about IR's method and scholarly rigour could hardly justify eliminating, rather than reforming, Gwladys Jones's international relations course.[16] Not everyone taught the subject in the 'dabbler' mode. At Oxford, 'one of the first, if not the very first, tutor to take up the subject' was Agnes Headlam-Morley.[17] She lectured on international law and international politics in the mode of diplomatic history.

Might Cambridge dons have rejected IR because it was a subject taught by women? Jones was a senior member of Cambridge's second women's college, Girton, its director of history, though not a member of the Cambridge Faculty of History. She authored the second book of *The New World History Series*, covering the period 1485 to 1688, though she was not a prolific scholar.[18] Jones was a spinster in love with Eileen Power at an institution with a reputation for misogyny. In 1920, even Oxford's dons voted to permit women to graduate from the university.[19] Cambridge's so-called 'lateness' to IR was not only because of its tendency, indeed Manning's *desire*, to produce 'dabblers'. It was also a product of accident and misogyny.

As already discussed, Newnham College lecturer F. Melian Stawell was set for an eminent career as a scholar of ancient Greece and the new international relations. Yet her influence on Cambridge teaching and research on international relations was severely limited by serious ill-health, leading her to resign her lectureship at Newnham. Later, during the 1920s and early 1930s, Stawell continued to write on contemporary international affairs, coining the term 'international thought' with her 1929 book, as we know. Whereas Stawell's mentor, Oxford's Regius Professor of Greek Gilbert Murray, only claimed for himself her idea for a book on the League of Nations,[20] Cambridge's leading diplomatic historian threatened to kick Elizabeth Wiskemann down a flight of stairs.[21]

H.W.V. Temperley was 'well known for his favours and antipathies' and offered Wiskemann limited supervision of her Ph.D. on Napoleon III and the Roman Question, single-handedly denying Wiskemann her a doctorate in 1928. Wiskemann's second examiner, F. A. Simpson, 'the great expert on the Second Empire', thought very highly of her work, she claimed, but 'was too timid to stand up to Temperley'.[22]

On being awarded the M.Litt. instead of the Ph.D., Wiskemann duly resigned her teaching position at Newnham, where she might have shaped the international thought of generations of graduates. Instead, outside the academy, she became one of the leading journalists and writers of her generation, her writing on contemporary international affairs becoming standard texts on IR syllabi into the 1960s.[23] Wiskemann returned to the academy toward the end of her career, taking the Montague Burton Professorship of IR at the University of Edinburgh in the late 1950s. Historian Martin Wight invited Wiskemann to help build a new interdisciplinary field of European Studies at the new and experimental Sussex University, founded in 1960. In 1971, at the age of 71, she took her own life due to sight loss. In 2017, the Political Studies Association created the Elizabeth Wiskemann Dissertation Prize for the Study of Inequality and Social Justice. Erased from IR's intellectual and disciplinary histories, Wiskemann only recently became the subject of the full-length biography she deserves.[24]

In the 1920s, the misogyny of Cambridge dons led figures of the stature of Eileen Power and Elizabeth Wiskemann to decline or walk away from academic positions at Cambridge and pursue highly successful careers elsewhere. We can only speculate whether Power, Stawell, or Wiskemann, had they remained at Cambridge, would have been additionally appointed to a more prestigious joint position with the faculties of Classics or History in addition to their affiliation with a women's college. Distinguished Cambridge historian Betty Behrens, a Fellow of Newnham, author of the official history of merchant shipping in World War II, and third wife of historian E. H. Carr,

FIGURE 4.1. Elizabeth Wiskemann c.1940s. Photographer
Unknown. Courtesy of Julian Brigstocke

thought the sexism in the Faculty of History was so extreme that 'the majority
on any appointments Committee' would 'turn down even the archangel Ga-
briel if he appeared in female form'. Writing in the late 1970s, she continued,

> If a woman is a good lecturer, it can be said that she hasn't written anything.
> If she has produced some distinguished piece of writing it can be said that
> she can't lecture. If she passes muster on these two counts it can be said
> that her subject, or her approach to it, is unsuitable. If none of these argu-
> ments is plausible then it can be said (as I gather, it has been, or will be said
> of Zara Steiner) that she is too old.[25]

Behrens was right. The American-born Steiner was never offered a faculty position at Cambridge or honoured with the title of professor despite her standing as the world's leading historian of interwar international relations. After moving to Cambridge with her husband, Steiner became a Fellow of New Hall, Cambridge's third women's college, founded in 1954 when Cambridge still had the lowest proportion of women students at any university in Britain.[26]

Behrens was vocal in her criticisms of institutional sexism at the History Faculty in Cambridge.[27] She appears briefly in IR's disciplinary histories only because of her ill-fated marriage to E. H. Carr, whom she thought exhibited a 'total absence of a sense of pity' and 'indifference to suffering . . . Various doctors, and other people . . . described him to me as a psychopath'.[28] According to David Pryce-Jones, Carr's 'nastiness' toward all three of his wives 'was unlimited'.[29] Yet Behrens matters to IR not only for what she might reveal of the character of E. H. Carr, but also in exposing the irony, even hypocrisy, of Herbert Butterfield's criticism of Gwladys Jones.

During the 1950s, Herbert Butterfield taught a General European History Course c.1492–1914, a sweeping outline or 'map' of what he saw as the major trends and pivotal moments across centuries.[30] His textbook-level outline of international history, necessarily drawing on second-hand knowledge, was consonant with the Rockefeller Foundation-instigated and funded British Committee on the Theory of International Politics founded in 1959 that Butterfield chaired, becoming a 'founder' member of the so-called English School of international relations.[31] Led by Behrens, members of the History Faculty complained that Butterfield's course was too elementary, full of generalisations and 'too detached from real historical study'.[32] As Behrens put it, the General Course allowed 'weak' students to 'merely accumulate a lot of generalisations which when questioned they can't defend or sometimes even explain, some of the others show an arrogance and lack of respect for facts bred by their being continually urged to make judgments on ridiculously inadequate reading'.[33] Behrens was articulating a critique of Butterfield that historians levelled against IR, and in terms not dissimilar to Butterfield's earlier criticism of Gwladys Jones's IR paper.

Because intellectual and disciplinary historians assumed that Cambridge had no role in IR's history until Butterfield chaired the British Committee, none of the Cambridge women are adequately addressed in existing historiography. As trained historians or classicists, Jones, Power, Stawell, Wiskemann, Behrens, and Steiner all have in common the kind of disciplined specialist training that would go out of fashion in the effort to forge IR as a separate university subject, both Manning's project at LSE to train 'Supermen' and Butterfield's British Committee, discussed in chapter 8. The Cambridge women were also profoundly shaped by their intimate relations, making their careers by never marrying (Wiskemann, Lucy Philip Mair), marrying very late (Power), following their husband to Cambridge (Steiner), or sharing their intimate lives with women (Stawell, Jones). As already suggested in chapter 1, these broader themes—the effects of marriage and non-marriage on intellectual trajectories, the importance of disciplinary training, the project of a separate IR, misogyny and the politics of erasure—also illuminate better-known locations of international thinking in the 'separate' IR departments in Aberystwyth. What of LSE?

Born the same year as Lilian Friedländer, Lucy Philip Mair (1901–1986) was the second woman appointed to an IR department in Britain, the new International Studies Department at LSE created in 1927, but the first to hold a permanent lectureship in the subject. She was responsible for a large proportion of LSE's IR teaching before World War II. A Newnham College graduate and trained classicist, like F. Melian Stawell, Mair retrained and researched colonial administration through anthropological methods. She thus additionally illuminates the entanglements between colonialism and IR, and the degree to which disciplined training allowed scholars to move in and out of the new field-in-formation.

Against the background of the Cambridge women, Lucy Mair, this other IR 'first', highlights the significance and limits of LSE as a location of women's international thought; of Manning's effort to conceive and justify the separate university teaching of international relations; the related politics and processes of erasing women, colonial administration, and anthropological method from IR's history; and some of the roots of British IR's eventual failure as an intellectual project.

## Colonial Administration as IR: 'I'm not a Margery Perham'

Lilian Friedländer's exact contemporary, Lucy Philip Mair was appointed to the new International Studies Department in 1927, three years before Manning. She became a professor in 1963, but in anthropology, the discipline in which she received her Ph.D. in 1932. Like Stawell, Mair was initially trained in classics, graduating with a first-class degree from Newnham College, Cambridge in 1923. For five years, she worked with Gilbert Murray, another classicist, at the League of Nations Union.[34] 'There is hardly an aspect of the League's work on which she could not lecture effectively', Murray wrote in his recommendation to LSE Director William Beveridge.[35] Like numerous inter-war internationalists, including Virginia Woolf and Eileen Power, Mair taught on the side at London's Morley College for Working Men and Women, including twenty lectures on 'Some Aspects of World Politics' in 1928.

Into the mid-1920s, Mair wrote on international relations in the mode of contemporary history. Her first book, *The Protection of Minorities*, was a study of the 'minority question' in Eastern Europe posed by the dismemberment of the Ottoman and Austrian empires.[36] Drawing on official documents, Mair analysed violence against minorities, uprisings, and international monitoring of minority protection in Poland, the Baltic States, Czechoslovakia, Austria, Hungary, Rumania, the Balkans, and Italy, as well as League actions taken under the Minorities Treaties. Foreshadowing Hannah Arendt's claims about the world-historical significance of interwar statelessness, Mair concluded that 'there are considerable numbers of persons who cannot make good a claim to the nationality of any country; while others, because on different grounds they can claim to be subjects of more than one State, are bandied about indefinitely between two Governments. These unfortunate persons do not possess the most elementary rights'.[37] Mair's book was still cited nearly three decades later in surveys of important IR works.[38]

With her Cambridge degree, experience at the LNU, and expertise on the core League question of minorities, Lucy Philip Mair was an obvious candidate to appoint to the LSE's new International Studies Department. She also had family connections. Though there is no suggestion of any impropriety in the appointment, Mair's mother was the LSE secretary, Janet ('Jessie') Thomson Mair Beveridge, whose second husband was the LSE director, William Beveridge.[39] William was an occasional chair of meetings of the British Coordinating Committee for International Studies (BCCIS), which Jessie also attended *ex officio*. Jessie 'dominated LSE for 18 years', according to sociologist Ann Oakley, which was not always appreciated by faculty. Eileen Power and Jessie regularly clashed over attempts to block Power's promotions and salary increases.[40] 'Miss Power's main interest is not in the School', Jessie claimed, 'which is merely for her a means to a life outside'.[41] The emergence of LSE as a major institution of higher learning was nonetheless an 'achievement almost entirely due to the efforts of the Beveridge–Mair collaboration'.[42]

Until 1940, when Lucy Mair took leave of absence to work for the British Colonial Office and Chatham House, she lectured extensively on colonial administration, with all courses listed under IR. During 1928–9, Mair taught or co-taught seven of the twenty IR courses, including 'Cultural Contacts between the West and Primitive Peoples', 'Economic Aspects of International Relations'; 'Problems of Colonial Government'; 'The International Labour Organisation'; and 'Review of Current International Events'. Most notably, on the eve of World War II, Mair taught 'Possession of Colonial Territory as an International Problem', covering topics all central to British colonial strategy in the context of rival empires and anticolonial resistance: colonial possessions as a source of international rivalry; current demands for redistribution; attempts at international regulation of administrative standards; League of Nations and International Labour Conventions; and the mandate system.

Colonial administration was both a core IR subject and an interdisciplinary field.[43] By the early 1930s, with the encouragement of her colleague and friend Audrey Richards, and through work on her doctorate with LSE's leading anthropologist Bronisław Malinowski, Mair's methodological approach became increasingly anthropological. Malinowski was pioneer of the ethnographic method of living with and observing the daily lives of those studied and the social anthropological theory of functionalism, in which societies are understood as structured wholes and all its elements functionally interrelated.[44]

Like many of his students, Mair drew on Malinowski's functionalist ideas and ethnographic methods to practise the science of colonial administration. Even Margery Perham took a course with Malinowski in the autumn of 1931. An historian by training and temperament, Perham was 'more at home among the archives', than living among colonised peoples, ethnographic style. She conceived empire in world-historical and comparative terms and from the perspective of colonial administrators and, at best, educated Africans.[45] Nonetheless, at times, Perham also turned to functionalist arguments, including to explain away the 1950s Mau Mau uprising in Kenya not as a political act of resistance to colonial oppression. It was the result of psychological maladjustment to a rapidly changing society.[46] However, in terms of shaping official and public opinion, there is no question that Perham's world-historical vision dominated wider British discussions of the empire and its management, overshadowing Malinowski's heirs, including Lucy Philip Mair.[47]

In the early 1930s even those in imperial circles were beginning to question the axiom that empire was justified by its benefits to the colonised. In 1931, Mair attempted an empirical demonstration of the effects of imperialism on 'native' peoples living in the East African village of Baganda and doing 'field' research with Rockefeller funds, the results published in 1934 as *An African*

FIGURE 4.2. Lucy Philip Mair by Lotte Meitner-Graf, c.1961. Permission from the Meitner-Graf Estate

*People in the Twentieth Century*. According to anthropologist and close friend Audrey Richards, with this book, Mair was 'the first investigator to turn her back resolutely on the romantic savage of the bow and spear, and to describe the new African who has taken its place'.[48] In her 1936 book, *Native Policies in Africa*, Mair also claimed that Lord Lugard's policy of Indirect Rule in Africa 'consists in an understanding of the structure of native society and the interrelation of its parts, which precludes the possibility of assuming that it can be suddenly modernised from the outside, and at the same time reveals the points at which changed circumstances call for readjustment'.[49] The most disastrous effect of imperialism was in the economic sphere, Mair argued. Her response to the so-called 'problem of social adaptation' in this context was functionalist.[50] 'There is nothing metaphysical about the statement that a human society which functions satisfactorily must be a co-ordinated whole'.[51]

In 1936, Audrey Richards encouraged Mair to return to Africa. She had 'to do a Margery Perham tour on the ground that I am not really an anthropologist', Mair averred. 'I fear that is true but it's unfortunately also true that I'm not a Margery Perham'.[52] In moving from contemporary history to anthropology, Mair would be completely overshadowed in the political and intellectual field of imperial management by Perham the historian. By the 1940s, the Colonial Office also came to view 'colonial problems' in less anthropological and more sociological terms, shifting from the 'native policy' of Indirect Rule and 'tribal customs' toward nation-building, developmentalism, urbanisation, and foreign investment.[53] However, Perham collaborated with colonial anthropologists, including Mair; they reviewed each other's work, made a joint funding application to Rockefeller, and supported a more liberal attitude toward 'native rights'.[54] Mair and Perham were in complete accord in rejecting calls in the 1930s to create a new colonial regime in which conflict with Nazi Germany could be displaced to Africa, as advocated by Oxford's future Montague Burton Professor, Agnes Headlam-Morley.

## Towards IR as a Separate Subject

As a core member of LSE's cross-disciplinary International Studies Department, Lucy Philip Mair, in contrast to Agnes Headlam-Morley, was actively involved in what would become a perennial discussion around IR's peculiar status. As discussed in chapter 7, from the 1950s Headlam-Morley was vilified for refusing to support the project for a separate IR with no method of its own, especially if this meant demoting disciplined historical work. Much earlier in 1934, in contrast, Lucy Philip Mair wrote an internal LSE university memorandum on 'International Relations as a Separate Subject', one of the earliest such documents but entirely ignored by IR's disciplinary historians. Like the men of the BCCIS in the 1930s, Mair was primarily interested in whether international relations constituted a separate *teaching* subject, not an academic *discipline*, in the context of internal LSE discussions of whether to combine IR and colonial administration in one unit with a single head of department. Mair asked whether the subject of international relations 'can be clearly differentiated from those of other branches, and whether it is too wide for the field to be satisfactorily covered by the student unless he makes it a special study'.[55] She concluded that IR met both these conditions.

Mair's memorandum began with one of the earliest and entirely overlooked critiques of what would later be known as the 'domestic analogy' in international theory.[56] She did not mince her words, dismissing as 'facile' the view that IR was already covered in the teaching of politics and economics. It did not follow that simply because 'the most extensive international contacts are economic, and that a high proportion of present-day international problems arise from political control of this form of international relation . . . that the nature of such problems will reveal itself simultaneously to the student as a by-product of his studies of the theory of government, or of international trade.'[57] 'Data' drawn from studying relations between individuals could not be transposed 'by a process of facile generalization' to 'relations between groups'. Simply because the 'name "government" is applied to the political organisation both of individuals and of states, an analysis of national government' cannot 'explain the international community'.[58] The 'dangerous fallacy of re-armament by analogy' must be rejected because the nature of international relations is 'absolutely sui generis'.[59]

In contrast to the later BCCIS men seeking to establish IR as a separate subject in the 1950s, Mair insisted that the methods and assumptions of sociology were also inadequate to understanding the special nature of international relations. For sociologists, she claimed, the 'relevant consideration in studying the relations between organised groups of individuals is just that they are groups, and that the nature of their organisation conditions their interaction'. 'The international institutions which we have owe their peculiar form to the circumstance that they deal with already existent organised groups, and this fact, together with the fact that the application of coercion to such groups is a process which must differ not only in kind but also in degree from the coercion of an individual within the state, means that their development or failure to develop must follow lines peculiar to itself', and not those covered under sociology.[60] International relations was also broader than the old field of international law because it was concerned with 'the whole range of relations between those organised political entities we call nations', and one 'must study this in the widest context'.[61]

Politics, economics, sociology, and law were all inadequate bases for analysing international relations. The one approach Mair did not feel the need to neutralise was history. Yet what is the subject of International Relations? Mair's answer here was shaped by her own work for the League of Nations Union, her book on minorities treaties, and interest in the administration of empire. Writing the same year that the Soviet Union joined the League of Nations, Mair concurred with her contemporaries Gwladys Jones at Cambridge and Lilian Friedländer in Aberystwyth. IR's central focus should be 'analysis of those organs of international government which were established at the close of the last war', specifically the League of Nations. 'In its present-day form', she states, 'the study must centre round the problem of the attempt to unite in a collective system a number of communities which are highly organised politically with a view of independent action.'[62] Significantly, Mair refers to relations between *communities* with a high level of political organisation, rather than relations between states, perhaps reflecting her sense of the political organisation of the communities administered by Britain as colonies, with Mair's and Perham's assistance. By 1937, Mair had taken over the LSE's colonial studies course for imperial administrators based in the Department of Anthropology.[63]

## Erasing Women and Colonial Administration, Re-Defining IR

For 1936–7, Lucy Philip Mair received a fellowship from the International African Institute for a field trip in the mandated territory of Northwestern Tanganyika, the same year she was approached to work for the Chatham House Africa Research Survey led by Lord Hailey, which became the basis of a major reform of colonial policy and research funding.[64] In 1937, writing on 'Colonial Policy and Peaceful Change', she was one of eight contributors to the International Studies Conference and book on peaceful change in world politics, edited by her LSE colleague, the Montague Burton Professor Charles Manning, who was appointed in 1930.[65] During her year in Tanganyika, Mair wrote to William Beveridge, proposing that she move departments, from international studies to anthropology, and suggesting she continue 'merely giving lectures on the international aspects of colonies which students taking International Relations could attend'.[66]

Like several men who eventually abandoned IR and returned to departments of history, including E. H. Carr, Martin Wight, and Sydney Herbert, Lucy Philip Mair could leave IR because she had received methodological training outside, in her case anthropological methods, and she was recognised as a scholar in this field. While Mair was 'not a Margery Perham',[67] she did become an accomplished anthropologist. She was insecure in her position in what she called the new 'Colonial department' at LSE. Still, in 1944, she was comparing herself negatively to Perham. 'I don't know how the colonial office is persuaded to come clean with its archives, though apparently Perham has the secret'.[68] But Mair nonetheless had the security and authority of ethnographic method, and increasing respect for her work in colonial administration, which remained part of international relations as an interdisciplinary field into the 1940s.

During the war, Mair worked at the British Empire section of the Foreign Research and Press Service at Chatham House. In 1944 she published what Perham referred to as a 'little book',[69] *Welfare in the British Colonies*, under the auspices of Chatham House. Another work of contemporary history drawing on government documents, it analysed existing British colonial welfare policy across education, labour, and health in Africa, Malaya, Hong Kong, Ceylon, Fiji, the Western Pacific Islands, and the West Indies.[70] Such a fact-based survey, Chatham House's defining genre, was intended to measure the empire's progress in meeting its obligations as the 'guardians' of colonised peoples.[71] Based on her now recognised expertise in this field, Mair was invited by the Australian government to lecture for twelve months on the colonial administration of New Guinea, becoming instructor at the Australian Land Headquarters Civil Affairs School. In 1948, she drew on this experience, and ten weeks in Papua, to publish *Australia in New Guinea*. Treating the recently combined territories of Papua and New Guinea separately, Mair argued that Australia's direct and hostile colonial domination of New Guinea, including forced labour and the neglect of social welfare, was much worse than in Papua and contrasted unfavourably to the British policy of native administration in its empire.[72]

Mair returned from Australia in 1946, to LSE's Department of Anthropology. As we have seen, she had indicated her desire to leave the Department of International Studies before the war, largely because of her desire for a coherent teaching and research profile centering on her methodological specialism, rather than any fundamental distinction between IR and colonial administration.[73] As already shown, Mair's work was considered core IR. On one level is it easy to explain Mair's neglect in IR's disciplinary histories because of the later erasure of colonial administration and the fact that she was a woman: seemingly a double exclusion. But the process of erasure occurred as early as 1950 by her own colleague, Charles Manning.

Born in South Africa in 1894 between the First and Second Boer Wars, Manning was educated in an elite school in Cape Town and, after military service in World War I, took up a Rhodes scholarship to study 'Greats' at Brasenose College, Oxford. He studied civil law and jurisprudence, becoming a barrister in 1922, and then worked at the International Labour Organization at the League of Nations, and as personal assistant to Eric Drummond, the

League's first secretary general. Manning was 'a man in the Smuts mould', a loyal supporter of racial apartheid in South Africa.[74] After a year as a Rockefeller Fellow at Harvard in 1925–6, Manning returned to New College, Oxford, teaching international law and diplomacy. In 1930, Manning became international legal expert Philip Noel Baker's 'somewhat surprising successor'[75] as LSE's Cassel (later Montague Burton) Professor of IR. He 'had no special qualifications for the job',[76] and certainly less than Agnes Headlam-Morley when she took the equivalent Oxford chair in 1949. Like her, Manning only published 'one really substantial book', *The Nature of International Society*, in 1962.[77] However, by 1970 Manning could be referred to as 'the doyen of the international relations profession in Britain'.[78] Headlam-Morley, in contrast, would be vilified for resisting Manning's project of separating IR from diplomatic history. First, however, IR needed to be separated from colonial administration and the study of empire.

In an undated memorandum known to be written after 1949, 'Note on the Nature of International Relations as the province of the Montague Burton Chair', Manning offered his version of the LSE's IR curriculum. In his words:

> Flanked, thus, on the one hand by International Law, on the other by International History, and with the economic factor a staple of the curriculum, the subject of International Relations, in its early days at the School, included also a necessary emphasis on international institutions, the technique and procedures of diplomacy, and the geographical factor in international affairs . . . It has been along these lines that, *since the middle of the twenties* the subject of International Relations has been pursued at LSE.[79]

He makes no mention of the fact that Lilian Knowles, Britain's first full-time lecturer in economic history, began teaching imperial and great-power economic history as early as 1904;[80] that his predecessor Philip Noel-Baker lectured on inter-imperial relations of the British Empire;[81] that Eileen Power taught world economic and social history through the 1920s and 1930s, or that from the middle of the 1920s, Lucy Philip Mair was teaching colonial administration as IR using the methodological techniques of anthropology, fieldwork, participant observation, and occasional works of contemporary history.

Mair's role was further buried when Manning explained why the proposal to combine colonial administration and IR was rejected. In his words, 'the two subjects were, if anything, cousins rather than twins, the one being concerned with a manifestation of government, the other with the processes and possibilities of diplomacy—man's traditional means of doing his public business on that extra-national level where government has not as yet come to apply'.[82] Manning makes no mention of the fact that the suggestion to create a united department arose because colonial administration was part of the IR curriculum, was taught primarily under IR, and was considered as an area for expansion at LSE, even in the context of wider budget cuts during the Great Depression of the 1930s. In contrast to Manning, Mair's earlier, subtler notion of relations between 'communities' that are 'highly organised politically' accommodated colonial and inter-state relations.

Manning was certainly aware of Mair's central role in IR teaching and her specialist subject; they were colleagues for thirteen years, and he included her work in an edited volume in 1937. Indeed, many years later at his retirement in 1962, Manning briefly mentioned Mair while discussing 'the depletion, replenishment and growth of the staff'.[83] 'Lucy Mair, moving out from her specialisation in the League mandates, had opted for a future in the teaching of Colonial Administration.'[84] But there was less a 'moving out' than a natural progression from working on League mandates to analysing the administration of colonies, and colonial administration was a cross-disciplinary intellectual field, as was international relations.

Based on her world-leading expertise, Lucy Philip Mair was a high-profile figure among both scholars and policymakers over a long period of time, a prolific writer, teacher, and advisor of governments on one of the centrally important IR questions of her day. She taught a large percentage of the early students of IR in what at the time was one of its largest academic centres in the world. She is honoured in the academic discipline anthropology, into which she migrated, recipient of an honorary degree, and the subject of two edited volumes.[85] In 2016, the Royal Anthropological Institute and the Marsh Charitable Trust inaugurated the Lucy Mair Medal. In IR we only have the highly gendered line in F. S. Northedge's essay, that she 'assisted the Professor generally',[86] reflecting Charles Manning's original and direct erasure of both Mair and colonial administration from his department's history, part of his project to define 'IR' in a very particular, highly gendered and racialised way.

What 'moved out' at this moment was Mair's anthropological method to study her international relations subject of colonial administration. Hence, Mair's erasure from IR's history was a triple not a double exclusion, of subject, gender, *and method*. Mair's was a case of a figure moving to work in a department—anthropology—that was also, unlike IR, its own discipline and method. There is thus some irony that, when in the early 1950s Manning was forced to respond to criticisms that IR was not a proper discipline because it had no method, he turned to the anthropological method of participant observation as set out in Malinowski's field-defining 1922 book *Argonauts of the Western Pacific*.[87]

## 'What Manner of Man is this Teacher?'

After World War II, IR was still a university 'subject . . . in the making',[88] and its fate was unclear. The United Nations Educational, Scientific and Cultural Organization (UNESCO) had superseded the International Committee on Intellectual Cooperation (IIIC), the League-era organisation led by Gilbert Murray and Alfred Zimmern, the two British internationalists and classicists already discussed. The interdisciplinary International Studies Conference (ISC) and its British Coordinating Committee for International Studies (BCCIS) had formed under the IIIC.[89] In contrast, UNESCO's drive to create international academic associations followed the American model. In 1949, UNESCO created the International Political Science Association (IPSA) and, mimicking the American Political Science Association, subsumed IR as a subfield of political science. In cutting funding for the interdisciplinary ISC and defining IR as a branch of Political Science, UNESCO not only 'killed' off the ISC but provided further institutional justification for those who were doubtful of IR's separate academic standing, including those in Britain's Political Studies Association (PSA), created in 1950.[90] Then as now, political science was the gravest threat to IR's interdisciplinary character and autonomy in Britain.

It did not look this way to a group of men in London. BCCIS's activities were suspended during World War II and resumed after the war when British IR's collective professional organising centered on what were referred to as the 'Bailey Conferences'. Because they were initially organised by S. H. Bailey, an LSE lecturer until his premature death in 1938 at the age of thirty-four, later BCCIS conferences were given his name.[91] The attempt to revive BCCIS began in earnest at an all-white, all-male four-day ISC meeting on the university teaching of international relations at Cumberland Lodge, Windsor Park in March 1950. Here the primary threat to BCCIS, certainly in the eyes of Charles Manning, was not from political scientists, who simply viewed IR as a subdiscipline of itself and succeeded in the power politics at UNESCO. It was historians, who were more doubtful of the scholarly standing of any 'separate' IR in the absence of a clear methodology and raison d'être for the new field.

At BCCIS's fourth conference in 1949, as we have seen, Cambridge historian Herbert Butterfield had already mounted a powerful critique of the project for a separate IR on grounds that, without imparting proper methodological training, the subject would become a playground of 'dabblers'.[92] The almost exclusive focus on contemporary international affairs also meant the subject was 'too immediate and direct in its utilitarian direction'.[93] To date, he claimed, much of the university study of international relations, at Cambridge and also LSE, had taken the form of imparting a 'certain body of information' that for practical reasons, 'it would be "a very nice thing" for students to acquire'. Such a view chimes,

> very well with the educational tendencies of the age . . . [But] I should press very strongly that our aim . . . should be not to provide students with information . . . but rather to train the mind, establish certain kinds of intellectual discipline, and produce certain techniques . . . a combination of a lot of different techniques in a general study of international relations will provide solid discipline or training in none of them, and is in danger of producing dabblers in a journalistic kind of thinking; and though it may provide students with a lot of information which we may think it "nice" for them to acquire . . . the information would come better organised (and without some of the pitfalls) if it formed part of the study of 'general history'.[94]

After Gwladys Jones's IR course was dropped, IR was incorporated into the undergraduate syllabus at Cambridge only to a limited extent and only after students had been trained in the rigorous 'study of the past'.[95]

Few classicists or historians, including even Aberystwyth's Woodrow Wilson Professors Alfred Zimmern and E. H. Carr, thought IR was an autonomous university subject, let alone a separate discipline or method. After leaving Aberystwyth in 1947, Carr effectively renounced IR as a separate university subject, later advising those interested in the subject to study history. As he wrote in 1977, 'I have long thought that International Relations is a rag-bag into which one is entitled to put anything one pleases'. The attempt by LSE's Montague Burton Professor Charles Manning 'to turn it into some sort of organized self-contained subject was a fiasco'.[96]

Given its earlier association with the political project of the League, it was not very clear what a 'separate' IR had to offer intellectually. Historians, such as Eileen Power, Margery Perham, and Agnes Headlam-Morley researched and taught international relations by drawing on historical training and methods to evaluate the quality of the scholarship produced. Moreover, as Ian Hall observes, in this period, IR specialists were 'far outnumbered and indeed outmanoeuvred, in bureaucratic and sometimes intellectual terms, in political life and in the press, by the far more numerous and powerful historians. When newspapers, serious periodicals, diplomats, or even prime ministers wanted comment on international affairs, it was to historians that they turned'.[97] By the 1950s, the relation between history and IR was not just a matter of undergraduate teaching, but intellectual quality. If IR was to be a university subject of high standing, then how should it be taught and what methods should it employ?

## Towards IR's Failure as an Intellectual Project

These were fundamental *intellectual* questions, never satisfactorily resolved by the three leading advocates for IR as a separate subject in 1950s Britain, all based in London. The most influential was Charles Manning, who pursued a 'virtually single-handed effort to establish International Relations in the curricula of British universities'.[98] He was assisted by another LSE man, his successor as Montague Burton Chair, the British economist and Foreign Office mandarin, Geoffrey Goodwin. German Georg Schwarzenberger, professor of international law and relations at University College London, was the third, another outlier in teaching IR with no historical training. Rather than focus on the most institutionally powerful opponents to their agenda to secure IR's standing—the political scientists at UNESCO, IPSA, and the LSE itself—these men, two lawyers and an economist, became obsessed with distinguishing IR from history, with disastrous intellectual, gendered, and racialised effects.

IR scholars did not require specialist methodological training, claimed Manning. Students would not be trained in how to approach international relations as an historian, a lawyer, an economist or a political scientist, even within an IR department. Instead, they would learn a little bit of one discipline and a little bit of another concurrently 'with' something called IR. Manning set himself the task of training students to be superior scholars capable of acquiring knowledge from across the disciplines and combining it all to theorise 'international relations', literally conceived as 'Superman', as already noted. But as IR scholar Roger Morgan pointed out more mundanely and accurately, Manning 'once defined an international relations specialist as "someone who wishes he knew more about psychology, economics, diplomatic history, international law, comparative constitutional law, sociology, geography, perhaps languages—and a few other things as well"'.[99] Lacking his own methodology, the IR Superman was defined by a longing for the impossible. Manning envisaged a field filled not with supermen but covetous dabblers.

Manning's effort to breed supermen was his displacement of the methods question onto a sociological definition of 'the international'. As with the sociologist Nicholas Spykman's project for a new IR at Yale, defined against Lucie Zimmern's cultural internationalism as practised in Aberystwyth and Geneva, for Manning IR's core subject matter was no longer understood historically and politically as inter-imperial relations and the management of capitalism and empire. Instead, Manning and his colleagues founded IR as a separate subject on the highly racialised notion of a 'society of states'. IR was a 'special kind of specialisation, "by problem," as opposed to' method, he claimed. As Roberto Ago, another international lawyer, proposed: 'if it is right for International Relations to exist as an autonomous discipline' that is 'neither law, not economics, nor history', then it must be *the general study* of international society viewed as a whole'.[100]

In making this move, Manning became the progenitor of the so-called English School's core concept of 'international society', which influenced the second generation of thinkers in this vein, especially Martin Wight and Hedley Bull. The notion of international 'society', for Manning, and in contrast to Lucy Mair, was distinctively sociological in that it referred to a rules-based collective order that needed to be analysed as a whole, a kind of 'group sociology' to be studied by 'sociological method'.[101] But what was this 'method'? Manning drew on socio-legal theory, the claim that social relations underpinned legal rules, to argue that something called 'international society' was underpinned by the social relations among its members. The society of states operated because the actors involved, members of the international family, *believed* it was operative. The task for the IR scholar was to understand the rules, norms and organising principles of the society of states as accepted and enacted by its main players.

Manning was never very clear by what method the 'society of states' could be analysed beyond his own philosophical musings. The closest he came to specifying a methodological approach was in his 1962 book *The Nature of International Society*, where he affiliated IR to the social anthropological method of his LSE colleague Bronisław Malinowski, an irony given Manning's erasure of the anthropologist of colonial administration, Lucy Philip Mair. Based on several months living with and studying the so-called 'native life' of the Trobriand peoples, Malinowski pioneered the method of 'participant observation', as outlined in his 1922 book *Argonauts of the Western Pacific*.[102] 'Let the student of International Relations think then of the international society as Malinowski did of his Trobrianders', Manning declared, 'and be content with nothing other than whatever may prove to be the nearest practicable approach to a personal participation—in the role, as it were, of a sovereign state—in the international family'.[103] The task of the IR scholar was to reveal 'what it was like to be personally a participant in the life' of the international family, to engage in 'exercises in empathy'.[104]

In Manning's 'interpretivist' method, the IR scholar would be like a social anthropologist examining the norms and rules of the 'society of states', as interpreted by the actors involved. In practice, Manning's method fetishised the norms and rules of the white 'society of states', erased the history and politics of imperial domination, and authorised empathy for racial apartheid.[105] Black people in South Africa, he claimed, were disenfranchised not because of the colour of their skin. It was because power was held by a political party whose purpose was to preserve Afrikanerdom from 'the danger of obliteration by a culture which was seen not as inferior but as different'.[106] The disenfranchised only 'happened to be black'.[107] To be sure, Europeans viewed African culture as 'essentially other' but this was not the same as holding African culture 'in disesteem'.[108] Apartheid was a nationalist policy of the Afrikaner *volk* who should not be blamed for resisting the 'merging of white society into a culturally uncongenial and in principle homogeneous all-African mass'.[109] If 'the white man' had the right 'to preserve his achievement', apartheid was inevitable.[110] The vehemence with which Manning denied any link between his approach to 'international society' and his own racist politics is further evidence of the connection.[111]

Georg Schwarzenberger, another lawyer drawn to the notion of 'international society', also admitted the real 'danger of dilettantism' in the new IR, if shorn of its grounding in history. However, to be able to generalise about the nature of international society it 'is quite sufficient' to understand the 'guiding principles' of, say, international law 'and to have a rudimentary acquaintance with legal tools. . . . In other instances, the student of international relations will have to rely on the specialist'.[112] That is, IR would import knowledge from other fields, relying on the original ideas and labours of others. In some ways Schwarzenberger was more genuinely sociological than Manning, turning to a tradition of German social theory as the grounding for IR. 'The study of international relations', Schwarzenberger agreed in 1951, 'is the branch of sociology which is concerned with international society'.[113] Sociology's main virtue, according to Schwarzenberger, discussed further in chapter 11, was its ability to address the complexity of modern society through typologies and ideal types.

For both Schwarzenberger and Manning, IR was a synthetic and integrating specialist field for a certain kind of group sociology. International relations was its own special aspect of the social world and the subject cut across all IR's constituent subjects, justifying its separateness both as a specialised subject and an academic department.[114] Sociology also provided the analytic framework for 'a more systematised conceptual framework' to study the society of states.[115] As with Charles Manning, the constitutive Other to Schwarzenberger's scheme was history, which, he claimed, could not 'do justice to the structure of present-day international society, to the typical patterns of behaviour on the international scene or to the forces by which the hierarchy of powers within international societies determined'.[116] Imperialism was reduced to a 'strategy of international politics',[117] and the management of colonial mandates one among many functions of the League's successor organisation, the United Nations. Like Manning's 'interpretivist' focus on the norms and perceptions of the society of white states, Schwarzenberger demoted imperialism at a time when Britain was still violently clinging on to its empire in Asia and Africa.

For 'institution-builder' and 'committee man'[118] Geoffrey Goodwin, sociology allowed IR scholars to shed 'light on the development, structure and functioning of international society, for example how power political systems have worked in the past, and on how they are working . . . in the present'.[119] Largely because of Manning's efforts, and Schwarzenberger's, discussed in chapter 11, Goodwin could claim that 'most' IR teachers in Britain 'look to either History or to Sociology for chief guidance in evolving the methodology'. Moreover, the History–Sociology distinction, he observed, was largely a distinction between Oxford and London. At 'Oxford', according to the LSE men, 'the method throughout is primarily that of the historian', which they portrayed as 'the *description* of the continuous process of causality, coupled with a keen awareness that each historical situation or event has its unique and unrepeatable features. Thus, the historically-minded teacher of International Relations will be more preoccupied with recounting *what* happened rather than in showing *why* . . . only rarely will he be bold enough to postulate the existence of quasi-permanent "fundamentals" or "patterns" of policy'.[120]

Needless to say, this distinction between Oxford as history and London as sociology misrepresented historical method, resting on an anachronistic distinction between description and analysis, and the elevation of one tendency of some historical work to its defining characteristic. But the caricature was necessary for the London men to define IR as a special branch of an abstract and functionalist sociology that was allegedly more 'analytical'. However, as discussed in the next chapter, it depended on the erasure of another LSE colleague, Eileen Power, who was already experimenting with sociological approaches to international relations as world social and economic history in the 1930s. Moreover, as discussed in chapter 7, it also relied on a misogynist dismissal of Oxford's Montague Burton Professor, Agnes Headlam-Morley, and a misunderstanding of the possibilities and potentialities of Oxford IR under her reign. Manning almost certainly had Agnes Headlam-Morley in mind when he claimed that 'the older British universities have their inherited conceptions of their task. "What was enough for our fathers, and for us . . .".[121] The Oxford as history and London as sociology distinction was also a distinction between IR's two Montague Burton Professors—Manning, the supporter of racial apartheid, and Headlam-Morley, the Tory supporter of Nazi appeasement.[122]

## Conclusion

During his entire thirty-two-year reign as LSE's Montague Burton Professor, Charles Manning appointed no women to a permanent faculty position, despite the large numbers of women writing on international relations, but married his own undergraduate student, Marion Somerville Johnson.[123] Only in 1965, after Manning's retirement, was Coral Bell appointed to a readership. In turn, Manning would suffer his own erasure of sorts, or at least an attempt at forgetting. Martin Wight and Hedley Bull, both of whom benefitted from his patronage, wrote for Manning's *Festschrift*, published in 1973.[124] Yet the earliest history of the so-called 'English School', published in 1998, and the 2003 volume surveying the history of IR at LSE, includes essays on some of its main figures like Wight, Bull, and Strange, but astonishingly no essay on the person who did more than anyone else to shape IR at LSE.[125]

Recently Manning was called 'the neglected child of the discipline', or better its neglected pater.[126] But there is little justification to resurrect Manning as an international theorist, only an as an historical figure whose work exemplifies what went wrong with British IR at mid-century. The value of considering Manning today is not as a proto-constructivist or originator of the English School concept of 'international society'. It is as a case study of the intellectual insecurities of a white male mediocrity and the gendered, racialised, and methodological Others on which he tried to found IR as a separate subject.

The most charitable thing we might say of Manning's 32-year tenure at LSE is that he took 'the subject, international relations, as he found it . . . a thing of bits and pieces . . . and welded it, if not perhaps into a wholly coherent subject,

at least into a clearly conceived focus of interest', that of 'international society'.[127] Yet even this clearly conceived focus was based on a series of constitutive erasures—methodological, racialised and gendered—including but not
limited to the caricature and erasure of women, first Lucy Philip Mair, then,
as discussed in later chapters, Eileen Power and Agnes Headlam-Morley. Yet
there is more than one way to develop a 'separate' university subject. For the
three London men, IR's subject matter should be defined 'sociologically' as
'international society', erasing empire, race, and colonial administration. They
caricatured historical work as descriptive and non-analytical, erasing or belit-
tling numerous women historians of international relations, literally British
IR's constitutive, founding Others. Herein were the sources of the intellectual
failures of twentieth-century British IR.

# 5

# Power's World

## INTERNATIONAL RELATIONS AS WORLD SOCIAL AND ECONOMIC HISTORY

For certainly the devil can quote history to his purpose and Clio has too often been a *vivandière* in the army of politicians and militarists, instead of a grave and just muse, whose equal gaze surveys the world and whose hands weigh man's deeds in the balance.

—EILEEN POWER[1]

NOT UNTIL SUSAN STRANGE did a figure as dominating and intellectually significant as Eileen Power emerge from IR as a 'separate subject' in twentieth-century Britain. Power was 'exceptional' in many ways, a story of almost un-mitigated success and recognition, at least during her lifetime. She was Britain's best-known medieval historian of the interwar period, as well known during her lifetime as her contemporaries R. H. Tawney and Marc Bloch.[2] Along with her friend, collaborator, and colleague Tawney, Eileen Power was pioneering in the fields of economic and social history, founding the *Economic History Review* and co-founding the Economic History Society.[3] She was also at the forefront of establishing women's history as a core university subject and in collaborations across historical and social science.[4] She received numerous honorary degrees, and job offers in the United States. As discussed in chapter 3, she was also a public historian and intellectual, committed to writing internationalist textbooks for children and broadcasting regularly for the BBC.[5] At her death, thousands of British children 'knew her voice and loved her lessons'.[6] According to her biographer, historian Maxine Berg, 'It is hard to overstate the academic status Power had achieved at such a young age'; 'there were virtually no precedents for the kind of mainstream recognition she achieved'.[7]

With the exceptions of Margery Perham and Susan Strange, no other woman international thinker in the early- to mid-twentieth century was permitted entry into the male academic elite to the same degree. Her male peers often said that she 'thinks like a man'; hence she could be an honorary member of their club, at least the club of historians.[8] Influenced by her training in Cambridge, Paris, and London, as well as the internationalist, socialist, pacifist and feminist circles in which she moved, Power's intellectual originality was in her combination of social, economic, world, and women's history to analyse medieval and early modern civilisations and their interactions and mutual influence. Power's conceptual and theoretical work was underpinned by detailed archival and primary source material and a literary and cultural sensibility.

With these tools, Power developed a new theoretical and methodological framework to integrate sociological and economic history into a large-scale analysis of world history and international relations, as a conscious alternative to traditional diplomatic history and political theories of the sovereign state. She wrote comparative and world history focusing on non-European polities and cultures, medieval traders and trade routes, and the so-called 'rising powers' of her day, particularly China. The medieval world Eileen Power depicted was commercial and international, including details of foreign trade, and accounts of political and financial elites, ordinary people, traders, merchants, and travellers. Social and economic history as practised by Power was international and world history, crossing countries, civilisations, and periods. She had a world-historical vision that—unlike her contemporaries H. G. Wells and G. P. Gooch—was not rooted in a view of universal progress towards 'Western' modernity.[9] Unlike Wells, she researched and wrote her own works.[10]

Power's world social history was far more developed and sophisticated than the attempt of her LSE colleague, Montague Burton Professor of IR, Charles Manning, to create a sociological theory of 'international society'. While Manning was pursuing sociological abstractions, Power was one of the earliest proponents of a genuinely historical sociology of world history, seeking to account for the passage from a medieval world of multiple and diverse empires to the rise of the modern capitalist and imperial state system. Through the 1930s, Power's lectures on world history at LSE were considerably more popular than Manning's on the structure of international society. With Tawney, Power 'easily dominated not just economic history teaching, but teaching in the social sciences generally at the LSE ... Students from all subjects at LSE attended'.[11] Manning, in contrast, 'held special seminars for hand-picked students, those he deemed would carry on a sort of academic "apostolic succession" ... of a "mystery" from the Master to Apprentice'.[12] Power's literary gifts, as well as the contemporary relevance of her lectures, were likely more appealing than Manning's 'bizarre' and 'impenetrable' prose.[13]

Both Power and Manning married former students; Power in 1937 and Manning in 1939. As noted in the previous chapter, no new woman was appointed to LSE's IR department during Manning's 32-year tenure, but he married his student, Marion Somerville Johnson. She is said to have 'looked after' Manning 'solicitously' during their long marriage, including secretarial work.[14] Johnson had studied for the International Relations Diploma at the LSE between 1931 and 1934 and attended lectures by Bertrand Russell, Eileen Power, and Manning.[15] In contrast to the fate of many women student-cum-spouses, Power married her research student, ten years her junior, Russian Jewish émigré Michael Postan, and he enjoyed a highly successful academic career.[16] In a gender reversal of the more common practice, Power nurtured and supported her husband's career. She did not apply for the Chair of Economic History at Cambridge, which she would almost certainly have secured, so that Postan might, which he did. In contrast to Manning, Eileen Power was open about the relations between political and scholarly work.[17] In the 1930s, she advocated for LSE's Academic Freedom Committee to support visiting lectureships for Jewish scholars.[18] Manning feigned to separate his scientific studies from his political project of supporting racial apartheid in South Africa.

Eileen Power was no more marginal to the study of international relations in Britain in the 1920s and 1930s than numerous and far less important male thinkers whose work is repeatedly analysed in international intellectual and disciplinary histories. Indeed, in this period international relations was taught across the LSE departments of history, law, politics and public administration by diplomatic and economic historians and lawyers, drawing on their disciplinary expertise to analyse questions of world politics and economy. Power moved in the same Cambridge, LSE and Bloomsbury circles and wrote and taught on the same core international relations subjects and same venues as other figures in IR's intellectual history.[19] She was a recognised expert at IR conferences, including at the Institute of Pacific Relations, joining Margaret Cleeve, Arnold Toynbee, Barbara Ward, and Charles Webster in Kyoto in 1929 as part of the 'British group'.[20] She was close to both Toynbee and Webster. Yet Power's LSE contemporaries seeking to establish IR as a separate subject,

above all Charles Manning, were too insular, too stuck on anachronistic assumptions about the nature of historical scholarship to learn from Power's
ground-breaking collaborations across historical and social science. Power
was one of LSE's most prominent and popular lecturers during the 1920s and
1930s and its second woman professor. She was as well-known as a writer and
thinker on world politics when 'international relations' was not fully formed
as a separate university subject. Despite this standing, Power's LSE colleagues
in 'IR' failed to engage with her ideas.

How was Power erased from histories of international thinking, even at LSE
before a separate International Studies department was established in 1927 and
during the period when economic history was 'the soul of LSE'?[21] Maxine
Berg's exemplary biography situates Power in the context of a cohort of interwar women economic historians and her LSE contemporaries, including
Beatrice and Sidney Webb, R. H. Tawney, Michael Postan, and Charles Webster. She has yet to be placed in the context of international thinking as it was
being institutionalised by a different set of LSE contemporaries and successors. Reading Power in this context not only further illuminates the significance and the limits of Power's international relations as world social and
economic history, but also the gendered exclusions in the formation of a certain kind of 'separate' IR. Power's cross-disciplinary collaborations across history, sociology, and economics offered exactly what her LSE colleagues in IR
claimed to seek. More than any other thinker of her generation, Eileen Power
totally belied their clichéd distinction between historical and sociological
scholarship as that between recounting what happened and then theorising
about it. Her example makes a mockery of claims that historians were unable
to theorise, or that sociology largely meant abstraction. Yet, as Power's friend
G. G. Coulton observed, 'many of her fellow-workers . . . came to the easy conclusion that a woman who showed so much life was a lively lady and little
more'.[22] This gendered marginalisation of Power surely contributed to British
IR's failure as an intellectual project.

## Relativising Western Progress; Medievalising the East

During World War I, Eileen Power was director of studies in history at Girton
College, Cambridge, and remained so until 1920, when her intellectual trajectory was fundamentally redirected. During 1920–21, Power held an Albert
Kahn Travelling Fellowship, which she called the 'great event of her life', yet
also her 'ruin, for my heart will stray . . . I think I shall have to compromise by

working at the trade between Europe and the East in the middle ages'.[23]
Founded in 1910 and administered by the University of London, the Kahn
Fellowship was explicitly internationalist and comparative.[24] French banker
and philanthropist Albert Kahn's (1860–1940) most famous project was the
Archive of the Planet, in which dozens of photographers and cinematogra-
phers travelled the world recording the lives and cultures being destroyed by
imperialism and capitalism.[25]

Eileen Power used the twelve months of her Kahn Fellowship, previously
held by Goldsworthy Lowes Dickinson, to tour and study India, China, Japan,
the 'Dutch' East Indies, and Egypt during the collapse of the so-called 'Wilsonian moment' and increased nationalist agitation and anticolonial
resistance.[26] 'The defeat of Russia by Japan, the Chinese revolution of 1911, and
the rise of the Young Turk party', Power observed, 'all acted as a stimulus to
the political aspirations of coloured races'.[27] While Power gave greater promi-
nence to women in her earlier and later historical writing on women in medieval Europe, she did not ignore women political activists in nationalist and
anticolonial movements of the early twentieth century, highlighting the prom-
inence of Egyptian women in the picketing, strikes, demonstrations, and pro-
cessions in Cairo.[28] According to historian Billie Melman, Power's emphasis
on women's agency was novel in white feminist engagements with colonialism
in this period.[29]

The information Power collected and the opinions that she formed during
her travels were distilled into a 62-page *Report* to the Kahn Fellowship trustees.
Power's 1921 report and other writings in the early 1920s represent her earliest
attempt to write large-scale comparative and world history with internationalist intent. They are also Orientalist texts, trading in the civilisational hierarchies
that Power believed she was challenging.[30] Unlike other British intellectuals
interested in world history at this moment, Power did not read the political
uprisings across Asia as evidence of the march of Western values. There is no
sense in which, for Power, peoples in India, China, the 'Dutch' East Indies, or
Japan were not yet 'civilised', requiring political and economic development
along Western lines. In her study of the Dutch colonial system, for example,
Power attempted to subvert racist stereotypes about the idleness of natives.
Linking progress to colonial and economic exploitation, the act of a man 'lying
in the sun', for Power, became an act of political and economic resistance.[31]
She described and justified the view of an imaginary Javanese man who questioned why he should be forced to 'work all day' to produce goods that he does
'not value' on land stolen by Europeans with their ships, 'snorting trains', and

closed houses. 'I was happy when I had my rice patch and my village and was not made to work all day for the white man'.[32] Power at once elevates what she sees as defining of peasant life ('there is nothing unnatural or unreasonable') and fixes it in time, essentialising peasant values as necessarily preferring 'lying in the sun' to 'rapid transit'.[33]

Anticolonial movements in the 'Dutch' East Indies rejected any evolutionary model of political development, a model Power implicitly endorsed in British India. In Java, she observed, the political struggle was founded on 'the intrinsic value of oriental civilization, and its criterion of the native fitness for self-government is something more than the degree to which the Javanese have become westernized'.[34] Indeed, Power insisted that the highest representation of civilisation and beauty was not found in London, Oxford, or Cambridge, but a classical dance performed by fourteen- and fifteen-year-old girls for the sultan in royal palaces of Djokjakarta.[35] For Power, the Srimpi, a slow, refined 'immemorial hereditary' dance represented the 'climax of a great and old civilization'.[36] In comparison, the Russian ballet so elevated in the West was not civilised at all; it was 'the dancing of Barbarians, of a young half-civilised people, which must express itself in violent movements'.[37]

It was impossible to measure Java's aristocratic form of dance, which Power elevated to the higher plane of cultural perfection, by the same criteria of progress by which modern education, forms of government, and technical achievements are measured in the West; 'you can no more gauge the value of either in terms of the other than you can solve a problem in trigonometry by the aid of a Greek lexicon'.[38] There was no basis on which to claim one was essentially more or less civilised. 'One is unmoving, a perfect achievement in the realm of pure beauty. The other progressive, moving from one triumph to another. One is compatible with lying in the sun; the other is not'.[39] As Power looked from the sultan and others of his 'race' to the Dutch colonial officials and 'their heavy wives', with whom she clearly racially identified, she experienced a terrible irony. 'We were barbarians seated there'.[40] While Power's Kahn report sought to relativise Western economic progress and subvert her English readers' assumptions about high culture and 'oriental civilization', her critique of Dutch colonialism mythologised the art of an unchanging Javanese culture and fat-shamed colonial wives.[41]

Underpinning Eileen Power's attempt to relativise Western progress was an attempt to subvert the oppositional, geographical and civilisational distinction between 'East' and 'West'. By the 1930s, Power would conceive East–West unity in terms of common origins, mutual influences, and connections through trade, travel, and conflict. Yet in the early 1920s, in the months after the student-led anti-imperial protests of the May Fourth movement, Power identified China as the one civilisation that could be neither Eastern nor Western yet both at the same time. China represented the possibility of a non-Eurocentric historical development. Keen to relativise East and West, Power again romanticised Chinese civilisation. She was well aware of the tendency among Western intellectuals to periodically fetishise China, as they had in the eighteenth and early twentieth centuries. In both periods China appeared to be 'in tune with what the West imagines that it wants'.[42] But the more fundamental source was China's rationalism, 'the sweet reasonableness of Chinese civilization'.[43] Yet Power could not convey what she so admired about post-revolutionary China, its 'intellectual renaissance' and 'ferment of creation', without denigrating India and Japan.[44]

Power had no hesitation in ranking 'Eastern nations'. She was most enamoured by the 'charm' of China and 'the immense potentialities of this race'.[45] Its towns were dirty, its government corrupt; the 'working man's idea of China is still a mixture of yellow peril [and] cheap labour'.[46] None of this mattered because Chinese civilisation is 'what human beings ought to be like'.[47] Power was least impressed by Japan, 'essentially an imitative race'. She hardly met anyone there with an 'original mind' or with a 'creative thought'.[48] It had adopted all the trappings of Western modernity and its civilisation borrowed from Indian and Chinese culture, yet had 'never created out of themselves'.[49] Japan's material achievements were impressive, but it had adopted the worst elements of Western 'progress' without any of its compensating features.[50] 'I always find myself being asked to admire Japan for the things I most dislike in Europe'.[51] Now an imperial power, Japan ranked alongside the Western empires, but this status and modern civilisation, Power prophesised, would be short-lived. The pace of Japan's adoption of materiality came at a terrible psychological price: 'they seem to me always the people on the verge of a nervous breakdown'.[52] Later in 1932, Power could identify the roots of her crude and visceral reaction. 'The profound uneasiness of the West, face to face with the East today is uneasiness of the *Doppelgänger*—the man who met himself and didn't like it'.[53]

Unlike Japan, China possessed 'that seed of originality' and thus 'may become almost anything'.[54] As the Middle Kingdom, Power read Chinese civilisation as occupying a 'midway' position between East and West. It was like all other Eastern nations in its 'carelessness of all that we mean by progress',[55] having no interest in aping Western-style modernity like Japan. This made China 'Oriental', or in Power's terms, 'medieval'. China also had a completely different understanding of the nature of civilisation that had nothing to do with progressing or developing into something else, something new, as in the modern West. Civilisation was something that China had already achieved; 'civilization was a state of being one thing, not a state of becoming'.[56] Thus China could isolate itself in the nineteenth century, protecting itself 'from the incursions of alien powers with alien standards of civilisation'.[57] Aware of civilisation's ontological rather than developmental status, and recalling that China had developed an advanced culture while Europeans were living as 'barbarians', this liberated contemporary China from anxiety about its relative lack of 'progress' during the period of European and American imperial expansion and domination in China.

Yet, where Chinese civilisation most strongly resembled the West, and was different from other Eastern nations, Power claimed, was in its 'essentially rational' and 'unreligious' basis. Thus, China could be read as basically modern with 'almost limitless potentiality'. In common with Lucie Zimmern's aestheticisation of world politics, Power thought China could teach the West 'a truer reading of civilisation, a more reasonable outlook, a greater perception of beauty'. Yet to create a completely unique synthesis between East and West, Power claimed, China also had to develop rights and protections for workers and overcome the extreme poverty of its vast population. Chinese individuals had to be freed from the oppressiveness of the traditional patriarchal family structure, and the Chinese state had to learn better, less corrupt ways of government.[58] Only then, if China wishes, could it become a great modern power.[59] Eileen Power was attempting to develop a distinctive way of thinking about East–West difference and modern 'progress' that was neither hierarchical nor dependent on a universal standard or ideal, idealising China. Alone, 'of all the nations of the East', she thought, China might in the long-distant future find a synthesis of that which was good in both East and West 'to make a third civilisation, which should be neither and yet both'.[60]

Power sought to delink civilisation and progress and, much later in the 1930s, attempted to 'provincialise Europe' by pointing to the non-European origins of modernity and Western civilisation. In the early 1920s, Power's primary method of subverting the East–West distinction was replacing the geographical and civilisational difference onto a distinction between social systems and temporality. Power's earliest world-historical comparative framework did not rely on a progressivist narrative about the transition from medieval to modern. Instead, geographical Othering was replaced by temporal Othering, a medievalisation of 'the East', particularly India; 'the historian', she wrote, 'is tempted to assert that there is no such thing as East and West; there is mediaeval and modern'.[61] Yet the definition and meaning of the medieval was intricately bound up with Orientalism. Collapsing of space into time was a common trope among European medievalists in the nineteenth and twentieth centuries. Yet the specifics of Power's medievalisation of the East must also be understood in relation to her 1922 essay 'A Plea for the Middle Ages'.

## Interregnum: Power's Plea for the Middle Ages

At first glance, Eileen Power's specialism in medieval history could account for her neglect in histories of international thought, a neglect she herself would have anticipated. Where F. Melian Stawell creatively reread the Greeks for internationalist purposes, Power was scathing of the contemporary Grecophilia and its modern manifestation that she saw as a leading cause of the 'cataclysm' of World War I.[62] Her 1922 essay, 'A Plea for the Middle Ages', described Greek political philosophy as a 'curse'.[63] No matter that Greek city states and economies were so small, simple, and unique. Greek-inspired Hegelian notions of the sovereign state dominated modern political theorising: individuals owed all their freedom to the state, which could claim total loyalty in return. Other forms of association had no 'organic life' and existed only by virtue of an absolute state subject to no higher authority but in a constant state of hostility with other states.[64] Singling out the German philosophers Hegel and Treitschke, and the German militarist and historian Friedrich von Bernhardi, Power accused T. H. Green of being 'only Treitschke with an Oxford manner' and English philosopher Bernard Bosanquet as 'only Bernhardi in kid gloves'.[65]

For Power, it was not just the Great War that discredited Greek political theory and its modern expression in the theory of state sovereignty. It was also the basic realities of modernity: 'now three-quarters of life is international and a man cannot sit down to breakfast or call in a doctor without being dependent upon other nations'.[66] As Lilian Friedländer had also pointed out, Power argued that new political and international theorising on 'multiple sovereignty' was a product of the increasingly obvious fact that states were 'part of a larger whole and their sovereignty must be limited by their relation to that whole'.[67] Advocates for domestic and imperial reform recognised the higher authority of international organisations and courts. New theories of 'home rule, devolution, regionalism' were 'nibbling' away the state's functional administrative authority from both inside and out. Guild socialists were developing plans for smaller workers associations to establish 'a balance of power between a guild congress' and the state.[68] Eileen Power read these new intellectual currents not only as rebuke to the influence of ancient Greek political philosophy, but as a revival of ideas from 'the despised and rejected Middle Ages'; they were 'resuscitating mediaeval conceptions in modern forms'.[69]

The Middle Ages were no golden age, Power conceded, and the ideal was never achieved in practice. Yet medieval political ideals were the best historical referent for modern politics and international relations because they addressed the basic problem of reconciling two fundamental and necessary forms of association, the universal and general, the local and particular, 'the world and the group'.[70] Citing legal scholars Otto von Gierke and Frederic Maitland, and political theorist Harold Laski, Power argued that in medieval Europe ordinary people lived and laboured in small local associations, self-governing towns and guilds, but were also wholly conscious of their obligations to the universal Church. They felt the force of living in 'a community of communities' enveloping both their local town or craft association and world Christendom.[71] The underlying ideal of medieval political life, then, for Power, was that it should 'combine the qualities of the parish pump and the world: it must be small enough to give the individual intensity of interests and to form his personality by constant interpenetration with the personality of others; and it must be large enough to give him width and to prevent the senseless destruction of war'.[72] The political philosophy underlying this dual association was the 'idea of unity' under the Holy Roman Empire, theorised by Dante as a cosmopolitan world empire.[73] 'Both Papacy and Empire', Power claimed, 'acted, at one time or another, as a court of international arbitration; and the Papacy continually sought by such institutions as the Truce of God to limit war'.[74]

Again, Power declared, the ideal was not achieved, yet medieval ideas were instructive in a context in which some aspects of medieval life were now found in modern form. The modern state 'has ousted the parish pump'. Yet capitalism had unwittingly 'made the world small again'.[75] Modern telecommunications and transport mitigated distance, restoring the forms of cross-communal solidarity provided by the universal Church, particularly in class relations. Medieval English and French knights and prelates had a greater affinity with one another than with their feudal tenants, and modern workers were increasingly conscious that class, not nation, was their primary affiliation.[76] Because it reflected real national sympathies, the modern state could not be abolished, but it was both economically too large and politically too small. For Power, the rise of the modern capitalist state was also the passage from a medieval world of diverse European, Persian, Chinese, and Mongolian empires to the modern imperial state system. Power's later lectures on the history of the modern world during the 1930s were also the story of the transition from a medieval world defined by a combination of small-scale and local political and economic grouping, cross-border trade and the unity of Christendom towards increasingly national political and economic organisation and a 'world of states and new diplomacy' centring on the 'national enmities of great powers'. 'Something gained, much lost'.[77]

## Medievalising India

As an exercise in political theory, Power's idealisation of medieval multilevel governance is no more problematic than Hegelian theories of the sovereign state. Yet it becomes more problematic in the context of Power's strongest medieval projection in the early 1920s. Travelling from Madras to Peshawar, and Bombay to Calcutta, in the wake of the Amritsar massacre and the rise of the non-cooperation movement, Power felt as if she had 'outwitted time, stolen back through forbidden gates and caught a glimpse of the far, far distant morning of the world'.[78] So much of what she 'found' during her travels and interviews in India, or so she believed, was familiar to her from historical research on medieval Europe. As Power wrote to fellow medievalist G. G. Coulton, 'I could not imagine why so much of it seemed so familiar to me and then I began to recognise that it was just the Middle Ages'.[79] An Indian village bazaar was 'very like the mediaeval town in the time of the guilds'.[80] The throng of pilgrims in medieval Europe are like the 'crepitating mass of humanity' travelling to India's many religious sites.[81] The 'cult of Gandhi' spread so quickly because 'the wandering holy men preach his doctrines . . . [in] just such a fashion in mediaeval Europe'.[82] Gandhi himself 'is simply Peter the Hermit preaching the first crusade'.[83] In a 1922 article in *Foreign Affairs*, Power described the 'gentle, ascetic little visionary' as 'nothing so much as a mediaeval saint'.[84] The current agrarian conflicts in India 'are an exact replica of the troubles in England during the fourteenth century'.[85]

Obviously, Power acknowledged, caste differences in India were more complicated than class distinctions in medieval England. Yet the basic reality of feudal relations, agrarian discontent, peasant uprisings, and the gruelling nature of peasant life were alike.[86] More importantly, underlying peasant uprisings in both locations and periods was more than the basic fact of feudal inequality, or 'historical parallels' in the rise and fall of the price of agricultural produce, Power claimed. Contemporary India and medieval England were 'fundamentally as well as superficially alike' because they were governed by the same three basic ideas and social forms: extreme religiosity, a static culture, and the patriarchal subjection of women.[87] Hence, the contemporary struggles between East and West were not between two civilisations as such, nor even just the inevitable resistance to Western imperialism, but India's transition to modernity, that is, 'the ferment of two periods of history existing simultaneously'.[88] What distinguished contemporary India from the modern West also distinguished medieval from modern Europe.

Later in the 1930s, Power attempted to develop a more sophisticated methodological framework of sociological cross-civilisational comparison and world history, representing about the best of the international thinking at LSE in that period and for a considerable time. However, the political and intellectual limits of Power's project are best revealed in her treatment of anticolonial politics in India. Power had been one of only six Europeans at the Nagpur Congress in December 1920 when the Indian National Congress adopted the policy of non-cooperation.[89] Power was unimpressed by its early achievements. In the face of labour and agrarian disputes, religious unrest, and the propaganda targeted at 'ignorant and excitable crowds', she accused the movement of steadily leading toward violence.[90] Despite Gandhi's pacifism, she refused to condemn the colonial government's repression of Indian resisters because the non-cooperation movement also relied on pressure and coercion. The decision to boycott elections and schools simply meant that no socialists were elected and children drifted back to classrooms because 'Gandhi could offer them no more solid occupation than propaganda and the spinning wheel'.[91] The most interesting thing about Gandhi, whom Power briefly met, she claimed, was that he was 'not a product of India at all. His gospel is all of returning to a pure Indian civilisation . . . but the form of his attack on western civilisation (machines, modern medicine and law etc. etc.) is pure western anarchism. He has not a single doctrine which he did not learn from Tolstoy, or Thoreau'.[92]

Eileen Power was not an anticolonial thinker; in the 1920s, she did not insist on the immediate end to Britain's imperial rule in India, or anywhere else. She praised the Round Table group for representing the 'high ideal of Empire as a Commonwealth of Free Nations' in her contemporaneous work on school textbooks.[93] Her *Foreign Affairs* article supported self-governing dominion status for India within the context of a reformed imperial federation.[94] Immediate self-rule was impossible because India could not 'leap necessary stages of constructive development'.[95] In India's newly formed legislative assembly, Power supported the Moderate Party as she thought it represented

FIGURE 5.1. Eileen Power c.1922. Photographer Unknown. Courtesy of LSE Library

'the more educated and politically experienced class', more aligned with gradual progress towards self-government.[96] Britain's violent repression of the non-cooperation movement was a product of its unreasonable demands. The other threat was Gandhi's alliance with pan-Islamists. In the most racist and uninformed comment in Power's entire work, she claimed that Muslims could not 'possibly disbelieve in violence'.[97] The centre of the 'Khalifat' movement was 'not Delhi but Constantinople'; the pan-Indian anticolonial alliance was how 'the Khalifat tail wags the non-co-operation dog'.[98] Power also evoked the spectre of violent Islam in the 'Dutch' East Indies, again revealing her preferred class of anticolonialists. She negatively compared 'native . . . Mohamedan agitators' to Chinese traders and sugar and rubber plantation owners who led 'the first movement of a coloured race in Java towards political freedom'.[99]

As a 'pacificist' and member of the Labour Party, Power had expected to feel more solidarity with Gandhi's movement, which had gained strength after the Amritsar massacre.[100] As if it was largely an aesthetic choice rather than a political decision, it was rather 'unpleasing' to have greater sympathy for her imperial hosts 'because in politics I do so much prefer a position . . . on the left'.[101] But she was not only sympathetic to her colonial hosts; she echoed the government line. While she sought to relativise East–West differences and critique modern ideas of 'progress', Power was profoundly Orientalist. She read Asian nations through the lens of the Middle Ages, selectively projecting a desire for a different kind of politics and international relations onto the 'Eastern' polities she observed. She was sceptical of Bengali writer Rabindranath Tagore's attempted synthesis of East and West if the East included India. India's religious mentality was so entrenched and more fundamental than in medieval Europe, or contemporary China, making a true synthesis impossible.[102] China stood for something that was or could be 'neither and yet both'.[103] Yet the basis of Power's accord between the contemporary East and Europe's past was another idealisation of medieval Europe. In her later writings on medieval society, Power read the Middle Ages through the Orient.[104] In other words, as now explained, Power's comparative world history of East and West, medieval and modern, was fundamentally sociological.

## Social History and Sociological Method

During her Kahn travels, Eileen Power 'reluctantly' accepted the offer of a lectureship in the History Department at LSE alongside economic historian of the British Empire, Lilian Knowles, who ensured Power's appointment in 1921. Like Margery Perham, Lilian Knowles opened doors to white women in her profession, and was one of the few married women of her generation to have both a child and a successful academic career. Halford Mackinder was not the first or only pioneer of neo-mercantilist and imperialist thought at LSE in the first decades of the twentieth century. Knowles had read history and law at Girton College, Cambridge, taking Firsts in both in 1894. Cambridge, like Oxford, did not confer degrees on women. Hence, Knowles became one of the seven hundred women from Oxford and Cambridge known as 'Steamboat Ladies'. Between 1904 and 1907, they travelled by boat to Trinity College

Dublin to have their degrees awarded *ad eundem* because, for a short time, women at Trinity, Oxford or Cambridge could receive their degrees from any of the three. In 1907, Trinity discontinued the arrangement, fearing an exodus of Irish women to Oxbridge women's colleges, the same year the Vatican gave approval for Catholic women to study at Oxford.[105]

Knowles specialised in the history of British imperial economic development, focusing on the relations between imperial states. Her core international relations belief was that 'England must be treated as part of a great Western civilization acting on other Powers and being reacted on in turn by them'.[106] She taught 'The Growth of English Commerce and Colonization', 'Economic Development of the Empire' and courses on the economic and political positions of 'the Great Powers', which Power later taught. While IR scholars have recently discovered the significance of the nineteenth century to global transformations, Knowles's 1932 book *Economic Development in the Nineteenth Century: France, Germany, Russia and the United States* was reprinted eight times.[107] Active on the LSE's Imperial Studies Committee, she also liked to remind Indian students 'how fortunate they were to be part of the British Empire. She was known as Britannia, for she had the same ample figure and always lectured holding her pointer like a Trident'.[108]

Where Knowles was a 'country tory, patriot, and imperialist',[109] Eileen Power was an urban liberal internationalist and imperialist. Yet she told G. G. Coulton 'the atmosphere of the LSE is so very utilitarian, whereas I am hopelessly humanistic and have a mortal distaste for the pure economist!'[110] Cambridge counter-offered, but Power was disgusted at male dons who had just voted against full university membership for women.[111] At the time, LSE was more politically progressive than either Oxford or Cambridge and was co-educational from its founding in 1895. The School was associated with social reform, social science history, and women's and colonial education, all of which appealed to Eileen Power. Cambridge's loss was LSE's gain. Power remained at LSE for the rest of her career, teaching economic, social and world history and the political position of the great powers. Before Susan Strange, Power made her name by founding her own subfield and was an active convenor of scholars across disciplines, including anthropology, economics, sociology, and history.[112]

Beyond calling herself a social and economic historian, Power did not identify with any theoretical 'school', nor did she seek to found one. This made it easier for later generations of IR scholars—many of whom were trained to organise their work around debilitating 'isms' and 'schools'—to ignore her. Nonetheless, Power was one of the leading pioneers of social, economic, and gender history, comparable to the first generation of the *Annales* School in France, particularly the work of Marc Bloch and Lucien Febvre.[113] As Berg has pointed out, the *Annales* is most often credited with pioneering long-term social history, integrating historical and social-science methods to understand long-term historical structures across the *long durée* and as an intervention into contemporary politics.[114] Power was simultaneously developing a comparable methodological approach at LSE. In 1934, Bloch travelled to LSE to seek a collaboration with Power and Tawney.[115] Bloch and Febvre were not as original as they or their male followers have claimed; Power anticipated the second generation *Annales* emphasis on regions, one of the founding moves of world systems theory.[116] The *Annales* men succeeded in the game of intellectual influence, securing their 'reputations in terms of the making of historical memory—the creation of a "founding father" figure on the one hand, and the forgetting of the feminine presence on the other'.[117] But the fact remains that in the earliest decades of the formation of international relations as a separate subject, we find an historian in a social science school making a plea for sociological theory in historical research on world history and contemporary international relations.

Eileen's Power's 'A Plea for the Middle Ages' was an historian's critique of Hegelian theories of the sovereign state as applied to politics and international relations. She also levelled a comparable critique at her own profession, particularly the fields of political and constitutional history. '"Let us now praise famous men", was the historian's motto' she declared, 'to speak of ordinary people would have been beneath the dignity of history'.[118] Obsessed with the conflicts in the council chamber, political historians were interested in ordinary people only in relation to their political or economic masters. Anticipating Agnes Headlam-Morley's later defence of diplomatic history, the primary interest of traditional historians, Power claimed, was the ruling class; they had no interest in 'the obscure lives and activities of the great mass of humanity, upon whose slow toil was built up the prosperity of the world and who were the hidden foundation of the political and constitutional edifice reared by the famous men he praised'.[119] Seventeen- and eighteen-year-old schoolgirls could write in detail on the political and ecclesiastical consequences of the Thirty Years' War and the 'clauses of the Treaty of Westphalia were . . . as familiar as the multiplication table'. But, Power lamented, 'they did not think . . . of asking what results the Thirty Years' War had upon the people of Europe; they were content to believe that territorial acquisitions and ecclesiastical settlements alone were the results of war and matter of history'.[120]

The 'new' historical writing of the 1920s and 1930s, of which Power was one of the leading practitioners, reflected a conscious shift away from the political and constitutional history privileged by new scientific historians in the academy during the nineteenth century. As historian Bonnie Smith has shown, the nineteenth-century professionalisation of 'scientific history' was established in opposition to so-called amateurism. This was a gendered opposition defined against and considered superior to the historical work of 'amateur' women historians. The 'development of modern scientific methodology, epistemology, professional practice, and writing has been closely tied to evolving definitions of masculinity and femininity'.[121] Eventually, the new documentary and archival methods were assumed to privilege forms of legal and political history, including diplomatic history, over the social, economic, and medieval history on which many women wrote. In turn, Eileen Power reasserted a form of world social and economic history in reaction to this privileged status of legal and political history. Just as 'allowances' had to be made, Power said, 'for the race which disguises the white man's dividend as the white man's burden', conventional historians 'will no doubt continue to meet the charge of writing sociology with the indignation of a Victorian matron defending her virtue'. Nonetheless, 'the best historians', Power insisted, would 'increasingly write under the name of social history'.[122]

In her project for a new social, economic, and international history, Power claimed a special place for her period. Compared to modern historians, medievalists were more attentive 'to the theoretical aspects of their work'.[123] However, in this context, Power was unique in combining large-scale world social and economic history of the Middle Ages (and beyond) with women's history.[124] In the first decades of the twentieth century, most women's history was written in non-academic contexts; professional academic history was defined precisely against such low, 'amateur' and feminised subjects.[125] According to Berg, Eileen Power created women's history as a university subject in Britain in the 1920s and 1930s, 'but it fell out of academic history after the Second World War, and only re-emerged in the 1970s'.[126] Her 1922 work, *Medieval English Nunneries*, uncovered the social and economic life and household organisation of women-centred religious communities, and was described as 'incomparably better in quality than anything of the kind that has been done on this subject before or since in any European language'.[127]

Power's most famous and highly acclaimed book, *Medieval People*, first published in 1924 and reprinted in ten editions, included lengthy discussions of women and ordinary people, prefiguring one of the central moves of feminist IR.[128] In Power's much quoted words:

We still praise famous men . . . but we praise them with due recognition of the fact that not only great individuals, but people as a whole, unnamed and undistinguished masses of people, now sleeping in unknown graves, have also been concerned in the story . . . As Acton put it, 'The great historian now takes his meals in the kitchen.' This book is chiefly concerned with the kitchens of History.[129]

Power's own intellectual life was supported by the women-centred educational initiatives such as Oxford High School, Girton College, Cambridge, and the Shaw Fellowship at LSE, as well as the benevolence of her spinster aunts who paid for her education. Power, in turn, helped to financially support her sisters, but her professional success was also dependent on domestic housekeepers.[130] Social history relied on and bestowed dignity on the lives of ordinary people, women and men. It also innovated analytical and comparative sociological methods.

Clearly shaped by her position in a university dominated by the social sciences, Power insisted that historians should combine the skill in technical archival and/or primary source research, the work of the 'bricklayer', with 'historical analysis and synthesis—the architect's job'.[131] Social historians, in particular, had to develop 'theoretical equipment' and should make 'wider use . . . of abstraction and comparison',[132] though not at the expense of historical and empirical precision. Power was highly critical of Max Weber's ideal type abstractions as applied to economic history, which Georg Schwarzenberger later employed to generalise about 'international society' as the basis for a 'separate IR'. She criticised Werner Sombart's work on the historical stages of capitalism, which superimposed a theoretical account of different economic systems ('feudal', 'capitalist') onto different historical epochs. This led to a periodisation in which 'medieval' economic relations were defined as 'pre-capitalist', and caricatured as static, local and self-contained natural economies.[133] For Power, this ideal type produced a major historical distortion of both medieval economic life and the history of capitalism. Her own work revealed that as early as the twelfth and thirteenth centuries, Flemish and Italian cloth towns instituted 'a wage system . . . and was run by big entrepreneurs for an international market . . . International trade and international finance, based upon an elaborate credit system, animated by the unbounded desire for gain and capitalistic to the tips of its fingers'.[134] Capital accumulated through trade was 'a large-scale international affair . . . and differing from modern international commerce only in its range'.[135] Power's posthumously published

*The Wool Trade in English Medieval History* demonstrated how these wool and textile trades and export markets were large scale and international; its 'area of exchange was a country, a continent, occasionally indeed a world'.[136]

In a critique that could still be applied to much contemporary international theory, Power insisted that scholars who relied too heavily on ideal type concepts used 'theory not to interpret but to manipulate the facts of history',[137] to distort 'concrete historical realities'.[138] For this she criticised Marxists as much as followers of Max Weber. Marxists were better equipped to develop a 'structural analysis of society', Power claimed.[139] They understood 'that all phenomena are social phenomena' and all of society's main 'institutions and activities' could be socially explained. She praised Marxism's emphasis on society as a whole, its centring of economic history and historical processes.[140] To the degree that Marxists combined 'sociological induction with deductive analysis', it was similar to the social historical method that Power wished to pursue.[141] Yet Marx and his followers were less than reliable in the interpretation of history itself; they 'have not infrequently used their position in the kitchen for the purpose of cooking the evidence'.[142] Marxist historical writing was too often an effort to validate a predetermined theory. It too directly transposed everything into economic terms and presented all history as 'class war'.[143] For Power, the task of the social historian was to strip away Marxism's overly determinist and dialectical analysis and take up its 'pure methodological' position: that 'correlations between . . . different social phenomena can be stated in terms of general laws', which she understood quite loosely as 'rough approximations'.[144]

For the social and economic historian interested in world history, then, the goal was to examine 'different combinations of circumstances at different periods in the hope of deducing therefrom laws of social behaviour'[145] as they may relate, for example, to transitions between historical epochs, contacts between cultures and discontinuities and breaks within different civilisations, as well as urgent contemporary international relations questions, such as the effects of industrialisation in Asia.[146] Power had sought to show that the 'fundamental institutions and functions of modern times' could also be found, in different form, in the Middle Ages.[147] Power's essentially comparative method was to look for and analyse 'repeatable aspects of social life', and then compare 'their operation in different surroundings and at different periods, to discover whether certain social phenomena are habitual'.[148] The closest she came to executing this approach was in her world history that attempted to distil social practices 'into a certain number of universal abstract relations' that were not

ideal types read into history but emerged out of historical study.[149] She combined world, comparative, and social history, medieval and modern, East and
West, as interlinked and co-constituted, emphasising the ordinariness of international connection and trade, not as necessarily and naively displacing war
and conquest, but as more common, more normal to the lives of the majority
of people in the world than conquest and war. Yet in contrast to overly struc-
turalist, economic, or ideal-type accounts, Power insisted that social history
should also draw on the 'artistic method', 'to reconstruct in personal terms the
life of the past . . . a perfectly vivid and definite picture of individual lives in
relation to their social setting.'[150]

## World History as Social and Economic History

Maxine Berg rightly suggests that the twenty-eight chapters of Power's unpublished manuscript 'An Introduction to World History', stand comparison with
the work of her friends' H. G. Wells's *Outline of History*, published in 1920, and
Arnold Toynbee's multivolume *A Study of History*, the first six volumes published
in Power's lifetime.[151] The scale and ambition of Wells's work appealed to Power.
Yet, Wells's *Outline* was not based on original historical scholarship, like Power's,
and may not even have been his own work at all. Produced in the space of nine
to twelve months, the best that can be said is that Wells drew from the *Encyclopaedia Britannica* and other secondary sources, and the labours of numerous
women. Certainly, Wells's wife, Jane Wells, wrote whole sections; his mistress
Odette Keun provided editorial and other writing assistance; and Amber Reeves
Blanco-White, with whom he had an affair (and daughter), ghost-wrote other
parts of the text.[152] There is also compelling evidence that Wells plagiarised an
unpublished manuscript written by Canadian 'spinster' Florence Deeks.[153]

Unlike Toynbee, Eileen Power did not prognosticate on civilisational rise
and decline. However, her account of the transition from a medieval pluriverse to Western domination and the contemporary upheavals in Asia was more
genuinely global than the accounts of either Wells or Toynbee, centring Arab
and Chinese civilisations, the importance of trade, and the mutual constitution and connection between civilisations.[154] For Power, Arab and Chinese
medieval civilisations were not simply regional but, in contemporary language,
encompassed 'universalising *world* ordering arrangements'.[155] Her work predates
by almost a century contemporary interest in the 'global Middle Ages'.[156]

The turn to comparative and world history in the interwar period was not
only an obvious reaction to World War I. In Eileen Power's case, it was the

necessary counter to the catastrophic dominance of political, legal, and nationalist histories. Political and constitutional histories not only ignored ordinary people, labouring classes, and women; they normalised war and political conflict. Just as ordinary people had to be understood in their own sociological terms, so nations had to be situated in wider comparative and international context.[157] Across her writings and teaching on world history, Power was scathing about 'conventional' modes of historical writing that exclusively focused on the 'abnormal, the kings, the wars, the high politics', and divided mankind into separate national units.[158] Disproportionate attention was paid to irregular political and military struggles compared to what happened most of the time, and shaped the majority of peoples' lives much more profoundly. It was precisely these social phenomena, if uncovered by proper and original historical analysis, that could be distilled into approximate 'universal abstract relations'.[159]

For convenience, Power claimed, historical scholarship may be divided into geographical and chronological periods, yet there was a unity of world time and space, 'a history that is the common possession of mankind and can in some sense be viewed as a whole'.[160] If Power was one of the early founders of social history and developed a genuinely historical sociological method, then she was unique in combining social and world history with an 'East and West' focus. She echoed her early work during the Kahn Fellowship, although 'East' and 'West' were not defined in opposition, but as mutually constituted through trade and/or armed aggression that was of 'almost immemorial antiquity'.[161] Power's writing on world history was as much an international political project as an intellectual one. Her political activism in the peace movement and support for the League of Nations was closely related to her approach to social history as world history.

Eileen Power's social and world history was founded on three interrelated themes, or 'general laws'. First was her essentially materialist and anthropological claim that humanity's most basic challenge was the same for all peoples everywhere and throughout time: how to conquer nature. Humans spent far more time pursuing the regular, habitual practices required to sustain life than in 'political and military struggle'.[162] As Power claimed in her lecture 'Introduction to the Study of World History':

> people who (whether black, yellow, white; whether under blazing sun, or amid almost perpetual snow) are always much more like each other than they are unlike . . . Everywhere man interests himself in the same things: he founds religions, he builds houses, he clothes himself . . . he makes verses.[163]

The unity of world history was found in the commonality of these ordinary economic and social practices to sustain life that were everywhere 'much alike' and thus could be the object of world and comparative historical analysis: 'infinitely more time has been spent by infinitely more people in the pursuit of the normal, and the likenesses between different nations engaged in the pursuit of the normal are infinitely greater than their differences'.[164] Recognition of ordinariness and likeness was not just a sociological method but the basis for cross-civilisational coexistence. Humans 'exchange things and people who exchange are dependent on each other'.[165] Unlike political and constitutional history, world history as social and economic history could identify the basis for humanity's moral development along cosmopolitan lines, claims Power also made in her history writing for schools, as discussed in chapter 3.[166]

The second general theme of Eileen Power's world social history was the fundamental importance attached to cross-border trade and travellers. Though it was downplayed in political and constitutional history, Power argued, 'trading ships in the long run are more important than . . . battleships'.[167] She was predominantly interested in East–West trade, particularly Arab, Ottoman and Venetian trade routes, the opening of trade to the Far East, and, in accord with her 'artistic method', travellers in China, Ceylon, and India. Power's highly acclaimed *Medieval People* emphasised both the economic lives and social conditions of ordinary people, including women, and long-distance travellers and trade during the century 1245 to 1345. She wrote of the famous Venetian Marco Polo, 'who first made Asia known to Europe' by travelling the 'silk road', but he could do so 'solely and entirely' because of caravan routes established by the Tartar Empire that spanned northern Asia and Persia.[168] In Venice itself, merchants 'were kings' because the seaport 'gathered . . . all the trade routes' between Egypt, Persia, Syria, and Central Asia.[169] This period was an 'epoch in the relations of East and West' that created a world economy.[170] In a 1933 BBC radio broadcast for schools, Power told British children that it was three Chinese inventions that were at the origins of the modern world. Paper, gunpowder, and the Mariner's compass, all invented in China, created printing, democratised the use of force, and permitted Columbus to locate America. China's inventions were 'carried to the West by the Arabs, and they changed the whole of European history'.[171]

Third, Power's world social history continually emphasised the debts that different civilisations owed to others, particularly Western debts to Chinese and Arab civilisations. In her Kahn Report, she had suggested that China,

India, and Egypt were three of the four original civilisations and Greece only counted if it was 'not too deeply indebted to Egypt'.[172] The history and culture of the West itself came from and was made outside itself; it was Greco-Roman, but heavily influenced by Islamic, Egyptian, Indian, and Chinese civilisations. In her later lectures on Arab trade and civilisations, Power emphasised the greatness and scale of the Arab Empire of the seventh and eighth centuries, stretching across the Mediterranean, Persia, and Central Asia to Bukhara and Samarkand. The 'golden age' of Arab civilisation c.750–1055 drew on Greek, Jewish, and Indian sources to produce 'a remarkable international culture' with Muslim learning foremost in history, geography, maths, medicine, and philosophy.[173] In turn, its 'far-flung commercial activities' were of enormous significance in 'stimulating travel, trade, the spread of ideas, the interchange of civilisations', influencing the development of Western nations via Spain, Sicily, and travel to the Holy Land.[174] In Power's words, 'the more we study the civilization of the medieval Europe the more we come to realise how profoundly it was affected by its intercourse with the world of Islam'.[175] From reading historians, IR scholars only belatedly realised that there was no endogenous economic development of 'the West'.[176]

Eileen Power admired the Mongolian Empire as well as the ability of later fourteenth century Mongol khanates to co-exist relatively peacefully. She praised China under the T'ang emperors for its religious toleration, and noted a similar period of relative tolerance between 1580 and 1720 under the Mings and then Manchu emperors.[177] Crucially, Power's story of the 'rise' of the modern West, its so-called 'discoveries' and the new age of ocean powers 'is not a cyclone before which the East bends'.[178] The so-called Age of Discovery is the story of 'a whole new world and little Europe only a fraction of it'.[179] A major stimulus to commerce, it led to the rise of new middle classes, chartered companies, an economic revolution 'of the first importance'. The model for the 'great state' was 'firms of wholesale merchants' who 'learnt to calculate their own power by their trade and to sweep the new forces into their service'.[180] Despite initial European incursions, Power declared, the three great Eastern dynasties—the Mogul empire, the Ming dynasty, and the Tokugawa Shoguns in Japan—granted trade concessions to Europeans, but all remained in territorial control during the sixteenth and seventeenth centuries. This was still the age of 'splendid despots', of expanding military states in Europe and Asia and the rise of personalist monarchies in England, Persia, and Constantinople.[181] There was no question of Western cultural superiority or Europe's 'territorial aggrandisement' in the East.[182]

Power's world-historical consciousness, her sweeping account of world history from the middle ages to the late nineteenth century, was shaped by the world crisis caused by Western imperialism and its world wars. It was through this lens that she historicised the contemporary 'reawakening of the East', the 1911 revolution in China, the emergence of Japan as a great power, and against the background of three 'epoch-making wars' that defined East–West relations at the start of the twentieth century, the Chino-Japanese War (1894–5), the Russo-Japanese War (1904–5), and the Great War (1914–1918), in which all the powers of the Far East fought with the European allies.[183] Power's history was also, crucially, a medievalist's account of what was lost in the transition from a pluriverse of medieval empires—Persian, Chinese, Mongolian, European—to the rise of the modern state and the West's global expansion. She would not have been surprised by the work of later historians showing a 'great divergence' between the wealth of European imperial powers and Asian and Middle Eastern powers in the nineteenth century.[184] It was also a declensionist narrative, written when Power's hopes for the League of Nations were plummeting in the face of renewed imperial and fascist aggression around the world.

In 1934, Eileen Power reviewed *Empire in the East*, a book published under the auspices of the Institute of Pacific Relations (IPR). Perhaps surprisingly for a volume associated with 'the most important research organization in international relations of the interwar years',[185] Power thought a better title would be a 'Plea for a Socialist State'.[186] Edited by IPR's executive director, Joseph Barnes, who was later attacked during McCarthy's anti-communist witch-hunts, most of its contributors, Power claimed, conveyed the impression that imperialism in Asia had been a waste of time and that the violent conflicts wracking Asia in the 1930s were primarily caused 'by strains and stresses' in the Western nations. Hence the solution to conflict in Asia was a revolution in the West, including the abolition of capitalism. This was 'a ruthless analysis', Power claimed, 'and there is a good deal to be said for it; but it does not offer any very helpful clue for immediate action' in the face of Japan's invasion and occupation of Manchuria, then in its third year.[187]

The colonial occupation of Manchuria seemed to entirely confirm Eileen Power's view of Japan formed during her Kahn travels. 'What we see in the East today is something much more profound than the external contest between East and West; it is the contest between two types of civilisations in which the Eastern type is giving way. Japan today stands not with the East but with the West. Industrialism has changed her into the counterpart of Britain. And for the Chinese today she is no more acceptable than England or any

Western power'.[188] As her own counter to Japan's colonial projects, Power helped found the China Campaign Committee, coordinated shipments of medical supplies, and supported a boycott of Japanese goods. Her fable 'The Little God', which first appeared in *Graphic*, was reprinted in an edited volume *China: Body and Soul*, alongside essays by Gilbert Murray, Arthur Salter, and Harold Laski. With the proceeds donated to China, the book intended to convey to British readers 'a sense of China as a fact: something . . . a man can see in relation to himself, homely, rational, of the nature of flesh and blood'.[189]

Just two weeks after the Soviet invasion of Finland on 30 November 1939, Eileen Power travelled to Geneva to attend the League of Nations Assembly. In expelling the Soviet Union for breaking the Covenant, the League had taken the absolute minimum action, Power argued, and had shown the League still had some life. 'Of the quality of that life it is still too early to speak'. However, at this point, Power's hopes for the League were crushed. Italy had invaded Ethiopia and Germany had bombed Spain. All the busy people working in the splendid halls of the League, 'the throng of delegates, attachés, secretaries, members of the Secretariat, journalists, photographers', all these 'little figures moving in those vast halls may be maggots on the body of a corpse or mayflowers of a new spring'.[190] Like Lucie Zimmern, Power thought the League's social and technical work was of profound importance: 'the enduring and unceasing work of the League in the economic and humanitarian spheres goes on'.[191] But she had already diagnosed the wider problem in a lecture to the Cambridge History Club in late 1938. 'Not once alone in the history of Europe has the triumph of a hostile rule in Africa and Spain spelt disaster to our civilization'.[192] Titled 'The Eve of the Dark Ages: A Tract for the Times', an edited version was reprinted and posthumously published as 'The Precursors', in the tenth edition of *Medieval People*.

Ostensibly a lecture on the decline of the Roman Empire, the lecture was Power's response to fascist appeasement ('each compromise . . . a link in the chain dragging them over the abyss'[193]), and a commentary on the materialist decadence of the contemporary West on the eve of World War II.[194] 'Their roads grew better as their statesmanship grew worse and central heating triumphed as civilization fell'.[195] The 'disease' that had destroyed Rome was multifarious: internecine wars, the decline of free trade, hyper-inflation, crushing tax burdens on middle classes, the masses of unemployed 'kept quiet by their dole of bread and circus'. Political and economic elites, 'haughty senatorial families and the great landowners', carried on unaffected having 'luncheon and tennis parties'. Superstition triumphed over reason and mysticism over

philosophy, while the 'little professors' carried on with their lectures.[196] Their
educational system, the 'fatal study of rhetoric', left them oblivious, discon-
nected from reality. 'The things they learned in their schools had no relation
to the things that were going on in the world outside', wrote the reviser of
school textbooks.[197] None could comprehend Rome's slow disintegration
because they 'suffered from the fatal myopia of contemporaries'. 'Barbarianism
within' became 'a wasting disease' because Romans misunderstood the nature
of civilization, thinking the luxuries of their material culture and their technical achievements were 'the very antithesis of barbarism'.[198] They believed
Rome was a 'condition of nature like the air they breathed and the earth they
tread'. They did not understand it as 'a mere historical fact with a beginning
and an end'.[199]

## Conclusion

Eileen Power's complete absence from IR's intellectual and disciplinary
histories cannot be explained by her historical training or subfields; no one in
Britain had an IR doctorate in the 1920s and 1930s and most teachers and researchers on the subject were historians like Power. When we consider the
degree to which IR scholars have purloined from almost every other discipline
and field to *fill the gap left by its departure from serious historical scholarship*, why
has IR never had a 'social and economic history turn', drawing on Power's
experimentation with historical and sociological methods to write a world
social and economic history emphasising cross-border trade, merchants, and
migrations? As already suggested in chapter 3, Power's gender performance,
her beauty and personal charisma, certainly shaped the way in which her work
was read and received. By the 1950s, Power's legacy for the study of international relations was further erased when her LSE colleagues created post-war
IR's most debilitating founding myth: that to establish IR as separate university subject required breaking away from 'history' and the embrace of a very
particular kind of sociological research.

As discussed in chapter 4, according to Charles Manning and Geoffrey
Goodwin, historians 'recounted *what* happened' but were uninterested in the
theoretical work needed to understand the fundamental nature of international relations. The BCCIS men, either ignorant of Eileen Power's work, or
feigning such, claimed that historians were not 'bold enough to postulate the
existence of quasi-permanent "fundamentals" or "patterns" of policy'.[200]
The study of international relations required 'a more systematised conceptual

framework', namely 'the kind of analytical approach and techniques developed by the sociologist'. By the early 1950s, many BCCIS men caricatured 'historians' as reluctant to engage in theoretical abstraction and assumed that sociology of a very particular kind, systemic and structural theorising, was how to create a new field. Both moves were highly gendered and intellectually devastating.[201] Manning's undergraduate LSE course 'The Structure of International Society' was taken to embody the analytical 'spirit of sociology'.[202] But his efforts were totally outdated, representing not only a struggle against accusations of dilettantism and the post-war realities of Britain's imperial decline. They were a conservative reaction to all that was intellectually challenging, even potentially exciting, about the turn to social history in the 1920s and 1930s.

The BCCIS men's caricature of historical scholarship laid the groundwork for the erasure of one of the earliest historians in Britain to take seriously the sociological project. According to historian of international thought Lucian M. Ashworth, the two major trends in post-war IR were the marginalisation of both feminist thought and international political economy (IPE) writing, both recognised parts of the emerging intellectual field in the first half of the twentieth century.[203] While her work is irreducible to either feminism or IPE, Eileen Power was a victim of both erasures. It is especially ironic that the LSE men claimed that 'Economic History is to Economics' as 'Political and Diplomatic History' is to 'International Relations'.[204] As suggested by Power's social and economic history, the analogy prefigures the failed intellectual projects of both IR and economics. The now thriving fields of global and economic history point again to the significance of Power's pathway to international thought: disciplined training in one or more method and then the pursuit and innovation of new interdisciplinary collaborations.

Perhaps Eileen Power was also lost to IR because she died so young, in 1940 at the age of fifty-one. Had she lived just for another three years, Power would have taught Susan Strange during her one and only degree, in economics at LSE, perhaps changing the course of Strange's career and the course of IR. One of Strange's overriding impressions of her undergraduate days was the number of male professors looking for acolytes, naming among others Harold Laski. That was not Power's style. Yet it was Power's lectures to which LSE students flocked. As Berg has pointed out, 'hers and Laski's were known as the lectures to attend'.[205] What would the young Susan Strange have made of this brilliant older woman that was not interested in disciples? Would an older Strange, as Queen Bee of British IR, have even acknowledged an intellectual debt to Eileen Power, had there been one?

'If you are women and wish to become pre-eminent in a field', wrote Joanna Russ in *How to Suppress Women's Writings*, 'it's a good idea to (a) invent it and (b) locate it in an area either so badly paid or of such low status that men don't want it'.[206] Both Eileen Power and Susan Strange made their names as leading LSE women by establishing their own fields of research, social and economic world history, and international political economy. However, in Strange's case, her field was based on overcoming an intellectual and methodological schism created by her male LSE predecessors, which depended, in turn, on the erasure of Power. In turn, both Power and her IR LSE colleagues defined themselves against the old diplomatic and political history, though for different reasons and in different ways, Power to establish a new social and economic history attentive to the historical significance of ordinary people, Manning and Goodwin to justify a separate IR. But a new approach to diplomatic history was already afoot in 1930s Oxford.

# 6

# Oxford's Failures

## FROM DIPLOMATIC HISTORY TO CRITICAL HISTORIES OF INTERNATIONAL RELATIONS

IN HER 1950 SURVEY of international relations research in Britain, Susan Strange claimed that Chatham House took such a leading role in early IR because Oxford and Cambridge were 'slow to encourage the development of a new and untried branch of study except in connection with the established faculties'.[1] But this was only true of Cambridge. Oxford was a place of opportunity for women international thinkers. From the 1930s to the 1970s, there were more women and more senior women employed at Oxford than any other comparable institution in British IR's formative years. Oxford's *relative* openness to the new field meant that international relations could claim its first woman professor and the first African–American to earn a graduate degree. Women's colleges offered positions to Margery Perham (St Hugh's), Agnes Headlam-Morley (St Hugh's), Sibyl Crowe (St Hilda's), Rachel Wall (St Hugh's and Lady Margaret Hall), Mary Proudfoot (Somerville), and Agatha Ramm (Somerville). Headlam-Morley escaped the very heavy undergraduate teaching burden when she took the Montague Burton Chair. Oxford IR's first faculty lecturer was Rachel Wall. Perham was 'the first woman don, in the history of Oxford and Cambridge, to break out of the purdah of the women's colleges', as Martin Wight put it, when she became the first Official Fellow at the graduate-only and gender-mixed Nuffield College.[2] International relations, colonial administration, and diplomatic and contemporary history were overlapping fields in which women could get ahead.

With its women's colleges and Montague Burton Professorship, Oxford was a place of opportunity for some women international thinkers. Yet the fate and reputation of Oxford IR women was quite cheerless. A few privileged white women had the prospect of university employment, but Oxford itself was a difficult and unforgiving place. Only Perham's career was a glittering success, though her field of imperial governance was marginalised in the formation of disciplinary IR. She had 'burst out of the [Oxford women's] college into the wide world, and came back to Oxford again with more prestige than most men dons, and was ready to exercise it in Oxford. Hence jealousy and backbitings', including from her assistant Martin Wight.[3] Somerville's Agatha Ramm had a substantial publication record and wide respect, but as a diplomatic historian she was easily ignored.[4] Agnes Headlam-Morley and Rachel Wall, more squarely 'in IR', were deemed 'failures', Headlam-Morley's the more embarrassing since she held the Montague Burton Chair, and for so long. Sibyl Crowe, Mary Proudfoot, and Wall did not escape the heavy teaching and pastoral load of their women's colleges. St Hugh's, Somerville, and St Hilda's gave opportunities to women international thinkers. However, their teaching-first philosophy also thwarted scholarly research.

The 'obscure' St Hilda's was 'very much the bottom of the list', claimed Sibyl Crowe, politics lecturer and then Fellow at Oxford's poorest and smallest women's college from 1938.[5] All Oxbridge colleges were 'remote worlds unto themselves', but St Hilda's was the most extreme, she thought. Crowe claimed to be the only person in the College with a radio when war broke out in 1939. 'I am acutely aware of my own academic as well as other shortcomings', she wrote to a friend in 1975.[6] However, the truth was that Crowe's scholarly life was crushed by the colossal burden of teaching and administration. On average, she taught eighteen hours a week, not including preparation and college and faculty meetings. The absolute priority was teaching. Despite never having taught economics in her life, she had to cover economics as well as politics, and politics was new as well. 'I just mugged up'.[7] She was St Hilda's only PPE tutor until 1964, overseeing its development and expansion 'until it reached a size and a level of respectability in the early sixties when other fellows should be elected, in philosophy and economics'.[8] In the college, Crowe was a 'legendary figure',[9] likened to 'some Nordic princess, charging into battle with flying locks and scythes on her chariot wheels'.[10]

But the reality was more mundane. Crowe's teaching burden limited her research. In 1969, she told her employer that she was 'in the last stages' of a book provisionally entitled *France and Algeria: a Colonial Perspective, 1830–1962*. The research built on archival and fieldwork initially carried out for the Colonial Office under the direction of Margery Perham between 1946–48, during which Crowe was arrested by the police.[11] The draft, which she astonishingly claimed numbered four to five hundred thousand words, only needed an introduction and work on the footnotes and bibliography and would be in the 'hands of a publisher by next summer'.[12] The book never materialised. *The Berlin West African Conference, 1884–1885*, based on Crowe's Cambridge Ph.D. in history, published in 1942 to critical acclaim, was the pinnacle of her scholarly career, discussed further in chapter 7.[13]

In contrast, Merze Tate, the only African–American woman and graduate researcher in the Oxford cohort, enjoyed a highly distinguished career at the intersection of international relations and diplomatic history. Yet she later regretted ever going to Oxford. As a Black woman writing on empire, race, and geopolitics, Tate was entirely ignored both at Oxford and in the wider IR field until the 2020s. According to her biographer Barbara D. Savage, Tate initially found Oxford to 'be a "dream of a place"; she revelled in its intellectual, cultural and social offerings'.[14] I read Tate's experience of Oxford as more ambivalent. Oxford was 'the first great failure' of her life.[15] She had 'misgivings' about Oxford from almost the start and, years later, concluded that she had been 'unwise' to go there at all.[16] Oxford's elitism, racism, and sexism, its institutional blundering and supervision failures cost Tate dearly. When Tate complained, once well-meaning white scholars and administrators, including Headlam-Morley, switched to racist and sexist criticism. In turn, the two books Tate wrote that drew on her Oxford research downplayed Headlam-Morley's formative role to credit Alfred Zimmern instead. Tate's three Oxford years illuminate one exceptional student's pathway into international relations, its transnational and Anglo-American context; the racism and sexism in the academy; the burdens of financial precarity and racial representation; the intellectual and personal risks of entering a new interdisciplinary field-information; the different pathways to critical historical research in British IR; and the politics of recognising, honouring, and not honouring Tate as an international relations scholar today.

## 'A Credit to My Race and My Sorority'

Merze Tate was born in Blanchard, Michigan in 1905, growing up on a large farm settled by her great-grandparents. Compared to most African–Americans in the Jim Crow era, Tate was relatively privileged, 'a little bit better than the average person . . . I was born in Michigan, not in Mississippi. That probably has made all the difference in my life'.[17] She graduated from the mostly white Battle Creek High School as a valedictorian, straight-A student. Because of extreme overwork, Tate became ill with tuberculosis in the last year of high school and her first year at Western Michigan College (later University, WMU). She studied history and social science, becoming the first Black person to graduate, the person with the highest grades ever achieved, and completing the four-year degree 'in three years and one summer', while working as a live-in home helper on the side.[18] Tate's employer described her as 'the most ambitious person I have ever known. Brutus would have withdrawn his accusation of ambition against Caesar if he had seen Merze first . . . She has . . . an aggressive personality, and evidently made-up her mind in childhood to scale the heights in spite of all the obvious obstacles in the path of a coloured child'.[19]

The state of Michigan refused to employ Black high school teachers, so in 1927 Tate moved to Indianapolis, Indiana. She claimed that this was the only time she 'felt segregation and discrimination in the same way that some people have . . . But it didn't make me bitter'.[20] Tate taught history at the new Crispus Attucks High School, founded for Black students to enforce racial segregation in a city run by the Ku Klux Klan. She took extension courses at Indiana University in French, German, and European history and spent her summers studying for an MA degree, travelling to the Teachers College at Columbia University, New York.[21] Tate's work ethic and academic brilliance meant that, once again, she earned her MA degree across three summers instead of the usual five, with a dissertation on the 'Reorganization of Social Science Curricula for Secondary Schools'.[22]

In the summer of 1931, Tate travelled to Europe—England, Geneva, France, Germany, Austria and northern Italy.[23] She had originally intended to study French in Paris in the summer of that year, but Tate met African–American Grace Walker, who had studied at Julliard, Cambridge and the Royal Academy of Dramatic Art in London, and was to lecture on African–American music and poetry at the Zimmern School of International Studies in Geneva.[24] As already discussed in chapter 1, racial questions were central to Lucie Zimmern's polyphonic internationalism and, as Tate herself noted, much 'attention was given to the American N——'.[25] Tate was drawn to the Zimmern School, she said, because it attracted 'scholars from all over the world . . . And that was my objective', so she took a diploma in international studies instead.[26] At Geneva, she attended lectures on the purposes of the Zimmern School, race relations in the United States, international relations, and the mandates system. The Zimmern School's 'deployment of African American culture', as Savage has pointed out, 'presented Tate with a concept of international relations that treated racial injustices in that instance, but which at the same time remained silent on the status and treatment of colonial peoples of color'.[27]

As a member of Alpha Kappa Alpha (AKA), the oldest and largest African–American sorority, Tate was eligible to apply for its Foreign Fellowship of 1000 dollars. Naively, Tate later believed, she had named Oxford in her application because Miss Glass, the high school teacher who inspired her interest in history, had spent a summer at Oxford. Tate had also read about the 'very ancient and learned institution'.[28] She wanted to do graduate work with Alfred Zimmern, the new and first Montague Burton Professor, with her ultimate ambition to become a professor herself at one of the 'large coloured universities' in the United States.[29] Tate won the AKA award, though she also needed the endorsement of the American Association of University Women (AAUW), which had refused to admit Black women. She was assessed not only in terms of her academic record but her racial deportment and assumptions about her racial standing at Oxford.[30]

According to the dean of women at Western Michigan, Tate behaved with 'dignity and good taste' in her relations with the majority white students, which 'overcame any problem of racial differences'.[31] The president of the Michigan Division of the AAUW saw Tate as 'one of these rare educated coloured women who knows how to adjust herself inconspicuously and tactfully'.[32] Another assessor read Tate in terms of 'colourist' norms in which African–Americans with lighter skin were more socially acceptable to whites. She described Tate as a 'woman of refinement and culture. She is not very dark skinned, has regular features, and beautiful hair. She is tall and slender, dignified in bearing. She dresses neatly and well. Her voice is good, her enunciation clear. Among English people she would be looked upon, I imagine, very much as are the high class Hindu students'. It was noted that a young Polish woman thought Tate so acceptable that she was invited to attend a reception at the Geneva home of Poland's former prime minister, Jan Paderewski.[33] Overall, Tate was read as 'a distinct credit to her race or any race'.[34]

Merze Tate was also 'anxious to bring credit' to the AAUW, and 'to my Alma Mater and country'.[35] She knew people in Indianapolis were gossiping about her bravado in applying to Oxford; 'whites and blacks' were taking bets on whether she would get in. 'I did. So that was it'.[36] On the SS Bremen, the German ocean-liner on which she travelled in the late summer of 1932, Tate used poetry to convey the measure of what she was doing.

'Thoughts on Entering Oxford'
When I consider what before me lies
A chance to make a name
A chance to die
A chance to gather from these ancient walls
Covered with Ivy, hiding famous halls
What this mother of learning is ready to bestow
On one who has the courage and strength to go
Through endless hours of toil and grief and joy
I think of constant strife without these walls
And wonder if our lives are worth the while we
     spend on earth nurturing petty wiles
Then I recall
Who best bear his yoke
May serve him best
This relieves my mind and then I rest
And make one big wish a prayer to be
A credit to my race and my sorority.[37]

## 'I Guess They Went Liberal that Year'

Tate was an exceptional figure in Oxford. She was 'the only colored American in the entire University, man or woman'[38] and she was a graduate student. In the 1930s, Tate later pointed out in her oral history, Oxford was 'primarily an undergraduate university. They do not . . . emphasize graduate work'.[39] Moreover, she was not admitted to a traditional women's college, Somerville or St Hugh's, rather the Society of Oxford Home Students (SOHS), established in 1879 to allow women to live in more affordable city residences.[40] Tate requested a hostel, yet if she was to stay in private residence she wanted a place 'where American students do not predominate'.[41] Oxford was 'a great city', she thought, for retired army men and those from the foreign and imperial service.[42] However, 1932, she noted, 'was a rather unusual year for women at Oxford. It was the first time that they admitted Chinese women. Two women from Turkey . . . There was one African woman from Lagos. But she was an undergraduate. Not a graduate student. I guess they went liberal that year'.[43]

Because her AKA fellowship was only for 1932–3, Tate had to apply for the diploma in economics, which was not a degree. As soon as she arrived, Tate requested to transfer to the two-year B.Litt. research degree in what she called a branch of 'pure history', such as International Relations, 'with special emphasis on post-war events and international affairs'.[44] She already had a B.A. from WMU and M.A. from Columbia, she explained, with a record of fifty-nine As and two Bs, and she wanted to become a professor.[45] However, the SOHS vice-principal and graduate tutor, Ruth F. Butler, noted that Tate's undergraduate degree was from a teaching college, which she considered 'rather an elementary sort of place, <u>not</u> recognised for senior status'. Moreover, Tate's 'preparation in modern history was not quite thorough enough' and 'judging from the work she has sent (two rather good, but juvenile essays on education and social science)', she may not be up to the task.[46]

For the first time in her life, Merze Tate's scholarly credentials were deemed lacking. The M.A. from Columbia did not offset the inferior standing of a teaching college in the American mid-West. Tate was without the academic pedigree necessary for graduate research at Oxford. Her economics tutor, C. Violet Butler, expert on social work and reform, was additionally frustrated with Tate's choice to forgo an economics diploma which covered topics that, she thought, had a 'very real bearing on present problems of international organisation'.[47] Alfred Zimmern recommended a probationary term of work primarily on the United Nations, his current preoccupation. C. Violet Butler promised to not 'inflict further economic theory . . . I only wish that I could have convinced you of its relevance to the study of modern international relations'. Butler was blunt in her assessment of Tate's work which, to date, was 'quite good,—very sensible and workmanlike; but with the best will, I can't find in your work on this (uncongenial) subject, evidence of your capacity for original work, though I have nothing to say in the opposite direction'.[48] The 27-year-old 'n——' was recognised as a 'remarkable and interesting young woman (Christian)', the 'sort of person who would make up her deficiencies if given the opportunity'.[49]

Though she had already lost one term, there was no reason that the valedictorian could not produce a graduate dissertation at Oxford and remain on track for a professorship in the United States if she received proper supervision on a well-chosen subject in her preferred field. In January 1933, the Board of Social Studies approved Tate's subject of 'Disarmament in the Nineteenth Century', suggested by Alfred Zimmern and to be submitted by the spring of 1934.[50] By disarmament, Tate meant not the total abolition of arms, rather efforts towards a general and coordinated reduction of armies and navies in a period when such efforts were an 'integral part of international relations'.[51] She examined the diplomacy of disarmament, the underlying reasons for governments to propose or refuse disarmament; the influence of media, peace societies, public opinion, jurists and international congresses; and the Hague Conferences in 1899 and 1907. After nine months of work, the Board of Social Studies determined that Tate's topic was too broad. On the advice of James Brierly, professor of international law, Tate had to narrow her subject to 'The Movement for Disarmament 1853–1914'. From October 1933, Tate proceeded to research the movement prior to the first Hague Conference in 1889, the conference itself, and Anglo-German negotiations on limiting naval armaments from 1900 until the outbreak of World War I. She had until spring 1934 to submit her dissertation but received limited, if any, supervision from Zimmern who was teaching in the United States in the autumn and winter of 1933–4.

Tate's financial position, already perilous, became even more so with the additional unfunded year. Just to get to Oxford, she had sold her house and furniture and given up her job.[52] In the middle of the Great Depression, she contemplated returning to the United States to earn money to finish her degree. Instead, she borrowed money from her sister, received additional loans from the Bertha Johnson Fund and Gentlewomen's Employment Association, and spent the small money left over from her house sale.[53] Zimmern helped Tate by securing some funds from the Phelps Stokes Foundation in the United States.[54] During the summers, she also tutored students in Europe, including the daughter of a count and countess in the Rhone Valley.[55] She was literally down to sixpence when a sorority friend sent a check for 125 dollars as if it 'just dropped from heaven'.[56] In the damp, rain, and cold of England where the heating was never turned on, Tate became addicted to tea and ate brussels sprouts 'all winter long'.[57] She learned that 'English scholars often do not cover the subject, they ramble' in their lectures.[58] Yet she also enjoyed much of Oxford student life. She bought a bicycle for 10 shillings, painted it and added a bell and basket, eventually selling it on for 20 shillings. 'No loss there'.[59] She was invited but declined to join the communist student society.[60] She punted, watched plays and boat races, royal ceremonies, a royal wedding, and debates. At an Oxford Union debate, she dropped a knitting needle from the upper balcony, where women were allowed. 'I feel someone doth dart me from above', proclaimed a debater, to Tate's immense embarrassment.[61]

## Merze Tate and Her Bicycle

The black-and-white image of Merze Tate was taken by an unknown photographer between October 1932 and May 1935. Tate sits on a bicycle wearing a black academic soft cap and university gown that she was expected to wear during all

FIGURE 6.1. Merze Tate. Photographer Unknown. Courtesy of WMU Archives & Regional History Collection

lectures and university ceremonies. The tip of Tate's cap points towards All Souls, Oxford's most prestigious college and the building that housed the Codrington Library, named for the slaveholder, coloniser, and All Souls Fellow. Under her formal gown, she wears a longer, lighter-coloured dress coat with large lapels, a wool skirt and a light patterned scarf over a black neck-high top, sheer tights, and black shoes with a small heel and lighter-coloured edge that matches the coat. Tate's left foot is on the left bike pedal; her right leg is not visible but likely resting on the stone wall to balance on her stationary bike. Tate's hair is short under her cap, in waves, framing the left side of her face and in the style of the independent woman of the period. Her facial expression is hard to read. She is not obviously smiling yet her eyes shine. She is looking very slightly to the right of the camera, an engagement that suggests a certain agency. Tate appears confident and relaxed, although her left hand seems to be tightly gripping the handlebar.

The academic gown, Oxford's most iconic buildings, and the bicycle, signify scholarship and academic success. For Barbara D. Savage, the most telling feature of the image is Tate's bicycle, which she did not know how to ride before Oxford. 'She taught herself how', relates Savage, 'bought the bike used, painted it and made it hers. In that image then is evidence of her determination, her daring, and her ability to make a place for herself in spaces not designed with her in mind. And that is how she went on to make a career for herself as a prolific scholar'.[62] Savage also points to the 'rarity' of the image, a Black woman 'at a place reserved overwhelmingly for white men'.[63] Tate was at the intellectual centre of the British Empire in the period of its greatest extent. Here is a pioneering Black woman studying for her third degree at one of the most illustrious academic institutions in the world. This is not just an image of Tate, but an image of Merze Tate at Oxford. Oxford itself is a location in Tate's successful intellectual journey through some of the leading centres of early IR research: Geneva, Oxford, Radcliffe-Harvard, and Howard University.

The image places Tate in the heart of Oxford. Yet she did not study in any of its famous buildings or even attend one of the traditional women's colleges in the north of the city. While those colleges were poorer and less glamourous than the men's, they were still prohibitively expensive. Tate's left hand tightly grips the handlebar. Perhaps she is anxious about the quality of the photograph. Perhaps her balance on the bicycle is unstable. It figuratively foreshadows Tate's coming fall and her discovery that the 'most difficult thing at Oxford is getting in and getting out'.[64]

On May 4, 1934, between submitting her dissertation on disarmament in the nineteenth century and her oral examination, Tate had a serious bicycle accident. She hurt her foot so badly that she stayed in a convalescent home for ten weeks and prepared for her oral examination without books.[65] The same day as the accident, the Social Studies Faculty Board met to consider written examiners' reports on Tate's dissertation. On a first reading of the image, Tate's bicycle signifies the determination, courage, and skill that defined her life and career. However, her tight grip on the handlebar points to what Tate herself saw as the 'first great failure' of her life.[66] Yet it is also why she thought she had been 'unwise' to go to Oxford at all.[67] It highlights Tate's precarity. But, more importantly, it reconceptualises, if not severely undermines, Oxford's place in Tate's otherwise uninterrupted story of success. To the extent that the image acclaims Oxford, then the bicycle and Tate's tight grip portend both Tate's accident and Oxford's institutional and intellectual failures.

## 'I Have Failed'

With E. L. Woodward, Agnes Headlam-Morley examined Tate's dissertation and was not impressed. The examiners were unsparing in their critique of the work, claiming that Tate had not made an original argument about the movement for disarmament or demonstrated sufficient awareness of the historical background to the debates. Tate was not fluent in German, so could not follow Anglo-German diplomatic negotiations in sufficient detail. Tate presented 'an industrious compilation' of mostly secondary sources on the question, thus could not demonstrate her technical historical skills. Even the secondary literature was analysed 'uncritically, and without proper cohesion and arrangement'. On the basis of the written work and oral exam, Tate was deemed 'intelligent, industrious, and ready to learn', but did not appear to be 'a candidate of first class ability . . . more enthusiastic than critical in temperament'.[68]

However, the main problem, Headlam-Morley and Woodward subtly implied, was that Merze Tate had been ill-advised by Alfred Zimmern and the Social Studies Board. Evidently troubled, the examiners twice referred to the board's decision to 'allow' Tate to write on such a vast subject. Given the breadth of the topic and the limited time, Tate could hardly be expected to do anything more than summarise existing work; the necessary 'critical examination of detailed minutes and collections of authorities was out of the question'.[69]

Woodward and Headlam-Morley, both of whom succeeded Zimmern as Montague Burton Chair, presented their 'report in unusual terms'.[70] They neither passed nor technically failed Tate. In June 1934, after she already publicised the fact that she had her Oxford degree, Tate unofficially learned that her thesis had not passed.[71] She was travelling in Europe, making tentative arrangements to enrol for an IR Ph.D. at LSE, and turned down two positions offered to her in Geneva.[72] Tate's plans dramatically changed.[73] She wrote to SOHS Principal Grace E. Hadow that she was 'prepared to defend everything in my thesis or I should not have written it', but admitted it was unwise to submit the work when she did. (Later, Tate also reflected that 'I've never been run off a platform. I can defend whatever I say, I can defend myself'.[74]) Tate also pointed to her financial woes and implored Hadow not to use her 'as a standard for judging others of my race'. White people had a propensity to 'judge the members of the coloured race by one or two whom they have known instead of each person individually . . . There are hundreds of coloured women who could come up to Oxford and be successful for they would have money enough to live free from financial worries . . . I am anxious that others should not suffer because of my failure'.[75] In a later essay for the AKA's *Ivy Leaf Magazine*, Tate reflected that 'throughout the three years I spent in England, I was ever conscious of being a pioneer representing AKA in particular and N—— womanhood in general'.[76]

Tate was officially informed of the board's decision six months after submitting her thesis. According to Hadow, they were 'anxious to give' Tate 'every consideration' and 'themselves time to reconsider' the work.[77] Yet the reasons for the board's decision were never officially given.[78] Tate complained to Hadow that she 'had misgivings since my first fortnight in Oxford, but I never thought matters would be carried so far'.[79] If the board determined that the project they had formerly approved was now too broad, then Tate wondered if 'they would consider permitting me to turn my subject into a D. Phil . . . [the Oxford Ph.D.]. Of course, I should be taking a great risk but I am prepared to do so'.[80] They were not, though in October 1934 Tate was invited to narrow, rewrite and resubmit her B.Litt. the following spring, and she was strongly encouraged to attend additional lectures in modern history. Tate's writing on the early years of the movement for disarmament was deemed to be the most promising. Zimmern also belatedly determined that Tate should limit her period to 1888–98 and focus solely on efforts to 'influence public opinion, not bringing in government policies except insofar as it bears upon this'.[81] Tate's revised thesis focused on the movement for disarmament primarily in England, including a history of ideas on disarmament among 'popular circles and among the leaders of political thought'.[82]

Tate got through and out of Oxford with the help of two women historians, Lady Margaret Hall's medievalist, Mary Coate, 'one of our best women historians',[83] and diplomatic historian Agnes Headlam-Morley, who had returned to Oxford as a tutor in 1932 to replace Margery Perham at St Hugh's. Headlam-Morley was not much older than Tate and would eventually become Oxford's Montague Burton Professor of IR. Coate, who had also tutored Margaret Lambert, met Tate three times to help 'sort out her material' and treat them 'more critically'. Unlike Zimmern, Coate tutored Tate in historical method and argumentation, such as not drawing 'too general assumptions' from the sources.[84] Headlam-Morley also went through Tate's materials as her new supervisor. Generally, Headlam-Morley found the long hours of tutoring gruelling, though many of her students remembered her as 'most reassuring—she was sitting/lying with her neck in the bottom of the chair in her study wearing slacks and with her feet on the mantelpiece. A highly intelligent, and to me, a most reassuring person. I admired her more than any other'.[85] Another student thought she was 'delightful, interesting, easy-going. In one of my tutorials a message came that the police wanted to see her. She said "they should know by now not to come for me in the mornings" (I think it was a parking offence)'.[86] Phyllis Crisp recalls that she 'usually arrived late for tutorials and sometimes not at all, but was so stimulating when we did have the privilege of a session with her that we could not resent the waiting'.[87] 'There she sat', recollected Eileen Tanner, 'with one leg over the arm of her chair and smiling (I think), dismissing one's essay with modified approval, then proceeding to open up entirely new aspects of the subject of the essay, till one's head whirled and one felt utterly incompetent, but inspired to do better'.[88]

It is unlikely that Tate felt similarly to these undergraduate students; she was later muted in her acknowledgement of Headlam-Morley's support during her Oxford years, making much more of the fact that she had been supervised by one of its most eminent professors, Alfred Zimmern. This may have been academic elitism or internalised sexism on Tate's part, or the fact that she had told people in the United States that she had passed her degree under Zimmern's supervision, which she had not. Headlam-Morley, in turn, thought Tate lacked some confidence and was unsure about what material to include or leave out, yet 'worked very hard all the time' and 'improves her work as a result of criticism and has on one or two occasions almost (but not quite) admitted that she was enjoying it'.[89] She rather harshly determined that Tate's work was interesting though not especially deep. The root of the problem was that Tate was 'uncritical and very susceptible to anything she reads or is told about—however as I get the last word I think I have been able to give her ideas a more realistic stamp. She is however capable of the most appalling howlers and banalities—I have, I hope, eliminated most of these . . . however let us hope that the examiners will not know enough either to notice' the rest.[90]

Though critical of Tate's work, Headlam-Morley also retained some sympathy toward the student overwhelmed by the vast quantity of the material she had accumulated and who was not well advised by her first supervisor. In a letter to Ruth Butler, Headlam-Morley noted that Tate admonished her if she was late with comments on draft work and had acquired a reputation for being 'rather difficult to deal with as every normal difficulty she encounters is transformed into a grievance'. She was causing a 'good deal of unnecessary trouble',[91] though this was entirely unintentional. The tone from the principal and vice-principal of SOHS was more severe and melodramatic. 'Miss Tate haunts me' was anonymously written in response to Tate's request, after she had just submitted her thesis, to have it back to double-check that the pages were in the correct order.[92] 'Another of these special misfortunes that only happen to Miss Tate'.[93] Grace Hadow was even less sympathetic. Tate was concerned that future employers in the United States would learn of her initial failure, and this would 'wreck her career'.[94] She may also have feared being ridiculed for telling people in the United States that she had passed her degree in 1934 when she had not. According to Hadow, it was 'pathetic to see how determined she is that everyone's hand is really against her'.[95] But Hadow could scarcely understand what was at stake for Merze Tate, and the professional and financial consequences of failure in Jim Crow America.

Tate had good grounds for her grievance against Oxford. In the summer of 1935, she requested a statement from SOHS that she might use, if necessary, to explain and contextualise the additional year she spent on her B.Litt. She wanted a statement on C. V. Butler's 'opinion of my limited capacity to do research . . . Professor Zimmern's opinion of my capacity to do research'; the decision of the board to agree to her topic; its determination nine months later that the topic was too broad; then another nine months later, after she submitted her thesis, the board's determination not to award the degree, and suggesting again that a topic it had previously approved was now too broad. She wished to know the reasons for this 'failure', including the statement from the secretary of the Faculties and her examiners; and the decision to readmit Tate to the B.Litt. in December 1934, six months after she first submitted her work, to write on an 'entirely different thesis'.[96]

Ruth Butler reasonably disputed Tate's suggestion that the revised project was entirely different. Instead, Butler wrote by hand on the side of Tate's request that the new thesis 'was meant to be a) short b) deprived of its diplomatic side, on which she was very bad', or so it was claimed.[97] SOHS nonetheless provided a statement for Tate, including that it was 'by no means unusual for candidates to fail at their first attempt and to try again'.[98] Tate's revised B.Litt. was examined not by two historians, but two scholars of international law. James Brierly, who had initially suggested Tate limit her study, and the recently appointed LSE Montague Burton Professor of IR, Charles Manning, previously discussed. Their report praised Tate's work for its 'due discrimination' in the use of primary and secondary sources and the several 'definite' if 'minor' contributions to existing knowledge. 'In our opinion her work besides showing industry and a sense of scientific responsibility shows a commendable degree of technical proficiency'.[99] Tate passed. Immediately after defending her thesis, Tate travelled to Europe at a 'frightening' time. Her German-language tutor at the University of Berlin 'regaled us in Nazi philosophy'.[100] In Geneva, she stayed with millionaire friends, and observed the League of Nations' first debate on Italy's invasion of Ethiopia.[101]

## A Permanent Place Among American Historians

Merze Tate had not intended to revise her Oxford B.Litt. and become the first African–American woman to receive a Ph.D. in government from Harvard; it was 'purely accidental'.[102] She returned to the United States in the autumn of 1935 to a position as dean of women at Barber-Scotia College for Black women in Concord, North Carolina. It was not the position she 'had hoped to secure', she wrote to Grace Hadow, 'but after the financial loss and worries of the past three years I am thankful for anything . . . The salary . . . is miserable', and much less than she was earning before she left for Oxford, however it would allow her to pay her debts.[103] Tate moved to Bennett College in Greensboro, North Carolina, the following year, where she taught history and chaired the Social Science Division, revising its programme.[104] In the summer of 1938, she agreed to drive a friend from North Carolina to their son's graduation ceremony at Harvard. Hearing the titles of the doctoral dissertations read out, Tate concluded that the topics were no more substantial than the study of disarmament she had written three years before. Tate 'started getting ideas'.[105] The following day, she met Bernice Brown Cronkhite, a scholar of international law, and the dean of the graduate school at Radcliffe, the women's college associated with Harvard.

Instead of returning to North Carolina, and with 'eight dollars in cash and a Shell courtesy card for the gasoline for my car', Tate enrolled in Harvard's summer school.[106] She returned to Bennett for the 1938–9 academic year and, on Cronkhite's advice, applied for and received the Julius Rosenwald Fellowship to study at Radcliffe for 1939–1940. Her Oxford B.Litt. was 'the entrée', considered 'the equivalent in many ways to, and in some ways more than a PhD' in the United States, Tate claimed. She stayed in a graduate hall of residence and 'life was comfortable there'.[107] The term studying economics with C. Violet Butler allowed Tate to claim she had met the economics requirement for her comprehensive examinations in political science. She could thus dodge an entirely 'theoretical economics' course based on 'mathematical formulas' that 'even the professor couldn't teach'. Tate got back to 'my diplomatic history and international relations and law' and resumed her impeccable academic record.[108] Following an exam on US diplomatic history, in which Tate was the only woman in the class of eighty, the instructor asked to see 'Mr. Merze Tate' who had scored a grade of 97.[109]

Formally under the supervision of an international legal scholar, Payson S. Wild, Tate quickly repurposed her B.Litt., both the dissertation itself and other writing she had cut from it. She 'had practically the dissertation' in hand before she enrolled in the Ph.D., only revising it 'here and there'. She added some additional materials from the Library of Congress, but used most of the new research not for the Ph.D., but for her second book, *The United States and Armaments*.[110] In 1941, Tate received her Harvard Ph.D. and, the following year, published *The Disarmament Illusion: The Movement for a Limitation of Armaments to 1907*, which was 'virtually identical' to the dissertation.[111] Payson Wild declined Tate's request to write an introduction to the book and suggested Alfred Zimmern instead.[112] Zimmern also declined on grounds that the task really lay with Wild 'since he has been in touch with you during the later stages of your work'.[113] In the end, neither Zimmern nor Wild troubled themselves to endorse Tate's work. Instead, Cronkhite wrote the foreword. She praised the book for explaining 'at least in part, how the world has come to its present grievous pass'.[114] Cronkhite had supported the book's publication with a subvention from the Radcliffe Bureau of International Research, which she had co-founded with Ada Comstock, president of Radcliffe College, in 1924.

Initially conceived as a liberal feminist project, Cronkhite and Comstock's original Rockefeller Foundation funding bid was for graduate research in international relations and law; courses in international relations for women teachers and other women professionals; and conferences on international relations open to the public.[115] Watered down by the Harvard men who insisted on removing the focus on women, the Bureau was nonetheless the best funded institute for the study of international relations in the interwar years in the United States. Tate later noted that most of the Bureau's money 'went to Harvard men because', not entirely accurately, 'they were the people who are writing in government and international relations'.[116] But as IR historian Joanna Wood has shown, until its closure in 1942, the Bureau supported the international relations work of numerous mostly elite white women, giving rise to the first generation of credentialed women IR scholars in the US academy.[117] They included Fannie Fern Andrews, M. Margaret Ball, Vera Micheles Dean, Eleanor Lansing Dulles, Louise Holborn, Sarah Wambaugh, Mary Parker Follett, and Merze Tate. Bureau subventions supported the publication of Tate's first three books, helping Tate achieve her goal of becoming a professor at the most prestigious African–American institution of higher learning, Howard University, where she taught from 1942 until her retirement in 1977.

Tate's core argument in *The Disarmament Illusion* was that the competitive system of power politics made arms limitation almost impossible. In an era of economic imperialism, none of the major European states seriously considered limiting their arms production. Large navies were necessary to acquire and defend new colonies.[118] Even Tsar Nicholas II's 'Rescript for Peace' in 1898, his shocking call for an international peace conference and a halt to the competition in arms, was motivated by Russia's political, economic, and strategic interests. Pacifists, jurists and international peace societies were too disorganised to alter state policy. Militarist army and naval officers like Sir John Fisher, Admiral Tirpitz, Colonel Gross von Schwarzhoff, General von Bernhardi, and Captain Alfred Mahan were 'trained to predatory habits of mind' and far more influential.[119] Finally, the pursuit of a balance of power and alliance system 'accentuated the armament competition'.[120] No one country, even Germany, was to blame for the competition and rivalry that 'made war inevitable'.[121] Germany wished only to acquire and defend colonies, just like Britain and France. 'None was innocent', Tate wrote, 'for they all lived in a perpetual state of mutual fear and antagonism, expecting war and always preparing for it. If none was innocent, therefore they were all more or less guilty'.[122]

Basing her argument on an exhaustive 'critical historical' study of the late nineteenth- and early twentieth-century efforts among European powers and publics to limit the competition in arms, Tate drew a series of more general conclusions.[123] 'The limitation of armaments is not a matter of mathematics nor of morals but of politics', she argued; 'states seek to give effect to their national policies through armaments as well as through monetary and immigration policies, tariffs and embargoes'.[124] The acquisition of large armies and navies was the means to the end of foreign policy. Competition in this domain was entirely related to the degree of political friction between states. Negotiated agreements to reduce arms were only possible when states were not in conflict because 'international disarmament standardises the relative diplomatic power of the countries involved and prevents the use of armaments competition to upset the political equilibrium'.[125] In general, states most satisfied with the status quo were more likely to agree to arms limitations, but that would lead to an intolerable situation for other states. 'No dissatisfied state will agree to perpetuate indefinitely the conditions prevailing at a given time . . . Satisfied powers are equally determined to retain by force what arms have so successfully gained for them. This is the simple explanation for the failure of most disarmament proposals'.[126] States could not acquire lasting security either through unilateral disarmament or alliances. 'There is no security for any state until it be a security in which all its neighbors share'.[127]

Tate's book was hailed as 'definitive' and marking a shift in IR scholarship away from its alleged utopian roots in pacifist, isolationist, religious and humanitarian sermons to a field more attentive to 'the realities of international politics'.[128] As Tate herself pointed out, the book was not 'peace propaganda', but an 'objective, impartial, complete and authentic account' of the problem of arms control at a pivotal historical moment.[129] William O. Shanahan, an expert on Prussian military reform, praised Tate for her objective treatment of imperial Germany.[130] Works like Tate's would be invaluable when the allies 'begin the task of organising the post-war world'.[131] According to Rayford W. Logan, later Tate's colleague and nemesis at Howard, *The Disarmament Illusion* should be 'required reading for all who are hoping that, approximately twenty-five years from now, mankind will not be in the throes of World War III. Tate has assured herself a permanent place among American historians regardless of their color'.[132]

Some of the highest praise came from Hans J. Morgenthau, later the most influential proponent of the so-called 'realist theory' of international relations. Morgenthau found Tate's work much more 'intelligent, sound, and erudite' than other recent books on international relations or international law.[133] Her account of the limits of international arbitration as an alternative to war was something Morgenthau claimed to have been saying for the past fifteen years. He agreed that regional not universal federation could limit arms competition yet disagreed with Tate's emphasis on public opinion as an influence on foreign policy. The book was likely the 'definitive history', but its more 'permanent value', claimed Morgenthau, was its 'implicit and explicit exposition of the disarmament problem' more generally.[134] Because he could read in Tate's book support for his own emerging general theory of power politics among nations, Morgenthau encouraged Tate's next work to be 'primarily systematic and analytical'. This was her 'peculiar gift. And rare a gift it is'.[135]

Like Morgenthau, diplomatic historian Louis Martin Sears frowned on Tate's analysis of public opinion, which he claimed was presented 'in almost tedious detail. There are pages, in fact, suggestive of the Old Testament genealogies in their rescue from oblivion of persons whose very names would perish but for the loving labour of an indefatigable research', as if that were somehow a bad thing.[136] Naturally, Tate's book had engaged with the international thought of Bertha von Suttner, with Tate describing her 1889 novel *Lay Down Your Arms* as 'perhaps the greatest peace novel of all times'.[137] Any study of late nineteenth-century efforts to reduce armament production must necessarily engage with Suttner. Yet as historian Madeleine Herren has observed, when Tate 'highlighted . . . the role of the many women's organizations active at the Hague Peace Conferences' this aspect of her otherwise celebrated work 'evoked critical reviews'.[138]

By far Tate's harshest critic was W.E.B. Du Bois. A trained historian, Du Bois praised *The Disarmament Illusion* as 'one of the best examples of thorough painstaking study of historical documents'. But he slammed the book as a work of 'scholarly delusion', of 'logical contradiction', for which Du Bois blamed 'the Harvard school of social science'.[139] Unaware of the book's origins in Tate's Oxford B.Litt., Du Bois was taking a dig at his own alma mater, for ignoring 'the epoch-making philosophy of Karl Marx'. To ignore the underlying colonial–capitalist causes of European militarism was 'to leave out Hamlet from his tragedy. Harvard . . . tries to study social science by ignoring the way in which men make a living and the bitter struggle which they continually carry on for food, clothes, shelter and security'.[140] The failure of European empires to limit their military expansion at the turn of the twentieth century was because of their dependency on the economic exploitation of colonies.

Clearly, Tate's early work gave precedence to power-political competition between empires and states. Economic imperialism obviously mattered in Tate's historical analysis, though it was not the central organising framework. However, racial conflict and imperialism became increasingly central categories in Tate's later work. In 1943, she wrote about the potential of global race war.[141] After her Fulbright Visiting Professorship at Rabindranath Tagore's World University in India in 1950–51, when she 'felt more like a human being valued for my worth than any time in my life', she turned more squarely to the history of empires.[142] But as Robert Vitalis has pointed out, when her Harvard supervisor Payson S. Wild was asked to comment on Tate's new research project, 'he thought historical work on imperialism in the Pacific had little value for the field of international relations in the United States'.[143] Empire was already being erased as a legitimate subject of IR as an American political science. But Tate prefigured by decades the contemporary interest among international and global historians and theorists in the Pacific world.[144]

Tate was no Marxist. In the mid-1940s, she joined a radical book club at Howard and resented that *The Disarmament Illusion* 'didn't mean a thing'.[145] In India, she was invited to a lecture by the head of the communist party but was too much of a 'coward' to go, she claimed, fearing repercussions.[146] At Howard, she had to sign a statement declaring that she was not a communist and was questioned on her links to communists in Hawaii. As a Black woman, trained at some of the major centres of early twentieth-century international relations, Tate would have paid an immense price for adopting Marxist frameworks, as did her contemporary, the radical journalist Claudia Jones, discussed in chapter 9.

What Barbara D. Savage identified as Tate's antiracist approach to geopolitics included, though did not centre, class antagonisms or the workings of the global capitalist system.[147] Tate was also too much of an historian to make the grand sweeping generalisations about international relations that Morgenthau wanted her to make. Oxford was a hard school, but from Headlam-Morley Tate learned the historian's technical craft and then broadened the boundaries of diplomatic history beyond anything Headlam-Morley could conceive. In Tate's hands, and with her training in history and social studies, diplomatic history was a 'bridge' between 'government and economics and even some sociology'.[148] Tate worked with the skill and originality of the historian. But she was more than willing to make broader, critical arguments about empire and race in the contemporary history of international relations than scholars of the old diplomatic history, which Eileen Power had also criticised. It was Tate's intellectual commitments to a new form of diplomatic history, in addition to her race and gender, that marginalised Tate from both US and British IR.[149] But it is also what makes her so relevant to critical histories of international relations today, to the belated, tentative, though still discernible effort of some IR scholars to pursue historical work that can be taken seriously.

## Conclusion

Unlike Rachel Wall, discussed in chapter 10, Merze Tate managed to overcome her 'trouble' at Oxford. Working harder than anyone else, gaining better grades than anyone else, Merze Tate secured her position by sheer academic brilliance and credentials.[150] As a Black woman, she needed four university degrees to enter the academic elite. Margery Perham and Susan Strange each received only one undergraduate degree, but as white women could still become the leading British international thinkers of their generation. As Tate pointed out years later, 'what if you have someone on the board that just doesn't even like the looks of you? . . . Or feels that here's a N—— woman and she hasn't any business with a Ph.D. in government. I mean, you could have people like that you see'.[151] Tate was never 'crushed' by the 'unhappy fact' of constant discrimination in the racist and sexist academy, or the fact that she had to work harder than her white peers.[152]

The fact that Tate completed her Harvard Ph.D. in a year while taking courses and sitting the comprehensive exam raises serious questions about the assessments of Tate's work at Oxford. To be sure, with limited supervision from Zimmern, Tate's 'expansive research' may have 'overwhelmed her analytic skills'.[153] Yet the book she published to wide acclaim in 1942 was almost identical to her Ph.D., which on her own account was a relatively minor revision of her Oxford B.Litt.[154] Headlam-Morley, James Brierly, and Charles Manning could not see the significance and potential of Tate's work for reasons that are easily surmised. Yet she arguably became far more distinguished than all three of them, receiving numerous national and international honours and awards in her lifetime, including six honorary degrees. The image of Tate at Oxford is an image of intellectual achievement and success not because Tate was at Oxford, but despite it.

In her preface to *The Disarmament Illusion*, Tate thanked the numerous institutions and people who had supported her research, including the AKA sorority, the Phelps-Stokes and Julius Rosenweld funds, and the Radcliffe Bureau for International Research. She thanked Alfred Zimmern for his 'kindly interest, advice and assistance . . . throughout my period of study in England', a highly generous note, reflecting his initial encouragement and support perhaps more than any hands-on supervision of her actual research. She then thanked James Brierly for offering 'supervision' and only then Headlam-Morley, her actual supervisor, 'for valuable suggestions in limiting the subject' and advice on different strands of public opinion.[155] The preface to the spin-off book, *The United States and Armaments*, which also included some reprinted material from *The Disarmament Illusion*, thanked Zimmern, but not Headlam-Morley.[156] Merze Tate omitted entirely any mention of the SOHS, Ruth Butler, or Grace Hadow from *The Disarmament Illusion*. Less than eighteen months after leaving Oxford, Tate had paid off her debts to SOHS and contributed a small amount to its Building and Endowment Fund.[157] That was the end of Tate's relationship to Oxford as an academic institution and her college. The contrast with her continued relation to the three other main academic institutions of her life, which all recognised and honoured her achievements during her lifetime, could not be starker.

Tate was deeply aware of herself as an historical figure and was highly attentive to her own legacy. In 1971, she endowed a Merze Tate Fellowship at Radcliffe specifically 'for foreign students' and signed the rights to her books to Radcliffe as it had supported the publication of her first two books.[158] In 1974, Tate donated her papers to Howard and established the Merze Tate Fund in 1977, when she retired from the institution. But the university she favoured most was the least prestigious, Western Michigan. In 1974, she funded a Merze Tate Scholarship and, six years before her death, donated 1 million dollars to an endowment fund. In 1980, Tate received the Radcliffe College Alumnae

Association Graduate Chapter Medal for distinguished achievement in history, and in 1986, Howard awarded Tate an honorary doctorate. In 1991, five years before she died, Tate received the American Historical Association Award for Scholarly Distinction. Already in 1981, WMU created the Merze Tate Center for Research and Information Processing and in 2021 it established the Merze Tate College.

During her lifetime, Merze Tate never received comparable recognition at Oxford, nor in IR or political science, the fields in which she received her last two graduate degrees. Belatedly, in 2016, the American Political Science Association posthumously renamed a Dissertation Award for Merze Tate. In 2022, the historical section of the International Studies Association inaugurated an annual Merze Tate Prize for the best article in historical IR. As part of Oxford's recent and belated reckoning with empire, and informed by Barbara D. Savage's careful scholarship, Merze Tate was claimed by Oxford's Faculty of History when it 'symbolically' named a seminar room in her honour, hanging a portrait and a plaque describing some of her many achievements. Fittingly, the portrait selected was not the image of Tate as a young scholar with her bicycle at Oxford, but a portrait of a mature Tate in her mid-seventies. In 2020, the Faculty of History also inaugurated the Barbara Savage Prize for a thesis in Black History, and All Souls College, in the background of Tate's Oxford image, removed the slaver Codrington's name from its library. Against the new tide, and this moment of recognition of Merze Tate, as of mid-2024, Oxford's IR graduate committee, where Tate would have received her Oxford degree today, had declined a proposal to name a dissertation prize in honour of Merze Tate.

# 7

# The 'Spinsters' and Diplomats' Daughters

A work of diplomatic history has to take diplomacy seriously.
—AGNES HEADLAM-MORLEY, C. MID-1950S[1]

THE CONSENSUS AMONG chroniclers of IR's disciplinary history is that the most high-profile historical woman before Susan Strange was in every sense an abject failure. Agnes Headlam-Morley may have been Oxford University's first woman professor and the longest holder of British IR's most prestigious chair. Yet her 1948 appointment to Oxford's Montague Burton Professorship 'is not an edifying story'.[2] Asked to comment on her candidacy, neither of her predecessors considered her a worthy successor. E. L. Woodward thought she was extremely competent with a 'quick honest and vigorous mind' and 'a good teacher'. But she was a 'strange candidate', 'below the standard required for an Oxford chair . . . I doubt whether she is likely to change her ways and publish very much'.[3] Alfred Zimmern thought she was only qualified for a Readership.[4] Nonetheless, the electors made the 'surprising decision'[5] to appoint Headlam-Morley because a better man, John Wheeler-Bennett, declined the position; another candidate, E. H. Carr, had a disreputable character; and Lewis Namier lost out to 'her citizenly claims'.[6]

The elevation of Agnes Headlam-Morley to the Montague Burton Professorship is said to have sent shockwaves in certain circles, taken as evidence of a 'disastrous decline'[7] not only of IR as a scholarly enterprise, but the fate of the Anglosphere itself. The original political project of the 'Milner group', the clique of men who created the Round Table movement, Chatham House, and dominated the British Coordinating Committee for International Studies (BCCIS), was to steer Anglo-America's progressive imperialism to safeguard the white (now 'Western') world order. In Carroll Quigley's polemical exposé of this group, when Oxford appointed this 'middle-aged spinster' to the Montague Burton Chair in 1948, the 'great idealistic adventure . . . had slowly ground its way to a finish of bitterness and ashes'.[8]

For most historians of British IR, Headlam-Morley's most important distinguishing characteristic was not her age or marital status—that she died 'unmarried'[9]—but her identity as the daughter of a famous diplomat and alleged co-founder of 'the academic disciplines of contemporary history, international history and international relations'.[10] Headlam-Morley's scholarly and teaching interests were assumed to be 'inherited' from her father, famed diplomatic historian, Foreign Office advisor, and propagandist, Sir James Headlam-Morley.[11] Accordingly, the daughter's failings and achievements could be measured in this light. She had only 'one published work to her credit' when appointed to the Burton Chair.[12] Zimmern's review praised her first book for 'hereditary thoroughness and acumen'.[13] She 'published little',[14] had a 'thin' record of writing, and left only 'a large quantity of unpublished and disorganized notes'.[15] She lectured on the Paris Peace Conference, according to one historian, 'presumably because she . . . had a family interest in teaching it'.[16] According to another, she 'scarcely ventured outside the interwar period in her few writings'.[17]

Slim records of publication, often forgiven in male dons, were in Headlam-Morley's case evidence of failure in another respect.[18] Her greatest crime for IR's storytellers was not that she inherited her interest in international relations, published little, or signalled the decline of the Anglosphere project. It was not even that she was a 'well-known Germanophile' and lifelong supporter of appeasement, 'a constant protagonist of these views through thick and thin, whom nothing that the Germans did would ever dissuade'.[19] It was her refusal to modernise and develop the subject of International Relations itself. She was a scourge to the project for a 'separate IR'.

Under Alfred Zimmern, Oxford's inaugural Montague Burton Professor, IR became Oxford's most popular undergraduate politics paper. Yet 'on Headlam-Morley's watch', it was overtaken by sociology.[20] Through the 1950s and 1960s, international relations as a separate subject slowly expanded as a teaching subject, especially in London. But the professor in charge of developing the subject at Oxford, or so it was alleged, refused to modernise her teaching. Headlam-Morley is alleged to have 'stuck to a restricted vision' of IR 'as recent European diplomatic history'.[21] She was accused of refusing to change her syllabi, thus her lectures were 'not as popular or famous as those of her contemporary A. J. P. Taylor'.[22] She was 'a staunch opponent of the study of contemporary international relations, let alone the use of newfangled social scientific methods'.[23] She exhibited a 'reactionary attitude' and 'was old-fashioned, even in her own time, in her refusal to consider a new theoretic framework for a separate discipline'.[24] She 'had no talent for administration or academic entrepreneurship'.[25] She was 'absorbed with college life and had a low academic and public profile'.[26] In 1953, when the Australian Hedley Bull arrived in Oxford as a student, he claimed not to have taken Headlam-Morley's IR paper because 'its coverage would be limited to Anglo-German relations before the First World War'.[27]

During the 1970s and 1980s, those leading the project for a separate IR, both those wishing to subsume it into political science and those advocating for an interdisciplinary field, piled onto Oxford IR, now usually without naming Headlam-Morley. Deputy director of studies at Chatham House, Roger Morgan, claimed that Oxford's 'purely historical approach' was 'notorious': 'international relations at Oxford consisted of the history of the League of Nations and the diplomatic history of the inter-war period, and it is only recently that this has changed', he claimed.[28] In 1988, Susan Strange repeated the claim that IR at Oxford 'changed hardly at all over almost half a century and went on thinking that international relations was just a fancy name for diplomatic history'. Headlam-Morley's successors, Hedley Bull and Strange's friend Alastair Buchan were appointed 'just in time'.[29] Further evidence of Oxford IR's alleged 'torpor'[30] during the Headlam-Morley years was that these male successors quickly established a taught graduate degree in IR, supported by 'better professors' of 'intellectual eminence', like Bull, who became Oxford's Montague Burton Professor in 1977.[31]

So much scorn heaped on Agnes Headlam-Morley. Quigley's plain and open nastiness, written in 1949, is so misogynistic and overblown it need not detain us. More curious is Headlam-Morley's role as a high-profile and gendered foil for the standard and misleading stories of British IR's disciplinary history and failure. Like most mid-century international relations scholars in Britain, Headlam-Morley counted herself among the historians rather than a pioneer for a new 'discipline' without a method. After three years in the Montague Burton Chair, historian E. W. Woodward did not create a separate IR graduate degree either, one measure of subject status. Headlam-Morley only intermittently attended meetings of the British Coordinating Committee for

International Studies (BCCIS). But this did not preclude *progressing* an academic subject. She had no shortage of students writing on international relations, Merze Tate among them, and she taught and wrote far more widely than her critics suggest. She was not 'a staunch opponent of the study of contemporary international relations'.[32] In 1953, when Bull arrived, the IR paper was not 'Anglo-German relations before the First World War'. She also taught 'International Law and International Politics', 'International Institutions and Prevention of War', 'The Peace Conference of Paris', and 'The Treaty of Versailles and its Consequences'. More importantly, her scepticism of the 'newfangled social science methods' was not so far-fetched.

One need not endorse Agnes Headlam-Morley's mid-century approach to diplomatic and contemporary history to question whether the alternatives realistically available to her were so attractive, or to critically examine her function in the telling of IR's past. What new methods adopted by other IR scholars at the time was she supposed to profess? What enduring insights did this 'separate' IR then offer? Did the project for a new IR succeed where Agnes Headlam-Morley's 'professorial leadership failed'?[33] As we have seen, for most IR scholars the main contemporary alternative to diplomatic and contemporary history was to import theories and methods from functionalist sociology, behavioural social science, and/or so-called 'realist' theory from the United States.[34] Few, if any, considered Eileen Power's social and economic history approach, though at least Headlam-Morley was explicit about her rejection of it. Headlam-Morley's critics may point to growing student numbers and degree programmes elsewhere. But if we judge her position on intellectual grounds, then her stance emerges as less apathetic than principled, and not without some justification. As already discussed, her strict approach to source interpretation helped to set Merze Tate on course for a career as a serious diplomatic historian of race and empire. None of the alternative intellectual approaches in the IR academy available to Tate at this time would have produced scholarship of the same quality. W.E.B. Du Bois criticised Tate for sidelining Marxism in her analysis of efforts to limit the build of arms, not the technical quality of her work, which he praised.[35]

To date, not a single disciplinary historian has examined, or even enquired into, Agnes Headlam-Morley's reasons for pursuing her intellectual approach as either understandable in her context, acceptable on its own terms, or justifiable *in the absence of realistic and desirable alternatives* offered by the men trying to establish IR as a separate subject. It appeared enough to them to point to her relative lack of productivity and her parentage. With

Headlam-Morley's scholarly interests allegedly bequeathed from her father, she is read first and foremost as a daughter, as offspring, and then middle-aged spinster, a teacher at best. She is never read as a scholar, thinker, or political and intellectual entrepreneur in her own right, nor her mother's daughter. Thus reduced, Headlam-Morley can stand in for a caricature of diplomatic history, the constitutive Other to the new more supposedly sophisticated ('theoretical') and separate IR. As already discussed in chapter 4, Manning and Goodwin's effort to establish a separate IR rested on a distinction between history and sociology that was also largely a distinction between Oxford and London, between Headlam-Morley and Manning.[36] Agnes Headlam-Morley is a case study of the gendered and constitutive marginalisation of historical research in the process of mythmaking about the origins of 'disciplinary IR' in Britain. The misogyny discloses a real and justifiable intellectual, social, and even psychic anxiety about British IR's impoverished intellectual standing.[37]

'Every historian', wrote Agnes Headlam-Morley, 'must write in the light of his own vision'.[38] If, like most of her contemporaries, she viewed international relations as 'a branch of History',[39] then what mode of historical research did she adopt? Examining her papers, initially held among her father's, as well as her published and unpublished work, reveal Headlam-Morley's intellectual and political interests as more wide-ranging, shifting, and sophisticated than her critics imagined. She wrote more and on wider topics than they imply. She left 'a large quantity of unpublished and disorganized notes' because, after her death, no one thought to organise them.[40] According to Kenneth Wheare, then Gladstone Professor of Government at All Souls, and expert on the constitutional structure of Britain's dominions, Headlam-Morley was perfectly appointable to the Montague Burton Chair, 'the best of the three' shortlisted.[41] She had published only one book, but this was because of her heavy burden of teaching and examining. If 'at times', Wheare claimed, likely referring to her support for appeasement, 'I think her views are a bit eccentric, I am saying too she is an individual of sterling capacity and an individual with whom people will differ from time to time'. She is not 'over-specialised', she had a greater capacity to supervise widely than the very 'narrow range' of Lewis Namier.[42] On taking the chair, she declared that it is 'a subject which I think would and should be developed at the university and I shall enjoy trying to do it'.[43] For unlike at Cambridge, where Gwladys Jones's IR paper was dropped in 1945, IR at Oxford was—and still is—a strong component of the tripartite Politics, Philosophy and Economics, and joint History and Politics undergraduate

FIGURE 7.1. Agnes Headlam-Morley with Kittilein. Oil on canvas. Robert Lutyens c.1964. Courtesy of the Principal and Fellows of St Hugh's College, Oxford

degrees, not least due to the efforts of Headlam-Morley's colleague Sibyl Crowe, who is also discussed in this chapter.

Agnes Headlam-Morley is in no way deserving of hagiography. But when read properly she emerges as far more interesting, and certainly no more flawed than contemporary men and women of a similar racial and class position: author of the right-wing counterpoint to Eileen Power and F. Melian Stawell's left and liberal pro-League writings for wider publics and schoolchildren; an experienced political campaigner, party activist, and would-be Tory MP; a lifelong supporter of Chamberlain's policy of appeasement, with 'no secret shame in being half German', nor in arguing for Germany's fair treatment after both world wars; a figure who strategically deployed her privileged position as daughter of an influential diplomat, but whose politics was more influenced by her mother, Else Sonntag, than her father; a shaper of post-war Anglo-German relations, translator of Bertolt Brecht, and author of a novella that prefigured attempts to represent German civilian suffering during World War II; a famed *salon* hostess, considered one of 'the best known social and academic figures in Oxford', 'one of the most popular and accomplished teachers in the field of European history',[44] and 'one of the most attractive characters ever to have strayed into the academic scene'.[45]

## From Comparative Politics to
## Popular Colonial Internationalism

Most scholarly attention on British women's political and intellectual work in the interwar period focuses on the circles in which Eileen Power and F. Melian Stawell moved: feminist, socialist–internationalist, and peace activist.[46] But Britain's largest and most active interwar political society was the Conservative Women's Organisation.[47] Often less concerned with disarmament and the League of Nations, conservative women in the 1920s were more invested in empire and anti-Bolshevism, which in the 1930s became the rationale for the appeasement of Hitler. After the extensions of the franchise in 1918 and 1928, these women were the loyalist backbone of the Tory Party; wooed, educated, and mobilised, including by a cadre of insider Tory women like Agnes Headlam-Morley.

Agnes's German mother, Else Sonntag (1865–1950), was an accomplished musician and composer, student of Franz Liszt and contemporary of Clara Schumann. She met James Headlam on his studies in Berlin in the late 1880s when he was working with the German historians Hans Delbrück and Heinrich von Treitschke. Marrying in 1892, Else moved to England, and from concert performance to composition; her music was performed in London, Bournemouth, Berlin, Munich, and Leipzig. She had two children, Kenneth in 1901 and Agnes in 1902, but was 'not very practical in domestic matters', according to her daughter.[48] James took the additional name Morley in 1918 by royal licence, at the request of his cousin and godfather, George Morley, last in his line.[49]

After attending Wimbledon High School for Girls, Agnes read modern history at Somerville, which had the reputation for being Oxford's brainiest women's college. She achieved a first in 1924, and the B.Litt. degree in 1926. Agnes's father was clearly supportive of his daughter's education and professional interests, and she accompanied him on his research trip to Palestine to report on Church of England schools at the request of his brother Arthur Cayley, Bishop of Gloucester. They stayed at the British Residency in Cairo, and then travelled through Palestine, Syria, and Transjordan, in what Agnes later described as the 'short period of peace under the firm but benevolent rule of Lord Plumer', High Commissioner to the British Mandate in Palestine.[50] She claimed that her father had always believed that the 1917 Balfour Declaration was 'not just an opportunist move but a genuine expression of idealism' and that Britain 'would succeed in establishing a successful multiracial state in Palestine'.[51] Agnes Headlam-Morley's explicit commentary on British imperialism was usually fleeting, and always justificatory. To avoid another war in Europe, she later argued, Britain should make 'colonial concessions' to Nazi Germany in exchange for 'a quid pro quo in the way of European security'.[52] Headlam-Morley's interests were familial.[53] They were also unapologetically Eurocentric.

Like other international relations scholars of her generation, Agnes Headlam-Morley's first book, based on her B.Litt., was less a study of relations between states and more a work of comparative politics and political theory in which the focus and nature of 'comparison' was determined by the rise and fall of empires.[54] The international–imperial context for *The New Democratic Constitutions of Europe*, published in 1928, was the collapse of the German and Austro-Hungarian empires during World War I. The familial background was her mother's German nationalism and father's work at Versailles on minority protection, plebiscites, and the sovereignty of small East European nations. James's 1915 book on the causes of the war, *The History of Twelve Days*, emphasised Austro-Hungary's conviction that 'war against Serbia . . . was essential for the survival of the monarchy'.[55] Britain's purpose in the war, Agnes later maintained, was not to fight 'for democratic freedom' or the 'right to independence' of '"oppressed" nationalities', rather the break-up of Austria-Hungary.[56] In turn, post-war British policy aimed to forestall any unification of German-speaking peoples into another even more powerful multinational empire at the centre of Europe. Hence Britain's interest in the success or failure of new constitutions in central and eastern Europe.

*The New Democratic Constitutions* was Agnes Headlam-Morley's evaluation of the emergent political systems in Germany, Czechoslovakia, Poland, Finland, Yugoslavia, and the Baltic states, almost a decade after their founding.[57] She surveyed the mechanisms and practical application of parliamentary government and state functions, including social and economic duties; territorial questions, federalism, local government, and the 'democratic principle', including popular sovereignty, universal suffrage, electoral systems, proportional representation, and political parties; and she surveyed the systems of checks on the power of Parliament, referenda, second chambers and presidencies.

Alfred Zimmern's *International Affairs* review was full of praise.[58] He later described Headlam-Morley's book as a 'model of clear thinking and lucid exposition'. In fact, the book was anti-socialist and paternalist, obsessed with the degree to which the new systems followed or departed from the English model. Nonetheless, nearly three decades later, the work remained 'a standard authority'.[59] Almost four decades later, Headlam-Morley would cite her own 'long-forgotten book'[60] as evidence against the view that Britain's 'first past the post' electoral system was biased in favour of her party, the Tories. The system was necessary for the stability of democracy. The 'very able men who drafted the Weimar Constitution' made the mistake of trying to better the British system with a form of proportional representation. Its failure to produce strong and effective leadership was one of Hitler's most successful arguments in discrediting parliamentary democracy.[61]

After her first degree, Agnes returned to the north of England to live with and campaign for her cousin, Cuthbert Headlam, the Conservative MP for Barnard Castle, a large and largely working-class constituency, between 1924 and 1929 and again between 1931 and 1935.[62] She was Cuthbert's electoral assistant and researcher on industrial issues and attended and spoke at election meetings, often in his place. As she wrote to her mother in 1929, 'Last week I spoke almost every evening and usually canvassed the whole day'.[63] She was an organiser and campaigner for the Barnard Castle Women's Unionist Divisional Committee, particularly in districts where socialists were ascendant.[64] 'I know the people thoroughly', she boasted, 'and have the organisation entirely at my fingertips'.[65] She collaborated with Cuthbert on a book on reforming Britain's unemployment insurance. She did much of the research for Cuthbert's 1932 book, *House of Lords or Senate?* Drawing directly on her expertise on constitutions, the book argued for the abolition of the Lords in favour of a Senate elected by local county councils.[66] She expected to inherit the Barnard Castle seat from her cousin and become an MP herself.

While her primary interest was Tory party activism, Agnes Headlam-Morley also researched and drafted an unpublished second book on the early settler colonial history of the United States, experimenting with a genre aimed directly at shaping public opinion on international affairs.[67] Planned as a school textbook, and told, in part, through the life of George Washington, the manuscript tells a story of heroic settlers, their encounters with French colonialists, and attempts to persuade Indians to side with the English settlers. Part military history, part hagiography, she wrote of 'great men' like General Braddock and Benjamin Franklin, of disciplined Indian fighters and their military tactics, of the Seven Years' War between Britain and France. Her account of the War of Independence was sympathetic to Washington and the continental army. There is no sustained discussion of slavery, only brief mention of enslaved persons on tobacco farms. She acknowledged and moved quickly past the dispossession of indigenous peoples in favour of a celebration of empire.

Agnes Headlam-Morley's unpublished textbook was the right-wing version of Power and Stawell's liberal pro-League writings for school-children. But it was also a counterpart to her father's contemporaneous work. In the 1920s, James helped 'lay the foundations of opinion "that mattered" between the wars: he was a vital link in the connection between government, journalism and scholarship'.[68] During World War I, he was assistant director of Britain's Political Intelligence Department, working with Zimmern, Toynbee, Carr, and Eyre Crowe, all men with, or soon to have, international thinkers as wives or daughters. After the war, he became historical advisor to the Foreign Office, a new role in publicity or propaganda created especially for him, which involved writing anonymous commentaries, reviews, articles, and essays on British foreign policy, the origins of the war and the peace settlement for the leading papers.[69] In this context, James Headlam-Morley was a central figure at Chatham House, serving on its Council, chairing its Publications Committee, helping to establish its press-cuttings bureau, and appointing Toynbee to oversee the annual *Survey of International Affairs*.

Agnes Headlam-Morley wanted to become a Tory MP, but political work for the party was intermittent. In 1930, when Margery Perham resigned her tutorial position at St Hugh's to spend more time in Africa, Headlam-Morley applied to be her successor. Arnold Toynbee owed his position at Chatham House to her father, and duly wrote a letter of support for Headlam-Morley, praising Agnes's intellect and pedigree. She 'took advantage of the opportunities which came to her through studying contemporary affairs at first hand'.[70] Her undergraduate tutor, Irish historian Maude Clarke, was more subtle: Agnes 'has an intellectual energy and a confidence in handling problems and materials which I rarely found in women . . . [She comes to politics] naturally, as part of the chief interests of her life'.[71]

St Hugh's principal, Barbara Gwyer, duly offered Headlam-Morley the position that she was to take up after lecturing at the Lucie and Alfred Zimmern School in Geneva. But her political ambitions put her university position in jeopardy; 'my whole interest is really in the political work', she explained to Gwyer, apologising for accepting the job on the eve of a general election.[72]

After initial support from the College ('a certain sacrifice was worth making to secure her'[73]), St Hugh's refused to approve another delay. Headlam-Morley persisted: 'the whole future of our country depends upon the return of the national government with a large majority . . . and . . . at such a time of national emergency it is the duty of everybody . . . to concentrate every energy upon it'.[74] Never had the Tories campaigned against such a powerful political left, and at a time when the National Government was enforcing austerity and welfare cuts as their preferred response to the Great Depression. The great difficulty of the 1931 election, Headlam-Morley lamented, was that it was 'fought on class lines'.[75] Once the election was over, Agnes promised, her political work would come to an end. 'I should not of course wish to spend the rest of my time as a Women's Organiser and there is nothing I should like better than tutorial work at Oxford'.[76] In fact, she found the excessive workload arduous and 'boring',[77] later claiming to have applied for the Montague Burton Chair to reduce her teaching load from twenty-two hours a week to fifteen.

## How is Policy Made? Diplomatic and Contemporary History

Diplomatic history and the desire to influence contemporary British foreign policy and public opinion influenced Agnes Headlam-Morley intellectual outlook and methods, much more than her earlier work in comparative politics and settler colonial history. In 1930, Agnes and her brother Kenneth co-edited a collection of their father's memoranda, *Studies in Diplomatic History*,[78] based on his decade at the Foreign Office, and in 1972, co-edited and published his *Memoir of the Paris Peace Conference 1919*. The earliest forms of diplomatic history in this mode were nationalist, often 'official history' accompanying the opening of government archives in the latter half of the nineteenth century. The increasingly professional practices of diplomatic historians were central to the establishment of 'scientific history', in which 'the dramas of nation-states and their archives were intertwined'.[79] The relations between states were best illuminated in accounts of the decisions and personalities of the primary decision-makers, elite political men, hence the priority given to the documentary and archival records.[80] The raw materials were official government documents, correspondence, minutes, and memoranda of foreign policy decision-makers and advisors. The meticulous work of collection and interpretation was carried out by empirically-minded, highly skilled professionals, men like Headlam-Morley's father as she described him: 'essentially rational, detached, objective'.[81]

In her introduction to James's *Memoir of the Paris Peace Conference*, Agnes claimed her father had made substantial contributions to the diplomatic history method, but also, unusually for a work of this kind, credited the skill and intellectual accomplishments of his secretary, Mary Hughes. 'In our parlance', she wrote, Hughes 'would have been called a research assistant'.[82] Her father's 'most important' methodological 'innovation', Agnes wrote, 'was the inclusion of private papers and of minutes written on the papers at the time'. She cited Sir Eyre Crowe's famous unsolicited memoranda of 1907, 'Memorandum on the Present State of British Relations with France and Germany'. Crowe was an influential diplomat, father of Headlam-Morley's Oxford colleague Sibyl Crowe, who worked at the Foreign Office for forty years and became Permanent Under-Secretary. His memoranda pointed to the rising threat from German expansion and argued that war with Germany could not be avoided for long. Crowe was an anti-appeaser and with the memorandum articulated Britain's balance of power thinking. 'The minutes written by officials, often briefly and in haste', claim Headlam-Morley, 'show better than anything else the reaction of those whose duty it was to advise the Secretary of State'.[83]

In 1925, Crowe died from overwork, leaving his youngest daughter Sibyl, then aged sixteen, 'shattered', and the family with no means of income and no pension.[84] Foreign Office friends raised money to support the family, though not enough to send all four children to university. Sibyl's oldest sister took her life. The middle sister became a secretary, and died by suicide as well.[85] Sibyl won a Senior Scholarship to read history at Girton College, Cambridge in 1926, where she was tutored by Gwladys Jones. With her family connections, Crowe subsequently worked in the Foreign Office, officially as 'typist', but she 'didn't type a word' and instead broke code.[86] With few prospects for professional advancement—women were only admitted to the British diplomat corps in 1946[87]—Crowe returned to Cambridge, taught history in private schools, and began thinking about doctoral research.

Like Coral Bell, Crowe's career in IR was shaped by the early death of her first love. After meeting and becoming engaged to Arthur Fraser, a research student of economic history, Crowe put her research plans on hold. She wanted to relieve the financial burden on her mother, 'contribute to the family kitty', and, she said, 'I thought I would like in any case to devote a little time to perfecting myself in some of the domestic arts, including cooking'.[88] Arthur died of cancer in 1934 at the age of twenty-eight after a long illness and a series of misdiagnoses. Broken and unable to imagine being with anyone else, Sibyl Crowe returned to what, for her, was the familial subject of British diplomatic history, winning Girton's Carlisle Research Scholarship for a Ph.D. in 1935. Later asked whether her 'interest in international politics' was 'inspired' by her father, she replied, 'Yes, it was the background really'.[89]

Crowe's Cambridge Ph.D., defended in 1938, was on the 'colonial background of European history' in the late nineteenth century.[90] Despite the extraordinarily high teaching burden at St Hilda's, and travelling to work in the Foreign Office during the week, Crowe revised her dissertation and published her first book in 1942, a more focused study, *The Berlin West African Conference, 1884–1885*, on how European empires arranged the partition and further conquest and exploitation of Africa and its peoples. Crowe was the first historian to use the conference papers on the trade in enslaved people and the first to use the letters of her paternal grandfather—the art historian, journalist, diplomat, and one of the British Conference delegates, Sir Joseph Archer Crowe—retained among her own private family papers.

Sibyl Crowe tried to show for the first time that far from being a disaster for British diplomacy, the conference was a triumph. Britain defended its core colonial interests around slavery, boundaries, free trade, and the doctrine of occupation, because Germany, 'the arbiter . . . of colonial destinies'[91] grew closer to Britain's position, and away from France. As one reviewer noted of the great powers at the conference (and this could also be said of Crowe's book), there was a 'total absence of . . . reference to the interests or rights of the colonial peoples themselves. The very idea that such rights existed . . . was so only in inverse proportion to the actual stake which their countries had in the territories of Africa'.[92] Crowe was her father and her grandfather's daughter in this regard, entirely focused on European power politics, the great power diplomacy of empire. With her 'inherited skill in unravelling the tangled webs of diplomacy', and within this narrow, colonial, nationalist remit, according to one reviewer, 'it is difficult to see how the book could have been improved'.[93] Although *The American Historical Review* misgendered Crowe,[94] the book was praised as a 'splendid monograph',[95] 'indispensable',[96] and 'well-conceived'.[97]

After the death of her first love, Crowe never married. She took a politics lectureship and then later Fellowship at St Hilda's, which gave her a home, as well as a job. She lived in college 'in a very nice room' for the remainder of her professional life. As already discussed, Crowe's research career was thwarted because of her excessive teaching burden in the poorest of Oxford's women's colleges. After retirement in 1981, Crowe published a short memoir of Arthur and a collection of their love poems.[98] She also began work on what was meant to be the authoritative biography of her father. As with her grandfather's letters, Crowe refused to make Eyre's private correspondence, 'the crown jewels',[99] available to other historians, retaining them for exclusive use in her own book. *Our Ablest Public Servant*, co-authored with Edward Corp, appeared soon after her death.[100] Intended as work of diplomatic, biographical, and personal history, it was really hagiography. Crowe was the best Permanent Under-Secretary in Foreign Office history. Previous work that even slightly criticised Eyre or played down his historical significance was refuted. Previously, Crowe had criticised Zara Steiner's book on the Foreign Office for misrepresenting Eyre's relationship with Lord Hardinge, Viceroy of India.[101] 'She picks up things from somebody else and then repeats them . . . The footnotes are wrong . . . Apart from that, really she's quite good'.[102] Steiner took her revenge in her review of *Our Ablest Public Servant*. 'Miss Crowe has tried to settle too many historical scores and thus distorts her father's story. She fights unnecessary battles' and 'admits of no mistakes on Crowe's part'.[103] As another reviewer put it, the book's appropriate subtitle was 'Daddy was always right'.[104]

Headlam-Morley similarly elucidated and praised her father's general methodological approach to diplomatic history in his 1915 book, *The History of Twelve Days*: the belief that the proximate and underlying causes of World War I were revealed 'by a detailed examination of the official documents issued by the belligerent Governments . . . The diplomatic correspondence of the last crucial days would reveal the purposes of the contestants both before and during the conflict'.[105] A close reading of 'the bare record of dispatches and telegrams', she later argued in a critical review of A.J.P. Taylor's work, 'allow the actors to speak for themselves'.[106] Headlam-Morley praised her own research students who were 'careful to give full quotations from their sources and they are cautious, sometimes over-cautious, in stating their opinions. The result can be fruitful if, as Lord Salisbury put it, one is anxious to find out not what the historians think about it but "what really happened"'.[107]

Without question, both Agnes Headlam-Morley and Sibyl Crowe understood themselves as diplomatic historians, not least because the more expansive field and language of 'international history' was not yet institutionalised.[108] In Headlam-Morley's mind, 'the fundamental questions' were these: 'how is policy made? What do we mean when we talk of France and Germany, Englishmen and Russians?'[109] Hence she prioritised detailed examination of the documentary record to understand the 'motive and purpose' of foreign policy. The practice of contemporary diplomatic history matched the fundamentally *contemporary* influences on a nation's foreign policy. 'The political actions and decisions of a nation are governed by the living memory of its own historical past', she claimed.[110] This living memory was the basis of the national 'traditions of policy', such as the British tradition of the balance of power which, contra Arnold Toynbee and Geoffrey Barraclough, Headlam-Morley maintained was still decisive in the world, even at a time of British decline.[111] But Headlam-Morley was not, or did not aspire to be, a narrow diplomatic historian as caricatured in much IR that is as a 'strict day-by-day diary of events divorced from the wider framework of the international political system'.[112]

After World War II, Headlam-Morley's major scholarly ambition was to write a book on her main preoccupation, Anglo-German relations. Yet her explicit aim was to go beyond 'pure' diplomatic history to 'attempt to show the interaction of domestic history and foreign policy. Some of the chapters on the internal conditions of Germany during the Weimar Republic', she claimed vaguely, were 'in advanced state of preparation. I hope to finish the first volume . . . the period of 1918 to 1932, in a few years'.[113] In 1948, she also claimed to be working on 'a short study' on international law and institutions.[114] Hardly the aspirations of a 'narrow' diplomatic historian.

For nearly four decades at Oxford, Headlam-Morley covered what would now be recognised as the conventional core of the IR subject in the period in which she worked: 'International Law and International Politics in the Post-War Period', 'International Institutions for the Prevention of War', 'The European System and the Impact of Revolution since 1919', 'International Co-operation since 1943', 'The Covenant of the League of Nations and the United Nations Charter', 'The League of Nations and the United Nations Organization', 'Collective Security and the Rule of Law', 'International Organization and the Problem of Security', 'Problems of Collective Security', 'Causes of War, 1919–39', 'From Peace to War 1919–1939', 'The Peace Conference in Paris and the Treaty of Versailles', 'British Foreign Policy Since the War', 'Anglo-German Relations, 1919–1938', and 'The Peace Conference of Paris'. She thus taught more widely than assumed. Even the records from the 1950 Windsor meeting of the British Coordinating Committee for International Studies noted that Oxford's IR provision was more diverse than 'diplomatic history', including international institutions, international law, and international community, international communism, and political thought 'as it affects international relations'.[115] 'Thus, though the historical content of the subject is taught at Oxford is usually emphasised, it is nevertheless sometimes regarded as having a close affinity with Politics'.[116] The graduate B.Phil. degree, Geoffrey Goodwin admitted, provides 'a well-balanced course for the postgraduate study of International Relations'.[117]

Agnes Headlam-Morley taught all the basic IR topics of her day, and did so well, despite finding the tutorial work gruelling and 'boring',[118] with 'so awfully many pupils I hardly have any time . . . I have to teach all the day and often also after dinner . . . awfully busy and no nice people'.[119] As an assistant tutorial fellow from 1932, Headlam-Morley taught on average twenty-two hours a week, more than the typical eighteen hours for college tutors at this time.[120] When she took the Montague Burton Professorship, her load was reduced to the more manageable fifteen hours a week.[121] She remained at St Hugh's College because Balliol, the usual home of the Montague Burton Professor, did not admit women as either fellows or students. 'I don't suppose any other college ever thought of wanting me'.[122] She did not, in fact, wish to upend her college or private life. She had 'to look after an invalid mother' in London and she had no desire to be 'pushed into a new college and made to waste time and energy on arranging how to live in Oxford'.[123]

Some distance from Oxford's city centre, scholars in the poorer women's colleges often stayed on the fringes of Oxford's academic life, but not Agnes Headlam-Morley. She hosted a weekly *salon* at St Hugh's and, by the mid-1950s, was considered one of 'the best known social and academic figures in Oxford . . . with Enid Starkie, she was then the outstanding hostess in the University . . . Oxford dons waited for invitations to her dinner table'.[124] Tutor of modern history Susan Wood recalled that 'the only room for manoeuvre' during the then-compulsory college dinners depended 'on a rapid calculation of which end of the table to make for, with the aim, often, of sitting next to Agnes Headlam-Morley (who would talk, enchantingly, about almost anything)'.[125] Headlam-Morley admired Lucie Zimmern and her *salons*, which she praised in her inaugural professorial lecture. Like Zimmern, she also blurred the boundaries between this feminised cultural form and scholarship in the early years of academic IR. And like Zimmern, she considered international relations as 'simply a part of life—and the same way as she thought of poetry and music and philosophy'.[126] At St Hugh's, 'without exception', according to its principal Rachel Trickett, Headlam-Morley was considered the most striking member of the College Senior Common Room'.[127]

The social life covered for Headlam-Morley's limited academic publications. Alluding to imposter syndrome in her inaugural lecture in 1949, she confessed to continued 'doubts and hesitations' when she learned of her appointment to the chair.[128] Already in 1930, when offered the post at St Hugh's, she admitted to Isaiah Berlin that she 'was half afraid you might think I ought not to have worked my way in in the first place'.[129] Shortly after her inaugural lecture, she again confessed to Berlin feelings of 'despair' when she was 'stuck' with the lecture she could not write, and to experiencing 'panic that it was too long'.[130] Replying from Princeton, Berlin assured her that he heard the lecture was received as 'a great intellectual and moral success'.[131] Headlam-Morley negatively compared herself to Somerville's prolific scholar of French poetry and literature, Enid Starkie. 'I know one must accept the external inequalities of fortune, but I can't help contrasting her fortunes with mine. Enid has far more learning and scholarship than I shall ever have and she has written a great deal more. I hope to write in time but at present my reputation is firmly . . .'.[132] The next page is missing, though it is not difficult to imagine how Headlam-Morley imagined her reputation.

## 'Great causes, great events—and how dull they are!'

The double standard in evaluating Headlam-Morley's productivity is clear. At Balliol, reports Martin Ceadel, 'the IR paper was covered during its first decade by Francis ('Sligger') Urquhart, a historian famed more for his social salon than his academic work'.[133] Charles Manning was also known for the 'comparative paucity of his published output'.[134] With an even heavier teaching burden, research time was limited; scholars were not expected to churn out the publications as regularly as later generations. The same grace is not afforded to Headlam-Morley; 'college men' are more acceptable than 'college women'. Before World War II, Headlam-Morley had been working on two further book projects, British Foreign Policy since the War and German Constitutional Developments since 1914. 'The first of these', she explained, 'would be a comparatively short book [and] is already well advanced. The second would be on a much bigger scale. I have done a good deal of the preliminary research and have written one section. The book would take a considerable time to complete since it involves a detailed study of German political life under the Weimar Republic'.[135] She made little further progress on either project because of her enormous teaching burden during the war, which contributed to her ill-health, including tuberculosis; 'her capacity for sustained work', noted her *Times* obituary, was never what it had been before World War II.[136] During the war, and in the absence of Alfred Zimmern, she did most of the IR lecturing and teaching at Oxford,[137] and received no term of sabbatical leave until 1956. Her application for leave mentioned 'the constant pressure of a heavy programme of teaching, lecturing and examining'.[138]

Agnes Headlam-Morley was not alone in refusing to establish IR as a 'separate' subject, even an IR graduate degree, if this meant severing her subject from its home in history, and possibly teaching even more. In her inaugural professorial lecture, she situated her work directly in the field of international relations as *contemporary* history. She praised her predecessor, E. L. Woodward, and her contemporary Lewis Namier for their 'confident assurance that it is possible to study scientifically the history of contemporary events. By contemporary', she continued, 'I do not mean, as Dr. Toynbee would, the history of the last three thousand years. Nor do I mean only the events of to-day or yesterday—but those that fall within the memory of living historians'.[139] She was obviously aware that some international relations scholars defined themselves against 'pure' diplomatic history, that is, a history of international relations that takes 'account of economic factors, movements of public opinion, all the complex motives by which men's actions are determined'.[140] She was also aware that others wished to pursue structural explanations of international relations as a kind of Hobbesian anarchy, and others more sociological accounts of international society as the justification for a separate IR. She explicitly engaged with and rejected A.J.P. Taylor's realism, Toynbee's philosophy of history, and Barraclough's contemporary history, all of which, to her mind, prematurely decentred Europe in world politics. She did not address Manning's sociological speculations, likely because she did not view them as worthy of serious engagement.

In an unpublished review, Headlam-Morley rejected A.J.P. Taylor's 'realist' explanations for great power war, exemplified in the famous opening claim of his *Struggle for Mastery in Europe*: 'In the state of nature which Hobbes imagined, violence was "nasty brutish and short". Though individuals never lived in this state of nature, the Great Powers of Europe have always done so'.[141] She criticised Taylor for offering so little evidence to support his 'particular conception of power politics . . . which he does not consider it necessary to prove'.[142] His account of the origins of 1914 'falls back on generalisations'.[143] Rather than criticise Taylor for not situating Europe's diplomatic history in wider social and economic contexts, she argued that he did 'not take seriously enough the reasons which the statesmen themselves give for their complicated manoeuvres', and 'he does not sufficiently distinguish between those who saw below the surface of events and those who did not'.[144] Taylor 'dismisses as irrelevant the problems which had been a constant preoccupation to Bismarck and Salisbury . . . His account of the final negotiations lacks the sense of tension and mounting tragedy that is to be found in the bare record of dispatches and telegrams. He does not allow the actors to speak for themselves, he does not let us see them in the stress of circumstance'.[145]

Agnes Headlam-Morley was aware of the international and global context for the post-war turn away from diplomatic history toward contemporary world history and philosophies in the manner of Arnold Toynbee and Geoffrey Barraclough, the first two directors of research at Chatham House. As she recounted in her inaugural lecture in 1949, the first half of the twentieth century was 'an age of great events, events that may be horrible, strange, fantastic . . . an age moreover which has produced an unusual number of great men'.[146] Given the scale of global transformations, and the sheer volume of material, Headlam-Morley recognised the temptation to import equally grand meanings, to 'make sense of it all'.[147] Yet the 'raw material of this history', the bare documentary record, was 'far more interesting', she claimed, 'than the books which the historians write'.[148] When historians attempt to go beyond the methods of diplomatic history 'to recount these events, to describe these personalities, for the most part we make a sorry business of it'.[149] To support her claim, Headlam-Morley turned to a feminised genre written by a woman and the words of the main protagonist, Catharine Moreland, who 'wished she were more fond of history'. In her 1803 novel, *Northanger Abbey*, Jane Austen's main character famously complained to Miss Tilney that she read a little history out of duty, 'but I find little that does not either vex or weary me. The quarrels of Popes and Kings, with wars and pestilences on every page—and yet I find it odd that it should be so dull, for a great deal of it must be invention'.[150] Missing from Headlam-Morley's lecture is Moreland's more famous next line, which might have been said of IR's conventional histories: 'the men all so good for nothing, and hardly any women at all—it is very tiresome'.[151]

Headlam-Morley turned to Jane Austen not to suggest that historians invented facts, but that they were terrible at fashioning a moral for the story they were trying to tell. Claiming Austen's authority, Headlam-Morley argued that when

> historians use their imaginations . . . they are so dull . . . The imagination as [Austen] knew it, as all artists know it, is a faculty which enables them to penetrate below the surface of events, to an inner truth, a deeper reality. But when we plodding historians indulge in flights of fancy, it is ten to one not because we have any deeper insight, but because we wish to fit the facts into

our preconceived ideas. The story must have a moral. The moral is not always easy to see. So we invent one. It is then that we become tedious. For truth is always more interesting than our invention.[152]

The art of diplomatic history, as Headlam-Morley understood it, was not 'to invent explanations' for events or 'attribute motives' to the actors.[153] It was to allow the actors to speak for themselves, to reveal them in their 'stress of circumstance', to show whether *they* were able to see below the surface of events.

The politics of Headlam-Morley's method, and its difference from Eileen Power's world social history, discussed in chapter 5, becomes clearer when she evoked another, less reputable fictional character in her inaugural lecture. As she struggled with the prospect of taking up the Burton Chair, and 'appalled by the amount of history that goes on . . . by the books which I might be expected to read; worse still by the books which I might be expected to write',[154] she identified with the 'disreputable Italian count' in Eric Linklater's satirical 1946 novel, *Private Angelo*, the story of an Italian soldier during World War II under the command of Count Pontefiore. Contemplating her inaugural lecture, Headlam-Morley's 'mind echoed' Pontefiore's *cri de coeur*: 'I don't want books stuffed full of the world's calamities—give me one book about a man who strangled his mistress with her hair on a dark night'.[155] Again, she left out the rest of Pontefiore's commentary and misquoted him: 'I am bored by the spectacle of people moving hither and thither in great masses. One cannot even be sorry for a horde of people. It is only the individual who rouses either interest or compassion . . . It is a day of Great Powers, great causes, great events—and how dull they are! . . . I want to read, not some great overstuffed history of the world's calamities, but the brief and well-told tale of one embittered man, moved by a single hatred, who cut his sweetheart's throat in a deserted house'.[156] Headlam-Morley's historical method was a conservative reaction against the forms of social history best represented not by British IR's early male practitioners, but world social and economic history from below as pioneered by Eileen Power, that linked the great masses and their great causes with stories of the great powers and the great events. It was also compatible with Headlam-Morley's support for appeasing Hitler.

## 'She Could be Given Satisfaction in Africa': Tory Appeaser

Agnes Headlam-Morley's political ambitions did not end with the formation of the National Government in 1931. In 1936, she succeeded her cousin Cuthbert Headlam as the Tory's prospective parliamentary candidate for Barnard

Castle;[157] however, the election was not called. According to L. H. Mates, Cuthbert Headlam had 'moved from almost a pro-fascist stance in 1936 to anti-Nazism soon after (though he remained a Franco supporter)' and 'was one of very few Conservatives, and unique in the Northeast, explicitly to condemn the attempt to forge a cross-party Popular Front' alliance between left and right in order to thwart fascism.[158] While she was an unrepentant supporter of appeasement, there is no evidence of Agnes Headlam-Morley's opinion of the Popular Front or of her holding fascist views.

At Margery Perham's 1937 Oxford University Summer School on Colonial Administration, Headlam-Morley analysed Germany's transition from republic to totalitarian state. 'Fascism', she claimed, 'sprang from a spirit of negation' and the totalitarian state 'is the product of a reaction against a weak and inefficient form of Parliamentary Democracy'.[159] Though she was one of many women to analyse the rise of Nazism, still today she is considered 'among the sharpest and most critical observers of Nazi politics', seeing more clearly 'than others how authoritarian leaders systematically ignored norms of government'.[160] Her cousin Cuthbert's diary entry for January 7, 1939 records that Agnes was 'full of Germany as usual—all the people she has just seen in Berlin, she says, are disgusted with the Nazi regime and ashamed of the treatment of the Jews, etc. etc.'[161] She was still pursuing a parliamentary seat, explaining to her Oxford employer that her political activities did not 'interfere with my work at all during term'.[162] The 1940 election was postponed until 1945, when Labour held the seat, defeating the Tory candidate.

It is not difficult to imagine Agnes Headlam-Morley's opposition to a Popular Front alliance with the left in the 1930s, or the relation between her lifelong anti-Bolshevism and her support for the 'Tory policy of peace'.[163] Her mother, Else Sonntag, was as influential on Agnes's substantive views on international politics as her father was on her historical method. Even prior to World War I, Agnes recalled, Else 'had already got into trouble with [James's] family for supporting unpopular causes'.[164] She was 'always sticking up for the under dog—women should have votes, all animals but especially cats should be protected, Boers should be saved from the English Imperialists'.[165] The children, Agnes recalled, 'spoke German to my mother but not amongst ourselves'.[166] 'Now in all seriousness', at the start of World War I, Else

turned in love and loyalty to her own country. She made no secret of it. She spent the war years in almost complete isolation and paid no attention to the background rumble of 'Hun' and 'bloody German'. We children did not take it too tragically. My Mother assumed that we would wish Britain to win the war, but we were brought up not to deny our German ancestry. It was an open battle. Unlike so many children of mixed marriages we had no secret shame in being half German.[167]

Perhaps bitter at losing the Oxford chair to her daughter, E. H. Carr, also a Nazi appeaser, accused Else of being 'an impenitent German nationalist', who never learned how to speak English fluently.[168]

Unlike many of her peers, Agnes Headlam-Morley never concealed her support for one of the most maligned foreign policies of the twentieth century. She believed that Nazi Germany should be accommodated, to a point, in the face of the greater and common threat of the domestic and international radical left. As late as January 1937, she noted, Hitler still claimed that he would stand 'firm as the Guardian of civilization against communism'.[169] In an unpublished, undated essay, likely written for her tour of Germany in 1953, Headlam-Morley defended Chamberlain's policy as a 'bold bid for peace' underpinned by a basic understanding of the requirement of international pluralism.[170] While different states had 'different characteristics', she explained, quoting Chamberlain, 'there is something which is common to them all', even if that was 'only self-preservation and the pursuit of economic self-interest'.[171]

To avoid another world war, Headlam-Morley claimed the Allies had to recognise the 'harsh and unjust' nature of the Versailles settlement.[172] Appeasement was 'not the complacent acceptance of acts of aggression but an attempt to discern and remedy the causes of discontent'.[173] For example, Nazi Germany could be incorporated into a 'new colonial regime'. In exchange for forgoing the use of force in Austria and Czechoslovakia, the Nazis 'could be given satisfaction in Africa'.[174] The creation of a German-controlled international chartered company or the transfer of Portuguese and even British colonies was an acceptable sacrifice to avert all-out 'modern war, with indiscriminate air bombardment' in Europe.[175] For colonial administrators like Margery Perham and Lucy Philip Mair, no transfer of colonial territories should occur without taking 'native' views into account.[176] But Headlam-Morley did not dwell, even for a moment, on the consequences for colonial peoples.

Headlam-Morley was an appeaser, yet she was also ahead of her time in representing German civilian suffering during World War II. Her 1960 novella, *Last Days*, is the story of a German mother and widow grieving the loss of her son killed in shelling on his third day of fighting in Russia. 'They had put a red cross on the roof, but one could scarcely expect . . . She had heard it all before'.[177] Though written in the third person, the story is narrated entirely through the eyes of the unnamed mother. In a late essay on Bertolt Brecht, she praised, and may have been influenced by, his revival of 'the third person singular as a mark of distance, formality, respect'.[178] In a letter to German historian Beate Ruhm von Oppen, Headlam-Morley described her novella as a 'true story. The chief character was a dear friend, the sister-in-law of Wilhelm Backhaus', German pianist, and an early supporter of Hitler.[179] Headlam-Morley reportedly 'protected and looked after' her German friend until she died.[180]

Existing in a state of controlled pain, the main character of *Last Days* travels between her Berlin apartment off Potsdamerstraße, one of the heaviest-bombed areas of the city, and a farm in the northern German landscape near Greifswald, fifty miles from the Polish border. The entire story is set between June 1944 and January 1945, ending with the sound of the 'distant guns' of the approaching Russian forces and in the few months before the fall of Berlin. There is oblique reference to the transport of Berlin Jews, 'what's left of them';[181] Ukrainian and French prison labourers on the farm; evacuated German children, soldiers, and a Gestapo man; German soldiers sleeping, 'silent men, huddled in corners, propped against the walls'.[182] The protagonist's friend, Frau Preskow, risks her life to leave food for Russian women prisoners and their children. 'Women, she thought, must be braver than men.—Yet one could scarcely say so'.[183] There is allusion to the liberation of Paris and 'the trouble in July', perhaps the German attack on Kursk. The overwhelming focus is the inner life of the traumatised, grieving mother; her 'sense of disintegration'; flashes of memories of her son as a child; watching Russian women prisoners clearing bomb rubble from Berlin's streets and then imaging 'a jagged lump of concrete forced down into her head'.[184]

The reviewer in the *Times Literary Supplement* claimed that if all Headlam-Morley 'wished to convey was that the "commonplace" humanity in any nation could survive a brutal war and that life, for all its hardship and loss, was worth the continuing, then she has written well and succeeded admirably. And yet, peeping or squeaking beneath the measured, exceedingly formal prose, there seems to be another idea, unhappily mute and incommunicable'.[185] Yet the unutterable idea is quite clear. Writing in the late 1950s, Headlam-Morley recounted the quiet misery of an 'ordinary' German mother, not overtly to elicit sympathy and certainly not to suggest any moral equivalence, not to convey just the humanity and small acts of kindness, but to convey the psychological suffering of an ordinary German in the war years. Not until the early 2000s, in W. G. Sebald's *Lutfkrieg und Literatur*, were literary discussions of German civilian suffering more widespread.

Both Agnes and her mother Else were named in A. L. Rowse's 1961 *All Souls and Appeasement*. In a long line of works in which women were blamed for Britain's appeasement policy, Rowse claimed that the Bishop of Gloucester emitted 'pro-German sentiments—no doubt under the influence' of his 'half-German' niece.[186] Agnes rejected Rowse's 'silly little piece'.[187] Yet Rowse was very clear on her class of appeasers: 'there was a fatal confusion in their minds between the interests of their social order and the interests of their country. They ... were anti-Red and that hamstrung them'.[188] They were unwilling to countenance an alliance with the Soviet Union to defeat the Nazis. 'This, and the essential pettiness of the National Government, all flocking together to keep Labour out, was deeply corrupting both to them and the nation'.[189]

For Headlam-Morley, the Nazis were a deviation from German history and culture, not its culmination.[190] Some blamed Fichte, Wagner, or Hegel for Hitler's rise, but 'this is obvious nonsense', she claimed in 1949. Without naming Elizabeth Wiskemann's *The Rome–Berlin Axis*, which claimed Nietzsche was 'the metal with which the Rome–Berlin Axis was forged', she noted that 'some put it all down to Nietzsche'.[191] Yet, for Headlam-Morley, 'there was more human feeling' in Nietzsche 'than Hitler ever showed ... what Nietzsche meant by the superman was not at all what Hitler meant by the Aryan race'.[192] None of Hitler's ideas derived from German intellectual or philosophical traditions. Foreign policy is 'governed by the living memory of its own historical past rather than by the speculations of its thinkers and philosophers'.[193] In turn, thinkers and poets should not be reduced to their politics. In an essay, 'The Poetry of Bertolt Brecht', she observed that Brecht 'wrote a lot of didactic verse intended to prove this or that Marxist moral. But all this asceticism did him no harm'.[194] She translated Brecht's poetry for an important 1976 English edition of his work.[195]

Agnes Headlam-Morley obviously rejected Fritz Fischer's thesis that Imperial Germany's expansion was entirely responsible for World War I. She stormed out of a talk he gave in Oxford in 1963 after he criticised Gustav Stresemann, chancellor and then foreign minister during the Weimar Republic.[196] A decade later, she wrote a sympathetic essay on Stresemann, praising his 'skilful' use of the Reichswehr to put down political revolts from what she called 'the extreme right and the extreme left'.[197]

After the war, Headlam-Morley remained aloof from the male-dominated British Coordinating Committee for International Studies (BCCIS). In 1952, she was meant to chair a session at the LSE's Sixth Bailey Conference, but pulled out owing to illness.[198] After World War II, her major political cause was Anglo-German understanding, which she advanced in her academic and literary writings, teaching, lecture tours, and advising. She lamented the 'anti-German tendencies' in the press and was a minor participant in the intertwined drama of archives and nation-states over whether to return Prussian and German official documents from 1871, which Britain had confiscated at the end of World War II.[199]

Under the leadership of Margaret Lambert, the Foreign Office tasked a small group of British, American, and French historians with narrating the Third Reich's foreign policy, through editing and publishing the documents in multiple volumes. Lambert was an expert on plebiscites, a major international issue in the 1930s, publishing *The Saar* in 1934, based on research for her doctorate at LSE in 1936, with a cover by her lifelong partner, designer Enid Marx.[200] After World War I, Weimar-era intellectuals were accused of misusing official documents to question whether Germany bore sole responsibility for World War I, playing into Nazi hands. As editor-in-chief of *Documents on German Foreign Policy*, Lambert's team used documentary records to tell the story of Hitler's foreign policy before post-war German historians had the chance.

Agnes Headlam-Morley's reputation as a 'well known Germanophile' meant that she was 'conspicuously absent' from the list of historians E. L. Woodward suggested the Foreign Office might consult.[201] Senior British historians, including Lambert and Elizabeth Wiskemann, opposed ceding to German requests to repatriate documents, at least until Lambert's team had done its work.[202] Headlam-Morley weighed in on the pages of *The Times Literary Supplement*, accusing the British, French, and American editors of 'slowness' and claiming there was no excuse for keeping archives prior to 1914.[203] She defended the German editors of *Die Große Politik* against accusations of manipulating and/or omitting texts, at least without proper evidence. The archives should be freely available 'to scholars of all nations'.[204] At least the German editors were independent scholars, not 'official' historians and, never missing a chance to mention her father, they, like him, included minutes as well as official documents in their collections.[205]

## Conclusion

As Montague Burton Professor, Agnes Headlam-Morley was painfully aware of the additional burden of expectation and her exceptional situation as Oxford's first and, for a considerable time, only woman professor. Still, by the late 1950s, Headlam-Morley was the lone woman among Oxford's ninety-seven statutory chairs.[206] The unnamed protagonist in her novella, *Last Days*, was the first woman regularly employed at the Reichsbank. 'She had been happy there, and proud of her position . . . She had forgotten the name of the man she worked for . . . He could not at first accommodate himself to having a woman about and he had quite exaggerated ideas of feminine weakness'.[207]

In addition to helping steer Merze Tate through her Oxford graduate degree, Agnes Headlam-Morley's main legacy to IR, her lasting gift to the field, was inherited from her mother: 'supporting unpopular causes'.[208] Given British IR's failure as an intellectual project, and the recent (re)turn to something called 'historical IR', Headlam-Morley was partly vindicated. Her indifference to the new 'IR' was justifiable. It 'failed' as 'an *intellectual* project'.[209] Today, much of the most significant and interesting international thinking in the academy is not by the inheritors of those who pursued sociological theories of the state system or society of states, but contemporary international and global historians, those whom we might think of as Headlam-Morley's successors. Few, if any, contemporary historians, or scholars from any other field, import methods and approaches from IR, or require any grand theory of the international system or international society to write important works. Instead, practitioners of the new international and global history are comfortable with and are innovating all the thematic, conceptual, and theoretical moves that IR scholars still import.[210] Agnes Headlam-Morley was a flawed heroine not for the scholarship she produced, rather in her refusal of the claims of the London men obsessed with creating a 'separate IR'. She held her ground and for this she was vilified.

Of course, the 'problems of international relations cannot be adequately answered by the use of any *one* method which is rigidly fixed in advance'.[211] But that was never the historians' claim. David Long refers to Charles Manning's 'apparently paradoxical nature of specialization in international relations. It is a generalist training involving study in a wide variety of subjects . . . without being reducible to any one of them'.[212] Yet it is more than paradoxical. It was fatal. It was not necessary for IR to be reduced to any *one* method. However, the work of individual scholars could and should have been held to the methodological standards of at least one constituent discipline and method. Without a good standard of its own, the 'interdisciplinary' nature of IR became a substitute for any discipline at all. Manning became obsessed with rejecting historical methods, believing that 'a man may know much, even of the past, while comprehending little. Or so at least the devotees of International Relations are prone to believe'.[213] Some of IR's early devotees traded knowledge for the hope of comprehension, but they comprehended little and knew even less.

For all her very many flaws, Agnes Headlam-Morley insisted that her students master the craft of history. She should also have supported a wider remit of methodological approaches to the study of IR. Though not as responsible as Manning, Schwarzenberger, or Goodwin, Headlam-Morley was, in her failure, complicit in IR's partial absorption into political science. They all left IR exposed to subsumption by the more institutionally powerful field. By the 1970s, IR in Britain was much more likely to be treated as a sub-discipline of political science with history treated the way 'other political scientists do', as a source on 'the nature of the international political process *in general*', and as a theoretical source for IR's all-male, all-white intellectual canon. As discussed in more detail in chapter 10, Herbert Butterfield, chair of the British Committee on the Theory of International Politics, admitted that historians were to be 'trapped' into more 'general thinking' via 'the history of historiography ... I think that the same is likely to be true of International Theory'.[214] As Roger Morgan pointed out in a paper for BCCIS, IR specialists should have a 'fairly good knowledge of recent international history' but then proceed to IR's real business of studying why states pursue certain foreign policies and 'why the international system of states operates the way it does'.[215] One could approach international theory scientifically, he claimed, by drawing on 'economic theory, games theory, the mathematical theory of bargaining', or 'historically' [*sic*], by examining the writings of 'Thucydides, Hobbs [*sic*], Marx etc.'.[216]

# 8

# 'The Restraint to Efface Ourselves'

## ASSIMILATING DECOLONISATION

'Consider the Africans' side'.
—MARGERY PERHAM, *COLONIAL RECKONING* (1961), P. 61

IF WE WISH TO UNDERSTAND the most significant transformation of world politics in two centuries, or even British colonial and anticolonial policy in the 1950s and 1960s, we do not look to the scholarship of those who tried to establish International Relations (IR) as a separate academic discipline in Britain in this period, nor the related project of the British Committee on the Theory of International Politics, founded in 1959.[1] The limited nature of British IR scholarship on the British Empire must account, at least in part, for the astonishing fact that outside Oxford neither imperialism nor decolonisation were widespread topics of instruction in international relations between the 1950s and 2010s. At the London School of Economics (LSE) and Aberystwyth, the two centres of IR as a 'separate' subject, empire was removed from core IR curricula in the 1940s and 1950s, an erasure which coincided with the turn away from diplomatic history. By 1972 and the publication of *The Aberystwyth Papers*, the discussion of empire was transmuted into an essay on the 'Problems of the Developing World' written by economist and journalist Barbara Ward.[2]

At Oxford, Agnes Headlam-Morley held out against the effort to found IR as a separate subject and the history of empire was taught as international relations to politics students as late as 1976. Diplomatic historian Sibyl Crowe, for example, taught colonial policy and the relations between imperialism and inter-state relations as a core member of Oxford's PPE faculty from the late

1930s to late 1960s. She lectured on 'The Importance of the Imperial Issue in International Relations 1870–1914', 'Some Colonial Issues in *Weltpolitik, 1870–1914*', 'The French in North Africa', 'Imperialism and the Great Powers', 'The Colonial Background to European Diplomacy, 1871–1914', 'Some Modern Theories of Imperialism', and 'France and her Empires, 1870–1962'. Crowe's first book was *The Berlin West African Conference*. Because of an excessive teaching load, she extensively researched but never completed her book, *France and Algeria: a Colonial Perspective, 1830–1962*. Margery Perham, of course, was Oxford's, and then Britain's, foremost white teacher and thinker on empire from the 1930s to the 1960s, teaching and writing on colonial administration and empires in world-historical and comparative perspectives.

Neither Crowe nor Perham can in any sense be described as anticolonial thinkers. But neither would have demurred from Headlam-Morley's resistance to the single largest determiner of empire's (and women's) erasure from core IR curricula, the effort to develop a sociological 'theory' of international relations and the demotion of historical research. As discussed in chapter 10, when Rachel Wall proposed a new undergraduate paper in international relations in 1966 that incorporated imperialism, non-Eurocentric world histories, anticolonial nationalisms, and their major intellectual underpinnings, she was radically reforming and updating rather than fundamentally departing from the trajectory of (white) women-led historical international relations teaching at Oxford. Wall's course proposal was not adopted and by the 1970s her male colleagues rushed to make Oxford IR's teaching more theoretical, though they did not entirely remove history from the subject. Nonetheless, empire and its aftermaths, decolonisation and racial conflict at home, were increasingly inconceivable as core subjects of international relations in Britain and only gradually and partially restored when postcolonial IR scholars forced a more serious reckoning with the legacies of empire, especially after the 9/11 attacks.[3]

At the beginning of the 1950s, as already discussed, London-based members of the British Coordinating Committee for International Studies (BCISS), led by Charles Manning, set out to establish the separateness of international relations by defining its subject matter as 'international society'. At this moment and in this context, IR's constitutive Other was a caricature of history. We might think of the British Committee on the Theory of International Politics as a response to the failure of Manning's project both to establish the intellectual basis and justification for IR as a separate subject and to develop a coherent theory of international politics. When IR scholars in the United States were consulted on Manning's application to the Rockefeller Foundation to fund several specialist IR scholars in 1952, they did not understand what Manning meant by IR as a 'separate discipline'. They also doubted Manning's quality as a scholar.[4] In the US, IR was a subfield of political science. The main players at the 1954 Rockefeller Conference to develop a theory of international relations wanted to counter the new dominance of behaviourism in political science, not dissociate from that discipline as such.[5] With more Rockefeller money, historian Herbert Butterfield, a darling of American realism who was not very fond of archival work, led the British Committee equivalent.[6] The Committee purposely excluded Charles Manning, though not his concept of 'international society'.

In historical perspective, the most interesting and consequential fact about the British Committee is not how it fretted over American behaviourism, advocating instead for a so-called 'classical' approach more attentive to philosophy and history.[7] Nor is it that its accounts of the so-called 'expansion' of international society were provincial, conservative, and Eurocentric.[8] Nor is it even that the British Committee was organised as a white old boys' club from Oxbridge, London and Sussex, excluding even women contemporary and diplomatic historians, let alone people of colour, until Coral Bell defined herself in its terms. The most interesting thing about the British Committee was its role in disappearing *political* and *historical* analysis of colonial and neo-colonial relations by reducing empire to the remote past and contemporary anticolonial claims to a question of applied ethics.

Consider what some regard as an 'iconic' text of mid-century British IR, Herbert Butterfield and Martin Wight's 1966 edited volume *Diplomatic Investigations*, which was turned down by Cambridge University Press and eventually published by Allen & Unwin.[9] Assembled at the height of decolonisation, there is nothing on the British Empire, its history, current form, and legacies. Yet numerous essays use secondary sources to generalise about the medieval 'universal empire', the Holy Roman Empire, the empires of Alexander the Great, the Ts'in, the Moguls, the Swedes, the Ottomans, the Hapsburgs, Napoleon, and Imperial Germany, the Krupp empire, and Lenin's theory of imperialism. If the British Empire 'was never central to the early work of the English School', then only a constitutive erasure could sideline something of such historical and political importance for the context and supposed content of this 'seminal' piece of work.[10]

Members of the British Committee did not entirely ignore the world-historical fact of decolonisation.[11] This was a period of deep postcolonial contestation around global economic and political inequality, of growing debate on how to properly address the legacies of colonialism and white supremacy, and of powerful ideas and proposals for 'worldmaking after empire', including a New International Economic Order.[12] It was precisely against such claims that Adam Watson developed his version of the concept of international society in which 'there were indeed important continuities between the colonial and postcolonial international orders that held out hope for Britain'.[13] Explicitly borrowing from the 'racist–realism' of Alfred Thayer Mahan's concept of 'have-not' powers, and in common with his patron Charles Manning, Martin Wight argued that the 'Bandung powers and the Axis powers' had much in common. The defining feature of the so-called 'Afro-Asian' states demanding global reform was their inferiority complex, sense of resentment, and self-pity.[14] Manning similarly condemned 'Afro-Asians' for their refusal to countenance the merits of apartheid in South Africa. The 'Bandung confraternity', he claimed, had reduced the 'moral authority of the United Nations . . . to zero'.[15] 'If those powers have not consciously adopted Hitler's language, it must at least be admitted that Hitler did anticipate some of theirs'.[16]

'God forbid', pronounced white Australian Hedley Bull, 'that we should turn away from Eurocentric international and imperial history towards so-called anti-imperialist or national liberation accounts of the past'.[17] Sometimes seconded to the Foreign Office with his 'reassuringly realist' views on defence, during the 1960s and 1970s Bull duly reconceived anticolonial demands in terms of a tension between 'justice' and 'order'.[18] For Bull, deep postcolonial contestation could be minimally addressed by a limited wealth redistribution sufficient to co-opt the more powerful states of the 'global South'.[19] To avoid direct intellectual engagement with anti-imperial accounts of the past, the British Committee sidestepped historical and political analysis of the bloody history and legacies of the British Empire.

## A Cautious, Respectable Radical

Queen Elizabeth II became head of the British Isles, the imperial realms and the Commonwealth while visiting Kenya only weeks before its Land and Freedom Army began a guerilla campaign to end white settler rule. It was 1952 and Britain had been managing a succession of imperial crises in Palestine, Malaya, Cyprus, Aden, Oman, and Darfur. The Crown was not a bystander to the post-war crises of imperial government and decline. During and after the dissolution of the empire, Elizabeth II actively cultivated an image of (post)imperial benevolence, revelling in colonial symbols and encouraging the empire's children to love her, if not the institutions she represented. 'I cannot lead you into battle', she famously claimed in 1957. 'I do not give you laws or administer justice, but . . . I can give you my heart and my devotion'. The monarchy's vast riches and jewels from slavery and empire were only the most visible element of this extractive institution. Yet, the pomp and symbolism of the Crown were central ideological cement during the transition from British Empire to Commonwealth. Elizabeth II represented and performed an acceptable version of this transition, receiving Prime Minister Kwame Nkrumah at Balmoral weeks after Ghana's independence and inviting him to join the Privy Council, her formal body of advisors.

During the 1940s and 1950s, both monarchical and imperial rule were redefined as public service under the guidance of two women. Elizabeth II oversaw the transformation of monarchy and Dame Margery Perham was the empire's most effective publicist and moralist. The 'heart of this empire', she wrote in 1944, 'must now express itself less in power than in service'.[20] 'How far is Margery Perham Miss Mother Country?', her successor as Oxford's Reader in Colonial Administration was asked.[21]

The scholar, broadcaster, advisor, and educator of colonial officials is credited with producing 'the most accurate and far-reaching critique of imperial rule', at least by a white British thinker.[22] She is most often read as 'Britain's conscience on Africa'.[23] In the public sphere, and for successive colonial governments, she was the most significant British thinker on the empire in Africa and on the wider process of decolonisation. With her 'encyclopaedic knowledge of the empire and its administration',[24] Perham's audiences were not only scholars, government officials, colonial administrators, and wider public opinion in Britain, but numerous African interlocuters and sometimes collaborators. She was active in official and unofficial colonial and sometimes anticolonial networks and organisations, both governmental and non-governmental. Her assistant Martin Wight thought 'her supreme merit' was 'that she never identified herself either with the C.O. [Colonial Office], or the Labour Party, or the Oxford ivory tower, or the African nationalists. Each of these has accused her, falsely, of being a stooge of the others, but she has maintained an essential detachment from and sympathy with all of them'.[25] As already discussed, she had connections with the League of Coloured Peoples, the African Bureau, the London Group on African Affairs, Friends of Africa, the Fabian Colonial Bureau, the League of Nations and United Nations, the International African Institute, the Royal African Society, and Chatham House.

Perham is usually read as a 'good British liberal' and 'fair-minded' in her early advocacy for African education and development, critique of white settlers, relatively early acceptance of self-government, and admission of 'some exploitation and oppression' in the colonies.[26] She was also the most effective thinker of British exceptionalism in the moment of imperial decline, initially and most often recasting decolonisation as the natural culmination of British rule rather than its repudiation. As 'both researcher and protagonist',[27] she most powerfully intellectualised and emotionally performed white Britons' moral reckoning with empire and its loss. She was quick to see the Queen as a powerful counter to anticolonial critique, which she conceived as a form of racial resentment.[28] Britain would have to 'go on paying the penalty of their former domination in patient understanding', claimed Perham in 1960, 'and in such gestures of respect between equals as the British Sovereign has recently paid to Dr Nkrumah in entertaining him at Balmoral. Altruism has, indeed, become the best policy. But something warmer than mere calculation will be needed to secure success'.[29] In 1961, Elizabeth II danced with Nkrumah in Accra.

Perham was *sui generis* in the ease and the degree in which she traversed academe, practical administration on the colonial ground, and high policy and public opinion. Martin Wight thought this made her 'a uniquely English figure. A female academic heavy-weight who has been an influence on public policy. America has had its Dorothy Thompsons and Eleanor Roosevelts, but they are mere journalists. Who has France or Germany had of the kind?'[30] Like Eileen Power, Perham was a prolific and experienced broadcaster, delivering over one hundred BBC broadcasts across four decades.[31] She wrote over 150 articles for and letters to *The Times*. Only Claudia Jones, discussed in the next chapter, had comparable influence on her main audience of Black Britons in the 1950s and early 1960s. Yet Perham enjoyed all the resources and prestige of a semi-official publicist. She was duly rewarded in the way of the British Establishment, receiving a CBE in the 1948 honours list and a Damehood in 1965 as commander of the order usually reserved for diplomats.[32] She received numerous honorary doctorates and, unusually for a British woman working on international relations, was elected a Fellow of the British Academy. The Royal African Society awarded her its Wellcome Medal and the Royal Scottish Geographical Society its Mungo Park Medal. She was elected President of the African Studies Association.

Beyond calling for more native welfare and self-government, there is a far deeper sense in which Perham was a 'good British liberal'.[33] She perfected the art of deflection on liberalism's trickiest subject of empire through performing the 'restraint to efface ourselves' in the face of loathing toward Britain.[34] Perham was both praised and condemned for acknowledging the obvious fact that, as Martinican poet, writer, and politician Aimé Césaire put it, 'no one colonizes innocently'.[35] Perham's task was to show that there was something called British idealism and it was not 'merely a cloak in which we try to hide our complete self-interest from the world, and indeed from ourselves'.[36]

Perham at once recognised and relativised some of the worst colonial crimes, particularly those of white settlers, through moralism, liberal antiracism, psychological introspection, and continual engagement with African critics of empire, executing a constant back and forth between admission of mistakes and self-praise. In the midst of white supremacist attacks on Black Britons in the early 1960s, she pointed to Martin Luther King, to the Black Muslim movement, and the writing of James Baldwin: 'all these have lately opened their minds and ours to what men can suffer for the offence of being black'.[37] As already suggested, no British IR thinker at mid-century attempted to engage so extensively with figures now associated with Black internationalist and anticolonial thought. Through this engagement, Perham developed a political psychology of anticolonial critique as racial humiliation and resentment.[38] In turn, Perham became the subject of anticolonial critique herself, and framed the politics and history of the empire's loss into a question of white British psychology: 'what does it mean to *us*? . . . Do we feel shrunken in the face of the last, almost final, African loss?'[39] Perham's gender was inseparable from her position as the Establishment's authoritative voice on empire, but equally important was her conscious racial positioning, as well as her persona as 'that rare and precious thing, a cautious, respectable radical'.[40]

## Mistakes Were Made: On Mau Mau

During World War II, Margery Perham accelerated her advocacy for a new phase of 'cooperation and friendship' with colonial populations, including attempting to raise up the voices of 'good' African nationalists while trying to model engagement with younger radicals who 'according to their habit', she claimed, were 'somewhat noisy and tiresome as they march along their road to self-government'.[41] Perham found her ideal collaborator in the post-war Labour Government, which had been developing plans to stabilise and sustain imperial rule through economic development in what Perham called 'tropical East Ends'.[42] Perham later reflected that 'Labour men', less tainted by the historic stain of empire compared to the Tories, could remedy colonial abuses and bring forward 'gradual emancipation' with more 'detachment, almost a sense of innocence', and were a vast improvement on the highly theoretical Marxist critics.[43] Perham thus happily cooperated with Labour's Colonial Sec-retary, Arthur Creech Jones, who became her close friend and appointed her to several committees, particularly those related to education. African students were the vanguard of the struggle for political rights and Perham devoted con-siderable energies to developing universities in Africa and facilitating travel to study in Britain.[44]

In her introduction to Nigerian journalist and lawyer Obafemi Awolowo's 1946 federalist book *Path to Nigerian Freedom*, Perham insisted that the youn-ger, more radical generation could not be ignored or dismissed and were en-tirely right to hold colonial authorities to account for 'any faults or mistakes'.[45] Britons should be reading and sympathising with future leaders like Awolowo, she claimed, who were 'relatively moderate' 'rational' and 'constructive'.[46] Because Britain imposed its will by force on 'once ignorant and helpless' Afri-cans, Britain was, in the end, responsible for their inevitable reactions to colo-nial rule, even the intemperate and violent.[47] But *educated* Africans must now be held to a higher political standard if they claim to have 'come up to an age of discretion', Perham tutored. They can 'no longer ask indulgence for irratio-nal, childish or reckless words or actions', by which she meant attacks on the British Empire *tout court*. The critique of 'imperialism' in general, though 'in-tellectually enervating', will 'depress' those allies in Britain who think 'Africans are ready for political progress'.[48] Still, in the mid-1940s, Perham thought Brit-ain should not be 'unduly distressed' if anticolonial critique was 'coloured by resentment or even enlivened with abuse'.[49]

Not so by the mid-1950s. With the Mau Mau's guerilla campaign in Kenya, Perham was much less sanguine, and occasionally expressed irritation at the 'often blind and dangerous discontents' who were agitating against British rule.[50] Local instances of anticolonial resistance, she observed, were now part of a 'slow expanding interlocking pattern' linking Africa, Britain, the Com-monwealth, and the wider world 'all affecting each other . . . suddenly quicken-ing to a speed almost beyond control'.[51] Perham joined other white British thinkers in the 1950s in viewing the UN as a forum in which Britain was con-stantly 'bayed at'. She listed an 'eager pack' of communist and Arab states, South American republics, India, Russia, 'and nearly all the ex-dependencies'.[52] It bothered Perham that hypocritical outside critics 'perpetually' forced Brit-ain to remind everyone about the fact of African backwardness 'at a time when all energies are needed for a vigorous partnership in building up united and self-supporting states'.[53] Such was the burden of late empire. If Britain wished to keep African states 'under predominantly western and Christian influence',[54] then the organised 'Third World' states at the UN and at the Afro-Asian Conference in Bandung was further evidence in support of Perham's agenda for imperial reform.

Britain was losing control of the pace of decolonisation, above all in Kenya. Reassessing her debate with Elspeth Huxley about the status and obligations of white settlers, discussed in chapter 2, Perham stressed that she had been right all along; settler domination was untenable, yet she did not expect that her 'fears would be justified so soon and so violently'.[55] White settlers were to blame for the armed revolt of the Kikuyu people, Kenya's largest ethnic group, but London must take its share of guilt; 'we . . . are very much responsible for what the Kikuyu are to-day'.[56] The settlers might feel under siege. However, as she pointed out in her foreword to Tom Mboya's *The Kenya Question*, this 'is a siege of the high citadel of privilege and domination'.[57] General secretary of the Kenya Federation of Labour, Mboya was a Kenyan economic reformer who played a central role in independence negotiations and in post-independence politics until his assassination in 1969.

For Perham, Mboya was an ideal African leader, 'rounded out' by a year at Ruskin College, the adult education centre in Oxford, and links to the Fabian Colonial Bureau. He was 'very rational', unemotional, a 'fluent speaker', with a 'quiet restrained manner'.[58] If Britons did not take men like Mboya seriously, then 'others, less rational and experienced . . . may be driven back to the underground method and blow up the hidden fires of discontent'.[59] The wider world 'was shouting at' Kenyan Africans 'that colonial rule was oppressive', as if Kikuyu had not already realised that themselves.[60]

As if to provide 'balance' to her critique of white settlers, Perham was unsparing in her characterisation of the Mau Mau. She repeated racist tropes about its 'bestial' initiation oaths and terror campaign against settlers on their 'isolated farms', 'women alone with their children'.[61] Perham frequently travelled to Kenya during Britain's pacification war and visited 'hard core' fighters in concentration camps. She recalled 'the dark look upon their faces, which seemed to add an extra darkness to the colour of their skin, and their look of settled hatred'.[62] Perham endorsed 'ethnopsychiatrist' J. C. Carothers's diagnosis that the Mau Mau guerilla campaign was a traumatic reaction to old Kikuyu ways of life coming into contact with the West's 'superior civilization',[63] which echoed her own views on anticolonial 'reaction'.[64] Mass discontent was a product of psychological maladjustment to 'the great facts of history

and geography that have exposed isolated and tribal Africa to the sudden dis-
locating effects of twentieth-century civilization'.[65] Ordinary Kikuyu could not
comprehend long-term modernising forces and thus attributed their inferior
social and economic status to 'the evil will of other men, of colonial rulers and,
above all, colonial settlers'.[66] Anticolonialism reduced to a 'revolt against
inferiority'.[67]

If the 'uncomfortable processes of de-colonization', Perham wrote in 1954,
was to be 'less negative, less abrupt, less of a retreat and more of a planned
manoeuvre', then Britain needed to learn the right lessons from the Mau Mau
uprising.[68] She thought something good might come from 'the agony of Mau
Mau', that is, vindication of her call for major imperial reform.[69] The British
might 'hate ever to admit that the black-mail of violence can pay', but this was
the truth.[70] '*Honesty demands the admission* that the Mau Mau movement has
to its credit' forced Britain to initiate 'a long list of reforms and of plans all
aimed at offering to Africans a fuller share in the new way of life'.[71]

Confusing her advocacy for reform with the reality in Kenya, Perham described the process of 'villagization', meaning the mass forced displacement of
over one million Kikuyu into eight hundred punitive camps and the burning
down of their former homes, as 'errant tribes' being 'coaxed to accept the best
of western European experience—the pride of ownership and the amenities
of village life centred round school, church, and village hall'.[72] In fact, over
150,000 Kikuyu were detained in prison camps and large numbers were tortured.[73] If released from interrogation, detainees were sent to transit and
labour camps and/or 'new villages', administered by prison and 'rehabilitation'
officers.[74] Even Kenya's British attorney general at the time described the British practice as 'distressingly reminiscent of conditions in Nazi Germany or
Communist Russia'.[75]

Nowhere did Perham give a full and proper accounting of the conduct of
Britain's military campaign in Kenya, despite her frequent visits during the
'Emergency' and lengthy discussions and correspondence with its principal
architects. Instead, she expressed 'regret' for British excesses, but only when
balanced against the Mau Mau's 'corrupted savagery' and Britain's 'rehabilitation' programme, which she never admitted was a sham.[76] Instead she could
only claim that Britain failed in its normally (relatively) higher standards of
imperial altruism and insisted that anything that could be construed as altruistic 'must be set on one side of our picture to balance the figures on the other,
the murdered and massacred, the thousand and more sent to the hangman and
the 50,000 [*sic*] behind the wires'.[77] She chided Kenyan intellectuals and

political activists for critiquing Britain's crimes. Mboya said it was 'absurd' to suggest the Mau Mau movement resulted from 'too rapid a transition from primitive to a modern complex society'.[78] Instead, his account centered on the land problem, with white settlers reserving the most fertile land for themselves, and on Britain's collective punishment of Kikuyu, arbitrary and mass arrests, and brutal screening methods. Yet, for Perham, Mboya failed to place Britain's empire in the context of the longer and universal history of domination of the weak by the strong nor discuss Britain's philanthropy: 'insofar as Britain has failed in Kenya', she claimed, 'it has been in applying those high standards of imperial altruism which the world owes mainly to her initiative'.[79] Because Kenyan academic Gatheru R. Mugo repeated 'the common exaggeration about Kenya Africans' loss of land' he was not yet able to 'apply his scholarly standards to colonialism'.[80]

Even by the early 1960s, when the scale of British atrocities in Kenya was widely known, Perham acknowledged and assimilated anticolonial critique by performing moral anguish at crimes that were increasingly impossible to deny. In 1963, she wrote the foreword to Josiah Mwangi Kariuki's book-length memoir of life in Kenya before, during and after the 'Emergency', including torture in British detention.[81] At the time, 'Mau Mau' Detainee was considered unique in the literature on Mau Mau as 'testimony of a Kikuyu who stood firm in his commitment to the revolt'.[82] Kariuki had been a liaison officer in Mau Mau and later became private secretary to Jomo Kenyatta and a member of parliament, and was assassinated in 1975.

For Perham, Kariuki was another ideal interlocuter, with his 'modesty', 'balance' and 'healing desire for reconciliation'.[83] She acknowledged that his book, and her own foreword, could be used as anti-British propaganda because, admitting what was already known, 'some of the authorities . . . were guilty of acts of negligence, harsh-ness and cruelty' with 'some incidents of torture' and 'violent abuses'.[84] The admission itself, in Perham's hand, becomes evidence of imperial benevolence. The real problem with the abuse was that it delayed the moment when Africans were finally able to 'distinguish the services and disservices' that Britain had 'brought to Africa'.[85]

In exchange for her performance of limited regret, Perham insisted that her African interlocuters adopt a 'balanced view'; recognise 'degrees of guilt', and the unprecedented and 'pathological atmosphere in Kenya'.[86] Yes, Kariuki was tortured by officers 'at their wits' end', but he had also appealed to British 'standards of law, justice and humanity'.[87] Abuses were not 'calculated', 'sustained', or 'planned', but random and only 'during *a few years* of exceptional fear and crisis'.[88] In Perham's words, '*if they were sometimes* treated with brutality . . . the sincere attempts to apply psychological and other redemptive methods should also be remembered'.[89]

With her direct engagement with Kenyan intellectuals, Perham's intention was not exactly to vindicate Britain, though she was happy to generate some sympathy. Torture, but some Mau Mau fighters 'ceased to be normal human beings'.[90] Brutality, but 'humanity tempered violence'.[91] This was Perham's constant rhetorical technique and political bargain: she would recognise wrongdoing, express regret, engage with, absorb, withstand anticolonial critique. This was always in exchange for a 'balanced' view that also centred colonial emotions. British 'people have struggled, admittedly with varying success, to maintain a standard of humanity in their empire'.[92] As she pointed out her famous BBC Reith Lectures in 1961, 'we too have our feelings . . . we are not political eunuchs'.[93]

## Explaining Anticolonial Critique at Empire's End

Margery Perham's BBC producer thought her finest radio broadcasts were when '*the agony shows through*', no more so than in her commentary on the Nigerian Civil War.[94] In 1968, Perham moved from supporting Biafran secessionists to calling for their surrender to the Nigerian state, leading Nigerian writer Chinua Achebe to accuse Perham of reducing genocide to 'a matter of papers which she already has in large quantities in her study'.[95] Perham was clearly hurt by Achebe's suggestion that 'the Biafran cause means no more to me than a vast pile of documentation in my study'.[96] She was 'Britain's conscience on Africa' because she performed emotional, as well as intellectual, labour. Members of the West African Students Union protesting her talks, African intellectuals accusing her of being an apologist for empire—this was all necessary to Perham's persona of stoically surviving and countering attacks, whether from white settlers or Black critics. She had admired Lord Lugard for his 'intense power to feel and to suffer'.[97] Now Perham could display the moral qualities she argued all Britons needed to display in the empire's dying days: 'the power of sympathy of understanding to reach across racial divisions—the patience to bear the attacks of crude young nationalistic groups—the restraint to efface ourselves'.[98]

Perham's Reith Lectures delivered on the BBC in October and November 1961, republished as *Colonial Reckoning*, are best known as her effort to reconcile Britain to the loss of empire. Her BBC editor thought that 'when the task of adjusting public consciousness and public debate to the end of empire was at its most urgent . . . her influence was supreme'.[99] But these and other broadcasts and writings in the 1960s can also be read as Perham's performance of emotional, intellectual, and psychological labour for what she saw as her other main audience and set of interlocuters, university-educated Africans. Perham repeatedly returned to the question of anticolonial critique, imploring white Britons to take seriously the psychology of racial difference and the effects of racial domination. In her own attempt to do so, Perham became a theorist of racial resentment. That Britain had 'relinquished' power to African nationalists was not enough—psychologically, politically, or racially. The anticolonial attacks kept coming. 'The cult of anti-colonialism could not be shrugged off', even after the empire's end.[100] Violent reaction against inferior status, Perham insisted, was shaping racial, class and international relations. 'There is no escape from the issues aroused by this attack' because it concerned the stability of the postcolonial world order. Erasing the political economy of reparations for colonial pillage, the age of self-determination was also the age of resentment. 'It is not enough now for nations to be independent: if they are poor and weak they blame the wealthier and stronger states, at once asking their help and at the same time trying jealously to undermine their power'.[101]

## 'Three-quarters of our problems today are psychological'

Margery Perham had long maintained that decolonisation was 'implicit' in Britain's imperial history; it was in the very nature of the British Empire to dissolve itself.[102] What better validation of the distinctiveness and the success of the imperial project than the desire and increasing ability of Africans to follow in the steps of the white dependencies and join an association, or family, of Commonwealth nations?[103] Still, in the early 1960s, she suggested Africans were following the precedent set by white dominions; their demands for self-governance rooted in political principles 'learned very largely from Britain herself'.[104] Yet, as postcolonial scholar Priyamvada Gopal has recently pointed out, the Mau Mau also forced Perham to admit that freedom was not given to Africans in an orderly process of 'colonial abdication'.[105] It was *seized*. Nkrumah, in particular, Perham wrote, must be given 'the credit of having broken the spell of African quiescence in Britain's leisurely constitutional programme'.[106] Nationalist leaders 'can congratulate themselves for forcing the pace. But'—and there was always a but—'much depends on the way concessions were made'.[107] Nonetheless, it was only a 'half-truth', she admitted, that decolonisation was 'merely the fulfilment of our own policy and promise'. Stating the obvious, Britain was 'obliged to make concessions we never meant to make so soon'.[108]

Perham duly contextualised African decolonisation as a confluence of overlapping local, regional, international, and global forces. Yet when Perham stated that newly independent Ghana could not be equated 'with the Tudors or the Congo with the War of the Roses', or that 'our immensely gradualist history cannot be exactly fitted into theirs',[109] she was not exactly acknowledging distinctly African political and intellectual traditions of resistance and freedom. She was exculpating Britain from the effects of the empire's end, drawing a distinction between the slow development of bourgeois freedoms in Britain and the emergence of postcolonial dictatorships in Africa. Africa's 'different historical trajectory'[110] was towards dictatorship.

For Perham, the speed and the nature of African decolonisation was above all a story of racial resentment, the 'mine' that had blown up colonialism.[111] Perham's concession, then, was also a moment of differentiation and deflection. She at once conceded the basic fact that African peoples had forced the pace and insisted on their psychological *need* to know that independence was not 'given but . . . taken'.[112] To admit the obvious, that colonised peoples had won their freedoms, was cathartic, to help heal what Perham saw as one of the most significant legacies of empire—Black racial resentment. This was why, even after independence, she claimed in 1951, Britain still had to deal with 'unvarying but highly spiced denunciation',[113] including the charge of 'neo-colonialism'.[114]

Perham's account of the pace and ferocity of anticolonialism repeatedly returned to what she saw as the shame of the Black 'racial experience'.[115] One of the most common themes across her writing, from the fascist invasion of Ethiopia to the Mau Mau uprising and after, was the 'shock and distress' of young Black men on discovering their 'retarded position among the peoples of the world'.[116] She never questioned the 'fundamental fact' of backwardness that made Africa's subjugation both inevitable and so apparently easy for the British. The 'un-conscious mass' of African peoples were largely acquiescent in the initial period of colonization;[117] 'revolts', she claimed, 'were very few, and there does not appear to have been much sense of indignity at being ruled'.[118] However, by the 1930s, educated Africans 'reached the stage of world consciousness'[119] and experienced a deep sense of shame, personal humiliation, and 'angry blame' at their standing in the world, especially their *racial* inferiority. They experienced an 'almost intolerable anger or sorrow'.[120] The resulting bitterness was projected onto the most obvious and easiest target, which Perham variously characterised as 'colonialism', the 'white man', and later 'the West'.[121] Anticolonial 'denunciation of the colonial régime' is 'essential to Africans both as a political springboard and as a racial assertion'.[122]

Seen this way, for Perham, anticolonialism and immediate self-government were questions of racial dignity. The problem for the new generation of nationalist or pan-Africanist leaders, Perham claimed, was that there was no real nation to mobilise. The basic political units were tribes, not nations, and African nationalism was entirely elite-led. However, charismatic and 'flamboyant leaders',[123] like Kwame Nkrumah, Julius Nyerere, and Jomo Kenyatta, understood that freedom from the 'stigma of inferiority' was 'a powerful world force'.[124] Their years of anticolonial activism and imprisonment had given them not so much political capital as 'racial capital'.[125] Hence, to destroy the passivity of the masses, to break 'the crust of habitual subservience', ordinary Africans were mobilised along the lines of 'racial feeling'.[126] Content enough with British rule for fifty years, Perham claimed, Africans were now told that their status was 'shameful'.[127] For African nationalists, 'it was not so much . . . that the British had come to rule the Ibo or the Luo . . . No, it was white men who had mastered black men . . . all over Africa and all over the world'.[128] The deeper and more sudden realisation of racial inferiority, Perham observed, the more violent the reaction. The quality of colonial government, lamented the tutor of colonial administrators, 'seems to make no difference to the violence of the new rejection'.[129]

This was Perham's explanation for why Britain was such a target of reaction. France had given educated Africans greater social and political status.[130] More than once, Perham pointed to the transnational Francophone literary and political movement of the 1930s, *négritude*, and its notion of a special African personality, suggesting there was nothing comparable in the Anglophone anticolonial tradition.[131] She cited poet–politician and then president of Senegal Léopold Senghor's claim that *négritude* emerged from French revolutionary traditions, and Jean Paul Sartre's assertion that Africans had turned the 'intellectual weapons' of the colonisers against them.[132] In the context of Perham's longstanding engagements with African nationalist thought it is not so astonishing that she read verses from Senghor and translated David Diop's *Coups de Pilon* in her Reith Lectures.[133] It supported her contrast between racial resentment in the French and British empires. It is also why she then turned to Indian writer Nirad Chaudhuri's *Autobiography* and his recollection of attending an opera in Calcutta among 'the well-dressed English audience . . . he was seized with such a ferocity of hate', Perham relayed to her British audience, 'that he longed to drop a bomb and kill them all'.[134]

Perham also read new African-led research on African civilisations through her terms of racial assertion and pride. In 1942, she had noted that everywhere British 'explorers' went in Africa, there was 'a fully functioning society which met all the main needs of man', however 'primitive': leaders, markets, manufactures, cultivation and the arts.[135] Yet in 1951, she argued that Africa was 'without writing and so without recorded history'.[136] She was thus the first target of critique in Nigerian historian K. O. Dike's essay 'African History and Self-Government'. Despite there being 'no people without a culture and civilization', Perham falsely assumed that 'no other culture or standard of progress is valid except' her own, Dike claimed.[137] In the early 1940s, Dike complained to his undergraduate tutors at the University of Aberdeen that there were no courses on African history. He declined the offer to attend summer classes with Margery Perham in Oxford, likely because her African history was really colonial administration.[138] Years later, Perham acknowledged that some of her writings could be criticised in light of new scholarship on 'the lineaments *here and there* of civilizations [in Africa], ancient, varied, shifting, obscure, isolated, but claiming our respect'.[139] Yet African writers were still more likely to rebuke Perham, she opined, because their 'individual self-respect and their necessary cult of a new pride and self-confidence . . . political and racial . . . demand the support of a high concept of the African civilisation which, they claim, colonial nations have both injured and defamed'.[140] She declined W.E.B. Du Bois's invitation to advise on his new encyclopaedia on African history, claiming lack of expertise.[141] Yet she was clearly doubtful that such African civilisation existed.

Anticolonialism, then, for Perham, was less about freedom than 'dignity', a dignity she understood in racial and highly sexualised terms.[142] She speculated that the 'supreme racial compensation' for young African men studying in the metropole was 'sexual intercourse' with 'white women'.[143] But sex, specifically fear of race-mixing, was also central to Perham's theory of racism and imperialism itself: 'the intrusion of Europe . . . caused the full awakening of the latent potentialities of Africa, the dark sleeping beauty, even though the intrusion was a rape rather than a kiss'.[144] In the 1940s, she tried to explain (away) racism as at least partially rooted in white male fear of 'race mixture' and an assumed desire of African men for white women.[145] In the 1950s, she pointed to the 'abnormal, haunting fear' among white South Africans about sexual assaults by Black men, which were not borne out by statistics.[146]

Still, in the 1960s, Perham characterised African racialism as a 'counter-racialism to the original, and *perhaps understandable*, racial attitude of the white man when confronted with tribal Africa'.[147] She identified white men's more general 'pathological, sometimes subconscious fear' for 'his women' combined with fear 'for the future of his race'.[148] White supremacy as white male sexual insecurity, which Perham attempted to allay: to ordinary, as opposed to educated, African men 'white women are not necessarily objects of desire' and African nationalism will likely produce an 'anti-white solidarity' stigmatising inter-marriage 'from the black as from the white side'.[149] The 'coloured world' should accordingly be more understanding of the racial anxieties of the 'very tiny' white 'minority' in Africa.[150] Nonetheless, for Perham, a generalised white male fear linked settler violence in South Africa, Rhodesia, and Kenya, and white mob violence in London, 'with the news of occasional retaliatory orgies of the raping of white women in the Congo'.[151]

Perham's broader point was that anticolonial critique was only political on the surface. Something deeper, more psychological, was at stake in this act of Black racial assertion, that 'only psychological treatment will satisfy'.[152] In 1952, she even argued that colonised Africans 'are not suffering from oppression or from such extreme poverty and congestion as in India. The problem is, above all, one of political psychology'.[153] Two years later, she claimed that 'three-quarters of our problems today are psychological'.[154] So conceived, anticolonialism was less a product of colonial exploitation, material and objective, than elite African men dealing with an inferiority complex. Anticolonial criticism becomes performative, expressive, and opportunistic, 'playing up on every possible cause of discontent'.[155] If the new unifying force was a general discontent at inferior racial status, then every grievance had to be reframed in racial terms.[156] Colonial crimes are reduced to a stage on which Black men assert themselves and their racial identity: anticolonialism as male *ressentiment*. This is why, Perham suggested, otherwise reasonable figures such as Tanzanian activist and politician Julius Nyerere occasionally posed as a radical anticolonialist, to 'prove his independence'.[157] Perham read Nyerere as psychologically ambivalent: 'Instead of being repelled, therefore, we should be understanding'.[158] If the burden on African people was racial inferiority, then 'it is *the burden of the Western powers* that they must pay for their century or more of domination . . . by being the objects against which their former political or economic subjects must lever themselves up into the desired equality'.[159] Perham took on this task as her own personal burden.

FIGURE 8.1. Margery Perham, by John Bulmer 1963. Permission Getty Images

Through the 1940s and 1950s, Perham had performed the necessary task of engaging with critics of Britain's empire. By the 1960s, there was also something therapeutic in her attempt to remedy anticolonial 'hatred'. Without a remedy 'there could be no redemption' for anticolonial leaders or, for Britain, no peace from the baying mob at the UN.[160] As she had already identified in 1935, Ethiopian freedom from Italian colonial rule could 'give Africans all through the world the thing they most need for their own sakes and our own—racial self-respect'.[161] Perham's admission that Africans forced the pace of decolonisation was a statement of the obvious. The way she framed the admission was inseparable from her diagnosis of Africans needing to 'strike the defiant posture of demanding, of taking, of never—this is surely understandable—of appearing to *receive* their freedom'.[162] But Perham also had to make this palatable for white Britons in their own racial identity crisis. Again and again, Perham explained anticolonialism as 'the desire to assert the new dignity of the race' and insisted that 'the psychological difficulties' were not 'all on the African side'.[163]

Perham mounted a defence of all that could be seen as constructive and noble in the empire ('we too have our feelings') even if only in historical and comparative perspective. In setting out a balanced 'colonial account', Perham might mitigate British shame but also free African leaders of their violent and self-destructive indignation. If anticolonialism was racial reassertion, then the discourse of empire as 'progression in virtue'[164] was necessary for the wounded white ego and white 'racial self-respect' at empire's end.[165] Perham was trying to exculpate Britain, yet she must also be read as attempting in her deeply flawed way to repair—psychologically and racially—what she saw as the damage of racial humiliation caused by white domination, a resentment at humiliation that was 'almost', though not entirely, 'incurable'.[166] 'African nationalism ... demands its compensation for this long inequality'.[167] Perham's series of admissions and acceptances of colonial wrongs can be read in light of her claim that 'the crushed mind and the wounded dignity have to recover', but only in exchange for exculpating Britain, which was dealing with its own dignity crisis.[168]

### The 'Balance Sheet': On Britain's Wounded Dignity

The moral and political 'balance sheet' approach to the history of the empire is controversial, to put it mildly. To look for the 'positive' about an empire built on the transatlantic trade in the enslaved, genocides of native populations, mass killing and death, theft of land and natural resources, and the long-term impoverishment of millions is to seek excuse for the inexcusable.[169] Yet this was Perham's method of defending Britain's imperial record: acknowledging, then contextualising, normalising, and relativising its crimes. She was clear that the single biggest crime of empire—slavery and the trade in persons— was an 'unquestionable, widespread, long continuing and highly profitable crime'.[170] Yet the real story, for Perham, was slavery's end, abolished not because it clashed with new free trade ideas, but due to moral progress in Britain.[171] The tradition of informed and liberal public opinion in Britain was a 'strong palliative, if not a cure, for the evils to which empire was prone'.[172] The horrors of slavery are repurposed to her overall claim that 'imperialism is a mixed and changing force': humane when it ended slavery; harsher during the nineteenth century; and more sympathetic by the 1940s.[173] An empire built on slavery becomes 'the most humane and considerate of modern colonial nations'.[174]

Blanket denunciations of 'colonialism', Perham insisted, conveyed nothing of the enormous variations in time and place of Britain's 350-year empire, nor its varying purpose: trade, security, immigration, power, prestige, and philanthropy. British empire was the most 'checked and softened by humane ideals' in history,[175] not only in ending the trade in the enslaved but in its infamous method of indirect rule, which she had popularised and updated in her 1937 book, *Native Administration in Nigeria*.[176] Indirect rule was 'a synthesis' between European and African culture; a 'mean between the extremes' of over-regulation and *laissez-faire*, a paternalistic 'compound of realism and humanity'.[177] Local chiefs were permitted to govern 'their' peoples, according to their own customs and rules, as long as they submitted to the overarching rule of the British, a form of 'decentralised despotism'.[178] What was 'remarkable' about a figure such as Lugard, Governor General of Nigeria, Perham claimed, 'was that he used punishment so rarely and with so much deliberation'.[179] The Elizabethans were cruel, though 'to-day Africans are subjected to our beneficence as well as to our power'.[180]

In *Colonial Reckoning*, Perham also turned to the old tradition of *realpolitik* as the ultimate justification for violent domination. In all recorded history, Perham claimed, it was the norm that the strong dominate the weak; the 'old law of the jungle . . . ruled international relations through all the years of our empire until the very latest'.[181] Yet these latest years redeemed much of what went before. Where the Roman Empire ended 'amidst cries of despair from the intelligentsia; ours ends among almost universal cries of satisfaction'.[182] In one of the most dishonest remarks across her entire body of work, erasing the scale and brutality of the violence in Malaya and Kenya, Perham claimed that decolonisation occurred 'with so little bloodshed and even disorder'.[183] The main problem was the timing and lack of preparation. The transfer of power came at 'ramshackle speed', a 300-year-old empire ended in the space of a lifetime.[184] Perham constantly lamented that anticolonialism 'cut short' Britain's 'slow and steady work'.[185] Again, she adopted a confessional tone, admitting it was wrong to think the British could regulate decolonisation's speed.[186] By 1970, she was willing to concede one serious error, failing to allow Africans 'to take over the senior posts', a policy she had advocated.[187] Yet she also praised Britain's skill in creating states able to take power 'from the very day of our abdication'.[188] The overall purpose of Perham's back and forth between self-criticism and self-praise was to assure Britons that 'we have little need to be ashamed of our record of emancipation'.[189] Once Africans had become politically and racially aware, little more could be done. In the end, Perham's balance sheet amounted to a defence of liberal despotism: 'If it was bad who would have done it better?'[190]

## Conclusion

The disappearance of political and historical analysis of colonial and neo-colonial relations in the more theoretical work of the British Committee on the Theory of International Politics was not by random chance, a product of Herbert Butterfield's preference to 'avoid the world of practical politics', a discomfort with 'policy relevance', and desire to take 'a broad brush' approach, which he did not consistently follow.[191] The British Committee and its heirs were practising avoidance behaviour, escapism into the discussion of foreign empire's past not Britain's present, to dodge the full implications of the encounter with anticolonial intellectual and political demands in Britain and around the world. Anticolonial demands were historically oriented conceptions of justice and internationalism premised on the continuing legacies of imperial and racial domination. Hedley Bull's turn to normative theory, in contrast, was a watered down (middle ground) approach to global justice, deflecting more radical contemporary demands for a transformation of global political and economic relations.[192] We might think of this as IR's less sophisticated version of liberal theory's Rawlsian turn in the 1970s.[193]

The men of the British Committee may have been averse to American-style political science, but their preference for the so-called 'classical' approach, their devotion to remote imperial history and ethics, occurred at a very particular moment of the British Empire's reconfiguration and homecoming. The committee's work began at the height of Britain's attempt to delay and subvert decolonisation in Africa, the Caribbean, and Asia, was premised on the fiction that the period after the end of World War II to the 1970s is best defined as the transition from a world of empires to a worldwide system or 'society' of sovereign states. The corollary 'domestic' fiction was that the first decades after World War II were defined by Britain's transition from an empire to a nation-state; decolonisation was something that happened elsewhere.

The sublimation of empire was also an erasure of the influence and ideas of the leading white British thinker on empire at its end, Margery Perham. The committee's allegedly deepest thinker, Martin Wight, first encountered Perham as an 'aunt-figure out of P.G. Wodehouse, whirling her nephew and his friends off to the river, or to an evening at Stratford, always pointing to the Higher Life'. He thought she possessed 'impeccable political judgement . . . I doubt that there is a single public political issue on which the opinion of posterity will show her as having been erratic. She was anti-appeasement, anti-Munich, coolly objective about Soviet atrocities . . . anti-Suez'.[194] She was the single biggest influence on Wight's views on empire; his first three books on colonial legislatures were written under her direction and patronage.[195]

As Bull acknowledged in a letter to Perham, Wight's work for her on colonialism 'relate to his view of International Relations'.[196] Wight himself claimed in a lecture edited and posthumously published by his wife, Gabrielle Wight, 'the "Theory of Mankind", for want of a better name, verges upon a theory of colonial administration . . . Non-self-governing peoples, colonial populations, were barbarians who had been absorbed into international society but not yet been digested . . . The question of relations with barbarians was a political problem forming a bridge between international relations and colonial administrations'.[197] More specifically, as IR scholar Robbie Shilliam has pointed out, Wight's ethical Christian emphasis on 'prudence, interdependency, trusteeship', honed while working for Perham, became 'a model to conserve good imperial governance in the end days of the European empire' and the slow and necessary transformation of empire to Commonwealth.[198] While Perham and her subjects of empire and decolonisation were erased as core IR subject matter, Wight became one of the most venerated British IR scholars. Yet Wight's own British version of IR's all-white all-male canon was an act of amicicide. The figure of greater intellectual significance at this moment of world-historical transformation was not Grotius, as Wight suggested.[199] It was Margery Perham.

# 9

# Is British International Thought White?

So much for backwardness . . . let us learn a few things from these so-called backward people . . . before we give them 'Big Brother' leads, advice, guidance and leadership.

—CLAUDIA JONES, APRIL 1957[1]

WHAT IS 'BRITISH' international thought? Is it white?[2] Does it only include those born on the group of islands off the northwestern coast of mainland Europe in the North Atlantic or does it incorporate all those sharing common citizenship and fate within the British Empire? The question answers itself. From the Act of Union in 1707, 'Britain' encompassed not a national and geographically limited location or identity but was something broader and more expansive, first empire, then Commonwealth. As an attempt to reassert British imperial unity and centrality to the white settler dominions as empire faltered, the British Nationality Act of 1948 explicitly classed all populations within the islands, the dominions and overseas colonies, as sharing a common status as British subjects of the Crown. Only the British Nationality Act of 1981 defined citizenship in limited national and geographical terms, tied exclusively to the British Isles.[3]

Thus, if 'Britain' is a multiracial and imperial formation, then why are there no Black and brown thinkers in intellectual histories of International Relations in Britain? The formation and reformation of intellectual fields mirrors imperial geography and racial logics. Britain's first cross-social-science national funding council, established in 1944, was the Colonial Social Science Research

Council. In a period when successive governments were seeking to reconfigure rather than end empire—from brutal counterinsurgency campaigns in Malaya, Kenya, and Aden to the rejuvenation of colonial developmental projects— imperialism necessarily continued to shape intellectual production.[4] Yet, in the 1950s and 1960s, while Britain was still violently clinging to its formal empire, the once core subject of imperialism was slowly disappeared from the academic study of international relations in Britain.

British IR failed as an intellectual project in the twentieth century, and British international thinking is imagined to be 'white', because its scholars failed to recognise, let alone receive, the real intellectual gift from across the Atlantic. Not positivist behaviourism or Euro-American 'realism', but the Anglophone thought of the Black Atlantic brought by West Indian migrants to Britain. According to postcolonial scholar Bill Schwarz, Trinidadian historian C.L.R. James was one of the first to identify how it was 'through the encounter with the formerly colonial peoples of the Caribbean that native white Britons were first able to see themselves in their true historical light: what had previously happened elsewhere was now happening *here*'.[5] This transatlantic tradition of international thought offered to British international relations similar intellectual and cultural resources being erased in the post-war re-founding of American IR.[6] As elaborated by Schwarz, this was the 'gift of a particular vantage from which to comprehend the civilization of the mother country',[7] which West Indians possessed by virtue of what Trinidadian essayist, journalist, publicist, activist, and educator Claudia Jones called their plight as 'the cockpit of Europe'.[8] IR's very 'white' conception of the content and form of international thought not only erased thinkers of colour, it impoverished IR's understandings of the categories, sources, quality, and range of international thought.[9]

## Organising Black Britain, Schooling White Marxists

Without question, Claudia Jones was one of the most influential international thinkers in 1950s and 1960s Britain, directly shaping how tens of thousands of ordinary people conceived of world politics. For her many admirers, Jones was 'unique—there was no woman like her in England, of any colour. She had no peer'.[10] It is easy to see why. If C.L.R. James is 'the magisterial, world historical intellectual of the twentieth century anglophone Caribbean',[11] then Jones is the even more impressive 'female political and intellectual equivalent'.[12] As a Black Marxist feminist woman from a British colony who worked through journalism, political essays, organising and campaigning, Claudia Jones's absence from

British IR's intellectual history is entirely over-determined. She could be considered the most historically significant figure examined in this book. She certainly offers the greatest challenge to IR's existing intellectual histories.

Lacking the prestige of a think tank or university affiliation or a role as publicist for an imperial state, like Margery Perham, Jones's intellectual work nonetheless created and mobilised an international political and historical consciousness among Black Britons. Certain of the revolutionary capacities of the Black masses, Jones mobilised thousands of Black and brown people to political action through her original thought, skilled oratory, writing, and organising. She is said to have effectively 'established political thinking for minority people in Britain'.[13]

Born in the British colony of Trinidad in 1915, Claudia Jones is as important as her better-known West Indian contemporaries George Padmore, C.L.R. James, and Eric Williams. Since she moved in multiple spaces of empire, her name also appears alongside African–Americans Frederick Douglass and W.E.B. Du Bois, or as 'the Harriet Tubman and Sojourner Truth of the 20th Century'.[14] She was internationally renowned during her lifetime, received by Chairman Mao on her last international trip in China. Diplomatic delegations from Africa, Asia, and Latin America attended her funeral in 1965, which was 'the first really big Black funeral that London ever saw'.[15] Hundreds of people gathered outside to listen to tributes on loudspeakers. She was laid to rest at Highgate Cemetery in the plot immediately to the left of Karl Marx, which, her biographer notes, literally and figuratively represents Jones's historical place in the development of radical left thought in the twentieth century.[16]

In the British context, Claudia Jones's primary significance stems from her creation of two major institutions of Black political and intellectual life, both of which are entirely missing from IR's intellectual history: the West Indian (later Notting Hill) Carnival and the *West Indian Gazette*. Jones founded, edited and wrote for Britain's most important organ of Black journalism. Most Pan-Africanists left Britain in 1946–8, as did Jones's fellow Trinidadian George Padmore, who moved to Ghana in 1957. In this context, the *Gazette*—and Jones—inaugurated 'a new kind of politics in Britain . . . there was simply no comparable public voice at the time'.[17] In turn, Jones rekindled an 'indigenous black British political leadership' at a time of anti-Black riots across England and pervasive discrimination in employment, housing, and everyday life.[18] As discussed in more detail below, Jones's arguments for West Indian federation in the *Gazette* and elsewhere were as sophisticated as those discussed in Adom

Getachew's important book on Black federalist thought, *Worldmaking after Empire*.[19]

In the always precarious economic context of a British colony, Claudia Jones's parents were relatively secure prior to the economic crisis of the 1920s; her mother's family owned land and her father worked in hotels. In 1922, her parents, Sybil Logan and Charles Cumberbatch, left Port of Spain for Harlem, New York; Claudia and her three sisters and aunt followed two years later when she was eight years old. But the family continued to live in extreme poverty and ill-health. Cumberbatch was an editor at the *West Indian American*, but lost his post in the Great Depression. In 1933, Jones's mother died of spinal meningitis at the age of thirty-seven. Jones spent the following year in a sanatorium with tuberculosis, which inflicted permanent damage to her lungs. Part of the Black proletariat too poor to buy new clothes for her high-school graduation, Jones initially took low-paying laundry and factory work.

In the context of Jim Crow America, extreme poverty, and fascist Italy's invasion of Ethiopia, it is easy to understand Jones's attraction to the communist movement; the 'science of Marxism-Leninism', she later said, was the 'philosophy of my life'.[20] At eighteen, Jones joined the Young Communist League (YCL) and very quickly worked her way up the hierarchy of the Communist Party of the United States (CPUSA). In 1937, she attended the CPUSA's training school in New York for six months. By 1941, she was the national educational director and by 1945, an elected member of the National Committee, and the secretary of the National Women's Commission and the Peace Committee. Jones always worked as part of collective efforts, from political parties and newspapers to education and grassroots anticolonial and women's organisations.

Unlike C.L.R. James, who was born fourteen years earlier and attended Trinidad's Queen's Royal College, modelled on an English public school, Jones did not receive any kind of elite education. Trinidadian historian, independence leader and first prime minister Eric Williams received his doctorate from Oxford. But Jones was educated to high-school level in Harlem, the centre of the Black political and intellectual world. Jones drew on Harlem's intellectual currents and institutional resources to make sense of the grinding poverty and racial terror all around her, a poverty and persecution that caused lifelong illness and led directly to her untimely death at the age of forty-eight.

Having rigorously studied both 'the Marxist-Leninist science of society',[21] and Black intellectual traditions, Jones operated in senior, often founding, roles in multiple organisations, including the National N——Congress, the

Congress of American Women, the National Council of N—— Women, and the National Peace Commission. Later, in Britain, Jones worked through the West Indian Forum and Committee on Racism and International Affairs, the Communist Party of Great Britain, the West Indian Students and Workers Association, the Caribbean Labour Congress, the Inter-Racial Friendship Co-ordinating Council, and the Committee of Afro-Asian-Caribbean Organisations.[22]

Bill Schwarz has identified 'a James, or a James–Lamming, or even a James–Lamming–Jones tradition of mid-century marxisant West Indian thought'.[23] There should be no qualified inclusion of Claudia Jones. Jones was a working-class intellectual steeped in the theoretical debates and political organising of the CPUSA, the African–American freedom struggle, and global anticolonial movements. But unlike British Conservative Party activist Agnes Headlam-Morley, Jones was at the leading edge of theoretical development and policy change in her party.

As senior member of the CPUSA, Jones supported the Comintern's Popular Front anti-fascist alliance with imperial powers, which temporarily demoted its anticolonial and antiracist work.[24] Yet racial, imperial, and gender oppression were at the core of her analyses of capitalist empire. As editor and writer for the party youth journal, *Weekly Review*, Jones read together the geopolitical, racialised, and anticolonial implications of the expanding Nazi empire.[25] Moreover, building on the Pan-Africanism of earlier Black women communists such as Grace Campbell and Williana Burroughs, Jones superseded the basic categories of Marxism to become an original theorist of the super-exploitation of working-class Black women.[26] In a series of essays in the mid-1940s to mid-1950s, Jones developed the core theoretical tenets of her anticolonial and feminist historical materialism.[27] Accounting for the inter-connected operations of class, gendered, and racialised oppression on a global scale, 'triple oppression' was Jones's defining analytical category, presaging by decades work on 'intersectionality', only recently and belatedly taught in IR.[28]

Jones drew on the intellectual resources available to her in Harlem, but her ideas were distinct from its other main intellectual currents. She supported the Communist International's 'Black Belt' thesis, that African–Americans in the South constituted an oppressed minority with the right to form their own state, though she was no Black nationalist.[29] She praised Jamaican Pan-Africanist Marcus Garvey and his Harlem-based Universal N—— Improvement Association for instilling Black peoples' 'pride in their ancient origin and African heritage'.[30] Moreover, as a close friend of Jamaican

Pan-Africanist Amy Ashwood Garvey, Marcus's first wife, she respectfully reported on the transfer of Marcus Garvey's ashes from London to Jamaica and published a summary of Malcolm X's address to the Council of African Organisations in London in 1964.[31] In solidarity with her friend Amy Ashwood Garvey, Jones also refused to publish an interview with Garvey's second wife, Amy Jacques, who was passing through London and interviewed by *Gazette* reporter Donald Hines.[32] But Jones rejected Black capitalism as the path to ending Black poverty and what she considered Marcus Garvey's 'divisive racialism' in supporting racial separation. 'Back to Africa' policies were unsuccessful, Jones claimed, because African–Americans did not accept 'that their ultimate destiny or solution of their oppressed status lay elsewhere than where they were born'.[33]

Though recognising its roots as a reaction to white supremacy, Jones was also sceptical of the Black Muslim Movement in the United States and what she saw as its rejection of 'everything in white American civilization in favour of black integrity and Mohammedanism'.[34] In contrast to her later embrace of cultural expression as political action, she reduced Jamaica's Rastafari religious and social movement to a purely culturalist programme, which in untypically reductionist terms she described as 'comment merely on the super-structure of the economic system of a society'.[35]

As a member of the National Committee of the CPUSA, Jones was an obvious target of 'fascist McCarthyism'.[36] She was repeatedly arrested and jailed, suffering heart failure and hospitalisations with hypertensive cardiovascular disease. In 1955, she was jailed for nine months and then, despite an international campaign led by communist, women's, West Indian, and civil liberties groups, Jones was deported from the United States; 'as a N—— woman Communist of West Indian descent, I was a thorn in their side in my opposition to Jim Crow racist discrimination'.[37] US officials wanted to expel Jones to Trinidad. However, the colonial governor objected, fearing she would radicalise local anticolonial movements, and 'become a source of infection amongst all Colonials in Britain' as well.[38] But claiming her right under the British Nationality Act of 1948, Jones chose exile in Britain, departing on the Queen Elizabeth steamer on December 9, and docking in Southampton on December 22, 1955.

The coming to Britain of a celebrated senior party leader, writer and theoretician from the United States should have been a boon to the Communist Party of Great Britain (CPGB). As an experienced organiser, journalist and editor, a pioneer of new forms of feminist, Black Marxist, and anticolonial praxis and thought, a famous US-trained organic intellectual with an international reputation and 'air of power', Claudia Jones was ideally placed to diagnose and transform provincialism on the British left.[39] According to CPGB member Trevor Carter, 'Claudia . . . towered over us by her American experience . . . Claudia was a leader, she was a leader of the only Western communist party that was steeped in the Black experience, a party which had the advantage of being informed and led by brilliant Black men and women.'[40]

At the request of the CPUSA, the CPGB initially helped with Jones's entry to Britain and supported her in the first few months; the first two of which she spent in hospital as she continued to deal with the health effects of poverty and political persecution. With no senior Black people in the CPGB leadership, and racism endemic, Jones had no intellectual or political peer on the British left. Thus, despite Comintern instructions to address racism and engage with colonial populations, the contrast between the CPUSA and CPGB was stark.[41] In turn, the largely white male CPGB leadership did not know what to do with one of the most senior women in the global communist movement and allocated her secretarial work. Jones responded in kind by launching a blistering critique of the CPGB at an address during its 25th Congress in April 1957 at a time when the British Empire was fighting brutal colonial wars in Malaya and Kenya.

Jones thanked British comrades for their solidarity and asked for even greater solidarity with anticolonial struggles around the world. There was an obvious common origin in workers' and anticolonial battles, she argued; 'the same monopoly capitalists . . . exploit the British working class, but . . . superexploit the colonies'.[42] The USSR itself showed that 'big-nation chauvinism does not automatically die' once socialism was achieved.[43] The test for white communists in Britain, 'the oldest and biggest imperialist power', was to radically distance themselves from colonial theory and practice. The supposedly most technically 'advanced' nations were 'steeped in the mire of backward imperialist ideology' while the so-called 'backward' peoples were the most revolutionary and had 'the most advanced ideology'. The peoples of Russia, China, now India and the Afro-Asian nations, in 'their new world historic unity' on display at the Bandung Conference of 1955 had much to teach the so-called 'advanced' world. 'So much for backwardness'.[44] Just as emancipation from colonialism was not a gift from the British Empire, neither were the colonised masses awaiting political instruction from white communists.

Claudia Jones schooled white British Marxists on capitalism's relation to racism, slavery, imperialism, colonialism, anticolonialism, and the agency of colonised peoples. Relations never recovered. The CPGB leadership could not handle the ferocity of Claudia Jones's critique of its racism and colonial mentality, which she had likened to an 'infection'.[45] When Jones deviated from the party line by supporting China's nuclear weapons programme, the CPGB asked for her resignation. (In 1964, Jones was vice-chairman of the programme drafting committee of the 10th World Conference Against Hydrogen and Atom Bombs.[46]) Despite petty factionalism, Jones never resigned from the party which, in turn, could not risk expelling such a high-profile and respected figure.[47] She was simply too important to be thrown out. Instead, Jones was frozen out of the CPGB, never permitted to rise to a position commensurate with her standing and ability and was then written out of histories of the British left. To its lasting shame, the CPGB is also implicated in undermining Jones's legacy. After her death, a party functionary reportedly rummaged through her personal belongings and removed some of Jones's voluminous personal papers, including drafts of an autobiography that were never recovered.[48]

## The International Thought and Pedagogy
## of the *West Indian Gazette*

Frozen out by the white mediocrities of the CPGB, Jones's loss to the party was Black Britons' gain. Like Susan Strange and Elizabeth Wiskemann, the central professional context of Jones's political and intellectual life was journalism. Before arriving in Britain, Jones had two decades' experience as a reporter and editor in leading institutions of the radical Black and left presses, including *Weekly Review, Daily Worker, Spotlight,* and *Negro Affairs Quarterly*. However, her most important legacy to Black journalism was *The West Indian Gazette*, which she founded, edited, and published from March 1958 until her death in December 1964. Described as 'the pioneering pinnacle of black publishing in Britain',[49] the *Gazette* influenced every subsequent Black newspaper.[50] It is difficult to overstate the political and cultural influence of what Jones called her 'people's paper'.[51]

The *Gazette* filled a major gap in Black-owned print media in Britain after the collapse of *Caribbean News* in 1956.[52] Edited above a music shop on the Brixton Road in South London, the paper was run on a shoestring and depended on Jones' unflagging labours and willingness to live precariously. Her financial worries were constant, beyond anything Elizabeth Wiskemann faced in her freelance journalism career. Jones was never paid for her editorial work—she died financially destitute—and is often described as working day and night to keep the paper afloat. Increasing production costs, attempted censorship from printers, and better financed competitors of 'the Ebony type magazine showing the rather rosy . . . picture' of Black life,[53] meant Jones was never sure whether the next edition would go to press.[54] The *Gazette* nonetheless survived during her lifetime on Jones's labour, national and international sales, local advertising, goodwill, fundraising, and donations from readers and Jones's extensive network of collaborators and friends. By May 1961, the paper's circulation was ten thousand, rising to fifteen thousand at its peak, with each copy read and shared multiple times. Circulation would have been much higher, Jones maintained, 'but for the usual welter of problems faced by most progressive journals.'[55] She refused to sell its independence.

Established to address what she saw as the lack of organisation among West Indians, and provide a platform for her political views, Jones and the *Gazette* were major institutions in anticolonial politics in late 1950s and 1960s Britain. In addition to a busy paper room and location for activist events, historian Marika Sherwood describes how the *Gazette* office 'served as an advice bureau for Black peoples as well as a discussion forum' and was 'the necessary port of call for visiting dignitaries from the black world.'[56] The paper was a leading voice in the defence of Black Britons against racial discrimination in employment and housing and racist immigration legislation. According to *Gazette* reporter Donald Hinds, 'People fearing for their life and property would come, waiting impatiently to pour out their troubles. They had little use for the Migrant Service Division of the high Commissioner's Office. What they needed was a godmother, not diplomatists. That was the role Claudia Jones played best.'[57]

Jones was godmother *and* diplomat. She once defended a young Black man who was racially harassed by police, spending a night with him in Notting Hill Police Station. They were released, Jones claimed, because the police were aware of 'the sense of organisation and unity that our paper represents and the fact that they had no case.'[58] She met with and interviewed West Indian political leaders visiting London; joined delegations to the Home Office; and helped the African National Congress to conceive and organise the movement to boycott apartheid South Africa. On his way to receive the Nobel Peace Prize in 1964, Martin Luther King met with Jones at her South London home.[59]

Journalism, organising, and oratory were the modes and means of Jones's intellectual and theoretical work.[60] Where Susan Strange and Elizabeth Wiskemann published in mainstream news outlets, and went onto careers in the largely white academy, Jones combined journalism in the radical Black and

Marxist press with what historian Ula Taylor terms 'street scholarship'.[61] In her reportage, opinion pieces, and editorial decisions, Jones related her ideas to the everyday struggles of ordinary peoples and directed them toward immediate practical ends more thoroughly than professional, university-connected Black intellectuals like W.E.B. Du Bois, C.L.R. James, or Merze Tate. Journalism was more than a job for Jones, or second choice to a career in academe as it was for Wiskemann. It was the vernacular expression of her international thought. Jones was more openly political than Strange and Wiskemann. But there should be no doubt about the theoretical depth and historical consciousness underlying Jones's intellectual production in this genre. In contrast to James's high-cultural and literary work, Jones produced a democratic people's paper with a Black Atlantic understanding of the historical past in the service of a postcolonial future. Like James, Jones had a deep historical consciousness and adopted a clear historical pedagogy. Claudia Jones was an historian too.

The *Gazette's* pedagogy, including its 'Know your History' feature, included reviews of academic works and other intellectual forms. Jones mocked the first and only prime minister of the West Indian Federation, Sir Grantley Adams, for claiming that the three 'most historical' events in West Indian history were Columbus's 'discovery', the abolition of slavery, and a recent visit by British Tory Prime Minister Harold Macmillan. Jones's counter-history incorporated the Maroons of Jamaica who freed themselves from slavery, the labourers who rose up in revolts in the 1930s, West Indian trade unionists, and the new initiative of the University College of the West Indies, to properly teach West Indian history.[62] She taught her readers about the Caribbean 'struggle of the ancestors', including George Gordon who had led the rebellion in Morant Bay. Always behind such heroes, Jones insisted, 'are the people of the Caribbean—the militant Caribs, the N—— population, the Indian, Portuguese, Chinese, Syrians, who make up the multi-racial peoples of the West Indies'.[63]

Jones worked with, published, and introduced to the mass of Black Britons the ideas of prominent anticolonial intellectuals such as W.E.B. and Shirley Graham Du Bois, Paul and Eslanda Robeson, Eric Williams, and Amy Ashwood Garvey.[64] She introduced Black Britons to the political ideas emanating from freedom struggles in the United States and academic scholarship on West Indian history, and contemporary politics in the period she always described in terms of world-historical transformation.[65] As discussed below, Jones condemned the emerging academic sociology of race relations in Britain, but also drew *Gazette* readers' attention to some of the better works of scholarship published by the Institute of Race Relations, including Katrin Norris's

*Jamaica, the Search for an Identity*. Jones credentialed Norris as 'a scholar of St Anne's college, Oxford', who had done three years' fieldwork in the United States, Cuba and the West Indies, and a year as a reporter for the *Daily Gleaner*, Jamaica's newspaper of record.[66]

Through her editing, journalism, and longer essay form, Claudia Jones was a major intellectual force making and shaping the Black counter-publics through which ordinary people were informed of and engaged with world politics. She was also thinking through alternative postcolonial political forms and the politics of resistance with the aim of transforming class and racialised relations in Britain and worldwide. Building on her historical vision and consciousness, Jones mounted a powerful intellectual analysis and critique of racist mob violence in Britain; US neo-colonialism in the Caribbean, Asia, and Africa; West Indian federation as a bulwark against US encroachments; the progress in the socialist republics, including Cuba, China, the USSR, and the non-aligned movement; and an account of world history that centred the agency of colonised and formerly colonised peoples.

## Critiquing the 'Sociology of Race Relations'

The most common economic context given for the arrival of large numbers of Caribbean and Asian migrants to Britain in the 1950s was the post–World War II labour shortage. The reforming Labour government invited colonial workers, many of whom had fought for Britain in the war, to help rebuild the national economy and create the welfare state. For Claudia Jones, the most relevant context for mass migration was the continued economic subordination of the West Indies. Despite living in territories rich in natural and mineral resources, Britain's looting and deliberate under-development of colonial territories meant that most Caribbean peoples lived in poverty. The entire regional economy, Jones wrote, was 'distorted to serve the interests of an accumulation of super-profits' by 'the big imperialist combines and trusts'.[67] In addition to the 1950 McCarran Internal Security Act that restricted Caribbean migration to the United States, Jones argued that the demise of the West Indian Federation also forced people to migrate. As discussed later, Jones vigorously supported the attempt to establish a new postcolonial political federation across the Caribbean islands 'in which freedom of movement would have absorbed some of our disinherited, disillusioned, and un-filled people'.[68]

On arrival, Britain's labour ministry allocated even highly skilled and educated West Indians to lower-skilled jobs in public transport, heath services, manufacturing and textiles. Black and brown people faced pervasive discrimination in employment and housing, as well as a 'patronising or paternal attitude' from well-meaning whites.[69] Increasingly organised far-right groups like the White Defence League and League of Empire Loyalists instigated anti-Black riots in Nottingham and Notting Hill in 1958, blaming West Indians for taking jobs and housing, and polluting Britain's racial stock. Both Nazis and the British Ku Klux Klan targeted *West Indian Gazette* offices with hate mail and propaganda on their project to keep 'England awake, keep Britain pure and white'.[70] With 'illusions' about the 'mother country',[71] Jones thought, many West Indians were shocked at their treatment. They had been taught in Caribbean schools that they too were citizens of the Crown. But the only British workers allowed to enjoy the new welfare state, employment, and the spoils of empire were the so-called 'white working class'.[72] Class became race via social welfarist distinctions between the deserving (white) and undeserving (Black and brown) poor.[73]

With rampaging white mob violence and increasingly organised resistance among racialised communities, several so-called specialists in overseas colonial administration refashioned themselves as 'experts' on metropolitan 'race relations'. Social anthropologist Sheila Patterson moved from work on 'coloured' people in white settler South Africa to the new Rockefeller Foundation-funded Institute of Race Relations (IRR) in Britain, which published her 1963 book, *Dark Strangers*.[74] Growing out of the Chatham House Board of Studies in Race Relations established in 1952, and led by a former colonial administrator, the IRR was founded in 1958.[75] 'Race relations' and 'community relations' emerged as domains of new sociological expertise in the 1950s and 1960s to attend to and manage the effects of race and class oppression in the imperial metropole. While there had been Black people in Britain for centuries, the post-war migration and racist backlash was of a different order in scale, permanence, and implication.[76]

As Margery Perham put it, race relations were 'no longer comfortably overseas'[77] and were also not obviously outside the remit of 'British IR' in this period. Historian Peter Calvocoressi, later Reader in IR at Sussex University, sat on the IRR's Management Council. But the slow transformation of 'race relations' discourse from a colonial question into one of domestic policy and global public relations obscured the imperial–international basis and relevance of racial violence against Black and brown populations, and hence the work of leading figures such as Claudia Jones for the post-war IR field.

Claudia Jones wrote one of the earliest and most powerful critiques of the new sociological discourse of race relations in a 1964 essay for *Freedomways*, the journal co-founded by W.E.B. and Shirley Graham Du Bois. Alongside essays by C.L.R. James, Eric Williams, and the poetry of George W. Lamming and Derek Walcott, Jones identified British race-relations discourse as 'neo-colonialist' and singled out Sheila Patterson's *Dark Strangers*, which, Jones noted, was 'financed by the Institute of Race Relations and the Nuffield Foundation'.[78] For Patterson, large-scale racial violence not only threatened race war at home; it also damaged Britain's alleged international reputation for multi-racial inclusivity, what historian Kennetta Perry calls the 'mystique of Britain's anti-racism'.[79] In her *Freedomways* essay, Jones quoted Patterson at length:

> The people of these islands face the need not only to reformulate their views of Britain's role and status in such a Commonwealth, but also to apply the new relationships in their dealings with colored Commonwealth migrants here at home. And not only the color-conscious migrants themselves, but the newly-independent Afro-Asian countries and the outside world as a whole, show an inclination to judge Britain's good faith in international relations by her ability to put her own house in order.[80]

Margery Perham had also vociferously argued that the new postcolonial international relations centred on 'the relations of white peoples with coloured peoples', with domestic political implications for Britain.[81] 'The growing contacts between all N——', she wrote, 'means that our treatment of these West Indians affects our relations with all black groups'.[82] Black people had 'suffered oppression beyond any measurement and some of it at our hands', Perham wrote in her typical semi-confessional mode.[83] 'Black people among us' were 'bred from this oppression', including thousands of African workers and students, as well as those who had migrated from the West Indies, whom Perham called 'the foster-children of our civilization'.[84]

White liberal women like Perham and Patterson argued that Britain needed to address its own 'deep-seated sense of racial superiority', the better to lead 'white nations' in the struggle for 'inter-racial tolerance'.[85] Yet Perham could not sustain antiracism without slipping into the white sociology of race relations. The British state should have done more to 'house them and initiate them into our society'.[86] But lest anyone forget, Perham persisted, 'Britain did more than any other nation, more than it is yet understood or acknowledged, to bring Africans forward to self-government'.[87] Moreover, she did not accept that Britain had greatly profited from 'plundering Africa's riches', a view 'no serious economist would support . . . Britain as a nation certainly did not build up her latest empire simply as a profitable investment'.[88] However, this requires a dubious distinction between slavery and empire and excluded the immense wealth gained from the eighteenth-century slavery colonies in the West Indies.

Patterson was even more sociological and problem-solving than Perham. Drawing on the categories of sociologists Georg Simmel and Robert E. Park, in which relations between racialised communities are conceived as an interaction between 'strangers', Patterson argued that all social groups operate in terms of insiders and outsiders, strangers and foreigners.[89] Some degree of prejudice towards maladjusted foreigners was thus natural, derived primarily from the fact of immigration and cultural difference, rather than race itself. The main problem in Britain, then, was that West Indians did not conform to contemporary English social and cultural norms since they had an 'outmoded nineteenth-century model of lower-working-class behaviour'.[90] The problem could be redressed by more 'community' interaction between the normal (white) community and the (Black and brown) 'immigrants', helping West Indians to adopt 'local *mores*', for example, in how to appropriately interact with (white) 'women in the street'. It would also help West Indians to understand that 'ignorant but well-meaning remarks' from white people 'about their colour or way of life' were not always 'deliberate insults to their race'.[91]

Claudia Jones's early appraisal of the 'plethora of new sociological and analytical works' from the race-relations industry was meant to alert Black and brown working-class peoples to how the imperial state and academy sought to portray and pacify them.[92] For Jones, the white sociology and ideology of race relations was obviously 'neo-colonialist', 'full of pragmatic assertions that xenophobia is the "norm" of British life, and hence, by implication "natural"'.[93] Its apolitical, ahistorical 'norms' discourse was entirely premised on a denial of the historical and material origins and political economy of both migration and racist violence. Jones used the *Gazette* to repeatedly insist that racism was not natural, an understandable response to the arrival of so-called 'dark strangers'. It was 'man-made', rooted in the deep-seated imperial and racist 'ideology and training' required to dominate, enslave, and colonise people for three hundred years.[94] Large-scale racialised violence was always caused by concrete economic and social conditions that were also the soil for contemporary fascists.[95]

Presaging more recent academic work on the role of imperial revenue and the economic basis of the post-war welfare state, Jones cited Winston Churchill's claim that Britain's imperial possessions 'lay the foundation of that commercial and financial leadership which . . . enabled us to make our great position in the world'.[96] In making this now-commonplace argument in the 1950s, Jones was one of the first to puncture the mythology of post-war Britain as defined by the age of unparalleled wealth and welfare for all. She highlighted successive economic crises caused by a series of post-war government's attempt to hang onto empire. Britain's social-services crisis and housing shortage were not caused by migration, but by economic, colonial, and international policies: 'in a desperate attempt to cling to the colonies and the "cold war" policy, the Tory ruling class is imposing new hardships on the British people by attacks on their working and living standards by the credit squeeze and unemployment'.[97] Social services were under-resourced because funds were diverted to the H-bomb, 'and to keep up the huge and unnecessary campaigns against people seeking freedom' from colonial rule.[98]

For Jones, the attempt to restrict further migration to Britain was 'an attempt to control access to the spoils of empire' that funded Britain's welfare state such 'that dispossessed peoples have no claims over what was stolen from them' through enslavement and continued colonial pillage.[99] The *Gazette* published the 1962 Immigration Act in full, which, Jones explained, 'applies primarily and solely to prevent the entry [and] also the ejection of coloured citizens'.[100] Migrants from the white settler colonies, such as white Australian IR scholar Coral Bell, discussed in the next chapter, were more likely to possess the requisite financial and skills qualifications. Jones accused British politicians of grotesque hypocrisy and scapegoating. To redirect class resentment and justify new restrictions on migration, they stoked racial tensions by blaming class oppression on a racialised and 'highly visible minority'.[101] This form of white supremacy in the metropole, Jones claimed, was rooted in the same colonial-capital and racialised conflict over the sharing of colonial plunder.

Jones presaged by decades more recent critiques of 'white sociology' and 'Black struggle' by cultural studies scholars such as Valerie Amos, Paul Gilroy, and Erroll Lawrence.[102] Her remedy to white mob violence was not limited cultural pluralism and restrictions on immigration, as advocated by white liberals, but class and cross-racial solidarity. Workers were exploited in both metropole and colony and could work in solidarity for social justice. Leading by example, Jones's supported white and Indian workers and spoke at white-dominated trade unions around Britain.[103] The *West Indian Gazette* can be read as Jones's extended refutation of and radical alternative to the sociology of 'race relations', with her insistence on the right of Black and brown people to live in and transform Britain and the meanings of British-ness.

## A Different Polyphonic Internationalism

In August and September 1958, white mobs rampaged in Notting Hill, London and Nottingham, attacking West Indian residents in so-called 'race riots' instigated by fascists.[104] Later in 1958, Kelso Cochrane, an aspiring law student and carpenter from Antigua, was stabbed to death by a gang of white men in Ladbroke Grove, London. With an immediate aim of creating a legal defence fund to support those fighting back, Claudia Jones established a Caribbean Carnival organising committee under the auspices of the *Gazette*, with the first event held in January 1959 in St Pancras Town Hall and televised by the BBC.[105] Conceived as an act of Black resistance and Black pride, Jones established the original ideas and themes of what would become one of the largest and most famous musical and cultural events in the contemporary world, the West Indian (later Notting Hill) Carnival. That is, Jones established one of the most powerful and effective forms of polyphonic internationalism in history and is rightly hailed as the 'mother' of Britain's 'contemporary black art' scene.[106]

While Jones analysed the mechanisms of British imperialism, colonialism, and class power in historical materialist terms, she was profoundly interested in cultural and artistic expressions of anticolonialism. Growing up during the Harlem Renaissance, Jones understood the political importance of contemporary Black cultural struggle for peoples under siege. In contrast to her earlier dismissal of Rastafarianism, Jones's later praxis moved beyond a crudely reductionist Marxist account of culture, with *Gazette* readers introduced to art, music, poetry and theatre from Harlem, including works by African–American writers James Baldwin and Lorraine Hansberry.[107]

Like Lucie Zimmern's polyphonic internationalism, discussed in chapter 1, Claudia Jones understood the significance of art and culture as political and international practice, the importance of cultural diplomacy, the need for affective as well as intellectual grounds for world-historical transformation. Zimmern drew on and appropriated Harlem's cultural production to support a liberal cultural internationalism of imperial reform. She sought to harmonise nations within a reformed British-led culturally pluralist 'post-racial Commonwealth', inviting classically trained Black artists to perform a Western cultural form, albeit revised and interpreted by African and African–American traditions.[108] In thinking that was infused with racial and imperial hierarchy, Zimmern's celebration of 'rich and beautiful diversity'[109] used music and culture to *depoliticise* national difference. On one level, Claudia Jones's carnival can be understood through harmonic metaphors, to 'infuse the carnival spirit of Friendship, Gaiety and Joy into every British home'.[110] Yet Jones's political and intellectual agenda was much more radical and democratic, a challenge to imperial and racial hierarchies, including white supremist aesthetics, in an elevation of West Indian mime, song and dance.[111]

The carnival was modelled on the annual event in Jones's place of birth. The earliest carnivals in Trinidad began under French colonial rule when enslaved persons were permitted to wear costumes, play music, dance, and impersonate the 'masters' during their own carnival of white supremacy. In contrast to Zimmern's classical musical training, Jones's polyphonic internationalism centred on performing arts, was a celebration of the masses, and brought together high and popular cultural forms. 'It is as if the vividness of our national life', she wrote in the first carnival's souvenir programme, 'was itself the spark urging translation to new surroundings, to convey, to transplant our folk origins to British soil'.[112] As one early carnival co-organiser put it, 'the spirit of the carnival came out of Claudia's political knowledge of what to touch at a particular time when we were scared, we were people in disarray'.[113] 'There is a comfort in this effort', Jones explained, 'for all West Indians who strained to feel and hear and reflect their idiom even as they strained to feel the warmth of the sun-drenched islands and its memorable beauty of landscape and terrain'.[114] Yet carnival was more than palliative. It was Jones's multipronged strategic political and cultural response to neo-colonial and fascist violence in Britain: a refusal to be intimidated; a reassertion of West Indians' presence not as temporary visitors, but permanent and large; and the demand of a right to federate in the Caribbean and decolonise metropolitan Britain.

Underpinned by her belief that 'a people's art is the genesis of their freedom', Jones drew on her extensive international networks to persuade musicians, singers, actors, entertainers, dancers, and mas-makers—makers of masquerade, traditional carnival costumes—from across the Caribbean, Africa, Britain, and the United States to stage a display of West Indian cultural power. As Trevor Carter describes, 'what Claudia went for was what today [cultural theorists] Stuart Hall and Paul Gilroy would call the cultural thing. Claudia recognised that as being revolutionary'.[115] This was cultural production as international thought and praxis, a radical form of anticolonial polyphonic internationalism. Like Lucie Zimmern, Jones achieved her intellectual goal through collective organising, intellectual work, and also her great 'personal magnetism',[116] 'charm',[117] and a 'charisma' that 'could make people do things that they never knew they could do'.[118] Also like Zimmern, Jones is remembered as 'laughing, brilliant, full of energy',[119] 'capable of absolutely mesmerising her audience'.[120]

She was an institution-builder, educator, political entrepreneur, informal diplomat and even a performer. Journalism was Jones's alternative to a career in acting, as it was for Susan Strange.[121]

In some ways, Claudia Jones is remembered in similar terms to Eileen Power, as unusually beautiful and glamourous. Both dying young, they were prone to aestheticisation. For some, Jones looked 'successful' and had 'the appearance of a woman who knew where she was going: everybody's headmistress . . . that leader sort of person'.[122] Jones was described as 'beautiful in every sense', not just her looks, as it was for Power.[123] Yet aesthetics was central to the constitution of Jones's political and intellectual work. She was unapologetic in mobilising beauty and personal care to draw women to the *Gazette's* politics, with features on beauty tips and beauty contests. Zimmern may have claimed that the 'beautiful has no nationality',[124] but white supremacist assumptions underpinned her polyphonic internationalism. Jones ensured that beauty pageants, and the naming of a Carnival Queen, were central parts of carnival's politics of radical Black pride. As Trinidadian–British actress and carnival co-organiser and judge Corinne Skinner-Carter recalled, 'Faye Craig won the first contest, and I'm telling you, Faye Craig was black, I mean really black. But pretty. But without Claudia we would not have known that, because then we used to judge everybody's beauty by the European standard', a white supremacist aesthetic.[125] In the decade before the rise of Black Power in Britain, Jones's politics of Black self-realisation was exceptional. She turned the popular cultural form of beauty advice and contests into a form of liberation politics.[126]

A Caribbean Carnival organised by the *Gazette* became an established event during Jones's lifetime. There was no carnival following her death in 1964, after which carnival's politics and legacy, and Jones's place in it, was briefly contested. In his 1993 book *Masquerade Politics*, the social anthropologist Abner Cohen dismissed the notion that 'somehow' Jones had founded the carnival because she 'had arranged a big party for West Indians somewhere in London', suggesting that 'interest' in Jones and the 'discovery' of her work on the carnival was only made in the 1980s by those pursuing a Black political agenda.[127] According to Cohen, East London social worker Rhuane Laslett had separately organised a multicultural festival in Notting Hill in 1966; its 'general cultural form' was 'essentially English . . . There was no suggestion that it would imitate a West Indian or any other foreign form of carnival'.[128] With these claims, Cohen was accused of making a 'mockery' of Jones.[129] Another likened the appropriation of carnival to an English form, as well as Jones's

FIGURE 9.1. Claudia Jones c.1960. Photographer Unknown. Courtesy of the Lambeth Archives

erasure, to 'the general robbery and rape of our people in the music and the entertainment world'.[130]

Certainly, an instantiation of 'Carnival Limited'[131] that centres Laslett's multiculturalism and erases Jones's anticolonialism is easily co-opted to a narrative in which Carnival became part of the domestication of Black Britons, a 'containment' of its youth, and a 'tourism product'.[132] By the early 1970s, Trinidadian performers and Black Power groups reclaimed carnival, and its original African-Caribbean roots and radical politics, restoring Claudia Jones to her rightful place as founder and originator of some of its most radical political possibilities.[133] In response to heavy-handed policing, and routine police harassment of young Black people, anti-police uprisings broke out during the carnival in 1976, and in the 1970s and 1980s there were frequent calls to shut it all down, though carnival, and Jones's legacy, survived.[134] It is now Europe's largest carnival and attracts over a million visitors every year.

## Another Federalist of the Black Atlantic

In convening multiracial groups of West Indian artists, many of them already politically active in anticolonial and anti-apartheid movements, Claudia Jones was supporting a panracial and multiracial West Indian consciousness in the Caribbean itself. Carnival was part of Jones's project for a socialist and non-aligned West Indian Federation. Accordingly, Jones enrolled support from the embassies and high commissions of Trinidad and Tobago, Jamaica, British Guyana, British Honduras, Ghana, Sierra Leone, Haiti, Nigeria and India.[135] 'A pride in being West Indian', she wrote in her programme notes for the first carnival, 'is undoubtedly at the root of this unity: a pride that has its origin in the drama of nascent nationhood, and that pride encompasses not only the creativeness, uniqueness and originality of West Indian mime, song and dance—but is the genesis of the nation itself'.[136] New cultural practices were generative of, and not just expressions of, new identities and political alliances. Hence Carnival was Jones's attempt to create a multiracial postcolonial West Indian culture, with the first carnival souvenir programme including an image of a Kathakali dancer, originating in North India.[137]

Jones is thus a neglected figure in what political theorist Adom Getachew describes as the 'federalists of the Black Atlantic'.[138] Thinkers in this tradition understood that the formal independence of African or Caribbean nations was meaningless under continued economic and political subordination. Federation would diversify the regional economic system and increase Caribbean influence on the world stage. While Jones's main focus was West Indian federation, the *Gazette* published pan-African news, including W.E.B. Du Bois's plans for an encyclopaedia of African history, and Shirley Graham's report on attempts to establish an African common market, bank and continent-wide citizenship.[139] At a Movement for Colonial Freedom conference, Jones spoke alongside leading Pan-Africanist Julius Nyerere, whom Margery Perham considered 'the most poised, confident, extrovert and, indeed, radiant of the African leaders'.[140] Like Trinidad's first prime minister, Eric Williams, Jones theorised regional federation as indispensable to meaningful 'anticolonial worldmaking'.[141] When Jones was initially denied a British passport in 1957, Jones wrote to Williams asking him to intervene to support her 'natural right' to receive one.[142] There is no record of a reply. By 1960, Jones identified and theorised beyond the limits of Williams's federalist thinking.

The British Colonial Office imagined Caribbean independence in federal terms primarily for financial reasons, given the declining strategic and economic benefits of continued direct colonial rule and the new era of US global hegemony. Larger and wealthier Caribbean islands could assume some of the financial burden of the smaller units that remained reliant on Colonial Development and Welfare aid.[143] Hence, with Britain's support, the ten islands of Antigua, Barbados, Dominica, Grenada, Jamaica, Saint Kitts, Nevis and Anguilla, Saint Lucia, Saint Vincent, and Trinidad and Tobago formed the West Indian Federation in January 1958. The federation had its own parliament and executive, but there was no independent source of revenue nor agreement on free trade, customs, or movement. Without a strong central authority, the federation operated more as a confederation and there was disagreement among its members on the degree of centralisation.[144] The federation collapsed in 1962 after Jamaica, the most populous and economically developed unit, voted in a referendum to withdraw. Jamaica and Trinidad became independent states in 1962. Even after the federation collapsed, Jones held out hope for an eastern Caribbean federation comprised of the smaller nations to raise their 'stature among the nations of the world'.[145]

Like Trinidadian intellectual and political leader, Eric Williams, Jones engaged with international political institutional design beyond the confines of the nation-state. She was also influenced by Williams's landmark historical work *Capitalism and Slavery*, based on his Oxford doctorate, which Jones reviewed in the *Gazette*.[146] However, unlike Williams, Jones did not model federation on an idealisation of the United States. As Getachew has shown, Williams was clearly 'conscripted to the terms of a newly emergent American hegemony'.[147] For Jones, the real betrayal was Williams's support for a 'half-way house of self-ownership' of Trinidad's 'productive resources'.[148] Trinidad may be the wealthiest West Indian unit, but this 'wealth springs from its great oil and asphalt reserves' controlled by US and British firms.[149] Williams's refusal to support economic nationalisation effectively condemned Trinidad to a '"half-slave, half free", limbo'.[150] Thus one could only see the 'shadow—not the substance' of Williams's vision of freedom; 'one cannot truly reject colonial control of one's political independence and simultaneously accept the BONDAGE of colonialist domination of one's productive resources'.[151] As her long essay 'American Imperialism and the British West Indies' explained, for the US, the West Indies was a mere adjunct to the wider global capitalist market.

West Indian economic freedom required socialism and an independent foreign policy. The movement of newly independent states to transform the international order was necessarily tied to the worldwide ideological struggle between capitalism and socialism. For Jones, then, Williams and his party, the People's National Movement (PNM), was anticolonial, but not fully anti-imperial.[152] Anti-Castro and anti-Soviet, Williams supported an alliance with the US despite its active and repeated interventions in the Caribbean and effort to undermine federation.[153] Jones concurred that an open affiliation with the Soviet Union or China was unrealistic, inviting further US military interventions. Yet newly independent states were increasingly declaring Cold War non-alignment and Jones was a major proponent of an Afro-Asian bloc. Despite her lifelong membership of the Communist Party and refusal to publicly denounce the USSR even after the 20th Party Congress condemned Stalin, she advocated a neutralist foreign policy for Trinidad; it should receive economic 'aid from all sides and especially where there are no strings attached.[154] Similarly Jamaica should align with African states, who were then creating an Organisation for African Unity. The largest West Indian states should pursue a unified foreign policy centring on a regional 'nuclear-free zone', the removal of foreign military bases, insistence on 'the inviolability of national sovereignty', and 'friendship and trade with *all* lands'.[155]

The failed project of a West Indies Federation, socialist or otherwise, was also an opportunity for Jones to settle old political scores and stake a claim to be among a new generation of West Indian intellectuals in Britain. Jones and Trinidadian historian C.L.R. James were on different sides in the Stalin–Trotsky dispute, with Jones remaining loyal to the party through which she had made her way. But their difference was also one of class, generation, and the politics of collaboration. In 1958, on the invitation of Prime Minister Eric Williams, C.L.R. James, with his wife Selma James, returned to Trinidad from Britain to edit the PNM party paper, *The Nation*, though they were expelled from the PNM in 1961. The following year James published *Party Politics in the West Indies* as a retort to Williams and as an apologia for his short-lived collaboration with a party he knew would never introduce socialism to Trinidad.[156] From an upper-middle-class 'respectable' Trinidadian family, James was a lover of cricket and Shakespeare, and once suggested that some Black people in Britain exaggerated racial discrimination.[157] Selma James was an American working-class feminist and antiracist organiser and intellectual, and later leader in the wages for housework movement.[158] More than simply settling old scores and continuing internal Marxist squabbles, Jones's review of James's book can be read as her critique of his middle-class and older male arrogance.

In the review, Jones was scathing of the conduct and manner of the much hailed 'real intellectual' who thought he knew it all and would 'put matters right' in Trinidad. 'Mr. James, the "Marxist"', Jones claimed, 'sings glories of British democracy, according to him the class distinctions of Britain help toward democracy'.[159] However, the big man was reduced to a 'nagging aunt' when he collaborated with the anti-revolutionary PNM, reduced to 'a continuous nagging interference in PNM's affairs'. Even the title of James's book was 'pretentious', she claimed. It did not deal with party politics in the West Indies, but James's own dealings with the PNM, and was filled with 'moaning' about his political status in Trinidad. James called himself a Marxist, but then insisted that socialism and neutralism be removed from the agenda of the PNM's national convention. Party supporters became his political 'enemies . . . Is it any wonder that' C.L.R. and Selma James 'came back to England embittered and disillusioned?'[160] Like the white British Marxists Jones critiqued on her arrival in Britain, she advised James to be a 'little modest' and learn 'from his own bitter experiences' in Trinidad. 'Instead of finding refuge in his so-called international activities, he should apply his "Marxism" and do the class analysis of the West Indies, which he has not done in this book'.[161] Jones reduced James to 'a very old, arrogant, bitter man' in contrast to what she called the 'young West Indian intellectuals', naming George Lamming, Jan Carew, Sylvia Wynter, Pearl Connor, and herself.

## Conclusion

British IR's constitutive failure in the second half of the twentieth century was its inability to receive the gift of thinking creatively and expansively about the world-historical significance of empire, all that it meant for 'the British world' and beyond. When C.L.R. James first migrated, he famously claimed the 'British intellectual was going to Britain'.[162] When Claudia Jones arrived in Southampton in 1955, she claimed her right to a British passport. It was the belated and ideological reconfiguration of 'British' to mean 'white indigenous' that thinkers of Jones's and James's intellectual and political significance could be erased from IR's intellectual histories of 'what engaged, interested intellectuals thought about world politics in the postwar years' in Britain.[163]

International Relations ought to have been the location of the deepest thinking on empire, its reconfigurations, and afterlives, but was one of its shallowest. It is no coincidence that a professional association for British International Relations was only founded when the metropole was territorially and racially defining itself as distinct from the remaining few colonies and the Commonwealth—that is, as post-imperial and white. The belated establishment of a (semi-)disciplinary identity in the 1970s, when Susan Strange founded the British International Studies Association, must be placed in its proper colonial and racial context, the context of Britain's slow transition from an imperial to a national concept.[164] The white men of British Coordinating Committee for International Studies and later the British Committee on the Theory of International Politics had bequeathed a neo-colonial, provincial IR, assuring that generations of British IR scholars were not properly educated about the world in which they lived and purported to explain. As discussed next, one white British IR scholar trying to retain a focus on legacies of empire and anticolonial thought in the 1960s, Rachel Wall, was forced out of academe.

# 10

# 'This is No Witch-Hunt'

I must admit, perhaps because I was not schooled in either of the old universities, that it gives me a special pleasure to think of all this subversion going on here, in Oxford.

—RACHEL WALL, JULY 1965[1]

AS A COUNTER TO THE denigration or erasure of women in intellectual histories, there is an obvious temptation to focus on stories of success. Look at the fame and recognition in her lifetime, how many books she sold, the importance and originality of her work and ideas. Yet not all women who make their way as intellectuals achieve glittering success, even with all the privileges of the academy. By most conventional measures, Rachel Wall was not a success story, described by one male disciplinary historian as 'Oxford IR's second unfortunate experience' with a Fellow of the women's college St Hugh's.[2] On this view, the proper maturation of IR at Oxford—from Alfred Zimmern to Hedley Bull—was interrupted not only by Agnes Headlam-Morley's alleged 'torpor', but also the 'wayward behaviour' of Rachel Wall.[3] In 1977, Oxford University determined that 'Miss Wall is either wilfully failing to discharge the duties of her office or by reason of mental infirmity unable to discharge them and it has decided therefore to delate her'.[4] In the autumn of 1978, Hedley Bull's first 'grim duty' as Oxford's next Montague Burton Professor of IR was to attend Rachel Wall's lectures and determine whether they were good enough for her to keep her job. 'She failed'[5] and was dead within a decade, at the age of fifty-five.

Until her arrival at Oxford in 1964, Rachel Wall's career as a budding IR scholar was successful: Rockefeller Foundation funding, a Montague Burton Studentship, a research position at Chatham House, publications including co-authorship of a *Survey of International Affairs*, attendance at major IR conferences in the United States and Europe, a Research Fellowship at Cambridge, culminating in becoming Oxford's first lecturer in IR appointed by the university, not a college. (All previous related appointments, except the Montague Burton Professorship, were made in Oxford's self-governing colleges rather than the university itself.) Wall was a talented linguist. She had a promising research agenda on the international relations of Asia. She gave inaugural lectures, and broadcast on the BBC. Rachel Wall also had a progressive vision for IR pedagogy and the wider field. In 1966, she was planning a new undergraduate paper at Oxford, 'International Relations 1860–1960' that broke new ground in British IR. Students would read Rosa Luxemburg, Nietzsche, Lenin, Mao, Nehru, Nasser, and Nkrumah as well as Darwin, Mackinder, Lugard, Kennan, and Morgenthau.[6] As a white British IR scholar, Rachel Wall was way ahead of her time, thinking seriously about how to teach and research non-Eurocentric world histories, the international relations of imperialism, global wars, anticolonial nationalisms, postcolonial states and their major intellectual underpinnings, approaches that only became mainstream in the 2000s.

In other words, Susan Strange was not the first figure on the British IR scene to represent something different to the white men of the British Coordinating Committee for International Studies or the British Committee on the Theory of International Politics. But Rachel Wall couldn't pull it off. The course proposal went nowhere, and her compounding personal and professional troubles combined to produce her downfall and banishment from Oxford. In contrast, the Australian Coral Bell, ten years Wall's senior, and the first woman permitted entry to the British Committee, managed to thrive and survive in British IR, often at the same institutions and often dealing with the same men as Rachel Wall. As easily and literally the most visible 'only woman in the room' before Susan Strange, and representing this new generation of young women IR scholars, Bell provides the main counterpoint to Wall in this chapter.

Feminists and queer theorists have long pointed to the importance of thinking about 'failure' as a method of challenging gendered, classed, ableist, and heteronormative definitions of success.[7] Seen this way, Rachel Wall's story is not a case of academic failure and certainly not 'wayward behaviour', but of overwork, heartbreak, mental illness, and unforgiving academic institutions and colleagues—*Oxford's* failure of care. Where Rachel Wall did err was in choosing whom to love. Lucie Zimmern, Mary Bull, and Veronica Boulter Toynbee made their mark on international relations through marriage to a prominent man who, in turn, made his way off her domestic, emotional, social, intellectual and sometimes childcare labours. Like Sibyl Crowe, Coral Bell's first and only love died young, and she remained unmarried for the rest of her life. At the age of twenty-three, Rachel Wall had the misfortune of falling in love with and becoming the long-term mistress of a 'great man' at Chatham House who was a better professional patron than a romantic partner.

## A Very Useful Person

Rachel Frances Wall was born in Blantyre, Nyasaland (now Malawi) in Central Africa in 1933 when indirect rule was re-established over the British protectorate. Her working-class father, Ernest, had been a Royal Engineer and captain during World War I. He wished to marry the upper-middle-class Catherine Hutton Jessie Greener and was expected to prove himself, so he joined the colonial service as an engineer after the war, with Catherine eventually joining him as a colonial wife. The family moved to Nigeria in 1938, but with another global war looming, the three children, Rachel and her older sister and younger brother, returned to England to live with a nanny. The children were evacuated to Herefordshire for most of the war, living with grandparents and an aunt, and Catherine remained in Nigeria until 1941. From 1942, Rachel Wall attended the private Malvern Girls College founded by spinster sisters in Worcestershire. She took A-levels in History, French, and Italian and became proficient in Russian, taught to her by two Russian nuns, in addition to her regular schooling. After VE Day, Rachel and her siblings were flown on a troop plane to briefly visit their father in Nigeria, where he remained until 1950.

With the post-war expansion of higher education, and the 'benevolent despotism' of the Professor of Government W.J.M. Mackenzie, Manchester University superseded Oxford and Cambridge as the leading institution for social and political studies in the 1950s.[8] Rachel Wall read politics and modern history at Manchester between 1952 and 1955, working with Mackenzie, philosopher Dorothy Emmet and historian Albert Goodwin.[9] She was taught Imperial History, International Relations ('really post-1914 international history', she claimed), and the origins of the Second World War by historians. Wall was highly active in student affairs and won an Alexis Aladin Bursary for travel to northern Italy, writing her dissertation on Italian diplomatic activity in the four months prior to World War II. She described the work as an explicit counter to Elizabeth Wiskemann's interpretation of the diplomacy of the fascist 'pact of steel', indicating once again women's presence, and only later erasure, as a focus for post-war IR teaching and research.[10]

Though coming from a middle-class family on her mother's side, Wall, like Wiskemann, was never financially secure and combined study with paid work. Sometimes she did not eat because she had spent her money on books. At Manchester, Wall reviewed school exam papers during the summers. Later, while at the London School of Economics (LSE), she worked on the side as a supply teacher for the London County Council. Wall was exceptional, both in being one of the few women to attend university and, like Coral Bell and Susan Strange, one of the few women scholars of IR in this period who did not take their first degree at an Oxbridge women's college. Mixed education and financial precarity, being forced to work for pay on the side, may account for Wall's degree, an upper second rather than a first. She earned first-class marks in her IR papers, and in Mackenzie's assessment she would 'be a very useful person in many jobs in the international field, whether in administration or teaching'.[11]

Wall initially appeared to accept this gendered trajectory. In her application for the M.Sc. in the IR Department at LSE, she described her ambition as administrative work at the Foreign Office or an international organisation or teaching international relations. She was offered a place at LSE but deferred entry after winning a Rockefeller-funded scholarship to study philosophy, history, and Italian foreign policy in the Spanish Civil War at the Institute for Historical Research in Naples. In Italy, she met 'some racy people', including communist partisans, whom she described to her niece, Cathie Wilson, as 'idealistic, handsome, young people forging a new world'.[12] After spending the summer in Vienna studying German, Rachel Wall enrolled part-time as an M.Sc. student at LSE with a Montague Burton Studentship of 40 pounds.

In the mid-1950s, and with Charles Manning still at the helm at LSE, IR's distinctiveness and value as a separate and coherent university subject remained an open question. Building on her early intellectual engagement with Elizabeth Wiskemann, Wall proposed to research the diplomatic history of fascist Italy. The LSE graduate committee accordingly 'expressed grave doubts' whether IR was the correct degree programme. It was determined that W. N. Medlicott, the Stevenson Chair in international history, should be consulted on whether Wall was more suitably registered in the Faculty of Arts, with the international historians, rather than economics, with IR.[13] Eager to build up the IR M.Sc., Manning pointed out that 'the inter-play of politics at the domestic and international levels' was a specialist option in IR, sidestepping the point that Wall's chosen methodology was diplomatic history.[14] On these dubious grounds, Wall was admitted to IR and, under Manning's guidance, predictably changed her topic to the more presentist question of 'the West's'

FIGURE 10.1. Rachel Wall, c.1955. Photographer Unknown. Courtesy of
Cathie Wilson

policy toward German reunification after 1945. Tellingly, Wall later applied for
a Ph.D. at LSE in international history, not IR. However, Medlicott only
agreed to re-admit her to the history M.Sc., an offer Wall declined.

Rachel Wall may have wished to pursue a doctorate in international history,
but she was well regarded by her IR teachers, including the then leading intellectual light of the department, Martin Wight, as well as Manning. In support

of Wall's 1957 Civil Service application, and in line with her undergraduate performance, Manning identified signs of first-class work. However, he repeated Mackenzie's judgement of Wall's place in the gendered professional and intellectual pecking order. Since she was 'not of all-round first class material', Manning determined, Wall 'would be more dependable as a collector of material for the evaluation of a more senior official than in formulating advice on higher points of policy'.[15] He may also have been describing what he mistakenly assumed Wall was already doing at Chatham House. Following the same path as the brilliant Australian Coral Bell, Wall combined her IR M.Sc. with a position on the Chatham House resident writing staff in December 1956, replacing Coral Bell after she resigned over intellectual differences with the new director of research, the man who contributed to Wall's downfall.

## History Just Waiting to be Written

Like Rachel Wall, though a decade older, Coral Bell was a child of the British colonies, born to a working-class Anglo-Irish family in the self-governing white settler dominion of Australia in 1923. When she was seven years old, Bell's mother died from a cerebral haemorrhage; her father lost his job as an electrical contractor at the start of the Great Depression. Sent to live with her middle-class aunt and uncle, Bell was educated by Catholic nuns at a 'little bush convent', where she claimed to have learnt about the 'contemporary uses of history'.[16] In preparation for senior school exams in both Catholic and Protestant schools, Bell learned to reproduce both a 'very Catholic version of events'[17] 'heavily oriented to the woes of Ireland', which she learned with the nuns, and the 'Protestant version', including 'the glories of the British imperial story'.[18] Bell claimed that these contrasting accounts taught her 'how different the flow of history looked depending on where you stood nationally and ideologically'.[19] Colonial and anticolonial history reduced to religion and simple relativism.

As a straight-A student, Bell won a scholarship to the selective all-girls (Protestant) high school and another to attend Sydney University in 1942. She read English, history and philosophy at night, and helped demagnetise warships for the Australian navy during the day. She recalled anxious bus rides home in the evenings as Eddie Leonski—an American soldier stationed in Melbourne—was loose terrorising, raping, and murdering women. At a time of heightened wartime anxiety, there was concern that the serial killer 'might turn his attention to Sydney'.[20] Bell was also mourning her first love who was killed during the landing of Australian forces on Papua New Guinea.

Like Sibyl Crowe, Bell never married after the death of her first love, claiming to have given 'up the idea' after joining the Australian diplomatic service in 1946. The foreign service operated a marriage bar for women that was only rescinded in 1966.[21]

With a relatively small foreign service, Coral Bell's tasks during her six years working on Australia's 'external affairs' were wide-ranging and 'quite heady stuff for a twenty-five-year-old'.[22] In a larger service, she noted with relief, 'you might be required to spend half your life on the problems of Burkina Faso'.[23] Not tasked with addressing the legacies of French colonialism, Bell instead worked on the implications for Australia of the Baruch Plan on nuclear weapons and the Arab–Israeli disputes; attended the 1951 signing of the ANZUS treaty between Australia, New Zealand and the United States; and unknowingly interacted with several members of a Soviet spy ring who attempted to recruit her. At one point, she was desk officer for the entirety of Southeast Asia, but also got 'the wooden spoon' posting to New Zealand. Bell found diplomatic work intellectually frustrating and was disgusted at the Labour Government's continued support for the White Australia Policy. 'I did not care to spend even a fraction of my time on such degrading nonsense'.[24]

Bell left diplomacy to pursue a more independent career in academe yet was unimpressed by Australia's IR scene. She thus took the slow boat via Egypt to England, which she entered as a 'British (Australian)' national and enrolled for the M.Sc. at LSE. She was, she claimed, 'one of the last generation or two of Australians to take it for granted that we might divide our working lives between Britain and Australia'.[25] Like Wall, Bell worked with Charles Manning (on Australia at the UN), and like everyone else, was far more impressed by the historian Martin Wight. She called Wight the 'star' of the IR Department and 'the chief intellectual influence of my life'.[26] As for so many others in British IR's impoverished intellectual landscape in this period, men and women, Wight became Bell's lifelong intellectual crush, the 'finest mind and spirit I ever knew'.[27]

Bell later described herself as part of the 'London group' interested in the history of international thought that revolved around Wight, who was also active in the British Committee on the Theory of International Politics, from whose histories Bell is usually excluded.[28] She admired Wight's approach to international theory as the history of thought 'from Thucydides to Henry Kissinger as a sort of shimmering tapestry of many figures, a tapestry mostly woven from just three contrasting threads, which he called realist, rationalist and revolutionist'.[29] It is not clear whether she was aware, or would have cared, that the British Committee's 'history of thought' approach was a way of 'trapping' historians into the Rockefeller-funded project for a general 'theory of international politics'. According to British Committee Chair, Herbert Butterfield, historians were highly sceptical of 'general thinking or scientific analysis'.[30] They were 'very chary of theory as such' and 'contemptuous of anything like a general theory of history'. Hence, Butterfield wrote to the American Kenneth Thompson, the man tasked with co-opting British IR scholars to the project of a 'theory' of international politics: 'it occurred to me that a more concrete study of the history of historiography would be away of trapping them unawares into the discussion of methods and principles—a policy which has had a lot of success. I think that the same is likely to be true of International Theory . . . Martin Wight seems to me to be just the man to produce what is on the one hand a piece of concrete history and . . . a revision of theory'.[31]

So influenced by Wight's parsimonious approach to the history of international thought that produced the British counterpart to American IR's all-white all-male canon, Coral Bell's first topic of doctoral research was not in the field of strategic studies or US foreign policy, the work for which she is best known and subject of her first book.[32] With Wight and leading Marxist sociologist, Ralph Miliband, Bell began doctoral research on the history of liberal and left international thought in interwar England. While she had gathered materials for her history of thought, writing was stalled by her work at Chatham House from 1951, first as rapporteur for a project on Britain and the UN and then for 'everyone's favourite scholarly grandfather', Arnold Toynbee, on *The Survey of International Affairs*.[33]

Close to his retirement, and preoccupied with the philosophy of history, Toynbee gave Coral Bell free reign on the *Survey*. He 'did no more than glance at the table of contents I proposed', she claimed, and remembered him as if he was always 'walking *backwards* to avoid seeming to throw his weight around'.[34] Though she became quite the intellectual insider herself, Bell claimed to have shocked some of the 'old hands' at Chatham House by placing 'two non-European issues' at the centre of the *Survey*.[35] She wrote about the significance of the battle of Dien Bien Phu in the Vietnam War, which resulted in a victory of Vietnam forces over the US-backed French colonial army, and included a section, 'Atoms and Strategy', on the implications of nuclear weapons for international relations. The profound intellectual and political conservatism of Chatham House is indicated in the fact that, according to Bell, 'some of the more dedicated Eurocentric members of the establishment were a bit sceptical, and without Toynbee's backing I might have had to change my emphasis'.[36] But it meant that Bell could pose at least as 'very radical and daring' for suggesting in the mid-1950s that nuclear weapons would be central to the superpower relationship and 'most of the sources of trouble might be in the Third World'.[37]

Rachel Wall's big break came when Coral Bell fell out with Toynbee's successor as director of research. Medieval historian Geoffrey Barraclough had entered Oxford not from a private school but from a selective state-funded grammar school for brighter children of all class backgrounds, though are often dominated by the middle class. Unlike Toynbee, who relied on Veronica Boulter and then Coral Bell to research and often write the *Survey*, Barraclough informed Chatham House that he would do most of the research and writing himself. He confessed to being 'rather nervous' of Coral Bell and was unable to envisage how 'anyone as junior as Miss Bell could possibly' work as an 'understudy' to the *Survey's* main author. He did not doubt her 'capabilities', yet after their first meeting Barraclough reported that 'I did not seem to speak the same language as she did, and the schemes she produced, meant virtually nothing to me'.[38] The feeling was mutual. Bell later claimed never to have understood Barraclough's appointment as Toynbee's successor, mentioning his background in medieval history as if other medievalists such as Eileen Power had never worked on international relations. After Barraclough published *History in a Changing World* in 1955, he became a leading advocate of new historical and global methods.[39] Nonetheless, their 'first conversation made it clear to me', Bell recalled, 'that our assumptions about the world were incompatible, and that I had better start looking for a new job'.[40]

The exact source of Barraclough and Bell's differences is not entirely clear from the correspondence and Bell's later commentary. It was certainly not Bell's alleged 'radical departure'[41] from the 'establishment' by decentering Europe; this was one of Barraclough's core approaches to contemporary history. However, Bell identified Barraclough as a man of 'strong Left convictions' at a time when her own politics were shifting further to the right. She was delighted when conservative political theorist Michael Oakeshott succeeded the socialist Harold Laski at LSE. She also admired Karl Popper's *The Open Society*, which she saw as a 'straw in the winds of change in the general intellectual climate of the world' away from 'Fabian assumptions', those of the main socialist organisation in Britain that had founded the LSE.[42] This wider rightward shift may have influenced Bell's decision to drop her international intellectual history of the liberal left and write on US foreign policy and crisis management instead. In 1956, Bell quit Chatham House to become the first dedicated IR lecturer at Manchester University, Rachel Wall's alma mater, and no longer attended Wight's graduate classes at LSE. Wight described this as 'an irreparable loss';[43] Bell was 'the most mature and able member of the post-graduate seminar'.[44] She was a woman of opinions and experience and could handle men like Barraclough who, in turn, was 'glad' she was leaving Chatham House. Yet he would still need 'a young person, presumably a graduate, and preferably a male, who would "devil"'.[45]

## Preferably a Male

Despite being only twenty-three years old, and not male, Rachel Wall was an ideal candidate to undertake the arduous research tasks, the 'devil' work, on the *Survey of International Affairs*. With her impressive language skills and IR training, Wall was more than a documentarian, reading foreign newspapers and excerpting materials for the *Survey*. Like Boulter and Bell before her, she was soon co-writing the *Surveys*. During five of his six years as Chatham House director of research, and despite his initial intentions, Barraclough delegated much of his *Survey* work to Rachel Wall and took credit for work that was based on her research and writing.[46] In the 1955–56 *Survey*, Wall was sole author of at least five chapters. They appear as co-authors of the volume that analysed the world-historical significance of the Bandung conference, defending its real achievements against criticisms from the West.[47] For 1956–58, Wall claimed to have written 'at least the chapters attributed to me', implying she wrote some that were not, including the section on Asia and the Far East in the 1959–60 *Survey*. What Bell had claimed to initiate in the *Survey*, a focus on the non-European world, was normalised under Barraclough and Wall.

Barraclough was not the first or last director of studies to depend on women's intellectual labour.[48] Susan Strange was deeply involved with and very likely helped Andrew Shonfield redraft and edit parts of *Modern Capitalism*, first published in 1965, the year after she joined Chatham House as a full-time researcher and while Shonfield was its director of studies. Shonfield only credited his wife, Zuzanna Shonfield, 'who took an active part in the research which went into several portions of the book', also noting that he was 'assisted by a great many people . . . it is hard at this stage to identify precisely which individual idea I owe to whom'.[49] But, in contrast to Veronica Boulter, and more like Coral Bell and later Susan Strange, Rachel Wall was using her Chatham Housework and contacts to make her way in IR as a path to an independent academic career. During this period, Wall was a prolific book reviewer, including works in German, French, and Italian. For the house journal *International Affairs*, she reviewed rival surveys on world politics and publications of foreign policy documents.[50] She thought the first Indian yearbook was 'Delhi-centric' and had a 'slant on coloured opinion".'[51] She later broadened her reviewing to works on twentieth-century international relations, foreign policy, and biographies of figures like Gandhi, the Dalai Lama, and Nkrumah and sympathetically reviewed American IR scholar Kenneth Thompson's *Christian Ethics and the Dilemmas of Foreign Policy*.[52] Much later, in 1968, Wall wrote an extremely long annotated bibliography-cum-review of almost two hundred works on the general history of the twentieth century that included J. P. Nettl's biography of Rosa Luxemburg and the reissue of Wiskemann's *The Rome–Berlin Axis*, which had so shaped Wall's early interest in world politics.[53]

Through the late 1950s and early 1960s, Wall attended IR teaching and research conferences and events in Britain, Europe, Canada and the United States, including the Conference on North Atlantic Community in Bruges in 1957; the first Anglo-Soviet conference of historians in 1958; and discussions on writing contemporary history at the Institut für Zeitgeschichte in Munich.[54] She attended a meeting of the Polish Academy of Sciences in 1961, and discussions on different approaches to the study of international relations in Geneva.[55] Wall twice studied at The Hague Academy of International Law and continued to learn Russian. She spoke at the Council on Foreign Relations in New York and attended the Conference on IR in the Mid-Twentieth Century at Northwestern University, where Wall was the only woman except Vera Michales Dean, head of research at the Foreign Policy Association and later academic at Harvard, Rochester and New York University.[56] Dean's books sold in hundreds of thousands and championed her progressive vision of collective security, a global defence force, economic development, anticolonialism, and a less offensive posture toward the USSR, which she claimed only delayed its democratisation. As a Russian–American, Dean was attacked by anticommunists for insisting that Soviet foreign policy was primarily defensive.

Like Lilian Friedländer and Rachel Wall, Coral Bell also found the United States a congenial atmosphere for new thinking on international relations, a place of intellectual development and career advancement. With Mackenzie's support, Bell spent a year in the United States on a Rockefeller grant, primarily at Johns Hopkins, during which she met the architects of US Cold War policy George Kennan, Dean Acheson, Paul Nitze, and Hans J. Morgenthau. She visited Columbia and Harvard, where she met and developed a lifelong admiration for Henry Kissinger. At Princeton, she met J. Robert Oppenheimer, director of the Manhattan Project that created the atomic bomb, who told Bell about the still top-secret document NSC-68. These were all contacts and materials for Bell's new doctoral research on US Cold War strategy in the 1950s. Published as *Negotiation from Strength: A Study in the Politics of Power*, Bell's highly praised first book was a study of US policymakers efforts to establish a viable alternative to the mere 'containment' of the Soviet Union.[57] Influenced by her early diplomatic work, and in line with the so-called 'interpretive' approach pursed by both Manning and Wight, Bell thought international relations was best explained by the ideas and beliefs of elite policymakers, centring how they saw the world and justified their actions.[58] Like them, she confused elite accounts of the world with the way the world actually worked.

For Vera Michales Dean, Coral Bell and Rachel Wall, think-tank work was a way into the professional field of international relations, but gendered assumptions about the nature of the work often prevailed. In his reference for Wall's application for a Eugénie Strong Research Fellowship in History at Girton College, Cambridge, historian Richard Van Alstyne thought that 'so young a person should be selected to write a sizeable portion' of one of the *Surveys* was 'a distinction in itself'.[59] Barraclough's letter pointed out that Wall was more than the conventional 'research assistant'. She possessed 'a true historian's . . . attitude of mind', able to 'stand above . . . partisan terms: whether colonialists and anti-colonialists . . . communists and anti-communists'. Writing on St Valentine's Day, he also noted she was a 'handsome girl' of 'obviously good breeding'.[60]

Asked by Girton to comment on Wall's work, Denis Brogan, the Cambridge historian and later mentor to Susan Strange, doubted its independent intellectual worth. 'The framework, the chronological limits, the allocation of topics, are not the result of her independent judgement', claimed Brogan, because 'Chatham House has its own "house style" . . . that would prevent Miss Wall from showing her originality if she had any to show'.[61] Writing summaries of international events under Barraclough's direction was no substitute for a doctorate. 'I am certain', Brogan continued, 'without any inside information, that [Barraclough] must have kept a firm hand on all parts of the book while it was in progress'.[62] Brogan may not have had inside information, but it was unlikely the affair between the fifty-year-old married man and the assistant researcher in her mid-twenties was a total secret at Chatham cathouse.

Like Toynbee and Boulter, Barraclough and Wall were not just collaborators on the *Survey*, they were lovers. (Toynbee divorced his first wife, Rosalind Murray in 1946, marring Veronica Boulter soon after.) When Barraclough was invited to conferences and professional meetings, he solicited an invitation for Wall too. Her family were aware of, and disapproved of Rachel's affair with a married man, whose children she looked after when they visited Barraclough in London.[63] Barraclough was divorced from his first wife in 1945 and promised Wall he would divorce Diana Russell-Clarke, his second. He eventually did, but not for Rachel Wall. Wall got her Cambridge Fellowship at Girton in 1961, and the following year Barraclough returned to Cambridge as a Fellow of St John's.[64] The relationship with Wall may have ended in 1965, when he 'took flight to America',[65] though Wall taught at a summer school in California when Barraclough was teaching at the University of California in San Diego. It is unclear when the affair ended and whether it later resumed. There are several photographs of Barraclough among Wall's personal papers, and a letter from him as late as 1972.

## Wall's Century: Towards IR as Contemporary World History

The electors for the Girton Research Fellowship set aside Brogan's assessment of the intellectual limitations of the *Survey* and selected Rachel Wall. Although Wall's early academic record 'was not particularly distinguished', Barraclough had claimed, due to her second-class degree, Wall was 'one of the most remarkable cases of a "late developer"' he had seen.[66] Wall repaid his patronage by constantly citing Barraclough as the leading and most articulate exponent of international relations as contemporary and world history, an approach Barraclough called 'international history on a global plane',[67] and Wall 'the whole international social milieu'.[68] At Chatham House, her research interests had moved away from European and diplomatic history toward what she called 'an Asian-based worldview of the 20th century'.[69] During the 1960s, Wall too was on an upwards trajectory towards becoming a new practitioner of this seemingly less Eurocentric IR.

At Cambridge, Wall's teaching reflected her new interests in imperial rivalry in the Far East, the origins of the emergence of Asia in world affairs, and eventually what she called 'the resurgence of the non-white masses' during the 'colour-conscious' twentieth century.[70] In addition to 'European History since 1485' and 'European Expansion Overseas since 1500', she taught the special subjects 'The Chinese in Southeast Asia' and 'The British in Malaya'. The latter course she taught immediately after Britain's brutal late-colonial military campaign, involving mass forced displacement and concentration camps, in which Wall's younger brother, Edward, fought as a Royal Engineer and which traumatised him for the rest of his life.[71] Wall continued with her Russian and taught for the Workers' Educational Association Summer School in 1963, the same year double agent Kim Philby, one of the 'Cambridge Five', defected to the Soviet Union. Wall's sister recalls her sending Marks & Spencer pyjamas to one of the defectors because he said he missed his 'home comforts'.[72] The same year Wall decided that she would bequeath her books to the John Rylands Library at Manchester and her estate to Geoffrey Barraclough, apart from a specific legacy 'to the female children of her brother Edward'.[73] In 1964, she participated in the Ranke-Gesellschaft Conference on the 1919 peace treaties and helped lead a group visit to educational establishments in Moscow and Leningrad on the invitation of the Soviet Union.[74]

Wall's most substantial single-authored work was *Japan's Century: An Interpretation of Japanese History Since the Eighteen-Fifties*, published by the Historical Association under Barraclough's presidency in 1964.[75] The short but very well-written overview of Japanese foreign and imperial relations over a century also incorporated Japan's influence on 'Europe itself—on its arts and literature, its politics and diplomacy, its economy and its wars, even perhaps on its standards of morality'.[76] Wall surveyed the national seclusion debate and the imperial restoration, economic and political developments in Meiji Japan, the search for international recognition at the turn of the twentieth century, Japan's signing of the first equal treaty between a European and non-European power, its policy of imperialism and the interwar China question, World War II and post-war reconstruction. The publisher Routledge approached Wall to write an expanded book-length version and Methuen sought her advice on a book series in Pacific and Far Eastern Studies. She was invited to write a book on 'internationalism' for Blackie's General Studies series on twentieth-century history.

However, Wall's interests had moved to China, the principal focus of her writing and specialist teaching through to the 1970s. At Cambridge, she had started work on a book on modern China in the world, including Britain's China policy during the nineteenth and twentieth centuries. Pointing to the relations between Hong Kong and Shanghai banks and the British government, she suggested there is 'evidence enough of economic imperialism to make even the most sceptical conscious of the relevance of a Marxist interpretation of the period'.[77] The publishers Hutchinson issued her a contract for *The Rise of China*. In an unpublished paper, 'China and the Asian scene', presented at St Anne's College Oxford in 1965, Wall argued that students of modern

Europe had much to learn from Chinese history, which was not the history of a nation-state but 'a multiracial empire with its many intricate relationships—in both internal and external affairs . . . In a period of history when the autonomous nation state has been superseded by multinational and super national groupings, the Chinese Imperial tradition with its carefully regulated political and cultural relationships, provides an interesting pattern of study'.[78]

At Cambridge, Wall established and ran an inter-collegiate seminar on twentieth-century history and contributed to reform of the Cambridge history syllabus. But a permanent position at Cambridge was unlikely given the residual distrust of IR as a separate and dilettante subject, and the misogyny of many of its male dons. With Manning not appointing women at LSE, few IR posts elsewhere, and a greater openness to international relations, Oxford was the main location for women international relations scholars. In 1963, Oxford advertised its first-ever faculty lectureship in IR in association with two women's colleges, St Hugh's and Lady Margaret Hall. Interestingly, Wall's application, and Barraclough's reference, emphasised her ability to teach both international history and, in her words, 'the theory of International Relations'. She was familiar with the work of American-based IR theorists Hans J. Morgenthau, Quincy Wright, Stanley Hoffman and Richard Snyder, all of whom Wall met at an IR conference in Northwestern University.[79] Barraclough confirmed that Wall had an 'eye for the overall patterns and the inter-connexion of affairs in different regions', which he attributed to 'her knowledge of and interest in the theory of international relations . . . She is au fait with American work on the theoretical side . . . and her broad foundation of historical knowledge . . . makes her a pretty trenchant critic of theory'. He claimed to 'honestly believe that she will make a real mark, if appointed'.[80]

In 1964, at the age of thirty-one, Rachel Wall was the unanimous choice of selectors to be Oxford's first faculty lecturer in IR. Agnes Headlam-Morley, on sabbatical and not involved in the appointment, made 'the strongest possible protest' against the fact that her preferred candidate of 'outstanding merit', fluent in Russian and with 'more experience in the use of diplomatic documents', was not selected for interview.[81] Yet Wall had the wider range of teaching experience. She was initially appointed for a period of five years, after which her position would be reviewed and likely made permanent. Barraclough was right to believe that she could make a mark at Oxford. She was clearly on an upward trajectory: a woman without an Oxbridge or even first-class degree making her way through the elite locations of British IR—LSE, Chatham House, Cambridge, now Oxford. She did so with the help of her lover, but also the opportunities for middle-class white women at Chatham House and Oxbridge women's colleges, as well as hard work and intellectual versatility. She was an historian by training and temperament and IR theory was not rocket science; it did not take much to claim an ability to teach it. As Coral Bell pointed out in 1968, despite 'the latest psychedelic gear of computer simulation and communication theory', international theory was at 'present a rather unimpressive growth. It is as though the plant which ought to be the centrepiece and glory of the garden . . . had obstinately refused to put on more than a few inches in height, despite much watering, pruning, tilling, crooning over, and feeding with rare and expensive nutrients'.[82] Like Wall, Bell was inclined to 'the view that international politics will remain largely a meditation on history'.[83]

More importantly, at this historical moment, when Susan Strange was being pushed out of University College London for inconveniencing her male colleagues by having too many children, it was Rachel Wall and Coral Bell, both historians of different political temperaments, that represented a new generation of international relations scholarship in Britain. Bell had resigned from Manchester in 1961, returning to Australia to rekindle family ties after her father's sudden death, becoming a senior lecturer and the first dedicated IR scholar at the University of Sydney. There she researched and wrote the highly praised *The Debatable Alliance: An Essay in Anglo-American Relations* which, according to one reviewer, placed Bell 'in the front rank of writers on power-politics'.[84] The book critiqued all sentimental notions about a 'special relationship'. Anglo-American relations were rooted in the 'central power balance' between the United States and the Soviet Union.

With Charles Manning recently retired, the way was open for Coral Bell to return to Britain for a Readership in IR at LSE, making her, in 1965, the first woman appointed to a permanent post in that department since Lucy Philip Mair in the late 1920s. As a white Australian, she entered Britain through its racist 1962 Commonwealth Immigrants Act, which, as Claudia Jones had vociferously argued, was designed precisely to exclude Black Commonwealth 'immigrants' like her but permit white ones like Bell.

Owing to a slight delay in Bell's arrival in January 1966, and Hedley Bull's secondment to the Foreign Office, Susan Strange did some occasional teaching for LSE.[85] Still, into the mid-1960s, as one IR M.Sc. student recalled, IR as taught at LSE was 'a really woeful subject', especially after Martin Wight left for Sussex University and abandoned IR for history. The lectures at LSE 'were pretty odd', 'unengaging', 'and you scarcely even knew what they were going on about'. Some of the teaching was so poor, Cornelia Navari recalled, that

FIGURE 10.2. The LSE International Relations Department, 1967. Photographer Unknown. Courtesy of LSE Library

'rhetorical questions had no answers.' She was enraged at the 'fairly dismal sort of education' she received. It was a little like anthropology, 'a nice way of getting to know something about the world . . . a kind of finishing school subject'.[86] It was still not a serious academic discipline. Navari took one course on NATO with Coral Bell, who 'seemed pretty sensible' but had appeared quite 'shocked' by the 'New Leftie' approach Navari adopted in one essay, because it questioned how NATO's enemies were defined. It is unlikely that Rachel Wall, a woman of the left interested in postcolonial and non-Western thought, an historian on top of her IR theory, would have been shocked in the slightest.

## Reforming Oxford IR

During the mid-1960s, Rachel Wall 'promised . . . a brilliant career'.[87] She was not as prolific as Coral Bell but she had a reputation for being a good writer as well as a linguist—'writes *really* well' wrote St Hugh's Principal Kathleen

Kenyon during Wall's job interview.[88] She was successfully teaching and presenting work on the contemporary and global history of Asia, a new and distinctive approach to international relations. To her niece, Cathie Wilson, Rachel appeared 'rather wonderful and glamorous, independent, clever, and beautiful . . . She wasn't dependent on a man . . . She sent me this amazing letter that said that if you're a single woman, as long as you had a newspaper and a Mars bar, you could travel all over the world . . . With a newspaper you could stand on it, you can put it down your coat to keep you warm, you could read it, you could hit a man with it if he was too familiar, and you just eat the Mars bar'.[89]

On one level, Rachel Wall's early years at Oxford went well enough. Intellectually, she continued her advocacy for a new approach to international history as world history, returning to themes set out by Eileen Power in the 1930s, but which Wall was more likely to attribute to her lover. In contrast to her St Hugh's colleague and the Montague Burton Professor, Agnes Headlam-Morley, Wall insisted that 'history cannot remain Walpole and Peel, the history of "great men", when world history was a discussion of problems of race relations'.[90] The very nature of the study of 'inter-relations' mitigated against constitutional history and the diplomacy of 'great men', again as Eileen Power had insisted.[91]

Wall's 1968 review of general histories of the twentieth century began by praising Barraclough's inaugural lecture as president of the Historical Association, which had eschewed the search for the personal motives of great men and centred the immediate and long-term effects of major historical events such as colonialism.[92] The basic premise of the post-war approach to contemporary and world history was that the first decades of the twentieth century inaugurated revolutionary transformation and required a similar change in the categories of historical research.[93] Wall was alarmed at the 'cult' of regional studies because regions 'no longer have any independent existence . . . If our history is to be relevant . . . then it must be world history'.[94] Declining sovereignty, new federalist solutions to world order, Europe's loss of political and ideological power, and the technological and economic shrinkage of space undermined diplomatic, national or even regional approaches to history.

Like the world historians Power, Toynbee, and H. G. Wells, Wall agreed that any attempt 'to deal with Europe as a distinct entity . . . will soon bring one back to a mere collection of national histories'.[95] But unlike these largely interwar thinkers, who surveyed 'the whole vista of the historic past in order to discover trends and patterns and general laws', Barraclough and Wall's post-war approach to world history was more modest.[96] They simply emphasised the interaction of world regions and the recognition of the significance of non-European peoples and politics, including the international relations of race.[97] In her 1966 BBC radio broadcast, Wall pointed to the significance of pan-African and pan-Arab unity which had been sneered at in the West, including by the LSE figures associated with the 'international society' approach to international relations, Charles Manning, Martin Wight, and Hedley Bull.[98]

Rachel Wall was fascinated by postcolonial leaders and intellectuals, with their proposals for reconstituting international order around regional federations challenging neo-colonialist orders in ways that were deeply threatening to British, French, and US foreign-policy visions.[99] But 'what's of interest to the contemporary historian', Wall maintained, is that Ghana's Kwame Nkrumah and Egypt's Gamel Abdel Nasser 'should have thought along non-national lines at all' and in terms of postcolonial unity, alliance, and even federation.[100] Wall's review of general histories of the twentieth century also singled out South African anti-apartheid activist and writer Ronald Segal's *The Race War*. The central fact of history was 'the domination of the coloured poor rebel by the white rich'.[101] In a typical act of white appropriation, Wall assimilated this commonplace of the Black Radical tradition into Geoffrey Barraclough's writing on 'the revolt against the west'.[102] Yet even this limited thinking still opened new possibilities for mid-century white British IR. At Cambridge, Wall helped to organise a petition opposing the apartheid regime in South Africa, and wrote to inform white South African activist and politician, Helen Suzman.[103]

Contemporary history emerged in parallel with, but then later diverged from, much of the work on 'international society'—driven more by so-called 'theory'—Eurocentric and male intellectual history, and dismissiveness toward Third World claims. All of those became more influential in British IR due to the influence of Martin Wight and Hedley Bull, a divergence between IR and contemporary history not helped by Wall's eventual fate. After her BBC address, Weidenfeld & Nicolson approached Wall to write a book-length study of contemporary world history. Her reputation was growing, including among teachers interested in curricula reform. In 1965, she attended the International Historical Congress of Vienna and the Economic History Congress in Leningrad. In 1966, she was the inaugural lecturer of the North Staffs Historical Association series to colleges of education.

Wall was also an intellectual and curricula reformer at Oxford. Sibyl Crowe recalled that the subject of politics had 'an appalling status' at Oxford in the 1960s and 1970s, and politics teachers in general had 'a professional antagonism against Historians', the field in which Crowe had trained.[104] In 1965, as noted in the epigraph to this chapter, Wall admitted to a 'special pleasure' at what she saw as the intellectual subversion of a conference at Oxford on world history 'because I was not schooled in either of the old universities'.[105] Her 1966 proposal for a new IR paper was intended to differ in style, scope, and method from the two existing papers, which under Agnes Headlam-Morley covered 1919–1941 and IR since 1941. She was on the committee to examine and revise IR teaching.[106] Wall correctly thought students needed to understand major international developments before 1919, including imperialism and the rise of non-European powers, and to broaden the intellectual approach beyond political and diplomatic history, again the dominant approach under Headlam-Morley. Most significantly, Wall wanted the new paper to centre what she saw as the most important fact of the twentieth century, the 'change from a Euro-centric world to one dominated by extra-European considerations'. She imagined such a course would be taught through both an historical narrative of major developments and themes, including 'race relations in the United States; the modernisation of Japan; and the attempt to bring China into the European-type international relations system', but also attention to major books and texts with 'widespread influence in the period'. Again, she listed works by Darwin, Nietzsche, Lenin, Mao, Mackinder, Kennan, Morgenthau, Nehru, Nkrumah, Nasser, and Lugard. In handwritten notes, she added Luxemburg and Ortega.[107]

Walls's proposal for a new IR paper was never adopted. At the Sub-Faculty of Politics, 'it was felt that the papers in International Relations were still unsatisfactory, and Miss Wall undertook to make a fresh proposal for the meeting in the fifth week of term'.[108] But there is no record of her formally proposing her new course. Four years later, she scrawled 'Imperial Relations' over her colleague Wilfred Knapp's proposal for the graduate IR B.Phil. degree (now M.Phil.).[109] It is not clear whether Wall's note was motivated by her call for the inclusion of imperial relations in the syllabus, most likely, or implying that the proposal itself was a form of imperial relations. Nonetheless, Wall continued to call for 'more variety in the International Relations field',[110] like some of her Oxford male colleagues, though in a more global and intellectually pluralist direction. There is no record of her views on Michael Howard and Alastair Buchan's plans to make the core IR paper more 'theoretical' (literally the international thought of white men, 'Machiavelli to Morgenthau'; Coral Bell would have added 'Kissinger'). However, Wall complained that it was ridiculous that the 'general purpose' she appeared to serve at Oxford was 'to bridge the gap for those interested in the 1870s–1970s period in history, social science and Oriental studies'.[111] Her colleagues outside the Politics Department did not always appreciate her criticisms and reforming agenda. Director of St Anthony's Centre for Far Eastern Studies thought that with 'her denunciations of the old exclusively European interpretation of "Modern History" she sometimes seems to be flogging a dead horse with excessive zeal'.[112]

## Making Herself Awkward

The point is that Rachel Wall was gaining a reputation among some of her Oxford colleagues, and not only for her vision for a new IR.[113] The Secretary of Faculties reported that the Gladstone Professor of Government, Max Beloff, was 'expressing some concern ... Apparently [Wall] has been making herself awkward'.[114] Things were particularly difficult at St Hugh's where the classics tutor had complained of Wall's 'unsuitability for a Fellowship', accusing Wall of 'hysteria', 'flurried speech and resentment'.[115] Wall had actually delivered the tutorials expected of her but was faulted for sometimes changing subjects mid-term, refusing to oversee College admissions or meet students out of class who wanted advice.[116]

Wall's main problem, as Sibyl Crowe found at St Hilda's, was not her awkwardness and 'hysteria', rather an excessive teaching load, which spanned the faculty and two colleges, St Hugh's and Lady Margaret Hall. For the faculty, she taught an extraordinarily wide array of general and specialist papers and lectures, including 'IR since 1918', 'World War II', 'The Cold War', 'Problems in Twentieth-Century History', and 'Imperialism in the Age of World Politics'. Her specialist teaching included 'China in the 20th century', 'IR and East Asia and the Pacific 1894–1931', 'IR in Asia 1955–65', 'China and the Rest: Facets of Chinese History', 'Mao's China', 'China in the 20th Century', and 'Reformers and Revolutionaries in Modern China'. But she was also responsible for politics teaching at St Hugh's and Lady Margaret Hall, the only colleges with no other politics tutor.[117] Already by the end of her first term, Wall found the situation impossible.

Exhausted 'after ten years of almost uninterrupted work',[118] Wall applied for a year of absence for 1966–7, partly without pay, to work on her China book, learn the language, possibly visit China, and a US university 'where modern Chinese studies are well-developed'.[119] This may have been the University of California in San Diego where Barraclough was teaching. The leave was agreed, and Headlam-Morley arranged for Eleanor Breuning, an expert on the Soviet Union and East–Central Europe, to cover Wall's teaching. Wall appeared to be making good research progress. She continued to attend national and international conferences, review manuscripts for presses, give invited lectures, including for the Historical Association, deliver courses at the Department of Education and Science and Surrey County Council, and Oxford University's Delegacy for Extra-Mural Studies. In 1968, Wall presented a paper on the limits of sovereignty at a conference at St John's and was 'in Prague when the Russian tanks rolled while her parents thought she was in Blackpool'.[120] In May 1969, Thames and Hudson offered Wall a contract for her China book, now called *Reformers and Revolutionaries in Modern China*.

In Rachel Wall's personal papers, an undated draft letter in her own hand-writing but meant to be from her GP explained the other context for her 1966–7 year of leave. Since 1965, Wall writes in the third person, she was 'troubled' by an undiagnosed condition that her doctor hoped would resolve after 'a year in a different environment'. With 'varying degrees of sympathy', her three employers (the university and two colleges) had agreed to her taking leave for a year of research, but which her GP thought was for rest and recovery. Instead, Wall was having private tuition in intensive Chinese, 'starting a new enterprise without a break'.[121] Wall later informed the university that, for medical reasons, she had not made progress on research during her sabbatical and did not visit China. She was managing with her teaching yet could not also sustain research and writing at this time.

In contrast, Coral Bell's career was thriving, with her more conservative intellectual agenda supported by the emerging generation of new big men in British IR. In 1965, she returned to the institution that awarded her doctorate, LSE, mentioning in her letter of application that her forthcoming book on the balance of power in Asia 'may prove a standard work in its field'.[122] Bell was always more squarely networked with IR's leading men, becoming a member of the British Committee. She now began to define her work more openly in its terms. In *The Conventions of Crisis*, Bell offered a trenchant critique of new-fangled behaviourist theoretical approaches emanating from the United States, 'game theory, content analysis, operational research, systems analysis, and simulation theory' which 'already have been in use for long enough to have demonstrated their limitations as well as their occasional (and marginal) usefulness'.[123] Bell preferred an historical approach that centred on how elite actors interpreted and acted in the world. Accordingly, *Conventions* argued that in a world of nuclear powers, Armageddon could only be avoided by a new concert of powers managed by a small number of elite decision-makers, a position she shared with both Wight and Henry Kissinger.[124]

FIGURE 10.3. Some founding members of the British Committee and others near Lake Como Italy, c.1973. Photographer Unknown. *Standing*: Kenneth Thompson, Hedley Bull, Maurice Keens-Soper, Robert Wade-Gery, Wolfgang Momsen (guest), *Seated*: Desmond Williams, Adam Watson, Coral Bell, Herbert Butterfield, Max Kohnstaam (guest). Courtesy of Polly Watson Black

By the time Bell arrived at LSE, Martin Wight had left not only LSE but IR itself, a telling abandonment from the figure often described as post-war British IR's most, perhaps only, first-class (male) mind. In 1960, Wight became founding dean of European Studies and professor of history at the University of Sussex, an exciting new experiment in multidisciplinary teaching founded in 1959. Wight persuaded Elizabeth Wiskemann to resign her Montague Burton Chair at Edinburgh to join Sussex as tutor in modern European history.[125] Asked who should be offered the IR professorship, Wight named Coral Bell and Hedley Bull, then at Australia National University. Bell was appointed at Sussex in 1972, delighted to be rejoining Wight who had invited her to join the British Committee in 1971.[126] However, he died suddenly before Bell arrived at Sussex, and his major contributions to IR theory were posthumously published and edited by his wife, Gabrielle Wight, and others.[127]

Bell's appointment at Sussex was extremely controversial among the radical student body, and efforts to dissuade her from taking up the post 'produced the opposite effect—a determination to come so as to oppose 'left-wing McCarthyism'' at the institution.[128] But Bell did not stay at Sussex long. In 1977, she returned to Australia, joining Hedley Bull as a senior research fellow at the Australian National University, where she remained for the rest of her career. As 'Australia's most distinguished analyst of contemporary international politics', Bell was posthumously honoured when ANU established the Coral Bell School of Asia-Pacific Affairs in 2015. She arrived at ANU the same year Rachel Wall was forced out of Oxford, in part due to the actions of Australia's second most distinguished IR scholar, Hedley Bull, Oxford's new Montague Burton Professor. Recall his statement that 'God forbid that we should turn away from Eurocentric international and imperial history towards so-called anti-imperialist or national liberation accounts of the past'.[129] In helping Oxford to remove Rachel Wall from her post, Bull—and Oxford IR—was even less likely to progress in this direction.

## 'This is No Witch-Hunt'

Rachel Wall's initial five-year period of employment at Oxford was reviewed in 1969, but the Faculty Board declined to make her position permanent and only renewed her contract for a further five years. After three years the board would either re-appoint Wall to retirement or give her two years' notice.[130] Justifying the decision, her colleague Wilfrid Knapp claimed that those on the review board 'most closely associated with her field . . . were uneasy at her tenure of a faculty lectureship'.[131] But that is not true.

The director of St Anthony's Centre for Far Eastern Studies reported that Rachel Wall 'has a good knowledge of the Far Eastern field of international relations and from what I hear she is a good lecturer'. Making her position permanent was 'quite justified'.[132] The principal of St Hugh's also pointed out that she had given the tutorials 'satisfactorily, and sometimes with enthusiasm. There are, however, reservations about her full academic contribution to the College'.[133] The Fellows of Lady Margaret Hall, the second college where she taught, had no objection to the renewal. She had been a 'little tiresome on the Library Committee but not in the way that one could possibly complain of'.[134] There is also a note in Sibyl Crowe's hand that says 'everything goes smoothly with Miss Wall . . . She is obliging, easy and takes trouble. (She has strong views about what the girls should be learning.)'[135]

However, Knapp, whose own research was 'modest in quantity',[136] determined that Wall had not published enough. The main reason for refusing her tenure was unease with 'certain idiosyncrasies of character and behaviour', which might be 'related to an immaturity of judgement, which would inhibit scholarly work'.[137] Knapp offered no details of these idiosyncrasies or alleged immaturity but observed that Wall had been ill for some of her lectureship. In fact, since 1967, Rachel Wall had been under treatment for 'nervous and other disorders'.[138] The real and unstated reason Wall was not made a permanent member of Oxford's faculty in 1969 was the stigma and inconvenience of mental illness.

By 1970, there was finally some recognition that Wall had an unusual and unfair teaching burden, with Max Beloff complaining to the principal of St Hugh's about the lack of another undergraduate politics tutor in that college or Lady Margaret Hall. The university's appointment of faculty lecturers was not meant to substitute for college tutors tasked with undergraduate teaching.[139] Wall was not only dealing with the stress of precarity and a higher teaching load at her women's colleges. In 1970, Geoffrey Barraclough took the Chichele Professorship of Modern History at Oxford's most prestigious college, All Souls. It is unclear whether their romantic relationship resumed. But Barraclough's arrival and abrupt departure in 1972 coincided with a significant deterioration in Wall's mental health. He had written saying he was looking forward to seeing her and had a little present that he did not 'entrust to the post'.[140] She offered to help pack up his books and asked if they might see each other again. Possibly to follow Barraclough to his new position at Brandeis, Wall applied to the British Federation of University Women for a small grant to support a sabbatical in the United States in early 1974. In quite the departure from her long-running book project on China, she proposed to study US–Mexican relations.[141]

At the three-year mark in 1972, the Faculty Board awarded tenure to Rachel Wall. There is no evidence that her review was 'carried out less stringently than would otherwise have been the case', as Martin Caedel suggests.[142] Rather, there were no legitimate grounds to deny her. Wall had also done something she had never done before. She presented to her employer a letter from her doctor outlining her mental illness and its effects: 'her problems and their treatment have necessarily cut into the time she has had for her work. Nevertheless, I understand that she has managed to keep her work going. She is still having treatment but is now getting better'.[143] Wall's position was reviewed at a time when faculty positions were being converted into university lectureships, overseen by the central administration. She was accordingly awarded more pay with her new permanent position. However, disastrously, rather than reduce Wall's workload to help her manage her mental health, her teaching for the faculty was increased from twenty-four to thirty-six lectures and classes per year with no reduction in her two-college teaching load.[144]

During the 1970s and 1980s, feminist scholars emphasised systemic sexism in the field of psychiatry and how mental illness was understood, as well as how gender hierarchy itself produced mental ill health.[145] By Wall's own account, her severe depression commenced in 'spasmodic bouts' in 1973 and became 'more prolonged and disabling' over time.[146] She had been desperately unhappy at Oxford, writing to Barraclough in 1973 that she was sometimes 'just too depressed for words. I really wish I had just taken off for the [Soviet Union] or Italy. I simply can't wait to get out of this hole it is and always has been here. It may be alright for the under-21s but, except with you I haven't had an intelligent conversation since I came here'.[147]

During the second half of 1976, Wall was under the care of the senior consultant psychiatrist at Westminster Hospital. Wall was diagnosed with a 'manic-depressive' illness and prescribed various medications including lithium carbonate, Valium and Mogadon, taking sick leave for psychiatric care as an in-patient.[148] Rather than organise teaching replacement and offer reasonable adjustments to support Wall's slow return to work, the university proceeded to force her early retirement. St Hugh's wrote to Wall in the summer of 1975 asking her to resign her Fellowship or explain why she 'did not undertake her tutorial duties during 1974/75'.[149] She resigned from St Hugh's in spring 1976. The university, which paid most of Wall's salary, had to tread more carefully not least due to 'the cloud of hearsay which surrounds this case'.[150]

Wanting to self-manage her condition, Wall discharged herself from Westminster in the autumn–winter of 1975, and refused the suggestion of her psychiatrist, Dr. O. S. Frank, that she be admitted to hospital in Oxford.[151] 'If one thinks it a waste of time to stick used Christmas cards onto match boxes or mime charades you don't have much likelihood of getting a pass degree. There it is. So much for my health'.[152] Without her permission, the university wrote to Frank requesting a new diagnosis of Wall's fitness to work. Frank refused, not having recently examined Wall or received permission to share her medical information. In response, the vice-chair of the university's General Board wrote to Wall insisting that because she had discharged herself, she must resume her 'duties forthwith', or be placed on unpaid leave.[153] In fact, she was permitted another period of sick leave in the spring of 1976 and special leave on half-pay for the autumn and winter.

The university's stated plan was to slowly reduce Wall's pay to nothing, and dismiss her, unless she could produce 'conclusive medical evidence of a miracle cure', which was obviously an impossible condition to meet. If there was 'substantial medical evidence' that Wall was improving, then the vice-chair of the General Board of the Faculties, D. M. Stewart, thought the university 'will have a difficult time; if not, they will have a fairly difficult time' in getting rid of her.[154] The university administration never enquired how it could support Wall's mental health but was concerned primarily with removing her. 'I think we have acted slowly enough already to pose as a Good Employer', Stewart declared.[155]

For understandable reasons, Rachel Wall did not wish to return to a psychiatric ward though she did agree to return as a day patient. However, she was running out of medication.[156] Wall experienced severe side-effects from her treatment, including loss of facial expression, rapid weight gain and tremors, which she said were so great 'that I couldn't hold a cup on a saucer or write other than with a huge, shaky hand which looked as if I were about 80'.[157] A female consultant, Dr Gomez, prescribed medication to reduce the tremors. Wall wished to remain under her care, but she was reassigned to Frank. Wall responded by ending all contact with Westminster Hospital. The medical officer to the university, Bent Juel-Jensen, wished now to 'pressure' Wall by saying that she would only be permitted to return to work if she received psychiatric care.[158] Concerned again with Oxford's image as a 'Good Employer', D. M. Stewart rightly thought the university could not be so directive.[159]

With the constant pressure from the university, Wall agreed to lecture in spring 1977, writing to the university that after such a long break she feared that her lectures 'will not be very good . . . Trying to write a day here and a day there doesn't make for the most coherent course'.[160] At this point, university managers outlined their worst-case scenario: Wall returned to lecture, 'obviously quite incapable of so doing, and claiming restoration of full stipend'.[161] In other words, 'the most difficult situation' was that she 'delivers lectures in a *minimally acceptable* manner' and she would be paid for her work.[162] Arrangements were made for a graduate student to attend and report on Wall's lectures.[163] By the second week, Wall had not shown up, claiming she had flu. However, she now agreed to meet a university hospital psychiatrist, Richard Mayou, who described their brief meeting as 'extremely acrimonious'.[164]

Given the additional distress caused by rapid and unwanted weight gain, Wall also made and then cancelled an appointment with a metabolic specialist who, based solely on an 'incoherent' letter from Wall, described her as 'extremely psychologically disturbed'.[165] In May 1977, Wall's GP confirmed that she 'is obviously not fit to be working'.[166] Within a few days, Rachel Wall received a hand-delivered letter informing her that the university had decided to retire her on medical grounds.[167] She appealed, claiming that her doctor thought she was now fit to work and that she wished to nominate herself to the ad hoc Appeal Board.[168] She did not want Frank on the board, accusing him of 'medical bias and spite'.[169] She had previously accused him of messing her about 'for two and half years' and of being 'an inveterate snob'.[170] Juel-Jensen, she thought, was biased due to Frank's negative influence. She would have nominated Dr Gomez, but the General Board would not ask her opinion 'because she is a woman'.[171] Instead, Wall nominated a woman Italian doctor and friend, Laura Pozzi, whom she first met as a teenager in the 1940s. During a telephone call with the University Offices, she also claimed to be 'tired of "white expatriate doctors" and, if she was to undergo' another 'medical examination', the university 'should find her a "coal-black female n———"'.[172] It is unclear whether Wall intended to shock, make a point about gender and race in the medical profession, or was being straightforwardly racist—likely all three. Unfortunately, Wall also rejected additional support from her trade union.[173]

The three members of the ad hoc board were the medically qualified chairman, Dr. J.M.K. Spalding, the magistrate Lady Barbara Franks, and Dr Pozzi.[174] They determined that Wall should be compelled to retire because she had not performed her duties since October 1975. However, since she intended to return to teaching in the spring, the committee also recommended that the quality of her lectures be used to finally determine whether she was able to work to a level expected of a university lecturer.[175] The university thought the board had gone 'beyond its terms of reference', but reluctantly agreed to their reasonable proposal.[176] Wall had already delivered one lecture that term, which the University Proctors had monitored, and her other lectures 'would need to be observed'.[177] Initially, Wall was not informed that her lectures would be assessed and what was at stake in her performance.[178] However, the vice-chancellor, the most senior university manager, belatedly realised that 'out of fairness' and, more likely, to 'prevent any subsequent comeback', Wall should be informed.[179]

Could she pull it off? During the summer, Wall's mental health appeared to stabilise. D. M. Stewart reported that she was 'not incoherent . . . Many of the points she made were quite rational'.[180] One of the university medics thought her 'mania' was less than before and 'could perhaps be undergoing some degree of spontaneous improvement'.[181] Despite the stress and exhaustion caused by her exceptionally high teaching load, Wall was considered 'a good lecturer',[182] an 'effective and able teacher'.[183] But she was also speaking on a topic she had not lectured on before, 'The United States and Japan since 1853'. She would be observed by the proctors and the quality of her lectures would be assessed by three of the most senior male professors in the faculty and across their three different fields of research: Hedley Bull, the newly arrived Montague Burton Professor of IR, whose background was philosophy, Nevil Johnson, Nuffield Reader in the Comparative Study of Institutions and Chair of the Faculty Board, and H. G. Nicholas, Rhodes Professor of American History and Institutions.[184]

According to Johnson, all three professors had misgivings about the process and their role. The question of Wall's 'performance and competence', he strangely claimed, 'are not strictly relevant to a medical judgement of Miss Wall's suitability for further employment', as if performance and competence were not, in fact, decisive in determining her fitness to work. The professors wished their reports to be 'treated as purely supportive of or ancillary to the medical grounds for the medical board's main recommendation'.[185] But how could their assessment of Wall's lectures be a mere supplement to a medical judgment? The university agreed that if the board 'certifies that her academic performance during Michaelmas Term 1977 is such that it expects from a university lecturer', then quite rightly the decision to retire Wall must be 'reviewed'.[186] Wall's performance and competence was entirely relevant to the academic, not medical, judgement of whether she adequately performed her professional duties. Yet the chair of the Faculty Board tasked with certifying whether her lectures were adequate had already determined that someone with Wall's medical diagnosis could not, by definition, function as a university lecturer. Wall was being set up to fail.

H. G. Nicholas's report stretched to one paragraph. Wall covered the subject, he noted, 'completing a chronological narrative', though 'the intellectual level . . . was low' with 'a persistent "1066 and All That" style of analysis, a sustained crudity of thought and treatment which would make such lectures of little value to any but the most elementary student of the subject'.[187] Yet that was her undergraduate audience. Nevil Johnson attended half the lectures and the comparativist did not like that Wall paid more attention to the diplomatic history of US–Japan relations, her defined subject, than the domestic context, which was his. She presented 'reliable factual evidence', but the political scientist thought the international historian 'failed to define her subject' nor go beyond what he assumed was available in existing surveys or draw on her own 'current and recent research'. It was unlikely she had done her own research in recent months as Wall had just returned from long-term sick leave, which Johnson nowhere acknowledged. He did note that Wall 'was clearly performing under serious stress', but 'was highly dependent on the chronology and notes, and her responses to occasional interventions indicated that she was not really sufficiently in command of the field'.[188] Nicholas too acknowledged the 'obvious strain' on Wall given the circumstances yet agreed with Johnson. Oxford 'has a right and indeed an obligation to expect more'.[189]

Hedley Bull attended six of eight lectures and his report was most detailed and sympathetic. While Rachel Wall was obviously 'nervous and unsure of herself', she became much calmer as the term progressed. She delivered the 'eight lectures she set out to give; she covered the period she set out to cover; and . . . she imparted some information about the subject'. Based on Bull's initial observations, then, it could be said that Wall's lectures were of a minimally acceptable standard and were the basis on which she could rebuild, the stated worst-case scenario for university management. However, the philosopher judged the lectures to be 'disjointed', 'essentially a chronology with comments', and underprepared. Bull speculated that, while the proctors and professors made the occasion more stressful, their presence was likely the reason she had completed the series at all. There was no guarantee, he ventured, that Wall could do so again without external pressure. Wall's lectures were 'below the standard to which we are entitled to expect'.[190]

An emergency meeting of the Faculty Board, which included Bull and Knapp, unanimously agreed what it had anticipated all along: it was 'unable to certify that Miss Wall's performance was such as it expects from a university lecturer'.[191] However, what were Rachel Wall's colleagues entitled to expect and what did Wall have a right to expect from the university and her senior colleagues? Had she not delivered what the university most feared, eight lectures that were *minimally* acceptable in that they covered the period and the topic? Considering the mitigating circumstances, Wall's performance was arguably a success; the appropriate response was to support her continued recovery. Contra Bull, she might have delivered better lectures the following term without the presence of senior male professors from multiple fields sitting in judgement of her and her approach.

This was Wall's own assessment in the six-day period between the Faculty Board decision and her receiving the news. She apologised to Stewart for suggesting that he 'had behaved improperly over communications between' Juel-Jensen and Dr Frank.[192] She thanked P. W. Jones for his kindness toward Dr Pozzi. She expressed gratitude to the registrar for restoring her full pay as she was 'in debt in every direction—even having to borrow to get my lecture photostatting done'.[193] She enquired about sabbatical leave and the procedure for

FIGURE 10.4. Rachel Wall, date unknown, c. late 1950s. Photographer Unknown. Courtesy of Cathie Wilson

inviting outside specialists to deliver occasional guest lectures, though 'not eight weeks of visitors'.[194] Her letters were coherent and hopeful. When the judgement came, it was not clear that Wall fully understood the decision was final.[195] She attended St Hugh's first Governing Body meeting of the term and began delivering her lectures on 'China's Foreign Relations since 1949'.[196]

What happened next is one of the most difficult aspects of Rachel Wall's case. After several days, Wall accepted that she was being forced out of Oxford at the age of forty-four and made the reasonable request to see the medical information on which the decision was based.[197] Wall was completely unaware of the written assessments of her lectures which finally determined her fate and could not have requested to see them. The university determined that it had followed the nationally agreed process which only requires communication of its decision. 'Moreover, there might be difficulty in defining what constitutes information "concerning her health"', the board conveniently noted. Extracts from doctors' letters 'may be misleading', especially as one of the most recent had observed a recent improvement in Wall's mental health.[198] Both the registrar and chair of the ad hoc committee agreed to inform Wall that letters from various doctors about her own mental health 'were confidential and could not be divulged to her',[199] but she was welcome to 'consult the doctors concerned'.[200] Rather than insisting on her basic (not yet legal) right to see her own medical information, information used to end her university career, Wall simply thanked the registrar.[201] There was no internal discussion within the university about the ethics of withholding medical information used to terminate employment.

A handwritten note in the pocket of Wall's university file claims that the documents therein 'provide an example of the lengths to which the University is prepared to go in order to respect the rights of the individual'.[202] This is doubtful. Its chief medical officer claimed that 'this is no witch-hunt', likely unaware that in 'delating' Wall the university resurrected a language that was commonly used to bring charges against witches.[203] Yet that is a low bar. Keen 'to pose as a Good Employer',[204] Oxford was nonetheless setting Rachel Wall up to fail. But it was not Wall that failed. Her lover, employers, colleagues, and, by her own account, some of her doctors failed to support Wall, just as IR's intellectual and disciplinary historians failed to adequately recount her story. Wall herself seemed to understand this and was looking for a way out from the late 1960s, exploring leaving St Hugh's and Lady Margaret Hall for another college, leaving Oxford IR for history, and even abandoning academe itself. She interviewed at the Home Office for a position as a Probation Officer and applied for a job at the Imperial War Museum.[205] She asked her friend Marjorie Chibnall, a medieval historian, about her prospects for a history position at Merton, which Chibnall thought would go to a man, and asked Oxford's Oriental Institute about temporary posts in Chinese history.[206] She sought advice on whether her insurance might be transferred to positions such as librarianship, or teaching in a school or technical college.[207]

## Conclusion

Rachel Wall's limited attempt to take seriously the agency of newly independent states and her plea for a less Eurocentric contemporary history was a distinctive response to decolonisation and the 'spirit of Bandung'. Wall's vision was limited by her excessive teaching burden, illness, and her own intellectual constraints, yet it was nonetheless superior to the efforts of her contemporaries now associated with the so-called 'English School'. But Wall's so-called 'failure'—in other words, her disability—is no less illuminating of IR's gendered intellectual and disciplinary history than the cases of thundering success, like Coral Bell. Wall was dismissed from Oxford in 1977, the year she inherited an old gamekeeper's cottage in Leysters near Leominster, bequeathed to her by an aunt which Rachel, in turn, left to her niece, who carefully preserved her personal papers.[208] There is no record of further contact with Barraclough, who married for a third time in the 1970s, although he returned to his second wife when he became seriously ill. He died in 1984.[209]

There were no other known romances in Wall's life. She was devoted to her spaniel, Peter, and maintained some contact with St Hugh's.[210] But she was bitter about Oxford, recounted her niece.[211] If she was capable of volunteering at a local homeless charity, then, she thought, she was well enough to deliver lectures. In 1989, at the age of fifty-five, Rachel Wall died from smoke inhalation in a house fire likely caused by faulty electrics in the old cottage, Rachel becoming trapped and unable to get out of the small bedroom window.[212] David Robertson, then St Hugh's politics tutor, attended the funeral on behalf of the college. There were no representatives from the university or the IR group. Her sister recalls someone from the university enquiring about Rachel's papers soon after her death, which the family did not share, and which at the time of writing remain in the cottage in Leysters.[213]

# 11

# 'These Women with Large Families'

## ON MOTHERHOOD

As soon as we actually get her resignation, I would like to propose the name of a man to replace her.

—G. W. KEETON ON SUSAN STRANGE, 1964

IN NO SENSE is Susan Strange marginal in IR's intellectual and disciplinary histories. She is the only historical woman afforded canonical status, to have received anything close to the recognition she deserves.[1] Her books are printed and reprinted in multiple editions.[2] There are numerous professional prizes, student grants, and a professorship in her name and there is a large secondary literature on her scholarship.[3] Since the 1970s, Strange was and remains the most honoured, revered, and influential figure in the history of British IR, a 'giantess'.[4] Martin Wight and Hedley Bull, the next most revered, are only honoured as foremost heirs to the British Committee on the Theory of International Politics. Susan Strange conceived of and co-founded British IR's first properly learned society, the British International Studies Association (BISA) and was intellectual 'midwife'[5] to a new hybrid scholarly field, International Political Economy (IPE). What then could be the value of thinking with and about Susan Strange today?

Most often, Strange's story is told in terms internal to academia, namely her critique of the abstract and formal models of economics, which sidestepped power politics, and of IR's obsession with great power politics and the balance of nuclear terror, ignoring how world politics is underpinned by capitalism and financial markets.[6] In response to the limits of economics and IR, she founded and modelled a new field of IPE, devoted to understanding the interaction between political power and the global movement of capital.[7] 'The symbiotic, conflictual and cooperative, asymmetrical and inconsistent relationship between states and markets, markets and states, seems to me to contain the key to the perennial political question, who gets what?'[8] IR scholars, Strange claimed, had 'to escape the confines of international relations', meant narrowly as relations between states, and explore 'the larger world of international political economy'.[9]

For scholarship, but also institution-building and mentoring generations of students, Susan Strange is best known as the 'founding mother' of IPE and BISA.[10] But her main intellectual contributions only make sense in wider historical context, of British imperial economic decline and attempted entry into the European common market. During the first two decades of her professional career, in the 1950s and 1960s, Strange was clearly shaped by, and thinking in terms of the economics of, the transition from the British Empire to Commonwealth and then membership of the European Economic Community. Now, for the first time, Britain had much of its postcolonial border and immigration regime and was ready for deeper economic integration with Europe. Strange's first book, written at Chatham House and published in 1971, was a political and economic history of the decline of pound sterling, not only as the dominant world currency but also of the sterling area as an imperial monetary system. Britain's diminished status was reflected in the decline of sterling but also in attempts to hang on to the remnants of empire through the Commonwealth. We might think of Strange's political project, helping Britain's elites come to terms with and respond to economic decline after empire, as the political economy equivalent to Margery Perham's project of managing imperial decline.

Yet Strange's importance today is less as the British political economy version of Margery Perham. Much less is it to recount—yet again—her much-analysed approach to and warnings about the 'casino capitalism' of financial services and prescience in predicting global financial crises.[11] Nor is it the necessary and overdue work of situating a figure too often presented as the exceptional woman among a wider and neglected cohort of women international thinkers.[12] Strange had a singular effect on the course of British IR, but she was not a single mother birthing British IPE.[13]

Rather the value of thinking with and about Susan Strange today is how and why she became Susan Strange. Central to this story is motherhood, a theme often noted yet quickly passed over in voluminous analyses of Strange's work and legacy. Historically, the most exceptional thing about Strange is not that she was and remains the most influential figure in British IR, a metaphorical founding mother. It is that she was the literal mother of six children born in a twenty-year period from 1943 to 1963. Most academic women who achieved Strange's extraordinary professional status in the early to mid-twentieth century were unmarried (Perham, Tate) or married very late and were child-free (Power). Almost unique among the cohort in this book, Strange was a mother who worked for pay. Yet she was anomalous not only due to her number of children, but that she refused the main trajectory for mothers in the 1950s and 1960s. She insisted on returning full-time to her first academic post at University College London (UCL) and was accordingly bullied and harassed by two male IR professors until she resigned.

This story, mentioned briefly in Strange's autobiographical reflections though never taken up or analysed in the large secondary literature, is key to understanding the persona of Susan Strange and the IR that she came to shape and dominate. On one level, it would be easy to read Strange's early and formative experience of working motherhood as a story of a singular woman's triumph over adversity, of a feisty journalist with no graduate degree and six children who published her first book at forty-eight, smashing the glass ceiling. This is the story Strange suggested herself in her autobiographical reflections and her International Studies Association (ISA) Presidential Address in 1995. She was an active agent in the production of her reputation as singular, iconoclastic, an unconventional woman. An analysis of how Strange fashioned herself, how she performed and how she was read as performing different gendered roles, suggests a great irony.[14] One of the most attractive and compelling elements of Strange's persona—her irreverence, her patricidal contempt for the white male mediocrities of British IR—was assimilated to support British IR's conservative gender and racial order in the 1980s and 1990s.

## Rebel Daughter, Journalist

Susan Strange was born on June 9, 1923 in Dorset, the daughter of a well-known flying ace in the Royal Air Force. Lieutenant-Colonel Louis Strange (1891–1966) was a pioneer of machine-gun aerial combat, one of the few pilots awarded a Distinguished Flying Cross in both world wars. His memoir, *Recollections of an Airman*, displayed all the optimism of interwar air mindedness.[15] Dedicated to a 'luckless but not fameless generation', the book looked forward

to a time when the expansion of civil flying would break down barriers between classes and nations, making 'war less difficult to avoid'.[16] Susan's mother,
Marjorie, née Beath, appears only intermittently in Louis's memoir, published
when Susan was ten, but also in Peter Hearn's 1994 biography of Louis. She is
remembered by Susan's oldest son as often in pain and forcing her two children
to exercise their eyes to combat myopia, which Susan and her brother hated.[17]
*Flying Rebel* includes a photograph of teenage Susan and her parents, smiling
and stylishly dressed after her father receives another military honour. As a
child, she enjoyed regular trips in the family three-seater Spartan aircraft.[18]
Throughout Hearn's biography, written with Susan's 'encouragement and material support',[19] she is presented as a 'spirited rebel, just like her father'.[20]

Like Power and Perham, Strange's family background was white middle-
class, but also supplemented by military networks in the metropole. With her
mother pushing her at school, Strange received an entrance scholarship to the
Royal School in Bath, a private boarding school for daughters of army officers,
and took Higher Certificates in history, English, and geography.[21] In both *Flying Rebel* and her autobiographical reflections, the narrative of the rebel
daughter begins with the outbreak of World War II, when Susan was holiday-
ing in Switzerland with her mother. 'Not a girl to be put off by a few Germans',
reported Hearn, she returned to a continent at war the next summer to work
as an au pair and secretary to a professor at the University of Caen.[22] She only
suspended her studies when she could literally hear the shelling of Rouen,
evacuating 'just before it fell to the Germans'.[23] Strange was 'highly indignant
at being forced to leave . . . bringing with her one of the last Camembert
cheeses to be evacuated from France'.[24] She reluctantly left from Cherbourg
on a ship carrying three thousand British soldiers. 'But for the British Army',
she later astonishingly claimed, 'I would have spent the rest of the war in
France, or a German concentration camp'.[25]

Unlike Power and Perham, Strange did not go to Oxford or Cambridge
because she did not have 'money or Latin'. Latin would have been enough with
a scholarship, but Strange still claimed that it was a 'lucky break . . . getting to
university at all'.[26] Her luck, she thought, was in getting into the London
School of Economics (LSE). The father of a school friend was LSE's careers
officer and persuaded her to apply for a scholarship from the Leverhulme
Trust. The LSE was housed at Peterhouse College, Cambridge for the duration
of the war, a move facilitated by LSE economic historian Eileen Power's husband, Michael Postan. As an economics undergraduate, Susan Strange would
have been taught by Power when, under her reign, economic history was LSE's

hottest subject. But Power suddenly died of a heart attack a few weeks before Strange began her degree.

Economics teaching at LSE was more eclectic in the 1940s than it is today, though it was still economics, not economic history. Hence Strange may have exaggerated her non-economics training when later applying for an IR lectureship at UCL, claiming to have specialised in international law and relations, political history and political and social theory. In comments that would certainly have appealed to Georg Schwarzenberger, the senior IR professor at UCL, Strange claimed in 1949 that some of her undergraduate studies were 'supervised by one kindly but ineffectual old diplomatic historian'.[27] 'We had to choose from a broad social science menu. My preference was for politics, but I found the Department dominated by a cliquey set of disciples of Harold Laski', Strange claimed. The Marxist intellectual, and friend of Eileen Power, was 'an entertaining lecturer, but I couldn't agree with some of his rather simplistic ideas, nor did I want to be anybody's disciple'.[28] Strange became secretary and then vice-president of LSE's Students' Union. During vacations and in addition to 'hitch-hiking about the country',[29] she researched East End air-raid shelters, worked at an engineering factory, and as junior reporter at the *Swindon Advertiser*.[30] In her final year, she won the Cecil Peace Prize, a national competition for the best essay on international peace, and got pregnant.

Though her father would not have approved had she asked for his opinion, she claimed, Susan Strange married Dennis Merritt, a medical student, in a shotgun wedding.[31] She was already in the second trimester when she sat her final exams, graduating with a first in July and giving birth to Giles Hugh in November 1943. Motherhood, she claimed, 'spared' her from regular war-time work at the Foreign Office, likely as an assistant to Romanian–British scholar David Mitrany, who was working on post-war planning and reconstruction and developing his ideas about functionalist cooperation in international institutions that Strange would later criticise.[32] She chose lower-paid though more stimulating employment as a journalist. In 1944, Strange became an editorial assistant at *The Economist*, working under foreign-affairs editor and writer Barbara Ward, later an influential development economist, who was then rooming with Elizabeth Monroe, at the time the paper's leader writer on the Middle East.[33] Monroe had headed the British government's Middle East Information Division during the war and worked later as a contemporary historian of the Middle East and the first woman Fellow of St Anthony's College, Oxford.[34]

Susan Strange received no further academic training after her first degree, later claiming that her time at *The Economist* 'was as good as any graduate course at a university'.[35] She specialised in Indian affairs, the international aspects of civil aviation, her father's trade, and wrote lead articles and the features 'Notes of the Week' and 'American Notes'.[36] Later, while in Washington, she initiated an airmail information service to *The Economist*'s US editorial team. The pay was terrible, so she moonlighted at the London Bureau of *Time* magazine, *Fortune*, and wrote film-scripts for the cinema newsreel and documentary series, *March of Time*. 'They paid twice as much for half the work—but were apt to murder truth without a qualm'.[37] Like Stawell, Power, Perham, and Wall, Strange lectured on international affairs at the Workers Education Association.

In June 1946, at the age of twenty-three, Susan Strange became the youngest White House correspondent for the most exciting British newspaper, *The Observer*, then known for its 'small staff' and 'radical reputation', at least in liberal circles.[38] It was an offer that she could not refuse despite temporarily leaving her two-year-old son, Giles, and husband, Dennis Merritt.[39] They later joined Strange in the US, but were based in segregated Tennessee where Merritt worked for Merck Pharmaceuticals, and Giles was looked after by a Black nanny.[40] Commuting between Tennessee and Washington DC, Strange networked with politicians and officials in the Department of State under the Truman administration and, as one of the paper's 'stars', wrote for *The Observer*'s Foreign News Service. This involved much more work and expertise on a wider range of topics than an ordinary foreign correspondent, she claimed, including two or three substantial articles a week. These appeared in papers of record in Canada, New Zealand, Holland, Germany, Belgium, Sweden, Iraq, Egypt, South Africa, and the US. From early 1947, and separately from *The Observer*, Strange wrote on the US economy for colonial India's first and leading financial weekly newspaper, *Capital*.[41]

After one year, Strange transferred from Washington to New York, becoming *The Observer*'s United Nations correspondent in the summer of 1947, covering the General Assembly and its backstage talks on the UN's partition plan for Palestine. She later wrote on Palestine for the *Yearbook of World Affairs*, where she was critical of Arab negotiating positions.[42] Her time in New York was also short-lived. In March 1948, Strange had her second child, Jane Franklin, and applied for doctoral research and an academic post more compatible with raising young children, hoping to combine journalism with academia. In 1949, she enrolled as a part-time doctoral researcher at University College London and became an assistant IR lecturer.

Susan Strange's full-time career as a journalist only lasted five years, though she combined part-time journalism with academe and motherhood for another eight. With Giles and Jane at boarding school, she continued as the economics correspondent and editorial writer at *The Observer* until 1957. Indeed, had she not eventually entered academe, taken up acting, comedy or painting 'and had no children', she later claimed, 'I would also have dearly liked to be an independent newspaper columnist'.[43] Though a relatively short period in journalism compared to Elizabeth Wiskemann and Claudia Jones, these years as a reporter were hugely formative of Susan Strange's personal and intellectual development. They were also central to how she would fashion herself as a risk-taking, sceptical, expressive, even dominant figure in IR. Proud of her apprenticeship at *The Economist* and *The Observer*, it was journalism that professionally credentialed Strange, substituting, even bettering in her opinion, the doctorate she enrolled for but never completed. Giles Merritt, Strange's oldest son, also a journalist, claims Strange always felt more like a journalist than an academic and had profound contempt for those who thought along 'tramlines', like too many academics, they both thought.[44]

Journalism was central to the creation of Susan Strange's professional 'persona' as 'a bluff, no-nonsense empiricist',[45] sceptical of abstract theorising and of dons 'building intellectual card-houses and playing academic word-games'.[46] She also thought journalism taught her how to teach and write better than most of her academic peers, and certainly her older male contemporaries in IR like LSE's Charles Manning and UCL's Georg Schwarzenberger, both trained lawyers and would-be sociologists of international relations. They 'have their faults', Strange pointed out, 'but few [journalists] inflict on their readers the sort of stodgy, long-winded, pretentious, jargon-ridden writing that too many academics inflict on their unfortunate students'.[47] She was also protective of her own writing, reportedly telling 'publishers that she would not accept copy editing by 22-year-olds with a BA in literary criticism making a mess of her text'.[48] Journalists were superior writers and clearer thinkers. They were also more likely to effect political change; 'the television crews who risked their lives to get pictures of Israeli conduct' in Palestine 'may well have had more effect on American policy-making in the long run than all the academic literature on Lebanon and the PLO'.[49] Journalists, like women, she thought, were more realistic about politics.

## 'The Feminist Case Still Had To Be Made'

Founded in 1826, UCL became one of the first British universities in 1878 to admit women on the same terms as men. However, the Senior Common Room was men-only until 1960. Susan Strange enrolled part-time in the Ph.D. degree in 1949 initially to write on the UN General Assembly, though she soon switched topics to the recently founded Council of Europe.[50] She was supervised by Georg Schwarzenberger, Britain's own German–Jewish émigré realist, who had taught Strange as an undergraduate, and whom she later described as 'a realist' before Hans J. Morgenthau, the founding father of American realism, 'was ever heard of'.[51] She continued at *The Observer* until 1957, but Strange's primary work was as an assistant, then full lecturer in IR. In her later reflections on her 'falling out' with UCL's IR professors, Strange singled out Schwarzenberger's 'bullying ways', their disagreement 'over the number of children it was reasonable for a lecturer to have', accusing him of trying 'to take away' her 'tenure on a technicality'.[52] Yet it was neither Schwarzenberger alone nor a technicality that pushed Susan Strange out of her first academic post.

Susan Strange entered the world of 'British IR' at a time when the men of the British Coordinating Committee for International Studies (BCCIS) were seeking to establish IR as a separate university subject. Strange was active and networked into these circles and, perhaps because her first degree was in economics, not history, was seemingly quite content with the idea of a separate IR led by LSE figures like Manning and economist Geoffrey Goodwin. In 1950, she wrote a report for the United Nations Educational, Scientific and Cultural Organization (UNESCO) on IR research institutions in Britain, lamenting that the universities generally 'treat international relations as the poor relation of other studies'.[53] Through the 1950s, Strange attended conferences and discussions on IR teaching, including in schools, and co-authored with two proponents of IR as a separate subject, Goodwin and Schwarzenberger, including summaries of the main 'sociological aspects' of international relations for Schwarzenberger and George W. Keeton's *Yearbook of World Affairs*, published by the London Institute for World Affairs.[54] Keeton was UCL's dean of the Faculty of Laws and Strange's direct line manager as head of the Law Department, in which IR was taught.

Like Charles Manning, Schwarzenberger was a central figure in the effort to move the study of international relations away from history and toward sociology, though he was less obsessed with the question of 'separateness' than Manning and more confident that IR was a 'distinct academic discipline'.[55] Influenced by German sociologists Max Weber and Ferdinand Tönnies, Schwarzenberger viewed sociology as offering IR a 'body of theory' and a model of methodological eclecticism. Specifically, different types of behaviour in the so-called 'society of states' could be classified and assessed by their relative importance for 'the evolution and structure of international society'.[56] The ability to abstract and generalise about 'international society' 'gives to the science of international relations the unity and coherence without which it would be nothing more than an ill-assorted conglomeration of disjointed pieces of knowledge'.[57]

Schwarzenberger's intellectual efforts were far more successful than Charles Manning's, not least due to the unpaid labours of his wife, who had a doctorate in law and was the first woman faculty assistant at the University of Heidelberg. In 1933, both Georg and Suse Schwarzenberger were dismissed from the University of Heidelberg and deprived of their German nationality, Georg because he was Jewish and Suse because she was a woman married to a Jew. After they emigrated to England, Suse never practised law again 'but supported the work of her husband'.[58] Strange read and commented on the full typescript and proofs of the second edition of Schwarzenberger's *Power Politics*, published in 1951. However, his 'severest and kindest censor', he claimed, was his 'wife'. 'Without her insistence, I might not have revised whole chapters and paragraphs which appeared to be clear enough to me, but which she— probably rightly—insisted would have been completely unintelligible to anyone apart from my closest friends and my own students'.[59] In addition to assisting her husband's career, Suse Schwarzenberger wrote a personal history of German academics in the twentieth century, including lengthy discussion of the Schwarzenbergers' life and work.[60] We do not know if Manning's wife, Marion Somerville Johnson, his student at LSE, thought similarly, and censored some of Manning's terrible writing in *The Nature of International Society*, because there are no acknowledgements in the book.[61]

In June 1951, Susan Strange was promoted from assistant to full lecturer for an initial period of five years. She withdrew from the Ph.D. programme, re-entering again in 1958 after she had finally left *The Observer*, changing her subject again to hegemony in international relations after 1945. At UCL, Strange never had 'tenure' as such, rather the normal expectation was a rolling five-year contract, at least initially. In the early 1950s, Strange was among a tiny minority of white middle-class, university-educated mothers working full time for pay, even in the supposedly more enlightened field of higher education. The academic job market, like the wider labour market, was fundamentally structured around gender difference and assumed a male household head and primary breadwinner. In 1955, Strange divorced her first husband and married Clifford Selly, a farmer and agricultural correspondent whose copy she had edited at *The Observer*.[62] They were 'a striking couple', recalled her later LSE colleague, Fred Halliday, 'gracious and ironic in the company of friends'.[63] At UCL, Schwarzenberger repeatedly referred to Strange's status and 'duties as a farmer's wife',[64] 'wife and mother',[65] 'the wife of a farmer and journalist with wide interests and commitments'.[66] However, George Keeton, as her line manager, was more directly involved in forcing Strange out.

Late in 1956, Strange became pregnant with her third child, taking her first period of maternity leave from UCL for a term in 1957–8. Schwarzenberger and Keeton's complaints began immediately, the administrative inconvenience of finding a temporary replacement apparently intolerable. Keeton wrote to Provost Ifor Evans, airing his and Schwarzenberger's complaints 'about the arrangements that will have to be made'. He could not 'think of a suitable deputy' and the college would have to advertise.[67] The finance secretary confirmed that if Strange took maternity leave, then it would 'break new ground'.[68] The college had never advertised for maternity cover before.[69] Mothers in full-time work were rare; ones taking out loans to buy a farm for their husband rarer.[70] In 1957, Strange secured the loan from UCL that allowed her and Selly to purchase a farm near Tring. Selly could farm, Susan could commute the 40 miles to London, and they could raise their family.

In the late 1950s and 1960s, most middle-class mothers rejoined the labour market part-time and only after their children started school. This was endorsed by the report of a 1956 government committee chaired by Strange's former editor-in-chief at *The Economist*, Geoffrey Crowther: part-time though not full-time work was possible for mothers of young children.[71] Much to the relief of UCL Secretary E.A.L. Gueterbock, who wanted 'these women with large families' to return part-time, Susan Strange once indicated that she might consider part-time work after her second maternity leave in 1960.[72] But this was the only occasion. 'With a good nanny at home to take charge there should be no problems', she explained to Schwarzenberger. It was only the following year 'when the child is 1-plus and is more liable . . . to get upset if the mother keeps disappearing too often . . . that concerns me a little'.[73] Schwarzenberger expressed great 'regret'. However, 'I can fully see that with growing family obligations and duties as a farmer's wife, this is becoming inevitable . . . It will not be easy to find someone of the caliber required to replace Susan Strange'.[74] Quite. However, Strange changed her mind or was just buying time.

Strange refused to accept a part-time position at UCL because she wanted to maintain her professional and intellectual independence. There was no question of flexible hours, support for re-entering the workplace, or, in her case, even being left alone during maternity leaves. She was never spared the internal university ponderings about the 'effects of the married state' on her work, and the implications for her male managers. Schwarzenberger and

Keeton's complaints escalated when both Strange and another 'lady member' of the Department, Valentine Korah, became pregnant at the same time in the spring of 1961. Keeton was livid that they had failed to coordinate their pregnancies, and the 'still further' disorganisation of the department's work.[75] In an angry letter to the provost, he called for an urgent investigation into 'whether "Miss Strange" with five children and Mrs Korah with four can work effectively'.[76] Although two of 'Miss Strange's' children were teenagers, Keeton asserted that it was 'obvious . . . that the care of such large families, all of them young, must be for them a constant preoccupation'.[77] Both Korah and Strange were registered for the Ph.D., and it was 'beyond question' that 'their domestic responsibilities' slowed down their postgraduate work.[78]

There is no indication that Strange was anything other than irritated by her treatment at UCL. Keeton wrote to Strange about her 'approaching confinement', suggesting that 'the attention which you must devote to your growing family' might necessitate part-time work; and the matter would be discussed at the next Appointments and Promotions Committee (A&PC).[79] She was likely being sarcastic when she thanked Keeton 'for putting the situation' to the A&PC 'as favourably as can be'.[80] She was not afraid to ask for what she wanted: longer maternity leave and a temporary teaching reduction while her children were young. Part-time university work, she pointed out, only suited those with additional employment elsewhere. Instead, Strange proposed that her teaching be reduced so that she could spend a day a week on research, 'which I feel to be most important indeed, and . . . a vital complement to teaching'. The cost of a replacement would come from her salary, and she would return to a normal teaching load when the children were no longer in 'the infant stage'.[81] Moreover, one term of maternity leave was too short: 'my husband and I both feel that—at my age and for the baby's sake—one term is not really enough'.[82]

Susan Strange duly took her third maternity leave in the 1961–2 academic year, by which time she had also permanently withdrawn from the Ph.D. programme. The provost was 'unhappy about the views she expresses in her letter', particularly her request for longer maternity leave and a temporary teaching reduction.[83] UCL Secretary Gueterbock had recently written a memorandum, 'Married Women Members of the Academic Staff with Family Responsibilities', that doubted whether women with children could really perform full-time academic work; the college 'will wish to know the ages of the children and the places which the two teachers [Strange and Korah] occupy in the Department'.[84] He advised the provost that they might take advantage of the impending renewal of Strange's five-year contract to push her out. The normal procedure was to re-appoint on the same terms until 1966. However, the rules were vague.[85] Gueterbock duly wrote to Strange while on maternity leave, informing her that she would be re-appointed for only one year because the 'terms of appointment' were under review.[86]

Like Oxford's repeated assertions that it was a 'Good Employer' while forcing Rachel Wall out, UCL was anxious about its reputation for liberalism. The problem was how to compel Strange onto a part-time contract without 'in any way' cutting 'across the liberal attitude which the College has always adopted towards the employment of married women'.[87] The A&PC reassured itself that the college's liberal attitude had 'worked admirably' to date by asserting the ultimate expression of its liberalism: this was a private matter. It was entirely up to women themselves how they managed the demands of family and paid work, which 'must depend largely upon the resources available to hire employees to take a part of the load of domestic work which would otherwise devolve upon the wife and mother'.[88] In Strange's case, her two oldest children attended boarding school; she was supported by a French au pair and mother-in-law for the three younger ones. The total privatisation of parenting responsibilities was convenient for the wider heterosexual gender order; no change was required in university practice, or domestic patriarchal relations. As historian Helen McCarthy explains, this model of wage-earning motherhood 'rested on women's acceptance of a bargain which opened up new employment opportunities without disturbing wider inequalities in the labour market and at home'.[89] A similar bargain permitted Strange's entry into the IR canon.

On the one hand, UCL claimed that it 'was no concern of the College' how married women arranged their domestic affairs.[90] On the other, as Keeton never tired of explaining, the employment of married women 'poses several problems in regard to the effect of the married state'.[91] There was an essential incompatibility between women's (not men's) ability to work in academe and 'the claims of child-bearing and post-natal duties'.[92] The A&PC took the view that Strange and Korah had both adequately performed at work to date and that Korah would do so in the future. Her maternity leaves were short, usually only in the vacations, and easily dealt with.[93] She 'does not let her family responsibilities interfere with her academic work'.[94] In contrast, Strange's maternity leaves were longer and more awkwardly timed.[95] The maternity leaves themselves, not Strange's work as such, were intolerable. If it inconvenienced male managers, then maternity leave itself constituted the failure to work full-time.

The A&PC resolved to retain Korah on full-time hours but to reduce Strange's to part-time. However, the decision was not clearly conveyed, and then UCL backtracked.[96] In January 1962, Strange was forced to interrupt maternity leave to attend the A&PC to explain and justify her domestic affairs, despite UCL's claim that her domestic arrangements were of no concern. She disclosed that she did not expect to have more than five children; that her family arrangements allowed her to carry on with her academic work; however her research would be affected for the next three to five years; her Ph.D., for example, had not progressed 'owing to domestic duties'.[97] She did not deny the special difficulties imposed on her as a mother working for pay, and repeated her request for a temporary teaching reduction to spend a day a week on research. The committee refused, yet allowed Strange to continue full-time and extended her contract for five more years to 1967. She duly returned to work and resumed her contributions to the *Yearbook*, edited by the two men still intent on forcing her out.[98]

The decision not to place Strange onto a part-time contract in 1962 was likely due to Schwarzenberger's reservations about employing another part-time member of faculty. This was 'the worst of all possible worlds', he explained to Keeton. Part-time teaching is 'unsatisfactory . . . Unless a teacher can be relied upon to undertake research work of his own, he is likely soon to use up his intellectual capital . . . If the College wants a part-time complement to Susan on a semi-permanent basis, we are likely to get the type of non-descript middle aged person who merely wants to supplement an unsatisfactory existing salary'.[99] By this logic, UCL needed to force Strange out completely. The opportunity came with Strange's sixth pregnancy in 1963–4. In a confidential memorandum that likened her pregnancies to 'emergencies', Schwarzenberger concluded that she now should resign from UCL altogether not only for the benefit of the college and himself but in her own interests, yet again, as 'the wife of a farmer and journalist'. Any continued arrangement, he thought, even part-time or casual, was undesirable if it jeopardised 'a second full-time appointment' in IR.[100]

Once again, during a maternity leave, Susan Strange attended a meeting of the A&PC to explain and justify herself.[101] She insisted that it was not very difficult to find temporary replacements and repeated that she 'was confident that . . . she could arrange her domestic life in such a way' that she could do her job.[102] Though it was not in the formal minutes, the committee permitted Gueterbock and Keeton to keep pressing the issue, euphemised as the desire 'to explore the long term problem of her continued family responsibilities'.[103]

According to Keeton, 'matters cannot be left as they are'.[104] Strange would not be permitted to demonstrate her capacity to work as both mother and scholar. A series of letters and meetings followed which, taken together, constitute sexist workplace harassment.

Keeton was now privately urging the provost to terminate Strange's appointment at the end of her contract in 1966, but this was never directly conveyed to her in writing.[105] Instead Gueterbock wrote to inform Strange that Keeton would be exploring 'the matter of your ability' to work full-time 'with your continuing large family responsibilities'.[106] She did not take the bait, writing to thank the committee for its sympathy and making no mention of the longer-term 'problem'.[107] Keeton replied expressing his deep concern with the state of IR teaching at UCL, mentioning Strange's previous assurance that she would not become pregnant again, and that her maternity leaves extended over two teaching terms.[108] Despite already being told twice, Keeton demanded to know Strange's 'own views' on her appointment.[109] In January 1964, they met in person 'without any clear result', according to Keeton, who reported to the provost that Strange 'has as yet not any clear idea of the course she wishes to adopt', as if she had not already conveyed her position multiple times.[110] Weeks later Keeton wrote to Strange asking her again to accept a part-time position, though in liberal and disingenuous fashion mentioning that the decision 'must obviously be yours'.[111]

Believing that the college was determined to fire her and after years of workplace discrimination, Susan Strange resigned from UCL. 'I am afraid I cannot really feel reassured' about the reality of part-time academic work. She did not want to end up primarily as a teacher rather than researcher. 'It also seems to me', she wrote, 'that if I am to work part-time, it would be better to spend the time writing'.[112] She never exerted a legal right to work full-time because she did not have one. She was bullied and harassed, in part, because there was no legal protection for maternity leave until Labour Prime Minister Harold Wilson's Employment Protection Act of 1975. 'One of my colleagues in the law faculty', she later reflected, 'offered to help by proving that if the real grounds were that I had had too much maternity leave, he could prove that the chances of heart disease striking any of the middle-aged teachers in the college was hundreds of times greater than my getting pregnant for the seventh time', as if that were her main legal and biological redress.[113] Even before UCL received Strange's formal resignation, G. W. Keeton had lined up 'a man to replace her, who is available, and would be willing to come', and presumably not encumbered by young children, even if he had them.[114] The man was British IR scholar A.J.R. Groom, later co-author of *International Relations Then and Now*, a disciplinary history published in 1991 in which of the approximately 146 historical international thinkers discussed, only seven were historical women, 4.79 per cent. The only British-based woman scholar was Susan Strange.[115]

The level of anxiety and stress that Strange experienced during these years at UCL is unclear. In addition to parenting and work, her elderly father was having regular bouts of depression and treatments by electric shock.[116] However, according to disciplinary historian Brian Porter, the way she handled Schwarzenberger's bullying 'testifies to her toughness'; 'whereas some staff suffered a nervous collapse under that academic Captain Bligh, she did not'.[117] We do not know the personal price that Strange paid for working in such a toxic environment, but in 1995 she said 'academic politics . . . is a pretty rough game'.[118] In what could be read as a further marginalisation of a figure such as Rachel Wall, mental toughness was elevated as a personality trait necessary to survive as a woman in academe. In the late 1980s, Strange had also suffered an unspeakable tragedy when her son Mark, her third child, died in his early thirties of HIV/AIDS.

The way that Strange was assumed to overcome misogyny at UCL was assimilated into a narrative about her singular personality which was, in turn, central to her ability to later shape and dominate the British IR field. Susan Strange was becoming Susan Strange. Later Strange also suggested that being driven out of UCL was one of several 'lucky breaks', though she briefly— once—lamented that the 'feminist case' had not yet been made in the professions and that with four of her six children still young at home she 'didn't relish' taking up the 'fight'.[119] But if the remedy to the harassment of working mothers was feminist struggle, then why did she later disparage the generation of feminists in the IR profession who took up that fight?

## Fashioning an Iconoclast: On the Non-Feminist Feminism of Susan Strange

There are at least three interrelated aspects to the self-construction and later reception of Susan Strange in the IR profession: her exceptional intellectual and institutional influence; her iconoclastic personality; and her gender and relation to feminism. 'I profess to be a Marxist no more than I profess to be a liberated woman—the two are both woolly and self-defined categories', she claimed in 1994.[120] And 'as for women studies', she is reported to have said,

'I think that women should study'.[121] Given her experience at UCL during the 1960s, Strange's disavowal of the women's liberation movement of the 1970s is puzzling, until it is understood in relation to how she fashioned her own persona as the exceptional 'founding mother' of IPE and a new British IR of the 1980s and 1990s.[122]

## Intellectual and Institutional Influence: Smashing the Patriarchy

While G. W. Keeton was lining up her replacement, Susan Strange was busy making her own plans. Prior to resigning from UCL, she had accepted a full-time research position at the Royal Institute of International Affairs at Chatham House in 1964. There she developed her powerful analyses of global political economy, critique of formal modelling and pretensions of contemporary international theory, publishing her first book, *Sterling and British Policy* in 1971, at the age of forty-eight. Strange joined and eventually led research teams at Chatham House that included numerous women international thinkers, including Miriam Camps.[123]

Strange also stayed well connected at LSE. She had tutored on the 'Economic Factor in International Relations' as early as 1959 and continued teaching there from 1965, initially due to the delay in Coral Bell's arrival as the new Reader in IR.[124] To say that UCL's loss was LSE's gain is an understatement. By 1978, Strange had become LSE's Montague Burton Chair, but despite being the department's most senior professor she was paid less than her colleague F. S. Northedge.[125] Though there is some (inevitable and gendered) debate over the intellectual depth of her work, Susan Strange came to mark a generational, institutional, and intellectual shift in the British IR scene.

This is nowhere clearer than in the way Strange deliberately killed off the British Coordinating Committee for International Studies (BCCIS) when she founded BISA, her main 'organisational off-spring'.[126] Strange claimed sole ownership of the idea. 'Money is power', she declared, as if there were any questions why she was not BISA's first chair, 'and as treasurer . . . I saw to it that we provided the members with a service . . . to the young lecturer as to the established professor, to the provincial polytechnics as much as to any of the older universities'.[127] Strange was quick to see the significance of the expansion of IR appointments in both the older universities and polytechnics in response to the growing interest among students in the 1970s, and to leverage this for her institution-building purpose.[128] Consciously modelled on the International Studies Association (ISA) in the US, Strange explicitly conceived BISA as an antidote to the conservative, intellectually stale, and clubby BCCIS. It had to 'quietly expire'[129] and 'fade out of the picture',[130] to be replaced by something 'more stimulating', 'lively, democratic, liberal', 'friendly and un-stuffy'.[131] Institutionally, BISA may have started as a BCCIS sub-committee, but it did not organically 'grow out' of BCCIS, as suggested on BISA's current website.[132] BISA was not just a 'modernisation' of BCCIS.[133] Strange founded BISA as an intentional and rather gendered act of patricide.

Susan Strange mocked BCCIS's 'dreadfully constipated and hierarchical Bailey conferences'.[134] She conceived BISA in opposition to the 'barons and the top brass' of British IR not only because she hated BCCIS conferences but also because she scorned their efforts at international theory. Like her con-temporary Coral Bell, and predecessor Agnes Headlam-Morley, Strange was particularly dismissive of so-called 'IR theory' by people who 'would rather fit the facts of life into international relations theories than question the validity of the theories'.[135] Strange is reported to have had 'something like contempt for Charles Manning's ingenious word-play and subtle philosophising'.[136] As disciplinary historian Brian Porter observes, she 'was well aware of the heritage she was entering', when she took the Montague Burton Chair, 'and had scant respect for it'.[137] This may be why she never delivered the core lectures on the 'International System', unlike her recent predecessors.[138] Even *Millennium*, the exciting student-run journal established at LSE in 1971, had 'a fair sprinkling of banal thoughts and pontifical clichés from the good and the great'.[139]

Strange was equally dismissive of Martin Wight's attempt at LSE to estab-lish a canon of so-called great thinkers as the foundation for the new field in the 1950s, the British equivalent to the project of Morgenthau, Kenneth Thompson and others in the United States. According to IPE scholar and Strange student Ronen Palan, she derided the attempt to establish an intel-lectual genealogy for IR 'spanning allegedly from Thucydides to Machiavelli, Hobbes, Rousseau and Morgenthau'.[140] Perhaps because she was aware of its contemporary provenance, it was easy for Strange to reject what became the 'conventional historiography of IR'.[141] As already noted, in the British case, and in collaboration with Thomson's Rockefeller Foundation project, this version of the history of international thought was conceived by Herbert Butterfield as a way to trap historians into engaging with general 'international theory'.[142] In this context, Strange's views of IR's so-called 'great traditions' may have been 'cavalier', but were certainly justifiable.[143]

Susan Strange thought that her vision of an open and radically interdisci-plinary IR exemplified by the new IPE also exposed the so-called 'second great debate' as 'arid'.[144] For Strange, the 'debate' between the 'traditionalist' men of the British Committee pursuing a more classical philosophical and allegedly historical approach and the 'new men' of American social science who adopted behaviourist approaches was completely 'outdated and uninteresting'.[145] She nonetheless used her ISA presidential address 'to deliver a characteristically "Susan-like" diatribe against rational choice theory', which had become increasingly dominant at UCL after her departure, as well as in the United States.[146] She loudly though vainly admonished those who were infatuated with rationalist methods, or who considered game theory as anything more than a 'pedagogic device'.[147]

All of it—the invented traditions and canons, the anxieties of 'traditionalists' and 'theorists' of what became the 'English School', rational choice approaches—they were all distractions from what really mattered about the modern world of states and capitalist markets. Mirroring the BCCIS men's need to establish hierarchies of fields, Susan Strange thought 'the study of international (that is, intergovernmental) relations was only a branch of international political economy, as diplomatic history had been a branch of international history'.[148] She was laying the institutional and intellectual groundwork for something else, what Palen calls a 'pragmatic, empiricist and critical school of IPE'.[149] She also supported a more genuinely historical IPE, which was inspired, in part, by her friend Robert Cox, a Canadian officer at the UN, history graduate and later academic and leading critical IR scholar.[150] Like Eileen Power, Margery Perham, and Coral Bell, Strange pursued successful scholarly partnerships with men, some of whom considered women, or at least these women, as intellectual equals.

Susan Strange stands as the only historical woman in the IR academy afforded canonical status, though today she is often recognised more as a name than for the substance of her work. Her legacy of an intellectually open and 'eclectic' IPE faltered, especially in the United States, ignored in the contemporary fad for hypothesis-testing.[151] Still, some canonise Strange for her role as a 'great intellectual "midwife"'[152] to cohorts of devoted graduate students mainly in Britain and Canada who, in turn, carefully tend to and honour her legacy. For others, she owed her fame to the fact that she was 'a theorist who invented analytical categories and they were categories that revealed truths'.[153] For still more, her eclectic approach was more journalistic than high theory, the alleged real measure of intellectual profundity for some in IR.[154]

Yet even here there is a (gendered) question mark around the depth of her intellectual labour. 'In purely intellectual terms', claimed American IPE scholar

Benjamin Cohen, 'Strange's contributions were limited. By her own admission, she was no theoretician. Indeed, she always had a suspicion of grand theory', 'grand' referring to the 'isms', realism, liberalism, Marxism.[155] In rejecting the 'isms', Strange presaged IR's contemporary post-paradigm era, in which the field is no longer organised around debating so-called 'grand theories'. It annoyed Susan Strange that she was criticised for not adopting one of those theoretical frameworks, for being primarily interested in the pragmatic and the empirical. For Strange, structural global power could not be understood through theoretical abstraction or systematic theory, but through an open-ended and eclectic framework for analysing power relations. In her 1988 book, *States and Markets*, Strange analogised the narrow concern of much abstract IR theory 'with relational power of one state over another' to accounts of male violence against women that ignored the structural power of patriarchy. 'It is as if you said, "This man has power in relation to this woman because he can knock her down", ignoring the fact of structural power in a masculine-dominated social structure that gives the man social status, legal rights and control over the family money that makes it unnecessary even to threaten to knock her down unless she does as she is told'.[156]

However, only in a posthumous imaginary dialogue is the gendered (and partial) connection between 'men' and so-called 'high theory' made explicit. Strange was 'fascinated by . . . the "theories" [men] dream up and consider so important and so exclusive, by your dreams of utopia. Women . . . know what really matters'.[157] Though Strange recognised its role in IR's intellectual failure, she did not see the gendered and racialised assumptions behind IR's distinction between theory (what her LSE colleague Philip Windsor referred to as the 'higher bullshit'[158]) and other intellectual labour as mere empirics.

## No One's Disciple

Susan Strange's dismissal of IR's 'good and the great',[159] her open contempt for the work of her predecessors and many contemporaries, was central to the gendered production and reception of her iconoclastic persona as a rebel and 'an all-time iconoclast'.[160] She was known for her 'irreverence',[161] for being one of IR's 'most creative and influential personalities',[162] for 'disturbing the peace, and [enjoying] irritating people who thought they wielded power'.[163] She had a 'confrontational, in-your-face approach to academic debate and teaching'.[164] She is frequently described as 'energetic and iconoclastic', 'forceful' and charismatic, flamboyant, and unconventional, tough-minded, candid, prophetic, a 'luminous presence',[165] a reputation that Strange clearly and assiduously cultivated. In her own words, she would offer something different to the 'boring babble of the barons', as 'I irreverently called them'.[166]

Drawing attention to her own impertinence, Strange fashioned her style and mode of intellectual engagement to differentiate herself from and surpass British IR to date. During her Leonard Schapiro Keynote Lecture at LSE in 1995, she mentioned that she never gave an inaugural Montague Burton Professorial lecture because 'I was afraid of upsetting my colleagues'.[167] This persona, just as much as her vision of IPE and radical interdisciplinarity, attracted generations of scholars to her orbit. She let it be known over and over that she was nobody's disciple. She 'questioned prevailing nostrums with ill-concealed glee'.[168] Clearly shaped by her experience with Schwarzenberger, she would not be reviving nor establishing any 'school' of IR or clique to parrot her thoughts. She would take seriously students' ideas and believed herself 'double lucky' to have a large family and students—'both have taught me a great deal'.[169] If she was an empire-builder, then it was despite herself, and of a different kind to her male peers.

Already during her undergraduate days, Strange developed a strong distaste for male professors compelled to cultivate cliques and surround themselves with devotees. On finishing her undergraduate degree, she could have become Harold Laski's research assistant, or David Mitrany's, but she had no interest in working with people who only wanted 'disciples'.[170] When she singled out and criticised Schwarzenberger, she noted that 'like many of his generation, his ideas of the role of the professor had been formed in his native country [Germany]. He tended to be overbearing and intolerant of contradiction, especially from his students'.[171] Transforming sexist bullying into a 'lucky break',[172] Strange being forced out of UCL meant that she also avoided Australian conflict studies scholar John Burton. Just 'like Laski', she claimed, Burton, a rational choice scholar, 'was more interested in recruiting disciples than teaching students to think for themselves . . . All reports suggested that Burton wasn't an easy man to get along with if you didn't agree with everything he said'.[173] Charles Manning, whose scholarship Strange mocked, was also known to favour a few 'hand-picked' students who would reliably follow his patrilineal–intellectual line.[174]

On one level, it is quite straightforward to read Susan Strange's iconoclastic persona and professional standing as an alternative 'founding mother' of IR as fundamentally related to her gender and career in journalism. As she declared in her autobiographical reflections, 'I am a woman and an ex-journalist'.[175] She

FIGURE 11.1. Susan Strange c.1980s. Photographer Unknown. Courtesy of LSE Library

entered academe relatively late and had no formal training beyond her under-graduate degree. 'By that time, I suppose I felt there was no point in being too conformist. To make any kind of mark, I had to develop ideas of my own, and take a chance that no one would listen'.[176] This was Strange's persona as an outsider, a woman and mother. She was not entirely socialised into the standard ways. She could show open contempt for the barons against whom she defined herself.

Where other women would have been punished for such dissension, Susan Strange got away with her iconoclasm. 'At times this could be a little wearing—especially . . . in her later years',[177] remembers one former assistant. Strange escaped any backlash not only because she revived the intellectually moribund field of British IR, but because she was read, and presented herself, as an exceptional woman who was not *that* radical. She 'was no revolutionary'[178] and knew how to operate. Strange claimed to be critical of conservative orthodoxies and 'increasingly impatient of The Establishment and all it stood for' because Britain 'still had brains, enterprise, and an unquenchable love of liberty'.[179] 'She had no time for any of the fashionable 1960s . . . protest . . . against the ills of the world economy'.[180] Strange's critical IPE was not that critical after all.

In the 1930s, the male club of elite historians admitted Eileen Power as an honorary member because she 'thinks like a man', her expressive femininity and obvious beauty precluding her entrance as an 'honorary man'.[181] Not so Susan Strange. Seriously failing as an intellectual project, British IR was too dreary and stale, too intellectually and institutionally insecure, for an intellectual 'elite' to exist. Yet Strange was still 'honorary man', leader of what in a different context she called the 'loyal opposition'.[182] This accords with IR scholar Cornelia Navari's recent identification of Strange's 'honourable man strategy', in which she 'accepted the ideal standard of her discipline and she worked up to it', which could also apply to Coral Bell, with the 'aim to be accepted as an equal or superior amongst those that she recognized as her peers'.[183]

Susan Strange's honourable man strategy aligns with her self-presentation as sexually free and comfortable talking about heterosexual sex. She rejected the discourse of women's liberation, had a shotgun wedding, but did not entirely disavow all aspects of the radical sexual politics of her age. Her short autobiography recounts her undergraduate days where 'Cambridge girls were locked firmly into their colleges every evening. We LSE girls were free and could go to the local pubs . . . The fact that London was being blitzed and that most of the boys would be drafted . . . and some would never come back sharpened our appetites for life and love'.[184] She did not seek her father's approval for her first marriage. She boasted that she got her first job in journalism because 'my brother picked up a girl in a London bar . . . Her mother sat on some committee'.[185] She tried to persuade John Burton of the wrongs of rationalist approaches in IR by asking whether 'he had ever quarrelled with his wife or his mother-in-law!'[186] 'No need for political correctness around me', one admirer has her posthumously announce.[187] One can imagine Strange in her grey pantsuit making mother-in-law jokes at BISA or the ISA, 'holding forth, pint in hand, in the bar'.[188]

## Disavowing Feminists, Performing Gender

As a graduate student in the early 2000s, the first thing I ever heard about Susan Strange was that she criticised unnamed 'feminists' in a now infamous 'confrontation' during her 1995 ISA Presidential Address.[189] I had never read Strange's work, nor knew anything else about her, but this was the folklore among IR graduate students in Britain soon after Strange died in 1998. The rumours of Strange's contempt for feminists were also widely and often gleefully reported as fact in secondary literature. Strange is variously said to have told feminists to stop 'carping',[190] or 'whinging',[191] or 'complaining',[192] or 'whining'[193] and just 'get on with it'.[194] The 'it' was either 'their work',[195] empirical 'research demonstrating that attention to women and gender' matters,[196] or have 'babies sooner rather than later'.[197]

Despite her experience of discrimination, Strange did little to challenge the academic culture that punished mothers. 'She made no special claims for women and no special claims for being one', according to Navari, 'except that she had produced six children while inventing the central theoretical pillars of IPE'.[198] She thought the concept of 'liberated woman' was 'woolly and self-defined'.[199] At UCL, of course, she did make a special claim, requesting a temporary teaching reduction that was refused. The conclusion she drew was not that academic and wider culture needed to change, but that overcoming workplace sexism was a matter of will and personality. After all, with hard work, mental toughness, and career 'lucky breaks', a working mother of six could transform an intellectual field.[200] Yet for childcare she relied on French au pairs, boarding schools, help from her mother-in-law and her companion, and her oldest daughter, Jane. When her stepfather, Clifford Selly, insisted that the girls but never the boys clear dishes and wash up, Strange's daughter, Jane, has no memory of her mother protesting.[201]

After Strange's death, at least two of her admirers lamented that her 'genuinely well meant exhortation to the female members' of the ISA 'was misunderstood by the more politically correct'. But Strange was not bothered 'one jot'. Assimilating the furore to Strange's all-round iconoclasm, the episode, to these men at least, was all just 'illustrative of the irrepressible way she lived her life'.[202] But as one department colleague recalled, Strange 'thought feminism was tiresome . . . She was SUPERWOMAN and never *the* woman in the department, in the School, in IR internationally or anywhere . . . It was left to lesser women to identify with women students and colleagues, and to represent them in the department and in the School'.[203] Though Strange's comment on feminists from her presidential podium was not reprinted in the published version, many of Strange's male admirers seem delighted by whatever it was, assuming it was disapproval. Yet all reports are from memory, hearsay, or apocryphal, the folklore feeding the legend of Susan Strange. Only Craig Murphy sounded caution, noting that Strange had also offered 'guarded support for the new scholarship on women and gender in international relations'.[204] IR feminists were clearly already 'getting on' with their work.[205]

Susan Strange's problem with the IR canon was not that it was all-male, let alone all-white, but that it was intellectual nonsense. BCCIS was stale not because it marginalised women, people of colour, and the study of empire, but because it was hierarchical and outdated. Strange may have seen all this in gendered, though not racial, terms. According to her LSE colleague Margot Light, she 'found most men lily-livered', meaning cowardly.[206] She pronounced on the nature of women and men; the former are 'more realistic about life and people', while men 'are often incurable romantics'.[207] She told a graduate student that men belong 'either . . . to cultures in which' they 'liked women and enjoyed their company or they belonged to cultures that did not'.[208] BCCIS clearly was a culture that did not like women, yet Strange never explicitly called out the misogyny of British IR. It literally took years of sexist discrimination for her to acknowledge that there was a 'feminist case' to be made 'in the professions'.[209] She dismantled elements of British IR's patriarchal order, though not as a patriarchal order.

Susan Strange's relation to feminism was not consciously strategic, a willed and knowing disavowal to gain acceptance by IR's male establishment. Yet it was also no accident or personality quark. I read Strange's criticisms of feminists not as an attempt to please her male colleagues, but because it would not displease them. Ida J. Koppen, who worked with Strange at the European University Institute, called it her '*ante*-feminist approach to survival in a male-dominated environment'.[210] But her '*ante*-feminism' was more than survival. It was a constitutive and political repudiation that cleared her path to the top of British IR. The way Susan Strange constructed her persona, her conscious distancing from feminism, while also regularly drawing attention to sex and gender, is more than the performance of iconoclasm and exceptionalism. Her iconoclasm—and its warm reception—*relied* on this gender performance, on how she presented herself as an exceptional woman, an honorary gentleman, but also a Queen Bee.[211] The infamous 'Susan-like'[212] diatribes, her dismissals and open contempt for the IR barons, were acceptable because she did not see, or did not draw attention to, its fundamental grounding in patriarchy. Susan Strange challenged IR's gender order in the limited way that being an exceptional woman, honorary gentleman, and a Queen Bee allowed, remaining loyal to many of the structures and standards of the field, if not individual male barons.

## Conclusion

In contrast to Margery Perham, Susan Strange mocked Britain's pretensions after the end of empire and had little time for the Commonwealth ('a kind of methadone to the heroin addict'[213]), yet she loved the United States, supporting its leadership role in world politics. With a longstanding connection to Chatham House, she was not outside the 'Establishment' but, like Perham, she was helping to reform it. Perham most successfully reconciled British popular and intellectual opinion to the realities of the loss of empire. She took the anticolonial claims at the Afro-Asian Bandung Conference of 1955 and the Tricontinental Conference of 1966 seriously, all better to counter them. Susan Strange was writing at a time when these movements of global economic reform were largely defeated. However, she was the Perham of Britain's international economic decline, the acceptable dissenter, a figure representing reformist improvement of the international economic and financial architecture against the radical transformative demands of those calling for a New International Economic Order.

The British IR that Susan Strange helped to build also did not fundamentally challenge the gender or racial order of which she, her patrons, students, and most of her male colleagues were the beneficiaries. Susan Strange became Susan Strange because she left IR's existing sexual division of labour intact. Strange would simply not have achieved the same fame and influence if she had been a different kind of feminist. In distancing herself from feminism, the mother of six also became the perfect alibi for others in the field who were resistant to analysing or radically changing the gendered hierarchies of IR.

Many of Susan Strange's admirers praised her alleged ability to 'puncture the pretensions of post-positivist and feminist theory, as well as, of course and as always, economists and their allies in political science';[214] she was 'a scourge of some of the more pretentious exercises in international theorising'.[215]

Strange's iconoclastic persona thus became an alibi for critiques of post-positivism, including feminism and postcolonialism, that helped to open the door to more women and/or scholars of colour. Her admittance to the IR canon as the only historical woman further contributed to the marginalisation of women in IR's intellectual history. In other words, the IR that Strange helped to build could recognise her as the exceptional woman but also delayed IR's reckoning with the intellectual legacy of the other figures in this book. The exception might be Coral Bell, but only due to her involvement with the British Committee on the Theory of International Politics.

Like many of her male IR colleagues, Strange was not interested in race, decolonisation, or imperial nostalgia. By the 1960s, and at Chatham House, she was arguing that Britain needed to move on from the empire and focus on the economic, political and geopolitical effects of economic decline, and the relations between states and markets. The defining global events for Strange was the Suez Crisis in 1956, less because Suez revealed Britain's inability to bully Egypt, or because it signalled the coming end of the British Empire, and more because of its exposure of the rupture in the relationship with the United States.[216] Britain turned from empire to European integration.[217] The core of Strange's intellectual production in the late 1960s and early 1970s was the international position of sterling as Britain struggled to reconcile its 'extra-European' (imperial) financial commitments with prospective member of the European Economic Community. With Susan Strange, the field of IR was now about relations between post-imperial states.

The alternative British IR that Susan Strange helped to build was vastly superior to what had come before and compared to BCCIS or the British Committee. It was less hierarchical, more nurturing of independent thought, freer from the old historiography, open and interdisciplinary, less intellectually insecure. 'International relations', Strange approvingly observed, 'stands as the one social science with barriers to entry so low that anyone can jump them.'[218] According to IR scholars Caroline Kennedy-Pipe and Nicholas Rengger, 'Strange, more than anyone else at the time' insisted that 'those interested in the international did (and should) include, historians, economists, lawyers and many others'.[219] But so did Charles Manning. Strange may have moved the field in a more open and exciting direction in the 1980s. She was responsible for a partial and important corrective to British IR's intellectual failures. Yet she did not address British IR's Achilles' heel, the question of methods.

# The Voice of Portia

'WHAT MANNER OF MAN IS this teacher' of international relations? asked Charles Manning in 1951.[1] The most influential figure in British International Relations (IR) before Susan Strange grudgingly accepted the virtues of historical training, the discipline of the technical analysis of sources, the requirement to evidence claims, the art of interpretation and writing style. The approach 'may well have all the advantages claimed for it', Manning pointed out; 'but there continue to be students who do not choose to take it up'.[2] Yet if the justification for IR as a separate university subject was student numbers, then this did not equate to an intellectual project capable of producing significant and original scholarship. After all, what were IR's practitioners to be trained in? By what standards would its scholarship be judged and progressed? As Italian international lawyer Roberto Ago replied to Manning, 'We must be careful not to say that the professor of International Relations should combine a little history, a little economics and a little international law'.[3]

One obvious possibility was that IR scholars could be trained in one or more of its constituent disciplines—as historians, political theorists, lawyers, classicists, anthropologists, economists, or political scientists—and draw on one or more of their ever-evolving 'methods and techniques' to research and write about international relations.[4] This was the radically interdisciplinary field as practised by F. Melian Stawell, Lilian Friedländer, Eileen Power, Lucy Philip Mair, Agnes Headlam-Morley, Margery Perham, Merze Tate, and Rachel Wall. We will never know what IR could have been had women, people of colour, and empire not been marginalised and then erased from its history. They should be recovered not only because they helped to create a new intellectual field and were later erased; because they illuminate the gendered history of knowledge; or because they challenge existing intellectual histories and founding myths. They also offered different potentialities for the field, even via some of the most problematic aspects of their work.

In the 1920s, Lucie Zimmern introduced students to the work and thought of Black intellectuals and artists, inviting them to reflect on their complicity in global racial hierarchies, though to the end of reforming rather than overturning the British Empire. She offered an alternative genealogy of international thought that centred the comparative analysis of gender, race, and class for imperial ends. Merze Tate's painstaking history of the European arms race neglected its basis in capitalism yet her historical training underpinned her later antiracist approach to geopolitics.[5] The Tory appeaser Agnes Headlam-Morley refused to develop a 'theory' of international relations to justify IR's separateness and defended historical methods against the claims of junk sociology. Eileen Power's Orientalist experiments in world social history prefigured by decades contemporary international historical sociology. Outside the academy, one of Britain's leading intellectuals, Claudia Jones, introduced tens of thousands of Black and brown Britons to Black Atlantic thinking on colonial and postcolonial worlds. A reformer at Oxford, Rachel Wall, wanted to teach imperialism, less Eurocentric history, and anticolonial thought but was hampered by an excessive teaching load, deteriorating mental health, and heartbreak. Susan Strange mocked IR's male mediocrities and created the British International Studies Association (BISA) as a conscious act of patricide, yet also sustained British IR's conservative gender and racial order into the 1990s.

The diverse intellectual and methodological commitments of this cohort, some highly debatable and some still inspiring, make them enormously relevant today. They carried out their work as diplomatic, social, and contemporary historians, as international lawyers, area specialists, classicists, anthropologists, comparativists, as scholars interested in the workings of international organisations and of the politics of empire and race. They addressed all of IR's main subjects and remained within or with at least one foot in their constituent discipline, and the quality of their work was determined by those methodological standards.

'This is the voice of Portia', Manning protested, evoking Shakespeare's cross-dressing heroine in The Merchant of Venice.[6] For IR to be taught in and through the established methods of its constituent disciplines, potentially in different departments, was like an intelligent and beautiful woman disguising herself as a male lawyer, a hoax. 'The point of the Shylock story is that any trick of phoney argument is good enough to defeat the horrid Jew'.[7] The chair of LSE's IR Department rejected the voice of Portia, reducing the methods

question to a territorial fight over teaching subjects. It jeopardised the little
fiefdom that he ran 'like an absolute monarch'.[8] Instead, IR should sit 'side by
a side with those of the older established disciplines, and particularly history',
he insisted. But it should do so without their specialist forms of methodological training.[9] Yet how could international relations be studied, and studied
well, if not using the methods of one or more of its constituent disciplines? As
the Norwegian historian Wilhelm Keilhau pointed out: 'History is a special
science because History has developed certain methods . . . to examine
sources and criticise sources. In this way, I do not think that International Relations can be called a discipline of its own, because I do not think it will be
possible for it to develop any specific method'.[10]

Manning was racist and misogynist. The not unrelated fact was his comfort
with the 'superficiality' of IR's methods.[11] 'Platitudes, these?', Manning asked
in a 1953 essay, 'The Pretensions of International Relations'. 'One must indeed
hope that they may be', he continued. 'Here are more'.[12] Instead of training IR
scholars in, and holding them accountable to, the methodological standards of
one or more of its constituent disciplines, Manning bequeathed to his successors what his critics feared would become of IR in his hands, 'the haunt of the
charlatan'.[13] In the obsession with distinguishing IR from history, in failing to
develop a coherent answer to the methodological question that was its Achilles'
heel, IR was redefined as a meta-discipline populated by imaginary 'Supermen'.
These men would be dabblers in all subjects; the IR teacher should be 'on terms
with them all'.[14] The result, as Susan Strange saw it, was a mid-century British
IR dominated by (white) male mediocrities. In viewing history as the main
intellectual threat to the autonomy of IR, Manning and his followers failed to
prevent British IR's partial subsumption into political science, which claimed
to be more methodologically 'rigorous' in its treatment of empirical 'data'.[15]


Considering the recent explosion of new feminist histories recovering historical women philosophers, artists, and historians, the more challenging question
is not the one posed in the book's introduction, why women? Recent popular
works such as Katy Hessel's *The Story of Art Without Men*, Benjamin Lipscomb's *The Women Are Up to Something*, and Clare Mac Cumhaill and Rachael
Wiseman's *Metaphysical Animals* suggest that feminist recovery and women's
history that interweave interpersonal, institutional, and intellectual histories
have wide appeal.[16] The real question is, why international thought? The
history of this intellectual field could seem entirely parochial, of concern only
to IR scholars in the academy. But this history is also part of the country's

reckoning and non-reckoning with empire. Today, the intertwined movements of Rhodes Must Fall, Black Lives Matter, and decolonising the curricula all point to the continuing significance of colonial history, slavery, and racial capitalism in shaping world politics and the fields that make world politics their subject, primarily history and IR. The history of IR matters because it is part of the intellectual and political struggle over the legacy of the British Empire, the conflicts over what is taught about empire in schools and about decolonising the institutions of British life.

As the intellectual field initially formed to understand and oversee the management and eventual decline and transformation of the empire, IR ought to have been the scholarly field at the forefront of contemporary conversations about empire and its aftermaths, including Britain's entry to the European Economic Community and its exit, known as Brexit. Instead, the academic field followed the path of the late- and post-imperial state. IR turned away from empire towards Europe and almost unwavering alignment with the United States. IR's past in colonial administration was marginalised; intellectual approaches in which women excelled, particularly history, were caricatured; some institutionally powerful men developed theoretical frameworks that made it impossible to think seriously about the empire and its legacies; and they created an all-male, all-white canon. The principal intellectuals questioning and rectifying the erasure of or nostalgia for the British Empire were not associated with IR, rather they were historians and cultural-studies scholars and, outside the academy, thinkers of the New Left.[17]

Later generations of IR students were taught that the field was always organised around debating 'grand theories'—realism, liberalism, Marxism, constructivism, latterly feminism, poststructuralism and postcolonialism. Women engaged with and contributed to all, and sometimes defined and critiqued, these theoretical approaches that came to characterise much of IR, but were written out of IR's canon and textbooks.[18] Few were interested in the disciplinary boundary-work that accelerated in the 1950s or in developing theories of the interstate system when discussion of 'international theory' dramatically increased in the 1980s. Women did not join those men seeking to bestow intellectual legitimacy on themselves through inventing a canon of intellectual greats and positioning themselves as its true heirs.

'There is no point in pretending', one leading IR scholar wrote in 1987, 'that British writers on International Relations have so far made as much of an impact on their foreign colleagues as have their equivalents in the arts, or ... political philosophy'.[19] Two years earlier, another complained that 'for much of its history the academic study of international relations has failed'.[20] In 2001, leading practitioners were still lamenting that IR was 'backward' and lacked the standing of philosophy or history.[21] Its 'big names' were 'virtually unknown outside' IR.[22] IR scholars continued to draw extensively and belatedly from other disciplines. Yet humanities scholars and social scientists cared little for IR scholarship, and even less for so-called IR 'theory'. This was recently (re)confirmed using bibliographic data, anecdotal evidence, and citations.[23] IR scholars do not contribute their share to the world of letters. Works by self-identified IR scholars are rarely reviewed in the *London Review of Books*, Britain's leading magazine of ideas.[24] Educated publics read books by historians and literary scholars on international relations, not those who profess IR.[25] Is there a field with a greater discrepancy between the significance and magnificence of its subject matter and the standing and intellectual reach of its scholarship?

The continuing neoliberalisation of the British academy, the explosion of casualised labour, the erosion of pay, pension and working conditions, and the pressure to churn out publications mitigate against scholarly work of the highest standards in all fields. But contemporary anxiety about IR's specific status also occurs in a wider political, and intellectual context. This is Britain's reckoning and non-reckoning with empire, of course, but also more extreme intellectual fragmentation and further encroachments from political science.[26] If, since the 1970s, many IR scholars framed their work around competing international theories, then the move away from grand theory and the concomitant increase in hypothesis-testing and causal inference since the 2010s removed the glue that held the field together.[27] More and more scholarship under the name of IR is closer in method and approach to comparative and quantitative political science than the wide-ranging historical and theoretical approaches of 'pluralist' IR, that is, the diverse and thriving scholarship represented by BISA, the European International Studies Association (EISA), and, indeed, many sections of the International Studies Association (ISA) itself.[28] There may be disquiet over IR's intellectual status, but British IR is a story of *institutional* success, with national and internationally linked associations, journals, networks, and new degree programmes. Its degrees recruit extremely well; there are jobs for IR scholars with doctorates. Yet the blurring of the boundary with comparative politics has contributed to the partial takeover of these positions by methods-driven political scientists concerned only with mining international relations for empirical data.

We still await an intellectual history of the rise of abstract theorising in IR and its replacement with hypothesis-testing that is comparable to recent histories of the emergence of global justice theory in the same period.[29] After a brief resurgence at the end of the Cold War, the so-called liberal international order appeared in terminal decline and the political–scientific credentials of 'liberal international theory' came under assault. It is no coincidence that just as postcolonial, feminist, and other critical and more genuinely historical approaches gained a stronger foothold in the field, some have sought to reduce IR's subject matter to a domain of empirical political science. One can test a simple hypothesis and sidestep historical and theoretical questions about the bloody history and legacies of imperialism on contemporary patterns of global wealth and violence. As the 'Historical IR' section of the ISA thrives, recent editors of the ISA's flagship journal, *International Studies Quarterly*, newly defined disciplinary history as outside its remit. Empirical political scientists mine international subjects with ever more sophisticated forms of data collection. They appear to show little interest in the historical, theoretical, epistemological or ontological questions and debates that have shaped and defined IR, nor do they share in its intellectual anxieties.

The roots of British IR's intellectual failure were the interrelated erasures of empire and race, the marginalisation of women and people of colour, and evasion of the question of methods. As measured by raw evaluations of its approaches and debates, the short shelf-life and narrow reach of its scholarship, its constant borrowing from—but inability to export original ideas to—other fields, it was white male IR that failed as an intellectual project. As this book has shown, the IR that failed was not just white and male, but British and American, intellectually narrow, and methodologically weak. Its failures will not be remedied by doubling down on the roots of failure, by adopting the approach to history and theory associated with the British Committee on the Theory of international Politics; by developing and testing 'grand' theories of the international system; by further absorbing IR into empirical political science; or by pretending to be a 'meta-discipline', bridging or filling gaps left by other disciplines, an entirely derivative purpose.[30]

IR's problems will not be solved by *transcending* disciplinary boundaries, rather, in part, by listening to the voice of Portia. That is, by offering graduate students advanced methodological training not only in political science, but in the methods of history, law, political theory, anthropology and so on, and for scholarship on international relations to be held to the highest standards of research in these fields. Those who profess IR in the British academy today still do so as university professionals and as professors of the importance of a subject—international relations—and its many objects of study: war, global economy, alliances, the rise and fall of empires and great powers, global racial, class, and gender hierarchies. Unless they define themselves as 'political scientists', IR professionals do not, generally, profess IR as practitioners of a particular method.[31] That should change.

This is not a question of IR 'borrowing' methods from other disciplines, rather of training and the quality of scholarship. Practised this way, international relations would remain an interdisciplinary field and the quality of its scholarship would be no better or—crucially—no worse than that of the disciplines and methods its scholars employed. When scholars of international relations test hypotheses or conduct survey experiments, they are not borrowing from but practising political science. When scholars of international relations use archival and other primary sources to rewrite world, intellectual, or disciplinary histories, they are not borrowing from history, they are international or intellectual historians. When scholars of international relations undertake close and original readings of canonical political texts, they are not borrowing from political theory, they are international political theorists. The intellectual question is whether the scholarship produced is good or bad. The professional question is whether the scholar is genuinely pluralist, whether they believe that their approach to the subject of international relations is the best and only valid one, whether they accept and value the field's intellectual and methodological pluralism or seek to destroy it.[32]

There is intellectual quality but also epistemic justice grounds for listening to Portia's voice.[33] IR scholars now have a much better sense of which intellectual fields were marginalised—and at what intellectual price—when IR was refigured as a certain kind of theoretical enterprise in the 1950s and further reified in the 1980s. Given the painstaking work of feminist and postcolonial scholars, it is now much harder to profess ignorance of IR's intellectual and disciplinary history, to research and teach that history in a manner that erases empire, women and people of colour. The field will never look the same again. To paraphrase Eileen Power, some of the best IR scholars will increasingly write under the name of critical history. The greater challenges today are to prevent IR's further absorption into political science and the tokenistic treatment of empire, race, and gender. In both scenarios, international intellectual and disciplinary history is defined as marginal to what counts as core IR research. As historian Helen McCarthy has recently suggested, women's international thought often 'lies beyond' the dominant concerns of disciplinary IR, 'possibly constituting a new field altogether'.[34] This is a strength yet also a risk in the power politics of inclusion and exclusion from an intellectual field.

# NOTES

## Introduction: The Gender of International Thought

1. F. M. Stawell, *The Growth of International Thought* (London: Butterworth, 1929). John Galsworthy's early work was only an eight-page League of Nations Union pamphlet. John Galsworthy, *International Thought* (Cambridge: W. Heffer & Sons, 1923).

2. Glenda Sluga, 'From F. Melian Stawell to E. Greene Balch: International and *Internationalist* Thinking at the Gender Margins, 1919–1947' in Patricia Owens and Katharina Rietzler (eds.), *Women's International Thought: A New History* (Cambridge: Cambridge University Press, 2021), pp. 223–43.

3. A. M. Allen, *Sophy Sanger: A Pioneer in Internationalism* (Glasgow: Glasgow University Press, 1958), p. 66.

4. Allen, *Sophy Sanger*, pp. 100, 274.

5. See especially Sophy Sanger, 'The International Labour Organisation of the League of Nations', *Transactions of the Grotius Society*, vol. 5 (1919), pp. 145–54.

6. Allen, *Sophy Sanger*, p. 54.

7. Allen, *Sophy Sanger*, pp. 195, 142.

8. Allen, *Sophy Sanger*, p. 117.

9. Allen, *Sophy Sanger*, p. 83.

10. In this regard the history of IR is more like the history of sociology, another feminised field from which women were only later erased. See Mary Jo Deegan, 'Early Women Sociologists and the American Sociological Society: The Patterns of Exclusion and Participation', *The American Sociologist*, vol. 16, no. 1 (1981), pp. 14–24; Mary Jo Deegan, 'Transcending a Patriarchal Past: Teaching the History of Women in Sociology', *Teaching Sociology*, vol. 16, no. 2 (1988), pp. 141–50.

11. Barry Buzan and Richard Little, 'Why International Relations Has Failed as an Intellectual Project and What to do About It', *Millennium: Journal of International Studies*, vol. 30, no. 1 (2001), pp. 19–39, here 29; Fred Halliday, 'International Relations and Its Discontents', *International Affairs*, vol. 71, no. 4 (1995), pp. 733–46.

12. Buzan and Little, 'Why International Relations Has Failed', p. 19.

13. For a quantitative analysis of the scale of historical women's exclusion that analyses sixty texts in the history of international thought, see Patricia Owens, 'Women and the History of International Thought', *International Studies Quarterly*, vol. 62, no. 3, pp. 467–81.

14. David Lake, 'White Man's IR: An Intellectual Confession', *Perspectives on Politics*, vol. 14, no. 4 (2016), pp. 1112–22; Kenneth W. Thompson, *Fathers of International Thought: The Legacy of Political Theory* (Baton Rouge: Louisiana State University Press, 1994); Kenneth W. Thompson, *Masters of International Thought: Major Twentieth-Century Theorists and the World Crisis* (Baton Rouge: Louisiana State University Press, 1980); Ken Booth, 'Master-Debating in International Relations', *Millennium: Journal of International Studies*, vol. 27, no. 1 (1998),

pp. 141–44. Cf. Iver B. Neumann and Ole Wæver (eds.), *The Future of International Relations: Masters in the Making?* (London: Routledge, 1997); Martin Wight, *Four Seminal Thinkers in International Theory: Machiavelli, Grotius, Kant, and Mazzini*, edited by Gabriele Wight, Brian Porter, and David S. Yost (Oxford: Oxford University Press, 2005).

15. For example, Hans J. Morgenthau and Kenneth W. Thompson (eds.), *Principles and Problems of International Politics: Selected Readings* (New York: Alfred Knopf, 1950); Arnold Wolfers and Lawrence Martin, *The Anglo-American Tradition in Foreign Affairs: Readings from Thomas More to Woodrow Wilson* (New Haven: Yale University Press, 1956); Stanley Hoffmann, *Contemporary Theory in International Relations* (Englewood Cliffs: Prentice-Hall, 1960); F. Parkinson, *The Philosophy of International Relations: A Study in the History of Thought* (London: Sage, 1977); Howard Williams, Moorhead Wright, and Tony Evans (eds.), *A Reader in International Relations and Political Theory* (Buckingham: Open University Press, 1993); David Long and Peter Wilson (eds.), *Thinkers of The Twenty Years' Crisis: Inter-War Idealism Reassessed* (Oxford: Clarendon, 1995); Ian Clark and Iver B. Neumann, *Classical Theories of International Relations* (Basingstoke: Macmillan, 1996); Edward Keene, *International Political Thought: A Historical Introduction* (Cambridge: Polity, 2005); David Armitage, *Foundations of Modern International Thought* (Cambridge: Cambridge University Press, 2012).

16. See, for example, Dale Spender, *Women of Ideas and What Men Have Done to Them: From Aphra Behn to Adrienne Rich* (London: Routledge, 1982); Joanna Russ, *How to Suppress Women's Writing* (Austin: University of Texas, 1983); Joan Wallach Scott (ed.), *Feminism and History* (Oxford: Oxford University Press, 1996); Linda K. Kerber, *Toward an Intellectual History of Women: Essays* (Chapel Hill: University of North Carolina Press, 1997); Bonnie G. Smith, *The Gender of History: Men, Women, and Historical Practice* (Cambridge, MA: Harvard University Press, 1998); Penny A. Weiss, *Canon Fodder: Historical Women Political Thinkers* (University Park: Pennsylvania State University Press, 2009); Lynn McDonald, *Women Founders of the Social Sciences* (Montreal: MQUP, 2013).

17. Chris Brown, Terry Nardin, and N. J. Rengger, *International Relations in Political Thought: Texts from the Ancient Greeks to the First World War* (Cambridge: Cambridge University Press, 2002), p. 3. For a critique see Kimberly Hutchings and Patricia Owens, 'Women Thinkers and the Canon of International Thought: Recovery, Rejection, and Reconstitution', *The American Political Science Review*, vol. 115, no. 2 (2021), pp. 347–59.

18. See, especially, Imaobong Umoren, *Race Women Internationalists: Activist-Intellectuals and Global Freedom Struggles* (Berkeley: University of California Press, 2018) and Barbara D. Savage, *Merze Tate: The Global Odyssey of a Black Woman Scholar* (New Haven: Yale University Press, 2023).

19. For other British-focused histories centring men see Long and Wilson, *Thinkers*; Timothy Dunne, *Inventing International Society: A History of the English School* (New York: Macmillan, 1998); Brunello Vigezzi, *The British Committee on the Theory of International Politics (1954–1985): The Rediscovery of History* (Milan: Edizioni Unicopli, 2005); Andrew Linklater and Hidemi Suganami, *The English School of International Relations* (Cambridge: Cambridge University Press, 2006); Ian Hall and Lisa Hill (eds.), *British International Thinkers from Hobbes to Namier* (New York: Macmillan, 2009); Casper Sylvest, *British Liberal Internationalism, 1880–1930* (Manchester: Manchester University Press, 2013); Ian Hall, *Dilemmas of Decline: British Intellectuals and World Politics, 1945–1975* (Berkeley: University of California Press, 2012). The male-centrism mirrors British intellectual history writing more generally. See, for example, the two volumes Stefan Collini, Richard Whatmore, and B. W. Young (eds.), *Economy, Polity, and Society: British Intellectual History, 1750–1950* (Cambridge: Cambridge University Press, 2000); Stefan Collini, Richard Whatmore, and B. W. Young (eds.), *History, Religion, and Culture: British Intellectual History, 1750–1950* (Cambridge: Cambridge University Press, 2000). Cf. Rachel Foxley, 'Gender and Intellectual History' in Richard Whatmore and

Brian Young (eds.), *Palgrave Advances in Intellectual History* (Basingstoke: Palgrave Macmillan, 2006), pp. 189–209.

20. Mia Bay, Farah Jasmine Griffin, Martha S. Jones, Barbara D. Savage (eds.), *Toward an Intellectual History of Black Women* (Chapel Hill: University of North Carolina Press, 2015); Keisha N. Blain, *Set the World on Fire: Black Nationalist Women and the Global Struggle for Freedom* (Philadelphia: University of Pennsylvania Press, 2018); Jennifer Forestal and Menaka Philips (eds.), *The Wives of Western Philosophy: Gender Politics in Intellectual Labour* (London: Routledge, 2021). Here I also extend the small but growing cross-disciplinary field on women and the history of international thought. In the British context, Gottlieb's study of the gendered politics of appeasement in interwar Britain is the most detailed to date, but university contexts are discussed only briefly: Julie V. Gottlieb, *'Guilty Women', Foreign Policy, and Appeasement in Inter-War Britain* (Basingstoke: Palgrave, 2015). On the wider field see Patricia Owens and Katharina Rietzler (eds.), *Women's International Thought: A New History* (Cambridge, 2021); Patricia Owens, Katharina Rietzler, Kimberly Hutchings and Sarah C. Dunstan (eds.), *Women's International Thought: Towards a New Canon* (Cambridge: Cambridge University Press, 2022); *Global Studies Quarterly*, vol. 3. no. 1 (2023), special issue on women and the history of international thought. Earlier forays in IR include Patricia Owens, *Between War and Politics: International Relations and the Thought of Hannah Arendt* (Oxford: Oxford University Press, 2007); Lucian M. Ashworth, 'Feminism, War and the Prospects for Peace', *International Feminist Journal of Politics*, vol. 13, no. 1 (2011), pp. 25–43; Helen M. Kinsella, 'Simone Weil: An Introduction' in Felix Roesch (ed.), *Émigré Scholars and the Genesis of American International Relations* (New York: Palgrave Macmillan, 2014), pp. 176–96; Craig N. Murphy, 'Relocating the Point of IR in Understanding Industrial Age Problems' in Synne L. Dyvik et al (eds.), *What's the Point of International Relations?* (London: Routledge, 2017), pp. 71–82; Molly Cochran, 'The "Newer Ideals" of Jane Addams's Progressivism: A Realistic Utopia of Cosmopolitan Justice' in Molly Cochran and Cornelia Navari (eds.), *Progressivism and US Foreign Policy Between the World Wars* (New York: Palgrave Macmillan, 2017), pp. 143–65; Jacqui True and J. Ann Tickner, 'A Century of International Relations Feminism: From World War I Women's Peace Pragmatism to the Women, Peace and Security Agenda', *International Studies Quarterly*, vol. 62, no. 2 (2018), pp. 221–33; Jan Stöckmann, 'Women, Wars, and World Affairs: Recovering Feminist International Relations, 1915–39', *Review of International Studies*, vol. 44, no. 2 (2018), pp. 215–35; Immi Tallgren, *Portraits of Women in International Law: New Names and Forgotten Faces* (Oxford: Oxford University Press, 2023).

21. Glenda Sluga, 'Add Women and Stir': Gender and the History of International Politics', *Humanities Australia*, no. 5 (2014), pp. 65–72; Glenda Sluga, 'Turning International: *Foundations of Modern International Thought* and New Paradigms for Intellectual History', *History of European Ideas*, vol. 41, no. 1 (2014), pp. 103–15; Madeleine Herren, 'Gender and International Relations through the Lens of the League of Nations (1919–1945)' in Glenda Sluga and Carolyn James (eds.), *Women, Diplomacy and International Politics since 1500* (New York: Routledge, 2016), pp. 182–201.

22. Leila J. Rupp, *Worlds of Women: The Making of an International Women's Movement* (Princeton: Princeton University Press, 1997); Catia C. Confortini, *Intelligent Compassion: Feminist Critical Methodology in the Women's International League for Peace and Freedom* (Oxford: Oxford University Press, 2012); Njoki N. Wane, Jagire Jennifer, and Zahra Murad (eds.), *Ruptures: Anti-Colonial & Anti-Racist Feminist Theorizing* (Boston: Leiden, 2013); Francisca De Haan, Margaret Allen, June Purvis, and Krassimira Daskalova (eds.), *Women's Activism: Global Perspectives from the 1890s to the Present* (London: Routledge, 2013); Glenda Sluga and Carolyn James (eds.), *Women, Diplomacy and International Politics since 1500* (London: Routledge, 2016); Mona L. Siegel, *Peace on Our Terms: The Global Battle for Women's Rights after the First World War* (New York: Columbia University Press, 2020); Elisabeth B. Armstrong, *Bury the Corpse of*

*Colonialism: The Revolutionary Feminist Conference of 1949* (Berkeley: University of California Press, 2023); Jan Stöckmann, *The Architects of International Relations: Building a Discipline, Designing the World, 1914–1940* (Cambridge: Cambridge University Press 2022).

23. Katharina Rietzler, 'U.S. Foreign Policy Think Tanks and Women's Intellectual Labor, 1920–1950', *Diplomatic History*, vol. 46, no. 3 (2022), pp. 575–601; on the 'new professions' as locations for women's international thought see Valeska Huber, Tamson Pietsch, and Katharina Rietzler, 'Women's International Thought and the New Professions, 1900–1940', *Modern Intellectual History*, vol. 18, no. 1 (2021), pp. 121–45.

24. I distinguish between the wider history of international thought and its subfield of IR's 'disciplinary' history. Although I do not view IR as a 'discipline', I reluctantly adopt the common language of 'disciplinary' history to denote scholarship on IR's *academic* history. See Brian Porter, *The Aberystwyth Papers: International Politics, 1919–1969* (Oxford University Press, 1972); William C. Olson and A.J.R. Groom, *International Relations Then and Now: Origins and Trends in Interpretation* (London: Harper Collins Academic, 1991); Brian C. Schmidt, *The Political Discourse of Anarchy: A Disciplinary History of International Relations* (New York: State University of New York, 1998); David Long and Brian C. Schmidt (eds.), *Imperialism and Internationalism in the Discipline of International Relations* (New York: State University of New York, 2005); Duncan Bell, 'Writing the World: Disciplinary History and Beyond', *International Affairs*, vol. 85, no.1 (2009), pp. 3–22; Nicolas Guilhot, *The Invention of International Relations Theory: Realism, the Rockefeller Foundation, and the 1954 Conference on Theory* (New York: Columbia University Press, 2011); Lucian M. Ashworth, *A History of International Thought: From the Origins of the Modern State to Academic International Relations* (New York: Routledge, 2014); Robert Vitalis, *White World Order, Black Power Politics: The Birth of American International Relations* (Ithaca: Cornell University Press, 2015); Amitav Acharya and Barry Buzan, *The Making of Global International Relations: Origins and Evolution of IR at Its Centenary* (Cambridge: Cambridge University Press, 2019; Jo-Anne Pemberton, *The Story of International Relations, Part One, Cold-blooded Idealists* (Palgrave: Basingstoke, 2019); Jo-Anne Pemberton, *The Story of International Relations, Part Two, Cold-blooded Idealists* (Cham: Springer International, 2020); Jo-Anne Pemberton, *The Story of International Relations, Part Three, Cold-Blooded Idealists* (Cham: Springer International, 2020); Vineet Thakur and Peter Vale, *South Africa, Race and the Making of International Relations* (London: Rowman and Littlefield, 2020); Alexander E. Davis, Vineet Thakur, and Peter Vale (eds.), *The Imperial Discipline* (London: Pluto, 2020); Knud Erik Jørgensen, *What Is International Relations?* (Bristol: Bristol University Press, 2022); Stöckmann, *Architects*.

25. Joanna Wood, doctoral dissertation in progress, University of Oxford.

26. Katharina Rietzler, 'Introduction: 100 years of women in *International Affairs*', Archive Collection, *International Affairs* (December 2022), pp. 1–15; also see Stephen Legg, 'At Homes: Political Hostessing and Homemaking' in *Round Table Conference Geographies: Constituting Colonial India in Interwar London* (Cambridge: Cambridge University Press, 2022), chapter 9.

27. But see Vitalis, *White World Order, Black Power Politics*, the only disciplinary history to centre an historically Black university.

28. Charles Manning, 'Metadiplomatics for the Modern Man', *The Universities Quarterly*, vol. 11, no. 2 (1957), pp. 155–163, here 160–61.

29. Carroll Quigley, *The Anglo-American Establishment: From Rhodes to Cliveden* (New York: Books in Focus, 1981), p. 310.

30. C.A.W. Manning, '"Naughty Animal": A Discipline Chats Back', *International Relations*, vol. 1, no. 4 (1955), pp. 128–36, here 133.

31. On '*thinking*' as a 'potentially more generous concept than *thought* in its canonical accommodations' see Glenda Sluga, What Do We Learn about War and Peace from Women International Thinkers?', *Global Studies Quarterly*, vol. 3, no. 1 (2023), pp. 1–10, here 2.

32. Helen Jeffrey, 'A Light-Hearted Memory of Chatham House', 1982. 3/11/14. Chatham House.

33. Owens, *Between War and Politics*; for self-critique see Owens, 'Racism in the Theory Canon: Hannah Arendt and "the One Great Crime in Which America Was Never Involved"', *Millennium: Journal of International Studies* vol. 45, no. 3 (2017), pp. 403–24.

34. Kimberly Hutchings, 'Doing Epistemic Justice in International Relations: Women and the History of International Thought', *European Journal of International Relations*, vol. 29, no. 4 (2023), pp. 809–31.

35. See, for example, Laura L. Doan, *Disturbing Practices: History, Sexuality, and Women's Experience of Modern War* (Chicago: Chicago University Press, 2013); Denise Riley, *'Am I That Name?' Feminism and the Category of 'Women' in History* (London: Palgrave, 1988).

36. Jane Haggis, 'White Women and Colonialism: Towards a Non-Recuperative History' in Clare Midgley (ed.), *Gender and Imperialism* (Manchester: Manchester University Press, 1998), pp. 45–75, here 46.

37. Oyèrónkẹ́ Oyěwùmí, *The Invention of Women: Making an African Sense of Western Gender Discourses* (Minneapolis: University of Minnesota Press, 1997).

38. Billie Melman, 'Under the Western Historian's Eyes: Eileen Power and the Early Feminist Encounter with Colonialism', *History Workshop Journal*, vol. 42 (1996), pp. 147–68, here 164, 161.

39. On gender as performance see Judith Butler's classic, *Gender Trouble: Feminism and the Subversion of Identity* (London: Routledge, 1990).

40. Eve Kosofsky Sedgwick, *Between Men: English Literature and Male Homosocial Desire* (New York: Columbia University Press, 1985), p. 1.

41. Kimberlé Crenshaw, 'Demarginalizing the Intersection of Race and Sex: A Black Feminist Critique of Antidiscrimination Doctrine, Feminist Theory and Antiracist Politics', *University of Chicago Legal Forum*, vol. 1989, no. 1 (1989), pp. 139–67.

42. Allen, *Sophy Sanger*, p. 94.

43. Others include Rebecca West, Miriam Camps, Eleanor Rathbone, Sylvia Pankhurst, Amy Ashwood Garvey, Ellen Wilkinson, Una Marson, Sheila Grant Duff, Elizabeth Monroe, Mary Proudfoot, Nancy Cunard, Barbara Wootton, Barbara Ward, Edith Penrose, Margaret Lambert, Agatha Ramm, Helena Swanwick, Vera Brittain, Ursula K. Hicks, Sudha R. Shenoy, Vernon Lee, Virginia Woolf, Caroline Playne, Sheila Kitzinger, Margaret Gowing. Many of these are discussed in Owens, Rietzler, Hutchings and Dunstan (eds.), *Women's International Thought*.

44. The notion that British IR fostered a 'classical' approach, attentive to history and philosophy, compared to the more positivist and behaviourist Americans, is most clearly stated in Hedley Bull, 'International Theory: The Case for a Classical Approach', *World Politics*, vol. 18, no. 3 (1966), pp. 361–77.

45. On the limits of canonicity in historical recovery projects see Meera Sabaratnam, 'In the Ruins of Canonicity: Women and Their Practices of Thought', *International Politics Reviews*, vol. 9, no. 2 (2021), pp. 246–50 and Kimberly Hutchings, Sarah Dunstan, Patricia Owens, Katharina Rietzler, Anne Phillips, Catherine Lu, Christopher J. Finlay, and Manjeet Ramgotra, 'On Canons and Question Marks: The Work of Women's International Thought', *Contemporary Political Theory*, vol. 21, no. 1 (2022), pp. 114–41.

46. On fascist British women see Julie V. Gottlieb, *Feminine Fascism: Women in Britain's Fascist Movement* (London: I. B. Tauris, 2003); Kye J Allen, '"A Pro-Fascist English Lady": The International Thought of Muriel Innes Currey', *Global Studies Quarterly*, vol. 3, no. 1 (2023), pp. 1–13.

47. On the strengths and limits of 'historical IR' see Mlada Bukovansky, Edward Keene and Christian Reus-Smit (eds.), *The Oxford Handbook of History and International Relations* (Oxford: Oxford University Press, 2023).

48. Duncan Wilson, *Gilbert Murray OM: 1866–1957* (Oxford: Oxford University Press, 1987), pp. 180–84.

49. Ashworth, *A History of International Thought*, p. 228.

50. The International Committee on International Cooperation (ICIC) was established in 1922 in Geneva as a consultative body of the League of Nations and is distinguished from the International Institute of Intellectual Cooperation (IIIC), founded in Paris in 1926. Alfred Zimmern was deputy director of the IIIC from 1926 to 1930.

51. Manning, 'Metadiplomatics for the Modern Man', pp. 160–61.

52. Guilhot, *Invention of International Relations Theory*; Vitalis, *White World Order*; Felix Roesch (ed.), *Émigré Scholars and the Genesis of American International Relations* (New York: Palgrave Macmillan, 2014).

53. Thakur and Vale, *South Africa*.

54. The WHIT Project Oral History Archive can be accessed at https://whit.web.ox.ac.uk /oral-history-archive. Sarah C. Dunstan, 'Women's International Thought in the Twentieth-Century Anglo-American Academy: Autobiographical Reflection, Oral History and Scholarly Habitus', *Gender & History*, vol. 33, no. 2 (2021), pp. 487–512.

55. Patricia Owens, 'Images of International Thinkers', *Review of International Studies* (2024), FirstView.

56. The three standout biographies are Carole Boyce Davies, *Left of Karl Marx: The Political Life of Black Communist Claudia Jones* (Durham: Duke University Press, 2008), Maxine Berg, *A Woman in History: Eileen Power, 1889–1940* (Cambridge: Cambridge University Press, 1996), and, as this book went to press, Barbara D. Savage, *Merze Tate: The Global Odyssey of a Black Woman Scholar* (New Haven and London: Yale University Press, 2024) was published. Also see the shorter treatment of C. Brad Faught, *Into Africa: The Imperial Life of Margery Perham* (London: I.B. Tauris, 2012), and the excellent Geoffrey Field, *Elizabeth Wiskemann: Scholar, Journalist, Secret Agent* (Oxford: Oxford University Press, 2023).

57. Vitalis, *White World Order*.

58. Davis, Thakur, and Vale, *Imperial Discipline*.

59. On the US case see Joanna Wood, doctoral dissertation in progress, University of Oxford. On other European contexts see Stöckmann, *Architects*.

60. See, for example, Shruti Balaji, 'From Colonial Subjecthood to Shared Humanity: Social Work and the Politics of "Doing" in Kamaladevi Chattopadhyay's International Thought', *Global Studies Quarterly*, vol. 3, no. 1 (2023), pp. 1–12; Jennifer Bond, 'Gender, Christianity, and Peace in Chinese Women's International Thought 1914–1953', *Global Studies Quarterly*, vol. 3, no. 1 (2023), pp. 1–12. Also see the work of the Association for Global Political Thought, https:// projects.iq.harvard.edu/globalpoliticalthought/home.

61. Jennifer Pitts, *A Turn to Empire: The Rise of Imperial Liberalism in Britain and France* (Princeton: Princeton University Press, 2009); Duncan Bell, *Dreamworlds of Race: Empire and the Utopian Destiny of Anglo-America* (Princeton: Princeton University Press, 2020).

62. Richard Symonds, 'Historians and Sentinels of Empire', *Oxford and Empire: The Last Lost Cause?* (Oxford: Clarendon, 1992), pp. 47–61.

63. Vitalis, *White World Order*.

64. Robin D. G. Kelley, and Stephen G. N. Tuck (eds.), *The Other Special Relationship: Race, Rights, and Riots in Britain and the United States* (New York: Palgrave, 2015).

65. Bill Schwarz, 'Crossing the Seas', in Bill Schwarz (ed.), *West Indian Intellectuals in Britain* (Manchester: Manchester University Press, 2003), pp. 1–30, here 18. IR scholars have only recently and belatedly engaged with Black Atlantic (and Pacific) intellectual traditions, but see Vitalis, *White World Order*; Robbie Shilliam, *The Black Pacific: Anti-colonial Struggles and Oceanic Connections* (London: Bloomsbury, 2015); Musab Younis, *On the Scale of the World: The Formation of Black Anticolonial Thought* (Oakland: University of California Press, 2022).

## 1. Aberystwyth 1919: A Love Story

1. J.F.F., 'Music and Words with Lucie Zimmern', *The Criterion*, vol. 6, no. 2 (April 1951), pp. 27–9, here 27, Bodleian Library, Oxford. MSS Zimmern 173, 11.

2. Brian Porter (ed.), *The Aberystwyth Papers: International Politics 1919–1969* (London: Oxford University Press, 1972). Olson and Groom claim that in Britain, at least, the 'field's beginning can probably best be dated' to the Wilson Chair: William C. Olson and A.J.R. Groom, *International Relations Then and Now: Origins and Trends in Interpretation* (London: Harper Collins, 1991), p. 62; Ken Booth, 'What's the Point of IR? The International in the Invention of Humanity' in Synne L. Dyvik, Jan Selby, and Rorden Wilkinson (eds.), *What's the Point of International Relations?* (London: Routledge, 2017), pp. 21–33.

3. University College Wales (UCW) Council Minutes 1916–1919, p. 339. Aberystwyth University Archives. Their wealth was inherited from a Welsh industrialist grandfather, David Davies (1818–1890), after their own mother and father died young.

4. There is a large secondary literature on Alfred Zimmern. See D. J. Markwell, 'Sir Alfred Zimmern Revisited: Fifty Years On', *Review of International Studies*, vol. 12, no. 4 (1986), pp. 279–92; Paul Rich, 'Alfred Zimmern's Cautious Idealism: The League of Nations, International Education, and the Commonwealth' in David Long and Peter Wilson, (eds.), *Thinkers of the Twenty Years' Crisis: Inter-War Idealism Reassessed* (Oxford: Clarendon Press, 1995), pp. 79–99; Julia Stapleton, 'Alfred Zimmern and the world "Citizen Scholar"' in *Political Intellectuals and Public Identities in Britain since 1850* (Manchester: Manchester University Press, 2001), pp. 91–111; Paul Rich, 'Reinventing Peace: David Davies, Alfred Zimmern and Liberal Internationalism in Interwar Britain', *International Relations*, vol. 16, no. 1 (2002), pp. 117–33; Jeanne Morefield, *Covenants without Swords: Idealist Liberalism and the Spirit of Empire* (Princeton: Princeton University Press, 2005); Tomohito Baji, 'Zionist Internationalism? Alfred Zimmern's Post-Racial Commonwealth', *Modern Intellectual History*, vol. 13, no. 3 (2016), pp. 623–51; Tomohito Baji, *The International Thought of Alfred Zimmern: Classicism, Zionism and the Shadow of the Commonwealth* (London: Palgrave, 2021).

5. Vineet Thakur and Peter Vale, *South Africa, Race and the Making of International Relations* (London: Rowman and Littlefield, 2020); p. 32. Erez Manela, *The Wilsonian Moment: Self-Determination and the International Origins of Anticolonial Nationalism* (Oxford: Oxford University Press, 2009).

6. Aberystwyth's own Department of International Politics was home to a lecturer in colonial history between 1935 and 1946, though his major works were on dynastic marriages and the letters of 'ambassadress at large', Dorothea Lieven: E. Jones Parry, *Spanish Marriages, 1841–1846: a Study of the Influence of Dynastic Ambition upon Foreign Policy* (London: Macmillan, 1936); E. Jones Parry (ed.), *The Correspondence of Lord Aberdeen and Princess Lieven, 1832–1854* (London: Offices of the Royal Historical Society, 1938). On the importance of Dorothea Lieven see Glenda Sluga, *The Invention of International Order: Remaking Europe after Napoleon* (Princeton: Princeton University Press, 2021).

7. 'The Case against Woodrow Wilson, After 100 Years' (May 28, 2019). https://the disorderofthings.com/2019/05/28/the-case-against-woodrow-wilson/.

8. Benjamin de Carvalho, Halvard Leira, and John Hobson, 'The Big Bangs of IR: The Myths That Your Teachers Still Tell You about 1648 and 1919', *Millennium: Journal of International Studies*, vol. 39, no. 3, (2011), pp. 735–58, here 745.

9. Booth, 'What's the Point of IR?', p. 26. Porter refers to 'David Davies and his Sisters'. 'Preface', *The Aberystwyth Papers*, p. ix.

10. See David Davies Memorial Institute https://www.aber.ac.uk/en/interpol/research /research-centres-and-institutes/ddmi/ (accessed July 26, 2023). This follows a pattern set as early as 1928, when the first official history of the Woodrow Wilson professorship also erased

them. See Sidney Herbert, 'The Wilson Chair of International Politics' in Iwan Morgan (ed.), *University College of Wales Aberystwyth: The College by the Sea* (Aberystwyth: The Cambrian News, 1928), pp. 185–7.

11. Booth, 'What's the Point of IR?', p. 28.

12. Booth, 'What's the Point of IR?', pp. 25–6.

13. Booth, 'What's the Point of IR?', pp. 25–6, emphasis added.

14. Booth, 'What's the Point of IR?', pp. 25–6.

15. Booth, 'What's the Point of IR?', p. 25.

16. Jan Stöckmann, *The Architects of International Relations: Building a Discipline, Designing the World, 1914–1940* (Cambridge: Cambridge University Press 2022), p. 29.

17. David Long and Brian C. Schmidt (eds.), *Imperialism and Internationalism in the Discipline of International Relations* (New York: State University of New York, 2005); Alexander E. Davis, Vineet Thakur, and Peter Vale (eds.), *The Imperial Discipline* (London: Pluto, 2020).

18. Arnold Wolfers and Laurence W. Martin, 'Introduction: Political Theory and International Relations' in Arnold Wolfers and Laurence W. Martin (eds.), *The Anglo-American Tradition in Foreign Affairs: Readings from Thomas More to Woodrow Wilson* (New Haven: Yale University Press, 1956), pp. ix–xxvii, here x.

19. For a summary of these so-called 'debates' see Peter Marcus Kristensen, 'Discipline Admonished: On International Relations Fragmentation and the Disciplinary Politics of Stocktaking', *European Journal of International Relations*, vol. 22, no. 2 (2016), pp. 243–67.

20. Peter Wilson, 'The Myth of the "First Great Debate"', *Review of International Studies*, vol. 24, no. 1 (1998), pp. 1–15.

21. Wilson, 'The Myth', p. 1.

22. 'M. Cortot at Aberystwyth: Visit of Famous Pianist', *The Cambrian News* (December 4, 1919), p. 5, MSS Zimmern 179, 8.

23. Some of the following discussion of Lucie and the Geneva School draws from my research and writing for a co-authored article with Katharina Rietzler. See Patricia Owens and Katharina Rietzler, 'Polyphonic Internationalism: The Lucie Zimmern School of International Studies', *The International History Review*, vol. 45. no. 4 (2023), pp. 623–42.

24. 'Shorthand notes of a statement made by Prof A. E. Zimmern at a meeting of the college council on Friday the 3rd day of June 1921'. Aberystwyth University Archives.

25. 'Lady Zimmern, 88, Educator's Widow', *New York Times* (October 19, 1963), p. 20.

26. Stapleton, 'Alfred Zimmern', p. 99.

27. Lucie Barbier, 'Correspondence: The Hallé Concerts', *The Manchester Guardian* (June 1, 1911), p. 9.

28. Lucie Barbier, 'French Concerts in Manchester', *The Manchester Guardian* (October 22, 1908), p. 4; also see Martha Elisabeth Stonequist, 'The Musical Entente Cordiale: 1905–1916', doctoral dissertation, University of Colorado, 1971, p. 18.

29. Lucie A. Barbier, 'Correspondence: Alsace-Lorraine', *The Manchester Guardian* (August 9, 1917), p. 3.

30. Lucie Barbier, 'Correspondence: The Hallé Concerts', *The Manchester Guardian* (June 1, 1911), p. 9. Ian Parrott, *The Spiritual Pilgrims* (Pembrokeshire: H.G. Walters, 1968), pp. 27–8. The department was discontinued in 1916, 'the outbreak of the war having made it impossible to carry out the object which the donor had in view'. University College of Wales Reports Submitted to the Governors, 1916, p. 79. For more on the sisters see Trevor Fishlock, *A Gift of Sunlight: The Fortune and Quest of the Davies Sisters of Llandinam* (Ceredigion: Gomer Press, 2014).

31. Lucie Zimmern quoted in J.F.F., 'Music and Words with Lucie Zimmern', p. 27.

32. Parrott, *The Spiritual Pilgrims*, pp. 27, 26.

33. Parrott, *The Spiritual Pilgrims*, p. 30.

34. J.F.F., 'Music and Words with Lucie Zimmern', p. 27.

35. Parrott, *Spiritual Pilgrims*, pp. 30–31.

36. E. A. Simonds (On Behalf of the Pupils of the School of Music), To the Editor of the Dragon, 'The School of Instrumental Music', *The Dragon*, UCW Magazine, vol. 37 (1914–15), pp. 149–50. Aberystwyth University Archives.

37. Parrott, *The Spiritual Pilgrims*, chapter 3. David Davies was vice-chair of the League of Nations Union and wrote extensively on international affairs, with works including *The Problem of the Twentieth Century: A Study in International Relationships* (London: Ernest Benn, 1930); *Force and the Future* (Westminster: New Commonwealth, 1934); *A Federated Europe* (London: Victor Gollancz, 1940); *The Seven Pillars of Peace: A Radical Scheme for a World League of Regional Federations* (London: Longmans, Green, 1945). For Lucie Zimmern's critical review of Davies's book calling for an international police force because it was a distraction from what she saw as the real work of educating the public about the League of Nations, see Lucie A. Zimmern, 'Force, by Lord Davies (Book Review)', *International Affairs*, vol. 14, no. 1 (1935), p. 128.

38. Noam Pianko, 'Cosmopolitan Wanderer or Zionist Activist? Sir Alfred Zimmern's Ambivalent Jewishness and the Legacy of British Internationalism', *Ab Imperio*, vol. 4 (2009), p. 230.

39. 'Shorthand Notes of questions put to and answers by Prof. Barbier at a Meeting of the College Council on Friday, the 3rd day of June 1921'. June 6, 1921. Aberystwyth University Archives.

40. I am grateful to Martha Stonequist, Lucie's granddaughter, for this correction. In 'Polyphonic Internationalism', Rietzler and I state that *both* daughters became financially dependent on Alfred and left Aberystwyth with Lucie.

41. Sir Francis Edwards Bart to Sir Evans Jones Bart, M.P., April 18, 1921. Aberystwyth University Archives.

42. Minutes of a Meeting of the Special Committee appointed at the College Council on Friday March 4th 1921 to enquire into certain circumstances relating to the position of Professor Zimmern as Professor of International Politics at U.C.W. Aberystwyth. Aberystwyth University Archives.

43. Minutes of a Meeting of the Special Committee.

44. Ruth Lewes to J. H. Davies, April 19, 1921.

45. Sir Francis Edwards Bart to Unknown, April 14, 1921.

46. Unknown to Principal Joyce, April 14, 1921.

47. 'Shorthand notes of a statement made by Prof A. E. Zimmern'.

48. David Davies to J. H. Davies, April 21, 1921. David Davies to J. H. Davies, May 9, 1921.

49. Sir Francis Edwards Bart to D. Lleufer Thomas, April 14, 1921.

50. Sir Francis Edwards Bart to Sir Evans Jones Bart, M.P., April 18, 1921.

51. Unknown to David Davies, April 25, 1921.

52. David Davies to J. H. Davies, May 3, 1921.

53. 'Shorthand Notes of questions put to and answers by Prof. Barbier'.

54. 'Shorthand Notes of questions put to and answers by Prof. Barbier'.

55. 'Shorthand notes of a statement made by Prof A. E. Zimmern'.

56. 'Shorthand notes of a statement made by Prof A. E. Zimmern'.

57. 'Shorthand notes of a statement made by Prof A. E. Zimmern'.

58. Reports Submitted to the Court of Governors, University College of Wales Aberystwyth, October 25, 1922, pp. 72–3.

59. Alfred Zimmern, *My Impressions of Wales* (London: Mills & Boon, 1921), pp. 31, 39.

60. Chaim Weizmann to Vera Weizmann in *The Letters and Papers of Chaim Weizmann*, vol.12, series A, August 1923–March 1926 (Rutgers: Transaction Books, 1977), p. 385; Chaim Weizmann to Vera Weizmann, *The Letters and Papers of Chaim Weizmann*, vol. 10, series A, July 1920–December 1921 (Rutgers: Transaction Books, 1977), p. 157.

61. Christopher Stray, *Oxford Classics: Teaching and Learning, 1800–2000* (London: Duckworth, 2007), p. 195.

62. James Patrick Sewell, *UNESCO and World Politics: Engaging in International Relations* (Princeton: Princeton University Press, 1975), pp. 83–4.

63. John Toye and Richard Toye, 'One World, Two Cultures? Alfred Zimmern, Julian Huxley and the Ideological Origins of UNESCO', *History*, vol. 95, no. 319 (2010), p. 313.

64. F. Cyril James quoted in Stanley Brice Frost, *The Man in the Ivory Tower: F. Cyril James of McGill* (Montreal: McGill-Queen's University Press, 1991), p. 91.

65. Margaret Sanger to Hugh de Selincourt, May 22, 1927, quoted in *The Selected Papers of Margaret Sanger: Volume 4: Round the World for Birth Control, 1920–1966*, edited by Esther Katz, Peter C. Engelman and Cathy Moran Hajo (Baltimore: University of Illinois Press, 2016), p. 112.

66. 'Sentiment in Work for Peace: Criticism by Lady Zimmern', unnamed newspaper and n.d., MSS Zimmern 179, 291.

67. J.F.F., 'Music and Words with Lucie Zimmern', p. 28.

68. Robert E. Stansfield, 'A New Impulse Toward World Harmony', *The Harford Courant Magazine* (January 2, 1949), p. 5. MSS Zimmern 106.

69. Reuben George, 'Swindon W.E.A. at Childrey. Address by Mrs. Zimmern on "The Situation in France"', *Swindon Advertiser* (May 13, 1932). MSS Zimmern 179, 172.

70. J.F.F., 'Music and Words with Lucie Zimmern', p. 27.

71. 'City Club, Kansas City, MO. *Ladies' Night, Thursday, February 2, 1922*', MSS Zimmern 106, 113.

72. 'No Opportunity Like England's—Mrs. A. E. Zimmern: Frenchwoman's Eloquent Appeal for Big Effort to Secure World Peace', *Oxford Mail* (April 1, 1933). MSS Zimmern 179, 217.

73. 'New World Weapon Boycott, Blockade says Dr. A. Zimmern', *The Herald* (March 7, 1925), MSS Zimmern 179, 110. Also see: 'Visiting Internationalist: Lady Zimmern Interviewed', *The Western Australian* (October 10, 1938), MSS Zimmern 179, 264; 'Nations "Too Gentle with Germany": World Crisis Seen as Result of Over-Sentimentality', *The Sun News-Pictorial* (September 29, 1938), MSS Zimmern 179, 260. The article appears in the women's section of the Australian tabloid. Also see 'Sentiment in Work for Peace: Criticism by Lady Zimmern', unnamed newspaper and n.d., MSS Zimmern 179, 291.

74. Markwell, 'Sir Alfred Zimmern', p. 280; Rich, 'Reinventing Peace', p. 120; Baji, *International Thought of Alfred Zimmern*, p. 127.

75. Markwell, 'Sir Alfred Zimmern', pp. 280–81. Baji's book-length study of Alfred briefly mentions 'Lucy [*sic*] Barbier' once: *International Thought of Alfred Zimmern*, p. 111.

76. Bonnie Smith, 'Historiography, Objectivity, and the Case of the Abusive Widow', *History and Theory*, vol. 31, no. 4 (1992), pp. 15–32, here 17.

77. Hans J. Morgenthau and Kenneth Thompson (eds.), *Principles and Problems of International Politics: Selected Readings* (New York, 1950), p. 18.

78. Kasper Monahan, 'Peace and Licorice are Interview Subjects: English Lecturer and French Wife Also Discuss "Babbits"', *The Rocky Mountain News*, p. 4, n.d., MSS Zimmern 179, 141; Katharina Rietzler, 'IR's "Power Couples"', October 28, 2018, https://whit.web.ox.ac.uk/article/irs-power-couples.

79. On occasion, some aspect of Lucie Zimmern's work at the Geneva School is noted but never discussed at length. Stapleton, 'Alfred Zimmern', p. 99; Stray, *Oxford Classics*, p. 195; Toye and Toye, 'One World, Two Cultures?', p. 314; Jo-Anne Pemberton, *The Story of International Relations, Part Two, Cold-blooded Idealists* (Cham: Springer International, 2020), p. 128; Daniel Laqua, 'Educating Internationalists: The Context, Role and Legacies of the UIA's "International University"' in Daniel Laqua, Wouter Van Acker, and Christophe Verbruggen (eds.), *International Organizations and Global Civil Society: Histories of the Union of International Associations* (London: Bloomsbury, 2019), p. 62. The exception is Owens and Rietzler, 'Polyphonic Internationalism'.

80. Lucie bequeathed these papers to her granddaughter and music historian, who donated them to the National Library of Wales and wrote her doctorate on them. See Martha Elisabeth Stonequist, 'The Musical Entente Cordiale: 1905–1916', doctoral dissertation, University of Colorado, 1971.

81. The Zimmern papers in the Bodleian also include those of the Geneva School of International Studies, including contemporary accounts of the school's cultural practices, student essays and retrospectives; and Lucie's published writings, including several essays for the school's journal that she edited, and her book on the League of Nations. For the wider context of the founding of the School see Pemberton, *The Story of International Relations, Part Two*, pp. 114–17.

82. Student lists, MSS Zimmern 31, 112–14.

83. Montague Burton became rich selling men's clothes and avoiding tax. His strategy was to submit 'negative super-tax returns up to 1927/8 through building up undistributed profits. Then, on the liquidation of his company (to turn it into a public company), Burton received almost the whole undistributed profits of £1,607,239 as tax-free capital assets'. Peter Scott, 'The Anatomy of Britain's Interwar Super-Rich: Reconstructing the 1928/9 "millionaire" Population', *The Economic History Review*, vol. 74, no. 3 (2021) pp. 639–65.

84. In the mid-1930s, philanthropist Louise Whitefield Carnegie became honorary president. Other members were Carrie Chapman Catt, Helen Clarkson Miller, Ruth Morgan, Alice T. L. Parsons, Anita McCormick Blaine, and Florence Lamont. Pamphlet of the Geneva School of International Studies, 1927, Bodleian Library, MSS Zimmern 8, 2.

85. 'Geneva School of International Studies Report on the Thirteenth Session, July–August', MSS Zimmern 92, 119.

86. There were 47 identified as men and 31 as women. Geneva School of International Studies Report on the Fourteenth Session, July–September 1937, MSS Zimmern 92, 135.

87. The main study on Spykman is Olivier Zajec, *Nicholas Spykman: L'invention de la géographie américaine* (Paris: PUPS, 2016); also see Colin S. Gray, 'Nicholas John Spykman, the Balance of Power, and International Order', *Journal of Strategic Studies*, vol. 38, no. 6 (2015), pp. 873–97; Antero Holmila, 'Re-thinking Nicholas J. Spykman: From Historical Sociology to Balance of Power', *The International History Review*, vol. 42, no. 5 (2020), pp. 951–66.

88. In 1925–6, travelling Secretary of the School, Everett V. Stonequist, was married to Lucie's daughter Edith. In 1928, requests for accommodation, and further enquiries were addressed to Miss E. Barbier, Lucie's younger daughter Evelyn. *Vox Studentiums*, April 1928, MSS Zimmern 180, 228. Alfred's older sister, Elsie Zimmern (1876–1967), General Secretary of the International Council of Women, contributed during in the 1930–31 fiscal year. MSS Zimmern 91, 26.

89. Philip L. Boardman, 'Thirty-Three Nations at School', *The Commonweal*, 12 December 1930, pp. 416–18. MSS Zimmern 180, 260.

90. In their correspondence, Lewis Mumford was exploring Patrick Geddes's (1854–1932) 'art of simultaneous thinking'. 'My friend Lucie Zimmern's musical name for this method, polyphonic thinking, was even better; but perhaps when it draws in other sciences one ought to conceive it as contrapuntal'. Lewis Mumford in Mumford, Patrick Geddes, and Frank G. Novak, *Lewis Mumford and Patrick Geddes: The Correspondence* (New York, 1995), p. 356. Also see Guido Adler, 'Internationalism in Music', *The Musical Quarterly*, vol. 11, no. 2 (1925), pp. 281–300.

91. Boardman, 'Thirty-Three Nations at School'. MSS Zimmern 180, 260.

92. 'Visiting Internationalist: Lady Zimmern Interviewed', *The Western Australian* (October 10, 1938). MSS Zimmern 179, 264.

93. Lucie A. Zimmern, 'Women's Part in the New Renaissance' in Joseph Bachelor and Ralph L. Henry (eds.), *Challenging Essays in Modern Thought* (New York: The Century Co., 1928), p. 96.

94. Biographies of the Zimmerns for the programme of Alfred's six lectures as part of the National Lectureship Scheme of the National Council of Education, Canada. MSS Zimmern 33, 134.

95. Lucie A. Zimmern, *Must the League Fail?* (London: M. Hopkinson, 1932), p. 85 (emphasis in original).

96. J.F.F., 'Music and Words with Lucie Zimmern', p. 27. To create the right atmosphere and harmony, the string quartet, her favourite music, ought to be 'played before every political meeting'. Ibid.

97. Zimmern, 'The Geneva School of International Studies'. MSS Zimmern 180, 208.

98. 'Lecture courses in Geneva this Summer', n.d. MSS Zimmern 93, p. 123.

99. Untitled report, n.d., MSS Zimmern 92, 141.

100. 'The Geneva School of International Studies, 1923–1939', n.d. MSS Zimmern 106, 3.

101. 'The Geneva School of International Studies, 1923–1939', n.d. MSS Zimmern 106, 5–6.

102. 'The Geneva School of International Studies, 1923–1939', n.d. MSS Zimmern 106, 5–6.

103. Merze Tate, 'The Geneva School of International Relations', *Ivy Leaf Magazine*, vol. 10, no. 1 (March 1932), pp. 35–6, here 35.

104. MSS Zimmern 90, 107.

105. 'Sentiment in Work for Peace: Criticism by Lady Zimmern' in the 'Social News' section of an unnamed newspaper, n.d., likely c.1938. MSS Zimmern 179, 291.

106. Translated from the French, '*chercher sans l'harmonie des sons les aspirations de ceux qui travaillent à l'harmonie des esprits*'. Lucie Zimmern, 'Canticum Scholae Genavensis, Words by Alfred Zimmern, Music by Henri Gagnebin', *Comprendre: Organe de l'Association des Anciens Elèves du Bureau d'Etudes Internationales* no. 6 (1933), p. 299, MSS Zimmern 92, 21. There is a large literature on cultural international and musical cultural diplomacy. See Akira Iriye, *Cultural Internationalism and World Order* (Baltimore: Johns Hopkins University Press, 1997) and a recent special collection of articles in *Contemporary European History* edited by Benjamin G. Martin and Elisabeth Pillar on 'Cultural Diplomacy and Europe's Twenty Years' Crisis, 1919–1939'. Also see Marianne Franklin, *Resounding International Relations: On Music, Culture, and Politics* (London: Palgrave, 2005); Frédéric Ramel and Cécile Prévost-Thomas (eds.), *International Relations, Music and Diplomacy: Sounds and Voices on the International Stage* (Basingstoke: Palgrave Macmillan, 2018).

107. *Comprendre: Organe de l'Association des Anciens Elèves du Bureau d'Etudes Internationales* (1933), no. 6, MSS Zimmern 87, 21.

108. G. B. Wilson, 'Geneva 1931–A Critical Retrospect' in *Comprendre*, no. 1 (1931), pp. 25–7. MSS Zimmern 87, 16.

109. 'City Club, Kansas City, MO. *Ladies' Night, Thursday, February 2, 1922*', MSS Zimmern 106, 113. According to one reporter, 'probably no private apartment in Hartford has more international overtones per cubic foot than the spacious one the distinguished couple occupies'. Robert E. Stansfield, 'A New Impulse Toward World Harmony', *The Harford Courant Magazine* (January 2, 1949), p. 5. MSS Zimmern 106.

110. Quoted in Sewell, *UNESCO and World Politics*, pp. 83–4.

111. J.F.F., 'Music and Words with Lucie Zimmern', p. 27.

112. Agnes Headlam-Morley, 'Idealism and Realism in International Relations', an Inaugural Lecture delivered before the University of Oxford', May 6, 1949. Papers of Sir James and Agnes Headlam-Morley, Churchill College, Cambridge, GBR/0014/HDLM, 815/32.

113. Sir Michael Saddler to Lucy Zimmern, July 19, 1925. MSS Zimmern 89.

114. Lucie A. Zimmern, 'Woman's Part in the New Renaissance' in Joseph M. Bachelor and Ralph L. Henry (eds.), *Essays in Modern Thought* (New York: Century Co., 1928), 102.

115. 'Report Submitted by the Tutors of the Geneva School of International Studies'. MSS Zimmern 89, 158.

116. Headlam-Morley, 'Idealism and Realism', p. 2.

117. J.F.F., 'Music and Words with Lucie Zimmern', p. 29.

118. Biographies of the Zimmerns for the programme of Alfred's six lectures as part of the National Lectureship Scheme of the National Council of Education, Canada. MSS Zimmern 33, 134.

119. 'Report Submitted by the Tutors of the Geneva School of International Studies'. MSS Zimmern 89, 161.

120. 'Errata and Addenda in Report of Deputy Director', n.d. MSS Zimmern 93, 186–7.

121. 'Memorandum for the Administration in Europe of the Geneva School of International Studies', MSS Zimmern 89, 149.

122. 'Errata and Addenda in Report of Deputy Director'. n.d. MSS Zimmern 93, 184. See Alfred Zimmern, *Learning and Leadership: A Study of the Needs and Possibilities of International Intellectual Co-operation* (Geneva: League of Nations, 1927).

123. 'Errata and Addenda in Report of Deputy Director'. n.d. MSS Zimmern 93, 184, emphasis added. Spykman's first book, based on his Berkeley doctorate in sociology, was a study of Georg Simmel. See Nicholas J. Spykman, *The Social Theory of Georg Simmel* (Chicago: University of Chicago, 1925). On the centrality of his early sociological work to his later more explicitly IR 'realist' and geopolitical work see Holmila, 'Re-thinking Nicholas J. Spykman'.

124. 'Report Submitted by the Tutors of the Geneva School of International Studies'. MSS Zimmern 89, 160. 'Errata and Addenda in Report of Deputy Director'. n.d. MSS Zimmern 93, 186.

125. 'Errata and Addenda in Report of Deputy Director'. n.d. MSS Zimmern 93, 185–6.

126. 'Report Submitted by the Tutors of the Geneva School of International Studies'. MSS Zimmern 89, 161.

127. 'Report Submitted by the Tutors of the Geneva School of International Studies'. MSS Zimmern 89, 158.

128. Notes on the programme for the 8th session in 1931. n.d. MSS Zimmern 91, 8.

129. 'Report Submitted by the Tutors of the Geneva School of International Studies'. MSS Zimmern 89, 161.

130. 'Errata and Addenda in Report of Deputy Director'. n.d. MSS Zimmern 93, 188.

131. Untitled report, n.d. MSS Zimmern 92, 141.

132. 'Report Submitted by the Tutors of the Geneva School of International Studies'. MSS Zimmern 89, 158.

133. 'Report Submitted by the Tutors of the Geneva School of International Studies'. MSS Zimmern 89, 161.

134. Frost, *The Man in the Ivory Tower*, p. 91.

135. Labour Party activist Silyn Roberts to Thomas Jones, November 5, 1924, quoted in Toye and Toye 'One World, Two Cultures?', p. 314, fn.

136. Martin Ceadel, 'The Academic Normalization of International Relations at Oxford, 1920–2012: Structures Transcended' in Christopher Hood, Desmond King, and Gillian Peele (eds.), *Forging a Discipline: A Critical Assessment of Oxford's Development of the Study of Politics and International Relations in Comparative Perspective* (Oxford: Oxford University Press, 2014), p. 188.

137. Zimmern, *Must the League Fail?*, p. 6.

138. 'What is wrong with the League of Nations and how to repair it. By Vigiles'. n.d., 215 leaves. MSS Zimmern 132. I am grateful to Timothy Rood for pointing this out.

139. Alfred Zimmern, *The American Road to World Peace* (New York: Dutton, 1953), p. 14.

140. 'Errata and Addenda in Report of Deputy Director'. n.d. MSS Zimmern 93, 187.

141. 'Errata and Addenda in Report of Deputy Director'. n.d. MSS Zimmern 93, 187.

142. Nicholas Spykman, 'Methods and Topics for the Teaching of International Relations', *Proceedings of the Fourth Conference of Teachers of International Law and Related Subjects held at Briarcliff Lodge, New York, October 10–17, 1929* (Washington: Carnegie Endowment for International Peace, 1930), pp. 38–43.

143. Lucian M. Ashworth, 'Realism and the Spirit of 1919: Halford Mackinder, Geopolitics and the Reality of the League of Nations', *European Journal of International Relations*, vol. 17, no. 2 (2011) pp. 279–301, here 279; Lucian M. Ashworth, 'Did the Realist–Idealist Great Debate Really

Happen? A Revisionist History of International Relations', *International Relations*, vol. 16, no. 1 (2002), pp. 33–51.

144. Hans J. Morgenthau, 'Another "Great Debate": The National Interest of the United States', *The American Political Science Review*, vol. 46, no. 4 (1952), pp. 961–88; Wolfers and Martin, *Anglo-American Tradition*.

145. Edward Hallett Carr, *The Twenty Years' Crisis, 1919–1939: An Introduction to the Study of International Relations* (London: Macmillan, 1939).

146. Wilson, 'The Myth', p. 1.

147. Robert Vitalis, *White World Order, Black Power Politics: The Birth of American International Relations* (Ithaca: Cornell University Press, 2015), p. 118.

148. Wolfers and Martin, 'Introduction', *Anglo-American Tradition*, p. x.

149. Morgenthau and Thompson, *Principles and Problems*, pp. 18–31.

150. Nicholas Spykman, 'The Study of International Relations', *Yale Alumni Weekly*, vol. 43, no. 22 (1934), pp. 491–493, here 491. Kenneth W. Thompson, *Political Realism and the Crisis of World Politics: An American Approach to Foreign Policy* (Princeton: Princeton University Press, 1960), p. 22. The only book-length treatment of Spykman discusses his relationship with Alfred Zimmern, but not Lucie: Zajec, *Nicholas Spykman*, pp. 178–84. According to Holmila: 'The extent to which Geneva experiences shaped Spykman's supposed "conversion" from "idealist" to "realist" . . . is open to debate not least since Zimmern's reputation in particular is characterised by [an] idealist approach to IR. According to Zajec there never was such conversion [from idealism to realism], since Spykman had already in his *The Social Theory of Georg Simmel* constructed the world and human relations which constituted it in relatively dark terms'. Holmila, 'Re-thinking Nicholas J. Spykman', p. 955.

151. In Spykman's programme, first-year students studied French, History 101, and the 'development of Western Civilization'. Second-year students took 'Classical civilization', 'Greek civilization', two courses in economics, two in government, and two in philosophy. Third years took four economics courses and two history courses. Seniors took one more general history and government course, and specialist courses in IR, US foreign affairs, and contemporary Europe. Spykman, 'The Study of International Relations', p. 492. While he was still deputy director in Geneva, Spykmann published one of his first writings on international relations, an article on 'The Social Background of Asiatic Nationalism'. In an early example of modernisation theory, he argued anti-imperial revolts in Asia were not fundamentally political but due to destabilising effects of aggressive 'Western penetration' of 'Oriental culture'. Nicholas J. Spykman, 'The Social Background of Asiatic Nationalism', *The American Journal of Sociology*, vol. 32, no. 3 (1926), pp. 396–411.

152. Tate, 'The Geneva School', p. 35

153. Wilson, 'Geneva 1931–A Critical Retrospect'.

154. Barbara D. Savage, 'Beyond Illusions: Imperialism, Race and Technology in Merze Tate's International Thought' in Patricia Owens and Katharina Rietzler, eds., *Women's International Thought: A New History* (Cambridge: Cambridge University Press, 2021), p. 268.

155. Charles Gittins, 'The Eighth Session of the Geneva School of International Studies', MSS Zimmern 87, p. 34; Barbara D. Savage, *Merze Tate: The Global Odyssey of a Black Woman Scholar* (New Haven and London: Yale University Press, 2024), p. 41.

156. Tate, 'The Geneva School', pp. 35–6.

157. Gittins, 'The Eighth Session', p. 34.

158. Gittins, 'The Eighth Session', p. 34.

159. Untitled report, n.d. MSS Zimmern 92, 142–3.

160. Tate, 'The Geneva School', pp. 35–6.

161. Memorandum, n.d. MSS Zimmern 93, 168.

162. Bruce H. Ziff and Pratima V. Rao (eds.), *Borrowed Power: Essays on Cultural Appropriation* (New Brunswick: Rutgers University Press, 1997).

163. 'Lecture courses in Geneva this Summer', n.d. MSS Zimmern 93, 123.

164. Alfred Zimmern, 'The Geneva School of International Studies', *The American Review of Reviews* (April 1927), pp. 385–8. MSS Zimmern 180, 208. Also see Daniel Laqua, 'Exhibiting, Encountering and Studying Music in Interwar Europe: Between National and International Community', *European Studies*, vol. 32 (2014), pp. 207–23.

165. 'Retrospective of the work of Madame Zimmern's group', n.d. MSS Zimmern 94, 80–81.

166. Charles Elford, *Black Mahler: The Samuel Coleridge-Taylor Story* (London: Grosvenor House Publishing, 2008).

167. Lucie also invited her son-in-law, Everett V. Stonequist, to speak on race relations. George Zimmern, Alfred's Hong Kong-based nephew, recalled a session in Geneva in 1931 when Stonequist 'emphasised the need to treat every one whatever colour or creed as human beings, as persons not chattels. This may seem quite trite today, but nearly fifty years ago this needed saying'. George Zimmern to Edith Stonequist, April 13, 1979. I'm grateful to Timothy Rood for drawing my attention to this letter in the possession of Martha Stonequist that, at the time of writing, will soon be deposited in the Bodleian Library.

168. Untitled report, n.d. MSS Zimmern 92, 142–3.

169. J.F.F., 'Music and Words with Lucie Zimmern', p. 28, emphasis added.

170. Baji, 'Zionist Internationalism?', p. 629.

171. 'Retrospective of the work of Madame Zimmern's group', 80–81.

172. 'Retrospective of the work of Madame Zimmern's group', 81–82.

173. Pianko, 'Cosmopolitan Wanderer', p. 220.

174. Brian Porter, 'E.H. Carr—the Aberystwyth Years, 1936–47', in Michael Cox (ed.), *E.H. Carr: a Critical Appraisal* (London: Palgrave, 2000), pp. 36–67, here 47.

175. Frank Goodlaw to Carnegie Endowment for International Peace, March 11, 1927. Columbia University Rare Book and Manuscript Library.

176. Friedlander, Lilian—358 (1927–1928). Division of International Law—Fellowships. Carnegie Endowment for International Peace. Columbia University Rare Book and Manuscript Library.

177. Lilian Friedländer, 'The Admission of States to the League of Nations', *British Yearbook of International Law*, vol. 9 (January 1, 1928), pp. 84–100, here 94.

178. By 1956, Margery Perham similarly argued that 'the old tenet of political science, that sovereignty is indivisible . . . no longer fits the conditions of the modern world with its complex distributions of powers between tiers of authorities, such as that which the western powers are now devising'. Margery Perham, 'Re-Assessment' in Elspeth Huxley and Margery Perham, *Race and Politics in Kenya: A Correspondence between Elspeth Huxley and Margery Perham* (London: Faber & Faber, rev. edn, 1956), pp. 265–83, here 275.

179. Lilian M. Friedländer, 'Labour Problems in Two Worlds', *Economica*, vol. 9, no. 25 (1929), pp. 4–14, here 6.

180. The Montague Burton Professorship in Industrial Relations was endowed at the universities of Cambridge and Leeds in 1930, the same year as Oxford's Montague Burton Professorship in IR.

181. Rockefeller Foundation records, fellowships, fellowship recorder cards, SG 10.2, Fellowship recorder cards, Subgrp 2 Humanities Fellows, Series 5 United Kingdom, Friedlander, Lilian H. Also: Vranek, (Mrs.) Lilian H. (United Kingdom). Rockefeller Archive Center.

182. Friedländer, 'Labour Problems in Two Worlds', p. 13.

183. E. M. Jackson Jr. (ed.), *Rat Tat 1926: Published Annually by the Junior Class of St. John's College Annapolis, MD*, vol. 28, p. 64.

184. Porter, 'E.H. Carr', p. 49.

185. Reports Submitted to the Court of Governors, University College of Wales Aberystwyth, October 21, 1931, p. 66.

186. The reasons for Lilian's sick leave are unknown. Aberystwyth University has not retained staff personnel files from this period.

187. But see J. Vránek, 'Plans proposés en vue d'une solution des Problèmes de l'Europe Centrale', *Affaires Danubiennes*, vol. 0(1) (July 1, 1938).

188. Reports Submitted to the Court of Governors, University College of Wales Aberystwyth, October 19, 1932, p. 67.

189. Reports Submitted to the Court of Governors, University College of Wales Aberystwyth, October 22, 1924, pp. 26, 76.

190. Porter, 'E.H. Carr', pp. 49, 66. Porter is quoting a letter from Mrs. J. Vránek, December 10, 1992, written to him before she died.

191. Porter, 'Appendix I: Holders of the Woodrow Wilson Chair' in *The Aberystwyth Papers*, pp. 361–9, here 366.

192. His lecture was published as E. H. Carr, 'Public Opinion as a Safeguard of Peace', *International Affairs*, vol. 15. no. 6 (1936), pp. 846–62.

193. United States Holocaust Memorial Museum, Holocaust Survivors and Victims Database, https://www.ushmm.org/online/hsv/person_view.php?PersonId=3064056.

194. Ceadel, 'Academic Normalization', p. 193.

195. 'Vranek, Lilian Marie Hilda; Czechoslovakia; Assistant in Books Department, British Council; The Cottage, Chaucer's Lane, Woodstock, Oxfordshire. 3 July, 1947.' *London Gazette* (August 22, 1947), https://www.thegazette.co.uk/London/issue/38052/page/3978/data.pdf. An asterisk indicates her re-admission to British nationality.

196. 'Lilian Marie, Mrs. VRANEK, Grade 9 Officer, Her Majesty's Embassy, Rome', https://www.thegazette.co.uk/London/issue/44484/supplement/23/data.pdf. In Britain, membership of the 'Most Excellent Order of the British Empire' (MBE) is an award within the 'honours system'.

197. I'm very grateful to Jenny Mathers for information on the prize and the next woman appointed after Friedländer.

198. Long and Wilson (eds.), *Thinkers of The Twenty Years' Crisis*. Cf. Robbie Shilliam, *International Relations and Non-Western Thought: Imperialism, Colonialism, and Investigations of Global Modernity* (London: Routledge, 2011); Lucian M. Ashworth, *A History of International Thought: From the Origins of the Modern State to Academic International Relations* (New York: Routledge, 2014).

199. Susan Moller Okin, *Women in Western Political Thought* (London: Virago, 1980); Carole Pateman, *The Sexual Contract* (Stanford: Stanford University Press, 1988); Jean Bethke Elshtain, *Public Man, Private Woman: Women in Social and Political Thought* (Princeton: Princeton University Press, 2nd edn, 1993).

200. Christine Sylvester, *Feminist Theory and International Relations in a Postmodern Era* (Cambridge: Cambridge University Press, 1994), p. 84.

201. J. Ann Tickner, 'Hans Morgenthau's Principles of Political Realism: A Feminist Reformulation', *Millennium: Journal of International Studies*, vol. 17, no. 3 (1988), pp. 429–40. Agathangelou and Ling extended IR theory's subject positions to '*Pater* (realism), *Mater* (liberalism), and *Caretaking Daughters* (neoliberalism, liberal and standpoint feminism), *Bastard Heirs* (neorealism), *Rebel Sons* (Marxism, Gramscian IPE, postmodern IR and constructivism–pragmatism), and *Fallen Daughters* (postmodern feminism and queer studies)'. Anna M. Agathangelou and L.H.M. Ling, 'The House of IR: From Family Power Politics to the Poisies of Worldism', *International Studies Review*, vol. 6, no. 4 (2004), pp. 21–50.

202. Steve Smith, Ken Booth, and Marysia Zalewski (eds.), *International Theory: Positivism and Beyond* (Cambridge: Cambridge University Press, 1996).

203. Roland Bleiker, 'The Aesthetic Turn in International Political Theory', *Millennium: Journal of International Studies*, vol. 30, no. 3 (2001), pp. 509–33.

204. Porter, 'Appendix I', p. 362; Jo-Anne Pemberton, *The Story of International Relations Part One, Cold-blooded Idealists* (Palgrave: Basingstoke, 2019), p. 115.

## 2. This White, English, Self-Loved, Cultivated Self

1. Vineet Thakur and Peter Vale, *South Africa, Race and the Making of International Relations* (London: Rowman and Littlefield, 2020).

2. Andrea Bosco, *The Round Table Movement and the Fall of the 'Second' British Empire (1909–1919)* (Newcastle: Cambridge Scholars Publishing, 2017); James Cotton, 'Chatham House and Africa c1920-1960: The Limitations of the Curtis Vision', *South African Historical Journal*, vol. 68 no. 2 (2016), pp. 147–62; Daniel Gorman, 'Lionel Curtis: Imperial Citizenship as a Prelude to World Government' in *Imperial Citizenship* (Manchester: Manchester University Press, 2007); Andrea Bosco, 'From Empire to Atlantic "System": The Round Table, Chatham House and the Emergence of a New Paradigm in Anglo-American Relations', *Journal of Transatlantic Studies*, vol. 16, no. 3 (2018), pp. 222–46.

3. See, for example, Thakur and Vale's discussion of William Archer's 1912 work, *The Great Analysis: A Plea for a Rational World Order* as capturing how the early twentieth-century discourse of 'international' captured the new sense of thinking of the globe as a single space. Thakur and Vale, *South Africa,* pp. 152–3.

4. George Martel, 'From Round Table to New Europe: Some Intellectual Origins of the Institute of International Affairs' in Andrea Bosco and Cornelia Navari (eds.), *Chatham House and British Foreign Policy, 1919–1945: The Royal Institute of International Affairs During the Inter-War Period* (London, 1994), pp. 13–40.

5. See Alexander E. Davis, Vineet Thakur, and Peter C. J. Vale, *The Imperial Discipline: Race and the Founding of International Relations* (London, Pluto, 2020). Thakur illuminates this point through returning to Olive Schreiner. He argues that the immediate precursor to *The Round Table,* one of the earliest IR journals, 'was invested in countering the force' of Schreiner's arguments who 'perhaps alone among her contemporaries . . . analyzed South Africa's race conflicts in terms of a global struggle between capital and labour'. Thakur in Adom Getachew, Duncan Bell, Cynthia Enloe, and Vineet Thakur, 'Theorizing the History of Women's International Thinking at the "End of International Theory"', *International Theory*, vol. 14, no. 3 (2022), pp. 1–25, here 19.

6. Meera Sabaratnam, 'Introduction: 100 years of Empire and Decolonization', Archive Collection, *International Affairs*, October 2022, pp. 1–11.

7. Edward Keene, *Beyond the Anarchical Society: Grotius, Colonialism and Order in World Politics* (Cambridge: Cambridge University Press, 2002); William A. Callahan, 'Nationalising International Theory: Race, Class and the English School', *Global Society: Journal of Interdisciplinary International Relations*, vol. 18, no. 4 (2004), pp. 305–23. But as Hall points out, British international thinkers conceived of decolonisation in terms of a 'revolt against the West'. Ian Hall, 'The Revolt against the West: Decolonisation and Its Repercussions in British International Thought, 1945–75', *The International History Review*, vol. 33, no. 1 (2011), pp. 43–64.

8. There is a relatively modest secondary literature on Perham by historians and Africanists but little to no engagement in IR or discussion of her relation to the new field of international relations. See, for example, Alison Smith and Mary Bull's special issue of *The Journal of Imperial and Commonwealth History*, vol. 19, no. 3 (1991), devoted to Perham. She is also the subject of a short biography: see Brad C. Faught, *Into Africa: The Imperial Life of Margery Perham* (London:

I.B. Tauris, 2012). Also see Patricia Pugh, 'Margery Freda Perham, 1895–1982', *Proceedings of the British Academy*, vol. 111, pp. 617–33.

9. Margery Perham, '*The Round Table* and Sub-Saharan Africa', *Round Table*, vol. 60, no. 240 (1970), pp. 543–55, here 551.

10. On Curtis as a founder of 'IR' see Thakur and Vale, *South Africa*, pp. 10–14, 24–39. Perham received fawning letters from Gilbert Murray. Gilbert Murray to Margery Perham, June 1, 1931. Bodleian Library. MSS Perham, 27/5 55; Gilbert Murray to Margery Perham, November 27, 1941, MSS Perham, 27/5 56.

11. Patricia Pugh, *A Catalogue of the Papers of Dame Margery Perham 1895–1982* (Oxford: Bodleian Library, 1989). Emphasis added.

12. The exception is Robbie Shilliam's brief discussion in *Decolonizing Politics: An Introduction* (Cambridge: Polity, 2021), pp. 128–9, 135. In a survey of sixty histories of international thought, Perham appears in only two volumes: Patricia Owens, 'Women and the History of International Thought', *International Studies Quarterly*, vol. 62, no. 3, pp. 467–81. Perham is mentioned briefly in Ian Hall, *Dilemmas of Decline: British Intellectuals and World Politics, 1945–1975* (Berkeley: University of California Press, 2012), pp. 132–3. Hayward suggests that Perham's work 'amounted to a comparative inductive political science of colonial administration'. Jack Hayward, 'Beyond Zanzibar: The Road to Comparative Inductive Institutionalism', in Christopher Hood, Desmond King, and Gillian Peele (eds.), *Forging a Discipline: A Critical Assessment of Oxford's Development of the Study of Politics and International Relations in Comparative Perspective* (Oxford, 2014), pp. 222–43, here 232.

13. See, for example, those thinkers discussed in the sections on Imperialism and Anticolonialism in Patricia Owens, Katharina Rietzler, Kimberly Hutchings, Sarah C. Dunstan (eds.), *Women's International Thought: Towards a New Canon* (Cambridge: Cambridge University Press, 2022), including Jessie Fauset, Lilian M. Penson, Anna Julia Cooper, Lilian Knowles, Perham, Sibyl Crowe, Amy Jacques Garvey, Mary Proudfoot, Jane Nadal, Dorothy Macardle, Una Marson, Nancy Cunard, Simone Weil, Suzanne Roussy Césaire, Eslanda Robeson, Claudia Jones.

14. H. O. Davies, *Memoirs* (Ibadan, Nigeria: Evans Brothers, 1989), p. 85.

15. Priyamvada Gopal, *Insurgent Empire: Anticolonial Resistance and British Dissent* (London: Verso, 2019), pp. 425–33.

16. Isabelle Napier, 'Recovering Racial Positioning in "White" Women's International Thought: Lady Kathleen Simon's International Abolitionist Crusade, 1927–1955', *Global Studies Quarterly*, vol. 3, no. 1 (2023), pp. 1–11.

17. Margery Perham, 'Introduction', *Colonial Sequence, 1930–1949: A Chronological Commentary upon British Colonial Policy Especially in Africa* (London: Methuen, 1967), p. xiv. Perham offers some autobiographical reflection in Margery Perham, *African Apprenticeship: An Autobiographical Journey in Southern Africa, 1929* (London: Faber and Faber, 1974).

18. Janet Howarth, '"In Oxford but . . . not of Oxford": The Women's Colleges', in M. G. Brock, and M. C. Curthoys (eds.), *The History of the University of Oxford: Volume VII: Nineteenth-Century Oxford, Part 2* (Oxford: Oxford University Press, 2000), pp. 237–308.

19. Pugh, 'Margery Freda Perham', p. 621.

20. Perham, *African Apprenticeship*, p. 26.

21. Quoted in Smith and Bull, 'Introduction', special issue on Perham of *The Journal of Imperial and Commonwealth History*, vol. 19, no. 3 (1991), pp. 1–20, here 7–8.

22. Wm. Roger Louis, 'Historians I Have Known', *Perspectives on History* (May 1, 2001), https://www.historians.org/publications-and-directories/perspectives-on-history/may-2001/historians-i-have-known.

23. Joanna Lewis, *Empire State-Building: War and Welfare in Kenya 1925–52* (Oxford: James Currey, 2000), p. 91; Kenneth Robinson, 'Margery Perham and the Colonial Office', *Journal of Imperial and Commonwealth History*, vol. 19, no. 3 (1991), pp. 185–96, here 186.

24. Robinson, 'Margery Perham', p. 186.

25. Louis, 'Historians I Have Known'.

26. Martin Wight to Mr Ferris, November 16, 1961. WIGHT/233/14. LSE Library. I have been unable to locate Mr Ferris's profile of Perham or ascertain whether it was published.

27. Quoted in Faught, *Into Africa*, p. 31

28. Faught, *Into Africa*, pp. 100, 26.

29. Jon Branch, 'A Brief History of the Norton 16H' (April 1, 2020), Silodrome Gasoline Culture. https://silodrome.com/norton-16h-history/#:~:text=It%20was%20in%201921%20that ,most%20places%20by%20that%20time. I'm grateful to Helen M. Kinsella for pointing this out.

30. Rosie Dias and Kate Smith (eds.), *British Women and Cultural Practices of Empire, 1770–1940* (London: Bloomsbury, 2019).

31. Perham in Anthony Wood, 'How a Don Served her African Apprenticeship', *Oxford Mail* (September 16, 1974).

32. Faught, *Into Africa*, p. 34.

33. Margery Perham, 'To The Editor Of *The Times*', *The Times* (October 5, 1935), pp. 13–14.

34. Margery Perham, 'War in the Colonies' in *Colonial Sequence, 1930–1949*, p. 192.

35. Margery Perham, 'Editor's Preface' in F. D. Lugard, Margery Perham, and Mary Bull, *The Diaries of Lord Lugard,* vol. 1, *East Africa, November 1889–December 1890* (London: Faber and Faber, 1959), p. 13.

36. Sibyl Eyre Crowe and Edward Corp, *Our Ablest Public Servant: Sir Eyre Crowe GCB, GCMG, KCB, KCMG 1864–1925* (Braunton: Merlin Books, 1993).

37. Mary Bull, 'Writing the Biography of Lord Lugard', special issue on Perham of *The Journal of Imperial and Commonwealth History*, vol. 19, no. 3, pp. 117–136, here 117.

38. Margery Perham and Lionel Curtis, *The Protectorates of South Africa: The Question of Their Transfer to the Union* (Oxford: Oxford University Press, 1935).

39. Perham, *African Apprenticeship*, pp. 40, 138–9.

40. Richard Symonds, *Oxford and Empire* (Oxford: Oxford University Press, 1992), pp. 56–7. Others 'sentinels' including H. E. Egerton and Reginald Coupland.

41. Quoted in Faught, *Into Africa*, p. 90.

42. In 1942, Perham asked Chatham House to urgently commission two works, a review of US press coverage and opinion on British imperialism and a short pamphlet on US imperialism, including its 'dealings' in Cuba, Puerto Rico, Panama, and elsewhere. Margery Perham to Margaret Cleeve, November 24, 1942. 4/PERH/a Chatham House.

43. Margery Perham, 'African Facts and American Criticisms', *Foreign Affairs*, vol. 22, no. 33 (1944), pp. 444–57, here 452, 454.

44. Perham, 'African Facts', p. 457.

45. Perham, 'African Facts', pp. 450, 452.

46. Perham, 'Introduction' in *Colonial Sequence, 1930 to 1949*, p. xi.

47. Perham, 'From Power to Service' in *Colonial Sequence, 1930–1949*, pp. 246–7.

48. Perham in Elspeth Huxley and Margery Perham, *Race and Politics in Kenya: A Correspondence between Elspeth Huxley and Margery Perham* (London: Faber and Faber, 1944, rev. edn, 1956), p. 200; Roland Oliver, 'Prologue: The Two Miss Perhams', special issue of *Journal of Imperial and Commonwealth History*, vol. 19, no. 3, pp. 21–6.

49. Perham in Huxley and Perham, *Race and Politics in Kenya*, p. 200.

50. But still, in 1951, Perham suggested that it was 'not a very bold speculation' that Britain's African colonies 'may become fully self-governing nation-states by the end of the century'. Margery Perham, 'The British Problem in Africa' (1951) in *Colonial Sequence, 1949–1969: A Chronological Commentary upon British Colonial Policy in Africa* (London: Methuen, 1970), pp. 26–7. Margery Perham, 'The Colonial Empire, I—The Need for Stocktaking and Review, A Challenge that Can be Met', *The Times* (March 13, 1942), p. 5.

51. Caroline Elkins, *Legacy of Violence: A History of the British Empire* (New York: Alfred A. Knopf, 2022), p. 317.

52. Perham, in Huxley and Perham, *Race and Politics in Kenya*, pp. 20, 24.

53. Elspeth Huxley, *White Man's Country: Lord Delamere and the Making of Kenya* (London: Macmillan, 1935); Perham, in Huxley and Perham, *Race and Politics in Kenya*, p. 17; also see Wendy Webster, 'Elspeth Huxley: Gender, Empire and Narratives of Nation, 1935–64', *Women's History Review*, vol. 8, no. 3, (1999), pp. 527–45.

54. Perham, in Huxley and Perham, *Race and Politics in Kenya*, pp. 25, 72, 153.

55. Perham, in Huxley and Perham, *Race and Politics in Kenya*, p. 18.

56. Perham, in Huxley and Perham, *Race and Politics in Kenya*, p. 18; Perham, 'Educating Africa', *The Spectator* (November 11, 1938), p. 806.

57. Perham, *East African Journey: Kenya and Tanganyika, 1929–1930* (London: Faber, 1976), p. 190.

58. Margery Perham, *The Colonial Reckoning* (London: Collins, 1961), p. 89.

59. Margery Perham, *Africans and British Rule* (London: Oxford University Press, 1941), p. 80.

60. Margery Perham, *Pacific Prelude: A Journey to Samoa and Australia* (London: Peter Owen, 1988), p. 47.

61. Martin Wight to Mr Ferris, November 16, 1961.

62. Quoted in Faught, *Into Africa*, p. 173.

63. Perham, *Pacific Prelude*, pp. 42–3.

64. In her review, Perham did not engage with Zora Neale Hurston's analysis of race and gender in the United States through Black folklore. Margery Perham, 'Both Sides of the Medal', *The Spectator* (March 6, 1936), p. 403; Zora Neale Hurston, *Mules and Men* (London: Kegan Paul, 1935).

65. W.E.B. Du Bois, 'Interracial Implications of the Ethiopia Crisis: A Negro View', *Foreign Affairs*, vol. 14, no. 1 (October 1935), pp. 82–92.

66. Perham, 'To The Editor Of *The Times*'.

67. Margery Perham, 'The Colour-Challenge', *The Spectator* (August 23, 1935), pp. 284–5, here 284.

68. Margery Perham, 'War and Colonies', *The Spectator* (October 6, 1939), pp. 465–6, here 465.

69. On white allyship in Pankhurst's international thought see Isabelle Napier, doctoral dissertation in progress, University of Oxford.

70. 'A modern-minded, prophetic and very cold-hearted ruler of Ethiopia might almost have planned such an event'. Margery Perham, *The Government of Ethiopia* (London: Faber and Faber, 1948, 2nd edn, 1969), p. 374. 'A dose of modernising imperialism was in accord with 'the world tendency in favour of more, and (let us hope) better, centralization'. Perham, in Huxley and Perham, *Race and Politics in Kenya*, p. 165.

71. Sylvia Pankhurst to Margery Perham, July 16, 1948. MSS Perham 599/1.

72. Sylvia Pankhurst to Margery Perham, April 21, 1950. MSS Perham 292/1.

73. Perham, 'The Colour-Challenge', p. 285.

74. Margery Perham, 'The Little Emperor', *The Observer* (October 11, 1964), p. 26.

75. Margery Perham, 'European Civilization in Africa', *The Spectator* (June 12, 1936), pp. 1088–9, here 1089.

76. Perham, 'The Colour-Challenge', p. 284.

77. These 'anti-imperial critics' are 'useful' because they 'keep us on the alert'. Margery Perham, 'From Power to Service' in *Colonial Sequence, 1930–1949*, p. 244.

78. George Padmore, *How Britain Rules Africa* (London: Wishart, 1936), pp. 4, 2. The book contains a 'special thanks for typing' note to Nancy Cunard, 'the editor of that important

anthology *Negro*, and one of the staunchest and most trusted white friends of the black race, for typing the manuscript and preparing it for publication'. Ibid., p. 17.

79. Perham, 'European Civilization in Africa', p. 1089.

80. Perham, 'European Civilization in Africa', p. 1089.

81. Despite Perham's negative review of his book, Padmore was courteous toward Perham, while also pointedly noting that the magazine suffered, in part, because its editors refused 'Moscow gold or Berlin or Rome subsidies', which is 'why we have contempt for the Colonial Office subsidised hostels in London . . . and the "Uncle Toms" who sacrifice their manhood and self respect for a piece of ribbon'. George Padmore to Margery Perham, January 31, 1939. MSS Perham 27/2, 17.

82. Quoted in Daniel James Whittal, 'Creolising London: Black West Indian Activism and the Politics of Race and Empire in Britain, 1931–1948', doctoral dissertation, Royal Holloway College, University of London, 2012, pp. 241, 212.

83. Perham, 'African Facts', p. 449.

84. Perham, *Africans and British Rule*, p. 79.

85. Perham, 'African Facts', p. 449.

86. Perham, 'The Colour-Challenge', p. 284.

87. Perham, 'European Civilization in African', p. 1089. Akiki K. Nyabongo, *Africa Answers Back* (London: Routledge, 1936).

88. Margery Perham (ed.), 'Introduction', *Ten Africans: A Collection of Life Stories* (London: Faber and Faber, 1936, 2nd edn, 1963), pp. 9, 16.

89. Kofoworola Aina Moore, 'The Story of Kofoworola Aina Moore, of the Yoruba Tribe, Nigeria, written by herself' in Perham (ed.), *Ten Africans*, pp. 323–43. Imaobong Umoren, 'Kofoworola Moore at the University of Oxford', Blog of the Race and Resistance Network at Oxford. October 2, 2015, https://www.torch.ox.ac.uk/article/kofoworola-moore-at-the -university-of-oxford.

90. D. Westermann, Review of *Ten Africans*, by Margery Perham, *Journal of the International African Institute*, vol. 10, no. 2 (1937), pp. 239–40, here 240.

91. Louis Mbanefo, 'Africa Speaks for Herself', *The Keys*, vol. 4, no. 2 (1936), pp. 25–6, here 25.

92. Marc Matera, 'Colonial Subjects: Black Intellectuals and the Development of Colonial Studies in Britain', *Journal of British Studies*, vol. 49, no. 2 (2010), pp. 388–418, here 407.

93. Davies, *Memoirs*, p. 85.

94. Perham, *Africans and British Rule*, p. iv.

95. Perham, *Africans and British Rule*, p. viii. Michael Twaddle, 'Margery Perham and *Africans and British Rule*: A Wartime Publication', special issue on Perham of *The Journal of Imperial and Commonwealth History*, vol. 19, no. 3 (1991), pp. 100–111.

96. Perham, *Africans and British Rule*, p. iv.; Parmenas Githendu Mockerie, *An African Speaks for His People* (London: Hogarth, 1934); Davidson D. T. Jabavu, *The Black Problem: Papers and Addresses on Various Native Problems* (Lovedale: Lovedale Institution, 1920).

97. Perham, *Africans and British Rule*, p. 61.

98. Perham, *Africans and British Rule*, p. 93.

99. Perham, *Africans and British Rule*, p. 25. In 1934, Perham similarly suggested that neither 'science nor history as yet gives us a clear-cut decision' on whether a Black person's 'brain is inferior in capacity and quality'. Perham, 'Future Relations of Black and White in Africa' (1934) in *Colonial Sequence, 1930 to 1949*, p. 86. By 1965, she acknowledged that 'it is the opinion of scientists that there are no inherent differences in the mental equipment of the different races and so in their potentialities'. Margery Perham, *African Outline* (London: Oxford University Press, 1966), pp. 34–5.

100. Perham, *Africans and British Rule*, p. vii.

101. W. Arthur Lewis, 'Africans and British Rule, by Margery Perham', *Newsletter* (September 1941), pp. 125–130, here 130. MSS Brit Emp s 25 (K20) Bodleian Library. For a discussion of the incident see Robert L. W. Tignor, *Arthur Lewis and the Birth of Development Economics* (Princeton: Princeton University Press, 2005), pp. 35–36; Matera, 'Colonial Subjects', pp. 407–8.

102. Perham, 'The British Problem in Africa', p. 39.

103. Perham, *Colonial Reckoning*, pp. 124, 126–27.

104. Perham, *Colonial Reckoning*, p. 128.

105. Anthony Kirk-Greene, 'Forging a Relationship with the Colonial Administrative Service, 1921–1939', special issue on Perham of *Journal of Imperial and Commonwealth History*, vol. 19, no. 3 (1991), pp. 62–82, here 63.

106. Margery Perham and Lionel Curtis, *The Protectorates of South Africa: The Question of Their Transfer to the Union* (London: H. Milford, 1935); Perham, in Huxley and Perham, *Race and Politics in Kenya*.

107. Louis, 'Historians I Have Known'.

108. Martin Wight to Mr Ferris, November 16, 1961.

109. Margery Perham, *Native Administration in Nigeria* (London: Oxford University Press, 1937), p. 218. However, in her monumental Lugard biography, Perham discusses Lugard's wife, Flora Shaw, at great length, including her influence on Lugard and her own career as Governor's wife. Margery Perham, *Lugard: The Years of Adventure, 1858–1898: The First Part of a Life of Frederick Dealtry Lugard* (London: Collins, 1956), pp. 234–41. Shaw was a well known expert on colonialism at *The Times*.

110. Louis, 'Historians I Have Known'.

111. Martin Wight to Mr Ferris, November 16, 1961.

112. Perham, *African Outline*, p. 45; Barbara Bush, 'Gender and Empire: The Twentieth Century' in Philippa Levine, *Gender and Empire* (Oxford: Oxford University Press, 2007), pp. 77–111, here 80. Also Barbara Bush, 'Feminising Empire? British Women's Activist Networks in Defending and Challenging Empire from 1918 to Decolonisation', *Women's History Review*, vol. 25, no. 4 (2016), pp. 499–519.

113. 'In the colonial office she has always been the outsider, and not tempted to use, or in need of using, the wiles required in the Oxford dog-fight. But the C.O. [Colonial Office] seldom liked the letters to the *Times*, and watched her warily. To them too (except her close friends at the top of the Service) she was a potentially meddlesome woman'. Martin Wight to Mr Ferris, November 16, 1961.

114. Perhaps realising the inappropriateness of his comments, Wight also suggested that 'No lover of the Marx Brothers can fail to see Perham in Margaret Dumont'. Martin Wight to Mr Ferris, November 16, 1961. However, Dumont was a classic typecast actress, who played the rich widow comic foil, in turn insulted and wooed for her money and never understanding the joke was on her.

115. Margery Perham, 'Life—or death—in a battery', *The Guardian* (November 7, 1968), p. 7.

116. Faught, *Into Africa*, p. 153.

117. Faught, *Into Africa*, pp. 100, 26.

118. Quoted in Smith and Bull, 'Introduction', p. 7.

119. Martin Wight to Mr Ferris, November 16, 1961.

120. Martin Wight to Mr Ferris, November 16, 1961.

121. Martin Wight to Mr Ferris, November 16, 1961. Rider H. Haggard, *She: A History Of Adventure By Rider Haggard* (London: Longmans, Green, & Co., 1887); Rider H. Haggard, *Ayesha: The Return of She* (New York: Grosset & Dunlap, 1905); also see Julia Reid, '"She-Who-Must-Be-Obeyed": Anthropology and Matriarchy in H. Rider Haggard's *She*', *Journal of Victorian Culture*, vol. 20, no. 3 (2015), pp. 357–74.

122. Martin Wight to Mr Ferris, November 16, 1961.

123. Mary Bull, 'Early Years: Sydney and Oxford' in Coral Bell and Meredith Thatcher (eds.), *Remembering Hedley* (Canberra: ANU E-Press, 2008), pp. 1–8, here 4.

124. Faught, *Into Africa*, p. 122.

125. Bull quoted in Faught, *Into Africa*, p. 122.

126. Coral Bell, 'Foreword' in Bell and Thatcher (eds.), *Remembering Hedley*, pp. xi–xii, here xii.

127. I'm grateful to Glenda Sluga for sharing this conversation. Mary Bull died on December 1, 2020 before I was able to talk with her.

128. F. D. Lugard, Margery Perham, and Mary Bull, *The Diaries of Lord Lugard* (London: Faber and Faber, 1959–63); Mary Bull, *The Medical Services of Tanganyika in 1955* (Oxford: Rhodes House Library, 1984); Bull, 'Writing the Biography of Lord Lugard'; Mary Bull, 'Indirect Rule in Northern Nigeria, 1906–1911' in Kenneth Robinson and A. F. Madden (eds.), *Essays in Imperial Government: Presented to Margery Perham* (Oxford: Basil Blackwell, 1963), pp. 47–87; Mary Bull and Alison Smith (eds.), *Margery Perham and British Rule in Africa* (London: Cass, 1991); Mary Bull, 'Book Review', *African Affairs*, vol. 83, no. 330 (1984), pp. 121–3.

129. Quoted in Smith and Bull, 'Introduction', p. 3.

## 3. The House that Margaret Built: White Women's Housework in IR's Backroom

1. Roger Morgan, '"To Advance the Science of International Politics . . .": Chatham House's Early Research' in Andrea Bosco and Cornelia Navari (eds.), *Chatham House and British Foreign Policy, 1919–1945: The Royal Institute of International Affairs During the Inter-War Period* (London: Lothian Foundation, 1994), pp. 121–36; Deborah Lavin, *From Empire to International Commonwealth: A Biography of Lionel Curtis* (Oxford: Oxford University Press, 1995); Inderjeet Parmar, *Think Tanks and Power in Foreign Policy: A Comparative Study of the Role and Influence of the Council on Foreign Relations and the Royal Institute of International Affairs, 1939–1945* (Houndmills: Palgrave, 2004); James Cotton, 'On the Chatham House Project: Interwar Actors, Networks, Knowledge', *International Politics*, vol. 55, no. 6 (2018), pp. 820–35; Vineet Thakur and Peter Vale, *South Africa, Race and the Making of International Relations* (London: Routledge, 2020).

2. Susan Strange, 'Research Institutions in International Relations in the United Kingdom', *International Social Science Bulletin (UNESCO)*, vol. 1 (1950), pp. 62–79, here pp. 70, 64.

3. Lavin, *From Empire to International Commonwealth*.

4. Helen Jeffrey, 'A Light-Hearted Memory of Chatham House', 1982. 3/11/14. Chatham House. Jeffrey worked at CH between 1929–33.

5. Sir Ivision Macadam, 'Miss M. Cleeve', *The Times* (March 20, 1967). Also see 'Presentation to Miss Margaret Cleeve, O.B.E. on the Occasion of the Twenty-fifth Anniversary of her Appointment to the Staff of the Institute' (June 14, 1946), p. 3. Chatham House 4/CLEE/1.

6. Strange, 'Research Institutions in International Relations'.

7. Margaret Cleeve, 'Meeting to Discuss a Proposal to Form a Newfoundland Branch of the Royal Institute of International Affairs (Chatham House), London', n.d. 4/CLEE/1.

8. Katharina Rietzler, 'U.S. Foreign Policy Think Tanks and Women's Intellectual Labor, 1920–1950', *Diplomatic History*, vol. 46, no. 3 (2022), pp. 575–601.

9. Katharina Rietzler, 'Public Opinion and Education' in Patricia Owens, Katharina Rietzler, Kimberly Hutchings and Sarah C. Dunstan (eds.), *Women's International Thought: Towards a New Canon* (Cambridge: Cambridge University Press, 2022), pp. 517–32.

10. For an excellent study of the LNU see Helen McCarthy, *The British People and the League of Nations: Democracy, Citizenship and Internationalism, c.1918–45* (Manchester: Manchester University Press, 2011).

11. Glenda Sluga, 'From F. Melian Stawell to E. Greene Balch: International and *Internationalist* Thinking at the Gender Margins, 1919–1947' in Patricia Owens and Katharina Rietzler (eds.), *Women's International Thought: A New History* (Cambridge: Cambridge University Press, 2021), pp. 223–43.

12. Erez Manela, *The Wilsonian Moment: Self-Determination and the International Origins of Anticolonial Nationalism* (Oxford: Oxford University Press, 2007); Adom Getachew, *Worldmaking after Empire: The Rise and Fall of Self-Determination* (Princeton: Princeton University Press, 2019); Mona L. Siegel, *Peace on Our Terms: The Global Battle for Women's Rights after the First World War* (New York: Columbia University Press, 2020).

13. Kathleen Conyngham Greene, 'Memorandum on "The British Public and the League of Nations"' by Kathleen Conyngham Greene, 9/2 a-l, Chatham House, p. 17. Figures who responded to Greene's report include Norman Angel, K. C. Boswell, G. Lowes Dickinson, Maxwell Garnett (Secretary of the LNU), Alexander Gordon, Miss Gore, Miss. J. M. Jackson, Mrs. Clifton Roberts, Mrs. M. E. Roberts, Captain Alan Thomas, and Alfred Zimmern. Greene was a prolific writer for children, but also see Kathleen Conyngham Greene, 'The Post-War Generation and the League of Nations', *The Spectator* (March 21, 1931), p. 447.

14. Greene, 'The British Public and the League of Nations', pp. 20, 18.

15. Margaret Cleeve, 'Meeting to Discuss a Proposal to Form a Newfoundland Branch of the Royal Institute of International Affairs (Chatham House), London'. In her 1950 account, Susan Strange also described Chatham House's origins in a 'project in contemporary historical research' entrusted to H.W.V. Temperley. Strange, 'Research Institutions in International Relations', p. 63. Strange was referring to the first major Chatham House publication, the six-volume *History of the Peace Conference of Paris*, overseen by Harold Temperley. Harold W. V. Temperley, *A History of the Peace Conference of Paris* (Oxford: Oxford University Press, 1920).

16. Power, 'A Foreword on the Teaching of History', *A Bibliography for School Teachers of History, Edited, With a Foreword on the Teaching of History* (London: Methuen, 2nd edn, 1921), pp. 13, 10.

17. Power, 'A Foreword on the Teaching of History', pp. 50–51; Florence Melian Stawell, *Patriotism and the Fellowship of Nations; a Little Primer of Great Problems*, with a Preface by F. S. Marvin (London: J.M. Dent & Sons, 1916), p. 85.

18. Stawell, *Patriotism*, p. 66.

19. Stawell, *Patriotism*, p. 76.

20. Karen Levenback, *Virginia Woolf, Melian Stawell and Bloomsbury* (London: Cecil Woolf, 2017), p. 14. F. Melian Stawell's mother wrote a memoir: Mary Frances E. Stawell, *My Recollections* (London: Private Circulation, 1911).

21. Levenback, *Virginia Woolf*, p. 19; K. L. McKay, 'Stawell, Florence Melian (1869–1936)', *Australian Dictionary of Biography*, vol. 12 (1990), pp. 55–6.

22. Stawell's works include *Homer and the Iliad* (London: J. M. Dent, 1909); 'History and the League of Nations', *History*, vol. 3, 12 (1918), p. 224; *The Price of Freedom: An Anthology for all Nations chosen by F. Melian Stawell* (London: Headley, 1917); and with F. S. Marvin, *The Making of the Western Mind* (London: Methuen, 1924).

23. 'Florence Melian Stawell, Sidgwick Hall, 1889–1893', *Newnham College Roll Letter* (Cambridge: Newnham College, 1937, pp. 77–81, here 80. Also see Jeanne Morefield, *Covenants without Swords: Idealist Liberalism and the Spirit of Empire* (Princeton: Princeton University Press, 2005).

24. F. M. Stawell, *The Growth of International Thought* (London: Butterworth, 1929), p. 21.

25. Stawell, *Growth of International Thought*, p. 20.

26. Stawell, *Growth of International Thought*, p. 18.

27. Stawell, *Growth of International Thought*, p. 19.

28. Stawell, *Growth of International Thought*, p. 19.

29. Stawell, *Growth of International Thought*, p. 7.

30. 'Florence Melian Stawell, Sidgwick Hall, 1889–1893'. The image was selected for the cover of Owens and Rietzler, *Women's International Thought: A New History*.

31. Levenback, *Virginia Woolf*, p. 19; 'Florence Melian Stawell, Sidgwick Hall, 1889–1893', p. 78.

32. F. Melian Stawell, 'Mary Parker Follett, *Sidgwick Hall*, 1890 to 1891', obituary, *Newnham College Roll Letter* (Cambridge: Newnham College, 1935), pp. 39–44, here 41. Joan C. Tonn, '"The Great Milepost and Turning Point"' in *Mary P. Follett: Creating Democracy, Transforming Management* (New Haven: Yale University Press, 2003), chapter 6; Brian C. Schmidt, *The Political Discourse of Anarchy: A Disciplinary History of International Relations* (New York: State University of New York, 1998), pp. 168–171; Katharina Rietzler, 'International Law and International Organization' in Owens, Rietzler, Hutchings and Dunstan (eds.), *Women's International Thought: Towards a New Canon*, pp. 246–7. Later, Follett was in a thirty-year relationship with Isobel L. Briggs Myers, creator of a famous personality test still widely used. Leona M. English refers to Follett as a 'gay woman': see Leona M. English, 'Re-Infusing Adult Education with a Critical Feminist Framework: Inspiration from Mary Parker Follett' in *Power and Possibility* (Leiden: Brill, 2019), pp. 97–105, here 104.

33. Eileen Power, *Medieval English Nunneries: c.1275 to 1535* (Cambridge: Cambridge University Press, 1922). The sisters burned most of Eileen Power's personal papers after her death.

34. Eileen Power to Lilian Knowles, April 3, 1921. Eileen Power file, LSE.

35. For the wider context see Ken Osborne, 'Creating the "International Mind": The League of Nations Attempts to Reform History Teaching, 1920–1939', *History of Education Quarterly*, vol. 56, no. 2 (2016), pp. 213–40. Eileen Power, 'On the Teaching of History and World Peace' in F. S. Marvin (ed), *The Evolution of World Peace* (Oxford: H. Milford, 1921), pp. 179–91; Akira Iriye, *Cultural Internationalism and World Order* (Baltimore: Johns Hopkins University Press, 1997) p. 76.

36. Eileen Power, 'Editor's Preface' and 'A Foreword on the Teaching of History', *A Bibliography for School Teachers of History, Edited, with a Foreword on the Teaching of History* (London: Methuen, 2nd edn, 1921), pp. 7–16. The first edition was published in 1919.

37. Power, 'A Foreword on the Teaching of History', p. 14, fn.

38. Eileen Power to William Beveridge, December 12, 1931.

39. G. T. Hankin, 'The International Study of the Problems of History Teaching', *History*, vol. 19, no. 73 (1934), pp. 30–36.

40. Programme for a League of Nations Union Summer School held near Worcester July / August, n.d. GBR/0271/GCPP Power, E 1/11, Girton College. Other speakers included Gilbert Murray and G. Lowes Dickinson.

41. Greene, 'The British Public and the League of Nations', pp. 20, 18

42. Eileen Power, *Medieval People* (London: Methuen, 10th edn, 1963), p. 19.

43. Power, 'A Foreword on the Teaching of History', p. 7.

44. Power, 'A Foreword on the Teaching of History', p. 8.

45. Power, 'A Foreword on the Teaching of History', p. 7.

46. Eileen Power, 'History Syllabus', Cambridge University Library Add. 8961 13/1/6; Eileen Power, 'The Little God', *The Graphic* (August 19, 1922). GBR/0271/GCPP Power, E 3/11, Girton College.

47. Francesca Wade, *Square Haunting: Five Women, Freedom and London between the Wars* (London: Faber & Faber, 2020), p. 215.

48. Eileen Power and Rhoda D. Power, *Boys and Girls of History* (Cambridge: Cambridge University Press, 1926).

49. Eileen Power and Rhoda Power, *Twenty Centuries of Travel* (London: London &C., 1926); Laura Carter, 'Rhoda Power, BBC Radio, and Mass Education, 1922–1957', *Revue française de civilisation britannique*, vol. 26, no. 1 (2020), pp. 1–16.

50. Eileen Power, 'World History: 'VI—The Rise of the Workers', p. 9. 'Thursday, 5th March, 1936. 2.30–2.50 p.m.' Add 8961, B/1/2-27. Cambridge University Library.

51. Eileen Power, 'World History: Talks for Schools Broadcasts—BBC 1933, 1935 and 1936', 'For Monday 26th June, 1933 at 2.30-2.55 p.m.' pp. 1, 3. Add 8961, B/1/2-27.

52. But see S. H. Bailey, *International Studies in Great Britain* (London: Oxford University Press, 1933); S. H Bailey, *International Studies in Modern Education* (London: Oxford University Press, 1938). Barry Buzan, 'Before BISA: the British Coordinating Committee for International Studies, S.H. Bailey, and the Bailey Conferences', *International Politics*, vol. 57 (2020), pp. 573–87, here 578.

53. Brenda Helt and Madelyn Detloff (eds.), *Queer Bloomsbury* (Edinburgh: Edinburgh University Press, 2016).

54. Jane Robinson, *Bluestockings: The Remarkable Story of the First Women to Fight for an Education* (London: Penguin, 2010), p. 9.

55. 'Few were more effective as teachers at LSE than Eileen Power'. Ralf Dahrendorf, *LSE: A History of the London School of Economics and Political Science, 1895–1995* (Oxford: Oxford University Press, 1995), p. 235.

56. M. G. Jones, 'Memories of Eileen Power', *Girton Review*, vol. 114 (1940), p. 4. GBR/0271/GCPP Power, E 1/8, Girton College.

57. G. G. Coulton, 'Memories of Eileen Power', *The Cambridge Review*, vol. 52 (October 18, 1940), p. 28. GBR/0271/GCPP Power, E 1/8, Girton College.

58. 'Obituary Dr. Eileen Power', *The Manchester Guardian* (August 12, 1940), p. 8.

59. Dahrendorf, *LSE*, p. 188.

60. Dahrendorf, *LSE*, p. 188.

61. J. H. Clapham, 'Eileen Power, 1889–1940', *Economica*, vol. 7, no. 28 (1940), pp. 351–9, here 355; also see Rozemarijn Van De Wal, 'Constructing the Persona of a Professional Historian: On Eileen Power's Early Career Persona Formation and Her Year in Paris, 1910–1911', *Persona Studies*, vol. 4, no. 1 (2018), pp. 32–44.

62. Dahrendorf, *LSE*, p. 155. Though he withholds from her the honorific of public intellectual, Stefan Collini could also 'easily imagine' falling in love with Eileen Power. Stefan Collini, 'Historian–Intellectuals? Eileen Power, Herbert Butterfield, Hugh Trevor-Roper' in *Common Writing: Essays on Literacy Culture and Public Debate* (Oxford: Oxford University Press, 2016), p. 244.

63. Maxine Berg, *A Woman in History: Eileen Power, 1889–1940* (Cambridge: Cambridge University Press, 1996), p. 43. On Jones and Power's relationship see pp. 48–50.

64. M. Gwladys Jones *The New World History Series: Second Book (1485–1688)* (London: Collins, 1920); Eileen Power, *The New World History Series: First Book (from the beginning to 1485)* (London: Collins, 1920).

65. M. G. Jones, *The Charity School Movement: a Study of Eighteenth Century Puritanism in Action* (Cambridge: Cambridge University Press, 1938).

66. William McNeil, *Arnold J. Toynbee: A Life* (Oxford: Oxford University Press, 1990), p. 150.

67. Eileen Power, *Report to the Trustees September 1920—September 1921, Albert Kahn Fellowship* (London: University of London, 1921), p. 62.

68. Ellen Jacobs, 'Eileen Power's Asian Journey, 1920–21: History, Narrative, and Subjectivity', *Women's History Review*, vol. 7, no. 3 (1998), pp. 295–319, here 308; for a good discussion see Billie Melman, 'Under the Western Historian's Eyes: Eileen Power and the Early Feminist Encounter with Colonialism', *History Workshop Journal*, vol. 42 (1996), pp. 147–68, here 158.

69. Jacobs, 'Eileen Power's Asian Journey', p. 306.

70. Eileen Power, *Time and Tide* (August 17, 1940), pp. 846–7.

71. McNeil, *Arnold J. Toynbee*, pp. 141–3.

72. Katharina Rietzler, 'Introduction: 100 years of women in *International Affairs*', Archive Collection, *International Affairs* (December 2022), p. 6.

73. Rietzler, 'U.S. Foreign Policy Think Tanks' p. 585.

74. 'Presentation to Miss Margaret Cleeve, O.B.E.', p. 6.

75. 'Miss Cleeve's Speech at her Farewell Dinner, 10 October 1956', pp. 1–2. 4/CLEE/2. Also see Sir Ivision Macadam, 'Miss M. Cleeve'.

76. Brian Porter, 'E.H. Carr—the Aberystwyth Years, 1936–47', in Michael Cox (ed.), *E.H. Carr: a Critical Appraisal* (London: Palgrave, 2000), pp. 36–67, here 49.

77. Macadam to Cleeve, Memorandum, November 15, 1937. 4/CLEE/1. On librarianship as a pathway to women's international thought see Valeska Huber, Tamson Pietsch and Katharina Rietzler, 'Women's International Thought and the New Professions, 1900–1940', *Modern Intellectual History*, vol. 18, no. 1 (2021), pp. 121–45.

78. 'Presentation to Miss Margaret Cleeve, O.B.E.', p. 3.

79. 'Margaret Cleeve Certificate of Candidate for Election'. May 23, 1930. Chatham House 4/CLEE/1.

80. W.N.M., 'Margaret Cleeve O.B.E.', *International Affairs*, vol. 33, no. 1 (1957), p. 1.

81. Margaret Cleeve to Elizabeth Wiskemann, June 21, 1956. Chatham House 4/WISK.

82. 'Miss Cleeve's Speech at her Farewell Dinner, 10 October 1956'.

83. Margaret Cleeve, 'Visit to Estonia, Latvia, Poland and Berlin. October 1934', November 6, 1934. 4/CLEE/3 'Reports of Visits Abroad'.

84. Margaret Cleeve, 'Notes on Visit to Brussels, Berlin, Hamburg, The Hague. September–October 1930', p. 2. 4/CLEE/3 'Reports of Visits Abroad'.

85. Margaret Cleeve, 'Notes on Visit to Brussels, Berlin, Hamburg, The Hague'.

86. Cornelia Navari Oral History. Leverhulme Project on Women and the History of International Thought. February 28, 2019. Available at https://whit.web.ox.ac.uk/oral-history-archive.

87. British Coordinating Committee for International Studies, 'Report of a Conference on "International Studies in Great Britain" held at the London School of Economics on Friday, 23rd June 1933', p. 5. 9/5b Group V. British Coordinating Committee, Chatham House.

88. Report of a Conference on "International Studies in Great Britain" held at the London School of Economics', p. 2.

89. 'Report of a Conference on "International Studies in Great Britain" held at the London School of Economics', p. 5.

90. 'Report of a Conference on "International Studies in Great Britain" held at the London School of Economics', p. 7.

91. 'Report of a Conference on "International Studies in Great Britain" held at the London School of Economics', p. 2.

92. Cleeve to Macadam, September 30, 1937. 4/CLEE/1; Cleeve to Macadam, 'Confidential', April 15, 1937. 4/CLEE/1. For Cleeve, the period of great expansion began in 1929 with the arrival of the Scot Ivison Macadam, member of the Round Table editorial board, and founder of the National Union of Students, with whom Cleeve worked closely.

93. Cleeve to Macadam, June 28, 1937. 4/CLEE/1.

94. K. G. Younger to Mrs. Marion A. Fryer, March 15, 1967. 4/CLEE/2.

95. Margaret Cleeve, 'Meeting to Discuss a Proposal to Form a Newfoundland Branch of the Royal Institute of International Affairs (Chatham House), London', 'Extracts from letter from Miss Cleeve to Mr. Macadam dated April 13th 1938'. SS Nova Scotia (en route to Boston). 4/CLEE/1.

96. 'Extracts from letter from Miss Cleeve to Mr. Macadam dated April 13th 1938'. SS Nova Scotia (en route to Boston). 4/CLEE/1.

97. Cleeve to Macadam, April 10, 1938. 4/CLEE/1.

98. They include Elsie Fairfax-Cholmeley (Secretariat I.P.R.), Kate Mitchell (Secretariat I.P.R.), Catherine Porter (American Council, I.P.R.), Jeannette Randolph (American Council, I.P.R.), Ona Ringwood (Librarian F.P.A), Ruth Savord (C.F.R.), Sydnor Walker (Rockefeller Foundation), Helen Wheeler (Librarian, League of Nations Association). Visit of Miss Margaret Cleeve to Canada and the United States, March 31 to June 3, 1938. 4/CLEE/1.

99. Visit of Miss Margaret Cleeve to Canada and the United States.

100. 'Extract from the Minutes of the 121st Meeting of the Finance Committee, held on Wednesday, March 30th, 1938'. 4/CLEE/1.

101. Lionel Curtis, Waldorf Astor, Ivison S. Macadam, 'Notice to Members: Presentation to Miss Margaret Cleeve, O.B.E.' April 1946. 4/CLEE/1.

102. Rietzler, 'U.S. Foreign Policy Think Tanks'.

103. 'Our History', https://www.chathamhouse.org/about-us/our-history.

104. Lavin, *From Empire to International Commonwealth*, p. 106. Also see Vineet Thakur, Alexander E. Davis, and Peter Vale, 'Imperial Mission, "Scientific" Method: An Alternative Account of the Origins of IR', *Millennium: Journal of International Studies*, vol. 46, no. 1 (2017), pp. 3–23.

105. Strange, 'Research Institutions in International Relations', p. 66. William Hailey, *An African Survey: A Study of Problems Arising in Africa South of the Sahara* (London: Oxford University Press, 1938).

106. Lucy Mair to Meyer Fortes, September 22, 1936. Cambridge University Library Add. 8405/1/44/7.

107. Cf. Thakur and Vale, *South Africa*, pp. 12, 103.

108. Oscar Jászi, 'Review of *Czechs and Germans: A Study of the Struggle in the Historic Provinces of Bohemia and Moravia*, by Elizabeth Wiskemann, and *Csehszlovákia 1918–1938*, by M. Halász'. *American Sociological Review*, vol. 4, no. 3 (1939), pp. 421–2. Also see R. W. Seton-Watson, 'Review of *Czechs and Germans: A Study of the Struggle in the Historic Provinces of Bohemia and Moravia*, by Elizabeth Wiskemann', *The Spectator* (July 1, 1938), p. 25.

109. Geoffrey Field, *Elizabeth Wiskemann: Scholar, Journalist, Secret Agent* (Oxford: Oxford University Press, 2023), p. 62; Elizabeth Wiskemann, *Czechs and Germans: A Study of the Struggle in the Historic Provinces of Bohemia and Moravia* (London: Oxford University Press, 1938).

110. Cleeve to Macadam. 4/CLEE/1.

111. Cornelia Navari Oral History.

112. Cleeve to Macadam, January 13, 1937. 4/CLEE/1.

113. Cornelia Navari Oral History.

114. Cornelia Navari Oral History. After an interview with Kenneth Younger and Donald Watt, Navari took a research position at Chatham House at the beginnings of détente and was initially rapporteur for the détente lectures, but then as research assistant to the *Documents* and *Survey*. In the mid-1960s, Navari was the 'documents person. I ran down documents, collected documents, edited documents, put these volumes together. They all appeared under multiple authorships but it was me that put them together'. She left Chatham House when the *Survey* and *Documents* were discontinued because they were too expensive to produce. For all its intellectual limitations, she found LSE to be 'a kindlier place than Chatham House'. Cornelia Navari Oral History.

115. Cornelia Navari Oral History.

116. Muriel Grindrod (1902–1994) worked at Chatham House as an assistant to Toynbee from 1927. She studied classics at Girton, later switching to Modern and Medieval Language, becoming a leading expert on Italian politics. See Muriel Grindrod, *The New Italy: Transition*

*from War to Peace* (London: Royal Institute of International Affairs, 1947); Muriel Grindrod, *The Rebuilding of Italy: Politics and Economics, 1945–1955* (London: Royal Institute of International Affairs, 1955); Federico Chabod and Muriel Grindrod, *A History of Italian Fascism* (London: Weidenfeld & Nicolson, 1963); Muriel Grindrod, *Italy* (Oxford University Press, 1964). With Ivison Macadam, Grindrod produced numerous editions of *The Annual Register of World Events* during the 1960s.

117. Veronica Boulter to Lois Whitaker, December 30, 1964, in Veronica Boulter Toynbee and Lois Wiegardt Whitaker, *The Gentle Giant's Lady and Her Friend: Selected Letters of Veronica Boulter Toynbee, 1964–1980* (Dubuque, Iowa: Kendall/Hunt, 1997), p. 15.

118. Veronica Boulter Toynbee, *Chronology of International Events and Treaties: 1st January 1920–31st December 1925* (London: Oxford University Press, 1928); P. E Baker, V. M Boulter, R.G.D. Laffan, Arnold Toynbee, and Veronica M. Toynbee, *Survey of International Affairs, 1938* (Oxford: Oxford University Press: London, 1941); Veronica M. Toynbee and Arnold Toynbee, *Hitler's Europe* (London: Oxford University Press, 1954); Arnold Toynbee and Veronica M. Toynbee, *The Realignment of Europe* (London: Oxford University Press, 1955); Veronica M. Toynbee and Arnold Toynbee, *The War and the Neutrals* (London: Oxford University Press, 1956); Veronica M. Toynbee and Arnold Toynbee, *The Initial Triumph of the Axis* (London: Oxford University Press, 1958).

119. Boulter to Lois Whitaker, November 10, 1965, in *The Gentle Giant's Lady*, p. 24.

120. McNeil, *Arnold J. Toynbee*, p. 205.

121. McNeil, *Arnold J. Toynbee*, p. 125.

122. Boulter to Lois Whitaker, June 13, 1966, in *The Gentle Giant's Lady*, p. 32.

123. Whitaker, in *The Gentle Giant's Lady*.

124. McNeil, *Arnold J. Toynbee*, p. 125; Veronica Boulter to Lois Whitaker, March 27, 1966, in *The Gentle Giant's Lady*, p. 29.

125. See, for example, Ian Hall, '"Time of Troubles": Arnold J. Toynbee's Twentieth Century', *International Affairs*, vol. 90, no. 1 (2014), pp. 23–6, where in a footnote Boulter is described as Toynbee's 'assistant'.

126. Sir Ivison Macadam, 'Miss M. Cleeve', emphasis in original.

127. 'Presentation to Miss Margaret Cleeve, O.B.E.'.

128. 'Presentation to Miss Margaret Cleeve, O.B.E.'.

129. Lionel Curtis, Waldorf Astor, Ivison S. Macadam, 'Notice to Members: Presentation to Miss Margaret Cleeve, O.B.E.'.

130. 'Extract from Chairman's Speech at A.G.M. 1967'. 4/CLEE/2.

131. K. G. Younger to Mrs Marion A. Fryer, March 15, 1967. 4/CLEE/2.

132. Helen Jeffrey, 'A Light-Hearted Memory of Chatham House', 1982. 3/11/14.

133. 'Presentation to Miss Margaret Cleeve, O.B.E.'.

134. Sir Ivison Macadam, 'Miss M. Cleeve'.

135. 'Presentation to Miss Margaret Cleeve, O.B.E.'.

136. Sir Ivision Macadam, 'Miss M. Cleeve', emphasis added.

137. Lois Simpson to Ivison Macadam, March 21, 1967. 4/CLEE/2.

138. Kenneth Younger, 'Margaret Cleeve', n.d. 4/CLEE/2, emphasis added.

139. K. G. Younger to Andrew Shonfield, April 5, 1967. 4/CLEE/2.

140. K. G. Younger to Alan Bullock, April 7, 1967. 4/CLEE/2.

141. K. G. Younger to Alan Bullock, April 7, 1967. 4/CLEE/2. Younger had previously refused a request from UCL historian Robin Humphreys to donate a small sum to the Dame Lillian Penson Memorial Fund to support travel for British-based scholars to research in the Commonwealth and Commonwealth-based scholars to work in Britain. 'On the whole we do not feel that this is the sort of thing for which we should fairly use the Institutes funds. So as far as I am concerned, quite frankly I knew her very little and she ceased to be on the Council here

several years before I became director, so that I am afraid I don't really feel that it is up to me to make a personal contribution'. Kenneth Younger to Robin Humphreys, February 19, 1964. Penson Papers, Royal Holloway College, University of London.

142. Andrew Shonfield to K. G. Younger, April 5, 1967. 4/CLEE/2.

143. K. G. Younger to Macadam, April 11, 1967. 4/CLEE/2.

144. Alan Bullock to Kenneth Younger, April 10, 1967. 4/CLEE/2.

145. Katharina Rietzler, 'Undercurrents: The History of Women at Chatham House' (March 7, 2019). Available at https://www.chathamhouse.org/2019/03/undercurrents-history -women-chatham-house.

## 4. No International Relations Without Women

1. C.A.W. Manning, 'International Relations: An Academic Discipline' in Geoffrey L. Goodwin, *The University Teaching of International Relations* (Oxford: Blackwell, 1951), pp. 11–26, here 20.

2. Brian Porter (ed.), *The Aberystwyth Papers: International Politics 1919–1969* (London: Oxford University Press, 1972); Harry Bauer and Elisabetta Brighi (eds.), *International Relations at the LSE: A History of 75 Years* (London: Millennium, 2003); Ian Hall, *Dilemmas of Decline: British Intellectuals and World Politics, 1945–1975* (Berkeley: University of California Press, 2012), p. 55; and most recently, Nicholas Sims, 'The Department of International Relations: Origins and Foundations'. Available at https://blogs.lse.ac.uk/lsehistory/2021/11/26/the-department-of -international-relations-origins-and-foundations/.

3. Eileen Power to Margery Spring Rice, July 31, 1921. Girton College, Cambridge. GBR/0271/ GCPP Power, E 2/1/5.

4. Georg Schwarzenberger, *Power Politics: A Study of International Society* (London: Stevens, 2nd edn, 1951), pp. 6–7; Susan Strange, 'Looking Back—But Mostly Forward', *Millennium: Journal of International Studies*, vol. 11, no. 1 (1982), p. 40; Hall, *Dilemmas of Decline*, p. 55.

5. Geopolitical thinker and expert on Friedrich Ratzel, Harriet Wanklyn (1906–1990) also taught 'Historical and Political Geography' in the Faculty of Geography at Cambridge from 1933 to 1966. She is named 'Mrs H. G. Steers' in *Cambridge University Reporter* but published in her own name. She graduated in history from St. Hilda's College, Oxford, and was an accomplished linguist and worked voluntarily for the LNU and Chatham House. Wanklyn was was offered but declined a fellowship at Girton College to focus on her family, having married her colleague Alfred Steers. See Harriet Wanklyn and Alan G. Ogilvie, *The Eastern Marchlands of Europe* (London: G. Philip, 1941); Harriet Wanklyn, *Czechoslovakia: A Geographical and Historical Study* (London: George Phillip & Son, 1954); Harriet Wanklyn, *Friedrich Ratzel: A Biographical Memoir and Bibliography* (Cambridge: Cambridge University Press, 1961). For a brief profile of Wanklyn/Steers see Avril Maddrell, *Complex Locations: Women's Geographical Work in the UK, 1850–1970* (Oxford: Wiley-Blackwell, 2009), pp. 205–7.

6. Meeting of the Faculty Board of History, November 10, 1935, and Meeting of the Faculty Board of History, November 7, 1933. Meeting of the Faculty Board of History, November 6, 1934. GBR/0265/UA/HIST 1/1/5. Cambridge University Library.

7. GBR/0271/GCAS 2/6/2/2/14, M. G. Jones file. Girton College, Cambridge.

8. Herbert Butterfield, 'How Far Should the Subject of International Relations be Included in the Curriculum for Undergraduate Students of History?', Butterfield MS 130/2, 2, 1, Cambridge University Library.

9. Geoffrey L. Goodwin, 'Teaching of International Relations' in Goodwin, *The University Teaching of International Relations*, p. 118.

10. Goodwin, 'Teaching of International Relations', p. 124.

11. Charles Manning, 'Metadiplomatics for the Modern Man', *The Universities Quarterly*, vol. 11, no. 2 (1957), pp. 155–63, here 160–61.

12. Butterfield, 'How Far Should the Subject of International Relations', pp. 1, 3.

13. Butterfield, 'How Far Should the Subject of International Relations', p. 2.

14. Susan Strange, 'I Never Meant to be an Academic' in Joseph Kruzel and James N. Rosenau (eds.), *Journeys through World Politics: Autobiographical Reflections of Thirty-Four Academic Travelers* (New York: Lexington Books, 1989), pp. 429–36, here 435.

15. Manning, 'International Relations: an Academic Discipline', p. 20.

16. According to the university archivist, the Faculty of History Board Meeting minutes from 1936–1948 are missing.

17. Alfred Zimmern to Douglas Veale, May 31, 1948. UR 6/MB/1, file 1. Bodleian Library, Oxford.

18. M. Gwladys Jones, *The New World History Series: Second Book (1485–1688)* (London: Collins, 1920).

19. On Jones and her relationship with Power see Maxine Berg, *Woman in History: Eileen Power, 1889–1940* (Cambridge: Cambridge University Press, 1996), pp. 42–43, 48–50.

20. Glenda Sluga, 'From F. Melian Stawell to E. Greene Balch: International and *Internationalist* Thinking at the Gender Margins, 1919–1947' in Patricia Owens and Katharina Rietzler (eds.), *Women's International Thought: A New History* (Cambridge University Press, 2021), pp. 223–43.

21. Geoffrey Field, *Elizabeth Wiskemann: Scholar, Journalist, Secret Agent* (Oxford: Oxford University Press, 2023), p. 15.

22. Elizabeth Wiskemann, *The Europe I Saw* (London: Collins, 1968), p. 8; Betty Behrens reported a different view of Temperley who she thought was 'anxious to give the women a fair deal . . . to hold out a helping hand to them. To the best of my knowledge and belief there has since 1945 been no one with any influence in the Faculty who has wished to do either'. Betty Behrens to Miss Tagg, 16 January 1985, BEHR/892 ADD/14. Churchill Archives Centre. Temperley also appeared to have a good working relationship with the London-based diplomatic historian Lilian Penson. Penson assisted Temperley and Gooch in the production of their influential work, G. P. Gooch and H.W.V. Temperley, *British Documents on the Origins of the War, 1898–1914* (London: H.M.S.O, 1926). Temperley was one of the few diplomatic historians, along with E. Jones Parry, to take Princess Dorothea Lieven seriously as an *ambassadrice*, editing her diaries for publication. See Dorothea Lieven and H.W.V Temperley, *The Unpublished Diary and Political Sketches of Princess Lieven: Together with Some of Her Letters* (London: J. Cape, 1925).

23. Elizabeth Wiskemann, *Undeclared War* (London: Constable, 1939); Elizabeth Wiskemann, *The Rome–Berlin Axis: A History of the Relations between Hitler and Mussolini* (London: Oxford University Press, 1949); Elizabeth Wiskemann, *Germany's Eastern Neighbours: Problems Relating to the Oder-Neisse Line and the Czech Frontier Regions* (London: Oxford University Press, 1956); Elizabeth Wiskemann, *Europe of the Dictators, 1919–1945* (London: Collins, 1966).

24. Field, *Elizabeth Wiskemann*; also see Geoffrey Field, 'Elizabeth Wiskemann, Scholar-Journalist, and the Study of International Relations' in Owens and Rietzler (eds.), *Women's International Thought*, pp. 198–220.

25. Betty Behrens to 'Jack', November 1, 1979, BEHR/892 ADD/14. Churchill Archives Centre.

26. The American-born Zara Steiner (1928–2020) was also an occasional lecturer for the faculty, including on 'theories of international relations' at the Centre for International Studies, founded in 1967. Her two most famous works are Zara Steiner, *The Lights That Failed: European International History, 1919–1933* (Oxford: Oxford University Press, 2005) and Zara Steiner, *The Triumph of the Dark: European International History 1933–1939* (Oxford: Oxford University Press, 2011).

27. C.B.A. Behrens, *Merchant Shipping and the Demands of War* (England: H.M.S.O., 1955). According to Joan Bakewell, Behrens was as 'the nearest' Newnham College 'came to chic'. Joan

Bakewell, 'A moment that changed me: my teacher said my work was trite rubbish—and totally destroyed me', *The Guardian* (September 8, 2021). Clare Hall College recently inaugurated the Betty Behrens Seminar.

28. Betty Behrens, 'The Panjandrum', pp. 3–4. 825 BEHR/99 Box 15, Churchill Archives Centre. For an account of the marriage that focuses almost entirely on the perspective of Carr see Jonathan Haslam, *The Vices of Integrity: E.H. Carr, 1892–1982* (London: Verso, 1999), pp. 242–5, 263–8, 271–3.

29. According to Pryce-Jones, Carr never bothered to read Behrens's work and she had a 'nervous collapse' because of their marriage, spending time in an 'asylum, whereupon Carr tried to take some of her considerable fortune'. 'Enclosed in his ego', continues Pryce-Jones, Carr 'paid no attention to any' of his three wives, 'discarding them like tissues, resenting any interruption to his work, loathing Christmas because libraries were closed, loathing opera, loathing parties and social occasions. The nastiness was unlimited. Anne developed a sarcoma, and, on the day that one of her daughters was due to have a very serious operation, Carr informed her that the marriage was over, that he was leaving her for Joyce. In due course he left Joyce for her closest friend, Betty Behrens'. David Pryce-Jones, 'Unlimited Nastiness', *New Criterion*, vol. 18, no. 4 (1999), p. 68. Available at https://newcriterion.com/issues/1999/12/unlimited-nastiness.

30. Herbert Butterfield to Betty Behrens, March 15, 1957, BUTT/327. Cambridge University Library.

31. Timothy Dunne, *Inventing International Society: A History of the English School* (New York: Macmillan 1998), p. 73; for another adulatory account of the Committee and its doings see Brunello Vigezzi, *The British Committee on the Theory of International Politics (1954–1985): The Rediscovery of History* (Milan: Edizioni Unicopli, 2005).

32. C. T. McIntire, *Herbert Butterfield: Historian as Dissenter* (New Haven: Yale University Press, 2004), p. 317.

33. Betty Behrens to Herbert Butterfield, March 6, 1957, BEHR 100 A-F. Cambridge University Library.

34. Mr. H. Rackmam to William Beveridge, n.d. 1927 LSE File Mair, Dr. L. P. 1927–1935 A. LSE Library.

35. Gilbert Murray to William Beveridge, n.d. 1927 LSE File Mair, Dr. L. P. 1927–1935 A. LSE Library.

36. Lucy Philip Mair, *The Protection of Minorities: The Working and Scope of the Minorities Treaties Under the League of Nations* (London: Christophers, 1928).

37. Mair, *Protection of Minorities*, pp. 220–21. Hannah Arendt, *The Origins of Totalitarianism* (New York: Harcourt, Brace & World, new edn, 1966).

38. Quincy Wright, *The Study of International Relations* (New York: Appleton-Century-Crofts, 1955).

39. Ann Oakley, 'Janet Beveridge' in *Forgotten Wives: How Women Get Written Out of History* (Bristol: Policy Press, 2021), pp. 135–73.

40. Berg, *Woman in History*, p. 147; Oakley, *Forgotten Wives*, pp. 7, 10.

41. Quoted in Ralf Dahrendorf, *LSE: A History of the London School of Economics and Political Science, 1895–1995* (Oxford: Oxford University Press, 1995), p. 155.

42. Oakley, 'Janet Beveridge', p. 141.

43. Lucy Philip Mair, 'Colonial Administration as a Science', *Journal of the Royal African Society*, vol. 32, no. 129 (1933) pp. 366–71.

44. Bronisław Malinowski, *Argonauts of the Western Pacific: An Account of Native Enterprise and Adventure in the Archipelagoes of Melanesian New Guinea* (London: Routledge, 1922).

45. Perham in Elspeth Huxley and Margery Perham, *Race and Politics in Kenya: A Correspondence between Elspeth Huxley and Margery Perham* (London: Faber and Faber, 1944, rev. edn,

1956), pp. 173–4; Alison Smith and Mary Bull, 'Introduction', special issue on Perham of *The Journal of Imperial and Commonwealth History*, vol. 19, no. 3 (1991), pp. 1–20, here 5.

46. Margery Perham, 'Foreword', in Tom Mboya, *The Kenya Question: An African Answer* (London: Fabian Colonial Bureau, 1956), pp. 1–11.

47. Some of the discussion of Mair in this section draws from Patricia Owens, 'Women and the History of International Thought', *International Studies Quarterly*, vol. 62, no. 3 (2018), pp. 467–81.

48. A. I. Richards, 'Review: An African People in the Twentieth Century by L.P. Mair', *Africa: Journal of the International African Institute*, vol. 7, no. 4 (1934), pp. 497–8, here 497.

49. Lucy Philip Mair, *Native Policies in Africa* (London: Routledge, 1936), p. 15.

50. Lucy Philip Mair, *An African People in the Twentieth Century* (London: Routledge, 1934), pp. 4–5.

51. Mair, *An African People*, p. 287.

52. Lucy Mair to Meyer Fortes, September 22, 1936. Add. 8405/1/44/7, Cambridge University Library.

53. George Steinmetz, 'British Sociology in the Metropole and the Colonies, 1940s–1960s' in John Scott and John Holmwood (eds.), *The Palgrave Handbook of Sociology in Britain* (Basingstoke: Palgrave, 2014), pp. 302–37, here 318.

54. Mair, Perham and Richards co-authored a paper for Chatham House on 'Some Problems in Ethiopia'. Perham later published *The Government of Ethiopia* in 1948. Patricia Pugh, 'Margery Freda Perham, 1895–1982', *Proceedings of the British Academy*, vol. 111, pp. 617–33, here 626. Margery Perham, 'The Diet of the Savage', *The Spectator* (November 17, 1939); Lucy Philip Mair, 'Book Review: "Lugard: The Years of Adventure, 1858–1898", by Margery Perham', *Africa*, vol. 27, no. 3 (1957), pp. 289–90; L. P. Mair, 'Reviewed Work(s): *Native Administration in Nigeria*, by Margery Perham', *Man*, vol. 37 (1937), p. 196.

55. Lucy Philip Mair, 'International Relations as a Separate Subject', February 20, 1934, p. 1. LSE\LSE School History\Box 10 Chairs. LSE Library. I'm grateful to Sue Donnelley, then LSE archivist, for tracking down this file.

56. Hidemi Suganami, *The Domestic Analogy and World Order Proposals* (Cambridge: Cambridge University Press, 1989).

57. Mair, 'International Relations', p. 1.

58. Mair, 'International Relations', p. 1.

59. Mair, 'International Relations', p. 1.

60. Mair, 'International Relations', p. 2.

61. Mair, 'International Relations', p. 2.

62. Mair, 'International Relations', p. 1.

63. Dahrendorf, *LSE*, p. 248.

64. William Malcolm Hailey, *An African Survey: A Study of Problems Arising in Africa South of the Sahara* (London: Oxford University Press, 1938).

65. 'Colonial Policy and Peaceful Change', 1937. LSE File, LNU/7/36. C.A.W. Manning (ed.), *Peaceful Change: An International Problem* (London: Macmillan, 1937).

66. Mair to William Beveridge, April 28, 1937. LSE File, Mair, Dr. L. P. 1935–1946, B.

67. Lucy Mair to Meyer Fortes, September 22, 1936.

68. Lucy Mair to Meyer Fortes, August 19, 1944. Add. 8405/1/44/27, Cambridge University Library.

69. Margery Perham to Margaret Cleeve, November 13, 1944. 4/PERH/a Chatham House.

70. Lucy Philip Mair, *Welfare in the British Colonies* (London: Royal Institute of International Affairs, 1944).

71. Felix M. Kessing, 'Reviewed Work(s): Welfare in British Colonies. by L. P. Mair', *Pacific Affairs*, vol. 18, no. 1 (1945), p. 108.

72. Lucy Philip Mair, *Australia in New Guinea* (London: Christophers, 1948).

73. Mair to William Beveridge, April 28, 1937.

74. F. S. Northedge, 'In Memoriam: Charles Manning; 1894–1978', *British Journal of International Studies*, vol. 5, no. 1 (1979), pp. 1–5, here 5.

75. David Long, 'Of Mustard Seeds and Shopping Lists: C.A.W. Manning and International Relations at the LSE', *International Politics*, vol. 54, no. 1 (2017), pp. 118–23, here 119; also see David Long, 'C.A.W. Manning and the Discipline of International Relations', *Round Table*, vol. 94, no. 378 (2005), pp. 77–96.

76. Northedge, 'In Memoriam', p. 1.

77. Northedge, 'In Memoriam', p. 3.

78. Roger Morgan, 'International Relations as an Academic Discipline: Outline for a Discussion at Warwick University, 15th October 1970', p. 2. BISA/10. LSE Library.

79. C.A.W Manning, 'Note on the Nature of International Relations as the province of the Montague Burton Chair'. n.d. p. 2. LSE\LSE School History\Box 10 Chairs.

80. LSE figures include Lucy Philip Mair, Lilian Friedländer, Eileen Power, Lilian Knowles, and Coral Bell, all discussed here. LSE excelled at training graduate researchers, including Persia Campbell, Rita Hinden, Eleanor Lansing Dulles, Rachel Wall, Louise Holborn, Barbara Wootton, Ursula K. Webb, Eslanda Robeson, Margaret Read, Margaret Lambert, and Sudha R. Shenoy. Many of these thinkers are discussed in Patricia Owens, Katharina Rietzler, Kimberly Hutchings and Sarah C. Dunstan (eds.), *Women's International Thought: Towards a New Canon* (Cambridge: Cambridge University Press, 2022).

81. F. S. Northedge, 'The Department of International Relations at LSE: A Brief History, 1924–1971' in Bauer and Brighi (eds.), *International Relations at the LSE*, pp. 7–27, here 12.

82. Manning, 'Note on the Nature of International Relations', pp. 2–3.

83. Charles Manning, 'Out to Grass—and a Lingering Looking Behind', *International Relations*, vol. 2, no. 6 (1962) pp. 347–71, here 350.

84. Manning, 'Out to Grass', p. 350.

85. John Davis (ed.), *Choice and Change: Essays in Honour of Lucy Mair* (London: Athlone, 1974); Maxwell Owusu (ed.), *Colonialism and Change: Essays Presented to Lucy Mair* (The Hague: Mouton, 1975).

86. Northedge, 'The Department of International Relations at LSE', p. 11.

87. Malinowski, *Argonauts of the Western Pacific*.

88. Manning, 'International Relations: An Academic Discipline', pp. 20, 17.

89. Zimmern failed in his bid to become the inaugural first director general of UNESCO, with Lucie Zimmern falsely accusing Julian Huxley of being a communist. John Toye and Richard Toye, 'One World, Two Cultures? Alfred Zimmern, Julian Huxley and the Ideological Origins of UNESCO', *History*, vol. 95, no. 319 (2010), p. 326.

90. David Long, 'Who Killed the International Studies Conference?' *Review of International Studies*, vol. 32, no. 4 (2006), pp. 603–22, here 611.

91. According to Buzan, because Bailey organised two conferences and two books on the university teaching of IR in Britain in the 1930s, he bequeathed 'the foundations of the project that would eventually become BISA'. Barry Buzan, 'Before BISA: the British Coordinating Committee for International Studies, S.H. Bailey, and the Bailey Conferences', *International Politics*, vol. 57 (2020), pp. 573–87, here 578–9. This is a stretch. For a discussion of the gendered and patricidal origins of BISA see chapter 11.

92. Butterfield, 'How Far and Should the Subject of International Relations'.

93. Butterfield, 'How Far and Should the Subject of International Relations', p. 2.

94. Butterfield, 'How Far and Should the Subject of International Relations', p. 2.

95. Goodwin, 'Teaching of International Relations', p. 113.

96. Quoted in Haslam, *The Vices of Integrity*, p. 253.

97. Hall, *Dilemmas of Decline*, p. 9.

98. Alan James, 'Preface' in Alan James (ed.), *The Bases of International Order: Essays in Honour of C.A.W. Manning* (London: Oxford University Press, 1973), pp. vi–viii, here viii.

99. Quoted in Morgan, 'International Relations', p. 2.

100. C.A.W. Manning, 'Report of the General Rapporteur' in Goodwin (ed.), *The University Teaching of International Relations*, pp. 27–73, here 70, emphasis added. Also see C.A.W. Manning, *The University Teaching of the Social Sciences: International Relations* (Paris: UNESCO, 1954). Barbara Wootton was not impressed with Manning's survey of IR teaching for UNESCO, nor those on political science: 'it is far from clear just what purpose this whole series of reports is intended to serve . . . One may perhaps suspect that the material provided in the national reports was rather thin, so that in the preparation of these commentaries the authors found themselves obliged to make bricks from a very poor supply of straw'. Barbara Wootton, 'The University Teaching of Social Sciences: Political Science (Robson); International Relations (Manning) (Book Review)', *The Political Quarterly*, vol. 26 (1955), p. 80. Also see C.A.W. Manning, 'The Teaching of International Relations', *The Listener* , vol. 51 (1954), p. 1317; C.A.W. Manning, 'The Teaching of International Relations', *Political Studies*, vol. 3, no. 1 (1955), pp. 75–7.

101. Manning, 'Report of the General Rapporteur', p. 29.

102. Malinowski, *Argonauts of the Western Pacific*.

103. C.A.W. Manning, *The Nature of International Society* (London: G. Bell and Sons, 1962), pp. 204–5.

104. Manning, *Nature of International Society*, pp. 204–5.

105. On Manning's 'interpretive' approach see Patrick Thaddeus Jackson, 'The Dangers of Interpretation: C.A.W. Manning and the "going Concern" of International Society', *Journal of International Political Theory*, vol. 16, no. 2 (2020), pp. 133–52.

106. Charles A. W. Manning, 'South Africa and the World: In Defense of Apartheid', *Foreign Affairs*, vol. 43 (1964), pp. 135–49, here 141.

107. Manning 'South Africa', p. 141.

108. Manning 'South Africa', p. 142.

109. Manning 'South Africa', p. 141.

110. Manning 'South Africa', pp. 147, 141. According to Jackson, Manning's 'interpretivist' methodology was problematic in relation to his theory of apartheid because apartheid itself is 'actively contested' but was 'relatively unproblematic in the case of international society' because the notion of a society of states is 'widely shared'. Jackson, 'The Dangers of Interpretation', p. 136.

111. Aalberts reads Manning as a proto-constructivist as his 'added value' to the 'English School' but makes no mention of his writing on South Africa nor his lifelong support for apartheid, as if the South African project had nothing to do with his international theory, or British IR more generally. Tanja E. Aalberts, 'Playing the Game of Sovereign States: Charles Manning's Constructivism Avant-la-lettre', *European Journal of International Relations*, vol. 16, no. 2 (2010), pp. 247–68. As Suganami has put it, in an otherwise sympathetic reading, 'there are some worrying linkages between his stance on South Africa and his views about international society'. Hidemi Suganami, 'C. A. W. Manning and the Study of International Relations', *Review of International Studies*, vol. 27, no. 1 (2001), pp. 91–107, here 105.

112. Schwarzenberger, *Power Politics*, p. 9. See also Georg Schwarzenberger, 'The Study of International Relations', *Year Book of World Affairs*, vol. 3 (1949).

113. Schwarzenberger, *Power Politics*, p. 8.

114. Manning, *The University Teaching of the Social Sciences*, p. 84.

115. Goodwin, 'Teaching of International Relations', p. 126.

116. Schwarzenberger, *Power Politics*, p. 6.

117. Schwarzenberger, *Power Politics*, pp. 185–7.

118. Peter Lyon, 'Obituary: Professor Geoffrey Goodwin', *The Independent* (May 8, 1995).

119. Goodwin, 'Teaching of International Relations', p. 118.

120. Goodwin, 'Teaching of International Relations', p. 118, first emphasis added.

121. Manning, 'Metadiplomatics', p. 163. Alan James, 'Manning, Charles Anthony Woodward (1894–1978)', *Oxford Dictionary of National Biography* (September 23, 2004).

122. Goodwin, 'Teaching of International Relations', p. 118.

123. There were nevertheless some women teaching for the IR Department. After Lilian Knowles's premature death from cancer in 1926, her student, Vera Anstey, taught 'Economic Development of the Overseas Dominions, India and the Tropical Dependencies' for the next decade and, from 1938 until 1950, 'Economic Development of the British Empire'. An economic historian of imperial India, Anstey also tutored IR Department students, though not as a permanent faculty member. See Vera Anstey, *The Trade of the Indian Ocean* (London: Longmans, Green and Co., 1929); Vera Anstey, *The Economic Development of India* (London: Longmans, Green, 4th edn, 1952). During World War II, the prominent feminist campaigner and broadcaster, Mary Stocks, taught LSE evening classes on the 'Political Position of the Great Powers'. From 1950 until the end of the 1960s, international historian and specialist on Malta's history as a British colony, Hilda Lee, co-taught 'Diplomatic Relations of the Great Powers since 1815', as a special subject of IR, as well as international history courses in 'The Mediterranean in International Politics, 1815–1914' and 'The Great Powers and Egypt, 1882–1888' up to the middle of the 1970s. Hilda I. Lee, *The Development of the Malta Constitution 1813–1849* (Valletta: Malta Historical Society, 1952); Hilda I. Lee, *Malta 1813–1914: A Study in Constitutional and Strategic Development* (Valletta, Malta Historical Society, 1973). The Department of International History at LSE was founded in 1954.

124. James (ed.), *The Bases of International Order: Essays in Honour of C.A.W. Manning*.

125. Dunne, *Inventing International Society*; Bauer and Brighi (eds.), *International Relations at LSE*.

126. Aalberts, 'Playing the Game of Sovereign States, p. 248.

127. Northedge, 'In Memoriam', p. 3.


## 5. Power's World: International Relations as World Social and Economic History

1. Eileen Power, 'The Teaching of History and World Peace' in F. S. Marvin (ed.), *The Evolution of World Peace* (Oxford, 1921), p. 179. *Vivandière*: French for women attached to military regiments as sutlers or canteen keepers.

2. J. H. Clapham, 'Eileen Power, 1889–1940', *Economica*, vol. 7, no. 28 (1940), pp. 351–9, here 356.

3. R. H. Tawney and Eileen Power, *Tudor Economic Documents: Being Select Documents Illustrating the Economic and Social History of Tudor England* (London: Longmans, Green and Co., 1924); see Maxine Berg, 'The First Women Economic Historians', *The Economic History Review*, vol. 45, no. 2 (1992), pp. 308–29.

4. See, for example, her posthumously published international and cross-disciplinary collaboration, J. H. Clapham and Eileen Power, *The Cambridge Economic History of Europe from the Decline of the Roman Empire. Vol. 1, The Agrarian Life of the Middle Ages* (Cambridge: Cambridge University Press, 1941).

5. Eileen Power, 'A Foreword on the Teaching of History', *A Bibliography for School Teachers of History, Edited, With a Foreword on the Teaching of History* (London: Methuen, 2nd edn, 1921), p. 7.

6. M. G. Jones, 'Memories of Eileen Power', *Girton Review*, vol. 114 (1940), pp. 3–13 (unnumbered pages).

7. Maxine Berg, *Woman in History: Eileen Power, 1889–1940* (Cambridge: Cambridge University Press, 1996), pp. 4, 180.

8. G. G. Coulton, 'Memories of Eileen Power', *The Cambridge Review*, vol. 52 (October 18, 1940), p. 29. GBR/0271/GCPP Power, E 1/8, Girton College.

9. Cf. Chika Tonooka, 'World History's Eurocentric Moment? British Internationalism in the Age of Asian Nationalism, c.1905–1931', *Modern Intellectual History*, vol. 18, no. 1 (2021), pp. 95–120.

10. A. B. McKillop, *The Spinster and the Prophet: A Tale of H.G. Wells, Plagiarism and the History of the World* (London: Aurum, 2001).

11. Berg, *Woman in History*, p. 155.

12. Brian Porter, 'A Brief History Continued, 1972–2022' in Harry Bauer and Elisabetta Brighi, *International Relations at the LSE: A History of 75 Years* (London: Millennium, 2003), pp. 29–44, here 32.

13. David Long, 'C. A. W. Manning and the Discipline of International Relations', *Round Table*, vol. 94, no. 378 (2005), pp. 77–96, here 77–8.

14. 'On 21 March 1939 he married Marion (Maisie) Somerville Johnston (1898/9–1977), daughter of John Bell Johnston, a farmer; she was a student of Manning, who looked after him solicitously . . . They had no children'. Alan James, 'Manning, Charles Anthony Woodward (1894–1978)', *Oxford Dictionary of National Biography* (September 23, 2004). Charles Manning, staff file, LSE.

15. Marion Somerville Johnston, Student Dossier, LSE.

16. LSE biologist and statistician Lancelot Hobgen thought Power 'an exceptionally charming woman, though intellectually far less gifted than her second-in-command'. Quoted in Ralf Dahrendorf, *LSE: A History of the London School of Economics and Political Science, 1895–1995* (Oxford: Oxford University Press, 1995), p. 261.

17. F. S. Northedge, 'In Memoriam: Charles Manning 1894–1978', *British Journal of International Studies*, vol. 5, no. 1 (1979), pp. 1–5, here p. 5.

18. Francesca Wade, *Square Haunting: Five Women, Freedom and London between the Wars* (London: Faber, 2020), p. 243.

19. Eileen Power, 'The Teaching of History and World Peace' in F. S. Marvin (ed.), *Evolution of World-Peace* (Oxford: Oxford University Press, 1921). Other authors included Arnold Toynbee, G. P. Gooch, and H. G. Wells.

20. Quincy Wright, 'International Affairs: The Kyoto Conference of the Institute of Pacific Relations', *The American Political Science Review*, vol. 24, no. 2 (1930), pp. 451–7.

21. Dahrendorf, *LSE*, p. 233.

22. Coulton, 'Memories of Eileen Power', p. 28.

23. Jones, 'Memories of Eileen Power', p. 7. Power to Coulton, September 5, 1925. Quoted in Berg, *Woman in History*, p. 108.

24. Whitney Walton, 'Making Internationalists? The Albert Kahn Around-the-World Scholars' Reports on France and the United States, 1898–1930' in *Internationalism, National Identities, and Study Abroad* (Stanford: Stanford University Press, 2009), chapter 2.

25. Trond Bjorli and Kjetil Ansgar Jakobsen (eds.), *Cosmopolitics of the Camera: Albert Kahn's Archives of the Planet* (Bristol: Intellect, 2020).

26. Erez Manela, *The Wilsonian Moment: Self-Determination and the International Origins of Anticolonial Nationalism* (Oxford: Oxford University Press, 2007).

27. Eileen Power, *Report to the Trustees September 1920–September 1921, Albert Kahn Fellowship* (London: University of London, 1921), p. 42.

28. Power, *Report to the Trustees*, p. 29.

29. Billie Melman, 'Under the Western Historian's Eyes: Eileen Power and the Early Feminist Encounter with Colonialism', *History Workshop Journal*, vol. 42 (1996), pp. 147–168; also see

Billie Melman, *Women's Orients: English Women and the Middle East, 1718–1918: Sexuality, Religion and Work* (Basingstoke: Macmillan, 1992).

30. Power, *Report to the Trustees*. There is a small secondary literature on Power's Asian journeys. See Berg, *Woman in History*, chapter 4; Ellen Jacobs, 'Eileen Power's Asian journey, 1920–21: History, Narrative, and Subjectivity', *Women's History Review*, vol. 7, no. 3 (1998), pp. 295–319; Melman, 'Under the Western Historian's Eyes'.

31. Eileen Power to Lilian Knowles, April 3, 1921. Power personal file, LSE. Also see Eileen Power, 'Professor Lilian Knowles', *Girton Review*, vol. 72 (1926), pp. 3–6.

32. Power, *Report to the Trustees*, p. 32.

33. Power, *Report to the Trustees*, p. 32.

34. Power, *Report to the Trustees*, p. 43.

35. Power, *Report to the Trustees*, p. 34.

36. Power, *Report to the Trustees*, pp. 35, 34.

37. Power, *Report to the Trustees*, p. 35.

38. Power, *Report to the Trustees*, p. 33.

39. Power, *Report to the Trustees*, p. 33.

40. Power, *Report to the Trustees*, p. 36.

41. Power, *Report to the Trustees*, p. 34.

42. Power, *Report to the Trustees*, p. 59.

43. Power, *Report to the Trustees*, pp. 58–59.

44. Power, *Report to the Trustees*, p. 59.

45. Power, *Report to the Trustees*, pp. 59, 58.

46. Power, *Report to the Trustees*, p. 58.

47. Power, *Report to the Trustees*, p. 58.

48. Power, *Report to the Trustees*, p. 60.

49. Power, *Report to the Trustees*, pp. 59–60.

50. Power, *Report to the Trustees*, p. 60.

51. Power, *Report to the Trustees*, p. 60.

52. Power, *Report to the Trustees*, p. 60.

53. Power, 'Europe and the East. Introduction. 1932', p. 3. Add. 8961, 17/1/2. Papers of Eileen Power, Cambridge University.

54. Power, *Report to the Trustees*, p. 60.

55. Power, *Report to the Trustees*, p. 49.

56. Power, *Report to the Trustees*, pp. 52, 49.

57. Power, *Report to the Trustees*, p. 52.

58. Power, *Report to the Trustees*, p. 62.

59. Power, *Report to the Trustees*, pp. 59, 56, 49.

60. Power, *Report to the Trustees*, p. 62.

61. Power, *Report to the Trustees*, p. 20. John M. Ganim, *Medievalism and Orientalism: Three Essays on Literature, Architecture, and Cultural Identity* (New York: Palgrave Macmillan, 2005); Kathleen Davis and Nadia Altschul (eds.), *Medievalisms in the Postcolonial World: The Idea of 'the Middle Ages' outside Europe* (Baltimore: Johns Hopkins University Press, 2009).

62. Cf. Glenda Sluga, 'From F. Melian Stawell to Emily Greene Balch', in Patricia Owens and Katharina Rietzler (eds.), *Women's International Thought: Towards a New History* (Cambridge: Cambridge University Press, 2021), pp. 223–43.

63. Eileen Power, 'A Plea for the Middle Ages', *Economica*, vol. 5 (1922), pp. 173–80, here 173, 174.

64. Power, 'A Plea for the Middle Ages', p. 179.

65. Power, 'A Plea for the Middle Ages', p. 179. For a discussion of the influence of Hellenism on early international thinking see Jeanne Morefield, *Covenants without Swords: Idealist Liberalism and the Spirit of Empire* (Princeton: Princeton University Press, 2009).

66. Power, 'A Plea for the Middle Ages', p. 178.

67. Power, 'A Plea for the Middle Ages', p. 180.

68. Power, 'A Plea for the Middle Ages', p. 180.

69. Power, 'A Plea for the Middle Ages', p. 174.

70. Power, 'A Plea for the Middle Ages', p. 179.

71. Power, 'A Plea for the Middle Ages', p. 177.

72. Power, 'A Plea for the Middle Ages', p. 176.

73. Power, 'A Plea for the Middle Ages', pp. 176–7.

74. Power, 'A Plea for the Middle Ages', p. 176.

75. Power, 'A Plea for the Middle Ages', p. 179.

76. Power, 'A Plea for the Middle Ages', pp. 179–80.

77. Power, 'History of the Modern World (West)', Add. 8961, 17/1/1. Papers of Eileen Power, Cambridge University.

78. Power, *Report to the Trustees*, p. 14.

79. Eileen Power to G. G. Coulton, March 20, 1921, p. 3. GBR/0271/GCPP Power, E 2/2. Girton College.

80. Power, *Report to the Trustees,* p. 6.

81. Power, *Report to the Trustees,* p. 12.

82. Power, *Report to the Trustees,* p. 11.

83. Power, *Report to the Trustees,* p. 27.

84. Eileen Power, 'The Trouble in India', *Foreign Affairs,* vol. 1 (March 1922), pp. 183–5, here 183.

85. Eileen Power to G. G. Coulton, March 20, 1921, p. 3.

86. Power, *Report to the Trustees,* p. 7.

87. Power, *Report to the Trustees*, pp. 19–20. Also see Power, 'Introduction to the Study of World History', p. 9, Add. 8961, Box 17, 17/1/14. Papers of Eileen Power, Cambridge University.

88. Power, *Report to the Trustees*, p. 20. Also see Sir Henry Sumner Maine, *Village-Communities in the East and West* (London: John Murray, 1876).

89. Eileen Power, 'Mahatma Gandhi's Boycott: Another View', Add. 8961', 4/4/4. Papers of Eileen Power, Cambridge University.

90. Power, 'The Trouble in India', p. 184.

91. Power, 'The Trouble in India', p. 184.

92. Eileen Power to G. G. Coulton, March 20, 1921, p. 1.

93. Power, 'A Foreword on the Teaching of History', p. 46. Yet the model schoolbook on imperial history had 'yet to be written'; existing works continued to display 'the pride of acquisition . . . rather than a sense of responsibility and pride in the development of a commonwealth of nations'. Ibid., p. 45. Among the books listed under 'more detailed work' (for the teacher) is Lionel Curtis (ed.), *The Commonwealth of Nations, Part I* (London: Macmillan, 1916).

94. Power, 'The Trouble in India', p. 185.

95. Eileen Power, 'Present Political Situation in British India', Lecture in Batavia 1921, p. 6. Add. 8961, 4/4/5. Papers of Eileen Power, Cambridge University.

96. Power, 'The Trouble in India', p. 185; also see Eileen Power to G. G. Coulton, March 20, 1921.

97. Power, 'The Trouble in India', p. 184.

98. Power, 'The Trouble in India', p. 184.

99. Power, *Report to the Trustees*, pp. 42, 47.

100. Power, 'Mahatma Gandhi's Boycott'.

101. Eileen Power to G. G. Coulton, March 20, 1921, p. 2.

102. Power, *Report to the Trustees*, pp. 30, 31, 20. On Tagore and international relations see Liane Hartnett, 'Love is Worldmaking: Reading Rabindranath Tagore's *Gora* as International Theory', *International Studies Quarterly*, vol. 66, no. 3 (2022), sqac037.

103. Power, *Report to the Trustees*, p. 62.

104. Berg, *Woman in History*, p. 86.

105. Susan M. Parkes, 'Trinity College, Dublin and the "Steamboat Ladies", 1904–1907' in Mary R. Masson and Deborah Simonton (eds.), *Women and Higher Education: Past, Present and Future* (Aberdeen: Aberdeen University Press, 1996), pp. 244–50.

106. C. M. Knowles, 'Professor Lilian Knowles, 1870–1926', in C. M. Knowles and L.C.A. Knowles, *The Economic Development of the British Overseas Empire*, vol. 2, (London: Routledge & Kegan Paul, 1930), pp. vii–xxii, here xv.

107. L.C.A. Knowles, *Economic Development in the Nineteenth Century: France, Germany, Russia and the United States* (London: Routledge & Kegan Paul, 1932).

108. Eveline M. Burns quoted in Berg, *Woman in History*, p. 145. She was 'one of the few female academics of her generation with a child'. Ibid.

109. Maxine Berg, 'The First Women Economic Historians', *The Economic History Review*, vol. 45, no. 2 (1992), pp. 308–29, here 316.

110. Eileen Power to G. G. Coulton, March 20, 1921, p. 3.

111. Eileen Power to Margery Spring Rice, July 31, 1921. GBR/0271/GCPP Power, E 2/1/5. Girton College; for an account see Sarah Watling, 'The Gender Riots that Rocked Cambridge University in the 1920s', *OUPBlog*, July 4, 2019. Available at https://blog.oup.com/2019/07/gender-riots-rocked-cambridge-university-1920s/. Women were not recognised as full members of the university until 1948. Power one day hoped to become the head of one of the women's colleges and 'two kinds of experience are better than one'. Eileen Power to G. G. Coulton, March 20, 2021, p. 4.

112. Eileen Power, 'On Medieval History as a Social Study', *Economica*, vol. 1 no. 1 (1934), pp. 13–29, here 16.

113. Natalie Zemon Davis, 'Women and the World of the *Annales*', *Traces: Journal of Human Sciences*, vol. 32 (May 20, 2017). http://journals.openedition.org/traces/6902.

114. Berg, *Woman in History*, p. 208; also see Lynn Hunt, 'French History in the Last Twenty Years: the Rise and Fall of the *Annales* Paradigm', *Journal of Contemporary History*, vol. 21, no. 2 (1986), pp. 209–224.

115. Maxine Berg, 'East–West Dialogues: Economic Historians, the Cold War, and Détente', *The Journal of Modern History*, vol. 87, no.1 (2015), pp. 36–71, here 45.

116. Fernand Braudel, *La Méditerranée et le monde méditerranéen à l'époque de Philippe II* (Paris: Colin, 1949).

117. Berg, *Woman in History*, p. 251. Those who 'bring in' world and now 'global' history today can mention Power's male contemporaries but never see themselves as heirs to Eileen Power. Barry Buzan and Richard Little, *International Systems in World History: Remaking the Study of International Relations* (Oxford: Oxford University Press, 2000), pp. 30–31; George Lawson, 'International Relations as Historical Social Science' in Andreas Gofas and Inanna Hamati-Ataya, and Nick Onuf (eds.), *The SAGE Handbook of the History, Philosophy and Sociology of International Relations* (London: Sage, 2018), pp. 75–89. Historians are more likely to pursue transnational labour and working-class histories. See, for example, the Berghahn series, 'International Studies in Social History' and Brill's series, 'Global Social History'.

118. Eileen Power, *Medieval People* (London: Methuen, 10th edn, 1963), p. 18.

119. Power, *Medieval People*, p. 18.

120. Power, 'A Foreword on the Teaching of History', p. 9.

121. Bonnie G. Smith, *The Gender of History: Men, Women, and Historical Practice* (Cambridge, MA: Harvard University Press, 1998), p. 1.

122. Power, 'On Medieval History as a Social Study', p. 15.

123. Power, 'On Medieval History as a Social Study', pp. 23, 22.

124. Eileen Power, 'The Position of Women' in Charles G. Crump, and E. F. Jacob (eds.), *The Legacy of the Middle Ages* (Oxford: Clarendon, 1926), pp. 401–35.

125. Smith, *The Gender of History*.

126. Berg, *Woman in History*, p. 253.

127. Coulton, 'Memories of Eileen Power', p. 28. Eileen Power, *Medieval English Nunneries: c.1275 to 1535* (Cambridge: Cambridge University Press 1922). At least Power knew about what happened in nunneries. According to Hedley Bull, in 'abstaining' from intuition, history and philosophy, practitioners of the positivist scientific approach to international relations 'are committing themselves to a course of intellectual pluralism that keeps them . . . as remote from the substance of international politics as the inmates of a Victorian nunnery from the study of sex'. Hedley Bull, 'International Theory: The Case for a Classical Approach', *World Politics*, vol. 18, no. 3 (1966), pp. 361–77, here 366. For a more accurate study of sexual exploration in convents see Rosemary Curb and Manahan Nancy, *Breaking Silence: Lesbian Nuns on Convent Sexuality* (London: Columbus, 1985).

128. See Cynthia Enloe's classic, *Bananas, Beaches and Bases: Making Feminist Sense of International Politics* (Berkeley: University of California Press, 2nd rev. edn, 2014).

129. Power, *Medieval People*, p. 19.

130. Wade, *Square Haunting*, p. 228.

131. Power, 'On Medieval History as a Social Study', p. 18.

132. Power, 'On Medieval History as a Social Study', pp. 17, 23.

133. Werner Sombart, *Der Moderne Kapitalismus* (Leipzig: Duncker & Humblot, 1902).

134. Power, 'On Medieval History as a Social Study', p. 25.

135. Power, 'On Medieval History as a Social Study', p. 20. She praised Belgian medieval historian Henri Pirenne's alternative attempt to identify within each period of economic history their different classes of capitalists. Henri Pirenne, 'The Stages in the Social History of Capitalism', *The American Historical Review*, vol. 19, no. 3 (1914), pp. 494–515.

136. Eileen Power, *The Wool Trade in English Medieval History: Being the Ford Lectures* (London: Oxford University Press, 1941), p. 2.

137. Power, 'On Medieval History as a Social Study', p. 20.

138. Power, 'On Medieval History as a Social Study', p. 20.

139. Power, 'On Medieval History as a Social Study', p. 14.

140. Power, 'On Medieval History as a Social Study', p. 22.

141. Power, 'On Medieval History as a Social Study', p. 21.

142. Power, 'On Medieval History as a Social Study', p. 22.

143. Eileen Power, 'The Marxian Interpretation of History'. Add. 8961, 13/1/6. Papers of Eileen Power, Cambridge University.

144. Power, 'On Medieval History as a Social Study', pp. 22, 21.

145. Eileen Power, 'The Study of Social History', n.d. Add. 8961, 13/1/6, Part 2. Papers of Eileen Power, Cambridge University.

146. Power, 'On Medieval History as a Social Study', pp. 24, 23.

147. Power, 'On Medieval History as a Social Study', p. 26.

148. Power, 'On Medieval History as a Social Study', p. 21.

149. Power, 'On Medieval History as a Social Study', p. 21.

150. Eileen Power, 'The Study of Social History'.

151. H. G. Wells, *The Outline of History* (London: Macmillan, 1920); Arnold Toynbee, *A Study of History* (Oxford: Oxford University Press, 1934–61).

152. William T. Ross. *H.G. Wells's World Reborn: The Outline of History and Its Companions* (London: Susquehanna University Press, 2002), p. 26; Berg, *Woman in History*, pp. 225–6.

153. A. B. McKillop, *The Spinster and the Prophet: A Tale of H.G. Wells, Plagiarism and the History of the World* (London: Aurum, 2001).

154. Berg, *Woman in History*, p. 235.

155. Ayşe Zarakol, *Before the West: The Rise and Fall of Eastern World Orders* (Cambridge: Cambridge University Press, 2022), p. 10. Emphasis in original.

156. Catherine Holmes and Naomi Standen, 'Introduction: Towards a Global Middle Ages', *Past & Present*, vol. 238 (2018), pp. 1–44. This work should be distinguished from 1990s work in IR on the 'new medievalism' allegedly caused by 'globalisation' and the fragmentation of political authority after the end of the Cold War. Ronald J. Deibert, 'Exorcismus Theoriae: Pragmatism, Metaphors and the Return to the Medieval in IR Theory', *European Journal of International Relations*, vol. 3, no. 2 (1997), pp. 167–92.

157. Eileen Power, 'Peasant Life and Rural Conditions (c. 1100–c. 1500)' in J. R. Tanner et al (eds.), *Cambridge Medieval History*, vol. 7 (Cambridge: Cambridge University Press,1932), pp. 716–40.

158. Power, 'A Foreword on the Teaching of History', p. 7.

159. Power, 'On Medieval History as a Social Study', p. 21.

160. Eileen Power, 'Introduction to the Study of World History', p. 1.

161. Eileen Power, 'Europe and the East. Introduction. 1932', p. 1.

162. Power, 'Introduction to the Study of World History', pp. 5–6.

163. Power, 'Introduction to the Study of World History', p. 2.

164. Power, 'A Foreword on the Teaching of History', pp. 7–8.

165. Power, 'Introduction to the Study of World History', pp. 5–6; also see Power, 'A Foreword on the Teaching of History', p. 12.

166. Power, 'A Foreword on the Teaching of History', p. 11.

167. Power, 'Introduction to the Study of World History', p. 5.

168. Eileen Power, 'The Opening of the Land Routes to Cathay' in Arthur Percival Newton (ed.), *Travel and Travellers of the Middle Ages* (London: Kegan Paul, 1926), pp. 124–158, here 158; Power, 'Europe and the East. Introduction. 1932', pp. 6–7.

169. Power, *Medieval People*, pp. 25, 31.

170. Power, 'Europe and the East. Introduction. 1932', pp. 6–7; Power, 'The Opening of the Land Routes to Cathay', p. 158.

171. Power, BBC Broadcast 'For Monday 26th June, 1933 at 2.30-2.55 p.m.', p. 5. Add. 8961, B/1/2-27. Papers of Eileen Power, Cambridge University.

172. Power, *Report to the Trustees*, p. 60.

173. Power, 'The Moslem World', n.d. p. 6. Add. 8961, 17/1/2. Papers of Eileen Power, Cambridge University.

174. Power, 'The Moslem World', p. 2.

175. Power, 'The Moslem World', p. 14.

176. Power, 'Introduction to the Study of World History', pp. 6–7. John M. Hobson *Multicultural Origins of the Global Economy: Beyond the Western-Centric Frontier* (Cambridge: Cambridge University Press, 2021).

177. Power, 'Europe and the East', p. 10.

178. Power, 'Europe and the East. Introduction. 1932', p. 3.

179. Power, 'History of the Modern World (West). I. The New World'.

180. Power, 'History of the Modern World (West)'.

181. Power, 'European History to 1848 (General)', Add. 8961, Box 17, 17/1/3. Papers of Eileen Power, Cambridge University.

182. Power, 'Europe and the East', p. 8.

183. Power, 'Europe and the East'.

184. Kenneth Pomeranz, *The Great Divergence* (Princeton: Princeton University Press, 2009).

185. Robert Vitalis, *White World Order, Black Power Politics: The Birth of American International Relations* (Ithaca: Cornell University Press, 2015), p. 17.

186. Joseph Barnes (ed.), *Empire in the East* (New York: Doubleday, 1934). Contributors included Pearl S. Buck, Owen Lattimore, Grover Clark, and Tyler Dennett.

187. Eileen Power, 'Review of *Empire in the East*, by J. Barnes', *Pacific Affairs*, vol. 7, no. 4, (1934) pp. 447–9, here 448.

188. Power, 'Europe and the East. Introduction. 1932', p. 4.

189. E. R. Hughes, 'Editors Preface' and Eileen Power, 'The Little God', *China: Body and Soul* (London: Secker and Warburg, 1938), pp. 7 and 107–15.

190. Eileen Power, 'Geneva Impressions', *The Spectator* (December 22, 1939), pp. 892–3.

191. Power, 'Geneva Impressions', p. 893.

192. Eileen Power, 'The Precursors' in *Medieval People*, p. 14.

193. Power, 'The Precursors', p. 14.

194. Michael Postan, 'Preface to the Tenth Edition', Eileen Power, *Medieval People*, p. ix.

195. Power, 'The Precursors', p. 16.

196. Power, 'The Precursors', pp. 3, 14.

197. Power, 'The Precursors', p. 16.

198. Power, 'The Precursors', p. 16.

199. Power, 'The Precursors', pp. 14–15.

200. Geoffrey L Goodwin, 'Teaching of International Relations in Universities in the United Kingdom', in Geoffrey L. Goodwin (ed.), *The University Teaching of International Relations* (Oxford: Blackwell, 1951), p. 118.

201. Tim Dunne, *Inventing International Society: A History of the English School* (London: Macmillan, 1998). The argument about the intellectual forebears of the so-called English School or 'classical approach' is distinguished from Blanchard's call for so-called 'English School' scholars to use gender as a category to analyse 'international society'. Eric M. Blanchard, 'Why Is There No Gender in the English School?' *Review of International Studies*, vol. 37, no. 2 (2011), pp. 855–79.

202. Goodwin, 'Teaching of International Relations', pp. 124, 126.

203. Lucian M. Ashworth, *A History of International Thought: From the Origins of the Modern State to Academic International Relations* (London: Routledge, 2014), p. 270. 'IR in the first half of the twentieth century *was* IPE. In short, the [post-1945] trend to limit IR to politics and security . . . cut out the predominantly politico-economic interpretation of the international that had been part of international thought since the mid-nineteenth century. This gap was later to be filled by the establishment of IPE, which was developed to fill and intellectual space that IR had dramatically abandoned'. Ibid., p. 254.

204. Goodwin, 'Teaching of International Relations', pp. 118–19. In Manning's formulation, 'in the sense in which Economics, though dependent on, is yet distinct from, Economic History, International Relations is as independent of International History as it is of International Law'. Manning, 'International Relations: an Academic Discipline', p. 17

205. Berg, *Woman in History*, p. 155.

206. Joanna Russ, *How to Suppress Women's Writing* (Austin: University of Texas, 1983), p. 101.

## 6. Oxford's Failure: From Diplomatic History to Critical Histories of International Relations

1. Susan Strange, 'Research Institutions in International Relations in the United Kingdom', *International Social Science Bulletin (UNESCO)*, vol. 1 (1950), pp. 62–79, here 62.

2. Martin Wight to Mr Ferris, November 16, 1961. WIGHT/233/14. LSE Library.

3. Martin Wight to Mr Ferris, November 16, 1961.

4. Agatha Ramm, *The Risorgimento* (London: Routledge & Kegan Paul, 1962); Agatha Ramm, *Germany, 1789–1919: A Political History* (London: Methuen 1967); Agatha Ramm, *Sir Robert Morier: Envoy and Ambassador in the Age of Imperialism, 1876–1893* (Oxford: Clarendon

Press 1973); Agatha Ramm, *Grant and Temperley's Europe in the Nineteenth and Twentieth Centuries, Vol.1, Europe in the Nineteenth Century, 1789–1905* (London: Longman, rev. and rewritten 7th edn, 1984).

5. S. E. Crowe, 'Dear Madam', April 30, 1935. Letter in application for the Amelia Gurney Scholarship. Girton College Archive, S. E. Crowe file. GCAC 2/4/1/4.

6. Sybil Crowe to Nita Watts, June 23, 1975. FA 9/2/219. St Hilda's College.

7. Sibyl Crowe interview with Jill Hosford Pellew, October 11, 1989, SA 1A20. St Hilda's College.

8. Remarks by Barbara Levick, Fellow of St Hilda's College, at commemorative reception at St Hilda's, November 22, 1993, p. 2. FA 9/2/219. St Hilda's College.

9. Remarks by Barbara Levick, p. 1.

10. Mary Bennett, 'Sibyl Eyre Crowe', *St Hilda's College Report and Chronicle, 1992–1993, Centenary Edition*, pp. 101–3, here 101.

11. Bennett, 'Sibyl Eyre Crowe', p. 102. Among Crowe's tasks for Perham was to find quotations from colonial government officials in the late 1930s to the effect that 'native policy' was intended for 'the advancement of the natives' and research for Perham's comparative studies of empire. 'Official Policy 1: Notes by Sibyl Crowe' 1919–1939. MSS Perham 683, 7. 'Other Empires 8, French 1, Notes by Sibyl Crowe, 1946'. MSS Perham 674, 7.

12. Sybil Crowe, report on initial period of office as university lecturer, January 10, 1969. Sibyl Crowe file, Bodleian Library.

13. Sibyl E. Crowe, *The Berlin West African Conference, 1884–1885* (London: Longmans Green 1942); W. P. Morrell, *History*, vol. 28, no. 108 (1943) pp. 222–3.

14. Barbara D. Savage, 'Professor Merze Tate: Diplomatic Historian, Cosmopolitan Woman', in Mia Bay, Farah J. Griffin, Martha S. Jones and Barbara D. Savage, eds., *Toward an Intellectual History of Black Women* (Chapel Hill: University of North Carolina Press, 2015), pp. 252–69, here 256.

15. Tate to Grace E. Hadow, June 15, 1934. Merze Tate file, St Anne's College.

16. Tate to Hadow, August 1, 1934. Merze Tate, Oral History, p. 35, Schlesinger Library on the History of Women in America, Black Women Oral History Project, 1980. Available at https://guides.library.harvard.edu/schlesinger_bwohp/interviews. Transcript provided by Schlesinger Library.

17. Tate, Oral History, pp. 174, 25.

18. Tate to Esther C. Brunauer, April 12, 1932. Merze Tate file.

19. Marion Paton Teperring to Esther C. Brunauer, n.d. Merze Tate file.

20. Tate, Oral History, p. 174.

21. Linda M. Perkins, 'Merze Tate and the Quest for Gender Equity at Howard University: 1942–1977', *History of Education Quarterly*, vol. 54, no. 4 (2014), pp. 516–51.

22. Tate to Esther C. Brunauer, April 12, 1932; Perkins, 'Merze Tate', p. 517.

23. Tate, Oral History, p. 35; Tate to Esther C. Brunauer, April 12, 1932.

24. Barbara D. Savage, 'Beyond Illusions: Imperialism, Race and Technology in Merze Tate's International Thought' in Patricia Owens and Katharina Rietzler (eds.), *Women's International Thought: Towards a New History* (Cambridge: Cambridge University Press, 2021), p. 268; Barbara D. Savage, *Merze Tate: The Global Odyssey of a Black Woman Scholar* (New Haven and London: Yale University Press, 2024), pp. 39–40.

25. Merze Tate, 'The Geneva School of International Relations', *Ivy Leaf Magazine*, vol. 10, no. 1 (March 1932), pp. 35–6, here 35.

26. Tate, Oral History, p. 34.

27. Barbara D. Savage, 'Beyond Illusions', p. 268. For further discussion of the racial politics of the Zimmern School see Patricia Owens and Katharina Rietzler, 'Polyphonic Internationalism: The Lucie Zimmern School of International Studies', *The International History Review*, vol. 45, no. 4 (2023), pp. 623–42; Tate, 'The Geneva School'.

28. Tate, Oral History, pp. 26–27, 35.

29. Tate to Ruth F. Butler, September 4, 1932. Merze Tate file.

30. Esther C. Brunauer to Grace E. Hadow, June 1, 1932. Merze Tate file.

31. Bertha S. Davies to Esther C. Brunauer, April 13, 1932. Merze Tate file.

32. J. W. Hornbeck to Esther C. Brunauer, April 15, 1932. Merze Tate file.

33. Unknown to Esther C. Brunauer, April 12, 1932. Merze Tate file.

34. D. L. Shilling to Esther C. Brunauer, April 13, 1932. Merze Tate file.

35. Tate to Esther C. Brunauer, April 12, 1932.

36. Tate, Oral History, p. 38.

37. Tate, Oral History, p. 62.

38. Tate, Oral History, p. 42.

39. Tate, Oral History, p. 38. African–American Alain Locke had been an undergraduate at Oxford between 1907 and 1910. Tate, Oral History, p. 39. It also bothered Tate when Americans declared that they were 'at Oxford', but never formally part of the university. Tate, Oral History, p. 50.

40. The Society of Oxford Home Students became St Anne's Society in 1942 and St Anne's College in 1952.

41. Tate to Ruth F. Butler, September 4, 1932.

42. Tate, Oral History, pp. 54–5.

43. Tate, Oral History, p. 42.

44. Tate to Ruth F. Butler, September 4, 1932.

45. Tate to Ruth F. Butler, October 11, 1932. Ruth F. Butler was tutor of B.Litt. students. Merze Tate file.

46. 'Merze Tate', n.d. Merze Tate file. Written in Ruth F. Butler's hand.

47. C. Violet Butler to Tate, November 23, 1932. Merze Tate file.

48. C. Violet Butler to Tate, November 23, 1932.

49. 'Merze Tate', n.d.

50. Merze Tate, The United States and Armaments (Cambridge, MA: Harvard University Press, 1948), p. vii.

51. Merze Tate, The Disarmament Illusion: The Movement for a Limitation of Armaments to 1907 (New York: Macmillan, 1942), p. x.

52. Tate, Oral History, p. 38.

53. Tate, Oral History, pp. 39–40.

54. Perkins, 'Merze Tate', p. 518.

55. Tate, Oral History, p. 135.

56. Tate, Oral History, pp. 40–41.

57. Tate, Oral History, p. 48.

58. Tate, Oral History, p. 173.

59. Tate, Oral History, p. 53.

60. Tate, Oral History, p. 179.

61. Tate, Oral History, p. 56.

62. Barbara D. Savage, 'Poster Audio Guide'. Public Exhibition on Women and the History of International Thought, 2022. https://web.archive.org/web/20220705172842/https://www.lse.ac.uk/library/whats-on/exhibitions.

63. Savage, 'Poster Audio Guide'.

64. Tate, Oral History, p. 38.

65. Tate, Oral History, p. 51.

66. Tate to Grace E. Hadow, June 15, 1934. Merze Tate file.

67. Tate, Oral History, p. 38.

68. Minutes of Board of the Faculty of Social Studies Meetings, May 4, 1934, Examiners Appointed, OUA/FA 4/18/2/2, Bodleian Library.

69. Minutes of Board of the Faculty of Social Studies Meetings, May 4, 1934.

70. On accepting the Montague Burton Chair, E. L. Woodward said he would now 'study C. Bronte again but I still maintain that she is not in the L. Carroll or Mark Twain or Charles Dickens, or even in the W. W. Jacobs or P. G. Wodehouse class', as if reading women novelists and asserting their inferiority to men was part of the job description. Quoted in Martin Ceadel, 'The Academic Normalization of International Relations at Oxford, 1920–2012: Structures Transcended' in Christopher Hood, Desmond King, and Gillian Peele (eds.), *Forging a Discipline: A Critical Assessment of Oxford's Development of the Study of Politics and International Relations in Comparative Perspective* (Oxford: Oxford University Press, 2014), pp. 184–202, here 192–3.

71. As Savage notes, one of the leading Black newspapers in the United States, the *Pittsburgh Courier*, announced the award of Tate's degree on June 30, 1934. Savage, *Merze Tate*, p. 62.

72. Tate to Grace E. Hadow, June 19, 1934. Merze Tate file.

73. Tate to Ruth Butler, October 1, 1934. Merze Tate file.

74. Tate, Oral History, p. 173.

75. Tate to Grace E. Hadow, June 15, 1934. When she travelled in India, where she went to lecture on geopolitics, she was also often asked to lecture on African–American struggles 'or something with the race relations'. Tate, Oral History, p. 175.

76. Merze Tate, 'Three Years in England', *Ivy Leaf Magazine*, vol. 14, no. 1 (March 1936), pp. 18–19, 40, here 40.

77. Ruth Butler to Tate, October 12, 1934. Merze Tate file.

78. Handwritten notes, likely Ruth Butler's, on the side of Tate's letter to Butler dated June 20, 1935. Merze Tate file.

79. Tate to Grace E. Hadow, August 1, 1934. Merze Tate file.

80. Tate to Ruth Butler, June 20, 1934. Merze Tate file.

81. Alfred Zimmern to Miss Butler, November 5, 1934. Merze Tate file.

82. 'Report of the Examiners', June 14, 1935, Minutes of Board of the Faculty of Social Studies Meetings, OUA/FA 4/18/2/2, Bodleian Library.

83. Unknown to Merze Tate, November 5, 1934. Merze Tate file.

84. Mary Coate to Ruth Butler, November 16, 1934. Merze Tate file.

85. Mary Healey, quoted in Priscilla West, 'Reminiscences of Seven Decades' in Penny Griffin (ed.), *St Hugh's: One Hundred Years of Women's Education in Oxford* (London: Macmillan, 1986), pp. 62–243, here 129.

86. Quoted in West, 'Reminiscences', p. 110.

87. Quoted in West, 'Reminiscences', p. 109.

88. Quoted in West, 'Reminiscences', pp. 109–10.

89. Agnes Headlam-Morley to Miss Butler, November 5, 1934. Merze Tate file.

90. Agnes Headlam-Morley to Ruth Butler, April 26, 1935. Merze Tate file.

91. Agnes Headlam-Morley to Ruth Butler, April 26, 1935.

92. Unknown, 'Miss Tate Haunts Me', n.d. Merze Tate file.

93. Unknown to Principal, May 12, 1935. Merze Tate file.

94. Grace E. Hadow to Ruth Butler, March 19, 1935. Merze Tate file.

95. Grace E. Hadow to Ruth Butler, March 19, 1935.

96. Tate to Ruth Butler, June 20, 1935. Merze Tate file.

97. Handwritten notes, likely Ruth Butler's, on the side of Merze Tate's letter to Ruth Butler dated June 20, 1935.

98. Unknown, untitled ('Miss Tate has been an'), July 3, 1935. Merze Tate file.

99. 'Report of the Examiners', June 14, 1935, Minutes of Board of the Faculty of Social Studies Meetings.

100. Tate, Oral History, p. 66.

101. Tate, Oral History, p. 69; Savage, 'Beyond Illusions', p. 269.

102. Tate, Oral History, p. 92.

103. Tate to Grace E. Hadow, September 3, 1935. Merze Tate file.

104. Merze Tate, 'A Proposed Social Science Program for Bennett College', *A Quarterly Review of Higher Education Among Negroes*, April 1937; Merze Tate, 'Justification of the Women's College', *Journal of the Association of College Women*, vol. 14 (1937).

105. Tate, Oral History, pp. 92–3.

106. Tate, Oral History, pp. 93–4.

107. Tate, Oral History, p. 95.

108. Tate, Oral History, pp. 97–8.

109. Tate, Oral History, p. 101.

110. Tate, Oral History, pp. 96–97. Merze Tate, *The United States and Armaments* (Cambridge, MA: Harvard University Press, 1948).

111. Savage, 'Beyond Illusions', p. 270.

112. Merze Tate to Alfred Zimmern, August 8, 1941. MSS Zimmern 46, folio 173. Wild's written explanation for not introducing Tate's book, which Tate enclosed with her letter to Zimmern, is missing from the archive.

113. Alfred Zimmern to Tate, September 11, 1941. MSS Zimmern 46, folio 177.

114. Bernice Brown Cronkhite, 'Foreword' in Merze Tate, *The Disarmament Illusion: The Movement for a Limitation of Armaments to 1907* (New York: The Macmillan Company, 1942), pp. vii–viii.

115. Committee on the Bureau of International Research in Harvard University and Radcliffe College, 'Proposal for Foundation for Instruction in International Affairs' and 'Foundation for Instruction in International Affairs' in Patricia Owens, Katharina Rietzler, Kimberly Hutchings and Sarah C, Dunstan (eds.), *Women's International Thought: Towards a New Canon* (Cambridge: Cambridge University Press, 2022), pp. 39–40.

116. Tate, Oral History, p. 115.

117. Joanna Wood, doctoral dissertation in progress, University of Oxford.

118. Tate, *Disarmament Illusion*, p. 351.

119. Tate, *Disarmament Illusion*, pp. 359, 356.

120. Tate, *Disarmament Illusion*, p. 356.

121. Tate, *Disarmament Illusion*, pp. x–xi.

122. Tate, *Disarmament Illusion*, p. 347.

123. Tate, *Disarmament Illusion*, p. x.

124. Tate, *Disarmament Illusion*, p. 346.

125. Tate, *Disarmament Illusion*, p. 346.

126. Tate, *Disarmament Illusion*, p. 12.

127. Tate, *Disarmament Illusion*, pp. x–xi.

128. Charles A. Timm, 'Tate, Merze, *The Disarmament Illusion* (Book Review)', *Southwestern Social Science Quarterly*, vol. 23 (1942), p. 186.

129. Tate, *Disarmament Illusion*, pp. x, ix.

130. William O. Shanahan, 'Tate, Merze, *The Disarmament Illusion* (Book Review)', *Review of Politics*, vol. 5 (1943), p. 388.

131. Timm, 'Tate, Merze, *The Disarmament Illusion*', p. 187.

132. Rayford W. Logan, 'Tate, Merze, The Disarmament Illusion', *The Journal of Negro Education*, vol. 12, no. 1 (1943), pp. 92–3. On the feud between Tate and Logan, including Logan's 'persecution' of Tate in his role as department chair at Howard, see Robert Vitalis, *White World Order, Black Power Politics: The Birth of American International Relations* (Ithaca: Cornell University Press, 2015), pp. 165–6.

133. Hans J. Morgenthau, '*The Disarmament Illusion* by Merze Tate', *The Russian Review*, vol. 2, no. 2 (1943), pp. 104–5, here 105.

134. Morgenthau, 'The Disarmament Illusion by Merze Tate', p. 104.

135. Morgenthau, 'The Disarmament Illusion by Merze Tate', p. 105.

136. Louis Martin Sears, 'Tate, Merze. "The Disarmament Illusion" (Book Review)', *Annals of the American Academy of Political and Social Science*, vol. 224 (1942), pp. 201–2, here 201.

137. Tate, *Disarmament Illusion*, p. 53.

138. Madeleine Herren, 'Gender and International Relations through the Lens of the League of Nations (1919–1945)' in Glenda Sluga and Carolyn James (eds.), *Women, Diplomacy and International Politics since 1500* (New York: Routledge, 2016), pp. 182–201, here 191.

139. W.E.B. Du Bois, 'Scholarly Delusion', *Phylon*, vol. 4, no. 2 (1943), pp. 189–91, here 189–90.

140. Du Bois, 'Scholarly Delusion', p. 191. In 1888, Du Bois had enrolled as an undergraduate at Harvard, receiving his B.A. and M.A. in history and then becoming the first African–American to receive a Harvard Ph.D., also in history.

141. Merze Tate, 'The War Aims of World War I and World War II and Their Relation to the Darker Peoples of the World', *The Journal of Negro Education*, vol. 12, no. 3 (1943), pp. 521–32.

142. Tate, 'Oral History', p. 216.

143. Vitalis, *White World Order, Black Power Politics*, p. 163

144. David Armitage and Alison Bashford (eds.), *Pacific Histories: Ocean, Land, People* (Basingstoke: Palgrave Macmillan, 2014); Robbie Shilliam, *The Black Pacific: Anti-Colonial Struggles and Oceanic Connections* (London: Bloomsbury Academic, 2015).

145. Tate, 'Oral History', p. 179.

146. Tate, 'Oral History', p. 179.

147. Savage, 'Beyond Illusions', pp. 277–80.

148. Tate, 'Oral History', p. 96.

149. On American IR's treatment of Tate and other Black scholars of race and empire at Howard see Vitalis, *White World Order, Black Power Politics*.

150. Radcliffe student records are closed for 80 years, which means her file is not accessible until 2024, after this book went to press.

151. Tate, 'Oral History', p. 99.

152. Tate, 'Oral History', p. 118.

153. Savage, 'Beyond Illusions', p. 269.

154. Tate, *Disarmament Illusion*, p. x.

155. Tate, *Disarmament Illusion*, p. xi.

156. Tate, *United States and Armaments*, p. vii.

157. Grace E. Hadow to Merze Tate, November 9, 1936. Merze Tate file.

158. Tate, 'Oral History', pp. 112, 40.

## 7. The 'Spinsters' and Diplomats' Daughters

1. Agnes Headlam-Morley, 'Book review of A.J.P. Taylor's *The Struggle for Mastery in Europe* and von Kürrenberg's *The Kaiser*', unpublished manuscript, p. 4. HDLM 815/44, Agnes Headlam-Morley papers, Churchill College, Cambridge.

2. Christopher Hill, quoted in Jonathan Haslam, *The Vices of Integrity: E.H. Carr, 1892–1982* (London: Verso, 1999), p. 133.

3. E. L. Woodward to Douglas Veale, May 21, 1948. UR 6/MB/1, file 1. Oxford University Archives, Bodleian Library.

4. Alfred Zimmern to Douglas Veale, May 31, 1948. UR 6/MB/1, file 1.

5. Christopher Hill, quoted in Haslam, *The Vices of Integrity*, p. 133.

6. Martin Ceadel, 'The Academic Normalization of International Relations at Oxford, 1920–2012: Structures Transcended' in Christopher Hood, Desmond King, and Gillian Peele (eds.),

*Forging a Discipline: A Critical Assessment of Oxford's Development of the Study of Politics and International Relations in Comparative Perspective* (Oxford: Oxford University Press, 2014), pp. 184–202, here 193.

7. Carroll Quigley, *The Anglo-American Establishment: From Rhodes to Cliveden* (New York: Books in Focus, 1981), p. 310.

8. Quigley, *The Anglo-American Establishment*, p. 310. According to Quigley, a coterie of public figures and intellectuals centering around Oxford, Chatham House, *The Times*, and the Rhodes Trust (the Milner group) influenced British foreign policy in the first half of the twentieth century. They controlled the Montague Burton Chair and were the decisive influence in the British Coordinating Committee for International Studies.

9. Adam Roberts, 'Morley, Agnes Headlam- (1902–1986)', *Oxford Dictionary of National Biography*, 2004; online edn, May 2006 http://www.oxforddnb.com/view/article/55358.

10. Alan Sharp, 'James Headlam-Morley: Creating International History', *Diplomacy and Statecraft*, vol. 9, no. 3 (1998), pp. 266–283, here 268.

11. Agnes Headlam-Morley, 'Stresemann', in Frank Pakenham Longford, John Wheeler-Bennett, and C. S. Nicholls, *The History Makers: Leaders and Statesmen of the 20th Century* (London: Sidgwick & Jackson, 1973), pp. 197–211, here 198; Ceadel, 'Academic Normalization', p. 189.

12. Quigley, *The Anglo-American Establishment*, p. 310.

13. Alfred Zimmern, 'Headlam-Morley: "The New Democratic Constitutions of Europe" (Book Review)', *Journal of the Royal Institute of International Affairs*, vol. 7, no. 4 (1928), pp. 275–77, here 275.

14. Ceadel, 'Academic Normalization', p. 194.

15. Roberts, 'Morley, Agnes Headlam-'.

16. Ceadel, 'Academic Normalization', p. 192.

17. T. G. Otte, '"Outcast From History": The Fischer Controversy and British Historiography', *Journal of Contemporary History*, vol. 48, no. 2 (2013), pp. 376–96, here here 381–2.

18. Ceadel, 'Academic Normalization', p. 195.

19. A. L. Rowse, *All Souls and Appeasement: A Contribution to Contemporary History* (London: Macmillan, 1961), p. 109.

20. Ceadel, 'Academic Normalization', p. 194.

21. Roberts, 'Morley, Agnes Headlam-'.

22. Roberts, 'Morley, Agnes Headlam-'.

23. Ian Hall, *Dilemmas of Decline: British Intellectuals and World Politics, 1945–1975* (Berkeley: University of California Press, 2012), p. 53.

24. Rachel Trickett, 'Agnes Headlam-Morley', *St Hugh's College Chronicle, 1986–87*, no. 59, pp. 26–32, here 31. This is the text of the address delivered by the principal of St Hugh's at the college memorial service for Agnes Headlam-Morley held on May 17, 1986.

25. Roberts, 'Morley, Agnes Headlam-'

26. Otte '"Outcast From History"' pp. 381–2.

27. Robert Ayson, *Hedley Bull and the Accommodation of Power* (London: Palgrave Macmillan, 2012), p. 21.

28. Roger Morgan, 'International Relations as an Academic Discipline: Outline for a Discussion at Warwick University, 15th October 1970', p. 1. BISA/10. LSE Library.

29. Susan Strange, 'Looking Back—But Mostly Forward', *Millennium: Journal of International Studies*, vol. 11, no. 1 (1982), pp. 38–49, here 40.

30. Ceadel, 'Academic Normalization', p. 196.

31. Ceadel, 'Academic Normalization', pp. 195, 185, 197; Roberts, 'Morley, Agnes Headlam-'; also see Daniel Norman Chester, *Economics, Politics, and Social Studies in Oxford, 1900–85* (London: Macmillan, 1986).

32. Hall, *Dilemmas of Decline*, p. 53.

33. Ceadel, 'Academic Normalization', p. 184.

34. William C. Olson and A. J. R. Groom, *International Relations Then and Now: Origins and Trends in Interpretation* (London: Harper Collins, 1991).

35. W.E.B. Du Bois, 'Scholarly Delusion', *Phylon*, vol. 4, no. 2 (1943), pp. 189–91.

36. Geoffrey L. Goodwin, 'The Teaching of International Relations in Universities in the United Kingdom', in Geoffrey L. Goodwin (ed.), *The University Teaching of International Relations* (Oxford: Blackwell, 1951), p. 118.

37. Joan Wallach Scott, *The Fantasy of Feminist History* (Durham: Duke University Press, 2011), p. 21.

38. Agnes Headlam-Morley, 'Book review of A.J.P. Taylor's *The Struggle for Mastery in Europe* and von Kürrenberg's *The Kaiser*', p. 7.

39. Trickett, 'Agnes Headlam-Morley', p. 31.

40. Agnes Headlam-Morley's papers at the Churchill Archives Centre only received collection-level description in 2021 because of the work of archivist Katharine Thomson.

41. See Adom Getachew's discussion of Wheare in *Worldmaking after Empire: The Rise and Fall of Self-Determination* (Princeton: Princeton University Press, 2019), pp. 122–3, 126–7.

42. Kenneth Wheare to Douglas Veale, May 24, 1948. UR 6/MB/1, file 1, Oxford University Archives, Bodleian Library.

43. Headlam-Morley to Douglas Veale, June 27, 1948. UR 6/MB/1, file 1.

44. Agnes Headlam-Morley, 'Stresemann', p. 198.

45. Trickett, 'Agnes Headlam-Morley', pp. 31, 28. There is a portrait of Headlam-Morley by Robert Lutyens in Mordan Hall, St Hugh's College. 'She sits, with Kittilein (for she loved animals) on her knee, looking tentatively, unresolvedly but in some sense confidently into an indistinct distance'. Ibid., p. 32. She was also a member of the Longford Committee Investigating Pornography, which argued for greater legal controls on pornography. The results were published as Frank Pakenham Longford, *Pornography, the Longford Report* (London: Coronet, 1972).

46. Ingrid Sharp and Matthew Stibbe (eds.), *Women Activists between War and Peace: Europe, 1918–1923* (London: Bloomsbury, 2017).

47. Julie V. Gottlieb, *'Guilty Women', Foreign Policy, and Appeasement in Inter-War Britain* (Basingstoke: Palgrave, 2015), p. 101.

48. Agnes Headlam-Morley, 'Introduction' in James Headlam, *A Memoir of the Paris Peace Conference 1919*, edited by Agnes Headlam-Morley, Russell Bryant, and Anna Cienciala (London: Methuen, 1972), p. xiii.

49. Headlam-Morley, 'Introduction', p. x.

50. Headlam-Morley, 'Introduction', p. xxxvii.

51. Headlam-Morley, 'Introduction', p. xxxvii.

52. Agnes Headlam-Morley, '"Approaches to Germany" 1937–1938', n.d. (c.1953), p. 54. GBR/0014/AGHM 3/1/52, Agnes Headlam-Morley papers. Also see Headlam-Morley, 'Was Neville Chamberlain's Policy Wrong?' *The Listener*, vol. 40 (October l4, 1948), pp. 551–3.

53. In 1948, the year she converted to Catholicism, Headlam-Morley wrote an introductory essay on her uncle's *The Fourth Gospel as History*: part biography, part essay on Christian theology and history. Agnes Headlam-Morley, 'Arthur Cayley Headlam: A Biographical Essay' in *The Fourth Gospel as History* (Oxford: Basil Blackwell, 1948), pp. ix–xli.

54. Robbie Shilliam, 'Comparative Politics' in *Decolonizing Politics: An Introduction* (Cambridge: Polity, 2021), chapter 4.

55. Agnes Headlam-Morley, 'Introduction', p. xvi. James Headlam, *The History of Twelve Days* (London: Fischer Unwin, 1915).

56. Agnes Headlam-Morley quoted in Arthur J. May, 'Seton-Watson and the Treaty of London', *The Journal of Modern History*, vol. 29, no. 1 (1957), pp. 42–7, here 42.

57. Agnes Headlam-Morley, *The New Democratic Constitutions of Europe: A Comparative Study of Post-War European Constitutions* (Oxford: Humphrey Milford, 1928).

58. Alfred Zimmern, 'Headlam-Morley: "The New Democratic Constitutions of Europe" (Book Review)', *Journal of the Royal Institute of International Affairs*, vol. 7, no. 4 (1928), pp. 275–7.

59. Alfred Zimmern to Barbara Gwyer, June 23, 1930, SHG/S/2/2/11/4 1/53, Agnes Headlam-Morley staff file, St Hugh's College.

60. Agnes Headlam-Morley, 'Value of Transferable Vote System', *The Times* (June 11, 1975), p. 15.

61. Headlam-Morley, 'Value of Transferable Vote System', p. 15. Agnes Headlam-Morley, 'The Conservatives and Electoral Reform', *The Times* (October 11, 1975), p. 13.

62. In 1928, Headlam-Morley delivered a lecture at a summer school organised by the Women's International League for Peace and Freedom on 'The Difficulties of Democracy'. 'International Summer School at Selly Oak', *Birmingham Post* (July 20, 1928). Agnes Headlam-Morley papers, GBR/0014/AGHM 3/1/3.

63. Agnes Headlam-Morley to Else Headlam Morley, n.d. c.1929. J18/4/11-13, Else Headlam-Morley papers, Durham University. Translated by Meike Fernbach.

64. Agnes Headlam-Morley to Else Headlam Morley, n.d. c.1931. J18/6/14-15, Else Headlam-Morley papers. Translated by Meike Fernbach.

65. Agnes Headlam-Morley to Barbara Gwyer, September 17, 1931. SHG/S/2/2/11/4 1/376, Agnes Headlam-Morley staff file.

66. Cuthbert Morley Headlam and Duff Cooper, *House of Lords or Senate?* (London: Rich & Cowan, 1932).

67. Agnes Headlam-Morley, 'Life of George Washington'. GBR/0014/AGHM 2, Agnes Headlam-Morley papers.

68. Gordon Martel, 'The Prehistory of Appeasement: Headlam-Morley, the Peace Settlement and Revisionism', *Diplomacy and Statecraft*, vol. 9, no. 3 (1998), pp. 242–65, here 260.

69. Martel, 'The Prehistory of Appeasement', p. 243.

70. Arnold Toynbee to Barbara Gwyer, June 20, 1930. SHG/S/2/2/11/4 1/55, Agnes Headlam-Morley staff file.

71. Note from M. V. Clarke, June 23, 1930. SHG/S/2/2/11/4 1/546, Agnes Headlam-Morley staff file.

72. Headlam-Morley to Barbara Gwyer, September 17, 1931, SHG/S/2/2/11/4 1/376, Agnes Headlam-Morley staff file.

73. Memo June 24, 1930, SHG/S/2/2/11/4 1/52, Agnes Headlam-Morley staff file.

74. Headlam-Morley to Barbara Gwyer, September 29, 1931, SHG/S/2/2/11/4 1/34, Headlam-Morley to Barbara Gwyer, September 17, 1931, SHG/S/2/2/11/4 1/376, Agnes Headlam-Morley staff file. Stuart Ball, 'Introduction', Cuthbert Headlam, *Parliament and Politics in the Age of Churchill and Attlee: The Headlam Diaries, 1935–1951*, edited by Stuart Ball (Cambridge: Cambridge University Press, 1999), p. 43.

75. Headlam-Morley to Gwyer, September 17, 1931.

76. Headlam-Morley to Gwyer, September 17, 1931.

77. Agnes Headlam-Morley to Else Headlam-Morley, February 21, 1932. J18/7/7, Else Headlam-Morley papers. Translated by Meike Fernbach.

78. James Wycliffe Headlam, Kenneth Headlam-Morley, and Agnes Headlam-Morley, *Studies in Diplomatic History* (London: Methuen, 1930).

79. Bonnie Smith, *The Gender of History: Men, Women, and Historical Practice* (Cambridge, MA: Harvard University Press, 1998), p. 117.

80. Cf. Glenda Sluga, *The Invention of International Order: Remaking Europe after Napoleon* (Princeton: Princeton University Press, 2021).

81. Headlam-Morley, 'Introduction', p. xxx.

82. Headlam-Morley, 'Introduction', p. ix.

83. Headlam-Morley, 'Introduction', p. xxxix.

84. Sibyl Crowe, 'Arthur Fraser: A Memoir' in Arthur Fraser and Sibyl Crowe, *Amoris Laus* (Oxford: Mouette Press, 1981), pp. 5–57, here 28.

85. Mary Bennett, 'Sibyl Eyre Crowe', *St Hilda's College Report and Chronicle, 1992–1993, Centenary Edition*, pp. 101–3. Sibyl Crowe file, St Hilda's College.

86. Sibyl Crowe interview with Jill Hosford Pellew, October 11, 1989, St Hilda's Sound Archive, 1A20. I'm grateful to the College archivist, Oliver Mahony, for access to Crowe's college file.

87. Helen McCarthy, *Women of the World: The Rise of the Female Diplomat* (London: Bloomsbury, 2015).

88. Crowe, 'Arthur Fraser: A Memoir', pp. 28, 30.

89. Sibyl Crowe interview with Jill Hosford Pellew.

90. Crowe's dissertation was supervised by Eric A. Walker, historian of white settler 'pioneers' in Southern Africa. Eric A. Walker, *The Frontier Tradition in South African History* (Oxford: Oxford University Press, 1930).

91. Sibyl E. Crowe, *The Berlin West African Conference, 1884–1885* (London: Longmans Green 1942), p. 7.

92. A. W. Southall, '*The Berlin West African Conference, 1884–1885* by S. E. Crowe', *Journal of the Royal African Society*, vol. 42, no. 167 (1943), pp. 86–7.

93. W. P. Morrell, '*The Berlin West African Conference, 1884–1885. Royal Empire Society Imperial Studies No. 19* by S. E. Crowe', *History*, vol. 28, no. 108 (1943), pp. 222–3, here 223.

94. Francis Williamson, 'Reviewed Work: *The Berlin West African Conference, 1884–1885* by S. E. Crowe', *The American Historical Review*, vol. 48, no. 4 (1943), pp. 787–8.

95. Stanley R. Thomson, '*The Berlin West African Conference, 1884–1885. S. E. Crowe*', *The Journal of Modern History*, vol. 15, no. 2 (1943), pp. 150–52.

96. Morrell, '*The Berlin West African Conference*', p. 223.

97. Williamson, 'Reviewed Work'.

98. Fraser and Crowe, *Amoris Laus*.

99. Zara Steiner, 'The Bird's Eye View—Our Ablest Civil Servant by Sibyl Crowe and Edward Corp', *The Times Literary Supplement*, no. 4748 (April 1, 1994), p. 24.

100. Edward Corp and Sibyl Crowe, *Our Ablest Public Servant: Sir Eyre Crowe, 1864–1925* (Braunton: Merlin Books, 1993). Also see Sibyl Eyre Crowe, 'Sir Eyre Crowe and the Locarno Pact', *The English Historical Review*, vol. 8, no. 342 (1972), pp. 49–74.

101. Zara Steiner, *The Foreign Office and Foreign Policy, 1898–1914* (London: Cambridge University Press, 1969).

102. Sibyl Crowe interview with Jill Hosford Pellew.

103. Steiner, 'The Bird's Eye View', p. 24.

104. Keith Neilson, 'S. Crowe, E. Corp, "Our Ablest Public Servant: Sir Eyre Crowe GCB, GCMG, KCB, KCMG, 1864–1925" (Book Review)', *Canadian Journal of History/Annales Canadiennes D'Histoire*, vol. 30, no. 1 (1995), pp. 141–142, here 142. In 1957, Crowe was moved to write for the *Journal of Contemporary History* on the controversy over the 'Zinoviev Letter', a letter purportedly from the Comintern to British communists but actually forged by an agent of MI6, that sought to encourage sympathetic members of the Labour Party to support an Anglo-Soviet treaty, a loan to the Soviet government, and even a violent overthrow of the British government. Four days before the 1924 general election, called after the Labour minority government lost a vote of confidence, the letter was leaked to *The Daily Mail* in order to influence the outcome of the election and contributed to the Tory landslide. Gill Bennett, *The Zinoviev Letter: The Conspiracy That Never Dies* (Oxford: Oxford University Press, 2018). Because it involved her father,

who made the decision to share the letter with the prime minister, believing the Secret Service advice that it was authentic, Crowe went into the minutest detail of Eyre Crowe's minutes, letters, and the Foreign Office decision to publish the letter, to defend him. Sibyl Crowe, 'The Zinoviev Letter: A Reappraisal', *Journal of Contemporary History*, vol. 10, no. 3 (1975), pp. 407–32.

105. Headlam-Morley, 'Introduction', p. xvii.

106. Headlam-Morley, 'Book review of A.J.P. Taylor's *The Struggle for Mastery in Europe* and von Kürrenberg's *The Kaiser*', p. 6.

107. Agnes Headlam-Morley, 'C. G. Jung', *The Times Literary Supplement*, no. 3206 (August 9, 1963), p. 615.

108. Zara Steiner, 'On Writing International History: Chaps, Maps and Much More', *International Affairs*, vol. 73, no. 3 (1997), pp. 531–46.

109. Headlam-Morley, 'Book review of A.J.P. Taylor's *The Struggle for Mastery in Europe* and von Kürrenberg's *The Kaiser*', p. 8.

110. Headlam-Morley, 'British Foreign Policy', p. 4. GBR/0014/HDLM, 815/32, Agnes Headlam-Morley papers.

111. Headlam-Morley, 'British Foreign Policy', p. 6.

112. F. S. Northedge and M. J. Grieve, *A Hundred Years of International Relations* (London: Duckworth, 1971), p. ix.

113. Agnes Headlam-Morley, Report, June 2, 1948. FA 9/1/152, Agnes Headlam-Morley file, University of Oxford.

114. Headlam-Morley, Report, June 2, 1948.

115. Quoted in Goodwin, 'Teaching of International Relations', p. 121.

116. Goodwin, 'Teaching of International Relations', p. 121.

117. Goodwin, 'Teaching of International Relations', p. 121.

118. Agnes Headlam-Morley to Else Headlam-Morley, February 21, 1932.

119. Agnes Headlam-Morley to Else Headlam-Morley, January 18, 1932. J18/7/2, Else Headlam-Morley papers. Translated by Meike Fernbach.

120. Ceadel, 'Academic Normalization', p. 185.

121. Agnes Headlam-Morley, Untitled Memorandum, n.d. (c.1939), FA 9/1/15, Agnes Headlam-Morley file.

122. Headlam-Morley to Douglas Veale, August 5, 1948. UR 6/MB/1, file 1, Oxford University Archives.

123. Headlam-Morley to Douglas Veale, August 5, 1948.

124. Trickett, 'Agnes Headlam-Morley' p. 28.

125. Quoted in Princilla West, 'Reminiscences of Seven Decades' in Penny Griffin (ed.), *St Hugh's: One Hundred Years of Women's Education in Oxford* (London: Macmillan, 1986), pp. 62–243, here 165.

126. Trickett, 'Agnes Headlam-Morley' p. 31.

127. Trickett, 'Agnes Headlam-Morley' p. 31.

128. Agnes Headlam-Morley, 'Idealism and Realism in International Relations', an Inaugural Lecture delivered before the University of Oxford', May 6, 1949, p. 3. GBR/0014/HDLM, 815/32, Agnes Headlam-Morley papers.

129. Agnes Headlam-Morley to Isaiah Berlin, n.d. (1927–40), papers of Isaiah Berlin 108 (fol. 199), Bodleian Library.

130. Headlam-Morley to Isaiah Berlin, May 28, 1949, papers of Isaiah Berlin 119 (fols. 73–4).

131. Isaiah Berlin to Agnes Headlam-Morley, June 11, 1949, papers of Isaiah Berlin (fol. 140).

132. Agnes Headlam-Morley to Isaiah Berlin, October 26, 1949, papers of Isaiah Berlin 120 (fol. 131).

133. Ceadel, 'Academic Normalization', p. 187.

134. F. S. Northedge, 'In Memoriam: Charles Manning 1894–1978', *British Journal of International Studies*, vol. 5, no. 1 (1979), pp. 1–5, here 4.

135. Agnes Headlam-Morley, Untitled Memorandum, n.d. (c.1939).

136. 'Professor Agnes Headlam-Morley', *The Times* (February 24, 1986), p. 14.

137. Agnes Headlam-Morley, Report, June 2, 1948.

138. 'The Visitatotorial Board, Agenda—27 October 1956', FA 9/2 407, Agnes Headlam-Morley file, University of Oxford. Document 620/56 VB/PC/672 is a statement from Headlam-Morley requesting that the university reconsider its decision to pay from her own stipend the costs of her deputy replacement during a period of sick leave for tuberculosis. The deputy was Mr J. B. Joll of St Anthony's College, Oxford.

139. Agnes Headlam-Morley, 'Idealism and Realism', p. 2.

140. Headlam-Morley, 'Book review of A.J.P. Taylor's *The Struggle for Mastery in Europe* and von Kürrenberg's *The Kaiser*', pp. 4–5.

141. A.J.P. Taylor, *The Struggle for Mastery in Europe, 1848–1918* (Oxford: Clarendon, 1954), p. xix.

142. Headlam-Morley, 'Book review of A.J.P. Taylor's *The Struggle for Mastery in Europe* and von Kürrenberg's *The Kaiser*', p. 7.

143. Headlam-Morley, 'Book review of A.J.P. Taylor's *The Struggle for Mastery in Europe* and von Kürrenberg's *The Kaiser*', p. 5.

144. Headlam-Morley, 'Book review of A.J.P. Taylor's *The Struggle for Mastery in Europe* and von Kürrenberg's *The Kaiser*', pp. 4–5.

145. Headlam-Morley, 'Book review of A.J.P. Taylor's *The Struggle for Mastery in Europe* and von Kürrenberg's *The Kaiser*', p. 6.

146. Headlam-Morley, 'Idealism and Realism', p. 3.

147. Headlam-Morley, 'Idealism and Realism', p. 3.

148. Headlam-Morley, 'Idealism and Realism', p. 3.

149. Headlam-Morley, 'Idealism and Realism', p. 3.

150. Headlam-Morley, 'Idealism and Realism', p. 3.

151. I am grateful to Isabelle Napier for drawing my attention to this point. Headlam-Morley's 'great men' in the contemporary age, all European or American, were Lenin, Hitler, Churchill, Roosevelt, Stresemann, Weizmann, and 'behind them is a host of others', Wilson, Masaryk, Brian, Benes, Brüning, Mussolini, Stalin, Tito, Neville Chamberlain. Agnes Headlam-Morley, 'Idealism and Realism', p. 3.

152. Headlam-Morley, 'Idealism and Realism', pp. 3–4.

153. Headlam-Morley, 'Idealism and Realism', p. 3.

154. Headlam-Morley, 'Idealism and Realism', p. 3.

155. Headlam-Morley, 'Idealism and Realism', p. 3.

156. Eric Linklater, *Private Angelo* (New York: Macmillan, 1946), pp. 226–7.

157. Agnes Headlam-Morley, 'Stresemann', p. 198. Agnes Headlam-Morley, 'Obituary: Sir Cuthbert Headlam', *The Times* (March 5, 1964), p. 16.

158. L. H. Mates, 'The North-East and the Campaigns for the Popular Front, 1938–39', *Northern History*, vol. 43, no. 2 (2006), pp. 273–301, here 299.

159. Agnes Headlam Morley, 'The Totalitarian State' in Reginald Coupland and Margery Perham (eds.), *Oxford University Summer School on Colonial Administration: St Hugh's College, 3–17 July 1937* (Oxford: Oxford University Press, 1937), pp. 31–35, here 31.

160. Jan Stöckmann, *The Architects of International Relations: Building a Discipline, Designing the World, 1914–1940* (Cambridge: Cambridge University Press 2022), p. 266.

161. Headlam, *Parliament and Politics in the Age of Churchill and Attlee: The Headlam Diaries 1935–1951*, pp. 146–7.

162. Agnes Headlam-Morley to Master of Balliol (Alexander Dunlop Lindsay), February 25, 1939. FA 9/1/152, Agnes Headlam-Morley file, University of Oxford.

163. H. N. Brailsford, 'The Tory Policy of Peace', *The Political Quarterly*, vol. 9, no. 3 (1938), pp. 325–33.

164. Agnes Headlam-Morley, 'Introduction', p. xix.

165. Agnes Headlam-Morley to Beate Ruhm von Oppen, October 9, 1969, p. 3, GBR/0014/AGHM 1/4, Agnes Headlam-Morley papers.

166. Headlam-Morley, 'Introduction', p. xv.

167. Headlam-Morley, 'Introduction', p. xix.

168. E. H. Carr, 'James Headlam-Morley', *From Napoleon to Stalin and Other Essays* (London: Macmillan, 1980), p. 165.

169. Headlam-Morley, '"Approaches to Germany" 1937–1938', p. 8.

170. Headlam-Morley, '"Approaches to Germany" 1937–1938', p. 2.

171. Headlam-Morley, '"Approaches to Germany" 1937–1938', p. 3.

172. Headlam-Morley, '"Approaches to Germany" 1937–1938', p. 6.

173. Headlam-Morley, '"Approaches to Germany" 1937–1938', p. 1.

174. Headlam-Morley, '"Approaches to Germany" 1937–1938', p. 38.

175. Headlam-Morley, '"Approaches to Germany" 1937–1938', p. 3. She was not alone in this view. See A. Edho Ekoko, 'The British Attitude towards Germany's Colonial Irredentism in Africa in the Inter-War Years', *Journal of Contemporary History*, vol. 14, no. 2 (1979), pp. 287–307.

176. Lucy P. Mair, 'Colonial Policy and Peaceful Change', in C.A.W. Manning (ed.), *Peaceful Change: An International Problem* (London: Macmillan 1937), pp. 81–98, here 88.

177. Agnes Headlam-Morley, *Last Days: June 1944 to January 1945* (London: Methuen, 1960), p. 69.

178. Agnes Headlam-Morley, 'The Poetry of Bertolt Brecht', c.1954–8, p. 1. GBR/0014/AGHM 3/1/19, Agnes Headlam-Morley papers.

179. Headlam-Morley to Beate Ruhm von Oppen, October 9, 1969, p. 6.

180. Trickett, 'Agnes Headlam-Morley', p. 31.

181. Headlam-Morley, *Last Days*, p. 9.

182. Headlam-Morley, *Last Days*, p. 82.

183. Headlam-Morley, *Last Days*, p. 74.

184. Headlam-Morley, *Last Days*, p. 73.

185. Michael Robson, 'Hitting the Hay', *The Times Literary Supplement*, no. 3046 (July 15, 1960), p. 445.

186. Rowse, *All Souls and Appeasement*, p. 109; Gottlieb, *'Guilty Women'*, p. 175.

187. Headlam-Morley to Beate Ruhm von Oppen, October 9, 1969, p. 3.

188. Rowse, *All Souls and Appeasement*, p. 116.

189. Rowse, *All Souls and Appeasement*, p. 116.

190. James Wycliffe Headlam's first book was *Bismarck and the Foundation of the German Empire*. Though he died before Hitler's rise, Headlam-Morley argued her father 'came to think that succeeding generations of German writers and politicians had betrayed the Bismarckian tradition of moderation'. Agnes Headlam-Morley, 'Introduction', p. xv; James Wycliffe Headlam, *Bismarck and the Foundation of the German Empire* (New York: G.P. Putnam's Sons, 1899). In October 1939, she wrote to *The Times* criticising an article that claimed it was the 'German mentality' which made antagonism inevitable, and that cited her father's writing on Treitschke's anti-British, pro-imperial, and anti-Semitic views. Her father would have disavowed so 'sweeping a generalization', she claimed. He thought the expression 'German mentality' was 'meaningless'. Agnes Headlam-Morley, 'Treitschke and Hitler', *The Times* (October 21, 1939), p. 4.

191. Headlam-Morley, 'Idealism and Realism', p. 7. Cf. Elizabeth Wiskemann, *The Rome–Berlin Axis: A History of the Relations between Hitler and Mussolini* (Oxford: Oxford University Press, 1949), p. 341.

192. Headlam-Morley, 'Idealism and Realism', p. 8.

193. Headlam-Morley, 'British Foreign Policy', p. 4.

194. Headlam-Morley, 'The Poetry of Bertolt Brecht', p. 3.

195. Bertolt Brecht, *Bertolt Brecht: Poems 1913–1956*, edited by John Willett and Ralph Manheim, with the cooperation of Erich Fried (London: Eyre Methuen, 1976). She translated at least 'Der Kirschdieb' (The Cherry Thief), though there were probably others in the collection. John Willett, 'The Hunt by Night', *The Times Literary Supplement*, no. 4180 (May 13, 1983), p. 489.

196. Hartmut Pogge von Strandmann, 'The Political and Historical Significance of the Fischer Controversy', *Journal of Contemporary History*, vol. 48, no. 2 (2013), 251–70, here 261.

197. Headlam-Morley, 'Stresemann', p. 206.

198. The conference included a paper by Lucy Philip Mair on the 'anthropological aspects of International Aid to Under-Developed Territories'. Papers of British Coordinating Committee for International Studies, 327/5, London School of Economics Library. In addition to Mair and Headlam-Morley, other attendees included Hilda Lee, lecturer in international history at LSE; Susan Strange, then lecturer in IR at UCL; and Mrs. J. M. Taylor, lecturer in modern history at King's College in Newcastle. At the seventh Bailey Conference in 1954, attendees included Strange; Taylor; S.E.M. Reynolds, Department of Adult Education, University of Hull; Mrs. I. Collins, lecturer of modern history at Liverpool; C.D.M. Ketelbey, lecturer in modern history at St Andrews. Papers of British Coordinating Committee for International Studies, 327/5, London School of Economics Library.

199. D. Cameron Watt, 'British Historians, the War Guilt Issue, and Post-War Germanophobia: a Documentary Note', *The Historical Journal*, vol. 36, no. 1 (1993), pp. 179–185, here 183; Agnes Headlam-Morley, 'Anglo-German Relations', *The Times* (August 25, 1959), p. 9.

200. Margaret Lambert, *The Saar* (London: Faber & Faber, 1934). Lambert and Enid Marx collaborated in research on English 'popular art'. There is a Marx–Lambert Collection at the Compton Verney Art Gallery. See Margaret Lambert and Enid Marx, *English Popular Art* (London: B.T. Batsford, 1951). Also see Clare Taylor, 'Margaret Barbara Lambert (1906–95)—"A thorough and energetic investigator"'. Available at https://blogs.lse.ac.uk/lsehistory/2018/03/09/margaret-barbara-lambert-1906-95-a-thorough-and-energetic-investigator/.

201. Watt, 'British Historians'.

202. Astrid M. Eckert, *The Struggle for the Files: The Western Allies and the Return of German Archives after the Second World War* (Cambridge: Cambridge University Press, 2012), p. 7.

203. Agnes Headlam-Morley, 'German Diplomatic Documents', *The Times Literary Supplement*, no. 2689 (August 14, 1953), p. 521.

204. Headlam-Morley, 'German Diplomatic Documents', p. 597.

205. James Headlam-Morley had been central to the negotiations around the opening of archives and publication of *British Documents of the Origins of the War* (World War I), doing much of the preparatory work for the main editors G. P. Gooch and Harold Temperley. Sharp, 'James Headlam-Morley', p. 275.

206. Laura Schwartz, *A Serious Endeavour: Gender, Education and Community at St Hugh's, 1886–2011* (London: Profile, 2011), pp. 82, 159.

207. Headlam-Morley, *Last Days*, p. 64.

208. Agnes Headlam-Morley, 'Introduction', p. xix.

209. Barry Buzan and Richard Little, 'Why International Relations Has Failed as an Intellectual Project and What to Do About It', *Millennium: Journal of International Studies*, vol. 30, no. 1 (2001), pp. 19–39.

210. See, for example, Vanessa Ogle, *The Global Transformation of Time: 1870–1950* (Cambridge, MA: Harvard University Press, 2015); Glenda Sluga and Patricia Clavin, *Internationalisms: A Twentieth-Century History* (Cambridge: Cambridge University Press, 2017); Olivette Otele, *African Europeans: An Untold History* (London: Hurst, 2020); Mira L. Siegelberg, *Statelessness: A Modern History* (Cambridge, MA: Harvard University Press, 2020); Natasha Wheatley, *The Life and Death of States: Central Europe and the Transformation of Modern Sovereignty* (Princeton: Princeton University Press, 2023); Leslie M. Alexander, *Fear of a Black Republic: Haiti and the Birth of Black Internationalism in the United States* (Urbana: University of Illinois Press, 2023).

211. Georg Schwarzenberger, *Power Politics: A Study of International Society* (London: Stevens, 2nd edn, 1951), p. 8.

212. David Long, 'C. A. W. Manning and the Discipline of International Relations', *Round Table*, vol. 94, no. 378 (2005), p. 86.

213. C.A.W. Manning, 'International Relations: An Academic Discipline' in Geoffrey L. Goodwin, *The University Teaching of International Relations* (Oxford: Blackwell, 1951), pp. 11–26, here 24.

214. Herbert Butterfield to Kenneth Thompson, December 14, 1956. BUTT/28. Cambridge University Library.

215. Morgan, 'International Relations', p. 2.

216. Morgan, 'International Relations', p. 2.

## 8. 'The Restraint to Efface Ourselves': Assimilating Decolonisation

1. But see Achille Mbembe, *On the Postcolony* (Berkeley: University of California Press, 2001); Achille Mbembe, *Out of the Dark: Essays on Decolonization* (New York: Columbia University Press, 2021); Caroline Elkins, *Britain's Gulag: The Brutal End of Empire in Kenya* (London: Bodley Head, 2014).

2. Barbara Ward, 'Problems of the Developing World' in Brian Porter (ed.), *The Aberystwyth Papers: International Politics, 1919–1969* (London: Oxford University Press, 1972) p. 264–80; also see Jean Gartlan, *Barbara Ward: Her Life and Letters* (London: Continuum, 2010). For a discussion of Barbara Ward's international thought see Or Rosenboim, 'State, Power and Global Order', *International Relations*, vol. 33, no. 2 (2019) pp. 229–45.

3. For earlier efforts to bring IR to postcolonial scholarship see Roxanne Lynn Doty, *Imperial Encounters: The Politics of Representation in North–South Relations* (Minneapolis: University of Minnesota Press, 1996); Siba N'Zatioula Grovogui, *Sovereigns, Quasi Sovereigns, and Africans: Race and Self-Determination in International Law* (Minneapolis: University of Minnesota Press, 1996); Jenny Edkins, *Whose Hunger? Concepts of Famine, Practices of Aid* (Minneapolis: University of Minnesota Press, 2000); Sankaran Krishna, 'Race, Amnesia, and the Education of International Relations', *Alternatives*, vol. 26, no. 4 (2001), pp. 401–24; L.H.M. Ling, *Postcolonial International Relations: Conquest and Desire between Asia and the West* (Basingstoke: Palgrave, 2002); Geeta Chowdhry and Sheila Nair (eds), *Power, Postcolonialism and International Relations: Reading Race, Gender and Class* (London: Routledge, 2002); Naeem Inayatullah and David L. Blaney, *International Relations and the Problem of Difference* (London: Routledge, 2004); Branwen Gruffydd Jones, *Decolonizing International Relations* (Lanham: Rowman & Littlefield, 2006).

4. David Long, 'Of Mustard Seeds and Shopping Lists: C.A.W. Manning and International Relations at the LSE', *International Politics*, vol. 54, no. 1 (2017), pp. 118–23.

5. Nicolas Guilhot (ed.), *The Invention of International Relations Theory: Realism, the Rockefeller Foundation, and the 1954 Conference on Theory* (New York: Columbia University Press, 2011).

6. Ian Hall, 'History, Christianity and Diplomacy: Sir Herbert Butterfield and International Relations', *Review of International Studies*, vol. 28, no. 4 (2002), pp. 719–36.

7. Timothy Dunne, *Inventing International Society: A History of the English School* (Basingstoke: Macmillan, 1998); Hedley Bull, 'International Theory: The Case for a Classical Approach', *World Politics*, vol. 8, no. 3 (1966), pp. 361–77.

8. Edward Keene, *Beyond the Anarchical Society: Grotius, Colonialism and Order in World Politics* (Cambridge: Cambridge University Press, 2002); John M. Hobson, *The Eurocentric Conception of World Politics: Western International Theory, 1760–2010* (Cambridge: Cambridge University Press, 2012), pp. 222–33.

9. Ian Hall and Tim Dunne, 'Introduction to the New Edition', in Herbert Butterfield and Martin Wight (eds.), *Diplomatic Investigations: Essays in the Theory of International Politics* (Oxford: Oxford University Press, new edn, 2019), p. 1.

10. Dunne, *Inventing International Society*, p. 185; William A. Callahan, 'Nationalising International Theory: Race, Class and the English School', *Global Society*, vol. 18, no. 4 (2004), pp. 305–23. Suganami draws the parallel between Manning, Wight and Bull on the threat the less 'civilised' new states posed to the European society of states. See Hidemi Suganami, 'C. A. W. Manning and the Study of International Relations', *Review of International Studies*, vol. 27, no. 1 (2001), pp. 91–107, here 98.

11. Ian Hall, 'The Revolt against the West: Decolonisation and its Repercussions in British International Thought, 1945–75', *The International History Review*, vol. 33, no. 1 (2011), pp. 43–64.

12. Adom Getachew, *Worldmaking after Empire: The Rise and Fall of Self-Determination* (Princeton: Princeton University Press, 2019).

13. Ian Hall, *Dilemmas of Decline: British Intellectuals and World Politics, 1945–1975* (Berkeley: University of California Press, 2012), p. 143. See Watson's pseudonymous work Scipio, *Emergent Africa* (London: Chatto & Windus, 1965). For a sympathetic reading of Watson see Filippo Costa Buranelli, 'Beyond the Pendulum: Situating Adam Watson in International Relations and the English School', *International Politics* (2023), online first.

14. Martin Wight, 'The Power Struggle within the United Nations', *Proceedings of the Institute of World Affairs*, 33rd session (Los Angeles: University of Southern California, 1956), pp. 258–59; Hobson, *The Eurocentric Conception*, chapter 5. Also see Martin Wight, 'Brutus in Foreign Policy: The Memoirs of Sir Anthony Eden', *International Affairs*, vol. 36, no. 3 (1960), pp. 299–309.

15. Charles A. W. Manning, 'South Africa and the World: In Defense of Apartheid', *Foreign Affairs*, vol. 43 (1964), pp. 135–49, here 149.

16. Manning, 'South Africa', pp. 135, 148.

17. Hedley Bull, 'The European International Order' in Kai Alderson and Andrew Hurrell (eds.), *Hedley Bull on International Society* (Basingstoke: Macmillan, 1980, new edn, 2000), pp. 170–87, here 175.

18. Hedley Bull, 'Order vs. Justice in International Society', *Political Studies*, vol. 19, no. 3 (1971), pp. 269–83.

19. Third World states' opposition to continuing Western military intervention is reduced to an endorsement of 'the pluralist theory of international society'. Dunne, *Inventing International Society*, p. 148. Bull could 'only authorize a partial recognition of Third World demands, captured in the clichéd language of justice'. Mustapha Kamal Pasha, 'Decolonizing *The Anarchical Society*' in Hidemi Suganami, Madeline Carr, and Adam R. C. Humphreys (eds.), *The Anarchical Society at 40: Contemporary Challenges and Prospects* (Oxford: Oxford University Press, 2017), pp. 93–4.

20. Margery Perham, 'African Facts and American Criticisms', *Foreign Affairs*, vol. 22, no. 33 (1944), pp. 444–57, here 457.

21. Kenneth Robinson, 'Margery Perham and the Colonial Office', special issue on Perham of *Journal of Imperial and Commonwealth History*, vol. 19, no. 3 (1991), pp. 185–96, here 186.

22. Joanna Lewis, *Empire State-Building: War and Welfare in Kenya 1925–52* (Oxford: James Currey, 2000), p. 11.

23. D. A. Low, 'Britain's Conscience on Africa', *African Affairs*, vol. 70, no. 279 (1971), pp. 172–5.

24. Caroline Elkins, *Legacy of Violence: A History of the British Empire* (London: Bodley Head, 2022), p. 316.

25. 'She's likely to appear an exceedingly sane and balanced judgement to the historian of a century hence. She is statesmanlike—she combines an intense will for the politically ideal with knowledge of what is politically possible'. Martin Wight to Mr Ferris, November 16, 1961. WIGHT/233/14. LSE Library.

26. Perham, 'From Power to Service' in *Colonial Sequence, 1930–1949: A Chronological Commentary upon British Colonial Policy Especially in Africa* (London: Methuen, 1967), p. 244. Roger Owen, 'The Colonial Reckoning by Margery Perham', *Commentary*, July 1963, available at https://www.commentary.org/articles/roger-owen/the-colonial-reckoning-by-margery -perham-and-africa-for-beginners-by-melvin-j-lasky/; Gerald L. Caplan, 'Review of *Colonial Sequence, 1930 to 1949: A Chronological Commentary upon British Colonial Policy Especially in Africa*, by Margery Perham', *The Canadian Historical Review*, vol. 49 no. 4 (1968), pp. 439–40; also see Sarah Stockwell, 'Imperial Liberalism and Institution Building at the End of Empire in Africa', *Journal of Imperial and Commonwealth History*, vol. 46, no. 5 (2018), pp. 1009–33.

27. Alison Smith and Mary Bull, 'Introduction', special issue on Perham of *The Journal of Imperial and Commonwealth History*, vol. 19, no. 3 (1991), pp. 1–20, here 2.

28. 'There is much we still share, the Queen, if not the crown.' Margery Perham, *The Colonial Reckoning* (London: Collins, 1961), p. 157.

29. Perham, 'The Psychology of African Nationalism' (1960) in *Colonial Sequence, 1949–1969: A Chronological Commentary upon British Colonial Policy in Africa* (London: Methuen, 1970), pp. 182–98, here 198.

30. 'There have been women dons eminent in scholarship and even in university administration, who may even have sat on a Royal Commission; but their home was (and is) the discreet seclusion of their colleges, and only the senior men dons would know of their work. And these seniors will of course "respect" these admirable women, because they are behaving as women dons ought'. Martin Wight to Mr Ferris, November 16, 1961.

31. Prudence Smith, 'Margery Perham and Broadcasting: A Personal Reminiscence', special issue on Perham of *The Journal of Imperial and Commonwealth History*, vol. 19, no. 3 (1991), pp. 197–200.

32. That is, Commander of the Most Distinguished Order of St Michael and St George.

33. The literature on liberalism and empire is vast, and typically focuses on the nineteenth century. See Uday Singh Mehta, *Liberalism and Empire: A Study in Nineteenth-Century British Liberal Thought* (Chicago: University of Chicago, 1999); Jeanne Morefield, *Covenants without Swords: Idealist Liberalism and the Spirit of Empire* (Princeton: Princeton University Press, 2005); Duncan Bell, *Reordering the World* (Princeton: Princeton University Press, 2016).

34. Perham, 'Christian Mission in Africa' (1947) in *Colonial Sequence, 1930–1949*, p. 304.

35. Aimé Césaire, *Discourse on Colonialism*, with an introduction by Robin. G. D. Kelley, translated by Joan Pinkham (New York: Monthly Review, 1955; new edn, 2007), p. 39.

36. Perham, *Colonial Reckoning*, p. 15.

37. Perham, *African Outline* (London: Oxford University Press, 1966), p. 43.

38. Perham, *Colonial Reckoning*, p. 39.

39. Perham, *African Outline*, p. 70.

40. Smith, 'Margery Perham and Broadcasting', pp. 199, 200.

41. Perham, 'Foreword to *Path to Nigerian Freedom*' in *Colonial Sequence, 1930–1949*, p. 307.

42. For an excellent discussion see J. E. Lewis, '"Tropical East Ends" and the Second World War: Some Contradictions in Colonial Office Welfare Initiatives', *Journal of Imperial and*

*Commonwealth History*, vol. 28, no. 2 (2000), pp. 42–66, here 55; also see Anthony Kirk-Greene, 'Margery Who? A Biography Waiting to Happen', *African Research and Documentation*, vol. 107 (2008), pp. 47–50.

43. Perham, *Colonial Reckoning*, pp. 43, 42; Perham, 'Introduction', *Colonial Sequence, 1930–1949*, p. xiv.

44. Perham was an observer on the 1937 Commission on Colonial Education in East Africa and the Sudan, a member of the Colonial Office Advisory Committee on Education in the Colonies, the Asquith Committee on Higher Education in the Colonies and the Irvine Commission on Higher Education in the West Indies. After the war, she was on the Executive Committee of the Inter-University Council for Higher Education in the Colonies.

45. Perham, 'Foreword to *Path to Nigerian Freedom*', p. 308; Obafemi Awolowo, *Path to Nigerian Freedom*, introduced by Margery Perham (London: Faber and Faber, 1946).

46. Perham, 'Foreword to *Path to Nigerian Freedom*', p. 307.

47. Perham, 'Foreword to *Path to Nigerian Freedom*', p. 310.

48. Perham, 'Foreword to *Path to Nigerian Freedom*', pp. 310–11, 308.

49. Perham, 'Foreword to *Path to Nigerian Freedom*', p. 306.

50. Margery Perham, 'Foreword' in Tom Mboya, *The Kenya Question: An African Answer* (London: Fabian Colonial Bureau, 1956), p. 1–11, here 6.

51. Margery Perham, 'Re-Assessment' in Elspeth Huxley and Margery Perham, *Race and Politics in Kenya: A Correspondence between Elspeth Huxley and Margery Perham* (London: Faber & Faber, rev. edn, 1956), pp. 265–83, here 268.

52. Perham, 'Re-Assessment', p. 269.

53. Perham, 'Foreword to *Path to Nigerian Freedom*', p. 309.

54. Perham, 'Re-Assessment', p. 280. In her 1955 introduction to Tshekedi Khama's 'practical and modest' proposal to include Bechuanaland, later Botswana, into the Union of South Africa, which was written with 'patience and restraint', Perham noted that 'whether we like it or not, all matters of race relations and of "colonialism" are world matters. We, upon our side, have nothing, or at least little, to hide'. Margery Perham, 'Introduction' in Tshekedi Khama, *Bechuanaland and South Africa*, with an introduction by Margery Perham (London: Africa Bureau, 1955), pp. 1–5, here 5, 3, 1.

55. Perham, 'Re-Assessment', p. 266.

56. Perham, 'Re-Assessment', p. 272; Perham, *Colonial Reckoning*, p. 95.

57. Perham 'Foreword' in Mboya, *The Kenya Question*, p. 3.

58. Perham, 'Foreword' in Mboya, *The Kenya Question*, pp. 1, 2.

59. Perham, 'Foreword' in Mboya, *The Kenya Question*, p. 2.

60. Perham, 'Re-Assessment', p. 271.

61. Perham, *Colonial Reckoning*, pp. 94–5.

62. Margery Perham, 'Foreword' in Josiah Mwangi Kariuki, *'Mau Mau' Detainee: The Account by a Kenya African of His Experiences in Detention Camps, 1953–1960* (London: Oxford University Press, 1963), pp. xi–xxiii, here xiv. She repeated the claim in *Colonial Reckoning*, where 'dark faces [were] made so much darker by their look of settled hate'. Perham, *Colonial Reckoning*, pp. 94–5.

63. Perham, 'Foreword' in Mboya, *The Kenya Question*, p. 1.

64. J. C. Carothers, *The Psychology of Mau Mau* (Nairobi: Printed by the Govt. Printer, 1954); Perham, 'Re-Assessment', p. 279.

65. Perham, 'Foreword to *Path to Nigerian Freedom*', p. 308. Here Perham was updating Henry Sumner Maine's explanation for native resistance, which he developed as a colonial administrator in mid-nineteenth-century India. Sir Henry Sumner Maine, *Village-Communities in the East and West* (London: John Murray, 1876); for an applicability to understanding twentieth-century counterinsurgency discourse and ideology see Patricia Owens, *Economy of Force: Counterinsurgency and the Historical Rise of the Social* (Cambridge: Cambridge University Press, 2015), chapter 4.

66. Perham, 'Foreword' in Kariuki, *'Mau Mau' Detainee*, p. xix.

67. Perham, 'Foreword' in Kariuki, *The Kenya Question*, p. 6.

68. Perham, 'Britain's Response to the End of Colonialism', *Colonial Sequence, 1949–1969*, p. 94.

69. Perham, 'Re-Assessment', p. 282.

70. Perham, *Colonial Reckoning*, p. 95.

71. Perham, 'Re-Assessment', p. 274, emphasis added.

72. Margery Perham, 'Kenya After Mau Mau', *The Times* (March 18, 1957), p. 9.

73. David Anderson, *Histories of the Hanged: the Dirty War in Kenya and the End of Empire* (New York: W.W. Norton, 2005), p. 5.

74. David Anderson, 'Surrogates of the State: Collaboration and Atrocity in Kenya's Mau Mau War', in George Kassimeris (ed.), *The Barbarisation of Warfare* (London: Hurst, 2006), pp. 159–74.

75. Ian Cobain and Jessica Hatcher, 'Kenyan Mau Mau victims in talks with UK government over legal settlement', *The Guardian* (May 5, 2013).

76. Perham, 'Foreword' in Mboya, *The Kenya Question*, p. 10.

77. Perham, 'Foreword' in Mboya, *The Kenya Question*, p. 10.

78. Mboya, *The Kenya Question*, p. 17.

79. Perham, 'Foreword' in Mboya, *The Kenya Question*, p. 10.

80. Margery Perham, 'The voice of the new Africa', *The Guardian* (March 20, 1964), p. 23; Gatheru R. Mugo, *Child of Two Worlds* (London: Routledge & Kegan Paul, 1964). Perham may have reviewed Mugo's book because, on the question of the origin of the Mau Mau rebellion, it describes *Colonial Reckoning* as offering an 'impartial view'. See ibid., p. 171.

81. Perham, 'Foreword' in Kariuki, *'Mau Mau' Detainee*.

82. Marguerite Ylvisaker, 'Book Review: *"Mau Mau" Detainee: The Account by a Kenya African of His Experiences in Detention Camps, 1953–1960*', *The International Journal of African Historical Studies*, vol. 9, no. 4 (1976), pp. 643–9, here 644.

83. Perham, 'Foreword' in Kariuki, *'Mau Mau' Detainee*, p. xii.

84. Perham, 'Foreword' in Kariuki, *'Mau Mau' Detainee*, p. xii.

85. Perham, 'Foreword' in Kariuki, *'Mau Mau' Detainee*, p. xix.

86. Perham, 'Foreword' in Kariuki, *'Mau Mau' Detainee*, p. xiv–v.

87. Perham, 'Foreword' in Kariuki, *'Mau Mau' Detainee*, p. xvi, p. xiv–v.

88. Perham, 'Foreword' in Kariuki, *'Mau Mau' Detainee*, p. xx, emphasis added.

89. Perham, 'Foreword' in Kariuki, *'Mau Mau' Detainee*, p. xiv-v, emphasis added.

90. Perham, 'Foreword' in Kariuki, *'Mau Mau' Detainee*, p. xiv.

91. Perham, 'Foreword' in Kariuki, *'Mau Mau' Detainee*, p. xvi. Also see Margery Perham, 'Struggle Against Mau Mau II: Seeking the Causes and the Remedies', *The Times* (April 23, 1953), p. 9.

92. Perham, 'Foreword' in Kariuki, *'Mau Mau' Detainee*, p. xx.

93. Perham, *Colonial Reckoning*, p. 158.

94. Smith, 'Margery Perham and Broadcasting', p. 199, emphasis added.

95. Chinua Achebe, 'Biafra's Reply', *The Times* (September 19, 1968), p. 9.

96. Perham, 'Biafra's Reply', *The Times* (September 21, 1968), p. 9. She later wrote in *International Affairs*, 'I was much distressed by an attack upon me . . . by Mr. Chinua Achebe. There is no African writer whom I more admire, and I had attended the moving farewell party given to him by his publishers upon his courageous decision to return to Biafra'. Margery Perham, 'Reflections on the Nigerian Civil War', *International Affairs*, vol. 46, no. 2 (1970), pp. 231–46, here 240.

97. Margery Perham, *Lugard: The Years of Adventure, 1858–1898: The First Part of a Life of Frederick Dealtry Lugard* (London: Collins, 1956), p. 29.

98. Perham, 'Christian Mission in Africa' (1947) in *Colonial Sequence, 1930–1949*, p. 304.

99. Smith, 'Margery Perham and Broadcasting', pp. 199, 200.

100. Perham, *Colonial Reckoning*, p. 14.

101. Perham, 'Re-Assessment', p. 269.

102. Perham, 'The Colonial Dilemma', *Colonial Sequence, 1930–1949*, p. 336.

103. Margery Perham, 'Britain's Response to the End of Colonialism', *The Listener* (December 10, 1954); also see Perham, 'The Colonial Dilemma', *Colonial Sequence, 1930–1949*, p. 336.

104. Perham, *Colonial Reckoning*, p. 22.

105. Perham, *African Outline*, pp. 16, 70; Perham, *Colonial Reckoning*, p. 79.

106. Perham, *African Outline*, p. 37.

107. Perham, *Colonial Reckoning*, pp. 130–31.

108. Perham, 'Britain's Response to the End of Colonialism', *Colonial Sequence, 1949–1969*, p. 94.

109. Perham, *Colonial Reckoning*, p. 70.

110. Priyamvada Gopal, *Insurgent Empire: Anticolonial Resistance and British Dissent* (London: Verso, 2019), p. 439.

111. Perham, *African Outline*, p. 24.

112. Perham, 'Britain's Response to the End of Colonialism', *Colonial Sequence, 1949–1969*, p. 94.

113. Perham, 'The British Problem in Africa' (1951), *Colonial Sequence, 1949–1969*, p. 30.

114. Perham, *Colonial Reckoning*, pp. 10, 12, 17; Kwame Nkrumah, *Neo-Colonialism: The Last Stage of Imperialism* (London: Nelson, 1965).

115. Perham, *Colonial Reckoning*, p. 156.

116. Perham, 'The Psychology of African Nationalism', p. 184.

117. Perham, 'A Changing Continent', *Colonial Sequence, 1949–1969*, p. 68.

118. Perham, 'The Psychology of African Nationalism', p. 184.

119. Perham, 'The Psychology of African Nationalism', p. 185.

120. Perham, *Colonial Reckoning*, p. 39.

121. Perham, 'Foreword to *Path to Nigerian Freedom*', p. 308; Perham, 'The British Problem in Africa', p. 39; Perham, *Colonial Reckoning*, p. 39; Perham, 'A Changing Continent', p. 68.

122. Perham, 'Introduction', *Colonial Sequence, 1930–1949*, p. xii.

123. Perham, 'The British Problem in Africa', p. 30.

124. Perham, 'Britain's Response to the End of Colonialism', *Colonial Sequence, 1949–1969*, p. 95.

125. Perham, *African Outline*, p. 29.

126. Perham, *African Outline*, p. 28.

127. Perham, 'Britain's Response to the End of Colonialism', *Colonial Sequence, 1949–1969*, p. 96.

128. Perham, *African Outline*, p. 21.

129. Perham, 'Britain's Response to the End of Colonialism', *Colonial Sequence, 1949–1969*, p. 96.

130. Perham, 'The Psychology of African Nationalism', p. 197.

131. Perham, *Colonial Reckoning*, p. 155; Perham, *African Outline*, p. 42.

132. Léopold Sédar Senghor, 'Négritude et Civilisation de l'Universel', *Présence Africaine*, vol. 46 (1963), pp. 8–13.

133. Cf. Gopal, *Insurgent Empire*, p. 438.

134. Perham, *Colonial Reckoning*, p. 63.

135. Margery Perham, 'Introduction' in Margery Perham and J. Simmons (eds.), *African Discovery: An Anthology of Exploration* (London: Faber and Faber, 1942, new edn, 1949), pp. 13–22, here 18.

136. Perham, 'The British Problem in Africa', p. 28.

137. K. O. Dike, 'African History and Self-Government' (1953) in Kenneth Onwuka Dike, *Issues in African Studies and National Education: Selected Works of Kenneth Onwuka Dike* (Nigeria: Kenneth Onwuka Dike Centre, 1988), pp. 71–9, here 72.

138. J. D. Hargreaves, 'African History: The First University Examination?', *History in Africa*, vol. 23 (1996), pp. 467–68.

139. Perham, 'Introduction', *Colonial Sequence, 1930–1949*, p. xvi, emphasis added.

140. Perham, 'Introduction', *Colonial Sequence, 1930–1949*, p. xvi.

141. Margery Perham to W.E.B. Du Bois, November 9, 1960. W.E.B. Du Bois Papers (MS 312), Special Collections and University Archives, University of Massachusetts Amherst Libraries. Available at https://credo.library.umass.edu/view/full/mums312-b152-i064.

142. Perham, *Colonial Reckoning*, pp. 136, 99.

143. Perham, *Colonial Reckoning*, p. 38. Perham had been advisor on *Colonial Students in Britain: A Report* (London: Political and Economic Planning, 1955).

144. Perham, *African Outline*, p. 35.

145. Margery Perham, *Africans and British Rule* (London: Oxford University Press, 1941), p. 80.

146. Perham in Huxley and Perham, *Race and Politics in Kenya*, p. 198.

147. Perham, *African Outline*, p. 26, emphasis added.

148. Perham in Huxley and Perham, *Race and Politics in Kenya*, pp. 197–8.

149. Perham in Huxley and Perham, *Race and Politics in Kenya*, p. 198.

150. Perham, *Colonial Reckoning*, p. 88.

151. Perham, *Colonial Reckoning*, p. 88. The French, again, were more 'open and unashamed' about the deep connection between colonial and sexual relations. She recalled a visit to a French colony when a colonial governor 'thought nothing of asking me to camp in half a house, the other half of which was occupied by a polygamous French official and his four African wives. My well-trained Nigerian servant was shocked and insisted upon sleeping across the doorway'. Perham, *African Outline*, p. 42.

152. Perham, 'The Psychology of African Nationalism', p. 197.

153. Perham, 'A Changing Continent', pp. 67–8; Margery Perham, 'Distressful Countries', *New Statesman*, vol. 74 (July 1, 1967), p. 557.

154. Perham, 'Britain's Response to the End of Colonialism', *Colonial Sequence, 1949–1969*, p. 93.

155. Perham, 'Britain's Response to the End of Colonialism', *Colonial Sequence, 1949–1969*, p. 95.

156. Perham, 'The British Problem in Africa', p. 30; Perham, 'Britain's Response to the End of Colonialism', *Colonial Sequence, 1949–1969*, p. 95; Perham, *African Outline*, p. 24.

157. Perham, *African Outline*, p. 28.

158. Perham, *African Outline*, p. 28.

159. Perham, 'The Psychology of African Nationalism', p. 197, emphasis added.

160. Perham, 'Britain's Response to the End of Colonialism', *Colonial Sequence, 1949–1969*, p. 95.

161. Margery Perham, 'The Colour-Challenge', *The Spectator* (August 23, 1935), pp. 284–5, here 285.

162. Perham, *Colonial Reckoning*, p. 65.

163. Perham, *African Outline*, p. 45.

164. Perham, *Colonial Reckoning*, p. 130.

165. Perham, 'The Colour-Challenge', p. 285.

166. Perham, *Colonial Reckoning*, p. 93.

167. Perham, *Colonial Reckoning*, p. 90.

168. Perham, *Colonial Reckoning*, p. 154.

169. For a good recent critique of the 'balance sheet' approach see Priya Satia, *Time's Monster: How History Makes History* (Cambridge, MA: Harvard University Press, 2000), pp. 277–8.

170. West Indians, especially, 'have a long ante-dated cheque in hand which we still ought to try to honour'. Perham, *Colonial Reckoning*, p. 105.

171. Cf. Eric Williams, *Capitalism and Slavery* (London: A. Deutsch, 1964).

172. Perham, *Colonial Reckoning*, p. 107.

173. Perham, *Africans and British Rule*, p. 56.

174. Perham, *Colonial Reckoning*, pp. 131–2.

175. Perham, *Africans and British Rule*, p. 61; A. Kirk-Greene, 'Margery Perham and Colonial Administration: A Direct Influence on Indirect Rule' in F. Madden and D. K. Fieldhouse (eds.), *Oxford and the Idea of Commonwealth* (London, 1982), pp. 122–43.

176. F. D. Lugard, *The Dual Mandate in British Tropical Africa* (London: William Blackwood and Sons, 1922).

177. Margery Perham, *Native Administration in Nigeria* (London: Oxford University Press, 1937), pp. 344, 356, 354. In her Lugard biography, Perham acknowledged the contemporary 'moral censure' of the scramble for Africa. But 'the constructive processes of civilisation could not begin until these tattered, moustachioed and bearded white men, supremely convinced of racial superiority and of the national and humanitarian mission of their own nations, had walked their hundreds of miles in the bush under rain and sun, swum their rivers, shot their game, planted their flags and sweated or died of malaria in their little tents'. Perham, *Lugard: The Years of Adventure, 1858–1898*, pp. 630–31.

178. On decentralised despotism see Mahmood Mamdani, *Citizen and Subject: Contemporary Africa and the Legacy of Late Colonialism* (Princeton: Princeton University Press, 2018). For Perham, the distinctly British approach to indirect rule drew on what she saw as the two main strands of British political thought, the conservative 'aristocratic tradition with its sense of the necessity of organic growth, and . . . the liberal abhorrence for arbitrary interference with . . . the rights of groups or individuals'. Perham, 'Education for Self-Government' (1945) in *Colonial Sequence, 1930–1949*, p. 268.

179. Margery Perham, 'Editor's Preface' in F. D. Lugard, Margery Perham, and Mary Bull, *The Diaries of Lord Lugard*, vol. 4, *Nigeria, 1894–5 and 1898* (London: Faber and Faber, 1963, p. 14.

180. Perham, 'Introduction' in *African Discovery*, pp. 20–21.

181. Perham, *Colonial Reckoning*, p. 23.

182. Perham, *African Outline*, p. 70.

183. Perham, *Colonial Reckoning*, pp. 130–31.

184. Perham, *Colonial Reckoning*, p. 54.

185. Perham, *Colonial Reckoning*, p. 135.

186. Perham, *Colonial Reckoning*, p. 114.

187. Perham, 'Introduction' to *Colonial Sequence, 1949–1969*, p. xvi.

188. Perham, *African Outline*, p. 70.

189. Perham, 'Introduction' to *Colonial Sequence, 1949–1969*, p. xvi.

190. Perham, *African Outline*, p. 36.

191. Dunne, *Inventing International Society*, p. 184–5; Hall, 'History, Christianity and Diplomacy', p. 728.

192. For a sympathetic analysis see Molly Cochran, 'Normative Theory in the English School' in Brunello Vigezzi, Daniel M. Green, Cornelia Navari (eds.), *Guide to the English School in International Studies* (Oxford: John Wiley & Sons, 2014), pp. 185–203.

193. Katrina Forrester, *In the Shadow of Justice: Postwar Liberalism and the Remaking of Political Philosophy* (Princeton: Princeton University Press, 2019); Duncan Bell (ed.), *Empire, Race and Global Justice* (Cambridge: Cambridge University Press, 2019); the discussion here draws on my engagement with this work in Patricia Owens, 'History, Race, and the Pitfalls of Ideal Normative Theorizing', *Cambridge Review of International Affairs*, vol. 34, no. 6 (2021), pp. 846–50.

194. Martin Wight to Mr Ferris, November 16, 1961. Wight was school and university friends with her nephew, with whom he went to Oxford in 1932. At a meeting in the autumn of 1936 in Rhodes House to discuss fascist Italy's invasion of Ethiopia, Wight recalled Perham there with 'all the liberal big-shots', and 'Perham like a Valkyrie, prophesizing doom. (Perhaps I mean a Sibyl. Anyway, anti-Baldwin, pro-sanctions)'. She was either Valkyrie, Old Norse for chooser of slain, and a foreboder of war, or Sibyl, the female seer or prophetess of Greek legend, 'with frenzied mouth uttering things not to be laughed, unadorned and unperfumed, yet reaches to a thousand years with her voice by aid of the god', according to Heraclitus.

195. Margery Perham, 'Editor's Preface' in Martin Wight, *The Gold Coast Legislative Council* (London: Faber and Faber, 1947), pp. 5–7. Also see Martin Wight, *The Development of the Legislative Council, 1606–1945* (London: Faber and Faber, 1946); Martin Wight, *British Colonial*

*Constitutions: 1947* (Oxford: Clarendon, 1952). Perham supervised, edited and prefaced several Nuffield book series, including *Studies in Colonial Legislatures, Studies in the Tropical Dependencies*, and *Colonial and Comparative Studies*. The latter included Mary Macdonald Proudfoot, *Britain and the United States in the Caribbean: A Comparative Study in Methods of Development*, with an introduction by Margery Perham (New York: Praeger, 1954) and Kathleen Sthal, *The Metropolitan Organization of British Colonial Trade* (London: Faber, 1951).

196. Hedley Bull to Margery Perham, January 30, 1974. MSS Perham 26–2 Correspondence B.

197. Martin Wight, 'Theory of Mankind: "Barbarians"' in Martin Wight, *International Theory: The Three Traditions*, edited by Gabriele Wight and Brian Porter (London: Continuum, 2002), pp. 49–98, here 50; also see Dunne, *Inventing International Society*, pp. 51–2.

198. Robbie Shilliam, *Decolonizing Politics: An Introduction* (Cambridge: Polity, 2021), pp. 128–9, 135.

199. Martin Wight, *Four Seminal Thinkers in International Theory: Machiavelli, Grotius, Kant, and Mazzini*, edited by Gabriele Wight, Brian Porter, and David S. Yost (Oxford: Oxford University Press, 2005).

## 9. Is British International Thought White?

1. 'No.14 Claudia Jones', pp. 1–5, here 4, 1957 Congress of the Communist Party of Great Britain, speech by Claudia Jones, Claudia Jones Memorial Collection Box 2 (3), Sc MG 692. Schomburg Center for Research in Black Culture, Manuscripts, Archives and Rare Books Division, the New York Public Library.

2. Cf. Meera Sabaratnam, 'Is IR Theory White? Racialised Subject-Positioning in Three Canonical Texts', *Millennium: Journal of International Studies*, vol. 49, no. 1 (2020), pp. 3–31.

3. This ideological move became central to the discourse of 'Brexit'. See Gurminder K. Bhambra, 'Brexit, Class and British "National" Identity', *Discover Society* (July 5, 2016).

4. Caroline Elkins, *Legacy of Violence: A History of the British Empire* (London: Bodley Head, 2022).

5. Bill Schwarz, 'Crossing the Seas', in Bill Schwarz (ed.), *West Indian Intellectuals in Britain* (Manchester: Manchester University Press, 2003), pp. 1–30, here 2.

6. Robert Vitalis, *White World Order, Black Power Politics: The Birth of American International Relations* (Ithaca: Cornell University Press, 2015).

7. Schwarz, 'Crossing the Seas', p. 2.

8. Claudia Jones, 'Books—Capitalism and Slavery', *West Indian Gazette And Afro-Asian Caribbean News*, vol. 6, no. 7 (November 1964), p. 4.

9. Britishness is far more expansive category. 'Whiteness' may be closer to an imaginary sense of 'Englishness'. Stuart Hall (with Bill Schwarz), *Familiar Stranger* (London: Penguin, 2017), p. 204.

10. Jan Carew in Marika Sherwood, *Claudia Jones: A Life in Exile, a Biography* (London: Lawrence & Wishart, 1999), p. 50.

11. Bill Schwarz, 'George Padmore' in Schwarz, *West Indian Intellectuals*, pp. 132–52, here 133.

12. Carole Boyce Davies, *Left of Karl Marx: The Political Life of Black Communist Claudia Jones* (Durham: Duke University Press, 2008), p. 2. Also see Carole Boyce Davies (ed.), *Claudia Jones: Beyond Containment, Autobiographical Reflections, Essays, and Poems* (Banbury: Ayebia Clarke, 2010); Buzz Johnson, *I Think of My Mother: Notes on the Life and Times of Claudia Jones* (London: Caria Press, 1985); Sherwood, *Claudia Jones*; Jennifer Tyson (ed.), *Claudia Jones, 1915–1964: A Woman of our Times* (London: Camden Black Sisters Publications, 1988); Jones, Claudia, 1948, Tamiment Library and Robert F. Wagner Labor Archives, Individuals, Pamphlets and Ephemera Collection, PE 030 Box 13; "Claudia Jones", special issue, *BASA Newsletter*, no. 44 (January 2006).

13. Quotation from trailer of 'Looking for Claudia Jones', a film by Nia Reynolds.

14. Paul Robeson quoted in 'Editorial: To Uphold Her Policy is to Honour Her Memory!', *West Indian Gazette And Afro-Asian Caribbean News*, vol. 8, no. 2 (February 1965), p. 1; Johnson, *I Think of My Mother*, p. 51; Herbert Aptheker, 'Loyalty and Negro History', pp. 8–9, Marika Sherwood/Claudia Jones Research—US Journals/Newspapers 1937–1958, Marika Sherwood/ Claudia Jones Research Collection Box 1 (2). Schomburg Center for Research in Black Culture.

15. David Rousell-Milner in Sherwood, *Claudia Jones*, p. 195.

16. This is conveyed in the title and the argument of Davies's definitive biography, *Left of Karl Marx*.

17. Schwarz, 'Crossing the Sea', p. 15.

18. Stephen Howe, *Anticolonialism in British Politics: The Left and the End of Empire, 1918–1964* (Oxford: Clarendon, 1993), p. 192. Jones was also more radical than both Harold Moody and James.

19. Adom Getachew, *Worldmaking after Empire: The Rise and Fall of Self-Determination* (Princeton: Princeton University Press, 2019), chapter 4.

20. Quoted in Johnson, *I Think of My Mother*, p. 7.

21. Claudia Jones, 'Hiding Behind Nature's Skirts', *Daily Worker* (February 4, 1946), p. 7.

22. Davies, *Left of Karl Marx*, pp. xxiv–xxvi; Inter-Racial Friendship Co-ordinating Council 1/27, Claudia Jones Memorial Collection Box 1 (3).

23. Schwarz, 'Crossing the Sea', p. 18. George Lamming was a leading Caribbean novelist, writer, and academic.

24. Jones and James took different sides in the spit between Stalinists and Trotskyists, with Jones remaining loyal to the official party and Popular Front line. For a critique of Jones's stance in this period see Cristina Mislán, 'The Imperial "We": Racial Justice, Nationhood, and Global War in Claudia Jones' *Weekly Review* Editorials, 1938–1943', *Journalism*, vol. 18, no. 10 (2017), pp. 1415–30. Unlike Padmore, Jones did not have a 'talented woman of independent views' who subordinated '"herself . . . entirely to George and his work", earning the bulk of the money that kept them going . . . [who] contributed vast amounts of editorial work . . . and [once or twice] claimed sole or partial authorship', which Schwarz calls an 'essentially . . . modern, cosmopolitan, London relationship'. Schwarz is citing James, 'Notes on the Life of George Padmore', *Nation* (January 15, 1960, in Schwartz, 'George Padmore', p. 146. The woman was Dorothy Pizer. See George Padmore and Dorothy Pizer, *How Russia Transformed Her Colonial Empire: A Challenge to the Imperialist Powers* (London: Dennis Dobson, 1946). For an extended discussion of Pizer, Padmore and 'white allyship', including a detailed study of Pizer's international thinking, see Isabelle Napier, doctoral dissertation in progress, University of Oxford.

25. For a fuller discussion see Sarah C. Dunstan and Patricia Owens, 'Claudia Jones, International Thinker', *Modern Intellectual History*, vol. 19, no. 2 (2022), pp. 551–72.

26. Claudia Jones, 'An End to the Neglect of the Problems of the Negro Woman!', *Political Affairs* (June 1949), pp. 28–42; Minkah Makalani, 'An Apparatus for Negro Women: Black Women's Organizing, Communism, and the Institutional Spaces of Radical Pan-African Thought', *Women, Gender, and Families of Color*, vol. 4, no. 2 (2016), pp. 250–73; also see Denise M. Lynn, 'Socialist Feminism and Triple Oppression: Claudia Jones and African American Women in American Communism', *Journal for the Study of Radicalism*, vol. 8, no. 2 (2014), pp. 1–20.

27. Jones was one of the main organisers of women's resistance to the US war in Korea. Her essay 'Women in the Struggle for Peace and Security' argued that the models for Black and white American women's resistance to US aggression were the anti-fascist and peace-activist women in the global South. Claudia Jones, 'Women in the Struggle for Peace and Security', *Political Affairs* (March 1950), pp. 3–16; Jones, 'An End to the Neglect'; Claudia Jones, 'Limits of Tyranny Are the Measure of Our Resistance', *West Indian Gazette And Afro-Asian Caribbean News*, vol. 8, no. 2 (February 1965), pp. 6–7.

28. Davies, 'Women's Rights/Worker's Rights/Anti-Imperialism: Challenging the Super-exploitation of Black Working-Class Women' in *Left of Karl Marx*, pp. 29–68. Also see Cristina Mislán, 'Claudia Jones Speaks to "Half the World": Gendering Cold War Politics in the *Daily Worker*, 1950–1953', *Feminist Media Studies*, vol. 17, no. 2 (2017), pp. 281–96. Also see Claudia Jones, 'Women's Organizations in the Struggle for Peace', *Daily Worker* (February 13, 1951), pp. 7, 8; Claudia Jones, 'The Rising Peace Demand at Women's Convention', *Daily Worker* (June 15, 1951), p. 7; Claudia Jones, 'Warmakers Fear America's Women', *Daily Worker* (August 7, 1951), p. 5.

29. Claudia Jones, 'On the Right to Self-Determination for the Negro People in the Black Belt, 1946' in Davies (ed.), *Claudia Jones: Beyond Containment*, pp. 6–70.

30. Cf. Keisha N. Blain, *Set the World on Fire: Black Nationalist Women and the Global Struggle for Freedom* (Philadelphia: University of Pennsylvania Press, 2018).

31. Claudia Jones, 'Garvey Shrine in Kingston', *West Indian Gazette And Afro-Asian Caribbean News*, vol. 6, no. 5 (August–September 1964), p. 1; Claudia Jones, 'Garvey's Last Journey Home to Jamaica', *West Indian Gazette And Afro-Asian Caribbean News*, vol. 6, no. 7 (November 1964), p. 1; Claudia Jones, 'Washington DC Centre of World Imperialism—Malcolm X', *West Indian Gazette And Afro-Asian Caribbean News*, vol. 8, no. 2 (February 1965).

32. Hinds in Sherwood, *Claudia Jones*, p. 197.

33. Claudia Jones, 'A Garvey Revival?', *West Indian Gazette And Afro-Asian Caribbean News*, vol. 4, no. 9 (September 1961), p. 5.

34. Jones agreed with James Baldwin, who questioned the origins of its wealth: 'rumour has it that the Birchites (the American fascist group) and certain Texan oil millionaires look with favour on the Black Muslim Movement'. Claudia Jones, 'The Fire Next Time', *West Indian Gazette And Afro-Asian Caribbean News*, vol. 5, no. 14 (October 1963), p. 4.

35. Claudia Jones, 'Is Jamaica in Search of an Identity?', *West Indian Gazette And Afro-Asian Caribbean News*, vol. 5, no. 8 (February 1963), p. 9.

36. Claudia Jones, 'The Precious Charters of Liberty', *Party Voice* (February 1954), pp. 7–8, Marika Sherwood/Claudia Jones Research—US Journals/Newspapers 1937–1958, Marika Sherwood/Claudia Jones Research Collection Box 1 (2). Also see Claudia Jones, 'Un-American Committee and the Negro People', *Daily Worker* (August 1, 1949), pp. 7–8.

37. Claudia Jones's interview with George Bowrin in *Caribbean News* (June 1956), cited in Johnson, *I Think of My Mother*, p. 132. Also see Claudia Jones, 'I was Deported Because I Fought Colour Bar', *Caribbean News* (June 1956), Marika Sherwood/Claudia Jones Research—UK Newspapers 1949–1997, Marika Sherwood/Claudia Jones Research Collection Box 1 (2).

38. Quoted in Sherwood, *Claudia Jones*, p. 25; Donna Langston, 'Claudia Jones: Valiant Fighter Against Racism and Imperialism', pp. 15–17, 'Jones, Claudia, 1938–1995', Tamiment Library, TAM132 CPUSA, Box no. 113; also see Unknown, 'Claudia Jones—Our Freedom Fighter', n.d., Memorial Service Speeches, MG692 2/16, Claudia Jones Memorial Collection Box 2 (3); also see Carole Boyce Davies, 'Deportable Subjects: U.S. Immigration Laws and the Criminalizing of Communism', *The South Atlantic Quarterly*, vol. 100, no. 4 (2001), pp. 949–66.

39. Eric Hobsbawm quoted in Sherwood, *Claudia Jones*, p. 108. Jones's published Hobsbawm's breathless first-hand report on the early achievements of Castro's rule in Cuba, Eric Hobsbawm, 'Eye Witness in Cuba', *West Indian Gazette And Afro-Asian Caribbean News*, vol. 3, no. 4 (December 1960), p. 3.

40. Trevor Carter in Sherwood, *Claudia Jones*, p. 190.

41. Jones sought US citizenship in 1940 but her application was declined because of her communism. Jones's initial application for a British passport was declined in January 1956. She eventually received a passport in 1962, when she travelled to the USSR, partly to receive medical care.

42. 'No.14 Claudia Jones', p. 1.

43. 'No.14 Claudia Jones', p. 2.

44. 'No.14 Claudia Jones', pp. 3–4.

45. 'No.14 Claudia Jones', p. 2.

46. Claudia Jones, 'Report on a Two Month Visit to Japan and China' (part 1), n.d., p. 1, 10th World Congress Against Atomic and Hydrogen Bombs (Tokyo, Japan) 2/13, Claudia Jones Memorial Collection Box 2 (3).

47. 'Extracts from speech by Rose Smith (founder member of the British Communist Party)', Peking, February 21, 1965, p. 2, Memorial Service Speeches, MG692 2/16, Claudia Jones Memorial Collection Box 2 (3).

48. Carole Boyce Davies and Charisse Burden-Stelly, 'Claudia Jones Research and Collections: Questions of Process & Knowledge Construction', *Journal of Intersectionality*, vol. 3, no. 1 (2019), pp. 4–9. According to Sherwood: 'She died in a room brimming with books, pamphlets and papers . . . Much remained in her room that was taken over by her friend Manchanda. He kept everything. When he died in 1985, Diane Langford, his ex-partner, sorted out his belongings. She kept what she could but some of the material was too fragile and mildewed. Diane remembers Manu complaining that "people had taken material and had not returned it"'. Sherwood, *Claudia Jones*, p. 18.

49. Claudia Jones Organisation Newsletter, no. 1 (March 1986), Photograph Copies, 2/21, Claudia Jones Memorial Collection Box 2 (3).

50. Johnson, *I Think of My Mother*, chapter 10.

51. 'Editorial: Freedom—Our Concern', *West Indian Gazette*, vol. 3, no. 1 (August 1960), p. 4. Bill Schwarz, 'Claudia Jones and the *West Indian Gazette*: Reflections on the Emergence of Postcolonial Britain', *Twentieth Century British History*, vol. 14, no. 3 (2003), pp. 264–85; Donald Hinds, 'The West Indian Gazette: Claudia Jones and the Black Press in Britain', *Race & Class*, vol. 50, no. 1 (2008), pp. 88–97.

52. Langston, 'Claudia Jones', p. 18. 'We are the *only* journal of the kind in this country', she told her readers, 'published and owned by and for the coloured people'. 'Editorial: Freedom—Our Concern'.

53. Claudia Jones to Eslanda Robeson, June 6, 1960, Claudia Jones Memorial Collection Box 1 (3). The new monthly magazine was *Tropic*, edited by Edward Scobie.

54. Claudia Jones Organisation Newsletter, no. 1 (March 1986).

55. Claudia Jones, 'The Caribbean Community in Britain', *Freedomways: A Quarterly Review of the Negro Freedom Movement*, vol. 4, no. 3 (1964), pp. 340–57, here 355.

56. Sherwood, *Claudia Jones*, pp. 40, 16

57. Donald Hinds, 'The West Indian Gazette', in Sherwood, *Claudia Jones*, pp. 125–49, here 142.

58. Claudia Jones, 'I Spent a Night in Notting Hill Police Station', *West Indian Gazette And Afro-Asian Caribbean News*, vol. 4, no. 14 (February 1962), p. 5.

59. Claudia Jones, 'Editorial—Claudia Jones's Last Editorial: Dr. Luther King's Warning', *West Indian Gazette And Afro-Asian Caribbean News*, vol. 7, no. 1 (1965), p. 4.

60. On Jones as an exemplary activist–intellectual see Davies, *Left of Karl Marx*, pp. 8–10

61. Ula Taylor, 'Street Strollers: Grounding the Theory of Black Women Intellectuals', *Afro-Americans in New York Life and History*, vol. 30, no. 2 (2006), pp. 153–71.

62. Claudia Jones, 'Editorial: Sir Grantley & West Indian History', *West Indian Gazette And Afro-Asian Caribbean News*, vol. 3, no. 6 (May 1961), p. 2.

63. '"These Islands are Yours"', *West Indian Gazette And Afro-Asian Caribbean News*, vol. 4, no. 7 (June 1961), p. 3.

64. Garvey described Jones as 'the pluckiest, and most loyal friend I have'. Amy Ashwood Garvey to Claudia Jones, February 7, 1964, Correspondence Misc.-U.K. (1956–1963) 1/17, Claudia Jones Memorial Collection Box 1 (3). Also see 'Gazette Diary: Mrs. Garvey on West Africa Tour', *West Indian Gazette And Afro-Asian Caribbean News*, vol. 3, no. 1 (January 1960), p. 3; her

last editorial described King's visit to London, and included a photo of King with Jones and Eslanda Robeson at a reception in his honour; 'Toast to a Freedom Fighter', *West Indian Gazette And Afro-Asian Caribbean News*, vol. 4, no. 12 (December 1961), p. 5.

65. Claudia Jones, 'Is Jamaica in Search of an Identity?', p. 7.

66. Jones, 'Is Jamaica in Search of an Identity?', p. 7. Katrin Norris, *Jamaica: The Search for an Identity* (Oxford: Oxford University Press, 1962).

67. Claudia Jones, 'Editorial: Elections and Racial Hypocrisy', *West Indian Gazette And Afro-Asian Caribbean News*, vol. 6, no. 6 (October 1964), p. 4; Claudia Jones, 'West Indians in Britain', *World News* (June 29, 1957), pp. 412, 416.

68. Claudia Jones, 'Caribbean Community in Britain' p. 342.

69. Jones, 'West Indians in Britain', pp. 412, 416.

70. A. Whiteman to the editor, West Indian Gazette, August 18, 1958, Committee for Inter-Racial Unity, West London, 1/28, Claudia Jones Memorial Collection Box 1 (3); 'W.I.G. Offices Called by "Nazi Movement"', *West Indian Gazette And Afro-Asian Caribbean News*, vol. 3, no. 1 (January 1960), p. 3.

71. Jones, 'London Letter', *The Worker* (November 2, 1958), p. 6. Marika Sherwood/Claudia Jones Research—US Journals/Newspapers 1937–1958, Marika Sherwood/ Claudia Jones Research Collection Box 1 (2).

72. Nadine El-Enany, *(B)ordering Britain: Law, Race and Empire* (Manchester: Manchester University Press, 2020).

73. Robbie Shilliam, *Race and the Undeserving Poor: From Abolition to Brexit* (Newcastle upon Tyne, 2018), p. 103.

74. Sheila Patterson, *Colour and Culture in South Africa: A Study of the Status of the Cape Coloured People within the Social Structure of the Union of South Africa* (London: Routledge and Kegan Paul, 1953); also see Chris Waters, '"Dark Strangers" in Our Midst': Discourses of Race and Nation in Britain, 1947–1963', *Journal of British Studies*, vol. 36, no. 2 (1997), pp. 207–38. Also see Paul Gilroy, *'There Ain't No Black in the Union Jack': The Cultural Politics of Race and Nation* (London: Hutchinson, 1987).

75. By the early 1970s, and in the face of internal and external criticism, the IRR tried to become less 'Establishment' and concerned with managing racialised populations, to more focused on questions of racial justice and the root problem of white supremacy. The house journal *Race* was transformed into *Race & Class*. See the IRR's account of its own history at https://irr.org.uk/about/.

76. Olivette Otele, *African Europeans: An Untold History* (London: Hurst, 2020).

77. Perham, 'Britain's Response to the End of Colonialism', *Colonial Sequence, 1949–1969: A Chronological Commentary upon British Colonial Policy Especially in Africa* (London: Methuen, 1967), p. 97.

78. Jones, 'Caribbean Community in Britain', p. 344.

79. Kennetta Perry, *London Is the Place for Me: Black Britons, Citizenship, and the Politics of Race* (New York: Oxford University Press, 2015), chapter 3.

80. Patterson in Jones, 'Caribbean Community in Britain', p. 344.

81. Margery Perham, *Colonial Reckoning* (London: Collins, 1961), p. 9. Most obviously, in Africa, she argued, there was the 'dangerous internal issue of black-ruled versus white-ruled states, and the competition of other nations, white and less white, democratic and communist, for political and economic influences over the still plastic continent'. Perham, *African Outline* (London: Oxford University Press, 1966), p. 2.

82. Perham, *African Outline*, p. 43.

83. Perham, *African Outline*, p. 43.

84. Perham, 'Britain's Response to the End of Colonialism', p. 97.

85. Perham, *African Outline* pp. 41, 43, 40.

86. Perham, *African Outline*, p. 43.

87. Perham, *African Outline*, p. 44.

88. Perham, *Colonial Reckoning*, p. 129.

89. Sheila Patterson, *Dark Strangers: A Sociological Study of the Absorption of a Recent West Indian Migrant Group in Brixton, South London* (Bloomington: Indiana University Press, 1963); one of the earliest such studies was K. L. Little, *Negroes in Britain: A Study of Racial Relations in English Society* (London: Kegan Paul, 1947).

90. Patterson, *Dark Strangers*, pp. 23–4.

91. Patterson, *Dark Strangers*, p. 17.

92. Jones, 'Caribbean Community in Britain', p. 343.

93. Jones, 'Caribbean Community in Britain', p. 344.

94. Jones, 'London Letter', p. 6.

95. Jones, 'London Letter', p. 6.

96. Jones, 'Editorial: Elections and Racial Hypocrisy', p. 4; see Vanessa Ogle, 'Archipelago Capitalism: Tax Havens, Offshore Money, and the State, 1950s–1970s', *American Historical Review*, vol. 122, no. 5 (2017), p. 1431; Gurminder Bhambra and Julia McClure (eds.), *Imperial Inequalities: The Politics of European Governance Across European Empires* (Manchester: Manchester University Press, 2022).

97. Jones, 'West Indians in Britain', pp. 412, 416.

98. Claudia Jones, 'Butler's Colour-Bar Bill Mocks Commonwealth', *West Indian Gazette And Afro-Asian Caribbean News*, vol. 4, no. 11 (November 1961), pp. 1–2.

99. El-Enany, *(B)ordering Britain*, p. 2.

100. Jones, 'Butler's Colour-Bar Bill Mocks Commonwealth'; Claudia Jones 'Commonwealth Immigration Bill', *West Indian Gazette And Afro-Asian Caribbean News*, vol. 5, no. 1 (May 1962), p. 13; also see Ian Sanjay Patel, *We're Here Because You Were There: Immigration and the End of Empire* (London: Verso, 2021), p. 17.

101. Jones, 'London Letter', p. 6.

102. Valerie Amos, Paul Gilroy, and Erroll Lawrence, 'White Sociology, Black Struggle', in D. Robbins (ed.), *Rethinking Social Inequality* (Aldershot: Gower, 1982), pp. 15–41; Errol Lawrence, *Common Sense, Racism and the Sociology of Race Relations* (Birmingham: University of Birmingham, 1981). Also see Robbie Shilliam, 'Behind the Rhodes Statue: Black Competency and the Imperial Academy', *History of the Human Sciences*, vol. 32, no. 5 (2019), pp. 3–27; Sarah C. Dunstan's section introduction for 'Population, Nation, Immigration' in Patricia Owens, Katharina Rietzler, Kimberly Hutchings and Sarah C. Dunstan (eds.), *Women's International Thought: Towards a New Canon* (Cambridge: Cambridge University Press, 2022), pp. 573–86.

103. Sherwood, *Claudia Jones*, p. 106; Perry, *London Is the Place for Me*.

104. These were not the first white mob 'race riots'. In 1919, white mobs rioted and attacked Black and brown communities in port cities around Britain, accusing them of taking their jobs. Jacqueline Jenkinson, *Black 1919: Riots, Racism and Resistance in Imperial Britain* (Liverpool: Liverpool University Press, 2009).

105. As Jones wrote, 'through our annual Caribbean carnivals, receptions, councils, et cetera, book reviews of West Indian novelists, and related themes, we have helped to fill a cultural gap existing among West Indians in England, we have brought to the English people some appreciation of our cultural heritage'. 'Editorial: Freedom—Our Concern', p. 4. For an excellent discussion see Davies, 'Carnival and Diaspora' in *Left of Karl Marx*, pp. 167–89.

106. Don Letts in 'Hidden Herstories: Claudia Jones', The UK Black Association Online Heritage Archive, https://www.youtube.com/watch?v=HTT1nKQpTIk.

107. Claudia Jones, 'Negroes In The Films And Theatre—Film Review', *West Indian Gazette And Afro-Asian Caribbean News*, vol. 4, no. 8 (July 1961), pp. 2, 7; Claudia Jones, 'Theatre Review—A Wreath for Udomo'. *West Indian Gazette And Afro-Asian Caribbean News*, vol. 4, no. 12 (December 1961) p. 7.

108. Tomohito Baji, 'Zionist Internationalism? Alfred Zimmern's Post-Racial Commonwealth', *Modern Intellectual History*, vol. 13, no. 3 (2016), p. 629; 'Retrospective of the work of Madame Zimmern's group', n.d. Bodleian Library, Oxford, MSS Zimmern 94, 81–2.

109. Lucie A. Zimmern, 'Thought and Action', *Comprendre: Organe de l'Association des Anciens Elèves du Bureau d'Etudes Internationales* (Geneva School of International Studies), no. 4 (1932–3), pp. 206–8, here 208. MSS Zimmern 87, 19.

110. *West Indian Gazette And Afro-Asian Caribbean News*, vol. 3, no. 1 (January 1960), p. 1.

111. Claudia Jones, 'A People's Art is the Genesis of Their Freedom' in Davies (ed.), *Claudia Jones: Beyond Containment*, pp. 166–7, here 166.

112. Jones, 'A People's Art', p. 166.

113. Trevor Carter, quoted in Colin Prescod, 'Carnival' in Sherwood, *Claudia Jones*, pp. 150–62, here 157.

114. Jones, 'A People's Art', p. 166. For a discussion of the wider context see Stuart Hall, 'Black Diaspora Artists in Britain: Three "Moments" in Post-War History', *History Workshop Journal*, vol. 61 (2006), pp. 1–24.

115. Trevor Carter in Sherwood, *Claudia Jones*, p. 191.

116. Sherwood, *Claudia Jones*, p. 89.

117. Johnson, *I Think of My Mother*, p. ix.

118. Corinne Skinner-Carter, quoted in Prescod, 'Carnival', p. 152.

119. Ranjana Ash in Sherwood, *Claudia Jones*, p. 48.

120. Sherwood, *Claudia Jones*, p. 80.

121. Susan Strange, 'I Never Meant to be an Academic' in Joseph Kruzel and James N. Rosenau (eds.), *Journeys through World Politics: Autobiographical Reflections of Thirty-four Academic Travelers* (New York: Lexington Books, 1989), p. 429. 'In 1936, [Jones] was awarded a place to study drama at an advanced institution but turned it down to take up a post as a technical worker at the *Daily Worker*'. Johnson, *I Think of My Mother*, p. 9.

122. Trevor Carter in Sherwood, *Claudia Jones*, p. 189.

123. Alex Pascall in Sherwood, *Claudia Jones*, p. 49; Bill Ash in Sherwood, *Claudia Jones*, p. 48; Davies, *Left of Karl Marx*, pp. xviii, xxi, 76, 228.

124. Lucie Barbier, 'Correspondence: The Hallé Concerts', *The Manchester Guardian* (June 1, 1911), 9.

125. Corinne Skinner-Carter, quoted in Prescod, 'Carnival', p. 158. 'Your Holiday Beauty Tips', *West Indian Gazette And Afro-Asian Caribbean News*, vol. 6, no. 1 (December 1963), p. 8. Jones also featured sport in a political context. Claudia Jones, 'Profile of the Month—Captain Frank Worrell'. *West Indian Gazette And Afro-Asian Caribbean News*, vol. 5, no. 10 (May 1963), p. 6–7. Her close friend, Essie Robson, served as a Carnival Queen judge in 1962. Prescod, 'Carnival', p. 152.

126. On the gendered politics of the 'global beauty economy' see Angela B. McCracken, *The Beauty Trade: Youth, Gender and Fashion Globalization* (Oxford: Oxford University Press, 2014).

127. Abner Cohen, *Masquerade Politics: Explorations in the Structure of Urban Cultural Movements* (Oxford: Berg, 1993), p. 77.

128. Cohen, *Masquerade Politics*, p. 11.

129. David Rousell-Milner in Sherwood, *Claudia Jones*, p. 211.

130. Pearl Connor in Sherwood, *Claudia Jones*, p. 212.

131. Alex Pascall in Sherwood, *Claudia Jones*, p. 212; also see Carol Tulloch, 'Claudia Jones: Mother of the Mas', *City Limits* (August 18–25, 1988), p. 14.

132. Everton A. Pryce, 'The Notting Hill Gate Carnival—Black Politics, Resistance, and Leadership 1976–1978', *Caribbean Quarterly*, vol. 31, no. 2 (1985), pp. 35–52; Nicole Ferdinand and Nigel L. Williams, 'The Making of the London Notting Hill Carnival Festivalscape: Politics and Power and the Notting Hill Carnival', *Tourism Management Perspectives*, vol. 27 (2018), pp. 33–46.

133. As Davies pointed out, Cohen 'has been refuted by almost all London activists and scholars of black culture and history in England'. Davies, *Left of Karl Marx*, p. 265, fn. 28.

134. Gary Young, 'The Politics of Partying', *The Guardian* (August 17, 2002), https://www.theguardian.com/culture/2002/aug/17/nottinghillcarnival2002.nottinghillcarnival. Since 2014 the Caribbean Philosophical Association has given a Claudia Jones Award for the best paper by a graduate student presented at its international conference.

135. Prescod, 'Carnival', p. 161.

136. Jones, 'A People's Art', p. 166.

137. Prescod, 'Carnival', p. 151.

138. Getachew, *Worldmaking after Empire*, chapter 4.

139. Shirley Graham, 'Africa's Hour—Exclusive', *West Indian Gazette And Afro-Asian Caribbean News*, vol. 5, no. 11 (June 1963), pp. 1, 12; 'Encyclopaedia Africana', *West Indian Gazette And Afro-Asian Caribbean News*, vol. 5, no. 2 (July 1962), p. 3; also see Claudia Jones, 'The Meaning of DuBois' Life'. *West Indian Gazette And Afro-Asian Caribbean News*, vol. 5, no. 13 (September 1963), p. 4.

140. Perham, *Colonial Reckoning*, p. 74.

141. Getachew, *Worldmaking*, p. 109; 'West Indians Discuss The Case For Nationhood', *West Indian Gazette And Afro-Asian Caribbean News*, vol. 4, no. 13 (January 1962), p. 12. Williams's ideas on federalism drew on the work of Oxford professor Kenneth Wheare, expert on federalism and member of the Federal Union, which was launched in 1938 to support European federalism.

142. Claudia Jones to Eric Williams, July 23, 1957. British Passport and Relating Letters 1/6, Claudia Jones Memorial Collection Box 1 (3).

143. David Killingray, 'The West Indian Federation and Decolonization in the British Caribbean', *The Journal of Caribbean History*, vol. 34, no. 1 (2000), pp. 71–88. Margery Perham was also a federalist. 'Everywhere the tide runs in favour of larger groupings round the few great power-centres, of greater control for metropolitan and federal governments. This, indeed, is one of the problems of our time—how to square this seemingly inevitable concentration of power at a few centres with the self-respect and initiative and freedom of individual men and their small traditional groupings'. Perham in Elspeth Huxley and Margery Perham, *Race and Politics in Kenya: A Correspondence between Elspeth Huxley and Margery Perham* (London: Faber & Faber, rev. edn, 1956), p. 164.

144. Claudia Jones, 'Books—Towards a W.I. Confederation', *West Indian Gazette And Afro-Asian Caribbean News*, vol. 4, no. 7 (June 1961), p. 2.

145. 'Will Eastern Caribbean Federate?', *West Indian Gazette And Afro-Asian Caribbean News*, vol. 4, no. 13 (January 1962), p. 2; the new entity 'would be a loose association for securing to their mutual advantages certain objectives of a more or less limited character such as common defence arrangements, an economic or customs union, or merely good neighbourliness . . . The question of external economic aid with no strings attached is vital'. 'West Indians Discuss The Case For Nationhood', p. 12.

146. Jones, 'Books—Capitalism and Slavery', p. 4.

147. Getachew, *Worldmaking*, p. 118. For an excellent discussion of Williams's turn to the US, and some of its limits, see pp. 110–19.

148. Claudia Jones, 'Profile: Dr. Eric Williams: Conscience of Caribbean Nationalism', *West Indian Gazette And Afro-Asian Caribbean News*, vol. 3, no. 4 (December 1960), p. 2.

149. Jones, 'Profile: Dr. Eric Williams', p. 2.

150. Jones, 'Profile: Dr. Eric Williams', p. 2.

151. Jones, 'Profile: Dr. Eric Williams', p. 2.

152. Jones, 'Books—Capitalism and Slavery', p. 4. 'Editorial: Trinidad "Goes it Alone"', *West Indian Gazette And Afro-Asian Caribbean News*, vol. 4, no. 14 (February 1962), p. 2.

153. Claudia Jones, 'American Imperialism and the British West Indies', *Political Affairs* (April 1958), pp. 9–28.

154. 'Editorial: 'Trinidad "Goes it Alone"'.

155. Jones, 'Editorial: US-Jamaica Military Assistance Pact Arouses Concern', *West Indian Gazette And Afro-Asian Caribbean News*, vol. 5, no. 12 (July/August 1963), pp. 1, 4, here 4.

156. C.L.R. James, *Party Politics in the West Indies* (San Juan, Trinidad: Vedic Enterprises, 1962).

157. Stephen Howe, 'C.L.R. James: Visions of History, Visions of Britain', in Schwarz (ed.), *West Indian Intellectuals in Britain*, pp. 153–74, here 159.

158. For a selection of her writings see Selma James, *Sex, Race, and Class: The Perspective of Winning: A Selection of Writings, 1952–2011*, preface by Marcus Rediker, introduction by Nina López (Oakland: PM Press, 2012).

159. 'Books by Critics: Long Lament of a Nagging Aunt', *West Indian Gazette*, vol. 5, no. 7 (December 1962), p. 10.

160. 'Books by Critics: Long Lament of a Nagging Aunt', p. 10.

161. 'Books by Critics: Long Lament of a Nagging Aunt', p. 10.

162. In Schwarz, 'Crossing the Seas', p. 5.

163. Ian Hall, *Dilemmas of Decline: British Intellectuals and World Politics, 1945–1975* (Berkeley: University of California Press, 2012), p. 3. Similarly, if Caribbean intellectuals in the metropole were among the leading anti-fascist thinkers and activists, then it is puzzling to exclude the Jamaican activist Una Marson from political and intellectual histories of women's anti-fascist political work in Britain. Cf. Julie V. Gottlieb, *'Guilty Women', Foreign Policy, and Appeasement in Inter-War Britain* (Basingstoke: Palgrave, 2015); see also Imaobong D. Umoren, 'Anti-Fascism and the Development of Global Race Women, 1928–1945', *Callaloo*, vol. 39, no. 1 (2016) pp. 151–65.

164. This has been done for the interwar period but not the period after World War II. See Alexander E. Davis, Vineet Thakur, and Peter Vale (eds.), *The Imperial Discipline* (London: Pluto, 2020).

## 10. 'This is No Witch-Hunt'

1. Rachel Wall, 'China and the Asian scene'. Unpublished paper presented at History Conference at St Anne's, July 26, 1965. Rachel Wall papers, now deposited at St Hugh's College.

2. Martin Ceadel, 'The Academic Normalization of International Relations at Oxford, 1920–2012: Structures Transcended' in Christopher Hood, Desmond King, and Gillian Peele (eds.), *Forging a Discipline: A Critical Assessment of Oxford's Development of the Study of Politics and International Relations in Comparative Perspective* (Oxford: Oxford University Press, 2014), p. 196.

3. Ceadel, 'Academic Normalization', p. 197.

4. Confidential. Visitorial Board. Miss R. F. Wall. May 13, 1977. FA 9/3/428, File 1, Rachel Wall university file. Bodleian Library, Oxford.

5. Caedel, 'Academic Normalization', p. 198.

6. Rachel Wall, 'Options in International Relations', 1966. Rachel Wall papers.

7. Jack Halberstam, *The Queer Art of Failure* (Durham: Duke University Press, 2011).

8. Dennis Kavanagh, 'Obituary: Professor W.J.M. Mackenzie', *The Independent* (August 26, 1996).

9. Application for Faculty Lectureship in International Relations Combined with College Lectureship in Politics. FA 9/3/428, File 1, Rachel Wall university file.

10. Rachel Wall, CV and Memorandum, September 27, 1977. FA 9/3/429, File 2, Rachel Wall university file. Elizabeth Wiskemann, *The Rome–Berlin Axis: A History of the Relations between Hitler and Mussolini* (London: Oxford University Press, 1949).

11. W.J.M. Mackenzie to A.M. Bohun, May 28, 1956. Rachel Frances Wall LSE student dossier.

12. Cathie Wilson reflections, May 2, 2017.

13. Rachel Wall, 'Proposed Scheme of Work'. L. C. Robbins to Charlies Manning, November 9, 1955. Rachel Frances Wall LSE student dossier.

14. Anon to L. C. Robbins, November 15, 1955. Rachel Frances Wall LSE student dossier.

15. Civil Service Commission, Rachel Wall, February 11, 1957. Rachel Frances Wall LSE student dossier.

16. Coral Bell, 'Journey with Alternative Maps' in Joseph Kruzel and James N. Rosenau (eds.), *Journeys through World Politics: Autobiographical Reflections of Thirty-four Academic Travelers* (Lexington: Lexington Books, 1989), pp. 339–50, here 339.

17. Bell, 'Journey with Alternative Maps', p. 339.

18. Coral Bell, 'A Preoccupation with Armageddon', unpublished memoir. Canberra, 2012, p. 2. I am grateful to Ian Hall for sharing a copy.

19. Bell, 'Journey with Alternative Maps', p. 339

20. Bell, 'Preoccupation with Armageddon', p. 3.

21. Bell, 'Preoccupation with Armageddon', p. 3.

22. Bell, 'Preoccupation with Armageddon', p. 4.

23. Bell, 'Preoccupation with Armageddon', p. 3.

24. Bell, 'Preoccupation with Armageddon', p. 11.

25. Bell, 'Journey with Alternative Maps', p. 343.

26. Bell, 'Preoccupation with Armageddon', p. 12.

27. Bell, 'Journey with Alternative Maps', p. 342.

28. See, for example, Timothy Dunne, *Inventing International Society: A History of the English School* (New York: Macmillan 1998) and Cornelia Navari and Daniel M. Green, *Guide to the English School in International Studies* (Oxford: Wiley-Blackwell 2014), both of which exclude Coral Bell.

29. Bell, 'Journey with Alternative Maps', p. 342.

30. Herbert Butterfield to Kenneth Thompson, October 17, 1956, BUTT/28. Cambridge University Library.

31. Herbert Butterfield to Kenneth Thompson, December 14, 1956. BUTT/28. Cambridge University Library.

32. Martin Wight, *Four Seminal Thinkers in International Theory: Machiavelli, Grotius, Kant, and Mazzini*, edited by Gabriele Wight, Brian Porter, and David S. Yost (Oxford: Oxford University Press, 2005).

33. Bell, 'Preoccupation with Armageddon', pp. 13, 14. Geoffrey L. Goodwin, *Britain and the United Nations* (New York: Manhattan Publishing Company, 1957). At Chatham House, Bell also met figures such as Michael Howard and Alastair Buchan, later founders of the International Institute for Strategic Studies (IISS).

34. Bell, 'Journey with Alternative Maps', pp. 342–3.

35. Bell, 'Journey with Alternative Maps', p. 343.

36. Bell, 'Preoccupation with Armageddon', p. 14.

37. Bell, 'Journey with Alternative Maps', pp. 342–3.

38. Geoffrey Barraclough to Christopher Montague (Monty) Woodhouse, June 11, 1956. Chatham House 4/BARR/1.

39. Geoffrey Barraclough, *History in a Changing World* (Oxford: Basil Blackwell, 1955).

40. Bell, 'Preoccupation with Armageddon', p. 14.

41. Bell, 'Journey with Alternative Maps', p. 343.

42. Bell, 'Preoccupation with Armageddon', p. 12.

43. 'Report for Postgraduate Students Registered Session 1955/56', Bell LSE File 2, n.d.; Coral Bell to LSE Academic Registrar, May 1965, Bell LSE File 1.

44. 'Student Record', Bell LSE File 2., n.d.

45. Barraclough to Woodhouse, June 11, 1956.

46. Geoffrey Barraclough, *Survey of International Affairs, 1956–1958* (Oxford: Oxford University Press, 1962); Geoffrey Barraclough, *Survey of International Affairs, 1959–1960* (Oxford: Oxford University Press, 1964).

47. Geoffrey Barraclough and Rachel F. Wall, 'The Uncommitted Peoples' in *Survey of International Affairs, 1955–1956* (Oxford: Oxford University Press, 1960), pp. 57–65.

48. See, for example, Geoffrey Barraclough, *An Introduction to Contemporary History* (London: Penguin, 1964) and Geoffrey Barraclough, 'Universal History' in H.P.R. Finberg's *Approaches to History: A Symposium* (London: Routledge, 1962), pp. 83–109, but also Geoffrey Barraclough, *European Unity in Thought and Action* (Oxford: Blackwell, 1963); Geoffrey Barraclough, *Turning Points in World History* (London: Thames and Hudson, 1979); Geoffrey Barraclough, *Worlds Apart: Untimely Thoughts on Development and Development Strategies* (London: IDS, 1980); Geoffrey Barraclough, *From Agadir to Armageddon: Anatomy of a Crisis* (London: Weidenfeld and Nicolson, 1982).

49. Andrew Shonfield, *Modern Capitalism: The Changing Balance of Public and Private Power* (Oxford: Oxford University Press, 1965), pp. xv–vi. Although her specific role went unacknowledged, Strange continued to work closely with Shonfield as he revised the book for its second edition in 1969 while she was completing her own related Chatham House projects on international monetary relations. I'm grateful to Louis Pauly and Roger Tooze for sharing their memories of Susan Strange's engagement with Shonfield at Chatham House.

50. Rachel F. Wall, 'Review of *The Year Book of World Affairs 1957*, edited by George W. Keaton and Georg Schwarzenberger (London: Stevens for the London Institute of World Affairs, 1957)', *International Affairs*, vol. 34, no. 3, p. 332; Rachel F. Wall, 'The Year Book of World Affairs 1960 Vol. 14', *International Affairs*, vol. 37, no. 4 (1961), p. 483; Rachel F. Wall, 'An Atlas of Africa', *International Affairs*, vol. 36, no. 3 (1960), p. 399; Rachel F. Wall, 'The Indian Year Book of International Affairs 1959. Vol. VIII', *International Affairs*, vol. 37, no. 3 (1961), p. 340; Rachel F. Wall, 'The Indian Year Book of International Affairs 1957', *International Affairs*, vol. 35, no. 2 (1959), pp. 198–9; Rachel F. Wall, 'Economic Survey of Asia and the Far East 1960', *International Affairs*, vol. 38, no. 3 (1962), pp. 405–6; Rachel F. Wall, 'Rettet die Freiheit: Gründungskongress am 20.2.1959 in Köln', *International Affairs*, vol. 36, no. 3 (1960), p. 379; Rachel F. Wall, 'Documents on Canadian Foreign Policy 1917–1939', *International Affairs*, vol. 39, no. 1 (1963), p. 150.

51. Rachel F. Wall, 'Current Events Year Book 1958: A Review of the Important Events of the year 1957', *International Affairs*, vol. 35, no. 1 (1959), p. 137; Rachel F. Wall, 'Germany and World Politics in the Twentieth Century', *International Affairs*, vol. 35, no. 3 (1959), p. 350; Rachel F. Wall, 'Weltgeschichte des 20. Jahrhunderts', *International Affairs*, vol. 35, no. 3 (1959), p. 51; Rachel F. Wall, 'La conduite des affaires étrangères en France', *International Affairs*, vol. 36, no. 3 (1960), p. 376; Rachel F. Wall, 'Lezioni di Storia dei Trattati e Politica Internazionale. I. Parte Generale', *International Affairs*, vol. 37, no. 4 (1961), pp. 483–4; Rachel F. Wall, 'Aufgabe und Verantwortung der politischen Parteien', *International Affairs*, vol. 36, no. 3 (1960), pp. 378–9; Rachel F. Wall, 'From Stalin to Khrushchev', *International Affairs*, vol. 36, no. 3 (1960), p. 390; Rachel F. Wall, 'Foreign Relations of the United States. Diplomatic Papers', *International Affairs*, vol. 38, no. 3 (1962), pp. 384–5; Rachel F. Wall, 'Japans Russlandpolitik von 1939 bis 1941. Der Schriften des Instituts für Asienkunde in Hamburg. Band X', *International Affairs*, vol. 39, no. 4 (1963), pp. 642–3.

52. Rachel F. Wall, 'Christian Ethics and the Dilemmas of Foreign Policy', *International Affairs*, vol. 36, no. 3 (1960), pp. 349–50; Rachel F. Wall, 'I Speak of Freedom: A Statement of African Ideology', *International Affairs*, vol. 37, no. 4 (1961), p. 535; Rachel F. Wall, 'Mr Gandhi', *International Affairs*, vol. 38, no. 1 (1962), p. 88; Rachel F. Wall, 'Tibet and its History and My Land and my People', *International Affairs*, vol. 39, no. 1 (1963), p. 139.

53. Rachel Wall, 'The Twentieth Century, 1914–1966', *Annual Bulletin of Historical Literature*, vol. 52, no. 1 (1968), pp. 89–115.

54. Philip E. Mosely to Rachel Wall, January 20, 1959, Rachel Wall papers; Richard C. Snyder to Geoffrey Barraclough, December 18, 1958, Rachel Wall papers.

55. Rachel Wall, CV and Memorandum, September 27, 1977.

56. On Dean's international thought see Andrew Jewett, 'Collective Security for Common Men and Women: Vera Micheles Dean and US Foreign Relations' in Patricia Owens and Katharina Rietzler (eds.), *Women's International Thought: A New History* (Cambridge: Cambridge University Press, 2021), pp. 306–26.

57. Coral Bell, *Negotiation from Strength: A Study in the Politics of Power* (London: Chatto & Windus, 1962).

58. Ian Hall, 'The Interpretation of Power Politics: Coral Bell's International Thought' in Sheryn Lee and Desmond Ball, *Power and International Relations* (Canberra: ANU Press, 2014), pp. 45–55, here 50.

59. Richard W. Van Alstyne to Kathleen Peace, February 9, 1961. GCAR 2/5/6/1/7, Rachel Wall file, Girton College.

60. Geoffrey Barraclough to Kathleen Peace, February 14, 1961. GCAR 2/5/6/1/7, Rachel Wall file.

61. D. W. Brogan to Mary Cartwright, February 13, 1961. GCAR 2/5/6/1/7, Rachel Wall file.

62. Brogan to Cartwright, February 13, 1961.

63. Cathie Wilson reflections, May 2, 2017.

64. Peter Linehan, 'Obituaries: Geoffrey Barraclough', *The Eagle*, vol. 70, no. 293 (1985) pp. 48–50, here 50.

65. D. H. Fischer, 'Barraclough, Geoffrey (1908–1984)', *Oxford Dictionary of National Biography* (September 23, 2004).

66. Geoffrey Barraclough to Kathleen Peace, February 14, 1961.

67. Barraclough, 'Universal History', p. 91.

68. Rachel Wall, 'The Teaching of World History', n.d., pp. 1–34, here 5. Rachel Wall papers.

69. Wall, 'Teaching of World History', p. 5.

70. Wall, 'Teaching of World History', pp. 13, 20; Rachel Wall to The Secretary, Girton College, January 9, 1961. GCAR 2/5/6/1/7, Rachel Wall file.

71. Cathie Wilson reflections, May 2, 2017.

72. Cathie Wilson, 'An Awkward Woman—Your Relative and Mine: Brave, Bookish and Kind', unpublished memories of Rachel Wall, November 2023. Written to be deposited with Rachel Wall's papers transferred to St Hugh's College, Oxford in November 2023.

73. Cathie Wilson reflections, May 2, 2017.

74. Wall listed her publications as an article, 'New Ways in History', in the special number of *The Times Literary Supplement* (April 7, 1966), 'dealing with new approaches to Asian history'; the 20th-century bibliography for the *Annual Bulletin of Historical Literature* for 1965 and 1966 (published in 1967 and 1968). 'Die Washington Konferenz: Ursachen und Folgen im Pazifischen Raum' in *Die Folgen von Versailles 1919–1924* (Göttingen: Musterschmidt, 1968), pp. 29–55 and 'Japan's Politik in der Vorkriegsjahren' in *Weltpolitik 1938–1939* (Göttingen: Musterschmidt, 1975), as well as reviews in *International Affairs, English Historical Review, History,* and *Das historisch-politische Buch.*

75. Rachel Wall, CV and Memorandum, September 27, 1977.

76. Rachel F. Wall, *Japan's Century: An Interpretation of Japanese History Since the Eighteen-Fifties* (London: Historical Association, 1964), p. 3.

77. Rachel Wall, 'Study: International Relations in East Asia'. GCAR 2/5/6/1/7, Rachel Wall file.

78. Wall, 'China and the Asian scene', p. 13.

79. Application for Faculty Lectureship in International Relations Combined with College Lectureship in Politics.

80. Barraclough to Secretary to the Faculties, Oxford. February 19, 1964, FA 9/3/428, File 1, Rachel Wall university file.

81. There were seven applicants, two interviewed, and the appointment committee was the Chairman of the Faculty Board and Warden of Nuffield Professor Max Beloff, and Wilfred Knapp. At the time of writing, the University is withholding the name of Headlam-Morley's preferred candidate because it cannot determine whether she is living or dead and thus the information falls under the the Data Protection Act 2018. 'Proposed correction to minute 17 of the meeting of the Social Studies Board held on 12 March 1964: communication from Professor. Headlam-Morley' Ref. No. LU/3/SS. See OUA/UR 6/LU/3/SS/H1, file 1. University Registry Correspondence Social Studies Board Higher Studies Fund faculty lectureship (1) 1963–1964. Bodleian Library, Oxford.

82. Coral Bell, 'The State of the Discipline: I.R.', *Quadrant*, vol. 12, no. 1 (January–February 1968), pp. 79–84, here 82. Bell endorsed Martin Wight's 'Why Is There No International Theory?', *International Relations*, vol. 2, no. 1 (1960), pp. 35–48.

83. Bell, 'The State of the Discipline', p. 83.

84. A. L. Burns, 'The Debatable Alliance: An Essay in Anglo-American Relations', *The Australian Quarterly*, vol. 36, no. 4 (1964), pp. 107–10, here 108.

85. Geoffrey Goodwin to LSE Director, October 19, 1965. Susan Strange LSE staff file, 1959–1974.

86. Cornelia Navari Oral History. Leverhulme Project on Women the History of International Thought. Available at https://whit.web.ox.ac.uk/oral-history-archive. Navari was born in Pittsburgh, Pennsylvania and studied history at Barnard Women's College in New York when the atmosphere, she described, was 'very blue stocking, intellectual women', a legacy of Virginia Gildersleeve's long tenure as the dean. After an internship on the Africa Desk at the Voice of America in Washington, Navari studied for an M.Sc. in IR at the LSE in 1966.

87. Rachel Trickett, 'Rachel Wall', *St Hugh's College Chronicle, 1988–89*, no. 62, pp. 33–4, here 33.

88. Trickett, 'Rachel Wall', p. 33.

89. Cathie Wilson reflections, May 2, 2017.

90. Rachel Wall, Untitled, n.d. Rachel Wall papers.

91. Wall, 'China and the Asian scene', p. 7.

92. Wall, 'The Twentieth Century, 1914–1966', p. 89.

93. Rachel Wall, 'The Nature of Contemporary History', BBC broadcast reprinted in Patricia Owens, Katharina Rietzler, Kimberly Hutchings, and Sarah C. Dunstan (eds.), *Women's International Thought: Towards a New Canon* (Cambridge: Cambridge University Press, 2022), pp. 69–74, here 72. For a discussion of the relationship between contemporary history and early IR in Britain see Geoffrey Field, 'Elizabeth Wiskemann, Scholar-Journalist, and the Study of International Relations' in Owens and Rietzler (eds.), *Women's International Thought: A New History*, pp. 198–220. Also see Wall, 'New Ways in History'.

94. Wall, 'Teaching of World History', pp. 9–10.

95. Wall, 'China and the Asian scene', p. 9.

96. Barraclough, 'Universal History', p. 89.

97. Wall, 'The Nature of Contemporary History', p. 71.

98. The BBC broadcast is reprinted as Wall, 'The Nature of Contemporary History'.

99. Adom Getachew, *Worldmaking after Empire: The Rise and Fall of Self-Determination* (Princeton: Princeton University Press, 2019).

100. Wall, 'The Nature of Contemporary History', p. 72.

101. Ronald Segal, *The Race War: The World-Wide Conflict of Races* (London: Jonathan Cape, 1966).

102. Wall, 'The Twentieth Century, 1914–1966', p. 90. Also see Ian Hall, 'The Revolt against the West: Decolonisation and Its Repercussions in British International Thought, 1945–75', *The International History Review*, vol. 33, no. 1 (2011), pp. 43–64.

103. Cathie Wilson reflections, May 2, 2017.

104. Sibyl Crowe interview with Jill Hosford Pellew, October 11, 1989, St Hilda's Sound Archive, 1A20.

105. Wall, 'China and the Asian scene'.

106. Report of the Committee on the International Relations Rubrics, November 24, 1966, OUA/FA 3/4/2/6. Sub-Faculty of Politics Meeting Minutes, November 1949 to October 1968, OUA/FA 3/4/1/1. Bodleian Library.

107. Rachel Wall, 'Options in International Relations'.

108. Sub-Faculty of Politics Meeting Minutes, May 2, 1968, OUA/FA 3/4/1/1.

109. W. F. Knapp, Proposal for B.Phil. in International Relations, February 27, 1970. Rachel Wall papers.

110. Wall to University Registry, July 2, 1973, FA 9/3/428, File 1, Rachel Wall university file.

111. Wall to University Registry, July 2, 1973.

112. Geoffrey Hudson to Wilfred Knapp, March 20, 1969, FA 9/3/428, File 1, Rachel Wall university file.

113. C. H. Patterson, Secretary of Faculties, January 11, 1965, FA 9/3/428, File 1, Rachel Wall university file.

114. C. H. Patterson, Secretary of Faculties, January 11, 1965.

115. Dorothea Helen Forbes Gray to Kathleen Kenyon, November 5, 1964, SGH/S/2/2/47/1 1/56, St Hugh's College.

116. Kathleen Kenyon to Wilfred Knapp, April 25, 1969, FA 9/3/428, File 1, Rachel Wall university file.

117. Headlam-Morley was at St Hugh's, but as Montague Burton Chair, she was relieved of all undergraduate teaching. I have found no record of Headlam-Morley's opinion of Wall, except that she thought another candidate better suited to her post, nor of Wall's opinion of Headlam-Morley.

118. Rachel Wall, Untitled, n.d., Rachel Wall papers.

119. Wall to Secretary of Faculties, April 28, 1966, FA 9/3/428, File 1, Rachel Wall university file.

120. Cathie Wilson reflections, May 2, 2017. This is confirmed by Wall's passport.

121. Rachel Wall, Untitled, n.d., Rachel Wall papers.

122. Coral Bell to LSE Academic Registrar, May 1965, Bell LSE File 1. Coral Bell, *The Asian Balance of Power: A Comparison with European Precedents* (London: Institute for Strategic Studies, 1968).

123. Coral Bell, *The Conventions of Crisis: A Study in Diplomatic Management* (Oxford: Oxford University Press, 1971), p. 6, fn. 4.

124. Coral Bell, *The Diplomacy of Detente: The Kissinger Era* (London: Martin Robertson, 1977).

125. Martin Wight, 'European Studies' in David Daiches (ed.), *The Idea of a New University: An Experiment in Sussex* (London: A. Deutsch, 1964), pp. 100–119.

126. Coral Bell to Martin Wight, July 29, 1971. WIGHT/233/61. LSE Library.

127. Wight, *Four Seminal Thinkers in International Theory: Machiavelli, Grotius, Kant, and Mazzini*.

128. Zdenek Kavan, 'Memories of IR at Sussex', Programme of the 50th Anniversary Conference, Department of International Relations, University of Sussex, 2015, p. 28.

129. Hedley Bull, 'The European International Order' in Kai Alderson and Andrew Hurrell (eds.), *Hedley Bull on International Society* (Basingstoke: Macmillan, 1980, new edn, 2000), pp. 170–87, here 175.

130. Wilfred Knapp, 'Untitled Memorandum', June 9, 1969, FA 9/3/428, File 1, Rachel Wall university file.

131. Knapp, 'Untitled Memorandum', June 9, 1969.

132. Geoffrey Hudson to Wilfred Knapp, March 20, 1969.

133. Kathleen Kenyon to Wilfred Knapp, April 25, 1969. Kenyon was not happy that the Faculty Board did not initiate a formal process for the renewal of joint appointments because 'much of the embarrassment of separate consideration and the passing of views from one body to another would be avoided'. Kathleen Kenyon to Wilfred Knapp, June 26, 1969, FA 9/3/428, File 1, Rachel Wall university file.

134. Unknown to Kathleen Kenyon, March 21, 1969, Rachel Wall file, Lady Margaret Hall.

135. Sibyl to Lucy Sutherland, March 20, 1969, Rachel Wall file, Lady Margaret Hall.

136. Ceadel, 'Academic Normalization', p. 194.

137. Knapp, 'Untitled Memorandum', June 9, 1969.

138. Andrew C. Boag to Sir Alexander Cairncross, January 7, 1972, FA 9/3/428, File 1, Rachel Wall university file.

139. Max Beloff to Rachel Trickett, July 2, 1970, SGH/S/2/2/47/1, St Hugh's College.

140. Geoffrey Barraclough to Rachel Wall, January 4, 1972, Rachel Wall papers.

141. Rachel Wall to British Federation of University Women, September 10, 1973, Rachel Wall papers.

142. Caedel, 'Academic Normalization', p. 197.

143. Andrew C. Boag to Sir Alexander Cairncross, January 7, 1972.

144. J.P.W. Ropel to Rachel Wall, January 3, 1971, FA 9/3/428, File 1, Rachel Wall university file.

145. Phyllis Chesler, *Women and Madness* (London: Palgrave, 1972); Joan Busfield, 'Sexism and Psychiatry', *Sociology*, vol. 23, no. 3. (1989), pp. 343–64.

146. Rachel Wall to J. H. Burnett, June 24, 1976, FA 9/3/428, File 1, Rachel Wall university file.

147. Rachel Wall to Geoffrey Barraclough, July 19, 1973, Rachel Wall papers.

148. Dr O. S. Frank to J. H. Burnett, December 3, 1975, FA 9/3/428, File 1, Rachel Wall university file.

149. A.D.D. to Rachel Wall, June 29, 1975; Rachel Trickett to Rachel Wall, February 14, 1975; SGH/S/2/2/47/11/22, St Hugh's College.

150. C. H. Paterson, Memorandum, July 20, 1975, FA 9/3/428, File 1, Rachel Wall university file.

151. Dr O. S. Frank to J. H. Burnett, December 3, 1975.

152. Wall to D. M. Stewart, December 5, 1976, FA 9/3/428, File 1, Rachel Wall university file.

153. J. H. Burnett to Rachel Wall, November 24, 1975, FA 9/3/428, File 1, Rachel Wall university file.

154. D. M. Stewart to Mr. Hall and C. H. Paterson, n.d. c.1976, FA 9/3/428, File 1, Rachel Wall university file.

155. D. M. Stewart to Mr. Hall and C. H. Paterson, n.d.

156. Wall to D. M. Stewart, December 5, 1976.

157. Wall to D. M. Stewart, December 5, 1976.

158. Bent Juel-Jensen to D. M. Stewart, December 28, 1976; Bent Juel-Jensen to D. M. Stewart, December 13, 1976; FA 9/3/428, File 1, Rachel Wall university file.

159. D. M. Stewart, Memorandum, January 5, 1977, FA 9/3/428, File 1, Rachel Wall university file.

160. Wall to D. M. Stewart, December 5, 1976.

161. D. M. Stewart to C. H. Paterson, December 14, 1976, FA 9/3/428, File 1, Rachel Wall university file.

162. D. M. Stewart, Memorandum, January 17, 1977. FA 9/3/428, File 1, Rachel Wall university file. Emphasis added.

163. Memo from CHP/JP, January 7, 1977, FA 9/3/428, File 1, Rachel Wall university file.

164. Wall was trying to sort 'out her copious documentation', he recounted, and 'I formed the impression that Miss Wall was in a mildly hypomanic mood as well as displaying considerable abnormalities of personality'. She 'will not accept any form of psychological help at present'. Richard Mayou to Bent Juel-Jensen, March 11, 1977, FA 9/3/429, File 2, Rachel Wall university file.

165. John Ledingham to D. M. Stewart, April 17, 1977, FA 9/3/429, File 2, Rachel Wall university file.

166. John Dunwoody to Bent Juel-Jensen, May 23, 1977, FA 9/3/429, File 2, Rachel Wall university file.

167. Geoffrey Caston to Wall, May 25, 1977; 'Miss R.F. Wall', May, 13, 1977; FA 9/3/429, File 2, Rachel Wall university file.

168. Wall to Geoffrey Caston, June 16, 1977, FA 9/3/429, File 2, Rachel Wall university file.

169. D. M. Stewart, Memorandum, July 4, 1977, FA 9/3/429, File 2, Rachel Wall university file.

170. Wall to D. M. Stewart, February 11, 1977: 'From my observation, I surmise that, putting it bluntly, he is an inveterate snob. I think it just possible that had Professor Burnett had his title typed under his name, he might have received a reply. My suggestion is try some such. String out a list of initials, typed under and after your name. The end of the Concise Oxford Dictionary is a rich source. What about L.I.F.O., L.W.M? (Last in first out and low-water mark); or M.V., M.R.B.M? (motor vessel and medium-range ballistic missile)'. FA 9/3/429, File 2, Rachel Wall university file.

171. D. M. Stewart, Memorandum, July 4, 1977.

172. Mr. P. W. Jones, Memorandum, September 23, 1977, FA 9/3/429, File 2, Rachel Wall university file.

173. Wall also rejected the inclusion of the trade union chairman Tony Honoré, because he was a professor of comparative and civil law and Wall only knew about international law. She thought Juel-Jensen 'was confused about the difference between International History and World History', perhaps from reaching William McNeill's book *Plagues and Peoples*. Rachel Wall to Geoffrey Caston, June 24, 1977; Geoffrey Caston, Memorandum, June 21, 1977; FA 9/3/429, File 2, Rachel Wall university file.

174. Her address was Dr Laura Pozzi of Via Crati, 10, 00199 Rome, Italy. A University Constable reported trying but failing to hand deliver the letter informing Wall of the date and time of the ad hoc medical board, noting there was 'Evidence of occupation in that the Washing Machine could be seen and heard operating in the kitchen'. University Constable, September 23, 1977, FA 9/3/429, File 2, Rachel Wall university file.

175. 'Report of the Ad Hoc Board to Consider the Case of Miss Rachel Frances Wall', September 29, 1977, FA 9/3/429, File 2, Rachel Wall university file.

176. Visitatorial Board Minutes of the Meeting held on October 17, 1977, p. 1, FA 9/3/429, File 2, Rachel Wall university file.

177. Visitatorial Board Minutes of the Meeting held on October 17, 1977.

178. Geoffrey Caston to Rachel Wall, October 17, 1977, FA 9/3/429, File 2, Rachel Wall university file.

179. P. W. Jones, Memorandum, October 21, 1977, FA 9/3/429, File 2, , Rachel Wall university file.

180. D. M. Stewart, Memorandum, July 4, 1977.

181. J.G.G. Leadington to Bent Juel-Jensen, July 28, 1977, FA 9/3/429, File 2, Rachel Wall university file.

182. Geoffrey Hudson to Wilfred Knapp, March 20, 1969.

183. Wall to J. H. Burnett, June 24, 1976.

184. R.E.R to Nevil Johnson, October 18, 1977, FA 9/3/429, File 2, Rachel Wall university file.

185. Nevil Johnson to University Register, December 9, 1977, FA 9/3/429, File 2, Rachel Wall university file.

186. 'Report of the Ad Hoc Board to Consider the Case of Miss Rachel Frances Wall', September 29, 1977.

187. H. G. Nicholas to Nevil Johnson, December 7, 1977, FA 9/3/429, File 2, Rachel Wall university file.

188. Nevil Johnson to University Registrar, December 5, 1977, FA 9/3/429, File 2, Rachel Wall university file.

189. H. G. Nicholas to Nevil Johnson, December 7, 1977.

190. Hedley Bull to Nevil Johnson, December 6, 1977, FA 9/3/429, File 2, Rachel Wall university file.

191. Minutes of an extraordinary meeting on December 16, 1977, FA 9/3/429, File 2, Rachel Wall university file.

192. Wall to D. M. Stewart, December 16, 1977, FA 9/3/429, File 2, Rachel Wall university file.

193. Wall to Geoffrey Caston, December 16, 1977, FA 9/3/429 File 2, Rachel Wall university file. Wall still did not wish to join the union as it might affect her ability to work in the United States.

194. Wall to Mr. Roper, December 18, 1977, FA 9/3/429, File 2, Rachel Wall university file.

195. P. W. Jones to Mr. Parker at the University Press, December 21, 1977, FA 9/3/429, File 2, Rachel Wall university file.

196. Rachel Trickett to Geoffrey Caston, January 17, 1978. Caston had informed Trickett that Wall 'has given no sign of acknowledging that her employment is to be terminated. I fear that her mental state continues to be greatly disturbed'. Geoffrey Caston to Rachel Trickett, January 13, 1978. FA 9/3/429, File 2, Rachel Wall university file.

197. Wall to Geoffrey Caston, February 12, 1978, FA 9/3/429, File 2, Rachel Wall university file.

198. Visitorial Board, Minutes of the Meeting held on February 24, 1978, FA 9/3/429 File 2, Rachel Wall university file. See, for example, J.G.G. Leadington to Bent Juel-Jensen, July 28, 1977.

199. Visitorial Board, Minutes of the Meeting held on February 24, 1978.

200. Geoffrey Caston to Rachel Wall, March 1, 1978, FA 9/3/429, File 2, Rachel Wall university file.

201. Wall to Geoffrey Caston, March 3, 1978, FA 9/3/429, File 2, Rachel Wall university file.

202. File Note, October 21, 1985, FA 9/3/429, File 2, Rachel Wall university file. It was not until the Access to Medical Reports Act of 1988 that individuals were allowed access to any medical report supplied by a medical practitioner for employment.

203. Bent Juel-Jensen to D. M. Stewart, December 13, 1976.

204. D. M. Stewart to Mr. Hall and C. H. Paterson, n.d.

205. Marjorie Chibnall to Rachel Wall, April 19, 1968, Rachel Wall papers.

206. Ray Dawson to Rachel Wall, March 22, 1971; Marjorie Chibnall to Rachel Wall, November 3, 1970; Rachel Wall papers. Later, in 1976, she applied for but missed the deadline for a job as a research assistant in the Imperial War Museum. She wanted the job, she said, because she did 'not have enough to do' at Oxford and, given her relatively few graduate students, she 'would welcome the opportunity to advise researchers on the use of the Imperial War Museum archives and communicate my enthusiasm for 20th century history without the pedantry of explaining who Anthony Eden was'. When asked whether she had any 'disease or physical defect', she wrote, 'overweight with intermittent depression'. Imperial War Museum Research Assistants, November 10, 1976, Rachel Wall papers.

207. Wall to Board of the Faculties, October 7, 1976, FA 9/3/429, File 2, Rachel Wall university file.

208. Cathie Wilson reflections, May 2, 2017.

209. Fischer, 'Barraclough, Geoffrey'.

210. Trickett, 'Rachel Wall', p. 34.

211. Cathie Wilson reflections, May 2, 2017.

212. Cathie Wilson reflections, May 2, 2017. The current notice in the *Girton College Register* is misleading, stating that Wall 'Died 1989, after a long illness'. At the author's request, this was since annotated by Matilda Watson, the College archivist, to note that the cause of death was smoke inhalation.

213. Elizabeth Thomas reflections, May 2, 2017.

## 11. 'These Women with Large Families'

1. In a survey of sixty histories of international thought, Susan Strange is the most recognised historical woman. Patricia Owens, 'Women and the History of International Thought', *International Studies Quarterly*, vol. 62, no. 3 (2018), pp. 467–81.

2. Susan Strange, *States and Markets* (London: Pinter, 1988). Later she published two more important book-length works, Susan Strange, *The Retreat of the State: The Diffusion of Power in the World Economy* (Cambridge: Cambridge University Press, 1996); Susan Strange, *Mad Money* (Manchester: Manchester University Press, 1998).

3. After her death in 1998, the International Studies Association (ISA) awarded the Susan Strange Prize to the figure who has most 'challenged conventional wisdom and intellectual and organizational complacency' in the field. Since 2010, the British International Studies Association (BISA) has awarded the Susan Strange Best Book Prize.

4. Christine Sylvester, *Feminist International Relations: An Unfinished Journey* (Cambridge: Cambridge University Press, 2002), p. 5.

5. Roger Morgan, Jochen Lorentzen, Anna Leander, and Stefano Guzzini, 'A Cake for Susan: Acknowledgements' in Roger Morgan et al (eds.), *New Diplomacy in the Post–Cold War World: Essays for Susan Strange* (Basingstoke: Macmillan, 1993), p. v.

6. See, for example, Thomas C. Lawton, James N. Rosenau and Amy C. Verdun (eds.), *Strange Power: Shaping the Parameters of International Relations and International Political Economy* (Aldershot: Ashgate, 2000); Susan Strange, Roger Tooze, and Christopher May, *Authority and Markets: Susan Strange's Writings on Political Economy* (Basingstoke: Palgrave, 2002); Morgan et al (eds.), *New Diplomacy in the Post–Cold War World*; Randall D. Germain (ed.), *Susan Strange and the Future of Global Political Economy: Power, Control and Transformation* (London: Routledge, 2016).

7. Susan Strange, 'International Economics and International Relations: A Case of Mutual Neglect', *International Affairs*, vol. 46, no. 2 (1970) pp. 304–15.

8. Susan Strange, 'I Never Meant to be an Academic' in Joseph Kruzel and James N. Rosenau (eds.). *Journeys through World Politics: Autobiographical Reflections of Thirty-four Academic Travelers* (New York: Lexington Books, 1989), pp. 429–43, here 435.

9. Susan Strange, 'Wake Up, Krasner! The World *Has* Changed', *Review of International Political Economy*, vol. 1, no. 2 (1994), pp. 209–19, here 209.

10. Paul Post, 'How Susan Strange Founded International Political Economy'. Twitter, May 8, 2022, https://twitter.com/ProfPaulPoast/status/1523264339234463745.

11. Susan Strange, *Casino Capitalism* (Oxford: Basil Blackwell, 1986).

12. Cf. Kennedy-Pipe and Rengger's inaccurate claim that 'people working in International Studies in the 1970s were not only white . . . they were also male'. Caroline Kennedy-Pipe and Nicholas Rengger, 'BISA at Thirty: Reflections on Three Decades of British International Relations Scholarship', *Review of International Studies*, vol. 32, no. 4 (2006), pp. 665–76, here 668.

13. One of the six speakers at the British International Studies Association (BISA) inaugural conference at Oxford in 1975, American-born British-based development economist and policy advisor Edith Penrose was instrumental in establishing development studies at LSE and SOAS and thinking seriously about new directions for IR in the 1970s. See Edith Penrose, Ernest Penrose and Peter Lyon (eds.), *New Orientations: Essays in International Relations* (London:

Cass, 1970). Other works include Edith Penrose, *The Economics of the International Patent System* (Baltimore: Johns Hopkins Press, 1951); Edith Penrose, *The Large International Firm in Developing Countries: The International Petroleum Industry* (London: Allen & Unwin, 1968); Edith and Ernest Penrose, *Iraq: International Relations and National Development* (London: E. Benn Publishers, 1978). See Angela Penrose, *No Ordinary Woman: The Life of Edith Penrose* (Oxford: Oxford University Press, 2018).

14. For a collection of historical essays on the construction and performance of gender see Joan W. Scott (ed.), *Feminism and History* (Oxford: Oxford University Press, 1996).

15. On air-mindedness see Tamson Pietsch, 'Elizabeth Lippincott McQueen: Thinking International Peace in an Air-Minded Age' in Patricia Owens and Katharina Rietzler (eds.), *Women's International Thought: A New History* (Cambridge: Cambridge University Press), pp. 115–35.

16. L. A. Strange, *Recollections of an Airman* (London: Greenhill Books, 1933), p. 5.

17. Giles Merritt reflections, September 14, 2022. Merritt is Strange's eldest son.

18. Strange, *Recollections of an Airman*, p. 16; Peter Hearn, *Flying Rebel: The Story of Louis Strange* (London: HMSO, 1994), p. 172.

19. Hearn, *Flying Rebel*, p. x.

20. Hearn, *Flying Rebel*, p. 167; also see Gautam Sen, 'Obituary: Professor Susan Strange', *The Independent* (December 9, 1998), p. 6.

21. Susan Strange, pp. 1–2, Susan Strange UCL file.

22. Hearn, *Flying Rebel*, p. 99; Strange, 'I Never Meant to be an Academic', pp. 429–30; Susan Strange, pp. 1–2, Susan Strange UCL file.

23. Hearn, *Flying Rebel*, p. 110.

24. Hearn, *Flying Rebel*, pp. 110–11.

25. Strange, 'I Never Meant to be an Academic', p. 430.

26. Strange, 'I Never Meant to be an Academic', p. 429.

27. Strange, 'I Never Meant to be an Academic', p. 430. The diplomatic historian's identity is unclear, but it was not Harold Temperley, who died in 1939.

28. Strange, 'I Never Meant to be an Academic', p. 430.

29. Hearn, *Flying Rebel*, p. 167.

30. Susan Strange, pp. 1–2, Susan Strange UCL file.

31. Hearn, *Flying Rebel*, p. 167.

32. See Susan Strange, 'The Management of Surplus Capacity: Or How does Theory Stand Up to Protectionism 1970s Style?', *International Organisation*, vol. 33, no. 3 (1979), pp. 303–35.

33. For rare discussions of Barbara Ward in the context of international intellectual history see Louis Fletcher, 'Barbara Ward and the Colonial Origins of Development', 29 September 2020, https://whit.web.ox.ac.uk/article/barbara-ward-and-colonial-origins-development.

34. Elizabeth Monroe, *The Mediterranean in Politics* (London: H. Milford, 1938); Elizabeth Monroe, *The Awakening Middle East* (Toronto, Behind the Headlines, 1948); Elizabeth Monroe, *Britain's Moment in the Middle East, 1914–1956* (London: Chatto & Windus, 1963).

35. Strange, 'I Never Meant to be an Academic', p. 430.

36. Susan Strange, pp. 1–2, Susan Strange UCL file.

37. Strange, 'I Never Meant to be an Academic', p. 430.

38. Strange, 'I Never Meant to be an Academic', p. 432.

39. Strange, 'I Never Meant to be an Academic', p. 431.

40. Giles Merritt reflections, September 14, 2022.

41. Susan Strange, pp. 1–2, Susan Strange UCL file.

42. Susan Strange, 'Palestine and the UN', *Yearbook of World Affairs: 1949* (London: Stevens, 1949), pp. 151–68.

43. Strange, 'I Never Meant to be an Academic', p. 429.

44. Giles Merritt reflections, September 14, 2022.

45. Chris Brown, 'Susan Strange', *Review of International Studies*, vol. 25, no. 3 (1999), pp. 531–5, here 534.

46. Strange, 'International Economics and International Relations', p. 315.

47. Strange, 'I Never Meant to be an Academic', p. 431.

48. Richard Higgott, 'Susan Strange, 1923–1998', December 3, 1998. Available at https://wrap .warwick.ac.uk/2107/1/WRAP_Strange_wp1898.pdf.

49. Strange, 'I Never Meant to be an Academic', p. 432.

50. Susan Strange First Entry Form, Session 1949–1950, Registry Record, University College London.

51. Strange, 'I Never Meant to be an Academic', p. 432.

52. Strange, 'I Never Meant to be an Academic', p. 433.

53. Susan Strange, 'Research Institutions in International Relations in the United Kingdom', *International Social Science Bulletin (UNESCO)*, vol. 1 (1950), pp. 62–79, here 66.

54. Susan Strange, 'Economic Aspects' in *Handbook of World Affairs* (London: Stevens, 1951), pp. 353–64; Georg Schwarzenberger and Susan Strange, 'Sociological Aspects' in *Handbook of World Affairs* (London: Stevens, 1951), pp. 341–52; J. Frankel, L.C. Green, Susan Strange and Georg Schwarzenberger, 'Sociological Aspects' in *Handbook of World Affairs* (London: Stevens, 1953), pp. 308–33. Also see Susan Strange, 'Truman's Point Four', *Year Book of World Affairs* (London: Stevens, 1950), pp. 264–88; Susan Strange, 'The Schumann Plan' in *Yearbook of World Affairs* (London: Stevens, 1951), pp. 109–30; Susan Strange, 'The Atlantic Idea' in *Yearbook of World Affairs* (London: Stevens, 1953), pp. 1–19; Susan Strange, 'The Economic Work of the United Nations' in *Yearbook of World Affairs* (London: Stevens, 1954), pp. 118–40; Susan Strange, 'British Foreign Policy' in *Yearbook of World Affairs* (London: Stevens, 1955), pp. 35–53; Susan Strange, 'Strains on NATO' in *Year Book of World Affairs* (London: Stevens, 1956), pp. 21–41.

55. Georg Schwarzenberger, *Power Politics: A Study of International Society* (London: Stevens and Sons, 2nd edn, 1951), p. 5.

56. Schwarzenberger, *Power Politics*, p. 3.

57. Schwarzenberger, *Power Politics*, p. 8. Also see Ian Hall, *Dilemmas of Decline: British Intellectuals and World Politics, 1945–1975* (Berkeley: University of California Press, 2012), pp. 41–2.

58. See Stephanie Steinle, 'Georg Schwarzenberger (1908–1991)' in Jack Beatson and Reinhard Zimmermann (eds.), *Jurists Uprooted: German-Speaking Émigré Lawyers in Twentieth Century Britain* (Oxford: Oxford University Press, 2004), pp. 663–80.

59. Schwarzenberger, *Power Politics*, p. xviii.

60. Suse Schwarzenberger, 'German Academics in the 20th Century: A Personal Story'. The Wiener Holocaust Library, Unpub. Mem 4121.

61. C.A.W. Manning, *The Nature of International Society* (London: G. Bell and Sons, 1962).

62. Clifford Selly, *Capital Budgeting* (Burgess Hill: Farm Business, 1969). In 1972, Selly wrote an influential critique of industrial farming. Clifford Selly, *Ill Fares the Land: Food, Farming and the Countryside* (London: Deutsch, 1972).

63. Fred Halliday, 'Obituary: Susan Strange, New World Orders', *The Guardian* (November 14, 1998), p. 24.

64. Schwarzenberger to G. W. Keeton, December 30, 1959. UCL file no. 29/1/17, part I, folio 91.

65. 'Married Women: Appendix 1 A&PC 16.10.61'. UCL file no. 29/1/17, part I, folio 149b.

66. Georg Schwarzenberger, 'Memorandum (confidential)', April 30, 1963. UCL file no. 29/1/17, part I, folio 178.

67. G. W. Keeton to The Provost, UCL, May 13, 1957. Susan Strange—Appointment (Laws), University College London Records Department. UCL file no. 29/1/17, part I.

68. H. W. Claxon, UCL, Finance Secretary and Accountant, Memorandum to the Provost, May 15, 1957. Susan Strange—Appointment (Laws), University College London Records Department. UCL file no. 29/1/17, part I.

69. Susan Strange returned to full-time work in the second term of 1957–8. She continued to publish in the *Yearbook*, including on Suez, strategic trade embargoes, and the 'Commonwealth and the Sterling Area'. Susan Strange, 'Suez and After' in *Yearbook of World Affairs* (London: Stevens, 1957), pp. 76–103; Susan Strange, 'The Strategic Trade Embargoes: Sense or Nonsense', *Yearbook of World Affairs* (London: Stevens, 1958), pp. 55–73; Susan Strange, 'The Commonwealth and the Sterling Area', *Yearbook of World Affairs* (London: Stevens, 1959), pp. 24–44.

70. George W. Keeton, *The Development of Extraterritoriality in China* (London: Longmans, Green, 1928); L. A. Sheridan, 'George Williams Keeton, 1902–1989', *Proceedings of the British Academy*, vol. 80 (1993), p. 333.

71. Helen McCarthy, *Double Lives: A History of Working Motherhood* (London: Bloomsbury, 2020), pp. 241–2, 247.

72. E.A.L. Gueterbock to Keeton, July 27, 1961. UCL file no. 29/1/17, part I, folio 148.

73. Strange to Schwarzenberger, December 28, 1959. Susan Strange—Appointment (Laws), University College London Records Department. UCL file no. 29/1/17, part I.

74. Schwarzenberger to Keeton, December 30, 1959.

75. Keeton to Gueterbock, The Secretary, UCL, May 27, 1961. UCL file no. 29/1/17, part I, folio 123.

76. Ifor Evans to G. W. Keeton, May 30, 1961. UCL file no. 29/1/17, part I, folio 125.

77. Keeton to the Provost, May 29, 1961. UCL file no. 29/1/17, part I, folio 124.

78. 'Married Women: Appendix 1 A&PC 16.10.61'.

79. G. W. Keeton to Strange, June 13, 1961. UCL file no. 29/1/17, part I, folio 141.

80. Strange to Keeton, November 20, 1961. UCL file no. 29/1/17, part I, folio 157.

81. Strange to Keeton, June 24, 1961. UCL file no. 29/1/17, part I, folio 142b.

82. Strange to Keeton June 24, 1961.

83. Ifor Evans to Keeton, July 10, 1961. UCL file no. 29/1/17, part I, folio 143.

84. E.A.L. Gueterbock to Miss Colyer, Finance Secretary, 'Married Women Members of the Academic Staff with Family Responsibilities', June 16, 1961. UCL file no. 29/1/17, part I, folio 136.

85. E.A.L. Gueterbock, Secretary, to The Provost, July 3, 1961. UCL file no. 29/1/17, part I, folio 140; E.A.L. Gueterbock to Keeton, July 10, 1961. UCL file no. 29/1/17, part I, folio 144.

86. Gueterbock to Strange, July 14, 1961. UCL file no. 29/1/17, part I, folio 147.

87. 'Married Women Members of the Academic Staff with Family Responsibilities'. UCL file no. 220/103, n.d.; UCL file no. 29/1/17, part I, folio 149a.

88. 'Married Women: Appendix 1 A&PC 16.10.61'.

89. McCarthy, *Double Lives*, p. 258.

90. 'Married Women Members of the Academic Staff with Family Responsibilities'.

91. 'Married Women: Appendix 1 A&PC 16.10.61'.

92. 'Married Women: Appendix 1 A&PC 16.10.61'.

93. 'Married Women Members of the Academic Staff with Family Responsibilities'.

94. 'Married Women: Appendix 1 A&PC 16.10.61'.

95. 'Married Women: Appendix 1 A&PC 16.10.61'.

96. Strange to Keeton, November 20, 1961. UCL file no. 29/1/17, part I, folio 157.

97. 'Married Women Members of the Academic Staff with Family Responsibilities—Miss Susan Strange' A&PC, January 15, 1962. Min. 8. UCL file no. 29/1/17, part I, folio 188.

98. Susan Strange, 'Changing Trends in World Trade' in *Yearbook of World Affairs* (London: Stevens, 1962), pp. 139–58; Susan Strange, 'Cuba and After' in *Yearbook of World Affairs* (London: Stevens, 1963), pp. 1–28.

99. Schwarzenberger to Keeton, November 17, 1961. UCL file no. 29/1/17, part I, folio 161.

100. Schwarzenberger, 'Memorandum (confidential)', April 30, 1963. UCL file no. 29/1/17, part I, folio 178.

101. A&PC, May 27, 1963. Min. 56. Susan Strange—Appointment (Laws), University College London Records Department. UCL file no. 29/1/17, part II, folio 193b.

102. A&PC, May 27, 1963.

103. 'File Note' from Gueterbock, May 28, 1963. Susan Strange—Appointment (Laws), University College London Records Department. UCL file no. 29/1/17, part II, folio 194. 'She might be given assurance that the College would consider restoring her to full-time when home commitments due to her young children had ceased'. Gueterbock to Keeton, 'Confidential: Staffing of the Department of Laws'. September 13, 1963. F UCL file no. 29/1/17, part II, folio 203.

104. Keeton to Provost, December 31, 1963. UCL File No.29/1/17 Part II. Folio 210.

105. Keeton to Provost, January 27, 1964. UCL file no. 29/1/17, part II, folio 214; Keeton to Provost, February 7, 1964. UCL file no. 29/1/17, part II, folio 217.

106. Gueterbock to Strange, June 4, 1963. UCL file no. 29/1/17, part II, folio 195.

107. Strange to Gueterbock, June 9, 1963. UCL file no. 29/1/17, part II, folio 196.

108. Keeton to Strange, December 10, 1963. UCL file no. 29/1/17, part II, folio 209.

109. Keeton to Strange, December 10, 1963. Keeton had also written to the provost, claiming 'it is abundantly clear that Miss Strange is only giving part-time service'. Keeton to Provost, October 21, 1963. UCL file no. 29/1/17, part II, folio 206.

110. Keeton to Provost, January 27, 1964. UCL file no. 29/1/17, part II, folio 214.

111. Keeton to Strange, February 8, 1964. UCL file no. 29/1/17, part II, folio 218.

112. Strange to Keeton, February 18, 1964. UCL file no. 29/1/17, part II, folio 219.

113. Strange, 'I Never Meant to be an Academic', p. 433.

114. Extract of letter from Professor Keeton dated March 28, 1964. UCL file no. 29/1/17, part II, folio 222.

115. William C. Olson and A.J.R. Groom, *International Relations Then and Now: Origins and Trends in Interpretation* (London: Harper Collins Academic, 1991). The women are Annette Baker Fox, Adda Bozeman, Jessie Bernard, Sonia Z. Hyman, Elizabeth Fischer Read, Margaret Sprout, Susan Strange. They also mention the contemporary scholar Cynthia Enloe.

116. Hearn, *Flying Rebel*, pp. 172–3.

117. Brian Porter, 'A Brief History Continued, 1972–2002' in Harry Bauer and Elisabetta Brighi (eds.), *International Relations at LSE: A History of 75 Years* (London: Millennium Publishing Group, 2003), p. 36.

118. Susan Strange, 'The Limits of Politics', *Government and Opposition* Leonard Shapiro Lecture, June 1, 1995. Available at https://digital.library.lse.ac.uk/objects/lse:gaq423fok.

119. Strange, 'I Never Meant to be an Academic', p. 433.

120. Strange, 'Wake Up, Krasner!', p. 215.

121. Strange quoted by Anna Leander, 'Contributors' in Morgan et al (eds.), *New Diplomacy in the Post–Cold War World*, p. 307.

122. Post, 'How Susan Strange Founded International Political Economy'.

123. On Camps see Katja Seidel, 'Miriam Camps and European Integration: Blurring Boundaries between Scholarship and Diplomacy', *Global Studies Quarterly*, vol. 3, no. 2 (2023), pp. 1–11.

124. LSE Director to Strange, December 8, 1959, Susan Strange LSE staff file, 1959–1974; Geoffrey Goodwin to LSE Director, October 19, 1965. Susan Strange LSE staff file, 1959–1974.

125. Ralf Dahrendorf to Strange, September 21, 1978. Susan Strange LSE staff file, 1975–.

126. Richard Higgott and Roger Tooze, 'Professor Susan Strange (Selly)', *Centre for the Study of Globalisation and Regionalisation Newsletter*, issue 2 (1998–99) pp. 4–6, here 4. Available at https://warwick.ac.uk/fac/soc/pais/research/csgr/newsletters/nl2.pdf.

127. Strange, 'I Never Meant to be an Academic', p. 435.

128. I am grateful to Roger Tooze, one of these new IR appointments, for highlighting the significance of this context in Strange's plan for BISA.

129. 'Susan Strange to university Vice Chancellors in 1975'. BISA/8. LSE Library.

130. Susan Strange, Letter to Department of Politics, University of Reading. BISA/8. LSE Library.

131. Strange, 'I Never Meant to be an Academic', p. 435.

132. 'Where did we come from? International relations in Britain before BISA', February 3, 2020. Available at https://www.bisa.ac.uk/articles/where-did-we-come-international-relations -britain-bisa.

133. Barry Buzan, 'Before BISA: The British Coordinating Committee for International Studies, S.H. Bailey, and the Bailey Conferences', *International Politics*, vol. 57, no. 4 (2020), pp. 573–8, here 583.

134. Strange, 'I Never Meant to be an Academic', p. 435.

135. Susan Strange, '1995 Presidential Address: ISA as a Microcosm', *International Studies Quarterly*, vol. 39, no. 3 (1995), pp. 289–95, here 295.

136. Porter, 'A Brief History Continued', p. 36.

137. Porter, 'A Brief History Continued', pp. 36–7.

138. Strange's courses included 'International Institutions', 'The Place of International Business Corporations in the International System' and 'The Politics of International Economic Institutions'.

139. Susan Strange, 'Looking Back—But Mostly Forward', *Millennium: Journal of International Studies*, vol. 11, no. 1 (1982), pp. 38–49, here 40.

140. Ronen Palan, 'Pragmatism and International Relations in the Age of Banker's Capitalism: Susan Strange's Vision for a Critical International Political Economy' in Bauer and Brighi (eds.), *International Relations at LSE: a History of 75 Years*, p pp. 117–38, here 119.

141. Palan, 'Pragmatism and International Relations', p. 119.

142. Herbert Butterfield to Kenneth Thompson, December 14, 1956. BUTT/28. Cambridge University Library.

143. Palan, 'Pragmatism and International Relations', p. 119.

144. Hedley Bull, 'International Theory: The Case for a Classical Approach', *World Politics*, vol. 18, no. 3 (1966), [pp. 361–77, here 362. Bull's exemplars of 'various twentieth-century systematizations of international theory' following the 'classical approach' are Zimmern, Carr, Morgenthau, Schwarzenberger, Aron, and Wight.

145. Strange, 'I Never Meant to be an Academic', p. 434. See Susan Strange, 'International Economic Relations I: The Need for an Interdisciplinary Approach' in Roger Morgan (ed.), *The Study of International Affairs: Essays in Honour of Kenneth Younger* (London: RIIA/Oxford University Press, 1972), pp. 63–84. This essay appeared alongside others by Rosalyn Higgins on international law at the UN and Caroline Miles on international economic relations, covering business and trade.

146. Halliday, 'Obituary: Susan Strange', p. 24.

147. Strange, '1995 Presidential Address', p. 290.

148. Strange, 'I Never Meant to be an Academic', p. 434–5.

149. Palan, 'Pragmatism and International Relations', p. 134.

150. Piers Revell, 'Supplement to States and Markets: an Investigation of the "Knowledge Structure" in the work of Susan Strange', doctoral dissertation, LSE, 2014, p. 9. See Robert W. Cox, 'Gramsci, Hegemony and International Relations: An Essay in Method', *Millennium: Journal of International Studies*, vol. 12, no. 2 (1983), pp. 162–75.

151. Susan Strange, 'An Eclectic Approach' in C. N. Murphy and R. Tooze (eds.), *The New International Political Economy* (Boulder: Lynne Rienner, 1991), pp. 33–49.

152. Morgan, Lorentzen, Leander, and Guzzini, 'A Cake for Susan: Acknowledgements', p. v; also see Thomas C. Lawton, James N. Rosenau, and Amy C. Verdun, 'Introduction: Looking Beyond the Confines' in Lawton, Rosenau, and Verdun, *Strange Power*, pp. 3–18, here 4.

153. Cornelia Navari, 'The IR thought of Susan Strange', *The Global Thinkers Series*, University of Oxford, March 6, 2020. Available at https://podcasts.ox.ac.uk/ir-thought-susan-strange-prof -cornelia-navari.

154. Nat Dyer, 'Susan Strange: a Great Thinker or a Journalist?', Sheffield Political Economy Research Institute Blog. February 27, 2019. Available at https://www.earthriseblog.org/susan -strange-a-great-thinker-or-a-journalist/.

155. Benjamin J. Cohen, *International Political Economy: An Intellectual History* (Princeton: Princeton University Press, 2008), p. 50.

156. Strange, *States and Markets*, p. 37. I am grateful to Nat Dyer for this point.

157. According to Louis W. Pauly, 'The Spirit of Susan Strange (1923–1998)' in Richard Ned Lebow, Peer Schouten, and Hidemi Suganami (eds.), *The Return of the Theorists: Dialogues with Great Thinkers in International Relations* (London: Palgrave, 2016), pp. 302–12, here 303.

158. Quoted in Justin Rosenberg, 'International Relations—The "Higher Bullshit": A Reply to the Globalization Theory Debate', *International Politics*, vol. 44, no. 4 (2007), pp. 450–82.

159. Susan Strange, 'Looking Back', p. 40.

160. Diana Tussie, 'Shaping the World Beyond the "Core": States and Markets in Brazil's Global Ascent' in Germain, *Susan Strange* pp. 55–68, here 56.

161. 'Professor Susan Strange', *The Times* (November 24, 1998).

162. Halliday, 'Obituary: Susan Strange', p. 24.

163. Pauly, 'The Spirit of Susan Strange', p. 303.

164. Cohen, *International Political Economy*, p. 56.

165. Brown, 'Susan Strange', p. 535.

166. Strange, '1995 Presidential Address', p. 289.

167. Strange, 'The Limits of Politics'.

168. Sen, 'Obituary: Professor Susan Strange'.

169. Strange, 'I Never Meant to be an Academic', p. 436.

170. Strange, 'I Never Meant to be an Academic', p. 433.

171. Strange, 'I Never Meant to be an Academic', p. 432.

172. Strange, 'I Never Meant to be an Academic', p. 433.

173. Strange, 'I Never Meant to be an Academic', p. 433. On Burton see Martin Griffiths, 'John Burton Versus International Relations: The Costs of Criticism', *Australian Journal of International Affairs*, vol. 67, no. 1 (2013), pp. 55–70.

174. Porter, 'A Brief History Continued', p. 32.

175. Strange, 'I Never Meant to be an Academic', p. 429.

176. Strange, '1995 Presidential Address', p. 295.

177. Brown, 'Susan Strange', p. 534.

178. Sen, 'Obituary: Professor Susan Strange'.

179. Strange, 'I Never Meant to be an Academic', p. 432.

180. Sen, 'Obituary: Professor Susan Strange'.

181. G. G. Coulton, 'Memories of Eileen Power', *The Cambridge Review*, vol. 52 (October 18, 1940), p. 29. GBR/0271/GCPP Power, E 1/8, Girton College.

182. Strange, '1995 Presidential Address', p. 294.

183. Navari, 'The IR thought of Susan Strange'.

184. Strange, 'I Never Meant to be an Academic', p. 430.

185. Strange, 'I Never Meant to be an Academic', p. 430.

186. Strange, 'I Never Meant to be an Academic', p. 433.

187. Pauly, 'The Spirit of Susan Strange', p. 307.

188. Halliday, 'Obituary: Susan Strange', p. 24.

189. Craig N. Murphy, 'Seeing Women, Recognizing Gender, Recasting International Relations', *International Organization*, vol. 50, no. 3 (1996), pp. 513–38, here 532.

190. Sen, 'Obituary: Professor Susan Strange'.

191. Navari, 'The IR thought of Susan Strange'.

192. Pauly, 'The Spirit of Susan Strange', p. 302.

193. Higgott and Tooze, 'Professor Susan Strange', p. 6.

194. Murphy, 'Seeing Women', p. 532.

195. Pauly, 'The Spirit of Susan Strange', p. 303.

196. Murphy, 'Seeing Women', p. 532.

197. Higgott and Tooze, 'Professor Susan Strange', p. 6.

198. Navari, 'The IR thought of Susan Strange'.

199. Strange, 'Wake Up, Krasner!', p. 215.

200. Strange, 'I Never Meant to be an Academic', p. 433.

201. Jane Streatfield reflections, September 17, 2022.

202. Higgott and Tooze, 'Professor Susan Strange', p. 6.

203. Margot Light, 'Studying and Working in the IR Department at LSE in the 1970s and 1980s'. November 28, 2019. https://blogs.lse.ac.uk/internationalrelations/2019/11/28/studying-and-working-in-ir-at-lse-in-the-1970s-and-1980s/.

204. Murphy, 'Seeing Women', p. 532; also see Craig N. Murphy, '"The Westphalia System" Fifteen Years On: Global Problems, What Makes Them Difficult to Solve and the Role of IPE' in Germain, *Susan Strange*, pp. 33–51, here 49.

205. The ISA's Feminist Theory and Gender Studies Section was five years old at the time of Strange's address. Elshtain's *Women and War* had been out for eight years; Enloe's *Bananas, Beaches & Bases* for six; Ticker's *Gender and International Relations* for three; and Sylvester's *Feminist Theory and International Relations* was published the year before. Jean Bethke Elshtain, *Women and War* (New York: Basic, 1987); Cynthia Enloe, *Bananas, Beaches and Bases: Making Feminist Sense of International Politics* (London: Pandora, 1989); J. Ann Tickner, *Gender in International Relations: Feminist Perspectives on Achieving Global Security* (New York: Columbia University Press, 1992); Christine Sylvester, *Feminist Theory and International Relations in a Postmodern Era* (Cambridge: Cambridge University Press, 1994). Colonial relations and racial hierarchies were not often at the forefront of early (white) feminist IR. But see Geeta Chowdhry and L. H. M. Ling, 'Race(ing) International Relations: A Critical Overview of Postcolonial Feminism in International Relations', *Oxford Research Encyclopaedia of International Studies* (Oxford: Oxford University Press, 2010).

206. Light, 'Studying and Working in the IR Department at LSE'.

207. Strange, 'I Never Meant to be an Academic', p. 428.

208. Sen, 'Obituary: Professor Susan Strange', p. 6.

209. Strange, 'I Never Meant to be an Academic', p. 433.

210. Ida J. Koppen, 'Contributors' in Morgan et al (eds.), *New Diplomacy in the Post–Cold War World*, p. 307.

211. For an extended discussion of these subject positions through a close reading of the portrait of Susan Strange in Figure 11.1. see Owens, 'Images of International Thinkers', *Review of International Studies* (2024), FirstView. On 'Queen Bee' as one of the female subject positions allowable in the early nineties legal academy see Margaret Thornton, 'Discord in the Legal Academy: The Case of the Feminist Scholar', *Australian Feminist Law Journal*, vol. 1 (1994), p. 53–71.

212. Halliday, 'Obituary: Susan Strange', p. 24.

213. Strange, 'I Never Meant to be an Academic', p. 432.

214. Brown, 'Susan Strange', p. 534.

215. 'Professor Susan Strange', *The Times* (November 24, 1998).

216. Giles Merritt reflections, September 14, 2022.

217. Susan Strange, *The Sterling Problem and the Six* (London: P.E.P., 1967).

218. Susan Strange thought that this was a good thing. IR 'has been and will remain the richer for keeping those barriers low'. Strange, 'I Never Meant to be an Academic', p. 435.

219. Kennedy-Pipe and Rengger, 'BISA at Thirty', p. 666.

## Conclusion: The Voice of Portia

1. C.A.W. Manning, 'International Relations: an Academic Discipline' in Geoffrey L. Goodwin (ed.), *The University Teaching of International Relations* (Oxford: Blackwell, 1951), p. 20.

2. Manning, 'International Relations: an Academic Discipline', p. 21.

3. C.A.W. Manning, 'Report of the General Rapporteur' in Goodwin (ed.) *The University Teaching of International Relations*, pp. 27–73, here 70.

4. Manning, 'Report of the General Rapporteur' p. 42.

5. Barbara D. Savage, 'Beyond Illusions: Imperialism, Race and Technology in Merze Tate's International Thought' in Patricia Owens and Katharina Rietzler (eds.), *Women's International Thought: A New History* (Cambridge: Cambridge University Press), pp. 266–85.

6. 'Let the shoemaker stick to his last! Let the International Relations teacher proceed with his subject. Who wants to stop him? Let him have his rights. Only, no Strategics, mind you; no Economics, no Law!' C.A.W. Manning, '"Naughty Animal": A Discipline Chats Back', *International Relations*, vol. 1, no. 4 (1955), pp. 128–36, here 133.

7. Manning, '"Naughty Animal": A Discipline Chats Back', p. 133.

8. Brian Porter, 'A Brief History Continued, 1972–2002' in Harry Bauer and Elisabetta Brighi (eds.), *International Relations at LSE: a History of 75 Years* (London: Millennium Publishing Group, 2003), pp. 29–44, here 31.

9. Geoffrey L. Goodwin, 'Teaching of International Relations' in Geoffrey L. Goodwin, *The University Teaching of International Relations* (Oxford: Blackwell, 1951), p. 124.

10. Manning, 'Report of the General Rapporteur', pp. 43–4.

11. Manning, 'International Relations: an Academic Discipline', pp. 20, 17.

12. C.A.W. Manning, 'The Pretensions of International Relations', *Higher Education Quarterly*, vol. 7, no. 4 (1953), pp. 361–71, here 363.

13. Manning, 'Report of the General Rapporteur', p. 32.

14. Manning, '"Naughty Animal": A Discipline Chats Back', p. 134.

15. Janet M. Box-Steffensmeier, Henry E. Brady, and David Collier (eds.), *The Oxford Handbook of Political Methodology* (Oxford: Oxford University Press, 2008). There is no equivalent handbook for the more intellectual and methodologically pluralist field of IR.

16. Clare Mac Cumhaill and Rachael Wiseman, *Metaphysical Animals: How Four Women Brought Philosophy Back to Life* (London: Chatto and Windus, 2022); Benjamin J. B. Lipscomb, *The Women are Up to Something: How Elizabeth Anscombe, Philippa Foot, Mary Midgley, and Iris Murdoch Revolutionized Ethics* (Oxford: Oxford University Press, 2022); Katy Hessel, *The Story of Art Without Men* (London: Hutchinson Heinemann, 2022).

17. Stuart Hall, *Selected Writings on Race and Difference*, edited by Paul Gilroy and Ruth Wilson Gilmore (Durham: Duke University Press, 2021); Paul Gilroy, *'There Ain't No Black in the Union Jack': The Cultural Politics of Race and Nation* (London: Hutchinson, 1987).

18. Patricia Owens, Katharina Rietzler, Kimberly Hutchings, and Sarah C. Dunstan (eds.), *Women's International Thought: Towards a New Canon* (Cambridge: Cambridge University Press, 2022).

19. Christopher Hill, 'The Study of International Relations in the United Kingdom', *Millennium: Journal of International Studies*, vol. 16, no. 2 (1987), pp. 301–8, here 302.

20. Fred Halliday, 'International Relations and Its Discontents', *International Affairs*, vol. 71, no. 4 (1995), pp. 733–46.

21. Barry Buzan and Richard Little, 'Why International Relations Has Failed as an Intellectual Project and What to do About It', *Millennium: Journal of International Studies*, vol. 30, no. 1 (2001) pp. 19–39, here 29.

22. Buzan and Little, 'Why International Relations Has Failed', p. 19. They list Hedley Bull, Hans Morgenthau, Robert Gilpin, Stephen Krasner, Robert Keohane, James Rosenau, and Kenneth Waltz.

23. Ilan Zvi Baron, 'The Continuing Failure of International Relations and the Challenges of Disciplinary Boundaries', *Millennium: Journal of International Studies*, vol. 43, no. 1 (2014), pp. 224–44, here 225.

24. Exceptions include Robert Vitalis, *White World Order, Black Power Politics: The Birth of American International Relations* (Ithaca: Cornell University Press, 2015), reviewed by Susan Pederdon, 'Destined to Disappear', *London Review of Books*, vol. 38, no. 20 (October 20, 2016), and Laleh Khalili, *Sinews of War and Trade: Shipping and Capitalism in the Arabian Peninsula* (London: Verso 2021), reviewed by John Lanchester, 'Gargantuanisation', *London Review of Books*, vol. 43, no. 8 (April 22, 2021).

25. Priyamvada Gopal, *Insurgent Empire: Anticolonial Resistance and British Dissent* (London: Verso, 2019); Adam Tooze, *The Deluge: The Great War and the Remaking of Global Order 1916–1931* (London: Penguin, 2015); Adam Tooze, *Crashed: How a Decade of Financial Crises Changed the World* (London: Allen Lane, 2018); Gurminder K. Bhambra and John Holmwood, *Colonialism and Modern Social Theory* (Cambridge, MA: Medford, 2021); Caroline Elkins, *Legacy of Violence: A History of the British Empire* (London: Vintage, 2022); Charlotte Lydia Riley, *Imperial Island: A History of Empire in Modern Britain* (London: Penguin, 2023). The exception that proves the rule is Robbie Shilliam, *Race and the Undeserving Poor: From Abolition to Brexit* (Newcastle upon Tyne: Agenda Publishing, 2018).

26. Synne L. Dyvik, Jan Selby and Rorden Wilkinson (eds.) *What's the Point of International Relations?* (London: Routledge, 2017).

27. John Mearsheimer and Stephen Walt, 'Leaving Theory Behind: Why Simplistic Hypothesis Testing is Bad for International Relations', *European Journal of International Relations*, vol. 19, no. 3 (2013), pp. 427–57; Tim Dunne, Lene Hansen and Colin Wight, 'The End of International Relations Theory?', *European Journal of International Relations*, vol. 19, no. 3 (2013), pp. 405–25; Peter Marcus Kristensen, 'Discipline Admonished: On International Relations Fragmentation and the Disciplinary Politics of Stocktaking', *European Journal of International Relations*, vol. 22, no. 2 (2016), pp. 243–67.

28. The EISA was founded in 2013 due to a schism in European Consortium of Political Research about the independent status of IR.

29. Katrina Forrester, *In the Shadow of Justice: Postwar Liberalism and the Remaking of Political Philosophy* (Princeton: Princeton University Press, 2019); Duncan Bell (ed.), *Empire, Race and Global Justice* (Cambridge: Cambridge University Press, 2019).

30. Buzan and Little, 'Why International Relations Has Failed', pp. 22, 38. Cf. Knud Erik Jørgensen, *What Is International Relations?* (Bristol: Bristol University Press 2022), which claims IR is a discipline and roaring success. Others have more creatively thought with 'failure' itself. See J. Samuel Barkin & Laura L. Sjoberg, 'The Queer Art of Failed IR?' *Alternatives*, vol. 45, no. 4 (2020), pp. 167–83; Clive Gabay, 'Ever Failed. No Matter. Try Again. Fail Again. Fail Better: IR Theory, Utopia, and a Failure to (Re)Imagine Failure', *International Theory*, vol. 14, no. 2 (2022), pp. 285–310.

31. This is generally true even among critical IR scholars who specialise in methods and/or take seriously interpretative and critical methods. See Brooke A. Ackerly et al (eds.), *Feminist Methodologies for International Relations* (Cambridge: Cambridge University Press, 2006);

Audie Klotz and Deepa Prakash (eds.), *Qualitative Methods in International Relations: A Pluralist Guide* (London: Palgrave, 2008); Claudia Aradau and Jef Huysmans, 'Critical Methods in International Relations: The Politics of Techniques, Devices and Acts', *European Journal of International Relations*, vol. 20, no. 3 (2014), pp. 596–619; Claudia Aradau et al (eds.), *Critical Security Methods: New Frameworks for Analysis* (London: Routledge, 2015).

32. For recent work on the indispensability of methodological pluralism and thoroughness see Patrick Thaddeus Jackson, *The Conduct of Inquiry in International Relations: Philosophy of Science and Its Implications for the Study of World Politics* (London: Routledge, 2011); Cecelia Lynch, *Interpreting International Politics* (London: Routledge, 2014); Samuel Barkin and Laura Sjoberg (eds.), *Interpretive Quantification: Methodological Explorations for Critical and Constructivist IR* (Ann Arbor: University of Michigan Press, 2017); Brooke A. Ackerly and Jacqui True, *Doing Feminist Fesearch in Political and Social Science* (London: Red Globe Press, 2019); Daniel Bendix, Franziska Müller, and Aram Ziai, *Beyond the Master's Tools? Decolonizing Knowledge Orders, Research Methods and Teaching* (London: Rowman and Littlefield, 2020).

33. Kimberly Hutchings, 'Doing Epistemic Justice in International Relations: Women and the History of International Thought', *European Journal of International Relations*, vol. 29, no. 4 (2023), pp. 809–31.

34. Helen McCarthy, 'Women's International Thought: A New Field?', *International Politics Reviews*, vol. 9 (2021), pp. 251–6.

# INDEX

Page numbers in *italics* denote illustrations.

Brecht, Bertolt, 164, 181–82, 354n195

Breuning, Eleanor, 252

'Brexit', 294, 363n3

Briggs Myers, Isabel, 89, 323n32

British Committee on the Theory of International Politics, 11–12, 16, 19, 90–91, 185–89, 206, 231, 233, 238–39, 265, 282, 296; Bell as member of, 253–54; 'English School' as heirs to, 62 (*see also* 'English School'); photo of, *254*; Rockefeller Foundation as funding, 46, 90

British Commonwealth of Nations, 51, 56, 67, 193, 198, 220, 223, 231, 266, 327n141, 337n93; transformation of empire to, 189–90, 207–8, 266, 289

British Conservative Party, 212

British Coordinating Committee for International Studies (BCCIS), 11–12, 19, 42, 66, 71–72, 86, 92, 95–96, 101–2, 134–35, 160–62, 185; 'Bailey Conferences', 72, 76, 101, 182, 281, 332n91, 354n198; Cleeve as secretary of, 76, 83; Strange/BISA and, 272, 280–82, 287–88, 290, 292

British Empire, 2, 5, 8, 18, 45, 51–52, 55–58, 98–99, 122–23, 146, 186, 188–90, 193, 205–31 passim, 292; and antiracism, 'mystique of', 220; and British imperialism, 166, 223, 317n42; and colonialism, 205, 214; and decolonisation, 198; end of/transition to Commonwealth from, 189–90, 207–8, 266, 289–90 (*see also* British Commonwealth of Nations); legacies of, 294; Perham on, 205; racial resentment in, 200; and whiteness, 208–31. *See also* indirect rule; *individual names; specific topics*

British exceptionalism, 191

British Institute for International Affairs. *See* Royal Institute of International Affairs (RIIA)

British International Studies Association (BISA), 47, 231, 265–66, 280–82, 287, 290, 292, 295, 380n3, 380n13

Brittain, Vera, 303n43

Brogan, Denis, 86, 243–44

Buchan, Alastair, 161, 251, 372n33

Buck, Pearl S., 340n186

Bull, Hedley, 189, 206–7, 265, 303n44, 339n127, 356n10, 356n19, 385n144, 389n22; at LSE, 104, 107, 250; marriage of (*see* Bull, Mary); Montague Burton Professorship (Oxford), 161–62, 232, 255, 260–61; photos of, *61*, *254*; and Rachel Wall, 232, 247, 250, 254–255, 255, 260–61. *See also* 'English School'; 'international society' approach to IR

Bull, Mary, 46–47, 50–51, *61*, 233–34, 315n8, 321n127; as Perham's research assistant, 46–47, 60–62

Bullock, Alan, 83, 327n141

bullying, sexist, 272, 278–79, 284

Burroughs, Williana, 212

Burton, John, 284, 286

Burton, Montague, 41, 309n83. *See also* Montague Burton Professorship; Montague Burton Studentship

Butler, C. Violet, 143, 151

Butler, Ruth F., 143, 149–50, 157, 343n45

Butterfield, Herbert, 86–87, 90–91, 101–2, 185, 206, 239, 254, 281; *Diplomatic Investigations*, 188. *See also* 'English School'

Buzan, Barry, 332n91

Calvocoressi, Peter, 219

Cambridge University, 17, 37–38, 96, 101–2, 110–23, 133, 137–40 passim, 163, 188, 233–34, 250, 286, 313n180, 338n111; Crowe's PhD in history, 139, 171, 350n90; IR at/lateness to IR, 72, 85–92, 186; Power at, 112–22; Stawell as lecturer at, 87–88; Wall at, 243–46. *See also* Girton College; Newnham College; Oxbridge; *individual names, e.g.,* Behrens, Betty; Wiskemann, Elizabeth

Campbell, Anne, 80

Campbell, Grace, 212

Campbell, Persia, 332n80

Camps, Miriam, 79, 280, 303n43

canon, construction of, 37; as all-white male, 3–4, 8, 185, 207, 239, 288, 294; and *The Growth of International Thought* (Stawell) as first of genre, 1–3, 8, 65, 67; influence as criteria for, 3, 17; Leverhulme Project on Women and the History of International Thought, xiii, 14; and Strange's inclusion, 265, 278–79, 282; women's absence from, 136

capitalism, 103, 113; and anticolonialism, 212–15; Black, 213; and colonialism/anticolonialism, 212–15; and European militarism, 155, 292; global, 156, 229; and imperialism, 56, 214; (Claudia) Jones on, 212–15; modern, 110, 118, 241, 265, 282; and

A NOTE ON THE TYPE

This book has been composed in Arno, an Old-style serif typeface in the
classic Venetian tradition, designed by Robert Slimbach at Adobe.